Economics Education
A Second Handbook for
Economics Teachers

Economics Education
A Second Handbook for Economics Teachers

Edited by
David J. Whitehead
Senior Lecturer in Education (Economics)
University of London Institute of Education

HEINEMANN EDUCATIONAL BOOKS

Heinemann Educational Books Ltd
22 Bedford Square, London WC1B 3HH

LONDON   EDINBURGH   MELBOURNE   AUCKLAND
SINGAPORE   KUALA LUMPUR   NEW DELHI   IBADAN
NAIROBI   JOHANNESBURG   PORTSMOUTH (NH)
KINGSTON

ISBN 0 435 33750 5
© David J. Whitehead 1986
First published 1986
Reprinted 1988

British Library Cataloguing in Publication Data
Economics education: a second handbook for
  economics teachers.
  1. Economics — Study and teaching
  (Secondary) — England
  I. Whitehead, David, *1943 Oct 18–*
  II. Handbook for economics teachers
  330′.07′1242   HB74.9.G7
  ISBN 0 435 33750 5

Printed and bound in Great Britain by
Thomson Litho Ltd, East Kilbride, Scotland
Phototypesetting by Georgia Ltd, Formby

Contents

Section 4: Ways of Teaching Particular Topics

PART THREE: RESOURCES, ASSESSMENT AND ORGANISATION

Introduction to Part Three

Section 5: Miscellaneous

List of Contributors

Alain Anderton	Adviser in Economics, Staffordshire Education Authority
Martin C. Brimble	Head of Social Science, Elizabeth Garrett Anderson School, ILEA
David R. Butler	Senior Teacher, Hailsham School, Sussex
Nigel Carr	Head of Economics and Business Studies, Brentwood School
Ian Chambers	Lecturer in Education (Business Studies), London University Institute of Education
Paul Clarke	Field Officer, Economics Education 14–16 Project
Lindsey Collings	Head of Economics and Politics, Coopers' Company and Coborn School, Upminster
Ann Cotterrell	Lecturer in Economics, Waltham Forest College of Further and Higher Education
Richard Dunnill	Department of Trade and Industry Fellow, Economics Research and Curriculum Unit, London University Institute of Education
Morag Ellingham	Formerly Economics teacher, Hayesfield Upper School, Bath
Graham Evans	Assistant Headteacher, Herries School, Sheffield
Tony Evans	16–19 Co-ordinator, ILEA Division Six
Bob Fryer	Head of Economics, Rutlish School, Merton
Steve Hodkinson	Lecturer in Education (Economics), Manchester University
Michael Houser	Formerly Head of Economics and Political Studies, The Blue School, Wells
Ray Jarvis	Head of Economics, Simon Langton Grammar School for Boys, Canterbury
Graham Jones	Economics teacher, Charterhouse
Barrie King	Head of School of Humanities and Business Studies, Barnfield College, Luton
Andrew Leake	Head of Economics, Latymer Upper School, Hammersmith
Peter Leech	Head of Middle School, King James's School, Knaresborough
Frank Livesey	Professor and Head of the School of Economics, Lancashire Polytechnic
Stuart Luker	Head of Economics and Computer Education, Charters School, Sunningdale
Ian Marcousé	Head of Business Studies, Esher College
Keith Marder	Formerly Head of Social and Economic Studies, Langdon School, East Ham
Claire Minogue	Formerly Economics teacher, Feltham School, Middlesex
Mike Morris	Head of Economics, Dulwich College
Danny Myers	Head of Economics and Sociology, New College, Swindon
Philip Negus	Head of Economics, Peel Sixth Form College, Bury
Robert Paisley	Head of Economics, Northwood School
Norman Perrin	Formerly English teacher at Waltheof School, Sheffield, now an independent film maker
Richard A. Powell	Adviser to TVEI Project, London Borough of Bromley
Trevor Regan	Head of Economics, Royal Grammar School, Newcastle-upon-Tyne
Malcolm Scriven	Economics teacher, Peel Sixth Form College, Bury
Linda Thomas	Lecturer in Education (Economics), London University Institute of Education
Richard Thorne	Head of Sixth Form and Business Studies Department, Swanley School
Andrew Tibbitt	Head of Economics and Business Studies, Watford Grammar School
Michael Tighe	Head of Economics and Business Studies, Gateway Sixth Form College, Leicester
Kevin Tinsley	Economics teacher, Winchmore School
Brian Titley	Economics teacher, Coopers' Company and Coborn School, Upminster
Nigel Tree	Visiting Lecturer, Sunderland and Newcastle Polytechnics
Nancy Wall	Head of Economics, Beacon School, Crowborough
Sara Wall	Head of Economics, Southgate School
Richard Welford	Head of Computer Education and Acting Head of Economics and Business Studies, Swanwick Hall School, Derbyshire
David Whitehead	Senior Lecturer in Education (Economics), London University Institute of Education
Roy Wilkinson	Professor of Economics, Sheffield University
Sarah Wilkinson	Head of Economics, West Hatch High School, Chigwell, Essex
Maurice Willatt	Formerly Head of Economics, Haberdashers' Aske's School for Boys, Elstree
Robert Wilson	Head of Economics and Business Studies, Aberdeen College of Education
Keith Wood	Lecturer in Education (Economics), University of Hong Kong

Preface

The first edition of this publication evidently met a demand: most economics teachers and lecturers either purchased a copy personally or arranged for their departments to buy one. This second edition is aimed at the same market, and is therefore intended to be complementary to the first. To that end, it has been completely rewritten, and most of the contributions are by new authors.

In the seven years since the first manuscript was delivered, many of the resources suggested have become outdated, so in this edition we bring all such information up to date, while concentrating less on ephemeral materials and more on perennial problems of teaching particular concepts. I hope that the first edition will continue to be consulted, as most of it is still very valuable. All seventeen simulations have been cut from the new edition, but several different ones have been included. New teachers should be able to consult a copy of the first edition in their department or library.

The Economics Association journal, *Economics*, has done much to raise the level of debate about the justification for and the meaning of economic literacy. Unlike some handbooks, we eschew fundamental questions in order to concentrate on 'how to teach' – but the inclusion of certain rarely treated topics and concepts manifests the editor's position and may help some teachers to steer their courses in appropriate directions.

While there may be no theoretical consensus on how to teach economics, much uniformity exists in practice. Although the suggestions proposed here will enable teachers to continue in accustomed ways – but more effectively – they will also upset some teachers'

equilibrium, and encourage divergent activities that may be more conducive to the currently emphasised development of skills.

I thank: my Editorial Board for suggesting changes for the new edition, and for reading some of the draft chapters; my ex-PGCE and MA students, sixteen of whom have been inveigled into writing for me; the twelve contributors to the first edition who agreed to rewrite their chapters: the six textbook authors who forsook more commercial writing for the sake of this publication; the four ex-Visiting Tutors in Economics to the London University Institute of Education who share their expertise here; Sarah, Laurence and Rachel, for helping me to get on with it.

Chiefly I thank all the contributing writers (most of whom are experienced, practising school and college teachers) who have so willingly shared their enthusiasm and professional competence with others.

The first edition set a pattern for this type of writing which made my task much easier for this edition. Nevertheless, teachers are not accustomed to being 'edited' or 'corrected', and I am grateful for their forbearance and understanding. No attempt has been made to impose a uniform viewpoint or style on the forty-eight contributors: such emasculation would result in a bland presentation. Instead, we have a stirring diversity of viewpoints, a cornucopia for which everyone listed is responsible.

David J. Whitehead
August, 1984

General Introduction

The division of the *Economics Education* into sections for teaching 13–16-year-olds and 16–19-year-olds is slightly artificial and limiting. Often the diversity of mental age and capability within a class is as great as the mean difference between classes of different aged students. So users are advised to consult the index carefully: many helpful teaching ideas straddle the age groups into which the *Economics Education* is divided, and teachers will use their professional judgement as to suitability.

The *Economics Education* is a compendium of diverse approaches, and several articles that have been published in *Economics* since 1976–7 deserve to be reprinted here. This co-operation with the professional association of economics teachers and lecturers is much welcomed.

The first two parts of the *Economics Education* are provided for teachers of the 13–16 and 16–19 age ranges respectively. Section 1 describes some courses suitable for classes below the fourth year, various teaching problems and general pedagogical strategies at this level, and a variety of other courses, for the core curriculum, for business studies and consumer education. Section 2 consists of thirteen chapters on the teaching of particular topics and concepts to this age range.

Section 3 ranges from a general diagnosis of A-level syllabus problems to practical tips on making overhead projector transparencies. Economics in non-A-level post-compulsory education is thoroughly discussed, and the special problems that arise in colleges of further education are considered. A variety of general teaching and learning activities are put forward, with particular emphasis on experiential techniques in relation to the world of work. Section 4 has fifteen chapters on teaching specific topics and concepts to this age range.

Section 5 provides advice on textbooks and other resources for all age groups, and how to economise on them. Methods of internal and external assessment are classified. With the growth of school-based curriculum development, the importance of meetings of groups of teachers is emphasised. Comprehensive advice is given on how to run an economics department, and how to use and catalogue a library. Finally, there is a list of useful addresses for economics teachers. Most of the addresses collected together in this chapter are relevant to resources that are described in Sections 2 and 4.

Some errors are bound to remain undetected in such an enormously detailed work, and apologies are given in advance for any that have bypassed the editor's scrutiny. Particular organisations are likely to change their portfolio of free pamphlets, for example. It might be advisable not to ask for specific publications when writing to such bodies, but to state the area of interest, and ask for any relevant materials available.

It is notoriously difficult to classify resources with respect to their suitability for various age groups, so if, for example, the reader is looking for information about what is available on money and banking, it is advisable to refer to *both* the relevant chapters (20 and 44).

Part One
Teaching Economics to the 13–16 Age Range

Introduction to Part One

'I think it is a great mistake to equate Economics with real life'.

Peter Middleton, Permanent Secretary to the Treasury, 1983

Economics is seldom taught as a discrete subject below the fourth year of secondary education. Nevertheless, it has reasonable claims for inclusion in a broad social-science curriculum, and in some schools a gentle introduction in the third year or below is a practical possibility. Richard Dunnill's suggestions should ignite any latent enthusiasm for expanding the school's economics curriculum.

The dissemination of the Economics Education 14–16 Project has revealed an underlying demand for the provision of an economics component in the core curriculum for this age range. Ray Jarvis relates his experience of such a course over the last decade, and suggests a possible *modus operandi*. Within most fourth- and fifth-year economics classes, the range of ability and attainment of literary and numerate skills is now so great that all teachers must find problems in managing such diversity. Linda Thomas and Sara Wall suggest a variety of methods for professional handling of such groups, and stress the importance of flexible forms of classroom organisation. One aspect they cover is the use of worksheets, and this theme is expanded by Alain Anderton who provides practical advice on how they may best be produced. Roger Gomm and Patrick McNeil, in their *Handbook for Sociology Teachers* (p. 237), state (with unintended irony) that 'Writing essays in social science is not the same activity as writing them in English, as students often find to their cost.' Graham Evans and Norman Perrin suggest a strategy for improving written communication skills in economics, based on a pilot project they have run. Such extended written work is often required for projects, and Ian Marcousé shows how students may be weaned from their insecure copying from textbooks by a more experientially based course. Other strategies for reaching out into the community are based on Martin Brimble's development of survey work in his

school neighbourhood. Although his examples are localised, they may easily be paralleled in most areas.

Also in South London, Tony Evans, together with a group of teachers, produced a local economy resource pack, and he indicates how this useful kit might be prepared by similar groups elsewhere. Steve Hodkinson broaches an original idea for employing photographs as stimuli in economics teaching: an example of collaborative work with his PGCE students. He also raises more general questions about the meaning and role of consumer education, and gives some examples of how his approach might be implemented.

Many economics teachers also teach business studies, whether or not they subscribe to Al Capone's view: 'Business? Dat's just de legitimate rackets'. The justified popularity of the recently launched O-level in business studies may be gauged from Ian Chambers's explanation of its rationale, methods, content and examination strategies. He provides an example of a simulation, and a very full and valuable annotated list of resources.

Section 2 on teaching particular topics is again introduced by Richard Dunnill, whose stimulating 'active learning' approach has demonstrated its effectiveness at his inner-city school. Prices and markets are universally taught in economics classes at this level, and Paul Clarke throws up many suggestions for lively treatment. Sarah Wilkinson's chapter entitled 'Auction' should reinforce basic principles. Continuing the 'learning activities' approach, Robert Wilson relates his personal experience of teaching the theory of the firm through simulated decision-making by the students. His fresh, carefully thought-out sequence should be attractive to many teachers. The division of labour is commonly treated, and Peter Leech offers a range of methods from which teachers may select appropriate activities for their classes. Morag Ellingham chooses some innovative tactics, such as 'crossnumbers' and 'wordsearches', to facilitate the teaching of industry. Population is a potentially very rewarding topic, not only for the exemplification of basic economic concepts, but also for the introduction of wider issues. David Butler suggests several approaches that will enhance numeracy skills. Kevin Tinsley discusses an unorthodox module for teaching about trade unions, and appends a comprehensive and most valuable list of resources.

Money and banking is a frequently encountered topic, and David Butler again provides a varied menu of approaches and deals with several common problems. Paul Clarke has modified David McDougall's chapter on

employment, unemployment and inflation from the first edition, and adds some exercises and a simulation. A range of perspectives on international trade issues are provided by Robert Paisley. Richard Thorne offers units of work on public finance, including the use of cartoons, a case study and a role play exercise. Alain Anderton's chapter on the welfare state fills a gap in many textbooks, and suggests a variety of teaching resources.

Section 1: General

1 Economics in the Third Year: Two Approaches
Richard Dunnill

Introduction

At a time when very few schools in Britain teach an economics-related course below the fourth year, and when many schools only offer the subject to A-level, a proposal to introduce economics/social science into the third-year curriculum is very likely at best to be met with a lukewarm, apathetic welcome or, at worst, with downright hostility and accusations of 'empire building' resounding across the staff room!

What follows is in no way an attempt to 'empire build' – it is a plan of action for the introduction of a degree of 'economic literacy' among 13–14-year-olds, based upon the experience of one South London mixed comprehensive in developing two such courses. Teachers obviously need to take into account the individual characteristics of their institution, but it is hoped that this chapter will provide a basis/springboard for developing more economics input into lower-school courses.

Why teach economics at 13 + – stating the case

It is possible to see two sets of arguments in favour of teaching economics at this level. The first set is basically philosophical, and is along the lines of:

The curriculum needs to be related to what happens outside schools ... students need to be given a better understanding

of the economic base of our society, and the importance to Britain of the wealth creating process.[1]

In simpler terms, the school needs to ask itself why history, geography and RE are taught, but not economics? Are we genuinely 'educating' our students if they have little or no knowledge of the economic system, and their place in it?

The second line of argument is more practical, especially if economics is represented on the fourth-year options list. This refers to the need for students to make an informed choice, thus creating the need for some sort of economics course in the third year. 'How can students choose wisely if they do not know what economics is?'

In practice, of course, such discussions need to be carefully undertaken, but encouragingly often a decision is made to introduce a course with an economics input into the curriculum. In the South London school previously mentioned, a social science course was proposed and introduced.

What should be taught? Designing a syllabus: two approaches

Drawing up a new course is a demanding occupation for teachers already overburdened with work. In practice, one of two approaches can develop. Either one or two staff design the course, and the school adopts the ideas and materials they present, or a deliberate decision is made by the teaching team involved to produce co-operatively the new syllabus and materials.

Table 1.1   Third-year social science course I

1 What is social science?	Definitions, justification, practical examples, etc.
2 Methodology	Scientific method, differences from other subjects, is it acceptable?
3 Family (+ Industrial Revolution) 4 Education 5 Work	Institutions, social pressures, socialisation + how they operate in these familiar structures of society, why they exist, how they work on us, how other countries operate, how they are changing and our views on them.
6 Work + the economy (+ Industrial Revolution)	How work 'helps the country'.
7 Circular flow	Classic exposition of economic flows.
8 Savings 9 Taxation 10 Prices	Look at how *we* are affected by these three economic factors, how to choose, how the government uses taxes and finally, a brief and very simplistic view of supply and demand.
11 Production + the firm	A chance to 'launch your own product'.
12 The political system	The curious 'unwritten' system of British politics.
13 Parties + philosophies	Fascism, Marxism, 'Democracy', etc.
14 Pressure groups	CND, BMA, media, unions, CBI, CLA.
15 How to change things	Issues like conservation, war, poverty, unemployment, etc.

First syllabus

Table 1.1 shows the first course drawn up, following the former approach, by two members of staff, and then adopted by the school and used for three years.

Its aims in economics terms
1 To establish a level of basic economic understanding in students.
2 To give potential examination-level students an introduction to such courses.
3 To show students their own part in the economic system, and how it affects them.

The content
This was largely drawn from existing O-level/CSE courses, and 'watered down' a little. Nevertheless, it did cover certain basic concepts and illustrated the essentials of 'practical' economics quite well. Another feature was the ability of sociology, economics and politics to flow into one another, thus creating a genuine social science perspective, not three separate viewpoints.

The methods and resources
The idea was to concentrate on the student's own experience, and then to develop outwards towards general concepts and explanations. Much use was made of free films, free literature, slides, etc., reinforced by structured worksheets. Role play and group project work was also developed, as illustrated by Figure 1.1, where 'launching a new product' is explained. Conventional textbooks at this level proved well-nigh non-existent!

'The Launch Of '?'' as shown in Figure 1.1. is a consolidation unit, to be used after the more abstract ideas of supply and demand, etc. have been covered. It is also an attempt to get the students to think imaginatively as well as to show the 'relevance' of economics in the 'real world'.

Examples of firms and products 'launched' by groups in past years are: 'Zye' – a rock band being marketed to teenagers; a toothbrush with integral toothpaste dispenser; hairpieces for balding teachers!; 'Kilo-Rat' – a firm producing food products from people's unwanted cats, dogs, etc. and many, more conventional, products and services!

All the 'end products' are displayed for the rest of the school to comment upon, and this generates much interest. Each group finally presents a 'prospectus' showing their ideas and achievements.

Assessment
Assessment was by means of a one-hour structured test at the end of each subject unit, and then, following help with 'revision techniques', a full two-hour examination, and coursework assessment of knowledge, understanding and analysis (and originality of thought via project work).

Conclusions on the first course
It is probably fair to say that the style of syllabus design, teaching methods and assessment is typical of many courses in schools. Certainly it proved very popular with students, who felt they were 'getting to grips' with the real world, and enjoying it too! It also seemed to improve performance among the fifth-year examination candidates. However, this scheme is very conventional/predictable, and a feeling that perhaps a more innovative kind of course is necessary may be growing in the reader's mind.

The great temptation, if a course appears to be running smoothly, is to 'leave well alone'. However, the underlying feature of the first course is its very predictability, and perhaps it made too little of the opportunity to provide third-year students with a broader education. Its content, the underlying concepts and its methods were all felt to demand too little from students. Thus the second course was developed, as outlined in Table 1.2.

Economics

The launch of '?'

Instructions:

Working in groups of TWO, THREE OR FOUR, using the work in your books to help, you now have the chance to FORM YOUR OWN COMPANY and LAUNCH YOUR OWN NEW PRODUCT. Follow the flow diagram for guidance, and read the Advice at the end......

1   COMPANY NAME + LOGO......................something catchy.

2   IDEA FOR A NEW PRODUCT.....look for a gap in the market.

3   ROUGH POSSIBLE DESIGNS ....then choose the best.

4   COST THE PRODUCT......exploded diagram showing costs.

5   RAISE CAPITAL.................letters etc. to sources of finance.

6   MARKET RESEARCH........questionnaires etc. for the public.

7   SUPPLY + DEMAND ANALYSIS..showing equilibrium price and quantity.

8   ADVERTISING CAMPAIGN.................posters, scripts, tapes, special offers.

Advice!

At the front of the room, you'll find...

*Rough Paper,

*Large + Small Plain, Writing + Graph Paper.

*Coloured Mounting Paper, Colouring Felts, Glue etc.

Make sure your group ends up with a collection of mounted pieces of work for each of the (8) stages !

GOOD LUCK !

Figure 1.1

Table 1.2 Third-year social science course II

First half-year's syllabus. (The second half-year was spent studying villages/towns/cities in Britain from economic, sociological and theological perspectives.)

1	Speech bubbles	Introduction to the different approaches of sociology, economics and theology.
2	Information on Britain and India and a comparison	A detailed comparison of size, population, religion, GNP and wealth distribution.
3	Film	'An introduction to India'.
4	Clothing	Taking the most immediate differences to be visual, these three units explore the reasons for wearing clothes, how different situations require us to dress differently, and finally show the variety of India and Britain, avoiding stereotype images.
5	Clothing extender	
6	Faces	
7	Using resources	Investigating the two countries' resources from an economic perspective, and seeing how using resources influences people's living. Finally, exploring how and why trade developed between Britain and India, and what happened to that trade as Britain incorporated India into the Empire.
8	Tunic trade	
9	Trade game	
10	Trade – who makes the rules?	
11	Khadi movement	The link between economics, sociology and politics is shown by Gandhi's passive resistance idea, which leads into an examination of belief systems, especially those of Hinduism and Buddhism, reincarnation and the attitude to life fostered by such beliefs.
12	Investigating belief	
13	Bloxham tapes	
14	Samsara/karma	
15/ 16	Caste + Gandhi	Lastly, the caste system is examined from the various social science perspectives to show how it affected/affects India.

Second syllabus (based on similar aims)

The second method of syllabus design was used, involving six staff (sociologists, economists and RE specialists) working co-operatively. The methodology for designing the syllabus and materials was also different, being based on the idea of collaborative learning. This is a learning strategy aiming to encourage students to work together in situations designed to stimulate their abilities, to gather information, consider it and make decisions about it, rather than simply relying on the teacher for everything. Thus the question of 'What should be taught?' was joined by the question 'How should it be taught?' Table 1.2 shows how the syllabus was designed.

Most courses are still content/fact based, as was much of the first course previously mentioned. Concepts, being very generally defined as 'general ideas', should help students to make more sense of a rapidly changing world than mere 'facts'. Moreover, facts are so numerous as to be impossible to cover fully. They are increasing daily, and 'in the time it takes to read this sentence, two hundred pages of book and news material will have added their quota to the world's stock of factual information'.[2]

Facts also rapidly become out of date and inaccurate. A fact-/content-oriented course has no realistic chance of educating students whereas concepts can give a framework from which to interpret the world:

Concepts and content – theme: Britain and India

1 Whole group (six staff) drew up key concepts, lists and definitions, discussed them and decided on a course 'concept base'.
2 Whole group then tied in content relating to these concepts.
3 Finally this was all organised into an order representing how the course would be structured.

All this took three months of weekly meetings. Then the team spent another six months developing:

Methods and resources

1 Group divided into pairs/individuals who produced sample materials for 'their' chosen unit of the course, and 'piloted' them.
2 The group discussed these samples and, after any necessary alterations, adopted them.
3 Finally, materials were duplicated and organised into class sets ready for use.

Again, weekly meetings were required. Thus, the whole process demanded a group of staff willing to spend a year developing a new course and devising new style resources to accompany it. Examples of an economic-based unit is given and explained in Figure 1.2.

Figure 1.2 'Tunic Trade', is a variation on many similar games, but it does show how simple ideas can be adapted to provide a very useful unit in a third-year course. The teachers' guide reminds staff of the reasons behind the game, and acts as a checklist for preparation. The students' guide tries to be both entertaining and rigorous, especially with regard to stealing other groups' resources, and about the quality of the final product. Once again, the discussion following this activity is very valuable, and far better argued than from a group who have simply read a textbook chapter on scarcity, resources, surplus and subsistence.

The theme 'Britain and India' was chosen in conjunction with new geography and history syllabuses being designed at the same time. The need for a multicultural influence across our whole curriculum was one reason for choosing a comparative element, as was the more general feeling that a broader 'world' perspective for education was beneficial. Again, different schools in different areas may well choose differently, but the idea of planning in conjunction with other subject teachers is certainly worth considering!

TUNIC TRADE   Teachers' Guide......

✱ AIM....   to reinforce the concepts of:SUBSISTENCE SURPLUS
to reinforce/introduce the concepts of: SCARCITY RESOURCES
SPECIALISATION/DIVISION OF LABOUR

✱ MATERIALS.....

Surplus Group

1   Lots of Paper
2   2 Pencils + Sharpener
3   2 Rulers
4   2 Round Objects
5   8 Pairs Scissors
6   2 Felt Pens

Subsistence Group

1   Lots of Paper
2   1 pencil (Stub!)
3   1 Short Ruler
4   2 Felt Pens

✱ PLAYING THE GAME.....

(i) Split the group into 2 '½s' according to the previous activity.....

(ii) Give-out Tunic Trade and Tallis Tunic giving groups 5 mins for problem solving. Meanwhile, place Resources at each end of the room..help solve any obvious problems.

(iii) Start the game.....give them a certain time.....15 mins minimum.....be strict about accepting PERFECT tunics.

(iv) After the game, use the follow-up sheet What Happened and Why to find-out the reasons for the success of the surplus group.

TUNIC TRADE !

✱ Your group is a FIRM producing COTTON TUNICS, using the RESOURCES provided.....
1   NATURAL RESOURCES.....(PAPER)
2   MAN MADE RESOURCES.....(PENCILS, SCISSORS, RULERS,ETC.)
3   HUMAN RESOURCES.....(YOURSELVES!)

✱ Your aim is to make the most money, by producing as many HIGH QUALITY TUNICS as possible, in a given time, and selling them to the MERCHANT (YOUR TEACHER).

✱ The price of a PERFECT SHIRT is £10, for an IMPERFECT SHIRT, £1, so it pays to take care !

REMEMBER ! !

✱ An EXACT COPY of your perfect shirt is needed to make £10.
✱ NO STEALING other groups' resources, or using your own pencils etc. is allowed!
✱ Work together to make the most tunics.
✱ The MERCHANT'S decision is FINAL!

GOOD LUCK

GET WEAVING YOU LOT____!!

Figure 1.2

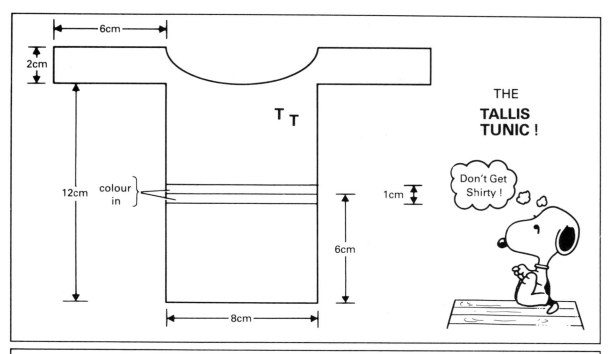

'TALLIS TUNIC' ......
What Happened - and Why?

✱ Why did the SURPLUS GROUP WIN?

....
....
....
....
....
....
....
....

✱ What problems did the SUBSISTENCE GROUP have ?

....
....
....
....
....
....
....
....

✱ Does this sort of thing really happen? If so, give examples of it.

....
....
....
....

Figure 1.2

The methods, using collaborative learning, encourage the use of pairs/small groups to handle data, understand and analyse them, and finally to discuss them, often with little need to refer directly to the teacher. This does not imply the 'redundancy' some may fear; instead, it allows more individual help to be given by the teacher.

Assessment

Assessment of the course is by means of a type of 'Profile' assessment, using a 'Standard Test' to examine knowledge, understanding, analysis and creativity. Then subject staff assess more subjectively, based on their knowledge of the student, on the following criteria: self-discipline, presentation, co-operation with peers, self-understanding, application.

This mode of assessment, which is used again in the third-year curriculum, is used because we felt that having spent a long time debating and reforming our *input* into the third-year curriculum, we needed to devote equal attention to assessment of *output*. A vaguely set exam and a generalised report seemed too undemanding an assessment of such a new syllabus.

Conclusions on the second course

This is radically different from the first syllabus. It makes very different and much greater demands on staff and students, but is also, dare it be suggested, more enjoyable!

After nearly two years of operation, the course is proving quite successful but, as might be expected, it has also thrown up several problems. New staff have found it difficult to adjust to, being so different to conventional courses. Existing staff find the production of so much original material very demanding. The excessive use of paper and written resources is also criticised. Finally, the students need time to adjust to a new style of learning, and the teacher may find this difficult to cope with.

Nevertheless, in terms of stimulating ideas and interest from students, the course has been very successful, and teachers are aware that they too are both more thoughtful and more enthusiastic about their work in the classroom.

Next year the syllabus is being reviewed, and no doubt revised in places in the light of experience, but any school and any economics teacher will find this style of teaching interesting, stimulating and even revealing, while students seem to gain a real interest in economics, as well as a much improved level of understanding.

Conclusion

The place of economics in the third-year curriculum must be argued and developed in different ways for different schools, but a strong case is capable of being made! Many types of syllabus, materials and learning activities can be devised which will have beneficial effects upon both staff and students. What has been outlined above is simply one line of development, but increasingly other schools are developing their own courses, and finding the experience a useful one!

The collaborative learning ideas are very demanding of the teacher, especially if the ethos of the school is very traditional. However, the benefits from stimulating students to begin really thinking for themselves are worth a little effort.

Over all, however, it is the development of more basic economic literacy among our students that is the important thing, whatever the type of course used. Teachers and students benefit, as do examination results[3]... why not try it?

Notes and references

1 DES/Welsh Office, *The School Curriculum* (HMSO, 1981) p. 16.
2 Elliott, G., *Teaching for Concepts* (Collins, 1976).
3 Sutton, C., (ed.) *Communicating in the Classroom* (Hodder & Stoughton, 1981).

2   An Economics Course for the Core Curriculum
Ray Jarvis

Introduction

Economics has been part of the core curriculum at my school since the early 1970s. The school is a three-form entry grammar school catering only for boys in the top 25 per cent ability range.

Originally economics was offered in the pre-O-level year (fourth year) for one period (40 minutes) a week. Various considerations were at work here including the genuine desire to give *all* students *some* experience of the subject before the daunting prospect of subject options. One period a week, however, proved to be unsatisfactory,

Table 2.1

	Autumn term	Spring term	Summer term	Periods per week
Fourth year	Core curriculum course ——————————→		O-level course covering items which are also of value to non O-level candidates, e.g. public finance.	3
Fifth year	O-level ————————————————→		Revision	5

mainly because it gave so little time for any detailed work, but also because continuity was difficult to sustain, particularly if the solitary period was lost for some reason. Alongside all the other subjects on three or more periods, economics appeared to be a timetable filler despite efforts made to devise an effective course.

Following curriculum reorganisation, economics was offered, compulsorily, for two periods a week from the mid-1970s until 1982–3. In September 1983, when a very limited option scheme was introduced, economics remained in the core[1] and was extended to three periods a week. At the end of this pre-O-level year, option choices are made for the final O-level year. Unlike many schools, a full option scheme is not introduced until the fifth (and O-level examination) year. This has implications for the type of course offered in the 'core curriculum course' (see later). This curriculum programme is summarised in Table 2.1.

This should be compared with the position in many other schools where fourth and fifth years are spent in option groups, often four periods in each year, but where economics students have had little or no experience of the subject before making their option choice.[2]

Current core curriculum: background thinking

Introduction

Implicit in the establishment of economics in the core is the belief that some sort of economics understanding is important. The justification for economics study in the core or in an option scheme has been explored elsewhere. Arguments in favour range from intellectual (improving analytical skills) to the practical (helping to prepare people for work). Recently, as part of the current educational debate, various official documents have stressed the need for economic awareness as an essential part of every school leaver's education.[3] However, once accepted in the curriculum, the most urgent question then becomes: What to teach? What sort of economics and to what level should it be taken? Again, various writers have expressed views on this question.[4]

At this school, students progress through a pre-O-level course (about two terms) to O-level (about four terms) and on to A-level (six terms). The pre-O-level core course is a self-contained unit which serves as an introduction to economics thinking for students who decide to drop the

subject at option time and as a base for further work for O- and A-level candidates.

In devising a core course, a major handicap was a lack of an adequate textbook. In our experience, students obtain reassurance from the possession of a course book. Most of the current books below A-level tend to be mainly designed for O-level exams. The attention given to basic ideas in economics is rather limited or, at most, fragmented across the whole book and tucked away inside chapters that are of marginal value to a student meeting the subject for the first time. One book worthy of special mention is F. Davies's *Starting Economics*. His statistics are rather dated and his stories rather far-fetched, but in a very real way he has managed to convey basic economics ideas simply and effectively. Used carefully, there is much helpful material in this book. The experience here (with a selective group of students, remember) is a willing acceptance of much of Davies's inventions. Other sources have been used, including video programmes and bank publications. For applied economics, students are supplied with *10 × Economics* by Peter Donaldson. Again this needs to be used carefully and selectively at this level.

The main bulk of the material used in the course has been teacher produced, supplemented where appropriate by extracts from books or viewing video programmes.[5] Charts and diagrams are used quite freely.[6] New resources[7] are being developed at this level and the hope is that they can be incorporated in the course outlined below.

Objectives of the course

1 To provide early experience of economics analysis. To begin to develop the 'economics way' of analysing a problem by showing that alternatives do exist, that they involve costs (open and hidden), and that the essential choices that have to be made spring from the scarcity of resources.[8]

2 To harness the student's own experience in an attempt at demonstrating and explaining the basic nature of the economic problem.

3 To provide a basis for further study which can be built upon at O- and A-level.

4 To increase awareness of the economic world which will be of some value to everyone as 'citizens'.

5 To give *some* indication to all students about the nature of the subject, vital if informed option choices are to be made. For students who decide to drop the

subject it is hoped that benefit would have been obtained from objectives 1, 2 and 4 above.

Above all, the objective is to establish a framework/technique for analysing *any* economic problem in an effective way. With such basic equipment, deeper/more specialised study of particular aspects of an economy can be undertaken at a later date: a base would have been established.

The core curriculum course

This is divided into two parts: 1 *introductory course* lasting about sixty periods of 40 minutes each, and 2 *O-level course* taking into account that about half of the students will not progress to the full O-level course in the fifth year.

1   The introductory course

This is the main part of the fourth-year work. It is intended to be a self-contained unit serving as a base for O-level and A-level work and as an introductory survey for students who will later drop the subject before O-level proper.

The main features of the course are (i) a limited use of textbooks, (ii) regular use of students' own experience and local information, (iii) use of charts, video programmes and recent national statistics, and (iv) provision of a basic course supplemented by an applied economics course.

At the heart of the basic course is an attempt to explain economics as a study of the choices that spring from the scarcity of resources. Items 1–4 in the seven-point programme are all related to this central theme. Items 5–7 pull the strands together and round off the introductory survey (see Table 2.2).

Table 2.2

Course item	Comments
1 *What is economics?* Class discussion plus teacher comments, e.g. scarcity and choice; Real and monetary – difference; list of 'economics' items; Davies, ch. 1, plus few of his questions; production options (see over); a few definitions including a *brief* look at Robbins. *Appendix:* The Factors of Production	An obvious starting point for any new subject – What is the purpose/meaning of the subject? The notion of scarce resources and unlimited wants is introduced very early with liberal use of family, school, local and national examples.
2 *Scarcity and choice* The basic economic problem. Opportunity cost: definition and examples. Production Possibility Curve; Robinson Crusoe as an example of Opportunity Cost (fishing net).	Students prepare their own examples of opportunity cost. Production Possibility Curve is introduced and both are linked to Davies's Crusoe Story.
3 *Five basic questions* Introduction: rich/poor countries; planned and market economies. All face same problems. What to produce (explain role of market and government). How much to produce (N.B. Margin). How to produce (labour intensive, etc.). For whom (share out of national income – labour and capital, etc.). Where? (Harvey's *Elementary Economics* is useful for 3 and 4 below.)	3 and 4 look at the way *all* economies face the same problems as a direct consequence of scarcity. By contrast, these same economies all deal with these problems in different ways. All are unique. The possible roles of markets and government administrative decision-making in resource allocation are stressed. Russia and the UK are taken as case studies.
4 *Various economic systems* Introduction: unique nature of each economy and broad division between planned–mixed–free. *Planned economy:* Russia (co-operate with Russian Dept). *Mixed economy:* UK – a survey using Lloyds Economic Profile (plus a study of the local economy).	

Table 2.2. continued

Course item	Comments
Foundations of wealth Ten video programmes illustrating basic economic problem, scarcity, opportunity cost, 'surplus' as a key to development; division of labour; living standards; barter; trade; money; markets; types of economy. Watch programmes...summary...exercises (Davies, ch. 3).	Ten video programmes, *Foundations of Wealth*, round off items 1–4, illustrating many of the ideas above and introducing the idea of economic development.

5 *Basic ideas in economics*
See Mini-chart: 'Basic Ideas in Economics'
Seven ideas:
    O/cost
    Market
    Specialisation   (boys prepare own
    Margin   chart with assistance)
    Circular flow
    Time preference
    Efficiency

Item 5 attempts to extract the main ideas in economics. Most have been met by now and it really only involves drawing them together.

6 *Micro- and macroeconomics*
Difference between them – examples of each (table).
Example of microeconomics:
    Supply and demand (useful background for O-level)
    Analyse demand (Davies, ch. 5)
    Analyse supply (Davies, ch. 6)
    Determination of price
    Why prices change
    How it works: CAP
    Ref: Davies, chs. 5 and 6
Example of Macroeconomics:
    Keynes and unemployment (useful background for O-level)
    Do a detailed circular flow model.

Item 6 shows economics analysis in action with a more thorough study of supply and demand and macroeconomics than previously attempted.

7 *History of economic thought*
Brief review from
Adam Smith ('invisible hand') → Ricardo → Marx → Marshall → Keynes → Friedman

Item 7 helps to put a historical perspective on the subject.

The introductory course is completed by adding an applied/descriptive element. The aim here is to discuss, perhaps for the first time, some of the economic issues of the day, within a specifically economics format. The hope is that some constructive comment and insight can be provided.

Applied economics would have been introduced in the 'mixed economy case study'; *What is economics?* would have provoked comment on current economic problems; and students are always asking questions about the economy. In addition to this, a deliberate attempt is made to encourage thinking about current issues (i) by asking students to present 'five-minute' talks on selected topics, and (ii) by using *10 × Economics* TV programmes and selected chapters from the accompanying book.

There is plenty of scope for development here. At this school, several weeks are given over to an applied economics approach serving as a convenient link with the O-level course proper.

Comments
Figure 2.1 is introduced very early. The comments inside the map of Great Britain can be used as a summary of economic activity.

The key point is to encourage students to begin to classify economic activity. A typical exercise would be for them to develop their own examples inside an empty sixteen-box framework provided beforehand.

Every economic activity which involves PRODUCTION (primary, secondary or tertiary) must result in the production of INVESTMENT or CONSUMPTION GOODS or SERVICES. Every resource which is claimed in the UK (by households, firms, governments or foreigners) is used for consumption or investment (goods or services). In addition every good or service (investment or consumption) must have been made by PRIVATE or PUBLIC operations and must be intended for DOMESTIC USE or for EXPORT.

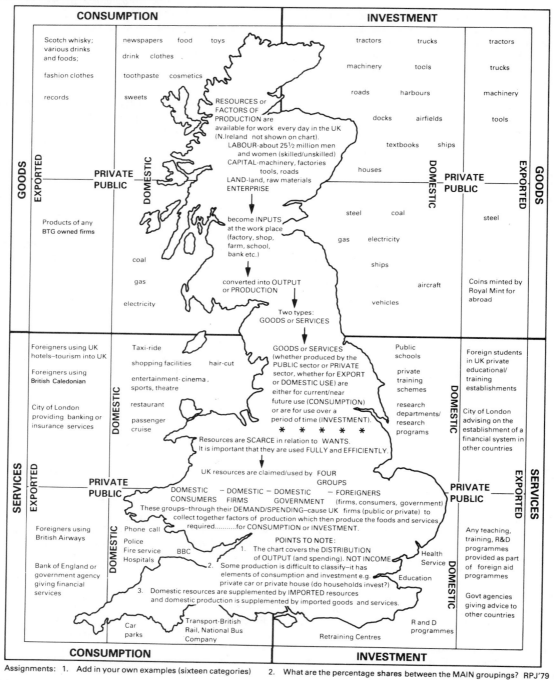

Assignments: 1. Add in your own examples (sixteen categories)   2. What are the percentage shares between the MAIN groupings? RPJ'79

Figure 2.1 Production options

2 The O-level course as part of the pre-O-level year work

This is an attempt at achieving a happy compromise between (i) need to begin the study of mainstream course material, (ii) the need to show further how early analysis can be applied to particular problems, and (iii) the need to give some general background to the problems all students will face as 'citizens'. It is hoped that such an approach will be of interest to potential O-level candidates and non-O-level students. Two topics are studied: economic management and public finance.

Economic management. The main aim here is to convey knowledge of how a macroeconomic system works and how it breaks down, as shown by unemployment and inflation. Both problems are considered quite fully. The possible role of government in dealing with such problems is then considered. In addition, the question of economic growth is studied, drawing particularly upon the *Foundations of Wealth* series.

Public finance. Analysis of the weapons of economic management raise the question of fiscal policy. A study of public finance is then undertaken, paying particular attention to the latest statistics and the most recent budget changes. Care is taken to explain the role of public expenditure and taxation with an attempt made to describe how some of the most important taxes work. All students can calculate simple income tax cases.

Conclusion

The course outlined above has evolved over the last decade. It is subject to constant change as new ideas and new material become available. Both the pre-O-level course and the O-level course were revised at the beginning of the current academic year (1983–4).

At the heart of the course is an attempt to show the economist's way of thinking about a problem. Much time is devoted to a specific study of scarcity and the problems connected with it. It is our belief that this is an important first stage in economics teaching. We have resisted the temptation to dash headlong into a 'topic-by-topic' approach to the subject. (This is left to O and A-level.) An attempt is made to study scarcity and its implications from various angles. The question of choice, how it is exercised and the costs resulting are central to this course. Clearly, real world, topical issues are relevant here. The course offered attempts to link the basic thinking above with real-world problems drawn from students' local experience and their knowledge of national problems. This happens throughout the introductory course. In addition, time is especially earmarked for a study of 'real-world' problems before the O-level course proper begins.

Response to the course has been quite enthusiastic, reflected in voluminous homework assignments, interesting student talks, out-of-period chats and an increasing number of boys choosing the subject at O-level.

End-of-term exams at Christmas and in July show that the majority have managed to cope with the course and some have developed their economics technique significantly. (The current courses – pre-O-level and O-level – have recently undergone changes (reflected in this chapter) so it is too early to identify any noticeable alteration in examination results.)

Notes and references

1 Again, the desire to give *all* students some glimpse of the subject was an important factor here.
2 There are distinct problems involved in getting economics into the core. Some headteachers are unconvinced of its merit and subject teachers are opposed to a loss of time to make room for the subject. The advice given here is to seize every opportunity as it arises; once allocated one period a week, a base has been established. When it was found in my school that one period a week was unsatisfactory a case was prepared for two periods. The headteacher – the most influential person in determining curriculum content – was finally won over when evidence was supplied from a variety of sources showing that economics provision elsewhere was generally much larger.
3 Recent studies/publications commenting on the role of economics in the curriculum:
   (a) Government documents:
       Education in Schools: A Consultative Document (HMSO, 1977)
       Curriculum 11–16: Working Papers by HM Inspectorates (DES, 1977)
       A Framework for the School Curriculum (HMSO, 1980)
       The School Curriculum (HMSO, 1981)
       17+: A New Qualification (DES, 1982)
   (b) In addition, various other writers have considered the value of economics education, including Oliver, J. M., *The Principles of Teaching Economics* (Heinemann Educational Books, 1973) ch. 4; Whitehead D. (ed.) *Curriculum Development in Economics* (Heinemann Educational Books, 1974) ch. 11; Lee, N., and Entwistle, H., 'Economics education and educational theory', in Lee, N. (ed.) *Teaching Economics*, 2nd ed. (Heinemann Educational Books, 1975) ch. 3.
   (c) The Economics Association has published two reports: *The Contribution of Economics to General Education* (December 1977) and *Economics in the Framework of the School Curriculum* (June 1980).
4 See Holley, B., 'The place of economics in the secondary school curriculum', in Whitehead, D. (ed.) *Curriculum Development in Economics* (Heinemann Educational Books, 1974) ch. 6; Christie, D., 'Economics in the early stages of secondary education', in Lee, N. (ed.) *Teaching Economics* (Heinemann Educational Books, 1975), ch. 10.
5 References useful for the pre-O-level course as outlined in the article: Davies, F., *Starting Economics* (Hulton, revised 1979); Donaldson, P., *10×Economics* (Penguin, 1982); Harvey, J., *Elementary Economics*, 5th edn. (Macmillan, 1984). Two free hand-outs containing useful statistics: *Economic Progress Report* (CSO) and Lloyds Bank's *An Economic Profile of Britain*. Video programmes: *10×Economics* normally shown in the autumn (ITV) and *The Foundations of Wealth* (available from Viscom), a series of ten programmes. Two other books that could prove useful are Christie, D., and Scott, A., *Economics in Action*

(Heinemann Educational Books, 1977) and Thorne, R., and Leeming, C., *Introducing Economics* (Economics Association, 1981). There is also a bibliography available: *An Annotated Bibliography of Pupils' Books in Economics for 14–16 year olds* (Economics Association, 1981).

6   See Chapters 4 and 31.
7   Probably the 14–16 project is the most notable newcomer. See Chapter 9.
8   See Thomas, L., 'Economics for all', *Times Educational Supplement*, 3 February 1984, p. 37.

3   Teaching Mixed-ability Groups

Linda Thomas and Sara Wall

Introduction

Do you find yourself teaching in circumstances that are imposed on you because it is the policy of your school to organise teaching groups without reference to ability and are these groups making excessive demands on you? Or have you instigated mixed-ability grouping in the school in which you teach because you regard it as an educational ideal? An observer might say that if the former, you are a teacher facing the tough reality of teaching mixed-ability groups, if the latter, an idealist giving little thought to the organisational difficulties of mixed-ability teaching.

Will mixed-ability teaching work in these circumstances?

It is certainly difficult successfully to teach mixed-ability groups without some appreciation of their educational value, even if this does not extend to conviction. The debate about mixed-ability grouping and teaching is amorphous and often conducted on an emotional level. It is therefore important to clarify and examine some of the more pertinent issues.

First, consider the foundation for the existence of homogeneous ability groups. As teachers we operate within schools that are increasingly pressurised by different sectors of the community to organise the day's work around the requirements of an examination system. The system uses conventional norm referencing, encourages the belief that success in examinations is the ultimate achievement, ensures that the majority of students fail and that they carry this label with them during and after school. It may be argued that individual teachers and schools have to accept this situation even if they are convinced first that most people emerge as

failures not because of personal inadequacies but because failure is a feature that is built into the design of the system, and second that students are not fulfilled in their educational needs if they must rebuild their self-esteem on leaving school.

But schools cannot evade all responsibility for their actions by reference to the long shadow of the examination system. On the one hand, it is possible for schools to exaggerate its importance, to allow its existence to dominate their curriculum and organisation, to adopt Draconian methods and structures which are more severe and more restrictive than any examination system and, whether by design or accident, to promote values and beliefs such as the following:

1   Learning and achievement are determined exclusively by ability and are not influenced by student motivation or the expectations of teachers and students.
2   Effective learning owes little to student interest but is the result of rote memorisation by students and drill and practice as teaching methods.
3   Academic pursuits are the province of the few.
4   The kind of learning that is involved in mastering snooker skills and the kind of excitement that is generated by it is different in kind to academic learning. Therefore it is irresponsible to apply to the second case the kind of teaching methods that work in the former case, e.g. student participation and involvement. Nothing will be gained, and students will become agitated and resentful when stability is threatened.

On the other hand, it is also possible for schools to mitigate the effects of the examination system by insisting that curriculum design, group organisation and teaching methods reflect a different set of beliefs. It is in this context that mixed-ability grouping is often advocated since it refutes the notions about learning, ability and achievement that are set out above.

Some degree of understanding of, if not commitment to, this rationale may be a necessary condition for successful mixed-ability teaching. But it is not sufficient. Romantic ideals are no substitute for proper planning and a realistic approach. It is as easy for meaningless activities and ineffective learning to occur in mixed-ability classrooms as in any other. No amount of conviction can justify the existence of situations where individual needs are ignored or where worksheets are used as a last resort in order to keep students relatively quiet. If mixed-ability teaching is to be made to work, it is important to consider practical matters such as methods and classroom organisation.

What kind of methods could the teacher use?

A great deal of work has already been done to develop, refine and extend different teaching methods, and this has occurred in response to pressure from many sources. For example, some teachers of 'homogeneous' groups have come to the conclusion that every class is mixed in composition – even the members of a class in a grammar school where streaming takes place will not always have their individuality removed – and that each individual contributes to the unique character and behaviour of the group as a whole. They have therefore been among the pioneers of methods which, because they take account of individual differences, are also appropriate in mixed-ability situations. For example, the suggestions and methods contained in some of the other chapters in this *Handbook*,[1] by actively involving each individual student, make the content of the lessons *accessible* to all students.

The most significant contribution in this context is the work of the second phase of the Economics Education 14–16 Project which is now based at Manchester University. The report of the first phase of the Project[2] recommended that, 'Particular attention should be paid to the needs of pupils for whom current provision is least satisfactory, viz: . . . pupils of average and below average ability.'

The members of the project team and of the teacher groups who designed the exemplar materials have interpreted this directive in the broadest way possible. Each unit of work contains stimulus material that is within reach of students of all abilities, while extension work suggestions cover a great breadth and depth of content. For example, the unit entitled *Consumers* uses two contrasting photographs as stimulus material:

> to stimulate reactions on the part of pupils, leading to discussion and associated pupil exercises about human wants and the connection between the satisfaction of these wants, the level of purchasing power and state provision of goods and services (introduction).

One of the extension work suggestions involves analysis of the differences between necessities and luxuries in different economic systems.

The units illustrate a wide range of different teaching methods. For example, *Prices, Price of a Perm* and *The Ice Cream Factory* use case study material; *Production Record Sheet, Journey to Work, Tiny Atom Radio, Community Expenditure* and *Land Use Planning in the Local Community* contain role-play exercises; *Alternatives, Lamb* and *Andy's Car* demonstrate that slides may be used imaginatively in different context; *Journey to Work* and *What is Work?* use videos; *The Rate for the Job* includes a simulation exercise; *Accident, Vandalism, Costs and Benefits, Wanting, Wages, Rate for the Job, Two Workers* and *Moving About* employ various kinds of visual stimulus material; *Price of Pop* and *Tiny Atom Radio* include surveys; *Lamb* describes a field visit, *Public Spending* and *Local Authority Rates* are based on textbook material.

The units also perform another function. They are not prescriptive; instead they contain suggestions for use of the stimulus materials. They are thus particularly useful for teachers of mixed-ability classes who wish to adapt the resources and materials to the needs of their own groups.

What forms of classroom organisation are effective in teaching mixed-ability groups?

1   It is possible to organise mixed-ability groups so that individual students work independently of one another. At best, this fosters individualised learning techniques, in which tasks are suited to the needs, abilities and achievements of each student. However, this form of organisation is rarely used in economics classrooms for various reasons. First, it depends on the availability of structured programmes of work such as the mathematics SMILE[3] scheme which allows students to progress at their own pace. Secondly, it demands a degree of interaction between student and teacher that is difficult if not impossible to sustain, especially if, as is the case in economics, structured programmes are not readily available. Thirdly, it reduces opportunities for students to interact collectively to explore a problem or issue and to learn from one another.

Teachers are therefore far more likely to define independently organised mixed-ability teaching as all students being exposed to the same work at the same time. At its worst this takes the form of the aptly named 'death by a thousand worksheets'[4] syndrome through which students are kept occupied (and relatively quiet) on routine meaningless tasks.

The strict application of some organisational criteria may be sufficient to prevent such distortion:

(a) the rules that apply to the use of worksheets are important enough to merit separate treatment (see next section);

(b) students should not be expected to work

independently for long stretches of time; they should be allowed to work in a variety of settings;

(c) independent work should be used only when it is appropriate, for example for routine practice of specific skills, when an individual student's knowledge and skills are being assessed, when the stimulus material is such that it is legitimate to expect individual students to give different responses, when students are expected to work with the material in a convergent way or when it is necessary to record the results of other activities;

(d) if students are asked to work independently, they should, whenever possible, be given opportunities to compare responses with other students.

2 It is also possible to organise mixed-ability classes into groups. This is particularly appropriate if students are asked to respond to stimulus material and classroom experiences in creative, exploratory or open-ended ways. Indeed, in many cases it is obligatory, e.g. if a role play or simulation exercise is being used. But it is also a useful technique if case study or other stimulus material is the focus for a lesson.

Less homogeneous small groups are also successful since students of different ability levels value and learn from one another's views and ideas. Teachers who successfully organise mixed-ability classes into small groups suggest that:

(a) activities must be carefully structured to challenge and involve students;

(b) steps should be taken to prevent dominant students from directing the work of a whole group. Students could be asked first to work out their own responses independently of other group members and then to discuss in groups; roles could be assigned by the teacher rather than by students, etc.

(c) it is important to encourage students to record the results of their activity. Therefore, since writing is an extremely frustrating business for many of them, other more imaginative ways should be explored. For example, groups could record results on computer printouts, supplementing these with a few extra comments; they could be asked to prepare a short report of their work for presentation to the rest of the class at the end of the lesson;[5] they could take up some of the ideas on the use of photographs in Chapter 9.

3 It is also possible for a mixed-ability class to work as a unit and to participate in a class lesson. Indeed, this is a natural form of organisation for the presentation of some stimulus material, for example, videos, films, examples, problem situations and tape slide sequences in which the tape presents information that is deliberately different from the evidence on the slides (see Chapter 51). It is also sometimes useful to engage the whole class in reporting or recording activity and in discussion of the results of individual or small-group work.[6]

What about the worksheets?

Worksheets are frequently regarded as being synonymous with mixed-ability teaching. The previous section argues that this need not be the case, and that other activities can and should be adopted since a single activity becomes dull and ultimately destructive, whether it involves working on a production line or doing endless worksheets. Indeed, HMI noted that, 'a diet of worksheets was observed to lead to growing boredom'.[7]

Such a conclusion was no doubt reached because:

1 Little or no interaction is allowed or expected between students while they work on worksheets.

2 Interaction between student and teacher is minimal, as the teacher distributes the sheets at the start of the lesson, and then goes around the classroom assisting those students who request help.

3 Worksheets tend to be similar in composition – a series of questions that students work through during the course of the lesson.

On the other hand, if properly used and imaginatively designed to incorporate a variety of tasks, worksheets are an important tool in any teacher's repertoire. In order to ensure that they are of a sufficiently high standard, it is necessary to consider the types of tasks that worksheets can perform, and to determine a general set of criteria that can be applied to assess the potential effectiveness of any worksheet.

The following are types of worksheet that do not adopt the conventional format, and are constructed so that their use can be dovetailed into many of the activities examined in the previous section. A worksheet does not necessitate individual learning; indeed, it can be used during group work or to draw the class together as a whole.

1 The basic structure of a flow diagram can be used to consolidate key words and ideas at the end of a topic. The teacher can direct the activity, but the boxes are left blank for the individual student to write as much as she feels is required.

2 A standardised table or the axes of a graph allow most students to attempt the compilation of data that they have calculated in an easier disintegrated form. An example of this appears in the Economics Education 14–16 Project unit entitled *Price of a Perm*. This prevents students becoming sidetracked by the task of drawing tables or devising appropriate scales on graphs; this is not to say that acquisition of such skills is not important but, in association with other activities, the task may become unnecessarily complex.

3 A record sheet (Table 3.1) can be used during a role playing exercise. After being given background information on the proposed siting of a chemical processing plant, students are divided into pairs with one assuming the role of an industrialist and the other an environmentalist. The teacher then specifies a time limit for each pair to discuss the issues from the view-

Table 3.1   Record sheet

Should the chemical processing plant be built?

1	As an industrialist/environmentalist, the three main points of my argument were: a) b) c) My opponent was an industrialist/environmentalist. The three main points of his/her argument were: a) b) c)

2	As an industrialist/environmentalist, the three main points of my argument were: a) b) c) My opponent was an industrialist/environmentalist. The three main points of his/her argument were: a) b) c)

3	If I were a town planner, and I had to make the final decision, I WOULD/WOULD NOT allow the chemical plant to be built because:

Table 3.2   Wordsquare

Location of industry

F	A	P	E	S	F	P	F	O	O	T	L	O	O	S	E
I	N	E	R	T	I	A	I	R	A	R	M	O	M	T	X
O	S	N	N	E	R	B	R	I	V	A	A	R	A	E	T
F	I	Z	C	T	C	D	M	E	O	N	R	I	N	E	E
I	N	O	L	T	E	A	A	T	S	S	K	E	U	F	R
R	D	P	Q	A	R	R	E	W	O	P	E	N	O	S	N
F	U	E	L	K	B	Z	P	A	B	O	T	T	R	E	A
P	S	I	E	A	C	O	O	R	T	R	R	E	E	V	L
S	T	T	B	S	N	Z	U	X	I	T	A	D	M	I	I
O	R	T	E	N	T	D	T	R	V	S	W	O	U	T	T
T	Y	R	T	S	U	D	N	I	L	E	E	T	S	N	I
R	A	W	M	A	T	E	R	I	A	L	S	Z	N	E	E
I	N	T	E	R	O	L	A	T	I	P	A	C	O	C	S
E	G	O	V	E	R	N	M	E	N	T	N	O	C	N	O
W	X	L	O	C	A	T	I	O	N	E	R	T	I	I	E

Market	Industry	Firm	Labour
Raw materials	Consumer	Government	Footloose
Incentives	Transport	Fuel	Steel industry
Location	Inertia	Externalities	Enterprise zone
Power	Capital	Land	Market oriented

point of their respective roles. After this, section 1 of the worksheet can be filled in. The process is then repeated with students adopting the opposite role, and if possible in new pairs, after which section 2 of the worksheet is completed. A public inquiry is initiated, with the roles of chairperson, industrialist and environmentalist assigned to three students. The length of the proceedings is set by the teacher, followed by questions from the floor being asked via the chair. Assuming the role of town planner, each student reaches an independent decision and records it in section 3. A vote can then be taken to find the actual outcome, and to illustrate that some individuals will disagree with the overall group decision. The use of the record sheet helps to overcome the difficulty in role plays of processing the abundance of information and ideas that emerge, while maintaining the spontaneity of the activity. Some students will reflect on their discussion, to draw out and summarise the main points, while others will be writing down a few words; all, though, will keep some form of record.

4   A wordsquare is an adaptation of a classification exercise (Table 3.2). It encourages the recognition of vocabulary in different settings, and the improvement in spelling of economic terminology. It can be used at various stages in a topic. At the beginning of a topic it allows students to familiarise themselves with key words. The activity can be pursued in small groups which will assist those with reading difficulties and encourage co-operation between students.

The feature that these worksheets have in common with the conventional worksheet is active participation by the student. The major difference is that they include activities that require student–teacher or student–student interaction. They therefore illustrate that completion of a worksheet need not be an isolated activity.

While a variety of worksheets will help to prevent boredom, a multiplicity of activities alone is insufficient. In addition, each worksheet should fulfil certain specified minimum requirements, which necessitate a threefold examination – first, of the reasons for using the worksheet, secondly, of the expectations that the teacher has of students, and thirdly, of the kind of features that will permit its effective use.

The reasons for using a worksheet will in the main be determined by circumstances that are unique to each particular class. However, there are two potential dangers:

1   The regular use of worksheets as the basis of a lesson is analogous to the perpetual lecturing of grammar-school students, the rationale being that it is expected and accepted by them. Work executed independently over a prolonged period provides little stimulus and a paucity of original thought. The 'one worksheet each lesson' trap means that the heterogeneity of the group is not recognised because some students are not stretched, while others lose motivation as they rarely complete work in the time designated. Thus students fulfil their own expectations and those of others instead of being involved in a variety of activities that provide motivation and help to promote the latent skills which all students possess.

2   Class control is an important aspect of teaching, and worksheets are often regarded as the panacea in a

disruptive classroom. A major cause of disruption is boredom, which will not be eliminated by bombarding students with a plethora of worksheets. At its worst this means that the work has little educational justification and the worksheet is being used purely as a means of social control. Even then problems arise, since the communication to be allowed will need an acceptable noise level to be specified and enforced. If such compromises are necessary to maintain a degree of class control, they may act as a distraction to work and put students in a position to usurp the ultimate control of the teacher. It is therefore dubious whether in the long run worksheets are an effective form of class control.

The use of worksheets as an integral part of a broader teaching programme will not immediately transform learning in the classroom. It is impossible to provide a foolproof list of recommendations that will guarantee successful use of worksheets, since the crux of mixed-ability teaching is the recognition of the unique needs of the group and of the individuals within it. However, the aim of the teacher is to ensure that the work is accessible to students, and the consideration of certain practical criteria will permit this:

1   The immediate potential barrier to accessibility is the level of language adopted. There will undoubtedly be the need to include an element of economic jargon but it is important to realise that it can obscure relatively simple concepts. General readability can be checked by examining the length of sentences, the use of clauses, sophistication of vocabulary and the number of syllables in words. In addition, data is frequently used as a means of communication in economics, but judicious use is essential. Collation, interpretation and presentation of data is a skill that is easier to foster using figures that do not run to six decimal places.

2   The inclusion of instructions on worksheets is usually to be avoided as they frequently go unread. The class will be drawn together at the start of the lesson if instructions are given orally (they can also be written on the board). After having ensured that the majority of the class understands the procedure, the teacher is then able to deal with personal difficulties on an individual basis.

3   In order to facilitate learning, the teacher aims to provide work that is new, appealing and stretches the student. A balance must be achieved since it is not productive constantly to bombard students with unfamiliar situations. To promote learning, the inclusion of a familiar feature, particularly a previously examined economic concept in another guise, will give the student confidence, and also provide continuity in the subject.

4   The cost of reproducing worksheets is an additional and necessary consideration, which is often in conflict with any educational rationale. The consequence of cramming information on to a worksheet is loss of impact, and students may find the worksheet too daunting even to start work. This type of worksheet is likely to be an independently pursued reading exercise, rather than a multi-activity sheet involving active participation by students and interaction with each other.

5   A title provides both an identity and a potential system for ordering the work. An excellent system of referencing is found in the Economics Education 14–16 Project, where on the top of each sheet the broad topic area, the title of the unit and the function of the individual sheet within that unit are given. If a system of referencing can be standardised and explained to students, it provides an initial entry point to the worksheet.

6   Clear delineation of tasks on one sheet can easily be obtained by constructing boxes around each section (see Table 3.1). This also simplifies and minimises the instructions that the teacher needs to give, as the section to be completed is readily identifiable.

7   Colour coding is a simple but effective way of illustrating links between tasks that are spatially divided on the page, while at the same time making the worksheet more attractive.

The increasing constraints on teachers imposed by ever decreasing resources, finance and time are clearly of great importance, and often cause more frustration than the activity of teaching. These suggestions are made in the hope that they will enable teachers to produce relevant, useful and cost-effective worksheets.

Notes and references

1   See Chapters 12–24.
2   Holley, B., and Skelton, V., *Economics Education 14–16 Phase One: Final Report* (NFER, 1980).
3   SMILE (Secondary Mathematics and Individualised Learning Experiment) materials available from Ladbrooke Centre, Middle Row School, Kensal Road, London W10 5DB.
4   Kerry, T., and Sands, M., *Mixed Ability Teaching in the Early Years of the Secondary School* (Macmillan, 1982).
5   In these cases, the kinds of techniques that allow groups of adults successfully to report to their colleagues may also be effective. For example, groups could be given large sheets of art paper and felt tip pens or OHP slides and pens. The former could be hung around the classroom walls; both could be used as a focus for group reports.
6   In order to control discussion and to allow all students opportunity to comment, it may be necessary to prepare charts or sequences on the blackboard or OHP slides and to complete them in response to student suggestions.
7   DES, *HMI Series: Matters for Discussion 6: Mixed Ability Work in Comprehensive Schools* (HMSO, 1978).

4 The Use of Worksheets and Self-instructional Material
Alain Anderton

Introduction

In many circles, teacher-produced worksheets have become a panacea, in others a symbol of all that is bad in teaching. The truth probably lies somewhere between these two extremes. Teacher-produced material won't solve discipline problems, won't initially be received with any more enthusiasm by students than a normal textbook, and won't necessarily be any better than bought material. However, there are very important advantages that can be claimed for worksheets:

1 Material can be tailored to suit the needs of the individual situation. Local interests can be catered for. It can be prepared with specific teaching groups in mind. The mixed-ability class can be more easily dealt with.
2 It is far less expensive to produce than to buy material. It is also more flexible as course sections can be added whenever necessary, and parts can be updated without having to throw the whole away. If worksheets are lost by students, the cost is minimal – certainly not the case with textbooks.
3 There might be no suitable commercially available material. This is especially true with experimental courses or many Mode IIIs.

There are, however, important disadvantages with worksheets:

1 However good the reprographic facilities, the best teacher-produced material can never be as good in terms of quality of reproduction as the best books available. It is possible to obtain colour, for instance, on worksheets produced with ink machines, but the process is so laborious and expensive that it is very rarely used. Modern textbooks are making very important strides in the quality of their presentation.
2 Producing worksheets is yet another burden on teachers' time. Worksheets that are worth producing do take a great deal of time to prepare.

The teacher in his or her own situation must make a choice, then, as to what to produce. Often textbooks will be used in conjunction with worksheets in the overall scheme of materials to be used. Teacher-produced worksheets can be used in a wide variety of ways:

1 As a text, as a substitute for part of a book.
2 As a short passage for use in discussion, comprehension or as an example. It might be a piece of contin-uous prose, or a set of figures, or purely visual material. Case studies would be included here.
3 As a set of questions and exercises, to be used in conjunction with other material.
4 As a set of instructions or explanations for a task to be performed. Instructions for fieldwork or games are examples.
5 As a guide to other resources available and where to find them.
6 As an individualised learning text, which would presumably contain elements of all the other five points mentioned above. Programmed learning is one way of approaching this.

The use of worksheets is for many teachers the least troublesome aspect; handling resources should be second nature to the teacher. A need arises where commercially produced material is unsuitable or unavailable; a work-sheet can fill the gap. Defining the need is simple, but producing a worksheet to meet it is far from easy. The following procedure, as summarised in Figure 4.1, might help in the production of worksheets.

The first step is to decide for whom the material is to be provided. The ability of the group being aimed at is crucial. If the material is for sixth-form use, for example, the language and presentation can be quite sophisticated. If it is for low-ability fourth and fifth years, then the language should be as simple as possible. Most worksheets assume far too great a competence on the part of students below sixth-form level. When writing for less-able children, try to keep sentences short with few subordinate

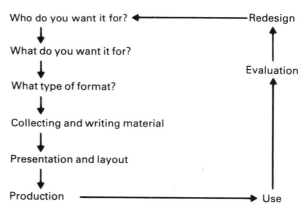

Figure 4.1

clauses. Technical terms and long words should be explained.

The next step is to decide on the purpose of the worksheet. Jot down key concepts or ideas. Formulate a set of objectives for the sheet. Think also of the context in which it is going to be used and other resources available which will be used in conjunction. This will lead on to thinking about the type of format to be used – a set of questions or a test perhaps. The format will also be constrained by the reprographic facilities available. A worksheet based on visual material will be difficult if not impossible without a stencil cutter or offset litho equipment. Then go ahead collecting or writing the material. While doing this, remember to bear in mind the ability range of the students. Pitching the work at the right level is probably the most crucial factor in the fate of a worksheet. Always take great care with presentation and layout of material. It is very important that the text should be legible. Students who have to decipher words are only being presented with additional difficulties in the learning process. Care should be taken with drawings and diagrams. Typed material is preferable unless the handwriting is excellent. Photographs should have plenty of contrast. Experience is the key to success: learning what the reprographic machines available will and will not do. Everything is now ready for production. Once used, the material should be evaluated. It can then be redesigned when the need arises. In most cases, the worksheets will be capable of improvement, however experienced the teacher. Fortunately, it takes little time to do this if the basic structure is sound.

Different types of machine will restrict what can be produced. Many schools now have banda machines, ink Roneo or Gestetner machines, offset litho and photocopiers.

The humble banda is still much used in schools, and for very good reasons. It can be produced quickly – writing or drawing on to a banda master sheet superimposed on to a banda wax colour sheet. Banda machines are fairly simple to operate. Variety can be obtained by drawing on different coloured sheets – a simple way of improving the quality of material but often ignored by teachers. The main disadvantages are that only about 100 to 150 copies can be obtained from one master, and the paper can only be printed on one side. If other means of reproduction are available the banda is useful for work wanted in a hurry and for short items.

Reproduction on Roneo or Gestetner machines is done through a cut stencil or skin, ink being pushed through the cuts on to the paper. It is possible to write or draw straight on to a skin, by using a plastic (or similar) sheet between the two layers of the stencil. Special pencils are available although most people use ordinary biros and pencils. The skin is delicate and can easily tear. For this reason, the banda is preferable if the teacher wants to write directly. Most skins in fact are used for printing. Typing straight on to a skin should be done with a typewriter whose keys are clean, preferably an electric typewriter. The cleaner the cut the better the quality of reproduction. Mistakes can be rectified by using a special correcting fluid. To reproduce photographs or pictures, use an electronic stencil cutting machine. This is invaluable. Don't expect miracles, but good well-contrasted material will be satisfactorily produced. The original copy is placed into the machine and a stencil is cut from that. The stencil is then used to reproduce material in the ordinary way. Text can be interspersed with pictures by typing the text on to paper and putting the pictures where desired. Many schools now have ancillary typing staff who will do the required typing, as well as reproduce the material – a great help to teachers.

Offset-litho equipment is a luxury. Its only real advantage over ink duplicating machines is the quality of reproduction, especially of the printed word. Paper or metal plates are used instead of stencils, a photocopier instead of a stencil cutter. The type of material that can be presented is no different from an ink machine with stencil cutter, and is prepared in the same way.

Photocopiers vary in quality. Although a good finish can normally be expected, the cost per item is often high. Photocopying twenty copies of a single-sided item is feasible, but photocopying 300 ten-sided booklets would be very expensive and time-consuming.

One problem that every producer of material must face is that of copyright. Most schools break copyright laws in one way or another. Despite some recent well-publicised cases, publishers are unlikely to prosecute an individual school for copyright infringement. Ultimately the question rests much on the morals of the teacher. Certainly copying material that is printed on single sheets (like some sets of case studies) is being unfair to the publisher and author. Reproducing magazine or newspaper articles is a minor infringement in comparison. Reproducing large parts of textbooks is, fortunately for the publishers, time-consuming, and probably as expensive as buying the textbooks themselves.

As has been mentioned before, worksheets are time-consuming to prepare. However, they can add a new dimension, and make for more effective teaching. This is being increasingly recognised as schools acquire more and more sophisticated reprographic hardware. It is unfortunate that in many schools these resources are underused.

5 Why Can't the English Teacher . . . ? A Programme to Improve Written Communication in Economics*

Graham Evans and Norman Perrin

*An earlier version of this chapter was published in *Economics,* vol. XVII, pt. 1, no. 73, spring 1981, pp. 20–2.

Introduction

This chapter proposes a strategy aimed at improving written communication skills in economics of students aged 14–16 years. It is based on a pilot project undertaken by the authors.

Language problems

It is a curious phenomenon that in many schools, while the English language teachers may boast continuously good results in public examinations, other teachers are only too conscious that when it comes to their subject, students face almost insurmountable difficulties in written expression.

A group of students will reveal a lively understanding of economic concepts in discussion and in oral questioning, and yet fail in varying degrees, some seriously, to display economic understanding in various written formats, the essay in particular.

Perhaps the textbooks are inappropriate or too difficult? But that does not readily explain poor written performance. To suggest that English language examinations are 'easy' and economics 'hard' is only to insult colleagues and students alike. What, then?

The explanation may well lie in two related factors: (i) the different demands made on students' language capabilities, by the very nature of communication in different subjects, and (ii) by the views taken of proper teaching priorities in those subjects. In short, the language of economics, it is suggested, is a very different beast from the language of creative expression and imaginative response: and the standard of students' written language performance is a reflection of this.

Students face the difficulty from the very start of their secondary school career: 'English' continues their development in basic skills; expands oral and written power in narrative, in analysing mood and tone, in handling metaphorical meanings, in detecting bias and manipulating point of view; it seeks to enlarge an ability in expressing personal opinion; it tries to deepen imaginative response, and so on. Meanwhile, the students go to other subjects for which the language work in English has not prepared them and, crucially, is not intended to. This is not to isolate the English teacher for sole blame. From day one of their secondary schooling, students enter the language worlds of a host of new subjects. The English teacher already faces an impossible task. And how many subject teachers see language skills as one of their major responsibilities when designing courses? In *Awareness of Language,*[1] Hawkins argues for a programme of language awareness with the specific aim of bringing teachers together across disciplines to plan and *teach* it, to confront the explosion of concepts and language introduced by the specialist secondary school subjects. In particular, he notes how frequently the lack of confident control of written English leads to failure for too many students.

Background

It was at this point of sympathy for the students' language mystification that the authors started to explore practical solutions for a group of fourth-year students, the majority of whom, by chance, formed a common English and economics class: the pilot group, from which developed the strategy proposed here.

Waltheof is an inner-city, mixed comprehensive school in Sheffield with 900 students. Within the school, both the English and Economics departments have, for many years, achieved notable successes in public examinations. The English teachers were, at the time of the pilot project, committed to the view that the creative and imaginative experience of personal writing and of literature should be fundamental to the timetable subject 'English'. Consequently, as the English department became uneasily aware of other voices and demands – from industry; from the 'falling standards' lobby; from advocates of the then new TEC and BEC courses (now BTEC) and from certain examination boards – such functional views of 'English' tended to get short shrift, and were seen as being mechanistic and stultifying.

Nevertheless, within the school, the English department was keenly aware of the expectations of other subject teachers, of the very real pressures on students' practical writing and reading skills across the curriculum, and of the need for the department to develop a 'service' role.

Language teaching

The teaching of written communication in British schools is almost solely confined to the English lesson – this despite repeated surveys showing the importance of writing in other curricular areas. Relying then on the English teacher, how many subject specialists inquire of their English colleagues what is done? Do *you* know what language/writing skills courses are run in your school? Have you asked?

Unfortunately, language work in the English classroom is almost exclusively directed at or below the level of the *sentence*. It is concerned with accuracy and correctness, in spelling, punctuation and syntax. Teachers of English are familiar with textbooks of 'common errors', in use in most departments, for the teaching or practice and correction of specific items. This concentration on sub-sentence accuracy is reinforced in the marking of students' written work – both in English and elsewhere. How commonly do *you* mark/correct spelling and grammatical errors? How rarely do you disentangle a whole paragraph – preferring to scribble 'muddled thinking', or some such, in the margin. (Note 'thinking' – not '*writing*'.) There isn't time, is there?

Above the level of the sentence, be it discursive essay or narrative, English teaching is largely unconcerned with matters of language. Attention is turned to content and to the organisation of content: to the pre-planning of ideas and of paragraphs. This, in reality, is frequently a rather limited, not to say negative aim: that of avoiding a mere jumble by establishing discrete paragraph-topics or a narrative sequence.

The result is that many, perhaps most, students do achieve a minimal competence, and are able to write *sentences* that are reasonably accurate grammatically, in more or less well-ordered paragraphs. What they cannot necessarily do – crucially for economics writing – is to produce complete written communications ('essays', if you prefer) that are internally cohesive and coherent.

Cohesion and coherence

Modern linguists identify two elements, cohesion and coherence, that together are vital for the continuous logical flow of sustained written discourse of the kind required in economics essays.

Cohesion may most easily be viewed as the grammatical links binding successive sentences, for example:

> Pension funds and insurance companies collect another big part of the nation's savings. They invest those savings mainly in financing the government or . . .

Here, 'they' in the second sentence clearly refers back to 'Pension funds and insurance companies' in the first. Had the writer said 'we' or 'you' the second sentence would have remained internally grammatical, but would not properly have linked to the previous sentence in this context. Coherence, on the other hand, is more elusive, and is most easily illustrated when it breaks down, for example:

> The downturn in the British economy is accounted for by three factors. The first of these is the high rate of interest and the second is the strength of the pound. The strength of the pound encourages imports and discourages exports, thus tending to create an adverse balance of payments.

The third sentence, here, does not follow happily from the previous two, producing a passage that is *incoherent*. The error does not lie in the grammar of the third sentence, nor do the three sentences lack cohesion. It is, rather, that in a series of statements such as these which are introductory to the essay, the reader expects the third factor immediately after the first two, or that the second factor should not be expanded upon in priority to the first before mention of the third. What is required is that the sentences follow at the level of *sense* as well as grammatical correctness and cohesion: in short, that they are coherent. Clearly, there is a strong conceptual element involved, but there is also a linguistic element – 'rules of language use' in academic discursive writing. There is no evidence that such rules of use come naturally. The majority of students need specific instruction and practice if they are to be coherent over longer stretches of discourse typically required in economics. Unfortunately, such instruction falls outside the present priorities of both the English and the economics teacher.

Should the economics teacher bother about language?

> Economics also helps to develop language in certain specific ways. . . . The secondary school phase of education supplies an admirable place in which to promote the careful use of the language of economics . . . will all help to develop the special language of economics understanding.[2]

In an article in *Economics*, Henderson writes of his experience in teaching Iranian students with English language problems: 'As an economics teacher I was made very aware of the importance of language (not jargon) as a prime vehicle for the development and communication of the subject. The way language is used in economics is an interesting subject for discussion in its own right.'[3]

Henderson reports an experimental approach at the University of Birmingham in teaching economics to Iranian students. The particular features of this new approach are that it specifically recognised language as a problem, rather than say innate intelligence, or cognition, or complex economics; and that it brought together economics and English teachers in what was clearly a successful venture.

In his conclusions, he somewhat modestly denies 'any wider implications for economics teaching in general arising from the partial experience of an unusual course'. However, the work described in his article suggests that many of the problems faced by his Iranian students may be parallel in the experience of English-speaking students in British schools studying economics for the first time.

Does economics pose unique problems of language use?

1 Vocabulary

The newcomer to the study of economics must learn a considerable terminology specific to the subject. This includes both wholly new words and terms (some of which signify very complex concepts, e.g. 'marginal utility'), as well as more familiar words, with shades of meaning particular to economics. Examples of the former might be *entrepreneur, clearing banks, public sector borrowing requirement*. An example of the latter: *good*, meaning 'a good', not the opposite of bad. A facility in the use of such terms is important to success in economics, as in other specialised areas of study.

2 The sentence

> The rules that govern language are known as grammar. . . .Yet the rules are not stifling. They are at times disconcertingly flexible. In short, although rule governed, language is creative. There is still an infinity of untapped sentences.[4]

The set of rules governing the grammatical construction of sentences is not unique to economics, any more than, say, are the rules of punctuation. As such, for better or worse, the grammar of the sentence is firmly the problem of the English teacher.

What is distinctive is the particular selection or balance of sentence functions, and of typical sentence *forms*. An illustration in punctuation may make this clear. Commonly in English lessons, the successful student is expected to handle the precise and subtle rules governing the punctuation of speech – not only inverted commas alone, but also the use and exact placement of such marks as capital letters, full stops, and commas, as well as question and exclamation marks. It is an important skill for a variety of English purposes. In economics discourse, on the other hand, such skill is largely redundant: the accurate transcription of sequences of direct speech being rarely, if ever, required. Thus, the selection and balance of required skills differs, in this instance, between English and economics writing. Is it possible to identify sentence forms and functions that are central to economics discourse? An examination of economics textbooks in standard use in schools and of examples of students' work that are well written suggests that this is the case. Henderson implies a similar conclusion: 'Economics discourse contains numerous instances of hypothetical language using If . . . then. . . . Other exercises that can be included in this section are economic comparisons, the making of locational and the making of temporal statements.'[5] A provisional list of sentence functions common in economics discourse would add: definition; evaluation; classification; exemplification; and description. Typical sentence forms would include: present simple active; future simple active; past simple active tenses; conditional and comparative structures. Clearly such functions and forms are not exclusive to economics, but are sufficiently characteristic in use as to be essential for the successful student to control.

3 Metaphor

Henderson highlights a further level of language difficulty: 'Teaching students with language problems made me aware of the use of *analogy* and *metaphor* in economics.'[6] In a later article,[7] Henderson expands on metaphor in economics:

> Metaphor is often considered either as a feature of personal style (i.e. of textual decoration) or as a misleading mode of thinking and writing that has no place in science. The language of economics contains many examples of descriptive terminology based on metaphor. Even predictive models have underlying metaphorical foundations.

Henderson exemplifies the 'horse' metaphors frequently used to describe rates of inflation with danger being suggested by the increased speed of the horse: e.g. 'trotting inflation'; 'galloping inflation'; 'run-away inflation' and even 'inflation – the riderless horse'.

4 Beyond the sentence

The functions listed under the heading 'The sentence' above are not solely restricted to statements at the level of the sentence. Perhaps more importantly they may be functions of a series of sentences in extended, connected discourse. The mastery of connected discourse is not merely a matter of 'clear thinking' but of the confident operation of the rules of language use that produce coherent discourse. The student needs the ability to control the resources of language to sustain a particular purpose over a sequence of sentences, and also to mark the alteration of that purpose in the flow of discourse. For example: an initial definition of the problem, moving to a provisional hypothesis that might be contrasted with an alternative, adducing evidence and exemplification, leading to a conclusion or summary.

It is all too easy, particularly for teachers, who have successfully mastered these skills, to underestimate the complexity and precision of the language rules at work in such an example – and the difficulty that confronts the newcomer to economics whose only previous experience of the English language has been for quite different purposes.

The intention of the English-in-economics programme is, therefore, to focus on the distinctiveness of economics discourse, on the functions that are typical of it, and to encourage in students a confidence in the coherent use of written forms.

English-in-Economics: the strategy

Introductory

The course is intended to run over ten weeks, though the timing is flexible and a matter for individual judgement. Considerable emphasis is placed on active classroom learning, the students being encouraged to work in groups, for argument and discussion. It is felt that the best results can be achieved through students engaging in the management of their own learning, rather than restricting lessons to question-and-answer sessions centred on the teacher and the blackboard. These developments in teaching methods may be most familiar to teachers engaged in 'life skills' and social and personal education courses. Although the aim of the course is to improve writing skills, the opportunity to practise oral skills in group work and in the plenary sessions provides an element of reinforcement and motivation. At the very least, such methods provide an enjoyable 'workshop-style' environment, which may be very different from students' normal classroom learning experience.

Lessons 1 and 2

Discussing the overall 'flow' in the content and argument of a standard essay makes a familiar starting point for student and teacher alike – mundanely, 'teaching them to write in paragraphs'. Nevertheless, it seems an effective lesson to revise. Suitable subjects seem to be those of topical or local interest, with some economic point: in South Yorkshire the debate over subsidising public transport from the rates is a topic of benefit to students and one that might be expected to provoke ready discussion.

Formed into groups, the students are issued with felt pens and large sheets of paper ('flip charts') and asked to 'brainstorm' – to throw out ideas, which are freely written down on the large sheets. When the groups are finished, the flip charts are displayed for discussion. The teacher might lead this, or preferably encourage each group to provide a reporter. Once all of the groups have explained their ideas, discussion is turned, either by the teacher with the whole class, or again in groups, to the ordering of the ideas in topical, balanced sequences. There will be many acceptable possibilities, which should be recognised by the class or group, before a final decision is reached and an individually preferred fair copy made by each student.

Two lessons are set aside in order to establish firmly the working method.

Lessons 3–5

Following the same methods as for lessons 1 and 2, this block turns to a repetition of two exercises concerned with cohesion and coherence. The exercises are based on academic articles, which should be *deliberately* selected to be well beyond the functional reading ability of the pupils – and even the teacher! *The Economist* and *Scientific American* are an excellent source.

The aims of the two exercises are to identify the syntactic indicators – the signposts, if you like – of discourse coherence, and for the students to see that this is very largely possible even when the subject-matter is not understood.

In Exercise 1, groups are given copies of the selected article and asked to underline those words and phrases that, in their judgement, seem to have more to do with the movement of the content than with the content itself. Some brief initial guidance in what to look for is helpful,

possibly with a short example. Afterwards, groups report their decisions, including problems and inevitable disagreements (there is no 'right answer' at this stage), which should be defended and challenged.

When reports are complete, it should be possible to draw out the idea that a number of devices are at work. For example (and this is *not* a linguistics lesson – the terms are unimportant):

> Time relaters: *earlier, until, at this point*
> Additive conjuncts: *moreover, equally, besides*
> Result conjuncts: *therefore, as a result, accordingly*
> Contrastive conjuncts: *by contrast, on the other hand*, etc.[8]

In Exercise 2, the groups construct a skeleton of the article from these underlined words and phrases, either by listing them, or by diagrams and networks. Where possible, they should begin to discuss and agree what the writer's functional purpose might be at each stage – an example, a classification, a contrast, or whatever – and the diagram labelled accordingly.

Again, reporting and discussion should follow, ending, as in lessons 1 and 2, with agreed structures and interpretations, each student making an individually preferred fair copy.

Lessons 6–9

Functions informally drawn out in previous lessons are now looked at specifically: *hypothesis, classification, exemplification, contrast* and *comparison*. In each case, examples of the individual functions are presented to the students and discussed, or the students are set to search textbooks, articles and even their own essays for them. The important questions are: How does the author introduce ('signpost') the function to the reader? Why does the author do so, at that point?

It is important that these exercises are not just analytic, but practical: the examples related to a context and practised. A fairly straightforward, current economics lesson topic can be taken, and in the groups the students asked to construct possible 'skeletons' from the given title. Again, reporting back, and final discussions follow.

Lesson 10

The final lesson is essentially summary: concluding with a return to overall structure; this time, not in terms of content but of language strategies for writing. Using new, or earlier, essay topics, deal with (i) openings and the setting out of main themes, (ii) establishing main points, (iii) introducing secondary points, (iv) concluding remarks – and overall, emphasising again the need clearly to sign-post the sequence of the argument.

Conclusions and implications

From the original project

1 Educationalists at any level must benefit if they join together to tackle a problem.

2   The students involved understood what was being done and why it was being done – and undoubtedly benefited.

3   Both teachers and students recognised the evidence of improvement in logically coherent written work, which was a source of further motivation in English and economics work.

4   An unforeseen benefit was that the work here provided a language in which the students' essay work could be discussed in later lessons.

5   It is fairly true to say that the vast majority of students in the 14–16 age group who study economics are assessed by some form of written examination. If, as the London Examining Board state on their O-level economics papers, 'candidates are reminded of the necessity for good English and orderly presentation in their answers', it is only sensible, it appears to us, that candidates are helped to meet these requirements.

6   Such assistance is in line with the explicit and implicit recommendations of the Bullock Report, chapter 12 in particular.[9]

Further thoughts

1   There is room for massive research in this area – not least into the specialised language of academic economics writing. It is unlikely that such research is possible for the classroom teacher, given the lack of time and financial resources.

2   The writers question whether, despite the valuable work on the *teaching* of economics, enough has yet been done on the *learning* of economics and the problems experienced by the student.

Notes and references

1   Hawkins, E., *Awareness of Language* (Cambridge University Press, 1984).
2   HMI Working Papers, *Curriculum 11–16* (HMSO, 1977) pp. 53–4.
3   Henderson, W., 'Teaching economics through the medium of a new second language', *Economics*, vol. XV, pt 3, no. 67 autumn 1979, pp. 85–9.
4   'Order from the tower of Babel', *The Economist*, 28 April 1984, p. 91.
5   Henderson, op. cit.
6   Ibid.
7   Henderson, W., 'Metaphor in economics', *Economics*, vol. XVIII, pt 4, no. 79, winter 1982, pp. 147–53.
8   For further discussion, see Quirk, R. *et al., A Grammar of Contemporary English* (Longman, 1972) ch. 10.
9   *A Language for Life.* Report of the Committee of Inquiry under the Chairmanship of Sir Alan Bullock FBA (HMSO, 1975).

6   Projects for 14–16-Year-Olds – A Positive Approach

Ian Marcousé

Introduction

The average 14–16-year-old student seems to think like a shorthand secretary; their job is to take notes that they can reproduce later. Exams are therefore a test of the students' ability to regurgitate all their notes from memory. Homework essays test the extra skill of selecting the right passages from textbooks to weave into their notes.

Projects give the teacher the chance to cut through this intellectual mediocrity. This is because the students start with a blank canvas, and have to think about how best to fill it.

So what does the term 'project' mean? There are three main types:

Type 1

A project based upon a group activity such as a factory visit or a field trip. This is relatively easy for the student, because the teacher makes the arrangements and discusses the findings in class afterwards.

Type 2

A project with a theme common to all the students, but where they must take individual decisions on content. For example, an advertising project where each must decide upon a new product to advertise. The teacher provides the understanding of concepts and the logical sequence of thought – and the students apply it. Research information can come from teacher or student.

Type 3

A truly individual project, in which each student must research and write up a topic of their own choice. The teacher may need to assist at almost every stage, but success depends almost totally on the student.

Which to tackle first

It is important to realise the extent to which some pupils dread the uncertainties and responsibilities of project work. The attempt to kick away their crutches of class notes and textbooks may indeed result in some students falling flat on their faces.

This makes it crucial for students to be eased gently into the right way of thinking. So it is wise to choose a group activity project (Type 1, above) for their first effort. A visit to a large retailer would be ideal, where concepts such as stock control or impulse buying can easily be related to their own experience. In addition, the guides at large stores tend to pitch their presentation at a rather shallow, PR level – making the material easy to cope with.

A mistake made in the selection of the first project can lead some students to say that they 'can't do projects'; this can be almost impossible to overcome later.

Practical considerations

Getting contacts for visits

Before deciding how to get contacts, the teacher must consider how institutional the project is to be. Is a guided tour by a tour guide adequate? There clearly is a gulf between the professional tour (glossy and safe) and the amateur, friendly company tour (faltering and revealing). Ideally, a mixture of the two types would be best.

There are four main sources of 'institutional' contacts:

1 the local careers service;
2 the Associated Examining Board (AEB) British Industrial Society O-level 'Notes for Teachers';
3 the Industrial Society – who could suggest a local, willing member;
4 the local chamber of commerce.

Possibilities for individual contacts include:

1 Students – probably the best potential source. Their part-time work can provide a good basis for individual projects, and their parents may be able to arrange group visits. Yet the obvious means of communication with parents – a letter – seems to provide insufficient stimulus. So it seems better to 'piggy-back' a project meeting with parents on to any convenient parents' evening. This provides a better opportunity to inform and motivate the parents, and even to pin them down to specific arrangements.
2 Local press – a letter or 'press release' to a local paper will probably yield one or two good contacts. It is quite an effective method (in time spent per visit arranged) and the constructing of a press release could be a useful and stimulating class activity.
3 Contacts through careers or work experience teachers – though this risks over-stretching the generosity of the local firms involved.

Briefing the firm

The firm needs to be provided with full details about the visit's objectives. Yet to send a full list of questions in advance can result in overly one-way communication. For once a finance director has spent 45 minutes lecturing on the suggested topics, most students will feel too saturated to ask anything else. Nor does advance notice guarantee advance preparation.

The key issue in preparation, then, is to ensure that the group will see the right people (and the relevant aspects of their work). If the objective is a general 'study of a firm', differing viewpoints are essential. Of course, an honest talk by a factory floor worker would be marvellous, but even a foreman or a production control manager may tell a very different story from the glossy views of the marketing or personnel management. Senior managers are prone to think that they 'can cover the other points perfectly well' – and of course they can to a great extent. Yet without differing views, students will only be able to contrast the one view with the evidence of their own eyes: a useful, but limited, approach. So it makes sense to stress in advance that differing opinions from within the firm are essential.

Preparing the students

When students' first drafts appear, they tend to suffer from three main faults.

1 A failure to state sources of information: the general pattern is to re-hash the hosts' talk so as to present it as a factual story.
2 Over-elaboration of certain aspects of the firm, with only a cursory look at others: often there seems no logical pattern to this selectivity.
3 Inadequate use of their own eyes and ears, both to convey important facts such as the physical actions of the workers, and to communicate the atmosphere of the different departments of the firm.

The fundamental reason for all three problems is the students' habit of note-taking from spoken information, and then treating these notes as 'the facts'. It is obvious how this explains 1 and 3, but it also covers point 2. This is because students start note-taking with a flourish at the beginning of each talk, but then flag. So their reports reflect this capricious note-taking.

All the above emphasises the need for good preparation of students before they visit the firm. To warn them against these pitfalls, a set of preparatory rules might help.

1 Keep taking notes selectively but consistently throughout the talks. Do not rush at the start; you will soon tire.
2 Always state the source of your information. Who said it? Get their name and job title.
3 Keep looking and thinking all the time; do not only take notes of what you are told. You will need to describe how a product is made, so you must note what you see.

4 Above all, keep wondering whether there are inconsistencies in what you are hearing and seeing. Is everyone telling the same story? And does that story square with what you see? If not, why not?

Yet even if they have tried to follow these guidelines, many will still revert to description unless care is taken. A useful trick, here, is to discuss what conclusions they draw from their visit, as soon as possible afterwards. Then get the students to write their conclusion before they write anything else. This demonstrates successfully how important the teacher thinks a conclusion is, and ensures far greater thought and effort.

Furthermore, better students can then build a theme into their earlier, more descriptive parts of the project in order to lead up to their conclusion. This injects not only a more analytic approach, but also more coherence and structure than one can usually hope for.

A good example of this device of writing the conclusion first, came in a recent project on Marks & Spencer. Three classes of 16-year-olds received the same tour and talk on two different occasions, and just one class was asked to write the conclusion first. The two 'control' classes produced rather predictable work with conclusions that were little more than summaries of their 'findings'. The other class produced several interesting conclusions, including the following:

Conclusion

Marks and Spencer, as far as I could tell from my visit, is a very well organised and administered organisation. This is good and makes Marks a very efficient store. But the organisation is so good that the staff do not seem to have any actual responsibility, i.e. the organisation caters for all the staff's requirements, which include social needs and heavily subsidised services, e.g. canteen, hairdressing etc. Yet when it comes to individual responsibility and the ability to use one's own initiative and intelligence, Marks and Spencer does not help. For the on-floor staff, life is made as easy as possible and very smooth flowing, boring even. But the middle management find this form of administration restricts the use of their skills, the main management of the Marks and Spencer group ('Head Office') dominate the whole system. This probably explains the large drop-out percentage of management trainees in Marks and Spencers (which our guide 'let slip' to us)!

These conclusions – which were based upon evidence given earlier in the project – constituted an interesting departure from the generous praise that most expressed for the company.

The development of educational skills through projects

The separation of fact and opinion

Although the teacher will need to warn in advance about the importance of distinguishing between these two concepts, it may well be that this will only be communicated successfully afterwards.

To illustrate this, an assistant store manager recently told a group of students: 'We have a Communications Group drawn from all sections of the store. It's very successful...they discuss things like changes in the uniform or the temperature of the store.' Afterwards, we discussed this statement in class, and most considered that a fair verdict (on the evidence we had) was 'a talking shop with no real power'. Most importantly one could stress the need to report the manager's comment as 'The manager said it was very successful', rather than just 'It's very successful.' Without discussion of these points, students would simply state the manager's comments as fact.

Criticism

Many students seem to have sound critical faculties. They can identify a bad teacher, for example, and analyse his/her faults. Yet this is usually within the students' own, oral world.

Projects offer a means by which the teacher can help them learn to use this skill in academic work.

The following extract is from a Type 3 (individual) project done by a 17-year-old student in the second year of O-level re-takes. His first draft was very well researched, yet read like a public relations hand-out for MacDonalds; discussion revealed and gave focus to his reservations. It cannot be over-stressed that most students think it impolite or even subversive to criticise. So they need positive encouragement.

This was from a section headed 'Behind the Scenes'; the project title was 'How a MacDonalds Branch is Run'.

MacDonalds perform a service to the public, with fast and pleasant service. This is being told to you all the time. People who have been aggravated by non-conforming customers are moved away from the front area immediately, for the person running that area knows he or she are tired and will not serve people in the MacDonalds way. Any waste, e.g. product that has been in the production bin for more than the holding time of ten minutes, or has hit the floor, is thrown in a red bin and waste counts are taken every hour. If weekly figures on wastage are high, MacDonalds will put a special emphasis on this factor and will make you get the figure down, e.g. by a threat, such as a verbal warning. There is no room for human error, working at the till front, if people are emotional and get carried away, they are immediately set upon and warned about their work.

Concepts

This opportunity to discover information, to analyse it, and then to criticise and evaluate it, is student-centred learning at its best. It also encourages students to think for themselves about how class-taught concepts relate to the outside world; and then provides feedback to the teacher on whether the concepts are fully understood. Later on in this project, the following sentence was a model:

Machinery is always kept clean, fitting in with cutting the cost of replacing machinery, therefore overheads will be lower and a larger profit will form.

Similarly, another individual project on a small clothes shop considered an obviously relevant topic: economies and diseconomies of scale.

> Compared to Marks and Spencers' 1983 turnover of £2505 million, Clementine's was very small – just £72 000 .... As the goods are almost unique for the area, they have to pay because they cannot benefit from the standardisation of clothes like Marks and Spencer. This means the prices of Clementine's goods seem high .... However, communication within the shop is no problem as there is only one assistant who is very knowledgeable.

Writing a conclusion

Students seem to see a conclusion as meaning a 'rounding off' paragraph; at best it is a summary or synthesis of the material presented, but often it is simply a repetitive winding-down process. Few can see that there exists another function: that of evaluating the question/topic set.

A key advantage of exam project writing is that it gives the teacher the chance to demand draft versions of students' work, and then to discuss and recommend alterations. The importance of this cannot be overstated; for in the normal course of events one might comment on a conclusion to an essay, but the student only receives the criticism passively. To rewrite a homework would be seen as a horrendous punishment. So it is often hard to develop their skills at synthesis and evaluation.

The following conclusion was a 16-year-old's third attempt. His first had been a dull summary of his findings; the second was overloaded with poorly substantiated personal opinions. This one seems quite well balanced:

> At present, there has been a lot of speculation about drug firms over-spending on doctors. Drug firms are now voluntarily cutting down on entertainment that seems lavish because of the poor publicity it's receiving in the media. This is justifiable, because it gives the impression that the drug firms are trying to 'crawl' to the doctors to prescribe their drug. Which they are.
>
> As there is such heavy investment in research, it is justifiable that drug firms would want a large share of the market. With enormous pressure on the firms, it can be seen that they will go to enormous lengths to promote their product. Given the medical need for informed (but not biased) prescribing, and the huge cost to the public of NHS drugs, it seems to me to be sensible for advertising to continue – but to be carefully controlled.

Motivation

Just as MacDonalds see motivation as the key to their business, so it is to ours. We need to motivate our students to learn and to stretch themselves; and to do that year after year we need to be learning new things ourselves.

At a recent parents' evening, a doctor offered to help his son with a project on 'Drug Companies' Sales Methods' (we had a fascinating discussion and the project proved just as interesting). The next parent was a self-employed plumber, who admitted to extensive experience of 'The financial problems of a one-man business'.

A teaching method that can stimulate and involve teacher, student and parent? Well actually, yes.

Progress

The AEB British Industrial Society O-level requires six projects for 40 per cent of the exam mark (from the 1986 exam this will change to four longer projects). Having several projects provides the teacher with the opportunity to develop the students' project-writing skills over time. For although some will do interesting work immediately, many others will produce dourly descriptive writing that needs a complete rethink. Given the demotivating effect of numerous rewrites, it often seems best to concentrate on one or two weaknesses at a time. With the first project one might emphasise the construction of an evaluative conclusion; later one can turn to critical analysis, or separating fact from opinion. Pressing weak students to assimilate all these skills at once would lead to confusion and resistance.

The 16-year-old author of the following passage had made such a bad job of her first project that it was still weak after two rewrites. Yet her later projects became far more logical and thoughtful, as in this evocative piece on a visit to a small manufacturing firm:

> The girls in the assembly room looked like robots; they pressed all the various parts together and had to do a stated amount of binders to get the basic wage. Anything on top of this would be on bonus rate. They can't have enjoyed their work much because it was so repetitive and the firm seems to do their utmost to get the maximum from them. This works well for the firm but not so well for the staff. An example of this is that to take the boxes of components from one place to another they have a conveyor belt. So they miss out on actually getting up and moving about, which is a good excuse to have a cup of tea or have a chat to fellow workers.
>
> The women have to make 3600 ring binders a day to get their basic wage and the bonus money is 35p per extra 800 binders – staggeringly little ...
>
> I don't really understand why the workers put so much effort into the job when they weren't going to receive very much more for it. They only explanation can be that their position as the dominant local employer keeps people on their toes.

Non-examination projects

However convinced the teacher may be that project work is valuable, it may be hard to generate and sustain sufficient student interest if the work does not contribute to an external exam.

Four possibilities present themselves:

1 Try to replicate exam motivation by introducing an independent and preferably awesome judge: a local bank manager would be suitable, and probably co-operative.
2 Only tackle irresistible topics such as advertising – though these are often the ones where students are especially 'expert' and therefore overly subjective.
3 Generate interest by using an alternative medium such

as sound or, ideally, video. Firms are flattered to have a film made of them, and students are fascinated by the idea; the constructing of the 'screenplay' becomes the project (from the teaching point of view) because of the preparation and thought that must go into it.

4 Change your exam syllabus. Whatever else, it would be awful if visits and fieldwork were to become a nightmare because of the dreaded follow-up project. For although projects often stem from visits, it would be wrong to confuse these two things. Projects are a test of initiative, observation, analysis, criticism and evaluation, whereas visits offer social and motivational benefits to the students and to the class as a unit. Examined projects combine these two elements because of the common goal that they provide.

Footnote

There is clear evidence that teachers are becoming less willing to put up with the 'inconvenience' of examined projects. For it is the teacher who must put in the preparation, the organisation, the suggested improvements and even – eventually – the moderation. The year 1983, for example, was the last year that AEB's Social Economics included a project and, as stated above, from 1986 the British Industrial Society course will have just four projects instead of six. AEB says that this is a response to teacher attitudes and demands.

This is as sad as it is short-sighted. Schools are and will be suffering increasing competition from MSC initiatives and from the private sector, at a time when the pupil population is shrinking. Interesting projects provide not only 'education', but also 'events' that students can talk about and remember with fondness. Furthermore, they can involve the parents in the kind of positive, self-

confident way that most parents seem to leave behind at primary or even nursery school. Thus, to the extent that any one subject can influence the image of a school, a course with examined projects can be of real benefit.

Resources

Exams including projects

Business Studies O-level, Cambridge Board. This has a core syllabus, plus six options – one of which must be chosen. Four pieces of project work constitute one option. For further information, contact D. H. Dyer, Cambridge Business Studies Project.

British Industrial Society O-level, AEB (Associated Examining Board). Currently six projects must be completed for 40 per cent of the exam total; from the 1986 exam, four projects (one of 2000 words, three of 1500 words) will be required. For further information, contact Mrs Gunningham, AEB.

Sources for contacts for visits

AEB 'British Industrial Society O-level: Notes for the Guidance of teachers concerning coursework'.

The Industrial Society.

Examples of recent 'individual study' titles submitted for examination

Advantages and Problems of Agricultural Co-operatives.
How TI Gas Spares Chose a New Computer System.
Financial Problems of a One-man Business.
Motivation and Training of Life Insurance Salesmen.

7 Survey Work in Economics: Investigating Industry
Martin C. Brimble

Introduction

Three basic approaches exist to using fieldwork in schools:[1] (i) the field study centre approach, (ii) the factory visit/museum approach, (iii) the local area approach. This latter method is of particular use if the school is, 'situated in the middle of a large town or industrial complex'.[2] Teachers in rural areas are advised to consider alternative strategies (small area statistics/ward profiles provide a possible starting point).[3]

Gathering survey materials and resources

The local area is the greatest resource, but it is important to gather a range of materials, initially by consulting a local reference or college library. These usually contain a variety of directories, for example, *Sells' Directory*[4] of products and services (this provides an alphabetical list of firms, which might help in identifying the number of branches of some of the more important firms in the area). Another directory (*Kelly's Manufacturers and*

Merchants Directory) lists what companies make and provides considerable information on subsidiary industries. Background books, usually geography textbooks with a regional section, provide a valuable overview.

The following will also be needed before starting survey work:

1　maps of the area;
2　film slides of local industry, a sensible fall-back for a 'wet weather routine';
3　letters of identification;
4　clip-boards and questionnaires;
5　tape-recorders and cameras.

Survey methods

The two methods most suitable are (i) the use of observation, (ii) questionnaires. Questionnaires can be partly completed using directories or observation, but they do provide opportunities for students to conduct interviews. At this point teachers of economics may well encounter problems. Firms are reluctant to release information, for business reasons. Advice on how to proceed can be sought from a range of sources, for example, local chambers of commerce, business studies inspectors/advisers and, where they exist, industry/school co-ordinators. It is important not to swamp a particular firm with repeated requests for information/literature. Students should visit a maximum of one or two and present a short report. The information can then be pooled for class use, with information on new firms added in later years.

Establishing aims and testing hypotheses

A useful first step in taking students out into the community is to construct an industrial trail[5] that allows the students to see a cross-section of the types of firms and industries nearby. It is also important to consider carefully whether local examples meet syllabus requirements, and how they can be used to illustrate more conventional lessons and schemes of work. Then a more selective approach may be adopted, using specific firms and situations to illustrate the concept that is being developed. Some examples follow.

Scarcity and choice

Most economics courses start with a discussion of the concepts of scarcity and choice. This early work can be linked to a study of production by taking a firm and identifying:

1　the product made;
2　the processes involved (are they labour-intensive or capital-intensive?);
3　the raw materials involved (are there alternatives?).

Students should be asked to consider how much the final product will cost and also the cost of the individual parts used to make the product. The difference will not all be profit, of course, and this opens up discussion of the other costs involved, both fixed and variable, as well as a discussion of the role of private enterprise in a mixed economy, and why economic goods exist and command a price.

Capital as a factor of production

Later on in their first term, students can proceed to a consideration of the types of firms that exist and the amount of capital required given their financial organisation. A small comparative exercise/survey, with the teacher as guide, can be undertaken. Three features – the size of the firm, the product/service provided, and the type of financial organisation of the firm – can be inter-related (this latter category giving a rough guide to the amount of capital available to the firm). Two areas can be contrasted. One might compare part of the local high street with a section of a neighbouring industrial area. Not more than thirty firms should be looked at in total. Two simple hypotheses can be put to the students (or, alternatively, the survey can be undertaken experientially, with conclusions arrived at afterwards):

Hypothesis 1
Firms with access to capital tend to be larger than firms without access to capital.

Hypothesis 2
Firms need greater amounts of capital if they are involved in certain forms of economic activity.

The students should be given clip-boards and then taken to each area. In order to get a fair comparison the same questions should be posed on each occasion:

Example of questions
1　What is the name of the firm?
2　What does it make/sell?
3　What is its financial organisation?
4　What is the size of the firm: large/medium/small?

On returning to the class, two charts can be constructed from the data, one for each area (see Figures 7.1 and 7.2). On the charts the horizontal axis records the type of firm and its size, and the vertical axis the number in each category.

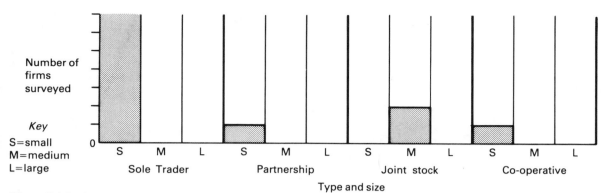

Figure 7.1 High street survey by type and size of firm

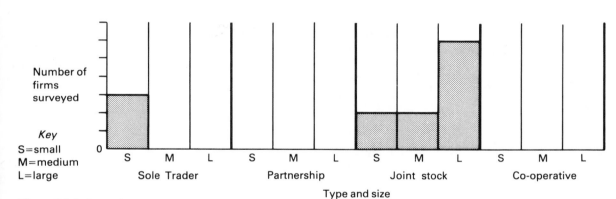

Figure 7.2 Industrial area survey by type and size of firm

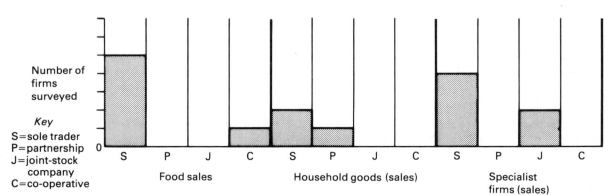

Figure 7.3 High street survey by type of firm and form of economic activity

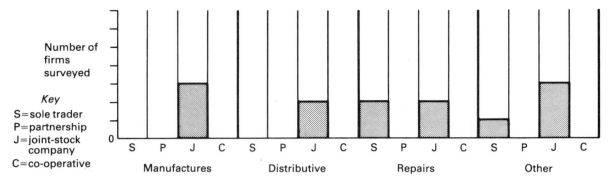

Figure 7.4 Industrial area survey by type of firm and form of economic activity

If you are able to compare a high street/shopping area with an industrial district, two distinct patterns should emerge. The high street, particularly if it is a minor one, will have a greater number of small firms. The industrial area will frequently have larger establishments. In a neighbourhood shopping area, in particular, most of the firms will be under sole ownership/some form of partnership, whereas in an industrial area factory units will tend to be owned by joint-stock companies. Once an area pattern has been recognised, students can be asked whether their findings prove or disprove their first hypothesis. A positive answer is soon forthcoming. The same data can be reworked in order to address the question, 'Why do certain firms seem to need large amounts of capital?'

A second set of charts can be constructed – this time with the product sold/service provided emphasised (see Figures 7.3 and 7.4). With this second set of charts you can examine the form of economic activity by type of firm. What do they suggest about economic activity? It should not take long for answers to flow:

You don't need much capital to sell things.
A one-man business is going to be more interested in selling, it's easier to set up.
They need machines, you need capital to buy machines.

Your second hypothesis is proved to be correct.

Location and costs of industry

Once the economics course is under way and students have gained an appreciation of the advantages and disadvantages of large-scale enterprises, it makes sense to proceed to a study of the location of a firm and its influence on the costs of production.

This area of our survey work has always begun with a visit to a large plant situated near us: Deptford Power Station. The visit immediately emphasises the importance of the location of the establishment, as well as its unique historical importance as the world's earliest commercial AC power station. Built by Ferranti, almost as much attention was focused by him on its location as on its

construction. He settled on Deptford because (i) there was an unlimited supply of water for cooling purposes, (ii) there were facilities to unload sea-borne coal, (iii) pre-National Grid power generation had to be located near the market. Similar local stories about the foundation of an enterprise can be unearthed in most industrial areas (see firms' brochures, local libraries, local newspaper archives).

During their visit to a firm and on return to the classroom, students should be encouraged to complete a questionnaire so that sufficient information can be retrieved in a structured way.

An example follows:

Industrial questionnaire (location/costs)
1 What is the name of the firm?
2 What type of business or financial organisation is the firm?
3 What product is produced by this firm?
4 How long has the firm been in the area?
5 What are the principal raw materials of the business?
6 Do any of the products reach the firm via waterborne transport?
7 What specialisation is involved in the manufacture of the product?
8 What links does the firm have with other firms in the same region?
9 What are the principal advantages gained from such links?
10 What are the main advantages of being based on the firm's present site?
11 What attracted the firm to the site in the first place?
12 What are the disadvantages for the firm of being located where it is?
13 What contacts exist with firms abroad?
14 How is the product distributed?
15 What stage of industry is involved?
16 What are the fixed costs?
17 What are the variable costs?

Table 7.1

	Name	Activity	Natural advantages	Acquired advantages	Disadvantages
1					
2					
3					
(cont).					

18 Briefly describe how the product is produced.
19 List the principal machinery used in the production process.
20 Give a brief outline of the firm's history in the area and its prospects.

Once students have looked at one firm, they should be encouraged to visit other firms. Careful organisation and a letter of introduction, preferably a phone call in advance to the firm, is essential at this stage. A range of firms should be chosen with students visiting only one or two. Information can then be pooled in class.

A suitable theme for classroom work is essential. The hypotheses we have tested are:

1 The area is a declining area.
2 Firms leave an industrial location when disadvantages begin to outweigh the original reasons for choosing the site.

Completed questionnaires can be photocopied and circulated around the class, with some of the information transferred to a grid designed to test these hypotheses (see Table 7.1).

Each student should be encouraged to talk briefly about the firm they have investigated. This takes time but is well worth the effort, oral skills being often overlooked in classrooms.

Students are now ready to complete a project related to the industrial survey and, if they proceed, they should be given a brief outline to help them:

Suggested outline

The aim of this project should be to relate work that you have done on the subject to examples that you can find in your local area. Organise your project in paragraphs and chapters. Illustrate it as well, where possible. Include a list of contents at the beginning and a list of books consulted at the end.

There is no right way to organise a project on industry in your area. The following is merely a guide-line as to what topics to include and a suggested ordering of these topics. The questions below can be used as headings for each section. If you get stuck on one section, because of lack of material, do not worry too much – leave the section until we can talk about it,

and in the meantime move on to another section. Do not forget to use examples that you have seen or read about and, where possible, include newspaper cuttings and other material (e.g. photographs) to improve your project.

Four golden rules:
(a) Write neatly.
(b) Underline all headings.
(c) *Do not copy whole chunks of material.* Express points clearly in your own words.
(d) Do not forget a list of contents and a list of references.

Contents:
1 Briefly explain what your project is about. Include a map to show where the area is.
2 How has the area developed? How has the use of the land changed?
3 What are the natural advantages that determine the location of industry in the area? You may also use regional, national and international examples of how and why industry is located.
4 What are the acquired advantages?
5 What are the disadvantages of concentration?
6 How can the government help a depressed region?
7 Describe your survey of firms. What were the advantages and disadvantages enjoyed by each firm you've looked at? What evidence of concentration can you find?
    What problems exist? Is there a case for firms leaving or staying in this area? What help should the area get? What would you recommend?

Construct a chart to show (i) the name of the firm, (ii) its natural advantages, (iii) its acquired advantages, (iv) its disadvantages, (v) the case for leaving or staying.

Further work in the classroom

At all times, students should be encouraged to draw conclusions from the work they have undertaken. Does the survey show that the natural advantages possessed by an area no longer apply? Is the area overcrowded or unattractive to the businessman for other reasons (e.g. rate bills)? A good student should be able to see that if circumstances affecting one industry change, other industries suffer and the social fabric of the community changes, with associated downward multiplier effects, and outward migration by the economically active. The exceptional student would probably be able to detail in writing or class discussion proposals to help the area, if it is experiencing decline or, if it is growing, proposals to manage, direct and control growth without stifling enterprise.

Where a complete list of firms can be found for an area, rates of decline using a base year can be plotted. Concentration ratios can be constructed. Using *Kelly's Directory*, subsidiary firms can be investigated and examined, and links established using 'chains of production' flow diagrams. The small area statistics/ward profiles of neighbouring but different areas can be used to examine and contrast how economic activity/inactivity affects the social structure, for example, numbers unemployed, percentage with cars, consumer durables, the percentage of elderly.[6]

Evaluation

Ideally, survey work should be evaluated as part of the final assessment of the student. This, as we have seen above, is usually achieved through the project mode, but there is no reason why room cannot be made available on the examination paper for students to express their findings. Self-evaluation is also important. Could I have saved time by collecting and tabulating some of the material? What areas were poorly organised? Has the project achieved the aims I set for it?

It is important to keep a balance throughout the survey work between collecting data and organising and interpreting the data collected. This is, as most experienced teachers realise,[7] a question of gut feel and fine judgement.

Notes and references

1   This summary of approaches is taken from Barden, P., 'The use of local field studies', in Whitehead, D.J. (ed.) *Handbook for Economics Teachers*, 1st edn (Heinemann Educational Books, 1979) pp. 45–8.
2   Ibid., p. 45.
3   Small Area Statistics, and in some areas ward profiles derived from these, are now available for the 1981 Census. Local libraries may well have copies. The SAS contain a range of social and economic data for each enumeration district–types of accommodation, age, sex, marital status, economic activity, household amenities. Copies can be ordered from Census Customer Services, OPCS, Tichfield, Fareham, Hants PO15 5RR. Ask for prospectus CEN/80/8, which contains an order form.
4   Suitable for work with a specific firm that has already been identified, available from Sells Publications, Sells House, 39 East Street, Epsom, Surrey.
5   See Hough, J.R., 'An economics trail', in Whitehead, D.J. (ed.) *Handbook for Economics Teachers*, 1st edn. (Heinemann Educational Books, 1979) pp. 136–40; and Brimble, M., 'Decline in Deptford', *Working Capital*, 1982, pp. 28–46.
6   See also Gomm, R., 'Finding out about local companies and the local labour market', in Gomm, R., and McNeill, P. (eds.) *Handbook for Sociology Teachers* (Heinemann Educational Books, 1982) pp. 160–2, for a range of other sources and for suitable investigations into the sociology of industry at a local level.
7   With reference to experienced teachers in mind, I am particularly indebted to my colleagues at South East London School, Roy Newman and Thomas Meehan, and to Brian Hoy of John Roan School. They will recognise much of what I put forward here.

8   Producing a Local Economy Resources Pack
Tony Evans

Introduction

In many areas of the curriculum, there is concern to relate the issues discussed in the classroom to the day-by-day reality of the community in which young people are living. Information on the local economy is of interest in a number of subject areas – social studies, geography, careers and environmental studies as well as economics itself. Indeed it was from a group of teachers covering just such a range of subject interests that the idea for the Greenwich Local Resources Park was conceived. This description of the compilation of the pack is designed to inform teachers in other localities of the process by which the Greenwich pack was produced and to encourage colleagues, where they are able to find the resources to back such a venture, to undertake similar work in their own locality.

The Local Economy Resources Pack is a fifty-page,

loose-leaf document providing information about the Greenwich community under the following main headings: population, industrial structure, employment/unemployment, transport, local studies. It was published in late 1982 after just under one year's co-operative work by teachers and local authority officers.

Identifying the need

Perhaps it is worth pointing out straight away that the production of this pack was not an isolated venture and that teachers working in areas where there is less of a history of collaboration between the schools of the area and between the various branches of the local government machinery will have additional preliminary groundwork to do in order to establish the network of contacts necessary for such an enterprise.

Greenwich is, of course, an inner London borough. This means that education is the responsibility of the Inner London Education Authority, while other main services are the responsibility of the borough council, the London Borough of Greenwich.

This separation of responsibilities might at first appear to offer obstacles in the way of a collaborative scheme such as this. There has, however, been a history of close co-operation in the area between the borough council and the ILEA which had been signified in such ventures as the sponsorship of a large-scale employment/education exhibition accompanied by supporting literature for school students, and of the production of a directory of local employers able to contribute in some way to the educational needs of young people. It may well be that in many unitary authorities the liaison between the education sector and the branches of the local authority administration is less well developed.

The need for a pack of teaching materials on the local economy was first discussed within this joint authority context. Interestingly, the first initiative came from careers educators who felt that in the explosion of youth unemployment of the early 1980s, they needed accessible information on trends in the labour market in the locality. Once the suggestion had been made that there was a need in this area of the curriculum, it soon became clear that it related to the interests and needs of other subject specialists and the original group of careers educators was widened to include economists, social studies teachers and geographers.

At this stage, then, there was a growing consensus among a group of teachers that it would be useful to have a resource giving accessible information on various aspects of the local economy. How did this 'good idea' get translated into the production of a pack?

There were clearly many questions that needed clarifying at this stage: What information would it be useful to bring together? What information was accessible? With what sort of ability ranges and age groups did teachers envisage such information being used, and in what format should it be presented?

The Borough Planning Department and the Employment Development Office already had close contact with a number of schools and, faced with this barrage of questions, it was decided that the way to proceed would be to undertake a survey of appropriate staff in the secondary schools. After all, the enthusiasm of a small group might not reflect the interests of a wider range of practitioners.

The survey

Twenty-eight teachers responded to the survey – twenty-seven of whom welcomed this initiative! The vast majority were already trying to incorporate local information into their teaching, though many expressed a wish for more systematic information than they currently had. For those who were using local information, the Borough Planning Department was the most popular source of information being used; other sources of information included student surveys, the careers service, the local press.

So far as the contents of a pack on the local economy were concerned, three areas had been put forward for consultation in the survey, and these were overwhelmingly endorsed as being relevant to the teachers' needs; these areas were employment/unemployment, industrial structure and local studies. An additional open-ended question invited suggestions for further topics on which information was needed. The most popular requests were for information on population, transport, recreation facilities, planning issues and retail patterns.

When asked with whom they envisaged using such material, there was a wide range of response which clearly demonstrated that, used appropriately, such information could support work in such different contexts as lower-school social studies and sixth-form economics. It was on account of this inability to specify a precise student target that a decision was made quite early in the process to make the pack a teacher resource, not a student resource. It would, however, be perfectly possible in other circumstances to have a more specific student target in mind, and produce a pack designed for student use.

Teachers were asked for their views on the format of a pack of teaching materials. It was from the responses on this that it was decided to use a loose-leaf format. This had two advantages. First, the publication would be free of copyright, and where a teacher made a decision that the data was appropriate to use with students, then it would be easy to photocopy material. Secondly, such a format allowed for updating of and addition to the contents of the pack. It was not possible within the budgetary constraints of the project to follow up suggestions on video accompaniment, but from the printed pack teachers in the schools have developed sets of overhead projection transparencies and older groups of students doing project work using the pack as a starting point have developed themes in a tape/slide presentation.

Meeting the need

The survey confirmed the view that a resource pack on the local economy would be welcomed by teachers in several disciplines in the schools. It had answered the question about the target group – in this case the teachers themselves rather than a particular range of students – and it had provided clarification on the issues of content and format, though practical concerns of money and the accessibility of information limited the possibility of responding to some of the more ambitious suggestions received.

This point to the publication of the pack took six months. The actual production became the responsibility of a relatively small group which strongly reflected the collaborative nature of the enterprise. The group was chaired by a teacher and included other representatives from the education authority, from the local teachers' centre and the careers service. From the borough council there were officers from the planning department and the employment development office. The specialist knowledge of the latter was heavily drawn upon, and most sections of the pack were produced in draft form by them. Drafts were then passed on for comments and suggestions by a wider group of teachers covering the range of subject specialist interests. While depending very much on the goodwill of the officers concerned, this system worked well in that it ensured that the teachers who would actually use the pack were able to shape the final presentation of the document.

The pack was jointly sponsored by the ILEA and the London Borough of Greenwich, who provided the resources for printing the pack. Schools, colleges and public libraries received an initial allocation of copies, after which further copies were available for purchase. Teachers in other parts of the country might find they would need to seek sponsors for such a venture.

Contents of the pack

Each section of the pack is self-contained and the page format was designed with boxed inserts to emphasise main points. Information is presented in tabular form, by graph, by pie-chart or in map form, as is most appropriate to the subject in hand (see Table 8.1 and Figure 8.1). Sources of information are stated on all occasions so that if further information is required by the teacher or by students a reference is available. Questions that can be raised with students are included in the text. Whenever possible, sources of additional information are specified.

The section on population drew heavily on the 1981 census figures which had recently become available at the time of printing. Population trends in Greenwich were compared with trends in Greater London and nationally. Some analysis of the population by age and by sex is offered, related to the local economy through analysis of present and future employment requirements of that population.

Table 8.1   Industrial structure

The manufacturing base of the Greenwich economy has suffered a severe decline in the past twenty years. Service-sector employment is increasingly dominant in the area even though total employment in Greenwich is on the decline.

1   *Total employment*

In 1981 total employment in Greenwich was about 75 000, although this is considered to be an under-estimate due to the way in which the figures were compiled.

Table A.1 shows that in 1966 there were 99 000 jobs in the borough and in 1981 only 75 000. On average, this meant a loss of 1600 jobs per year.

Table A.1
Jobs in Greenwich

Year	1966	1971	1976	1981
Total number of jobs	99 000	85 000	*78 000	*75 000

*Figures for 1976 and 1981 are not directly comparable with earlier years.

2   *Structure of employment by sex and hours of work*

In 1976 about half the jobs were taken by males in full-time employment and a quarter of females in full-time employment. A quarter of all the jobs were part-time.

Table A.2
Structure of employment by sex
Hours of work in 1976
(100% = 77 800)

	Part-time %	Full-time %	Total %
Males	4.3	53.0	57.3
Females	20.2	22.5	42.7
Total	24.5	75.5	100.0

Women took four out of ten jobs in the borough. About half of all the jobs taken by women were on a part-time basis. In contrast, less than 9 per cent of jobs occupied by men were part-time.

The section on industrial structure delineates the shift in the employment base in Greenwich away from manufacturing to the service sector, using Census of Employment data from 1966 onwards. Information on the structure of employment by sex and on part-time employment is given. Major local employers from the 1976 Census of Employment are identified and analysed by sector.

The section on employment/unemployment uses Department of Employment statistics and locally produced figures from the careers service to establish

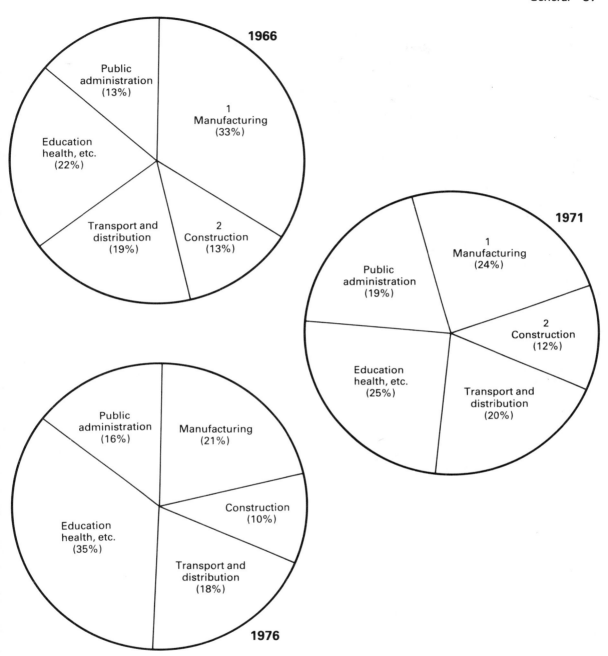

Figure 8.1 Changes in employment pattern, 1966–76 Sources: 1966, 1971, 1976 Census.
Note: Definition of sectors used (from 1968 Standard Industrial Classification)
1 Manufacturing (SIC 2–19).
2 Construction/utilities (SIC 20–21).
3 Transport, communications and retail distribution (SIC 22–23).
4 Education, health, financial, professional and miscellaneous services (SIC 24–26).
5 Public administration and defence (rest).

trends in unemployment from 1979 to 1982 by overall rates, by duration of unemployment, by sex and by age. Comparisons with national statistics are given in all cases.

The section on transport considers the patterns of journey to work, establishing the interdependence of the Greenwich economy with that of the region. At the time of the preparation of the pack, the 1971 census provided the most recent reference on this, though the information was already ten years old. The sections on road transport and public transport summarise the main proposals for development in the area.

The final section on local studies brings together information on related topics through focusing on three specific areas within the borough – (i) Woolwich town centre, a significant employment and retail centre undergoing redevelopment, (ii) Thamesmead, the largest area of new building in London, and (iii) the Industrial Riverside area, the area most affected by the shift in the local economy over the years. By focusing on smaller areas, this section aims to bring an economic dimension to more traditional environmental approaches. Suggestions are made on ways of relating the issues raised to other localities within the borough.

range of courses, including lower-school social studies and as a resource for project work both in the 14–16 curriculum and for courses for the 16–19 age group which require local investigations.

The experience in Greenwich is certainly encouraging in suggesting that a valuable resource can be produced by local collaborative arrangements. Even in localities where such an enterprise may not seem immediately feasible, approaches to the policy section of the local planning department ought to prove fruitful. In some areas there will be other local initiatives such as urban studies centres, SCIP projects or established school industry liaison co-ordinators who could also act as a resource for teachers.

The next issue to be tackled in Greenwich will be the updating of the pack. There is further information on the resident population now available from the 1981 census, and workplace information should be forthcoming soon. The establishment of an accepted format for providing local schools with information on economic developments and the close relationships that have developed as a result of the work undertaken will enable future projects to develop from this starting point.

Conclusion

Discussions with teachers using the Local Economy Resources Pack confirm that it has proved of use in a wide

Note

Copies of the Greenwich Local Economy Resources Pack are available for £2.50 including postage and packing from the Gordon Teachers' Centre, Craigton Road, London SE9 1QG.

9   On the use of Photographs in Economics Teaching

Steve Hodkinson

Introduction

Much of the information received these days comes from visual images. Opinions, stereotypes and attitudes developed about people, institutions, events and issues are given form through pictures. Educational research into the effects of a variety of forms of image on learning has led researchers to argue:

that the picture can no longer be ignored nor even confined for long to the peripheral status of an optional aid. Pictorial stimuli and responses, e.g. mental imagery, have penetrated deeply the invincible world of verbal learning, and are challenging the venerated provinces of concept learning, problem solving and thinking.[1]

And yet, at a time when the visual images reproduced on videotape or computer software are the vogue, the potential of the simplest and most cost-effective visual image, the photograph, seems to remain little explored in economics teaching, at least as far as the UK is concerned. Economics teachers appear to rely largely on commercially produced filmstrips and tape-slide sequences – and for many, even the use of these is not commonplace.[2] Textbook writers too have largely restricted themselves to line drawings, cartoons or to photographs designed only to break up the text.[3]

Using photographs: benefits

There are, however, real benefits to be gained from the use of photographs and photography, not only as the stimulus resource on which teaching and learning is based but also as part of the student's personal record of his/her educational experiences:[4]

1 Photographs offer a medium through which students can be helped to document and understand the often harsh realities of our economic environment because they can be used to introduce complex themes and provide concrete situations for discussing abstract concepts.
2 Photographs provide an opportunity for students to recognise and challenge their own stereotypes.
3 Photographs can help students to develop skills of evaluation and the ability to distinguish between fact and fiction in pictorial information.
4 Teachers are provided with a very useful means for diagnostic assessment at the beginning of a teaching topic or theme.
5 Students of all academic abilities are given a real opportunity to succeed because thinking is stimulated and reflection encouraged visually rather than through the written word.
6 An alternative/additional means of recording the outcomes of project work, industrial visits, fieldwork, etc. is provided, especially where students are encouraged to produce their own portfolios of work.
7 Photography provides one way of utilising the practical skills developed in students/teachers in many art/design courses or as a result of a hobby.
8 Using photographs is cost-effective because equipment is relatively inexpensive, most young people have access to a camera, and the outcomes of student work or even holiday camera work can serve as visual aids for general use.

Using photographs: available published resources

Unfortunately, the tendency for filmstrips or lengthy slide sequences to be used has meant that there are few published examples of individual or pairs of photographs devised specifically for use in economics lessons. In America, the innovative Economics in Society team pioneered the use of contrasting pairs of photographs as the stimulus for brainstorming activities.[5] In the UK, however, it is only now that similar techniques are being developed by the Economics Education 14–16 Project for use across the ability range of students aged 14–16 years.[6] Similar work for older students has yet to be explored, but there is every reason to believe that the outcomes of such pilot work would be positive.

Other disciplines and curriculum themes, on the other hand, are a rich source of examples of the use of photographic stimulus. For instance, in the field of development education *Learning for Change in World Society: Reflections, Activities and Resources* and *Priorities for Development: A Teacher's Handbook for Development Education*[7] provide a variety of photographic-based student activities and hints for the teacher. *Developing Cities*, one in a series produced as an extension to the Schools Council Geography for Young School Leavers Project, is an excellent example of student text in which an informative range of stimulus black and white and colour photographs is a key feature.[8] The Centre for World Development Education, with its extensive resource bank and satellite centres outside of London, provides access to a massive range of photographs on free loan or for purchase.[9]

Using photographs: some examples

The pointers towards the possible use of photographic stimulus and photography in economics teaching that follow are from the work of Post Graduate Certificate in Education students at the University of Manchester in 1983–4. The photographs illustrated were composed after six hours of photographic tuition. The students had not previously considered using photographs other than in the form of tape/slide sequences or filmstrips as part of their teaching.

1 Pairs of photographs as stimulus

Contrasting pairs of photographs provide an ideal way of getting into an issue or problem. One photograph reinforces the image portrayed in the other, triggering off a range of responses on the part of students without the initial need for the teacher to provide the lead. Whitehead gives a simple account of 'brainstorming', a technique well suited for use with photographic stimulus.[10]

Take, for example, the powerful images represented by the deserted coastal resort and the hustle and bustle of the shopping centre (Figures 9.1 and 9.2). Introduced in juxtaposition or separately, these two photographs provide the vehicle for students (working individually, in pairs, in small groups or as a full class) to consider the implications of seasonal variations in demand for employment, price, output, etc. Student responses can be recorded on a blackboard by the teacher or jotted down by the students themselves. Careful follow-up discussion or extension activities are very important, for the initial stimulus-response activity is intended to be no more than that.

In this case a series of photographs or newscuttings of particular goods and services (or even the goods themselves) could form the basis for worksheet activities as illustrated (Shopping worksheet 1).

Figures 9.3 and 9.4, on the other hand, raise one of today's crucial issues, that of advancing technology. The contrasting historical photographs can be used with effect to analyse the implications of the decision to introduce new techniques of production and indeed to expose the value judgements that underpin that decision. In this case

Figure 9.1 The beach, Herne Bay, Christmas 1983

Figure 9.2 Christmas shoppers in Chester High Street

Figure 9.3 Dough mixing   Source: United Biscuits plc.

Figure 9.4 Dough mixing

Figure 9.5 Christmas collage

Figure 9.6 Ashton Canal, Manchester, 1984

Figure 9.7 Ashton Canal, Manchester, 1984

Figure 9.8 Ashton Canal, Manchester, 1984

Figure 9.9 Ashton Canal, Manchester, 1984

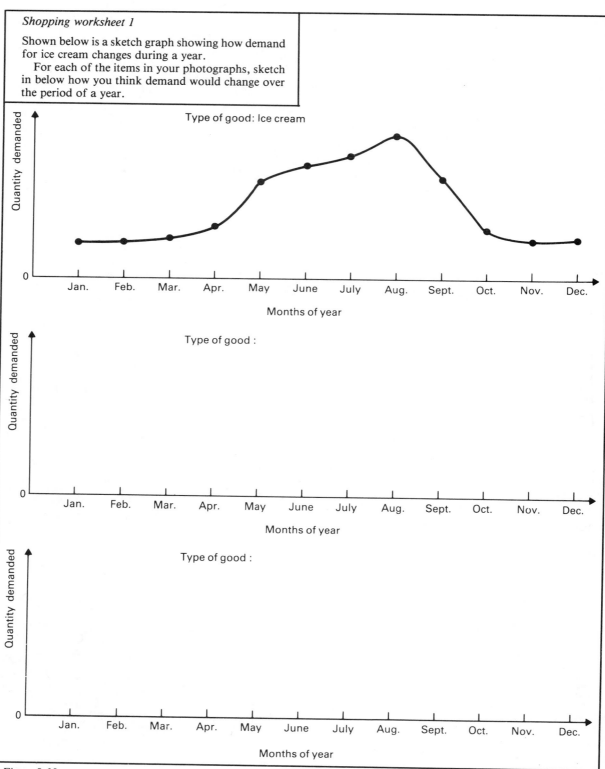

Shopping worksheet 1

Shown below is a sketch graph showing how demand for ice cream changes during a year.

For each of the items in your photographs, sketch in below how you think demand would change over the period of a year.

Type of good: Ice cream

Type of good :

Type of good :

Figure 9.10

Shopping worksheet 2

The questions below are for discussion in your working groups. Choose one person to write down the points you raise and to explain them later to everyone.

1 Why does demand for the products in your photographs change during a year?
2 Do the changes in demand over the Christmas period appear to affect the price of the products?
3 How do the shops and businesses concerned try to make up for the fact that they sell more at certain times of the year?
4 Does Christmas affect employment?

etc.

the manufacturer has concluded that marginal benefits from the changes exceed marginal costs, but are there other costs involved? To what alternative uses could the resources be put? Is society involved in any costs as a result of the decision? Are there additional private costs to be taken into account? Is the decision a 'best' decision? What is 'best'?

Figures 9.3 and 9.4 were selected from a slide set produced as an outcome of a factory visit. Companies often have historical photographs available which can be used to add a dimension to what students observe in a modern factory. Follow-up work to visits of this kind is crucial and a photographic record of a visit can be used, as here, to form the basis of analysis. An interesting technique, and one tried and tested by geography teachers, is to encourage students to record responses around the border of a photograph or sketch, giving a permanent record of their initial thoughts alongside the stimuli that triggered them off.[11]

2 Photographs and collage work

Processing photographs for individual use in class can be an expensive business for all but the most accomplished amateur photographer. For schools with fairly sophisticated printing equipment, reproducing photographs is less costly. However, one way round the problem, and an interesting variation in teaching style both for student and teacher, is to use photographs as part of a collage. In this way students, working individually, in pairs or small groups, can make use of a single set of processed photographs. An added advantage is an improved classroom appearance, at least for a short time.

Figure 9.5 is one of a series of collages which was displayed around a room for students to study and respond to. A simple worksheet (Shopping worksheet 2) provided the focus for responses with groups commencing their work at different points on it.

3 Photographs as a record of activities

From time to time attention has been drawn to the usefulness of economics trails and field studies in the teaching of economics. Student reporting of such activities is usually seen in written and statistical forms. Rarely are student observations captured in photographic form to provide a permanent 'action replay' of experience for analysis and discussion. And yet there is perhaps much to gain from the practice, for photographs will contain student rather than teacher perceptions of what is important in the 'real' economic environment that surrounds them. This is of crucial importance, since any approach to the teaching of economics that can encourage students to reveal what sense or nonsense they have made of their economic environment can only help the teacher to plan student activities accordingly.

Figures 9.6, 9.7, 9.8 and 9.9 are part of a photographic record of an urban canal trail. They expose the dynamics of industrial change – the long abandoned canal warehouse a monument to the Victorian age; one time prime industrial land now left to the weeds and the illegal rubbish dumpers; the endless task of keeping the canal pollution free; and the emerging leisure facility as canal and society at last come to terms with industrial change. For A-level students there is here the basis for investigations into the economics of deindustrialisation, transportation, leisure or even pollution. The photographic record brings out the students' observations and provides the focus for research activities, general analysis or the preparation of case-study material. For non-A-level students, the stark message that adjustment to changes in our range of products, where we produce them, and who produces them can take a lifetime, is a lesson in itself.

Conclusion

Space has precluded all but a skimming over the surface of a potentially stimulating experience for both student and teacher. The use of photographic resources and photography in economics teaching is not widespread. However, evidence emerging from the work of the Economics Education 14–16 Project indicates that teachers are quick to recognise the value of what for them is a new teaching aid.

Notes and references

1 Fleming, M. L., 'On pictures in educational research', *Instructional Science*, September 1979, pp. 235–51.
2 For a selected list of such items suitable for economics in the 'core' curriculum 14–16, see *An Annotated List of Non-Textbook Resources* (Economics Association, 1985).
3 Comments on the use of these techniques in some 130 textbooks is to be found in Economics Education 14–16 Project, *An Annotated Bibliography of Pupil Books* (Economics Association, 1985).
4 For a discussion of the role of photography in schools, see Mann, S., 'Photography in schools', *British Journal of Photography*, vol. 130, nos. 6415, 6416, 6417 and 6418.
5 Helburn, S. W., Sperling, J. G., Evans, R. G., and Lott, E. J., *Economics in Society: Concepts and Institutions*

(Addison-Wesley, 1974); and Helburn, S. W., Sperling, J. G., Evans, R. G., and Davis, J. E., *Economics in Society: Strategy and Methods* (Addison-Wesley, 1974).

6   The Economics Education 14–16 Project has developed five teaching units based on photographic stimulus resources, see *Understanding Economics* (Longman, 1985).

7   World Studies Project, *Learning for Change in World Society: Reflections, Activities and Resources* (World Studies Project, London, 1979), Development Education Centre, *Priorities for Development: A Teacher's Handbook for Development Education* (Development Education Centre, Birmingham, 1981).

8   Jones, M., *Developing Cities* (Thomas Nelson, 1982).

9   Centre for World Development Education, 128 Buckingham Palace Road, London, SW1W 9SH.

10   Whitehead, D. J., 'Learning processes and teaching strategies in economics education', *Economics*, vol. XIX, pt. 4, 1983, no. 84 pp. 141–8.

11   See, for example, an illustration of this technique in World Studies Project, op. cit., p. 48.

Acknowledgements

This chapter would not have been possible without the patience and enthusiasm of the University of Manchester PGCE group 1983–4 – Peter Bailey, Ruth Corderoy, Wendy Griffin, Neale Perrins, Nigel Royden, Deborah Sharples and Gillian Wells.

David Griffiths (photographer, University of Manchester) provided expert tuition and guidance throughout.

United Biscuits plc kindly provided Figure 9.3.

10   Economics Teaching and Consumer Education

Steve Hodkinson

Consumers – is there a problem?

All young people are consumers. From the very early years they are involved in choosing how to use their resources of time and income on a range of goods and services. Until recently the steady growth of economies in the developed world has led, among other things, to a sharp rise in standards of living and to changes in consumer habits.[1] In addition, however, changes in the balance of power between consumers and producers/distributors have also occurred because:

1   technical progress has led to the marketing of an increased variety of highly complex products;
2   both public and private services have become increasingly diversified;
3   there has been a rapid development of sales and sales promotion techniques;
4   production and distribution have come increasingly into the hands of fewer and larger companies.

These factors have combined not only to make individual consumer decisions more difficult but also to give producers and distributors a greater opportunity to determine market conditions than consumers.

Pressures on individual consumers have also been expressed in terms of their responsibilities as citizens living in a community. Consumer decisions, it is argued, should take into consideration the quality of the environment, energy usage, the consumption problems of low-income groups and of famine-ridden developing economies.

Individual consumers in countries like the UK have experienced a long-term easing of income constraints, but at the same time other constraints (institutional, ethical, social, etc.) have intensified.

Consumer education – what do we mean?

It is tempting to pretend that a consensus exists on the meaning of consumer education. However, even a cursory glance at the different perspectives advocated by Maclean,[2] Jensen,[3] the Commission of the European Communities,[4] and the National Consumer Council[5] is sufficient to dispel such a thought.

Of these differing approaches, the problem-solving perspective put forward by the European Commission carries considerable appeal. Consumer problems are considered to fall into one of five categories:

1   problems related to the situation of an individual consumer (e.g. inadequate information, making unconsidered choices);
2   problems related to the situation of consumers in general (e.g. belonging to a certain age group or social category, having a certain level of income);
3   problems related to an individual producer or distributor (e.g. misleading advertising, defective products, monopoly pricing);

4 problems related to production and distribution structures in general (e.g. concentration of the means of production, international competition);
5 problems stemming from society at large (e.g. choices between market goods and public infrastructures, polluting and non-polluting consumption).

On the basis of this problem-solving approach, the European Commission argues that young people should be helped:

(a) to identify consumer problems;
(b) to be aware of the roles of the various parties involved in the economy and of the possibilities for and effects of individual or collective action;
(c) to act responsibly as autonomous individuals recognising the constraints on choice presented by economic and social reality.

The European Commission is not therefore advocating the creation of passive consumers, but rather (and controversially) that young people should be concerned with examining and critically evaluating the values upon which our economic system and mass consumpton society are based. To this extent the European Commission is joined by Maclean (1981), Jensen (1981) and the National Consumer Council (1983).

Economics teaching – a role for consumer education?

Few proponents of consumer education have made special claims for it as a separate subject within the curriculum, preferring to emphasise how a consumer context can be infused into the framework of existing curriculum subjects. Maclean, for example, argues that:

> Although it is appropriate that economics continues to occupy a central place in consumer education programmes, no one discipline can lay claims to this subject area, for many subject areas have much to contribute that is of value.[6]

The European Commission, on the other hand, sees a multi-disciplinary approach as a way of avoiding the difficulties of introducing a new subject into an already overcrowded curriculum. It does, however, foresee potential hazards with such arrangements:

> if such an approach is not to appear facile and fragmentary, consumer education needs to be incorporated systematically into the traditional curriculum. There is also a risk that it may not give pupils an overall view of consumer problems and may remain dependent on the distribution of specialised subjects in the education system.[7]

And yet, in whatever way consumer education becomes infused into the curriculum of all young people, it is difficult to see how it can be effectively pursued without economics. Much of what is proposed for young people by the supporters of consumer education is dependent upon economics, for it is only through economics that young people will develop the objectivity, autonomy and tools of analysis to enable them to examine and evaluate those experiences of life that relate to aspects of the economic system and its operation which bear directly on consumer issues and problems.

The links between consumer education and economics education goals are nowhere more strongly reinforced than in the aims set out for the 'economic literacy' programmes which are fast becoming part of the 'core' studies for students aged 14–18 years in schools and colleges.

At 17 + , for example, the article 'Working Party Report on the 17 + ' describes the major economics education aims for a 17 + course in the following terms:

1 Activities should help students to develop a critical awareness of the way the economic system works.
2 Activities should help students to develop an understanding of their own economic experiences and thus to appreciate their relationship with the economic system, the importance of their personal contribution to that system and the strength of its influence on them.
3 Activities should help students to develop the skills which, in conjunction with the other expected outcomes, allow them, at worst, to survive after school, and, at best, to operate in the economic system with competence and understanding – communication skills, information skills (ability to search for, extract, process, evaluate and use information for their own purposes), numerical/graphical/data handling skills, decision-making skills and problem solving skills.[8]

The report then provides teachers with a framework of objectives that seeks to ensure that students are given access to the kind of investigative processes, economic concepts and information that will meet these goals.

At the 14–16 stage, too, strong links with consumer education are apparent in the work of the Economics Association's Economics Education 14–16 Project. The Project has developed exemplar teaching units specifically related to the economic experience of young people as consumers but set within a framework of key economic ideas:

> The Young Person as Consumer module seeks to provide an insight into the economic process. It is intended to cast light on the basic problems encountered in most aspects of economics and which stem from the existence of *SCARCITY* and the need for *CHOICE*. Since purchasing power is inadequate in relation to desired consumption (of better food, clothing, leisure facilities etc.) choices have to be made as to which wants to satisfy and to what level. The decision to have one thing rather than another has an *OPPORTUNITY COST* in terms of forgone alternatives. Particular decisions are motivated by the desire to secure an optimal solution to the problem of *EFFICIENT ALLOCATION* of purchasing power. Personal economic decisions have implications and consequences for other individuals, groups and institutions in the economy (local, national and international) whose decisions in their turn have implications. In being aware of the costs and benefits, both personal and social, of these decisions the young person is led to consider *INTER-DEPENDENCE* within the economic system.[9]

Emphasis on consumer matters in current examination syllabuses in economics is more difficult to assess. The only study available is that carried out by the National Consumer Council and reported in *A Better Class of Consumer*, a study limited to an analysis of the frequency with which key words in consumer education appear in Mode 1 A-level, O-level and CSE examination syllabuses.[10]

At A-level, most syllabuses refer to 'nationalised industries', 'organisation of production and distribution' and 'consumer behaviour'. At O-level, key word frequency is highest with 'money and banking' and 'organisation of production and distribution'. At CSE level the number of Mode 1 economics syllabuses is too few for meaningful data to be collated.

What is significant in the examinations field is that as a result of the introduction of the General Certificate of Secondary Education and the implementation of the *National Criteria*, the aims of all GCSE syllabuses in economics will have to meet the following requirement: 'to prepare students to participate more fully in decision making processes as consumers, producers and citizens'.[11]

There is, then, at least in this writer's view, a clear and valuable contribution to be made by economics teachers to consumer education. Moreover, the choice of a consumer context for learning experiences may to some extent help to convince young people of the relevance of their school or college work for their futures as independent people.

Consumer education – some examples and references

1 The Working World: a non-examination course for 14–16-year-olds: Parrs Wood High School, Manchester (abridged)

A Aims
The Working World is set in the context of the current and potential future experiences of students as consumers and producers. It is concerned with developing in each individual some understanding of the economic facts of life in order to allow him/her to better contribute to, and to participate in, society's further development. Course aims are therefore:

1   to provide individual students with information, skills and concepts that will enable them to better understand the workings of their own economy and its effect on their lives;
2   to develop a basic grasp of economic forces and institutions with which they will come into contact as producers and consumers;
3   to help students to develop the capacity to participate more fully in the decision-making processes of the working world.

B Objectives
(i) Knowledge and understanding

By the end of the course students should have a knowledge and understanding of:
(a) the terminology of economics concerned with their experiences as producers and consumers;
(b) the major concepts used in economics, e.g. scarcity, choice, efficiency, opportunity cost;
(c) specific concepts concerned with their experiences as producers and consumers, e.g. demand, supply, price, budgeting, value added;
(d) the methods of inquiry used in economics to provide evidence for generalisations about the working of the economy.

(ii) Skills
The course should contribute to the development of the following skills:
(a) the development of logical thinking;
(b) data processing – the collection, collation, presentation and interpretation of data;
(c) communication – written and verbal expression of factual and conceptual understanding in a clear and accurate manner;
(d) group process – advocating and listening in a group situation. Role playing as consumers, producers, wage earners and union members and in interview situations.

(iii) Attitudes
The course should develop the attitudes of students in the following ways:
(a) by helping them to distinguish between facts and value judgements;
(b) by helping them to appreciate the values held by individuals in society;
(c) by encouraging a willingness to participate in group activities and to listen to other people's views;
(d) by promoting a more balanced view in economic decision-making.

(iv) Methods
The course is 'activity-based' and should involve the use of a wide range of media and activities. Surveys, case studies, visual aids, simulations and games are essential teaching techniques.

(v) Assessment
The course will not be examined by external agencies. Emphasis in assessment will be placed on the students' own record of work and willingness to participate fully in course activities.

2 Using an economics framework to teach the topic 'saving': Linda Thomas, University of London Institute of Education

The autumn 1983 edition of *Money Management Review* is devoted to the theme 'saving'.[12] Linda Thomas's article sets out a series of general principles and checklists which, when used by teachers to derive aims and procedures, ensure that 'economic literacy' is furthered. The general principles are then used to develop a teaching scheme for the topic 'saving'.

3 Multi-disciplinary teaching in France

Some extremely successful multi-disciplinary project work by economists, historians and geographers has taken place at the Collège Hohberg, Strasbourg. These are fully illustrated in *L'Education du Consommateur* by P. Callet, G. Seiller, M. Spisser (Scodel, Paris, 1981).

4 Consumer education through basic economic concepts: an American example

Economics and the consumer (Joint Council on Economic Education, New York, 1966) is an attempt to marry personal consumer experiences with economic analysis. Opportunity cost, price determination, inflation, advertising, government services, borrowing and insurance are included.

5 Examples of strategies for teaching consumer aspects of economics at intermediate level: an American example

Master Curriculum Guide in Economics for the Nation's Schools – Part II: Strategies for Teaching Economics (Joint Council on Economic Education, New York, 1978) gives examples of teaching approaches and student activities, many with a consumer emphasis. In three volumes (primary, intermediate and secondary), the strategies are designed to show how a conceptual structure of the economics discipline can be used to assist in more effective economic decision-making.

6 A resource book for consumer education

A *Consumer Education Bibliography* has been published by the Scottish Consumer Council (1984). The Consumer Association's *Consumer Education: A Resources* *Handbook for Teachers* (Hodder & Stoughton, 1979) is a comprehensive UK reference book for resources in this area.

Notes and references

1 These arguments are rehearsed succinctly in Commission of the European Communities, *Working Document of the Commission to the Council: Reflections on Consumer Education in Schools,* X1/488/81-EN-rev. 1, 1981, paras 5–8.
2 Maclean, R., 'A case for consumer education in schools', *Economics*, vol. XVII, pt. 2, no. 74, summer 1981, pp. 45–50.
3 Jensen, H. R., 'Some reflections', ibid., pp. 50–1.
4 Commission of the European Communities, op. cit., paras 18–21.
5 National Consumer Council, *A Better Class of Consumer: An Investigation into Consumer Education in Secondary Schools* (NCC, 1983).
6 Maclean, op. cit.
7 Commission of the European Communities, op. cit., para. 31.
8 Economics Association, Working Party Report on the 17+, *Economics*, vol. XX, pt 2, summer 1984.
9 Economics Education 14–16 Project, 'The young person as consumer: general teacher guidance', unpublished draft manuscript.
10 National Consumer Council, op. cit., pp. 33–6.
11 GCE and CSE Board's Joint Council for 16+ National Criteria, *The National Criteria: Economics*, January 1985.
12 Thomas, L., 'In the classroom', *Money Management Review* (the Life Offices' Association/Associated Life Offices) no. 9, autumn 1983.

11 Cambridge O-level Business Studies

Ian Chambers

Why business studies at O-level?

Many organisations now exist whose objectives are to influence young people's understanding of business and to create closer links between schools and industry. The Industrial Society organises conferences that involve managers, trade unionists and students in case-study and discussion work. Young Enterprise facilitates direct experience by operating mini-companies, sponsored by local firms, within schools and colleges. Understanding Industry brings managers into the classroom to explain how companies evolve and work. The Schools Curriculum Industry Project encourages the development of work experience programmes and school/industry links as an integral part of the school curriculum. The unique contribution of the Cambridge Business Studies Project has been to pursue this common aim of encouraging a greater understanding of the role of business activity through the central academic curriculum of schools and colleges.

The initial focus of the Project work was on developing the syllabus and resources for Cambridge A-level business studies but, with a favourable climate of interest in business education and with growing demands from schools and colleges, in 1978 the O-level was started, with a syllabus developed by a group of teachers experienced in the teaching of the A-level course. The course was developed to provide for the following needs of students at 16 + or 17 + :

1 for information about the world of work which the students will shortly be entering;
2 for an integrated body of knowledge which cuts across existing subject boundaries;
3 to relate classroom work to the industrial and commercial community in which students live;
4 to bring the outside world into the classroom;
5 to develop students' own attitudes and perceptions about the business world.

Thus, the O-level is concerned with developing important life skills. It encourages the understanding and use of both qualitative and quantitative information; it aims to give students relevant experience of the external working environment; it helps develop important communication skills and improve confidence of students in contact with business and commerce; it helps students build up their own ideas and opinions about the outside world.

We are in an educational climate that is sympathetic to the aims and objectives of the Cambridge Business Studies course. The Secretary of State has called for more breadth and relevance in the secondary school curriculum, taking up earlier demands from industry, commerce, parents, students and teachers. New initiatives in pre-vocational education, and technical and vocational education in schools, as well as the new academic examination at 16 + and A/S level, will all provide a context in which an integrated business studies course will have an important role to play.

An integrated course

What does O-level Business Studies look like? As in the BTEC courses, Cambridge adopted a core plus options approach as the most appropriate for business studies at 16 + and 17 + . The core contains five themes that are central to any study of business and commerce, while the options allow students to explore in greater detail one important aspect of business studies. Many teachers come to this course from a background of commerce, accounts, office skills or economics teaching and the option choice reflects this and provides familiar territory from which

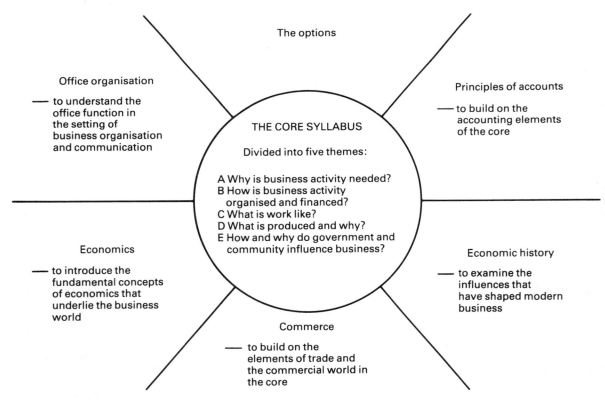

The options

Office organisation

— to understand the office function in the setting of business organisation and communication

Principles of accounts

— to build on the accounting elements of the core

THE CORE SYLLABUS

Divided into five themes:

A Why is business activity needed?
B How is business activity organised and financed?
C What is work like?
D What is produced and why?
E How and why do government and community influence business?

Economics

— to introduce the fundamental concepts of economics that underlie the business world

Economic history

— to examine the influences that have shaped modern business

Commerce

— to build on the elements of trade and the commercial world in the core

Figure 11.1 O-level business studies

they can approach the core. Emphasis in designing a teaching syllabus must be on integrating option teaching with core teaching, so that the students gain a unified view of the subject, with the option growing out of the core rather than being separate from it. Thus one hopes to get away from business studies as discrete subjects and skills taught by specialists with little co-ordination or integration. An outline of the course is given in Figure 11.1.

A detailed breakdown of both core syllabus and option syllabuses can be found in the University of Cambridge Local Examinations syndicate syllabus booklet for Economics and Business Studies.

How is it examined?

The core syllabus is examined by a combination of short-answer questions, essay and structured questions, some with a numerate element. With the option areas there is a choice between an examination based largely on structured questions, or four short pieces of coursework (of which one piece may be based on a core topic) assessed by the teacher and externally moderated. The balance of marks between the core and the options is 70 per cent to 30 per cent. The flexibility of the syllabus is therefore reflected in the examination.

Coursework will be new for many teachers and has not been a popular choice. This seems a pity because it allows experiential learning and, in schools and colleges where it is undertaken, it helps motivate the students and improve their comprehension of elements in the core syllabus. A popular choice for coursework in the economics options has been a study of prices and the factors influencing demand in a local shopping precinct. As well as the need to design and carry out their own research, students have also been studying sales promotion, advertising, consumer protection and much more. Imaginatively selected coursework may give students a learning experience of great value for the course and their general education.

Further details of the examination structure can be found in the University of Cambridge Local Examinations Syndicate booklet, including some assessment criteria for the coursework.

A two-year course or a one-year course?

Over two years, the course allows ample opportunity for student-centred, participative activities, whether or not coursework is being examined. There is also enough time to follow up interesting areas and to build into the syllabus a programme of visits or talks, business games or simulations – such as the running of a small enterprise or company.

If teaching this course at 17 +, over a one-year period, one's flexibility is somewhat reduced by the time constraint, but in other respects the course is ideally suited to sixth-year students. Often they have extra maturity and

experience on which to build. Many will have first-hand experience of the world of work through part-time jobs or through careers work. Many who have failed at traditional subjects find new challenges and motivation from business studies. Students at 17 + also find the participative approach easier to come to terms with and thus teachers can be quite ambitious in their teaching approaches. The time constraint can also be eased by using coursework to cover the option area, freeing more teaching time for core-based work. The course has also proved attractive for A-level students seeking to widen their studies.

Teaching approaches

By its aims, syllabus and examination, this course encourages the use of a variety of teaching techniques, and the Cambridge Business Studies project has developed an O-level teaching file that uses this variety. Some of the major approaches encouraged are examined below, together with illustrations of project material.

1 Simple exposition and questioning

There is a body of factual knowledge that provides the basis for understanding business problems, ranging from the structure of different business organisations to the different advertising media that exist; from the conventions of the accountant to the laws of consumer protection; from the cost structures of firms to the needs of individuals, and so on. In order to develop this important factual understanding in students, two considerations are vital.

First, understanding must be built on the students' own experiences, on their own view of the world. Thus an exposition on consumer law should start by relating to students' experience as consumers; an exposition on the income and expenditure of an organisation should start by looking at their income and spending, at the school's income and expenditure or at the accounts of their local fishing club or church.

Secondly, students will understand better when they are involved in learning. Communication in the classroom must be two-way, with the students having some chance to provide a feedback. In its simplest form, this might be question and answer sessions, or written exercises and worksheets. Alternatively, students can be encouraged to research and discover. The following example might be used to help students build up their understanding of small businesses and the problems they face:

Small business survey
(a) Walk around your local community and try to list all the small business organisations in your area. What activities are they taking part in?
(b) Go and talk to the owner of a small business. There are many questions that you could ask, among them:

(i) Advantages in being a small business?
(ii) Disadvantages compared to larger businesses?
(iii) How is the business organised?
(iv) How is capital raised?
(v) Why do customers deal with this business rather than a larger one?
(vi) How much time does the business take up?
(vii) Did the possibility of business failure ever worry?
(viii) Does the government help your business?

Write up your interview in the form of an article that could appear in a local newspaper.

Such an exercise both helps to create a degree of background experience (for the student) and involves students in their learning.

2 Problem solving

The course encourages students to apply their understanding of this basic knowledge to simple problems and situations. Here is one such situation that the teacher can use to apply knowledge of market research:

Assume that you are the marketing manager of a firm producing bicycles. The firm has decided to investigate the possibilities of producing a new model of bike, or producing something that bicycle owners would consider buying, which is not already on the market. As the marketing manager, you have to produce details for the next meeting of the board of directors, on how you would go about this investigation.
  Present your ideas in the form of a report and include the following:
(a) the areas to be researched;
(b) whether you would use questionnaires or interviews or both;
(c) examples of questions you would ask;
(d) how you would prevent a biased conclusion being reached;
(e) the method of sampling you would use.

In this problem, the student can take a broadly qualitative approach to market research although one could consider the possible cost of a large survey. It is likely to be in teaching the numerate elements of the course that explaining techniques in simple problem-solving terms would be most common. In teaching numeracy in the O-level course, it is important to use simple but real problems set in a business situation, where the students can see that a solution is needed, and that a simple numerate approach will be useful in helping to arrive at a solution. Emphasis should not be on the mathematical technique itself, but on how and when it can be used, and on the limits to its use. Very often it is useful to include a qualitative element in a problem, so as to show that a numerate technique is often only an aid to decision-making. The following problem could be used to show the value of contribution costing in business:

A company has been making and selling 1000 calculators a year at £6 each. Its costs are:

	£
Direct labour	1000
Direct materials	1500
Factory indirect expenses	2000
Administrative expenses	500

A large store makes an offer, stating that they will buy 300 calculators if the price can be reduced to £4. *Should the company accept this order?*
  At first glance it would seem it should not, as the present average cost per calculator is £5. But considering the figures more carefully:
(i) Direct costs will obviously rise in direct proportion to the rise in production.
(ii) Factory indirect expenses may rise, but not necessarily in proportion – a reasonable estimate might be an extra £250.
(iii) Administrative expenses would probably not rise at all.
Therefore costs would be as follows when the new order is included:

		£
Direct labour $1000 + (1000 \times 30\%)$	=	1300
Direct materials $1500 + (1500 \times 30\%)$	=	1950
Factory expenses $2000 + 250$	=	2250
Administrative expenses 500	=	500
		6000

Profit before accepting the order was:

$$\text{Profit} = \text{Revenue} - \text{Costs}$$
$$= £6000 - £5000$$
$$= £1000$$

Profit when the new order is included:

$$\text{Profit} = \text{Revenue} - \text{Costs}$$
$$= (£6000 + £1200) - £6000$$
$$= £7200 - £6000$$
$$= £1200$$

So the profit made by the firm would increase as the new order helps *contribute* to fixed overheads of the firm as well as covering variable costs. The value of marginal or contribution costing has thus been illustrated. But perhaps a further question could be asked – will the firm's existing customers, paying £6 per calculator, be happy that it is supplying another company at only £4?

3 Case studies

Although the use of case studies in the O-level course is not explicitly encouraged by setting a formal case examination (as in A-level Business Studies), they should form an important and regularly employed tool for the O-level teacher. The key to the successful use of case studies is that the teacher has a specific objective or set of objectives in mind when developing the case material, which will often be adapted from real situations.

These objectives should not be seen in terms of transferring information about the outside world from the teacher to the student via the case study. It is the learning skills that should form the starting point for using case materials (and this will also be true of games and simulations). Skills that can be developed by using the case method include:

(a) Information handling – where various kinds of information about an organisation are given and the students have to classify, organise and perhaps evaluate that information. Alternatively, students might have to think about how to collect and interpret information.

(b) Application skills – where students have to apply the ideas and techniques they have learnt to sort out and find the solution to a problem.

(c) Analysis – often the case will take the form of a simple story line which asks the student either to analyse what went wrong (or right) or to look at how they think the case will develop. Real-life problems would be especially suitable for this type of use. The ability to be creative and generate new solutions is one that should be encouraged, but may well be beyond most school students.

(d) Social skills – a recognition that by discussing cases in groups, by communicating with others, by reporting back either verbally or in written form, students will be practising important social skills. The development of such skills should be a conscious aim of teachers and the use of case studies gives an opportunity.

An abundance of good case material exists that can be tailored to the specific aims of the O-level teaching syllabus. The 'Launch of Persil Automatic' produced by Unilever, and the marketing of 'Yorkie' by Rowntree-Mackintosh are two cases that provide an excellent stimulus for students in the marketing/production area; both the positive and the negative side of industrial relations and participation can be illustrated by work based on the long-running *Times* dispute, British Leyland's experience, the Meriden experiment, the Saab and Volvo group working schemes or Sony's quality circles; and magazines like *Which?* provide a continual fund of good consumer protection cases.

Tailor-made case material is less readily available for the financial and accounting work, so it is probably necessary for the teacher to create it, perhaps by following a small business through the financial trials and tribulations of their first year's trading, so that the students learn the role of finance and accounting within the context of business operations. Alternatively, many companies now produce very useful annual reports which can be used as the basis for case material, with BP leading the way by providing a worksheet on their annual report.

4 Games and simulations

It is probably the motivational effect of using simulations that is of most value within the O-level course, although, as with case studies, they do allow students to practise the skills of application, analysis, communication and decision-making. A game can, and in fact should be used as the basis for aiding further understanding of a topic, and thus should not be used as an 'end of term' morale booster. Within this area, emphasis should be on the simple type of game or simulation which can be incorporated into a teaching programme, perhaps taking up one or two double lessons, rather than the large-scale simulations run over a series of weeks, although the latter can provide very effective support material for those following the O-level course.

Four examples might best illustrate the role that games and simulations can play. 'Survival' is described in the first edition of this *Handbook* and has proved most successful as a practical way of encouraging students to think about what business activity involves and why it is needed. It can be played right at the start of the O-level course and will provide a chance for the class to interact, and it functions as a good motivator for the early work in the course.

A simple production game can provide the starting point for looking at the way production is organised, simple costing and pricing, and perhaps marketing and collective bargaining. The example given below involves the construction of paper bricks (paper hats or paper planes would be two other alternatives) and entails the students in organising production, actually producing the goods, deciding on pricing and output levels, quality control and industrial relations. Teachers can choose, in their debriefing and the work they set to follow up the exercise, which aspect they wish to emphasise.

The paper brick game

'Geesentax' Ltd are world famous for their paper bricks – to be found propping up buildings from Tibet to Timbuktu. You are the management, and the workers of Geesentax.

Your product is drawn (not to scale) below. It is built to the strictest specifications.

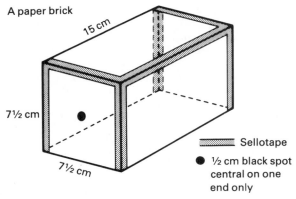

A paper brick

15 cm

7½ cm

7½ cm

▦ Sellotape

● ½ cm black spot
central on one
end only

What you have to do:
To start, the management must decipher how to make
each brick.
It must then decide how many bricks to make in each
production run.
There will be two production runs, with a tea break in
the middle. It must also decide at what price to sell the
bricks to the Paper Brick Purchasing Company.

Raw materials and machinery
These are available at the following prices:
RULERS   – 20 Money Units (MUs) per period
SCISSORS   – 50 MUs per period
PAPER   – 5 MUs per sheet
SELLOTAPE   – 50 MUs per roll

Production
This is only done by the workers. It is up to the workers
to negotiate their own wages. The managers must devise
and keep a record of expenditure and income. All
finished bricks should be delivered to the Purchasing
Company at the end of each product run, and the
agreed price will be paid, provided the quality is good.
Your objective is to maximise your profits!

Collective bargaining simulations are probably the type
most frequently used by business studies teachers, and
their value lies in giving students a chance to experience
the different roles. Teachers need to devise a scenario
relevant to the experience of their students, perhaps
locating the firm or organisation within the local
community, or else building on the situation developed in

the paper brick game. Try to ensure that there are a variety
of roles to play in the bargaining and that students gain a
view of both sides of the bargaining table. It is also useful
to have one group as independent arbitrators who can be
called in, and perhaps another group as journalists
reporting the bargaining (perhaps not so independent).
Although the simulation is likely to be built around a wage
conflict, one might also build in some more positive
elements, such as discussion on health and safety or
training schemes.
    A different type of simulation may be used in teaching
about organisation and communication in the section on
'What Work Is Like?' in the core. Communication in
groups can be explained by using the concept of the
communication network, and the students can be given
the opportunity of experiencing for themselves the
strengths and weaknesses of the different types of net that
might exist in an organisation. Each group is given a
simple problem to solve, about which each member only
receives one piece of information. They can only
communicate with each other by writing one message at a
time and passing it on. The students are arranged
according to one of the standard networks in groups of
five – perhaps two different groups at a time is ideal so
that comparisons between the two networks is possible –
while the rest of the class act as observers. Possible
problems and networks that can be used are given below:

Communication nets – problems and networks
Problem 1 Each member has a list of colours. Find the
           common colour and pass this information
           to each member of the group.

A	B	C	D	E
Blue	Yellow	Pink	Blue	Pink
Red	Brown	Blue	Brown	Red
Yellow	Red	Yellow	Purple	Yellow
Purple	Blue	Brown	Orange	Orange
Orange	Purple	Orange	Yellow	Brown

(A similar exercise could be carried out using symbols
or numbers.)

Problem 2 You are members of a small company
           moving from one office building to
           another. There are four types of equipment
           that must be moved: chairs, desks, filing
           cabinets and typewriters. Find out how
           many truckloads the move will need and
           communicate the information to each
           member of the group.

Networks:

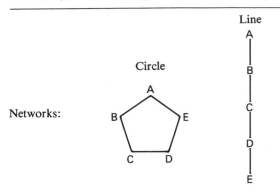

Circle

Line

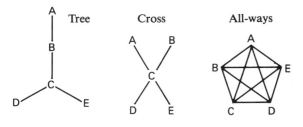

Tree   Cross   All-ways

A The company has twelve desks. Five filing cabinets is a truckload.

B The company has forty-eight chairs. Each truck holds six pot plants.

C Twenty-four chairs will go into a truck. The company has twelve typewriters.

D A truck holds four bookshelves. The company has fifteen filing cabinets.

E A truckload would be twelve typewriters or three desks.

As follow-up to the exercise the students should assess each type of net under a number of possible criteria:

(a) speed of decision-making – during the exercise time how long each group takes to solve each problem;

(b) number of messages sent – this could be the role of the observers to see how many messages had to be sent before the problem was solved;

(c) speed in correcting mistakes;

(d) involvement of those in the group – was anyone not able to take part because of their position in the net?

(e) who is the leader?

The students could then look at the appropriateness of these nets for use as organisational models in a number of different business situations, e.g. 'brainstorming' for a new product, emergency procedures in case of fire, wage negotiations, consultation, meetings between management and workforce, etc.

5 Contact with the outside community

The O-level syllabus places emphasis upon understanding of, and ability to refer to, the industrial and commercial community both nationally and locally. Teachers must build their lessons around the range of experience of their students but they can do a lot to widen that range either in the classroom by using case studies and simulations, or by taking their students into the local community (or bringing it into the classroom).

If the teacher decides to follow the coursework option, then students will, by necessity, have the opportunity to go outside the school into the local community and apply their classroom work to some aspect of commercial activity going on there. If one takes the commerce option, assignments could be based on the retailing activity of the town, on how local business is financed, on how it is insured, and on the trading documents used by a local firm. One assignment could also be chosen from the core area – perhaps a study of a local trade union or a look at the launch of a new product. All these activities will help build up the understanding and experience of the students.

Project-type activity has an important place in the syllabus, whether or not the coursework option is followed. Designing and carrying out a local questionnaire, a field study of the local industry and commerce, visits to local employers to look at training or the local careers office, studying the organisation of the local council or hospital, studying the accounts of the local fishing club – all this and much more can form part of the teaching syllabus and can bring relevance to the classroom study. The only constraint is the teacher's time. It is important to remember that non-profit-making organisations, such as clubs, charities, councils or schools, can provide as fruitful and useful a source for visits and illustrations as commerce or industry.

Contacts established in this way can lead to representatives from these organisations coming into schools to bring their experience into the classroom. Here the best way of ensuring a successful visit is to get the managers to run a case study or simulation so that the students can divide into groups and talk to the visitor in a less formal atmosphere.

16 + Business studies – the future

It is envisaged that the aims and approach of the Cambridge O-level will have an important influence on the development of curricula for 16 + business studies. It has been recognised that the O-level course already serves a wider range of ability than more traditional O-levels, and that students who are not academically gifted have been able to benefit from the more relevant and practical work that business studies offers, often building on careers and work experience programmes in their schools. In addition, a CSE in Business Studies has been successfully introduced by the East Anglian Examination Board, adopting an integrated approach to business studies which is very close in spirit to the Cambridge O-level course. The 16 + National Criteria for Business Studies produced in October 1983 by the Joint Council identified three different approaches to the examining of business studies at 16 + :

1 on the basis of separate single subjects (e.g. accounting and commerce);

2 as a single integrated subject – business studies;

3 as a core syllabus in business studies with an option, or options;

It regarded these approaches as equally acceptable, thus providing a framework that allows for sufficient flexibility while ensuring that syllabuses have sufficient common content. The Cambridge 'core + options' approach can be seen to be in a strong position in relation to the Joint Council's thinking, and this is further confirmed in the detailed aims, assessment objectives and content for business studies which the Joint Council set out. The general educational aims for all business studies courses were:

1 to develop knowledge and understanding of business and its environment both in general terms and in relation to those roles and interrelationships that are part of commercial and economic activity locally, nationally and internationally;

2 to develop relevant skills and techniques as an integral part of general education and as an appropriate foundation for further study;

3 to develop knowledge and understanding of the co-

operation and interdependence that participation in society entails and to encourage the confidence and awareness of young people in their approach to such participation through group activity within the classroom and direct experience outside it.

From what has been said about the aims and approaches of the Cambridge course, it can be seen that it embraces these aims, and students who have followed the course over the last five years have been having the type of educational experience envisaged by the Joint Council. Whether one could say the same about students who have been following existing accounting, commerce or office practice courses is open to doubt. In a similar way, much of what the National Criteria consider to be the content of such courses is already included in the Cambridge O-level course.

Examinations at 16 + will bring radical changes in the methods of assessment used by examination boards, but there is a good opportunity to build on the practice of the different ranges of ability, to bring in more teacher assessment and coursework and, the most difficult area, to develop grade-related criteria specifying skills and knowledge expected for award at each grade. Teachers who have been involved in the development and teaching of the Cambridge O-level course and the East Anglia CSE will already have experience of many of the skills that will be needed in successfully developing and organising a 16 + business studies examination and, given the time constraint that exists if the first examination is to be in 1988, this experience should form the basis for the future development of business studies as part of the academic syllabus in schools and colleges.

Resources

The Cambridge Business Studies Project

University of London Institute of Education, 20 Bedford Way, London WC1 0AL. (01 636 1500 Ext. 309/311/798). Director: D. H. Dyer, Assistant Director: I. H. Chambers. The services of the Project are available to all who teach or who are preparing to teach the Cambridge Business Studies courses, parallel courses for CSE and those developing a business studies input to teacher training. A team of experienced teachers act as regional officers to provide advice and information at the local level. The Resource Centre for the Project is at the Director's home and is run by the Resources Officer: Mrs M. E. Dyer, 22 Nene Crescent, Oakham, Leicestershire (0572 2557).

The O-level file

The basic teaching aid for the core part of the syllabus, it contains both student material and teachers' guides for each section of the core. There are also plenty of problems and exercises, and suggestions for participative work. It can be obtained from the Resource Centre. An O-level text is currently in preparation and, when it is complete, the O-level file will be revised to complement the textbook.

Books

The Longman Understanding Business Series (Editor: Richard Barker)
There are eight books in this series, accompanied by eight teachers' guides. Although primarily produced for the Cambridge A-level course, some of the series can be of use to teachers of the O-level course:
Financial Decisions by D. R. Myddleton – very good for the types and sources of finance;
Accounting and Decision Making by P. Corbett – a good introduction to the accounting model and the final accounts. Most value for the Principles of Accounts option;
Production Decisions by J. Powell – especially for its introduction to costing and location;
Marketing Decisions by P. Tinniswood – a valuable aid for the marketing mix part of the core;
People and Decisions by N. Worrall – will help with the human relations aspects of the core, especially the needs of workers, motivation and communication.

In all the aforementioned books each chapter is accompanied by checklist questions, case exercises and problems, and suggested essay titles, and the teachers' guides contain further suggestions about approaches, timing, etc. as well as solutions to any problems set. All titles are published by Longman.
Understanding Industry by J. M. Baddeley (Butterworth) – produced in association with the Industrial Society, this provides a good student resource, especially for 17 + . It contains plenty of cases, simulations and games and is particularly strong in the human element of business. A teacher's guide is also available.
Understanding Industrial Society by A. P. Sanday and P. A. Birch (Hodder & Stoughton) – aimed at the course of the same name, it sets out to involve students in their learning and to look closely at their outside community. Not a detailed text, but it contains a lot of participative ideas. Most suitable for fourth and fifth years. A series of tapes and a teacher's guide is also available.

General book list

A wide range of books exists which would be of value to a business studies teacher, and the Project has produced a detailed list indicating which books or series are most suitable for student, teacher or library use. The list is included in the O-level file and is also available separately from the Resource Centre.

Booklets

An Introduction to Business Studies – a series of six booklets produced by Unilever Market Research, Advertising and the Launch of Persil Automatic. They are of great value, therefore, in the marketing area of the course. Available from Unilever Education Section, PO Box 68, Unilever House, London EC4P 4BQ.

Industry in Close Up and *Industry in Perspective* – two booklets that examine how the various functions in a company are organised and the role of business in society. Sponsored and published by a consortium of companies, with the support of the Industry Education unit of the Department of Trade and Industry, they are available in packs of thirty from Motivity Ltd, PO Box 6, Hampton, Middlesex TW12 2HE.

Understanding British Industry – the Resource Centre produces a series of booklets for teachers which cover topics such as visits to schools, teaching materials, visits to industry, trade union resources, and micro-electronics; these will give the teacher an unending source of ideas and materials to use in the classroom. UBI's main resource centre is Sun Alliance House, New Inn Hall Street, Oxford OX1 2QE, but they also have satellite resource centres and liaison officers organised on a regional basis.

Careers Research and Advisory Centre – CRAC publications provide excellent resource material for studying the world of work, especially their Survival and Job Skills series, their Work Experience series and Job Quiz series. Fuller details are available from CRAC Publications, Hobsons Ltd, Bateman Street, Cambridge CB2 1LZ.

Schools and Industry – a simple booklet produced by the DTI Industry Education Unit which lists the major organisations involved in developing schools-industry links and briefly describes their role and the resources they produce. The Unit is at Ashdown House, 123 Victoria Street, London SW1E 6RB.

BP Annual Report and Accounts Resource Pack – includes both the up-to-date BP accounts and also an educational guide to the accounts with question and discussion points. Available in class size batches from BP Educational Service, PO Box 5, Wetherby, West Yorkshire.

Case studies and simulations

CRAC case studies and business games – most suitable for using with students following the course in the sixth form, CRAC have produced a series of ten business experience case studies covering organisation, industrial relations, communication, finance, production and marketing. Their five simple business games, including the famous 'Gorgeous Gateaux' and 'Fresh Oven Pies', are well suited for mixed-ability groups and for a range of ages, and evaluation exercises are also included. Available from same address as above.

BP Paraffin File – now in a computer pack, this game gives students a taste of how the economic environment affects business as each group represents an oil company. A numerate exercise probably better suited to sixth form groups. Available from BP Educational Service, address as above.

The Mini Co. Kit by Elizabeth Bray (Longman) – a do-it-yourself business package that allows students to create and run a company or co-operative in miniature. Very much building on the experience of Young Enterprise in encouraging direct experience and participation. Having such an enterprise running alongside the academic course would give an excellent source of illustration and practical problems.

Videos and tapes

Business Matters – ten programmes considering general aspects of business activity, as well as specific topics such as the problems of small businesses and information technology. First broadcast by BBC radio in 1982–3. A book *Business Matters* by Jenyth Worsley (Cassell) was published to accompany the series.

A Head for Business – produced for the DTI Industry Education unit by John Cleese and made available free to all schools, this video is also accompanied by *Self Starters* which looks at some young entrepreneurs, and a full teacher's guide. Now available from CFL Vision Distribution Centre, Chalfont Grove, Gerrards Cross, Bucks.

Foundations of Wealth – a series of videos sponsored by Esso, ICI and Unilever aimed to bring to life some of the basic principles of economic and business activity, such as the division of labour, mechanisation and the market. Teachers' notes are also available. Available from Unilever Education Section, address as above.

This list cannot hope to be comprehensive and a good teacher of business studies will be able to find many more useful resources and organisations to help, especially at the local level where organisations are often willing to lend to schools or colleges some of their own resources that they use for training, induction, etc. There is also a growing list of computer simulations relating to the way industry and commerce works, although as yet most would only be suitable with A-level students.

Section 2
Ways of Teaching Particular Topics

12 'Starting Off!': Suggestions for Beginning a Two-year Course
Richard Dunnill

Introduction

Old educationalists' joke:

Philosopher to student: 'Good Morning'
Student's reply: 'Define what you mean by "Good"'
Teacher to class: 'Good Morning'
(No reply): Students all writing down 'Good Morning'!

All too often, teachers are seeking to develop the positive and critical attitude shown by the philosophy student above, only to find that they have to be satisfied with the second situation illustrated. This chapter outlines one approach to this problem, tried out in a south London comprehensive school with a fair degree of success.

An outline of the problem

The problem is one common to most schools. Groups are fairly large, and contain students with wide ranges of ability, motivation and attitudes towards both education in general, and economics as a subject. They also have virtually no previous knowledge of the subject. Staff, meanwhile, have to teach to the CSE and O-level syllabuses, cope with the above factors, and try to develop some enthusiasm for economics among the students, with all the usual constraints of time and money! Thus, the following question is posed: 'What should my fourth year economics students be doing for the first part of their course?' It may be useful for readers to pause at this stage, and consider their answers to this question.

The answer to their question? Traditionally, teachers start teaching the first item on the syllabus, for no other reason than that it is first on the list. Why not, instead, consider what you really want the students to do over the two years, and then think carefully about how those vital first few lessons can establish a worthwhile standard? In addition, do not just consider *what* is to be taught, but consider *how* it should be covered.

Suggested aims

Aims for the two-year course should be:

1 Exam success – for obvious reasons;
2 Hard work – a positive, hard-working attitude;
3 Motivation – a desire to do well, and to learn;
4 Enjoyment – for staff as well as students!

Few (if any) teachers would disagree with these aims – the real question is how to achieve them. ('Enjoyment', of course, is very rarely mentioned in connection with education. A pity, since a course that combines 'relevance' and 'fun' to stimulate learning will inevitably succeed.)

Traditionally, economics teaching has been 'formal':

1 Students work as a class, or as individuals.
2 Heavy reliance is placed on a textbook that preordains the approach to the subject.
3 The teacher does most of the thinking.
4 The student simply records information.

Thus, an essentially *passive* approach to economics is developed. However, in the light of the new London University O-level syllabus proclaiming, 'The Examiners are anxious to destroy the belief that Economics is a mere textbook subject',[1] and the fact that both teachers and students are becoming increasingly dissatisfied with such passive methods, an alternative approach is outlined below.

Suggested method

'Active learning' is where students are more involved in their own learning:

1 Students work in groups/pairs, as well as in classes or as individuals.
2 Materials are varied, as are tasks and assignments.
3 Discussion and argument are encouraged, and students' ideas are respected by teacher and fellow students.

4 Thus the students are encouraged to think rationally, using an economics perspective.

Of course, the teacher is still 'in charge'! Active learning is simply an attempt to mix the best elements of traditional learning with the best parts of progressive methods.

What follows is a suggested 'Introduction to Economics' for a fourth-year group, combining active learning with the overall aims set out previously and with some attempt to make the whole experience 'enjoyable' for both teacher and students.

The first four weeks: an 'active' introduction to economics

Aims
1 Obvious academic coverage.
2 Establish discipline and behavioural guidelines for the course.
3 Develop students' confidence and ability to reason, examine and analyse.
4 Observe how group works together.
5 To show the relevance of economics to the 'real world'.

Methods
1 Teacher-centred learning, initially whole group.
2 Audio/visual resources from their own experiences.
3 Simulation/game – pairs/groups.
4 Research/opinion piece for homework.

		Week one
(a)	'The economic problem'	Teacher-centred introduction on scarcity, choice, opportunity cost.
(b)	'Resources'	Friends of the Earth materials and a video of The News item. Worksheet and discussion.
	'Homework'	Explain a current news item concerning resources.
		Week two
(a)	'How can we solve "the economic problem"?'	Game about the adventure holiday and the Arab in the desert. Brief discussion.
(b)	'Three methods to solve the problem'	Worksheet consolidation. Then into three systems, terminology, etc., information sheets.
	'Homework'	Each group produces a description of a system.
		Week three
(a)	'Report back'	Each group reports on 'their' system to the class. Worksheet consolidation.
(b)	'Current economic problems'	Newspapers and structured discussion on

		problems in each of three systems.
	'Homework'	Revise all terms and ideas covered.
		Week four
(a)	'Springboard session'	Using video on Keynes, look at issues leading us into rest of the course.
(b)	'End of topic test'	Designed to examine 'recall understanding' *and* analysis.

Two lessons per week, each of approximately 1 hour's length.

This introduction gives a varied and stimulating programme of activities. These activities are designed to achieve the specific aims stated, and more general long-term aims, together with a thorough coverage of the topic necessary for examination success.

In Figure 12.1 a simple game is outlined, designed at the time Mark Thatcher was lost during a car rally. As well as allowing the group a change from formal learning, it also enables students to form their own idea about distributing scarce resources. The usual answers develop after about fifteen minutes of intense discussion. Going around the groups, three ideas arise – an auction of watches, jewellery, other valuables and cash; the Arab choosing the people to survive; a mixture of these two.

Figure 12.2 is a straightforward consolidation worksheet to be completed after the discussion of these three ideas.

Figures 12.3, 12.4 and 12.5 develop the three ideas into 'systems', the advantages and disadvantages are meant to be debatable! A session at the end of a lesson simply going through the terms and concepts used on the sheets is useful, enabling the students to go away and produce a description of 'their' system for homework, and for use next lesson.

Finally, Figure 12.6 consolidates all this, after the group has discussed the three systems and listened to each other's descriptions. The posters or newspaper articles are designed both to improve the students' understanding and analysis of each system, and to allow another change in the learning techniques employed.

The originals of the materials shown were produced using drawing pens and were deliberately not typewritten. Handwritten (if good!) materials often work better as a stimulus to thought and action. Typewritten materials are generally used for in-depth information, supplements, etc. They are reproduced using an offset litho or high-speed photocopier at a cost of only a few pence a sheet.

Conclusion

The ideas and materials outlined in this chapter are open to criticism and revision, but they do represent a practical attempt to provide a stimulating, relevant and challenging

SO HOW CAN WE SHARE SCARCE RESOURCES?

✱ Work in groups of three-five people

You are leading a **group** of fifteen tourists on an ADVENTURE HOLIDAY, driving through the Sahara Desert in a Land Rover, camping at night.

The Land Rover has broken down, and after some days, your water has run out, and you are in real trouble!

An ARAB rides into view on his camel, leading two more camels. He stops, you explain the problem, and he agrees to help...

The ARAB only has enough water for himself and SIX of you to survive until you reach the nearest oasis...

HOW DOES THE ARAB DECIDE WHO SHOULD HAVE WATER?

Discuss this, and decide what he would do...write down his decision here, giving reasons for his choice.

....
....
....
....
....

Figure 12.1

introduction to a fourth-year economics course, working within fairly tight demands on teacher time, energy, money and limited school resources.

The keys to success have been careful planning of each syllabus topic, detailed planning for each lesson, and a large degree of enthusiasm for economics by the staff concerned. This latter often proves 'infectious' enough for the students to be stimulated towards both a real economics perspective, and excellent examination results. Incidentally, the teacher usually enjoys teaching more, too! Why not try some of these ideas? They may 'infect' you!

Further reading

Sutton, C. (ed.) *Communicating in the Classroom* (Hodder & Stoughton, 1981). London Regional Examining Board, *Model Economics Syllabus* (LREB, 1984).

Notes and references

1   University of London, *O-level Economics Syllabus* (London University, 1984).

METHODS of sharing out resources

* So, there are three main methods of sharing scarce resources

    i...

    ii..

    iii...

* For each method or **ECONOMIC SYSTEM** fill in the details in each box below, making notes.

i.
   a Name of system...

   b How is it decided who gets what?...

   c What do you think of this system?...

   d 5 Countries who use it..

ii
   a

   b

   c

   d

iii
   a

   b

   c

   d

Now....write up these notes properly into your books using as your title: 'THE THREE ECONOMIC SYSTEMS'.

Figure 12.2

THE FREE-MARKET SYSTEM

Outline ....

All resources are privately owned, and PRODUCTION is by private firms aiming to make a PROFIT. The forces of supply and demand fix the PRICES of goods + services, e.g. The more apples there are, the lower the price. The more people wanting apples, the higher the price. The GOVERNMENT just keeps the country safe with an Army, Navy, Air Force, Police, Courts, etc. and does very little else.

ADVANTAGES.........
1 Consumers get the products they want, through supply and demand.
2 No massive bureaucracy.
3 Profits ensure efficiency, enough production and the right sort of production.
4 Competition ensures low prices and new technology.
5 Monopolies won't last—other firms will join in.

DISADVANTAGES...........
1 The inequality of rich + poor continues.
2 Profits become more important than people.
3 Some goods and services won't be produced well.
4 Competition can cause waste and inefficiency.
5 In real life, monopoly does exist.
6 Pollution, noise, smell, ugliness, etc. all get worse.

Figure 12.3

THE PLANNED SYSTEM

OUTLINE ....

The government/state owns all RESOURCES, and takes the job of estimating people's NEEDS + WANTS, and of organising production to satisfy these needs + wants. Prices are thus fixed by the government, not by market forces (supply and demand).

ADVANTAGES ....

1 All basic necessities produced for everyone, as are essential services.
2 No bureaucracy wasting money—they're only making sure the system works properly.
3 People don't need profits as an incentive; working for the community is enough, and will prevent pollution, etc. as well as inefficiency.
4 No waste on luxuries until everyone has the basic essentials, or on useless competition.
5 The people control the economy...so no unemployed.

DISADVANTAGES ....

1 It is difficult to estimate people's needs and wants.
2 The bureaucracy needed to organise production will be large and inefficient.
3 No profits will mean laziness, and people not trying as hard as they might.
4 People lose their freedom to choose.
5 Technology will not advance very fast, and prices will stay high because of no competition.

Figure 12.4

THE MIXED SYSTEM

OUTLINE ....

The RESOURCES are mostly owned by private companies, who organise most of the production of goods and services but....The government owns and controls the basic industries and spends money on helping people with health, education, unemployment benefit, etc. The idea is to combine the best points of the other two systems. People are free to choose what is produced and consumed, but the government makes sure problems are minimised while social welfare is maximised.

AIMS ....

1 To produce goods and services, a free market system ignores.
2 To provide more efficiently than other systems.
3 To avoid great inequalities of wealth, to give everyone a minimum standard of living and equality of opportunity.
4 To protect people from monopolies.
5 To control pollution and social problems.
6 To get full employment and low inflation.
7 To help the regions.
8 To improve our trade.
9 The achieving of constant economic growth.

BUT IN THE REAL WORLD.....

since the mid 1960s, we have seen 1 HIGH INFLATION, 2 HIGH UNEMPLOYMENT and 3 LOW ECONOMIC GROWTH.......things don't seem to be getting much better!

Figure 12.5

ECONOMIC SYSTEMS

HAVING READ AND DISCUSSED THE THREE ECONOMIC SYSTEMS, USE YOUR NOTEBOOKS/FILES TO DO THE FOLLOWING QUESTIONS..........

1   Explain the following words..........

PRIVATE FIRMS	COMPETITION	MINIMISED AND MAXIMISED
PROFIT	TECHNOLOGY	MINIMUM STANDARD OF LIVING
SUPPLY AND DEMAND	MONOPOLIES	EQUALITY OF OPPORTUNITY
GOVERNMENT	INEQUALITY	ECONOMIC GROWTH
CONSUMERS	GOODS AND SERVICES	NECESSITIES/ESSENTIALS
BUREAUCRACY	RESOURCES	INCENTIVE
EFFICIENCY	BASIC INDUSTRIES	LUXURIES

2   Explain SIMPLY (in your own words) how each system is organised, by writing a PARAGRAPH on each.

3   Write a sentence or two to explain each advantage and disadvantage.

4   What countries would you think of for each system? How do you think the systems work... well/badly...why? (Your own thoughts, not the teacher's/your friend's...)

5   Which system would you support? Design a poster and leaflet explaining your system and its advantages over other systems...ie.why is it best?

OR.

Write a newspaper article describing the three systems, trying to convince the reader that your choice is the best....

Figure 12.6

13   Prices and Markets

Paul Clarke

Introduction

The nature of supply and demand and their interaction represented by price is fundamental to most economics courses. While teenagers know something of demand, albeit implicitly, few will have had the opportunity to explore 'market demand' in any systematic way. Supply is a subject more remote from their experience, while the first encounter with price changes is usually in textbooks best suited to more able groups. There is an obvious need for lessons allowing students to operate some kind of market, and it is unrealistic to adopt too theoretical an approach.

It is also likely that market analysis in some shape or form will appear many times throughout an economics course. Suggestions for teaching a 'topic' should not imply 'one bite at the cherry', but rather an introduction to the basic ideas, ready for use in a variety of situations.

Content

The teaching of prices must include demand, supply and their interaction, and the students should ultimately be able to explain and analyse changes in demand, supply and prices. The teaching of markets at this level can cover the behaviour of producers in three different situations: (i) where there are many producers, (ii) where there are a few producers, and (iii) where there is only one producer.

Teaching methods

The following methods could be used either separately or in a series of lessons. Some will be very basic activities, intended as stimuli to further thought; others involve more ambitious activities and can serve as an end in themselves. Most aspects of prices and markets are covered adequately in textbooks from the teacher's point of view, but have to be broken down into a form usable by younger students.

1   The demand curve

(a) Consumer satisfaction

The subjective nature of consumer satisfaction can be made very clear by showing students a variety of advertisements for products favoured by that age group (e.g. a scarf of a particular football club, a packet of cigarettes, music cassettes of two or three different groups, packet of crisps, a can of soft drink, etc.). Students are then asked to rank the products according to the satisfaction they would gain from them, giving three points for most satisfaction down to zero for the least. In pairs and then in fours, and finally on a class basis, students can compare the scores given to different products, and try to explain the reasons for the most obvious differences. It does not take long to collect the advertisements if students bring in their own magazines, and photos provide a very accessible resource for any age.

(b) Diminishing satisfaction

This can be illustrated in similar fashion by asking students to decide on a scale of, say, one to five, how many units of satisfaction they would receive from the consumption of one product (e.g. a packet of crisps or a bar of chocolate). The teacher asks how many points would be awarded to the consumption of one packet; the points are totalled and noted. The procedure is repeated for a second packet and for several more packets until the students have been offered, say, ten packets. A graph of the totals is then constructed (see Figure 13.1). An overall picture of diminishing satisfaction with each successive unit of consumption will emerge and provides the basis for considerable class discussion.

(c) Class demand

It is now quite easy to show the links between consumer satisfaction and market demand by emphasising that demand reflects both 'wanting' a product and the willingness and ability to pay for it. Students are asked how many packets of crisps they would buy if the price per packet was 2p. The price is then increased successively through several price levels to, say, 25p. This allows a class demand curve to be drawn (see Figure 13.2). Even at this stage it is possible for students to discuss what they think might happen to the graph if they all had more spending money, or the price of a rival product fell. It is possible to highlight the need for a precise definition of demand by comparing the quantity of crisps demanded at any one price during a day, a week, a month, etc.

(d) Elasticity of demand

Although it may not be necessary to use technical words for a younger age group, students could look at the significance of elasticity using graphs. Class demand curves could be constructed for products like a tub of salt, or a specific brand of chocolate bar, and students could

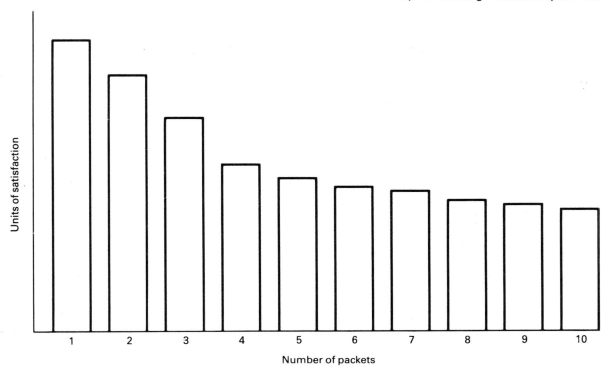

Figure 13.1 Consumption of crisps

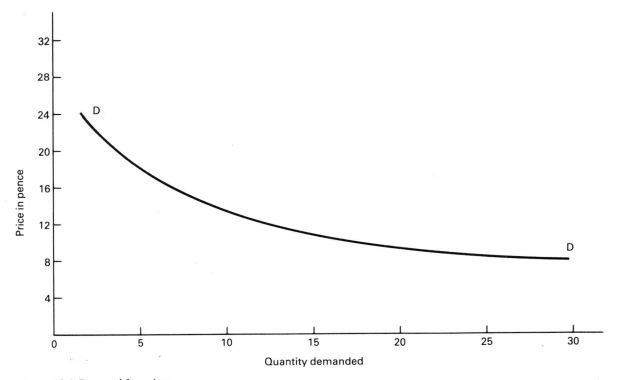

Figure 13.2 Demand for crisps

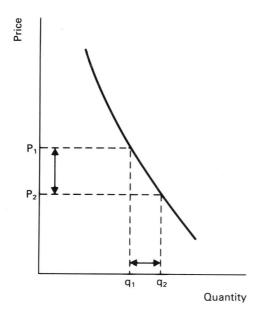

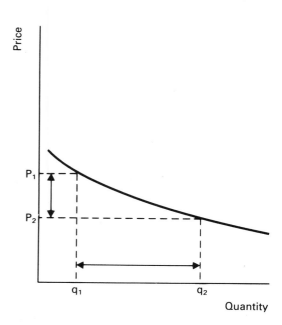

Figure 13.3 (a) Demand for tubs of salt

(b) Demand for 'Tiger' chocolate bars

then be asked to observe the change in quantity demanded as prices change. They could be asked to consider why the responsiveness of demand matters to different groups, e.g. producers, government, an importer (see Figure 13.3).

(e) Market research
The class could conduct a survey within school to investigate the demand for a product over a range of prices. This can have a quite topical impact where, say, lunchtime provision offers a choice of self-service meals or a visit to a local café. A group report can offer the chance for a degree of creative work and thoughts about the value of market-demand information.

(f) Derived demand
Extending analysis to the labour market reminds students that demand exists for services as well as for goods. It also stresses the interdependence between the demand for factors and the demand for final goods/services. A look at the job ad pages of a local newspaper provides a guide to vacancies within different wage levels. A visit to a local firm's personnel department can serve as an introduction also to the reason why demand for workers may change regardless of wage levels.

(g) Shifts in demand
The class is given a demand schedule and asked to draw the demand curve from it on graph paper. They then calculate the effect of (i) a 10 per cent increase, and (ii) a 10 per cent decrease in the level of demand at each price level. They draw the new demand curves on the same graph

paper and try to suggest factors that might have caused the shifts in the curve. This could be done also in case-study fashion. The original demand schedule could represent the number of rolls bought in a local café at a range of prices. Background details of a few customers could be made up, including a variety of reasons why each person is ordering more/less rolls. Students could be asked to identify the reasons and assess their importance for the café owner. They could look for changes that might be short/long term; those that might produce large/small shifts in demand. The case study could then be extended at a later date to consider how the café owner might meet these changes in demand.

(h) Simulated demand
Several computer programs suitable for a younger age group have demand-related content. Two programmes from the Economics 14–16 Project computer materials serve as examples. A modest business game requires students to estimate the demand for vacuum cleaners over a range of prices so that the company can produce an appropriate number. The computer's ability to offer a vast range of responses to students' own inputs is a distinct improvement on one demand schedule drawn in class. Another program gives students a map of a town with a number of houses for sale in particular sites. Students try to act as estate agents and price each house according to site, condition and a degree of subjective taste. It is a good introduction to non-price influences on demand and readily lends itself to further research by groups visiting local estate agents (Figure 13.4).

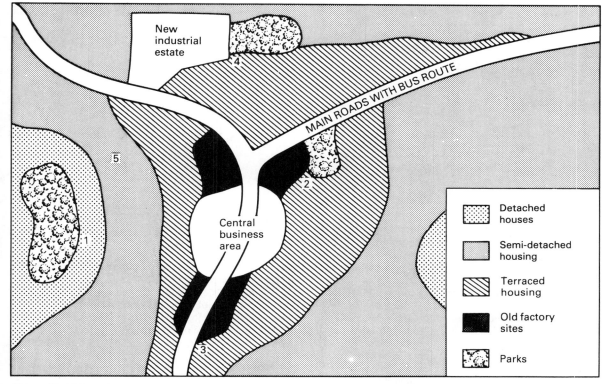

New industrial estate

MAIN ROADS WITH BUS ROUTE

Central business area

	Detached houses
	Semi-detached housing
	Terraced housing
	Old factory sites
	Parks

Figure 13.4 Map of town centre and suburbs (numbered boxes illustrate house sites)

2 The supply curve

(a) The basis of supply

Students are asked to put themselves in the place of a corner shop proprietor selling crisps. They are told that crisps are bought from a wholesaler at 4p a bag and are asked how many packets they would stock if the market price was 3p, 4p, 5p, etc. By totalling the crisps supplied at each price, a class supply curve could be drawn. Such a crude simplification may well cause dissatisfaction among students wanting to know more detail of costs, but is a useful starting point for discussion. Is profit the main consideration for a corner shop? Would the wholesaler give a discount on larger quantities, etc.? The simplification also has the merit of identifying clearly the difference between price and cost; this is a source of confusion for many younger students.

(b) Shifts in supply curve

A variety of examples can be given for the corner shop illustrating non-price influences on supply – the wholesaler wants 5p a bag; a new method of packaging gives longer shelf life to the crisps; the interest rate on the credit used by the shop owner to buy products increases, etc.

As with demand, there are many ways of exploring changes in supply in detail: a case study and/or a visit to a local store; a look at the supply of labour in the local area using census information. The factors affecting the supply of housing for sale is well explained in a tape/filmstrip produced by Mary Glasgow Publications (1979).

3 The interaction of supply and demand

(a) Graph work

Having constructed class supply and demand for crisps, it is now a short step to drawing them both on the same graph. Students are asked questions about quantities supplied and demanded above and below the equilibrium point. Discussion about shortages or surpluses and the likely effects on behaviour lead towards the idea of an equilibrium price. Students can then be given a new supply or demand schedule and asked to consider the effects on the equilibrium price. The separation of supply and demand changes is artificial and students often have difficulty understanding why a spending tax, for example, is seen to affect supply initially rather than demand. It would probably be adequate for younger students merely to suggest these are like snapshots of a process that is happening very quickly. A glance at a typical range of prices for commodities over a number of months, of the sort that appears frequently in diagrams in the *Financial Times*, will raise questions about the stability of equilibrium prices (Figure 13.5).

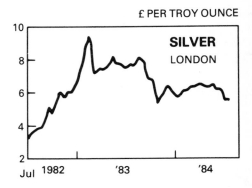

Figure 13.5 Source: Financial Times *10 June 1984.*

(b) Case studies

There are many ways of using case studies so that students can develop their use and understanding of supply, demand and price. The local housing market is easy to research given the usual number of estate agents with leaflets describing a range of house prices in a variety of locations. It provides a welcome opportunity to set economic analysis into a social and historical context; students find out when some estates are considered more 'desirable'. Given the impact of interest rates on the market, the seasonal variations in building and the large disparities of house prices in different regions, the housing market can be an effective link to wider economic issues.

A visit to a local firm is frequently part of an introductory economics course. A few shrewd questions on the teacher's part focusing on marketing can provide sufficient ammunition for later lessons on supply and demand.

The written materials from the Economics 14–16 Project contain several examples of the way in which case studies can be used. Background notes on a local hairdresser's business provide both personal interest and economic data. Follow-up exercises involve both comprehension and data-handling; open-ended questions about the future success or failure of the business allows scope for divergent thinking! A few photos or pictures showing the change in price of one product over a certain time period provides a lively stimulus without the need for a mass of information (Figure 13.6).

For the more able students, a comprehensive case study linked to radio programmes was published by the BBC in 1982. *The Potherbridge Challenge* illustrates the questions a young producer of 'shlurp bowls' asks when he realises that satisfying a market involves something more than guesswork. The presentation is lively and takes students through a carefully planned set of exercises. There are many ideas that teachers could also apply to their own examples (Figure 13.7).

(c) Stock Exchange game

The purpose of this game is to illustrate the effects of changes in demand and supply on market prices, and

perhaps to give the students a simplified introduction to the buying and selling of shares. Each student has £10 to spend and the object is to make as much money as possible by trading in shares. These are four companies whose shares are available, with different prices attached to each company's shares, e.g. £2, £1, 75p and 50p respectively. Each company's shares are looked after by a different 'broker', whose job is to distribute share certificates to buyers and collect certificates from sellers. Buying and selling can only take place through a broker.

Each student is given a sheet divided as shown in Table 13.1. Each broker has a supply of about twenty certificates for his company and, in each time period, the students are not allowed to buy more than one share in each company. (The teacher has to decide the method of allocation if demand exceeds supply.) The teacher announces the prices at the start of each time period. If demand is high (i.e. many buyers) the price will rise in the next time period, but if there are many sellers, the price will fall in the next time period. Eventually the brokers may be able to fix their own prices, determined by market forces, and it may be possible to introduce several other 'sophistications' to make the game more realistic.

Table 13.1

Time period	Price of A	Price of B	Price of C	Price of D
1	£2.00	£1.00	75p	50p
2				

4   Different types of markets

(a) Stock Exchange game

The Stock Exchange game can be extended to introduce students to the idea of different types of markets. Instead of having four companies, it is possible to operate with only one company's shares available, but with a larger number of brokers. This introduces a greater degree of competition and can allow experiments to assess the effects on price of a market where there are many buyers and sellers. The same kind of experiment could be tried where there are only, say, four sellers all competing with

Figure 13.6
Source: Davies, B. and Hender, D.,
Production and Trade (Longman, 1982).

Exercises

1a What happens to the demand curve
if demand increases?
b If demand decreases does the demand
curve shift to the left or the right?
c If quantity supplied increases
at each and every price what happens
to the supply curve?
d If the supply curve shifts what has
happened to supply?
e If price falls what do you predict will
happen to demand and to supply?
f If price rises what do you predict will
happen to demand and to supply?

2a Write down a definition
for ceteris paribus.
b Make a list of any variables, other than
price, that will:
cause demand to change
cause supply to change
c Study the cartoons below. Each one
shows a variable that will influence the
demand or supply of the good in question.
Identify the variable and predict what effect
it will have on demand or supply.

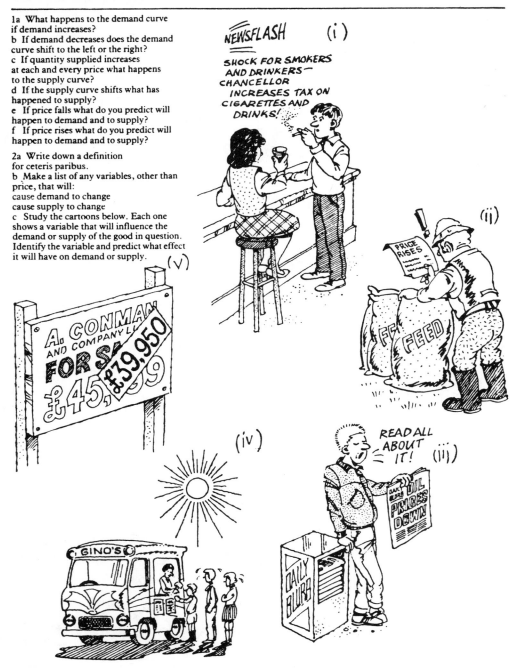

Figure 13.7

Source: The Potterbridge Challenge *(BBC, 1982) written by Linda Thomas and illustrated by Richard Geiger and reproduced with the permission of the British Broadcasting Corporation.*

each other. If the sellers do not of their own volition introduce practices such as collusion or price fixing, the teacher can discreetly suggest to one or two of them that these practices might be adopted. Eventually it is possible to experiment with only one seller who is trying to maximise profit. This may lead to some interesting results if the teacher can resist the temptation to interfere, because the seller may at first raise prices so high that demand for the product disappears. In order to make any money, the seller is forced to reduce his prices and take account of the demand for the product. This again raises possibilities for considerable class discussion.

(b) Trade simulation

There are several mock-up trading games available from agencies like CWDE. Students are divided into groups and are given a box of 'resources' with which they are to make a product for sale. In a classroom, these resources might be paper (raw materials), pencils, rulers, scissors, etc. (capital goods), and the product for sale could be certain paper shapes cut to a required degree of accuracy and decorated with certain colours. The teacher alone knows that the different groups have unequal resources (e.g. one group may have everything, another only raw materials). Students are given a time period to produce goods, with the teacher giving points to any group that hands in quality finished goods. After one or two periods of 'manufacture' and attempts to trade, the inequalities become apparent and groups adopt different strategies. Some continue to compete as if the room were full of buyers and sellers on equal terms; others find they have a resource that is much in demand and charge high prices; the less successful traders often form cartels. Prompts from the teacher where appropriate can encourage different kinds of market structure. Most classes are easily motivated by the 'game' but the real value lies in the debriefing sessions with groups. It may help at this stage to have appointed an observer to each group or asked someone to keep some record of the group's trading decisions.

(c) Case studies

Many of the case studies used in the development of supply and demand analysis can lead into discussion about market structure. The very existence of council housing raises questions about failures in the private market. The process of tendering bids for estate development by large firms offers an interesting view of market structure at work.

A study of the local labour market can raise queries about the impact of large firms on the demand for labour, and of trade unions on the supply side. The English Football League provides another fruitful basis for study with the contrasting fortunes of large and small clubs, and the very different earnings for footballers in different divisions.

(d) Market research

It is possible for students to gain some insight into the market structure across a range of products by local surveys. Questionnaires put to consumers of a chosen product can be an interesting exercise in itself in data collection but should give students ideas about the nature of demand and the factors most likely to change existing spending patterns. A survey of shop shelves would give some impression of the product range available. Polite requests to shopkeepers can usually identify manufacturers as opposed to brand names; most libraries carry a directory of UK firms that can also help in identification of the supplier. Students should then be able to report about the type of market structure for their chosen product and, on the basis of their 'consumer report', discuss how satisfactorily the market is operating.

(e) Historical survey

The class studies the development of one industry that has progressed from having a large number of relatively small producers to having only a few firms competing with each other. The UK motor industry could be used as an example. The teacher then asks questions about the behaviour of the buyers and sellers in different market situations, and with some classes it may be possible to draw diagrams to illustrate the different markets. This type of survey allows the class to consider the costs and benefits to consumers, as well as producers, of the markets, and provides the basis for studying other related topics such as economies of scale, costs of production (and cost curves), government intervention and types of integration.

(f) Computer models

There are several published programs aimed mainly at the A-level market but which may have some application for more able students in this age range. *Competition, Mergers and Control of Monopoly* (Longman, 1984) and *Paraffin File* (BP, 1981) contain some vocabulary and concepts that would be way beyond the ability of most 14-year-olds, but it is possible for them to understand the importance of market shares without worrying too much about more complicated cost theory.

(g) Social costs and market intervention

It is probably enough for students of this age to appreciate that most intervention in markets is justified where market prices are not a genuine reflection of all the costs to society. A stimulus for discussion could be no more than a photo showing a queue for a bus in a local shopping centre. Students could first consider the costs facing any bus operator and the kind of custom they can expect at different times of the day, the week, the year. If an operator has to make a profit at all times, what kind of service would be provided? What of the benefits to private motorists in reduced congestion because of the bus service? Ultimately this will be a cost benefit study which is likely to raise many questions and value judgements that might otherwise not appear in more traditional market analysis.

Conclusion

The general tenor of this chapter is to suggest that very little of the existing published material is aimed at students in the 13–16 age range, though there are signs of improvement. As a result, little of this material can be used directly to help students in their understanding of prices and markets. The teacher can use parts of textbooks, but only if these are adapted for younger students. The chapter tries to show ways in which existing resources readily available to the teacher may be used in an interesting manner without losing sight of the essential economics.

Resources

Textbooks

As has been pointed out, very few textbooks simplify their treatment of prices and markets sufficiently to be very useful to 13–16-year-olds. Among the better attempts are *Production and Trade* by B. Davies and D. Hender in the Longman Social Science Series (2nd edn, 1982). The factors affecting supply and demand are introduced in a simple and interesting way.

Written material

The Potherbridge Challenge (BBC, 1982) is a booklet to accompany five radio programmes aimed at introducing supply and demand up to O-level standard. The text is lively, the vocabulary precise and the booklet is full of student activities. The Economics Education 14–16 Project is publishing many exemplar materials related to supply and demand with ideas for further development.

For case studies, books like Peter Waymark's *The Car Industry* (Sewell, 1983) provide valuable background information for teachers.

Audio-visual materials

Some slightly old-fashioned-looking tape/filmstrip sequences are still available from Audio Learning Ltd with titles like *Scarcity and Choice, Demand, Supply and Price*. Topic tape sequences, like *Housing* from Mary Glasgow Publications, again provide interesting applications of market analysis.

14   Auction
Sarah Wilkinson

Introduction

This auction is designed to demonstrate a number of economic principles. It may be used with mixed-ability classes and a variety of age groups.

Aim

To allow students to experience market forces in operation.

Key ideas

1   that price is determined in the market;
2   that demand exists when wants are combined with the ability to pay;
3   that a market is any situation where demand and supply are in contact;
4   that some prices are determined in the market;
5   that prices can be determined both before, and at, the point of sale;
6   that consumer surplus may exist and can be eliminated;
7   that income may be distributed unequally.

Skills

1   written and oral responses to stimuli;
2   co-operation with others in a group.

Organisation

There are various ways that an auction can be introduced and organised:

1   During an introductory session, students could be introduced to the basic economic problem. This leads

to the development of markets where supply and demand come together and where the price is determined.

Students can be asked to give examples of markets where the price is determined at the point of sale. They will probably suggest the following:

(a) jumble sale;
(b) antique shops;
(c) auction;
(d) street markets.

Another possibility would be to present the list and ask students what those markets have in common and how they differ.

2 Four or five items should be available for sale. One of them should be attractive – e.g. a bar of chocolate – others could include an empty match box, a jam jar, a paper clip, etc.

Students could be asked to think of different ways of selling the items, for example, cost price, cost plus profit, auction, subsidised price.

This could be followed by asking which method would allow the seller to obtain the highest price possible – or alternatively, asking for the advantages of each method both to the buyer and the seller.

3 At this point students could be allocated different sums of money with which to bid. Two things nearly always happen:

(a) Someone says 'It's not fair – she/he's got more money than me.' This point can be followed up by looking at the distribution of income and wealth and discussing whether or not it is 'fair'. If it is to be followed up later, it is probably a good idea to draw everyone's attention to the comment.

(b) Students inevitably want to get into groups, pool their money and then share the chocolate if that group succeeds in purchasing it. It is obviously up to the teacher whether or not this is to be allowed.

It is interesting to observe how they divide the chocolate between the members of the group and two opposing viewpoints generally come to light: (i) division of the chocolate according to the amount of money each person contributed, (ii) division of the chocolate equally. There is quite a strong case for this since even if someone contributed only a small sum of money, their contribution was probably crucial in allowing that particular group to buy the chocolate.

This, too, can be related to follow-up work on the distribution of income.

4 The goods could then be auctioned – use of a proper gavel is desirable – and the prices could be recorded on an OHP or blackboard.

Students could also record the price that each good fetches and use that as a basis for written work and group discussions.

5 Possible follow-up questions might include:

(a) When was the price of each good actually determined?

(b) Which good was sold for the highest price? How many students wanted this good? Who bought this good? Why did this particular good fetch the highest price and why did student X buy it?

(c) Which good was sold for the lowest price? Explain as fully as possible why this was the case.

(d) Why is selling by auction an advantage to the seller?

(e) List some goods that are normally sold by auction. Do these goods have anything in common?

(f) Why aren't all goods sold by auction?

(g) Why may auctions be described as markets?

15   A Task-oriented Approach to Teaching the Theory of the Firm

Robert Wilson

Introduction

The approach set out below has been used for many years for teaching rudiments of the theory of the firm to secondary school students. For less-able 13 to 16-year-olds it has frequently been used as the only approach; for candidates attempting O-level it is used as a way into a difficult area of the syllabus prior to tackling the graphical interpretations required by many examination boards. The rationale for the approach lies in the following beliefs: that a great deal of economic knowledge has been absorbed by students by the time they reach secondary school; that much of an economics teacher's time can gainfully be used up in helping students to articulate, formalise and bring coherence to what they already know (but may not realise that they know or, knowing it, see no relevance, use or worth in that knowledge); that students of all ages tend to prefer activity to passivity; that for many students reading and writing present greater barriers to progress (and hence to motivation and interest) than do listening and talking.

A consistency of approach across a wide range of ages and abilities should not be confused with a uniformity of presentation. Account has to be taken of the age of the students, and adjustments made to the volume of material presented, the length and quality of response expected, and the language and syntax used in the oral and written activity. The other main variable is the allocation of time. Such adjustments within the overall framework presented here should not be beyond the wit of practising teachers, who may also wish to change some or all of the examples used in order to fit in with local conditions and with the particular experiences of their classes in the 13–16 age range.

In introducing the theory of the firm, it is assumed that the students have already become acquainted with the concepts of scarcity, choice, production, consumption, economic efficiency and technical efficiency – though not necessarily with the terminology – and as a result have some hope of appreciating the significance of questions such as 'Does the degree of competition faced by producers have any influence on how well an economic system uses its resources to meet the needs of consumers?', towards which the latter part of the work presented here is addressed. The approach is set out in five stages.

Stage 1

The aim of this stage is to establish that in production processes, costs are incurred in advance of revenues being received. Students are issued with the following exercise:

Exercise 1

1 Write down the name of:
 EITHER your favourite product in your role as consumer;
 OR   the product you would most like to produce or help produce;
 OR   the product that some member of your family helps to produce.
2 List the main raw materials, components, labour and machinery used in its production.
3 Make a note of the main production processes and their sequence.
4 Jot down your guesstimate of the time taken from deciding to introduce that product to making your first sale and receiving payment for it.
5 Make a guess at the size of the sum of money needed to develop the product to the stage of being ready for sale.

Together with the exercise, students receive an undaunting A5 sheet of scrap paper. The use of moderately sized scrap

paper usually results in the correct signal being given to the class, namely, the exercise is not a formal test, no marks will be recorded, spelling and presentation are not at a premium, and there are no uniquely correct answers that only the cleverest students will manage to attain. If the teacher is seen to prepare a piece of his own 'work' at the same time, the level of class opposition to being asked to do something is likely to be reduced. The teacher's effort may well come in handy later on in any event (see below). When the allotted time has elapsed, each student is asked in turn to identify the product chosen, and a list of products is compiled on the blackboard or similar display board. This open-ended approach runs the risks associated with working with teenagers but it is important that all efforts are recognised at this preliminary stage if at all possible. A few of the potentially more economically interesting products can then be selected for scrutiny. If the class list is unduly narrow, the teacher's own effort can be incorporated into the list and, if necessary, it can be refabricated instantaneously in order to inject breadth into the exercise.

Products can then be selected that exemplify wide differences in methods of production, in size of financial outlay and in lead times. Ideally, consideration should be given to services as well as to goods. With a typical class of 14-year-olds, it is likely that a significant number will have chosen a product about which they are particularly well informed, and for some students, it might well be the first time that they have had an opportunity to demonstrate their expertise to their peers. With the combined efforts of people in the class, a series of product profiles can be built up and made available to everybody. Useful products to hold in reserve in case the class effort is unduly restricted in scope include the manufacture of rosettes worn by supporters of particular sports teams (short lead time, low outlay, unskilled labour) and Concorde (long lead time, huge outlay, skilled labour). By the end of the exercise, students usually have become aware not only that costs are incurred by businesses in advance of revenues being received but also that certain expensive, high-risk projects require venture capital on a scale and for a length of time so great that only consortia and/or governments supported by well-organised financial markets can sustain them.

Stage 2

During the first stage, students will have demonstrated the extent to which they already have a grasp of the notions of costs and revenues. In Stage 2 an attempt is made to establish the notion of profit as (unsophisticated) a net return or residual and (more sophisticated) as a return to a factor of production and, therefore, a cost to a business. Use is made of a rudimentary role play, in which students have to imagine that they have an economic role to play as a producer. They are given the following exercise:

Exercise 2

Imagine that you are the owner/manager of a successful general store. Your new assistant, keen to impress you, suggests that your store ought to stock luminous mousetraps. Write down the questions that you would most like to ask him/her about the idea.

Some students might well find it difficult to formulate questions, since for the greater part of their school lives they are required to provide answers – *we* ask the questions! Not all questions suggested will be overtly economic in nature, but few will lack an economic dimension. Once again this exercise is a scrap-paper exercise and open-ended. It is advisable to set a ceiling and a floor to the number of questions that the class members are expected to create. The floor sets a realistic target for the weaker students and the ceiling obliges able students to exercise restraint and judicious selection. Between them, a group of students are likely to suggest without prompting the following questions among their combined offerings – wording is only approximate and many variants are acceptable. Once other questions suggested have been adequately dealt with, the following four questions concerning the luminous mousetrap are highlighted:

1 Where can I inspect one? Who makes them? Are you able to show me one?
2 How much will they cost the business to purchase?
3 At what price do you think they might reasonably be offered for sale?
4 How many could the shop hope to sell at that price in a week/month/year?

Once these questions have been concentrated upon, students should be able to explain why the answers to them are of particular importance to a retail business, and what assumptions are being made about the objectives of the business if it is agreed that these questions are important to it. The questions form the basis of the next task:

Exercise 3
Suppose that your new assistant comes up with the following answers to your questions:
1 Here is a luminous mousetrap – I make them myself.
2 They can be supplied at a cost to the store of £2.00.
3,4 If the store offered them for sale at £2.20, it seems likely that they would sell at a rate of ten a week each week for the next five years.
What would be your response? Would you be keen to stock the mousetraps?

It is seldom that this exercise produces a unanimous response. While a large number of students see advantages in stocking a product which can be sold for more than it cost to purchase, a few can usually be relied on to take a jaundiced view of a 10 per cent mark-up, and draw on their experiences as sales assistants, forecourt attendants, etc. to argue that a bigger profit is required. This opens the way for identifying some of the main items that the 20p 'profit' has to help pay for, and the class can be asked to draw up a list of the main financial outlays, other than the purchase of stock, associated with owning and running a small retail store. Wages of shop assistants, heating, lighting, rates, insurance, maintenance and repair, and advertising commonly feature in the majority of lists prepared.

Stage 3
The way is now clear to establish the distinction between fixed and variable costs, and thereafter the major learning difficulty lies in establishing the relevance and importance of this distinction to decision-making on the part of firms. A tape-slide programme published by Audio Learning[1] might prove useful in this regard with some above-average 13-year-olds; alternatively, the following exercise can be used:

Exercise 4
George Burns owns an ice-cream parlour. One week, his takings were so poor (only £150) compared with his business expenses for that week (£400) that he decided that he would be better off closing down for a week and going on holiday. So he did. To his dismay, he discovered that in the week in which he was on holiday his business lost £300 – a worse result than when he had been keeping it running. He is trying to understand how this could possibly have happened. Offer Mr Burns some possible clues to his problem.

For some classes, this task will prove too demanding unless some structured assistance is provided. The following guideline usually does what is required of it:

George Burns – Ice-cream parlour
1 Some things that George's firm still had to pay for even though it was closed.
2 Some things that George's firm no longer had to pay for while it was closed.
3 The income that George's firm no longer received while it was closed.

It is not hard to devise numerical exercises offering unique solutions which further demonstrate the relationship between cost structures and short-run production decisions and which point up the particular difficulties of firms with a high proportion of fixed costs.

Stage 4
So far no reference has been made to marginal analysis, and yet even an elementary course on the theory of the firm requires its inclusion if students are to appreciate aspects of decision-making in business. It is not essential that all students come to appreciate that profits are maximised or losses minimised at an output level where $MR = MC$, but some attempt should be made to instil in students the idea that, whatever a firm's present predicament, the next decision taken about output will have some bearing on profits/losses. A structured exercise can help establish this point:

Exercise 5

Mrs Jones supplies shops with dolls that she makes out of coloured paper. Each doll uses up five sheets of paper, which costs Mrs Jones 24p a sheet when purchased in a pack of 500 sheets. Each doll takes 40 minutes to make, and Mrs Jones prices her labour at £3.00 per hour to cover all the other expenses incurred as well as giving her a wage. She receives an inquiry from a shop and is asked to supply a quotation for producing 120 paper dolls. She has no paper in stock. What price should she quote (per doll) for completing the order?

It is tempting to provide a framework for this exercise to help weaker students towards a solution, but the danger of so doing is that it tends to point them in only one direction, whereas left to their own devices, they will adopt more than one approach and produce more than one possible answer. The answers received are normally £3.20 and £4.00. Ownership of calculators has taken the chore out of doing the arithmetic, so the different answers reflect genuine differences of approach. The point of divergence is over the answer to the question 'Who should pay for the purchase of the paper which has to be purchased but is not used on this particular batch of dolls?' In the absence of a unique solution, some students lose interest and find uncertainty unsettling and unnerving, but in some instances the debate that ensues from the emergence of two 'camps' can be rewarding. Advocates of £4.00 argue that Mrs Jones may never receive an order from anyone else and so must recoup her total outlay from the one job: this response reflects a feel for average cost pricing and a strategy based on cautious pessimism. Protagonists of £3.20 argue that she should charge whatever it cost her to make these particular dolls: for them price reflects short-run marginal costs and strategy reflects optimism with regard to future custom. Occasionally a student will argue that the price charged by Mrs Jones should be based not on estimates of cost but on her view of what the customer might be willing to pay. If this customer will accept a price of £4.00, it leaves the way open to charge the next customer as little as £3.00 for any quantity up to eighty units. Even 12-year-olds have been known to offer this solution, albeit rarely. Clearly, however, the principles of discriminating monopoly may be appreciated long before the terminology is met. Once this exercise has been used to the full, a follow-up exercise can be used to point up the concept of the margin.

Exercise 6

PLASSYDAFFY is a firm that specialises in the manufacture of plastic daffodils. Each year 100 000 units are produced, at a total cost to the firm of £96 000. The firm has annual fixed costs of £56 000.

1   What is the cost on average of each daffodil produced?
2   All the daffodils produced are sold, at an average selling price of £1.20. How much revenue is received from selling daffodils?

3   How much profit is made in the year?

A customer asks for a special order of 1000 red; 1000 white; and 1000 blue plastic daffodils, but states in his letter that he is not willing to pay more than 60p for each daffodil.

PLASSYDAFFY calculates that to produce the daffodils will add £1500 to its costs that year.

4   State whether or not you think that PLASSYDAFFY should agree to supply the order on the terms set out by the customer, and justify your answer.

This exercise is capable of producing some interesting responses from students. Those *against* fulfilling the order draw attention to the fact that the suggested selling price (60p) is well below the average cost of production (96p) for normal production; the additional output will cost more on average (50p) to produce than the cost of producing additional units of the normal product (40p), so the firm is being asked to sell at half the normal price a special product that costs more than usual to make. Even for some who manage to see the advantages of accepting an order that brings in more in revenue than it incurs in costs, the prospect of a price only half the usual price becomes an overwhelming consideration and grounds for rejection. ('How would regular customers for the normal product react if they found out about the special deal?') After having experience of a few more similar exercises, most students are usually willing to accept that additional units of output are worth producing provided that they add more to revenue than to costs, and not worth producing if they add more to costs than to revenue, for as long as maximising profits is the firm's objective.

This conclusion has been reached without recourse to graphs and without reference to any particular type of competitive environment, since its validity is universal. Whether the terms 'marginal cost' and 'marginal revenue' are introduced is a matter for individual teachers' discretion. The arithmetic used to reach the conclusion involves skills learned in primary school. The numbers used are large enough to appear realistic without being unduly complex. The main requirement for the teacher is to create a learning environment in which students cease to worry about revealing in discussion their misconceptions. The main challenge thereafter is to identify and eradicate the sources of doubt and confusion.

Stage 5

The aim of Stage 5 is to establish the following ideas:

1   Not all firms operate in the same competitive environment.
2   The degree of competition faced by firms affects their ability to make their own independent decisions on price and output.
3   Consumers' knowledge of product markets varies widely from product to product.
4   Higher levels of ownership of telephones and cars has

enhanced consumer's knowledge of, and influence in, product markets.

5 Consumers' ability to influence producers' decisions on price and output varies enormously from product to product.

6 In relation to satisfying consumers' needs and the need to conserve scarce resources, no one form of competitive environment is inherently superior in all respects to any other form.

Students are issued with the following sheet of twenty-one questions and it is suggested to them that by discovering the answers to these questions in relation to a particular business or firm, a great deal can be learned about how it operates and why it operates in the way that it does:

A questionnaire for a firm/business

1 What do you produce?
2 What are the five biggest rivals to your product(s) in order of importance?
3 How many other firms produce things identical or very similar to what you produce?
4 What share of the total market for your type of product does each firm have on average?
5 What share of the total market does *your* firm have?
6 If you stopped production, what difference would it make to consumers in general?
7 Can anyone set themselves up in business in your industry?
8 Can you or anyone else leave your industry if they wish?
9 Do all firms in your industry find it equally easy to obtain all the things they need to use in your industry, such as land, premises, labour, raw materials and components?
10 Do all firms in your industry have the same opportunity to find buyers for their products?
11 In a typical week, how many people buy the products of your firm?
12 What proportion of your weekly/annual output does a typical customer purchase?
13 Can a typical customer influence the price that you charge?
14 Do you know what price your rivals are charging for their product(s)?
15 Do your customers know the prices being charged by your main rivals?
16 If you wish to sell more of your product, will you have to lower your price(s)?
17 How can your industry as a whole hope to increase its sales?
18 How similar are the products of your closest rivals?
19 In what ways do you compete for business?
20 Are all firms in your industry equally efficient?
21 Do you have a view on how much profit you need to make each year in order to be prepared to stay in that line of business?

After students have been given an opportunity to seek clarification of the meaning of any of the questions posed, the class is given the task of providing the answers in the case of a business of which it is reasonable to expect them to have some knowledge and experience, and in which they might well have an interest.

A retail outlet makes a suitable source of study, provided that it represents an example of a fairly competitive industry. A local record shop or a hairdressing salon usually work adequately, but regional specialisms can also play a part – a retail fishmonger yields fulsome responses in Aberdeen. Answers are prepared in rough and collated, and findings are then transcribed into a profile which serves as an exemplar. A profile prepared from specific questions/answers is set out below:

A profile of George Tullos – retail fishmonger

George Tullos sells fish in Aberdeen to the general public. So do more than eighty other fishmongers, who are his biggest rivals, particularly the four within half a mile of his shop. He sees fish and chip shops, supermarkets, butchers and poulterers as competition too. In Aberdeen he has about 500 regular weekly customers, representing about 2 per cent of the total market. His is a skilled trade, but anyone can set up in it and George can give up being a fishmonger any time he feels so inclined. If he closed down, his customers would not find great difficulty in obtaining fish elsewhere. He's lucky in that his father set him up in business and the shop is in a good area where customers are plentiful and comparatively well off. Some fishmongers in the city are much less favoured. Most of George's regular customers make a small weekly purchase and accept his prices with little question or complaint, but a few that own freezers haggle for a special deal on a bulk purchase. George knows that many of his customers own telephones and cars and feel no particular loyalty towards him, so he checks up from time to time on his rivals' prices. Experience has taught him that lowering his prices does little to boost his own trade at the expense of other fishmongers, and that sales of fish are more sensitive to quality of fish and standard of service than anything else. Higher meat prices have helped a little to increase sales of fish too. George doesn't worry too much about what his rival fishmongers are doing. His own shop is modern, clean and attractive, he stocks a wide range of fish, and parking is easy outside his shop. Moreover, he prides himself on knowing his customers' names and on being a shrewd buyer at the local wholesale fish market, so that fish seldom remain unsold at the end of a day's trading. If things turn difficult, he can always go back to being a joiner, where business is currently brisk.

Experience has shown that whereas this exemplar is not exceptional in its level of economic content – all of its basic information will be forthcoming from a collective effort with a typical class of 14-year-olds – the level of presentation in terms of flow and lucidity is beyond the reach of the great majority of 15-year-olds. Some teachers may well feel that to present students with a standard of work that they feel to be beyond their reach is counter-productive. It is a moot point. A great deal depends on the manner and spirit in which it is done. In the course of falling short of this standard, much highly commendable work might well be produced. In some instances, however, it might well be politic to set the target performance for a class as a collective discussion of a particular firm, or as the production of twenty-one discrete sentences (see Appendix 15.1).

A minimum portfolio of case studies is normally three – examples of imperfect competition, near monopoly and near perfect competition in that order. An oligopoly makes a very useful fourth study. In addition to industries indicated above, study has been made of:

Railway passenger services, letter-delivery services, electricity generation and supply	Near monopolistic
Market gardeners, window cleaners, secondhand car dealers, painters and decorators	Highly competitive in many areas
Petroleum retailing, television rental, detergent manufacture, brewing	Oligopolistic

For some classes, the study of business competition may well cease at this stage. For others, the extremes of the spectrum remain to be investigated. Penultimately, students are asked to imagine a business environment in which a firm is faced with a complete absence of any form of competition. In such circumstances, what will be the answers to the twenty-one questions?

Provided that the previous work has progressed satisfactorily, students usually make a good attempt at answering the questions on page 77 in relation to the (undeclared) model of pure monopoly (see Appendix 15.2). There is no reason why they should not invent a product name for themselves, with the faithful blodgett standing by for the unimaginative to use.

Once again, the exercise need not be conducted in a formal manner. Since students are venturing into new territory, there is much to be said for encouraging them to work in pairs so that they can discuss possible answers. Not all twenty-one questions are of equal importance and, in the case of pure monopoly, a teacher's main interest lies in what the students suggest as the answers to questions 2, 3, 5, 6, 7, 13, 16, 17. At the end of the exercise, students should be aware that an ability to restrict entry into an industry is a powerful means of retaining market share, but that even a sole supplier has his activities constrained by consumer sovereignty.

Finally, students can be asked to imagine working in a business environment in which a firm faces so much competition that the only decision it feels able to make for itself is the quantity it will supply – it has no element of monopoly power. What will its profile look like? This is much the hardest task for the class, and setting the class in action can be difficult. Here is a possible form of words which usually gets most people started:

Exercise

Imagine that you produce modgetts and are aware that you face enormous competition from vast numbers of other modgett producers compared with whom you have no particular advantage. What would your business profile look like? (see Appendix 15.3.)

By the end of the exercise, there are several aspects of a highly competitive environment that students should have begun to grasp: the inability of the individual producer to influence market price; the transfer of power and influence from producers to consumers that results from increasing consumers' knowledge of the market (product availability and prices); the uncertainty with regard to future prices that can result from unilateral uncoordinated decisions with regard to output.

It is sometimes advisable to omit consideration of some of the twenty-one questions on page 77. In the case of perfect competition, questions 20 and 21 are fraught with difficulties. Most students instinctively assume that in a perfectly competitive environment, all producers will be equally efficient on the grounds that if this were not the case then some producers would be advantaged compared with others. The great majority of undergraduates entering teacher training answer 'Yes' to question 20, but then have to admit that when they learned about perfect competition it was with reference to high-cost, low-cost, and marginal firms, implying that the answer to question 20 must be 'No'. This answer then raises the question as to why firms of widely disparate efficiency should share a common view of what constitutes normal profit. Should not firms that know themselves to be more efficient producers look for higher returns? The virtue of assuming that firms are not equally efficient lies in being able then to give an accurate impression of what happens in highly competitive industries when market price collapses: some firms are forced out sooner than others. The other major aspect of a competitive environment to stress is the right to freedom of entry – in such circumstances those already in the industry know the risks they run in organising their affairs too much to their own advantage at the expense of consumers.

The approach to introducing aspects of the theory of the firm set out above makes heavy demands on the teacher. Emphasis has been placed on encouraging students to make use of the knowledge and experience that they already possess. In some instances their knowledge and experience of particular types of economic enterprise will be superior to that of the teacher. In other instances, open discussion will lead to an airing of prejudices presented with a vigour that almost defies challenge or correction. In any event, the learning process that stems from this approach is most unlikely to be one-way. The experience can be mutually rewarding.

Appendix 15.1: A profile of British Rail

1   British Rail operates *railway passenger services* and freight services.
2   On *long haul*, competition comes from coaches, private cars and airlines.
    On *short haul*, competition comes from private cars, buses and taxis.
3   Only British Rail operates national rail services.
4   It controls the whole of the national railway network.
5   It has the railway market to itself, but only a share of the passenger transport market.
6   Many people rely heavily on rail services to get them to and from work.
7   Nobody may set up in direct competition with British Rail without parliamentary approval.
8   British Rail cannot abandon passenger services without going through a process of consultation and inquiry.
9   British Rail finds it harder in some parts of the UK than in others to obtain the land, labour and capital that it needs.
10 British Rail finds it harder to attract passengers in some parts of the UK than in others.
11 Millions of people travel by train each week.
12 Each passenger represents an insignificant proportion of total sales.
13 Customers are expected to accept the prices set by British Rail, though a users' committee can make complaints and observations about prices.
14 British Rail is aware of the prices being charged by its main competitors.
15 Customers can find out the price of rival passenger services, but finding out can be very time-consuming.
16 To attract more customers, British Rail may introduce special offers (lower fares).
17 Lowering prices tends to lower revenue rather than increase it.
18 Rival passenger services differ in terms of their speed, frequency, reliability, convenience, comfort and price.
19 British Rail competes through advertising, price reductions and product improvement.
20 The efficiency of British Rail varies in different parts of the UK.
21 Performance targets for British Rail are set by the government. The target may be a financial one (return on capital employed) or an output/efficiency target (e.g. number of employees per passenger mile operated).

Appendix 15.2: A profile of a blodgett maker who faces no competition of any kind

1   I produce blodgetts.
2   I have no rivals.
3   No firm produces anything remotely similar to a blodgett.
4   I've the blodgett market to myself.
5   I have a 100 per cent market share.
6   Customers depend entirely on me for their supply of blodgetts. Without me, they would be in great difficulty.
7   Nobody is allowed to set up in competition. I have sole rights to blodgett production.
8   I can leave the industry if I want, but why should I want too?!
9   I can obtain all the resources I need.
10 I've no difficulty in finding buyers for blodgetts in all parts of the country.
11 Millions buy blodgetts from me each week.
12 I've no big customers to be dependent upon. All my customers are 'minnows'.
13 I set the price charged. The customer can take it or leave it.
14 I've no rivals to worry about.
15 My customers know that they are unable to buy elsewhere.
16 Some people get by without buying blodgetts. To make them interested in buying, I would probably have to lower my price.
17 I suppose that advertising might also boost sales.
18 I have no rivals. Nobody is producing similar products.
19 I'm not greatly aware of having to compete for business.
20 There are no other firms in the industry. I am the industry! I don't have to worry about other firms' efficiency.
21 I know how much profit I expect to make each year – and make it.

*   *What disadvantages might there be for consumers in allowing a producer to be the sole supplier of a particular product?*
*   *Are consumers bound to be worse off as a result?*
*   *What might you find attractive about being the sole supplier of blodgetts?*

Appendix 15.3: A profile of a modgett maker who faces an enormous amount of competition

1   I produce modgetts.
2   My closest rivals also produce modgetts.
3   Thousands of other firms also produce modgetts.
4   Each of us has a tiny share of the total market.
5   My share is so small as to be insignificant.
6   If I stopped production, most people wouldn't even notice and the customers I have would simply go elsewhere at very little trouble to themselves.
7   Anyone can set up business as a modgett maker.
8   Any of us can leave the industry too.
9   All of us in the industry have the same opportunity to obtain the resources we need.
10 All of us have the same opportunity to find customers for our product.

11 Many people buy modgetts from me each week.
12 Each customer buys an insignificant proportion of my total output.
13 No single customer affects the price of modgetts.
14 I know the price at which my rivals are trying to sell their modgetts.
15 My customers know the price being charged by all my rivals, and are free to buy from them if they wish.
16 I can't affect the market price of modgetts. I have to accept the ruling market price.
17 If all of us are to increase our sales at the same time, market price will have to fall.
18 Other firms' modgetts are identical with the modgetts that I make.
19 Unable to influence the market price and trying to sell the same product as everybody else, I try to stay in business by producing modgetts more efficiently.

20 Some of us seem to produce modgetts more cheaply than others, and so can cope with low prices more easily than others.
21 If I can't make an adequate living out of producing modgetts, I'll switch to producing something else.

*   *How keen would you be to become a modgett maker?*
*   *What steps might you be tempted to take in order to increase your market influence?*

Notes and references

1   Wilson, R. D., *Production – Fixed and Variable Costs of Production* (Audio Learning, 1980).

16   Division of Labour
Peter Leech

Introduction

It is virtually impossible to find a syllabus in economics, or related subjects such as commerce, that does not contain reference to the concept of division of labour. This is as true of courses up to CSE and GCE O-level as it is at other levels. The reasons for this are clear. It is not only a precondition for trade to take place, and hence a precondition for the existence of economics, but along with the development of language it is probably one of the key factors separating human beings as social animals from creatures of lower orders.

Given the importance of this topic, it is hard to appreciate how it can be treated in a cursory way by many teachers of economics, often on the shallow justification that students find it 'boring'. Might it not be the case that the topic is, in fact, very interesting but that the presentation of it in the classroom is dry and uninspired? It is on this assumption that this chapter is written. It aims to give a very brief outline of the various components of the topic before going on to describe a number of methods that have been used to teach it. It is important at this stage, however, to point out that the approaches mentioned will vary enormously in their suitability for particular groups of students and particular courses. The right blend of methods for any given teacher in a specific context will need to be chosen with care.

Areas of content

History and development

The historical development of the division of labour is often the basic organising principle of the classroom teacher in this area. It is common to trace the development of the concept of specialisation right back to the dawn of civilisation. The main stages in this development are as follows:

1   No specialisation: Usually presented as a caricature of a primitive pre-civilised existence.
2   Product specialisation: Often seen as the first step towards civilisation and used in the classroom to introduce the concept of exchange.
3   Process specialisation: This is seen as the link between the early ideas of specialisation and the further splitting up of the process of production of a product. It is at this stage that students tend to find it easier to relate to the idea.
4   Mass production: This stage is often presented as the

pinnacle of the development of the idea and it is at this stage that the concepts of efficiency and automation are commonly introduced.

Extent of the division of labour

Having built up a picture of the development and refinement of the idea of the division of labour, the students can be shown what relevance the concept has to everyday life in the world around them. Many students are surprised at the extent to which the division of labour is practised. When put in the context of the world of work, and the implications for careers are pointed out, the students see the relevance of the concept in a way that they might not have done had it been presented to them in the age-old style of the 'Robinson Crusoe' approach.

Advantages of the division of labour

Having been told that the division of labour is the key to civilisation and the creation of wealth, it is not unreasonable to expect them to ask why. The teacher will need to find methods of showing students how the use of the division of labour can make a business more efficient in the following sorts of ways:

1 By the application of comparative advantage theory.
2 By the reduction in costs of training and skill development.
3 By the reduction in costs of capital equipment.
4 By an improvement in individual productivity rates through practice.
5 By increased standardisation of products.

When presented as real-life practical benefits, rather than as a list learnt from a textbook, students readily grasp the significance and importance of specialisation in modern industry.

Disadvantages of the division of labour

While it is important that students are made aware of the potential gains from increased use of the division of labour, they must also be given the other side of the picture. The division of labour has some negative implications as well as the sort of advantages just mentioned.

From the point of view of the producers it could be shown that greater use of the division of labour increases boredom, reduces pride in work and, as a result, may lead to a fall in the quality of the products. In addition to the limits imposed on the extent of the division of labour by the market for the product, there may be limits imposed by the alienating effects on the workforce, often showing itself through a poor record in the field of industrial relations.

Equally, as consumers the students should be made aware of the implications of the division of labour. The reduction of standards of quality and limitations of choice for consumers are costs to set against the gains mentioned.

Other key concepts

Having outlined the various areas of content related to the teaching of the concept of division of labour, it should not be assumed that this topic need be taken in isolation. Indeed there are various links to other 'key concepts' in economics. It would be giving a false picture of the nature of the discipline if it were not related to the other key concepts in this area, such as exchange, interdependence and allocation. Fortunately, there are a number of points at which these concepts can be related to that of division of labour, allowing students to see a wider tapestry without the distortions and artificiality of some attempts to provide a conceptual 'framework' for economics.

Teaching approaches

As has already been mentioned, there is no single 'wonder method' guaranteeing the successful teaching of this topic to all students in this age range. It is intended that the following general approaches be used by the teacher as the starting point for providing a package specific to the needs of his or her context. The examples given, however, do allow the teacher to start this experimentation from the basis of a selection of approaches, each of which has been tried in an actual teaching situation.

Games and situations

Division of labour is very much a practical concept. It is to do with the organisation of how we carry out certain tasks. It makes sense, therefore, to illustrate its use by getting students actually to carry out a practical task. The description that follows concerns a simulated production line. The products are toy trucks made out of 'Lego' bricks. Such simulations usually gain a great deal by having outside 'experts' for briefing sessions and as advisers during the running of the game.

The class is split into four equal teams with any spare students acting as 'recorders', checking the quality of the products of each team and keeping a tally of their production levels. One person in each team is the Parts Manager responsible for giving the correct set of parts to each assembly-line worker. How these sets are decided upon could be a team decision. (The more workers are able to perform a simple part of the complete task, the greater the advantages to be gained from the division of labour, because of less need for training.) Another student acts as a Production Manager, supervising and organising the flow of production. Other members of the team act as the assemblers. In two of the teams the processes are split between workers in such a way that each worker completes the whole process of production.

The instructions for each of the processes involved is put on a role card, and one set given to teach team. In the first two teams, this means that workers have to learn all the tasks and may experience delays while learning these instructions.

In terms of organisation, a simulation such as this has

certain implications. First there is the timing of each part of the simulation. The briefing might be quite short, but the actual production should last up to an hour. The debriefing sessions are vital and should last a similar amount of time to the actual game and should be structured in such a way as to raise as many of the issues involved as possible. Students could be asked about such qualitative aspects as the relative boredom in two types of groups as well as the quantifiable items such as rates of production, number of 'rejects', and so on.

If the 'trucks' are given a selling price and the parts given a cost, then the comparisons of value added by the various teams can be made, with the consequent implications for relative wages in the two firms. A cost for the 'patent' (i.e. the instructions) could become the team's fixed costs.

In the debriefing sessions, it is a good idea to have outside experts (from local firms, parents, etc.) to expand upon points made by relating them to their own personal experiences of working in industry.

Exercises similar to this one could just as well be done by the use of a 'product' involving drawing on paper, cutting out, sticking in objects and, more attractively as far as the hard-pressed classroom teacher is concerned, by students performing some necessary routine chore such as folding PTA letters and addressing envelopes.

Factory visits

All too often a visit to a factory is seen as an 'end-of-term treat' by students and teachers alike. Happily, this is far less true now than it used to be, and much greater thought and preparation tends to go into the typical visit. This is especially important for younger and less-able students who cannot be expected to organise what they observe on such a trip without a great deal of support and clear structure from the teacher. This is really only possible if the aims of the visit are not only very clear but few enough to be achievable.

Although there may be other reasons for going on a particular visit to a factory, a study of the use of the division of labour in practice is obviously one possible one. As students go around the sections of the factory they should be asked to note a number of different points. The names of parts of the factory (administration, assembly line, warehouse, storeroom, canteen, etc.) give some indication of the extent of the division of labour. The work done by the people in each of these sections could also be observed and noted, along with any job 'titles'. Students could be allocated different workers on whom to write a detailed job description, and if possible they should interview the worker. This would provide the class with a number of worker profiles, but would, of course, need careful guidance.

Factory visits invariably have an embarrassing question session during which students are too shy or too bewildered to think of questions to ask. This could be prepared for by asking students prior to the visit, to make sure that they complete a checklist of information about the firm. This could be used to extend the knowledge of the division of labour beyond what students might see in a single factory by including items that refer to the relationship between the work done there and the work done elsewhere in the chain of production for that particular product. Students might, for example, be asked to find out about sources of raw materials, distribution systems, associated companies and so on.

Resource packs

Division of labour is practised all around us. Even in schools, there is no shortage of examples from which to choose. Given this easy accessibility of the applications of the concept, it should be relatively straightforward to produce a pack of resources that can be used on a class basis or for individual student research. Two main points to consider when producing such a pack are first, its contents and how it is produced, and second, how it might be used in the classroom.

On the first of these questions, much has been written. The scope is almost endless, and in this chapter only a few of the possibilities will be exemplified as a model for others.

A factory visit by a group of students is one way to use the resources of local industry. An alternative to taking students to the workplace is to bring the workplace into the classroom. Instead of the whole class going round the factory, the teacher might go round it equipped with a 35 mm camera and plenty of slide film. Another useful tool on such a visit is a small portable cassette recorder. The results of interviews, questions and commentaries can be put on to tape and used later in a number of ways. They could be edited to produce a soundtrack to accompany the slides as a tape–slide package. They could be edited to form a tape resource in their own right. Equally, there is no reason why something initially put on to tape should remain in that format. The cassette could act as a dictaphone and the outcome could be printed worker profiles, or descriptions of the scene in the factory.

Going around a factory is obviously not the only way that such resources can be obtained. The school itself is a good case study. In this case, much of the resource material may already be in existence (maps of the school, staff lists, timetables, etc.). Although such resources may be readily available in a school, they may be even more easily obtained elsewhere. The classified ad pages of the local newspaper, for example, contain a wealth of information on the extent of the division of labour in the local area. The same is also true of the *Yellow Pages*. Newspapers also contain articles that mention specific firms, jobs and so on. A collection of these could be made and mounted on card as the basis of a comprehension exercise.

Many more such resources could be put together to form a resource bank, the only limit to what is possible being the imagination of the teacher. Having got such a bank of resources, however, there still remains the question of how it can be used. Some of these resources will lend themselves automatically to a traditional class presentation. The tape-slide sequence is probably the best example. Even a tape-slide sequence, however, can be used as the basis of individual or small-group work. As an alternative to using the resources in a teacher-directed way, it is possible to split the class into small groups, each with the task of preparing a short presentation to the rest of the class on a specific aspect of the content of the topic of the division of labour. This splitting up could be carried even further by asking individual students to produce a short project on the division of labour as a whole or on some particular aspect of it. However, in using small groups, the teacher must take care that some way is found to ensure that all students are given the full range of information and experiences set out as the aim of teaching the topic.

Stories

On the one hand, the division of labour is to be seen all around us and is a classic case of a topic that can be dealt with by using real-life examples. On the other hand, it is so omnipresent that in order to understand its significance by imagining its absence, we are forced to move right away from reality. It is in this sort of area that the charismatic teacher has always been able to keep his students' attention by telling a story. For the typical classroom teacher, however, this is not a flash of inspiration, but a well-planned exercise with a lot of thought, and possibly technology, involved.

The type of story used may vary. It may be a traditional 'castaway' approach. The Video Arts films/videotapes on this topic use the idea of a story to great advantage by using a Stone Age village as the setting for their cartoon. At the other end of the scale, the story could be based on a science fiction theme, such as the use of a time machine by people on this planet or by visitors from outer space. Whatever the type of story chosen, all those mentioned so far concentrate on trying to provide a potted history of the way in which the use of the division of labour has developed. The story could, of course, be a real-life one. The teacher could illustrate the extent of the division of labour by talking about the people that he came across during his journey to work. This approach could also be based on student experiences of the jobs done for them during, for example, a Saturday shopping trip.

The medium used to present the stories can also vary. Mention has already been made of a commercially available film or video cassette. The story approach is also used in some textbooks (such as Davies's *Starting Economics* published by Hulton Education) and could obviously be produced in printed form by the teacher. Printed stories allow for the placing of questions and other exercises at appropriate points. Although this is less easy to do with tape-recorded stories, these do have other counterbalancing advantages. A tape-recorded story allows the use of actors (possibly sixth-formers or students studying drama courses) to provide feeling and emphasis in the story. Equally, it is possible to increase the realism of a tape-recorded story by the use of sound effects (often available at teachers' centres and resource centres).

Role playing

Closely related to the idea of using stories to allow students to gain some insights into situations with which they cannot easily be made familiar, is the use of role-playing exercises. This sort of exercise might be very much akin to the story approach. Simply ask the students to imagine themselves in a particular situation. They may, for example, be asked to imagine that they are castaways. Equally, they might be asked to put themselves into a 'post-nuclear situation' or on an army training exercise.

In contrast to the very loose structure suggested by the 'situation' approach, it may be felt preferable to be more specific about the context. The students may be asked to deal with a particular problem. Examples of this might be to decide on how to organise a small production team or come to a group decision on how best to use their talents to solve a particular problem.

Worksheets

Worksheets are a well-established way to teach students any topic, whether in economics or in other subjects. The example given below illustrates how the story approach previously outlined can be used as the basis of a worksheet showing a variety of exercises and activities.

Bill and Ben

Mrs Jones and Mrs Smith were next-door neighbours. Mrs Jones had booked a fortnight's holiday in Crete. Mrs Smith did the same. Mrs Jones asked for a builder to build a garage while she was away. Mrs Smith did the same. Mrs Jones asked her builder if he would also paint the outside of the house. Of course, when she found out Mrs Smith did the same. (A few weeks later the holidays and the builders arrived.)

Bill: 'Well, hello Ben. Long time no see.'

Ben: 'Well, if it isn't Bill Brown! What are you doing here?'

Bill: 'I've come to build a garage and paint the house for Mrs Jones. How about you?'

Ben: 'I've come to do the same for Mrs Smith. How long do you reckon on taking?'

Bill: 'The building shouldn't take long – my speciality you know – say three days. Mind you, the painting I'm not so keen on. That'll take me a good seven days.'

Ben: 'I reckon on ten working days too. The difference is that I love the painting. Always been good at it. I should get through that in three days. It's the building that I'm slow at. That'll take me the rest.'

Bill: 'Hey, Ben, I've just had a great idea!'

Exercises

1 Questions:
   (a) What do you think Bill's idea would be?
   (b) How many 'man days' were they planning to have to use?
   (c) How many 'man days' would they have to use if both went along with Bill's idea?
   (d) Think of as many reasons for the difference as you can.
   (e) Will Mrs Jones and Mrs Smith be happy with the result?
   (f) What else could Bill and Ben do with the time saved?

2 Replay:
   Suppose that Bill was more experienced and more skilful than Ben, and that as a result he could do both the building *and* the painting faster than Ben could. Say he could paint the house in three days compared with Ben's four days and that he could build the garage in three days compared with Ben's six.
   (a) What would be the total time taken if Bill and Ben worked separately on the two houses?
   (b) What would be the total time taken if Bill did the painting and Ben the building?
   (c) What would be the total time taken if Bill did all the building and Ben the painting?
   (d) Which way is most efficient and why?

3 Graph work:
   Draw a block to represent each of the first three answers in the previous exercise. Split each block into the share of hours worked by Bill and by Ben. Shade each section in a different colour. Write a short paragraph to describe what this diagram illustrates.

4 Chart work:
   Design a poster that will illustrate at a glance the reasons why Bill and Ben would do the work in a shorter total time if they each specialised.

Diagrams

The worksheet in the preceding section ends with an exercise asking students to draw a poster to illustrate the advantages of the division of labour. It might be criticised on the grounds that it is unrealistic to expect this level of conceptualisation and transfer from students so young. This criticism is far less likely to be upheld if they have been used to drawing and interpreting charts, posters and diagrams of this sort as a normal part of their work.

There are a number of different approaches to the production of a wall chart in this area of economics. The first general approach might best be described as the 'chain of production' approach. It involves putting the concept of the division of labour into the context of a flow of processes in the production of a good, going through primary, secondary and into tertiary industry. The easiest way for this to be approached is by choosing a particular product and charting its progress through these various stages. This might be done for a product with which

students are familiar or possibly one that they have come across after a factory visit. Figure 16.1 gives an example of this.

Box	Description	Jobs
Flour making → Bread baking → Bread retailing	The wheat is grown on the farm and ground at the mill into flour. It is transported to the bakery to be baked into bread. The loaves are then transported to the shops where the bread is advertised as being for sale.	Farmer Lorry driver Miller Baker Packer Van driver Orders clerk Warehouseman Shelf stacker Check-out girl Advertiser

Figure 16.1 Bread production

A variation of this general theme would be to provide such a wall chart as the outcome of a visit to a factory, being more specific about the way that the production process is broken down between workers.

This linear type of wall chart is not, of course, the only possibility. It might well be that a poster showing, for example, the advantages and disadvantages of the division of labour could be produced by the students themselves as the outcome of a small-group project. Equally, there is no reason why the poster need be a single wall poster. It could be a series of teacher- or student-produced A4 posters that could be duplicated and developed into a worksheet.

Visual material

Posters can be used to stimulate student interest in just the same way as a good textbook. This is particularly the case if they contain rich visual material. Such material might be photographs, cuttings, drawings, etc. Exercises could then be developed based on these.

Another important technique with visual material of this sort is to provide students with contrasting pairs of photographs and get them to 'brainstorm' differences and similarities between them. This may be the contrast between a wealthy family of a highly specialised worker compared to the poorer conditions of a self-sufficient peasant. The Third World element could also then be used to advantage to bring out teaching points.

As well as the photographs or drawings used in pairs or singly in this brainstorming way, they could be used as a series. The sorts of techniques used in modern language by which a series of drawings has to be made into a story could be used to a great advantage in this area of economics. The series could show the development of division of labour, the process of producing a good on an assembly line, the chain of production, etc.

Computers

The computer is an invaluable tool for teaching areas of content that involve repetitive calculations or the need for quickly handling a single complex relationship. There are programs available commercially that show the gains to be made from specialisation, but these tend to be written for A level. At levels below this, however, the level of analysis is simpler, and so are the programming problems. Many schools now have members of staff who can write short, simple programs to a specific brief. Often this method of producing programs creates a teaching tool that is less polished than the commercially available programs, but one that is more effective in a particular classroom context.

In order to allow the person writing the program to do so easily, the economics teacher should be able to specify the following:

1　What relationships are involved and what outcomes are expected.
2　What screen layouts are required.
3　What student/teacher inputs there should be.
4　What graphics are required.
5　What limits need to be put on variables.
6　Whether the program is to be 'interactive' or 'demonstrative'.
7　How it is hoped to use the program in a classroom setting.

This sort of information is the minimum that could be used. More will help get the program you want.

Resources

The topic of division of labour is the sort that is dealt with in most textbooks of economics and commerce. There would not be much to be gained from cataloguing these here, although examples of the main approaches to the topic in a selection of books might be helpful.

The storybook style is perhaps best illustrated by *Starting Economics* by Davies (Hulton Educational) which tells the story of Fred Flinthead. This is particularly suitable for the lower-ability groups. The same might be said of *Daily Economics* by Nobbs and Ames (McGraw-Hill), although their presentation of the topic is far more descriptive and structured. This book does, however, contain a number of interesting questions and exercises at the end of each chapter. Perhaps the best example of a similar structured descriptive approach aimed at high-ability students is Stanlake's *First Economics* (Longman). A book that puts the idea of division of labour into the context of production as a whole is *Everyday Economics* by Davey (Macmillan). This book is specifically produced for a 16+ target and is suitable for quite a range of abilities of students.

An article well worth reading is that by Campbell called 'Teaching division of labour to less able pupils – a role playing approach', which appeared in *Economics*, vol. 8, no. 6. In this article there is an extended example and discussion of the sort of simple task-performing exercise mentioned in the section above on the advantages of division of labour. As well as giving an outline of the organisation of the exercise, there is some discussion of the points that were made by his students and suggestions of areas of extension and integration into other parts of the course.

A cassette/filmstrip pack from Audio Learning is *Production – Primary, Secondary and Tertiary Activities* (ECO 002).

Edward Arnold has a series of audio cassettes aimed at this age group called *A Question of Economics* and tape no. 1, 'What a Way to Work', deals in a lighthearted way with this topic.

ICI and Unilever have collaborated with Video Arts to produce a video cassette about division of labour which takes the form of a cartoon strip story of a primitive village discovering the benefits to be gained from the division of labour. These very useful cassettes can be purchased or hired for a nominal charge and are suitable for even the lowest ability groups.

17　Industry
Morag A. W. Ellingham

Introduction

Economics is still an area of growth within the curriculum, and this indicates a heightened awareness of its potential in providing students with the ability to make rational informed choices in their adult lives. For the 14–16 age group, the content of economics courses at both CSE and O-level can be broadly grouped in three main areas. Three roles may be identified:

1　the consumer;
2　the producer;
3　the voter.

The discipline of economics may be used for problem-solving, and as such the decision-making process has been identified by Leech[1] as proceeding from the definition of economic problems, to the application of theory, and then to decision-making. However, depending on the nature of the syllabus, the emphasis will obviously vary. Not only will the level of the course determine emphasis, but also the process of learning activities may well be altered, resulting in an approach such as that exemplified in Figure 17.1 when conveying ideas and information to 14–16-year-olds.

The role of the producer within economics/commerce-related courses frequently occupies a significant block of time. Certain features may be identified: What is production? Costs; types of firms; business organisation/structure; business finance; location.

To sustain interest, a wide variety of materials and techniques is essential. Not only will this make lessons livelier for students but it will also be more stimulating for the teacher, whose enthusiasm and interest can only be of benefit to those on the receiving end.

Bearing in mind this particular model of the process of economic thought, the topics included under 'Industry' may be approached and developed. The aim of this chapter is to suggest alternative methods of covering the material demanded by the syllabuses, that is, to cater for the varying needs of students at this age.

Teaching methods

What is production?

It is vital that students are familiar with economic terminology and are equipped with precise definitions. It is valuable to draw upon their existing knowledge to extract a definition of this term.

A useful starting point for the teacher is a dictionary definition:

Production – producing, thing produced.
Product – thing produced by natural process or manufacture.

Once group discussion has produced a satisfactory definition, the idea could be represented pictorially, as shown in Figure 17.2.

This technique can be used to emphasise the idea of the flow of production. It also has the advantage of being readily adaptable, depending on the level of the group, and indeed can be developed to encompass the rewards to the factors of production (financial flows) and other production processes (see Figure 17.3).

It is also important that the structure of the economic system is understood. Therefore industry should be placed in context and its relationship to production and commerce and direct services should be explained. Diagrammatically this could be as shown in Figure 17.4.

Considered in this way, students' personal experience and knowledge is the starting point – and their contributions provide the definition of production. This is

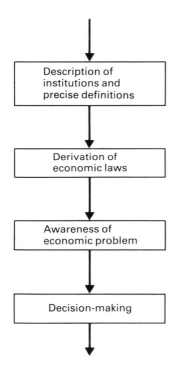

Figure 17.1 The process of problem-solving

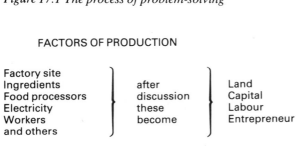

Figure 17.2 The manufacturing process

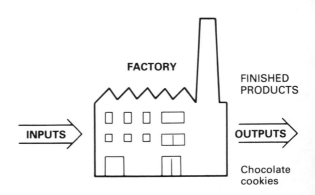

then developed to provide a structure of industry and production; and economic laws may be derived from this.

A useful conclusion to this topic would be to provide students with a vocabulary list and ask them to provide definitions:

production	extraction	manufacturing
industry	services	commerce
primary	secondary	

Costs

Having encountered the idea of the flow of inputs into the industrial process, this may be built on to, again from students' own experience. A role play exercise may be designed where the student is placed in the position of considering the materials required to perform a particular activity and is also asked to cost the exercise. Content may be negotiated so that students choose an item with which they are familiar.

However, the teacher should prepare her/his own selection to provide general guidelines to spark off the imagination of the students:

rag doll;
wooden box;
honey biscuits;
bottle garden;
vegetable/flower garden.

The costs that arise may then be classified in a move from student- to teacher-centred activity. Similar costs may be grouped, and students may be asked to give an explanation of such a classification, and the related terminology of fixed and variable costs may be extracted and clarified.

Many students find the actual calculation of costs and the related concepts of price and profit a struggle. The development of such skills may be aided by the use of either number chains or 'crossnumbers' (see Figure 17.5).

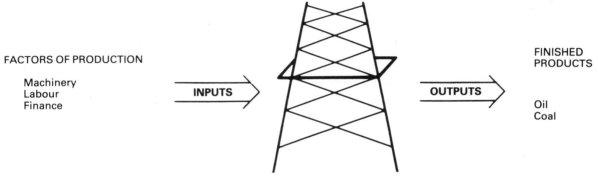

FACTORS OF PRODUCTION

Machinery
Labour
Finance

INPUTS

OUTPUTS

FINISHED PRODUCTS

Oil
Coal

Figure 17.3 The extraction process

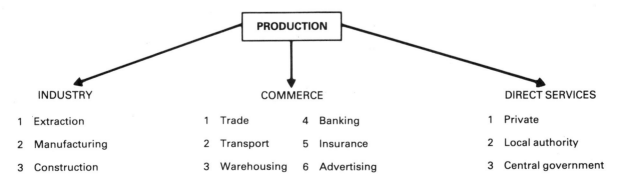

INDUSTRY	COMMERCE		DIRECT SERVICES
1 Extraction	1 Trade	4 Banking	1 Private
2 Manufacturing	2 Transport	5 Insurance	2 Local authority
3 Construction	3 Warehousing	6 Advertising	3 Central government

Figure 17.4 Production   Source: S. Hodkinson.

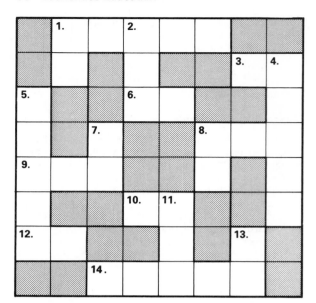

Figure 17.5 Costs 'crossnumber'

ACROSS

1   You are the owner of a business producing titanium jewellery. Your fixed costs are £3000 per year and your variable costs are £10 per article. You wish to produce 1200 articles per year. What is the average cost per article?

3   At what price should the article be sold in order to make a total profit of £3000 per year?

6   Calculate total profit of an organisation that wishes to make a 25 per cent profit, and faces the following costs of production:

Number of articles produced	20;
Fixed costs	£100;
Variable costs	£7 per article.

8   Calculate the profit or loss made by a firm using the information below:

Number of articles produced	75;
Price	£8;
Fixed costs	£400;
Variable costs	£2 per article.

9   Calculate the profit per article from the following figures:

Number of articles produced	200;
Fixed costs	£200;
Variable costs	£3 per article;
Price	£4.95.

10   From the following figures calculate the average cost:

Quantity	1500;
Fixed costs	£1500;
Variable costs	£20 per article.

12   Use the given figures to calculate the price per article, on a cost plus profit basis:
2000 articles to be produced;

Fixed costs	£2500;
Variable costs	£5 per article;
Anticipated profit	£1500.

14   If the total costs of producing 200 articles are £2500, how much will the firm have to charge in order to make a 10 per cent profit on each article?

DOWN

1   If fixed costs are £100 and variable costs are £10 per article, what is the average cost if fifty items are produced in a year?

2   Use the given figures to calculate the price per article, on a cost plus profit basis:
500 articles to be produced;

Total costs	£200;
Anticipated profits	15 per cent.

4   Calculate the cost per article from the figures below:

Quantity	300;
Fixed costs	£10 000;
Variable costs	£25 per article.

5   You are the owner of a small business. Your fixed costs are £2000 per year and the variable costs are £20 per article. You wish to produce 800 articles per year. What is the average cost?

7   At what price must the article be sold in order to make a total profit of £2000 per year?

8   Calculate the price per article, on a cost plus profit basis from the following figures:
1000 articles to be produced;

Fixed costs	£32 000
Variable costs	£15;
Anticipated profit	£8000.

11   Calculate the profit or loss made by a firm using the information below:

Number of articles produced	20;
Price	£5;
Fixed costs	£50;
Variable costs	£2 per article.

13   Calculate the average cost from the given figures:

Quantity	2000;
Fixed costs	£50 000;
Variable costs	£50 per article.

Types of firms

Students are required to gain knowledge of the types of establishments and their characteristics. Once again, they have a great deal to offer, and a successful way to approach this topic is to begin with a brainstorming session. The general guidelines to any brainstorm should be adopted. The title of the session should be placed centrally on a blackboard or flip-chart. Students are introduced to the exercise and asked to proffer any ideas that come to mind. The teacher transfers these ideas to the chart in their entirety – ideas should be neither shortened nor edited for there should not be any element of judgement entering at this stage. If this is the first occasion on which this technique has been used, students will initially be slow to respond. However, once they see that all ideas are accepted without criticism, even the quieter members of the group will invariably contribute. With a large group, there is a tendency for ideas to flow rapidly, as different word associations arise – but students are only too willing to repeat their ideas in order that they too are placed on the chart.

The content of the exercise is frequently diverse. The length of the brainstorm may vary between 10 and 15 minutes; the session should be brought to a close when ideas peter out. Vital to the success of the brainstorm is the follow-up where ideas are grouped. Given the nature of this brainstorm, a useful categorisation would be as follows:

Sole trader
Partnership
Joint-stock companies – Private limited companies
                                   Public limited companies
Co-operatives
Nationalised industries
Multinationals

These sub-titles may be added at the end.

Students will certainly have provided a long list of names of firms – both national and local. Thus it is essential that the teacher running the session be well informed concerning local companies so that the categorisation is accurate. However, obvious guidelines can be used – for example, the full title of the local firm can give a direct clue to its identity. In Plantscape Ltd, the word 'Limited' in the title indicates that it is a private limited company. Additionally, the use of *Yellow Pages* or a local directory can clarify names of firms and hence they can be allocated accordingly.

Alternatively, it is often valuable for the teacher to complete the categorisation for a subsequent lesson and to produce a handout containing all the ideas arising from the session. This may be a more effective use of time.

A useful visual aid to clarify the ideas behind the classification system would be a series of pictures representing each type of firm.

Having introduced the various organisations, each will need to be developed further so that students have precise information concerning the financing of the firm, size, liability and disclosure.

Apart from approaching this material from the point of view of each type of firm, a supplementary approach can be adopted taking common features, for example owner-ship or control, and making clear the differences between the various business organisations. This is the approach adopted by Anderton.[2]

Finance

The term 'finance' is specifically related to the sources of finance of firms. With this in mind and given the changing nature of both the banking system and government schemes, it is an ideal area of the syllabus in which to call upon the individual expertise of a representative of the financial system. As an introductory exercise, the simple role play technique can extract the various sources of finance available to an individual or firm. The banking sector is bound to arise as a potential source, and hence a visit to a local branch of one of the primary commercial banks, or to invite a guest speaker from one of the banks, is an excellent development. Whichever is chosen, it is essential that both students and the other party are fully

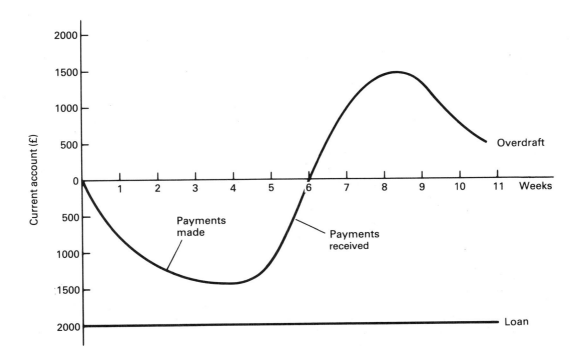

Figure 17.6 Graph to illustrate the distinction between a loan and an overdraft

prepared for the session. Specific objectives should be outlined to ensure syllabus coverage. Ideally, a meeting with the speaker prior to the talk or visit is desirable.

An area for emphasis is obviously the various loan and overdraft facilities provided by the banks as well as the wide variety of other services that they offer small businesses.

The loan/overdraft distinction is an issue that is often confusing to fourth- and fifth-years who often have no experience to call on. Apart from a verbal explanation, the graphical presentation shown in Figure 17.6 has proved successful in clarifying the benefits of each source of finance.

Figure 17.6 shows the stability of the loan and how the overdraft facility varies on a weekly basis. It is more readily apparent with the aid of the visual description that interest is paid on the entire sum of the loan until repayment, whereas the overdraft interest is only charged on the amount outstanding.

In addition, government schemes of finance can be highlighted as an area of interest. It is advisable, when first approaching a bank to request its assistance, to outline your requirements as clearly and in as much detail as possible, so that a suitable employee may be selected who will be knowledgeable in this field.

There are many leaflets containing information on the wide range of government schemes available. These can be a very useful source of up-to-date information for the teacher and can also be made available to students if placed on the subject notice board along with the *Financial Times* Share Index.

A visit to the Stock Exchange is of obvious benefit but, failing this, the Council of the Stock Exchange does publish a wide range of material for schools. Perhaps the most effective teaching aids are the postcards and slides of

the 'Trading Floor' and the entrance to 'The Building' which help to create a certain atmosphere within the classroom and make an impression on the students. Also available are share certificates; these help when making the distinction between par and market valuations which students find so difficult to understand.

A fine way to conclude this section is with a vocabulary list, to ensure that students have complete understanding of the new jargon that has arisen during the sessions. With this in mind, the presentation can be made amusing by the use of a 'wordsearch', whereby students are asked to find as many words or terms as possible associated with business finance, and to give definitions. Another useful exercise is for them to write sentences using the vocabulary in the 'wordsearch'. The merit of the approach is its novelty but it also allows more able students to develop their ideas.

In the 'wordsearch', words may be found horizontally, vertically, diagonally, as well as at right angles (see Figure 17.7).

Management structure

Students belong to the school organisation and have knowledge of its hierarchy, so this is a very useful starting point. The class may be asked to compile a tree diagram showing the structure of the school. Alternatively, a successful way of covering the same ground is to provide them with a skeleton tree diagram which they are asked to complete by inserting the names of the teaching staff. Irrespective of which approach is adopted, the tree diagram will need to be branched into academic and pastoral bands. The benefit of adopting the second approach is that students can be asked to work in small groups, which allows them to co-operate rather than compete and to pool their ideas and knowledge of the school – which invariably is incomplete.

Once the school staff have been positioned on the tree diagram, a parallel to the structure of companies may be drawn. The headteacher is in a similar position to the managing director; the separation of the staff into pastoral and academic fields is similar to the departmental split that is evident in many companies. The final exercise is then to produce a structure that has general relevance and to identify the advantages and disadvantages that can arise from large organisations.

Many firms produce tree diagrams for their staff notice boards, and it may be possible to use students' family connections to obtain such materials, which could serve as very useful visual aids to introduce at this final stage – showing students the relevance of the ideas covered.

A word of warning: if use is made of the school's internal structure, it is vitally important that it is correct in its order of seniority, although this may be open to dispute!

At this juncture, it can be extremely helpful to organise a school visit to a local firm, whether or not the course is project-based. It would be advisable when selecting the venue to choose a large firm as it is more likely to have

L	I	M	I	T	E	D	L	B	P
W	N	S	H	A	R	E	I	U	R
D	T	C	A	P	I	T	A	L	E
I	E	B	E	A	R	A	B	L	F
V	R	R	S	G	P	R	I	C	E
I	E	O	T	I	M	I	L	L	R
D	S	K	O	L	P	S	I	O	E
E	T	E	C	T	A	K	T	A	N
N	S	R	K	S	R	D	Y	N	C
D	F	A	C	E	V	A	L	U	E

Figure 17.7 Business finance 'wordsearch'

adopted precise communication channels and promotion ladders so that the internal organisation may be explained. Also, large firms are more likely to be able to provide detailed information on costs, finance and location material. Students need to be briefed before the visit, with either a questionnaire or a list of items to look out for. Cooke[3] has designed a list of questions that has a universal relevance and this may be used in its entirety or as a guideline.

Following the visit, students are invariably full of enthusiasm, and to capitalise on their feelings as well as clarifying certain observations, a debriefing session is of great value. The teacher needs to have knowledge of the firm and a clear idea of salient points relating to the firm's operations.

Location

A direct benefit arising from an industrial visit preceding this section is that the firm visited may be used as a case study either formally or informally. The location information could be written as a piece of stimulus material and accompanied by a set of structured questions to extract the locational factors considered by firms when deciding on suitable premises. This has proved to be successful in conveying the locational factors considered by firms, and the use of resources from the local economy helps to introduce an element of reality:

Herman Miller – office furniture
'An empty room,
A person,
A need
An expectation . . .
We are Herman Miller'

Herman Miller Limited, Bath, was established in 1970 on a site lying alongside the main Bristol Road. In the late 1960s Herman Miller US was faced with an expanding European market and it was thus desirable to expand abroad.

A London warehouse was selected as a temporary location, owing to easy access to Europe. Two Herman Miller representatives were then directed to decide on a suitable permanent location. They were on their way to Wales, attracted by the government grants that were available in this Development Area, when they stopped overnight in Bath. By chance, in an estate agent's window, they saw details of their present location, viewed it, and put their proposals to the parent company in the USA.

The site was away from the centre of Bath, so rent and rates were reasonable. The communication facilities were ideal for easy road access to the Bristol docks and the M4/M5 network leading to the North as well as Heathrow and the London docks. This was essential for the movement of hide and fabrics from Europe and the USA, wood from Finland, and the completed office furniture and systems.

The village of Twerton provided a local workforce that was familiar with the craft of furniture manufacture, owing to the presence of Arkana and Bath Cabinet Makers.

In 1974 a second factory unit was built on a site positioned across the river from the first factory unit. However, when further factory space was required in 1980, a new site at Chippenham was selected, since no further room for expansion was available in Bath.

Over the years, Herman Miller's Bath reputation has grown and much goodwill now exists within the local community.

Questions
1 In what country is the parent company?
2 What were the reasons for Herman Miller's expansion into England in the 1970s?
3 Why was a site in Wales thought to be desirable?
4 Where in England did Herman Miller establish its permanent factory location?
5 What are the advantages of this site?
6 Are there any disadvantages arising from the size of the Bath site?
7 Is there anything to suggest whether or not Herman Miller Limited has been successful?
8 What has happened to reinforce Herman Miller's location decision in Bath?

Teachers might adapt these ideas to produce a case study of an organisation in their area.

Conclusion

Syllabus coverage of industry as a topic is very broad, with considerable scope available for the teacher to develop novel approaches to stimulate and heighten students' awareness of economic life. Most of the content is descriptive and hence coverage is as important as understanding. A lively and imaginative approach has therefore a great deal to offer.

Notes and references

1 Leech, P., *Teaching Economics to the 14–16 Year Age Group* (Anforme, 1979) p. 1.
2 Anderton, A. G., *An Introduction to Social Economics* (Heinemann Educational Books, 1980) pp. 83–4.
3 Cooke, R., 'The firm, as in the "Understanding Industrial Society Project" ', in Whitehead, D. J. (ed.) *Handbook for Economics Teachers,* (Heinemann Educational Books, 1979) pp. 53–62.

Resources

Baddeley, J. M., *Understanding Industry* (Butterworth, 1980).
Baron, D., *Economics – An Introductory Course* (Heinemann Educational Books, 1976).

Concise Oxford Dictionary (OUP, 1961) p. 957.

Donnelly, G., *The Firm in Society* (Longman, 1981).

Information and Press Department, The Stock Exchange, London EC2N 1HP.

Lloyds Bank Finance Series.

National Federation of Self Employed and Small Businesses.

Nobbs, J., *Social Economics* (McGraw-Hill, 1977).

Nobbs, J., and Ames, P., *Daily Economics* (McGraw-Hill, 1975).

Sanday, A. P., and Birch, P. A., *Understanding Industrial Society* (Hodder & Stoughton, 1983).

Small Firm Information Service.

Wales, J. H., 'Industry – organisation, finance, location and government influence', in Whitehead, D. J. (ed.) *Handbook for Economics Teachers*, op. cit., pp. 79–85.

18   Population

David R. Butler

Introduction

Population is frequently included in economics and commerce GCE and CSE syllabuses. It may also be an element in many integrated social science and humanities courses and is often an aspect of geography and history courses. Population does not normally form part of mainstream economics (there is little emphasis on it at A level) and the teacher is tempted into either complete avoidance or at best a rather cursory look at the bits that might crop up in the compulsory question. This is a pity as the topic can be taught in a stimulating way and has potential for introducing to the student some of the basic tools of economic analysis.

Content

Most syllabuses have traditionally concentrated upon the UK's population structure in terms of its growth rate, changes in birth and death rates, and the age, geographical and occupational distributions of the population. More recently, there has been an increasing trend to look at more global population problems. This is certainly true of some of the integrated courses referred to above. Thus this is becoming one of the few areas in economics where students need to involve themselves in looking at comparative systems and there is a strong case for including a section on Third World population problems and the 'ghost of Malthus'.

Methods

1 A statistical approach

It has already been indicated that population could provide the ideal vehicle for introducing some of the basic

methods of analysis early on in the course. Thus there is great scope for the use of graphical interpretations, demonstrations of the difference between relative and absolute changes, the idea of growth rates and simple model building. Many of the relatively simple ideas that teachers often take for granted when drawing graphs and handling statistics are so often misunderstood by the young student of economics. How many students really appreciate the implications of a changing slope in a graph? A simple graph such as the one illustrated in Figure 18.1 could be used to introduce a number of important ideas.

Questions

1 How has the *rate* of population increase changed from 1960–80?
2 How is the 'estimated' part of the graph constructed?
3 What factors might cause the estimated figure for 2000 to be different from the actual figure?

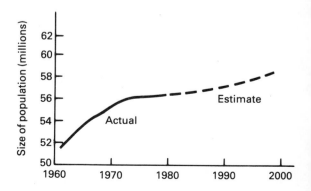

Figure 18.1 Britain's population 1960–2000

More-able students might, with the aid of calculators or microcomputers, attempt to make their own estimations of population growth. Example: Assuming a current world population of 4000 million and a birth rate of 28 per 1000 population per annum and a death rate of 12 per 1000 population per annum, what will be the population in 1990, 2000, 2010? Students will then be able to see the effect of small changes in either the birth or death rate on population estimates. The exercises could be repeated for the UK (see Resources on p. 95 for available statistics) and followed up with discussions on the problems of making accurate estimations in economics and the implications of this for planning.

2 A local survey approach

Most local libraries will have a copy of the census pertaining to that particular area. This will contain a wealth of statistical information which could form the basis of local population surveys. It is interesting and valuable to compare local statistics with national trends and to discuss the reasons for any notable variations. Local age/sex pyramids can easily be constructed – inner-city patterns can be compared to outer boroughs, rural areas with urban, etc.

Students themselves might provide the resource base for looking at local migration patterns by comparing their place of birth with that of parents and grandparents. Changing family size could be examined by comparing the students' families with parents and grandparents. (The teacher will need to be sensitive to personal situations to avoid causing embarrassment here.)

3 A data-response approach

Population is a good area in which to use data-response questions and examination boards quite commonly set questions involving the interpretation of population figures. The teacher might find the exercises that follow useful. (See also Anderton, A., *An Introduction to Social Economics*, 2nd edn. (Heinemann Educational Books, 1984) ch. 27, for some excellent examples of questions.)

Baby boom over?
Twenty years ago population experts were predicting a major increase in the UK's population by the year 2000. These predictions have been drastically revised downwards and the expectations are that the population will only increase by some 5–10 million in the next 100 years from its current level of 56 million.

World population explosion still on?
If current trends continue, the world's population is expected to triple by the year 2000 from its current level of around 4000 million. Twenty years ago warnings were being given about the problems that such an explosion would cause and these now seem increasingly to be becoming a reality.

Questions
1 The two statements above seem to conflict with one another – is it possible to explain how they may both be correct?
2 Why have predictions of the UK's size of population for the year 2000 been revised?
3 What types of problems are likely to be caused by a tripling of the world's population? Who is most likely to be affected by these problems?
4 Assuming that the world's population does triple by 2000, what steps could be taken to prevent the kinds of problems you have mentioned in answer to question (c) from occurring?

Match the population pyramid
The graphs in Figure 18.2 (overleaf) show the age and sex distributions for four countries: France, the USA, Mexico and Sweden. (i) Match the country to the graph. (ii) Explain your reasoning. (iii) Which graph most closely resembles the pattern you would expect for the UK?

Answer: A Mexico, B Sweden, C France, D USA.

Areas where students have problems in understanding

1 Interpretation of statistics

Students given population figures to discuss will very often make wild and exaggerated claims as to what they show. Given recent birth and death rate statistics, students are apt to make statements such as 'There must have been a recurrence of the Black Death'. Students frequently confuse absolute and relative changes when discussing statistics (an error not uncommon in other aspects of economics). A change of growth rate will often be confused with a change in total size. Clearly, practice in handling population statistics in the ways mentioned above is essential and extremely useful for the student.

2 Occupational distribution of population

A frequent examination question at this level is 'How and why has the occupational distribution of population changed in the last fifty years in the UK?' Candidates in answer to this question will frequently become too involved in discussing the changes in individual industries and fail to discuss overall trends. Students should thus be made aware of the main changes that have taken place in the primary, secondary and tertiary sectors of the economy before individual industries are considered. Individual industries very often show reverse trends to those of the overall sector and this leads to confusion among less-able students. Again, this is a very useful way of introducing some very simple ideas about statistical interpretation. Another frequent error here is to assume that a fall in the proportion of people employed in a particular sector is the same as a fall in the total number. Reference needs to be made to the size of the total 'cake' and the shares within it.

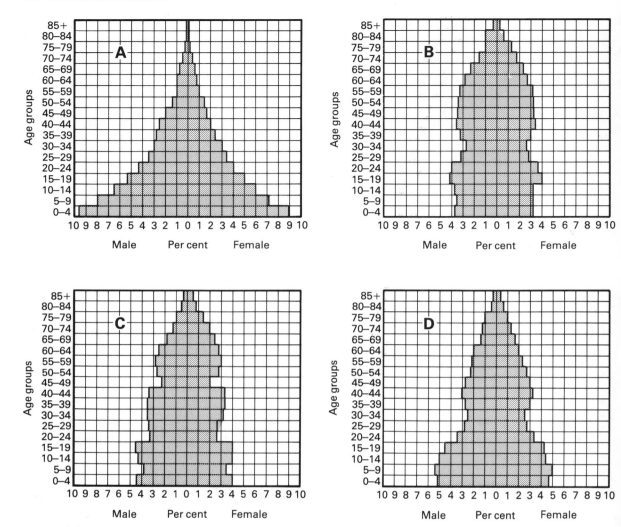

Figure 18.2

3 The 'ageing' of the population

Another frequent examination question might be 'What is meant by the ageing of the UK's population, what has caused it and what are its economic effects likely to be?' Many textbooks are themselves misleading as to the causes of the ageing of the population. Clearly, changes in both birth and death rates may influence the age distribution but, in the case of the UK, the only significant factor is the birth rate. Students find this difficult to grasp and will normally place the emphasis on the death rate. A useful way of demonstrating this is by taking an extreme case: if there were 1000 babies born in 1985 and none born at all in the next ten years then the population will 'age' as this 'bulge' moves up the population pyramid. In answer to the question on effects, candidates will often fail to take account of 'other factors' that will help offset the influence of an ageing population. There may well be less people as a proportion of the total population under the age of 16 in ten years time but will there really be a fall in the demand for pop records?

4 The size of population and unemployment

A popular misunderstanding (often reinforced by the media) is that unemployment is directly related to the size of population, that is, 'Unemployment could be reduced if the UK's population was reduced'. The size of any one cohort may have implications in terms of their chances of employment but the relationship is certainly not a simple one. International comparisons may be useful here; or reference to the 1920s, when the working population was smaller but the proportion out of work was higher, may help to illustrate that 'other factors' will also be significant. More-able students might like to illustrate this by discussing the effects of population growth on Third World countries compared to industrialised countries. Reference to the Industrial Revolution period in the UK (the history department may well be able to assist here) might aid the discussion.

Resources

Books

Books dealing with the descriptive aspects of population have a tendency to be almost out of date when they are printed and need to be constantly kept up to date by using one of the statistical sources mentioned below.

Anderton, A., *An Introduction to Social Economics*, 2nd edn. (Heinemann Educational Books, 1984) ch. 27. A lively, interesting and comprehensive coverage of this topic, including data-response questions based on newspaper articles.

Powell, R., *Population* (Longman Economic Studies, 1982). Small booklet on UK population with questions and 'activities'.

Stanlake, G. F., *Introductory Economics,* 4th edn. (Longman, 1983) pt. 4, ch. 13.

Pamphlets

The UK in Figures (Press and Information Service, Central Statistical Office). Available free and in multiple copies for distribution to students. UK vital statistics presented annually on a pocket card.

An Economic Profile of Britain (Lloyds Bank). Available free in multiple copies for distribution to students. Small booklet giving many basic UK statistics including birth and death rates.

Films/videos

The Foundations of Wealth (available on free loan from Viscom). Ten 10-minute films, partly in cartoon format, concentrating on the division of labour and specialisation but raising population questions. Suitable for younger students but also with application to older students.

Other resources

Office of Population Census and Surveys. Leaflets and wall charts about different aspects of census.

Malthusiana (Longman, Schools Council General Studies Project). Simulation on population problems. Also available in computer software as *MALTH: Computers in the Curriculum Project* (Longman). A model to examine population dynamics in relation to food and energy supplies.

Oxfam. Various pamphlets and stimulus materials on Third World population problems.

19 Trade Unions

Kevin Tinsley

'Without doubt, the most important feature was the extent to which, and the way in which, teachers enabled their students to participate in the teaching programme'. Some apparently lively discussion turned out to be simply rigid question and answer stuff: the teacher, well prepared, asking questions only as a cue for a correct factual answer or a conventional response from a narrow range of options and opinons. Such 'closed-reasoning' surely has little to do with, indeed could actually harm, political literacy or competence of any kind.[1]

Introduction

To teach trade unions to 13–16-year-olds as an economic concept is also to teach the subject as a political concept – hence the above quotation, which illustrates that certain teaching methods can be functionally useful in developing students' political literacy. Economics education can (and sometimes must) be political education, and there is no reason why this should not be so. The key, therefore, is to identify the role of trade unions in the *political* processes that produce *economic* decisions.

Most teaching of trade unions for this age range could be said to cover two basic areas: the history of trade unions, and the micro- and macroeconomic functions of trade unions. Other related areas, for example the structure and organisation of trade unions, can be dealt with as secondary material to the main areas. This chapter will deal mainly with the functions of trade unions, on the assumption that the history section is more fully covered in the subject of history itself, or through interdisciplinary projects (this, of course, will depend on the orientation of the school's curriculum). The history of trade unions should therefore be dealt with in the context of O-level, CSE or 16+ courses as an exposition of the origins of the functions of trade unions.

The most practical use of this chapter would be to illustrate a potential model 'Teaching Trade Unions' module, designed to cover, say, four double periods and which would highlight the possible teaching methods and their relationship with the ideas and information in question. This takes up the next section; the following section is a guide to resources and information centres. Finally, there is an appendix consisting of a trade-union/industrial-relations simulation, which can be used as an integral part of the module.

Module: 'Teaching Trade Unions'

1 The first lesson

This is based on the activity change cycle which is essential for maintaining student attention. The first stage could be a 'brainstorming' session (see, for example, Whitehead,[2]) to help get some idea of the students' various attitudes to the issue. A second stage may be story telling: demanding silent attention while the teacher dramatically recounts the story of the Tolpuddle Martyrs (see Booklets, next section). The third stage is extraction and comprehension – from the specifics of the Tolpuddle case to extracting from the students the general reasons for forming a trade union, and thus a preliminary identification of at least some of the functions of trade unions. The final stage can thus be a discussion, with note-taking, of the historical reasons, together with a comparison with some of the words and phrases that arose in the brainstorming section. An alternative way of discussing and defining key phrases could be the use of stimulus material, for example, part of the TUC Teacher's Kit is a glossary of terms on trade unions, the meanings of which could be blanked out, leaving the list of words and blank spaces as a handout.

2 The second lesson

This might consist of a role playing exercise of the type shown in Appendix 19.1, where the class is divided into two sections; the two groups can then be brought together *en masse*, or by a meeting of delegates from both sides – management and trade unions. The simulation illustrates some of the microeconomic functions of trade unions, and the political environment in which they take place. The teacher, recording points as the game unfolds, should be able to adopt a 'classroom manager role', and a discussion period at the end of the lesson should bring out the noted points.

Alternatives to a simulation could be to act out a play (see Resources on p. 97) if it is felt that the simulation is unsuitable for some students.

3 The third lesson

This could consolidate the experiences of the simulation, by various methods – for example, by showing a filmstrip or a video. Another way would be to invite a local shop steward or trade-union organiser to address the class, and to give his or her views as to how the simulation could have proceeded – or involve your visitor in the simulation itself! Another possibility would be to take the students to a place of work and hold discussions with trade unions and management on site.

There may be other aspects of trade unions that need to be taught; for example, the types of trade unions, their national organisation or the macroeconomic functions of trade unions. For the latter subject it is easy to use recent newspaper cuttings on some interaction between government and trade unions at a corporatist level as stimulus material, and other simulations could be devised to illustrate the national role of the trade-union movement.

4 The final lesson

This lesson depends on the way the learning process has developed during the first three periods and the associated homeworks. It may be useful at this stage to apply the new knowledge to case-study situations, which can be an ideal opportunity to use a group-teaching method, dividing the class into various groups and allocating different – or similar – case studies to each group, and then comparing conclusions.

Generally, it seems that the study of trade unions and their role in society and industry can best be achieved by a set of active teaching methods which involve students, and which as far as possible give the teacher a manager's role – hence the predominance in this module of activities such as brainstorming, simulations and group teaching.

Resources

Textbooks

There are two core books, both of which are lively and entertaining. The first of these is more suitable for lower-ability students:

Nobbs, J., and Ames, P., *Daily Economics* (McGraw-Hill, 1975) pp. 45–58.

Nobbs, J., *Social Economics*, 3rd edn (McGraw-Hill, 1981) pp. 37–51.

Booklets

What is a Union? Althea (Dinosaur Publications, 1981). This is simple and well-illustrated, and covers the history, functions and workings of trade unions.

Leigh, F., *Trade Unions – Checkpoint 10* (Edward Arnold, 1978). Contains cartoons and statistics, thus a good source/handout material.

The Story of the Dorchester Labourers (TUC, 1980). Resource for the story-telling lesson on the Tolpuddle Martyrs.

Plays

Walker, D., *Working Starts* (Edward Arnold, 1980) pp. 65–71. A book of plays exploring 'the world of work', with a play called *Unions*.

Simulations and role playing

Essex Raspberry Zooglebar Company Ltd (see Appendix 19.1).

Trade Union Simulation (Cockpit Arts Workshop/ILEA and Wandsworth Industry Schools Project, 1980). Superb set of three simulations, compiled with the advice of trade unionists, and raising many relevant issues (e.g. piece work, fixed wages, sexism in work). Write to Cockpit Arts Workshop, Gateforth Street, London NW8 8EH, price £2.00 + postage, or telephone 01 262 7907.

Unions and You (Clydebank EEC Project for the Strathclyde Area Department of Education, undated). Comprehensive set of action-based learning resources in seven sections with titles like 'Why do we need trade unions?', 'Trade unions and the future' and 'Case studies', the final section, which contains role playing exercises. Write to Clydebank EEC Project, Dalmuir Educational Resources Centre, Singer Road, Dalmuir, Clydebank G81 4SF.

Young Worker (British Youth Council, undated). Kit of materials aimed at the school leaver; includes a simulation based on a dispute called 'Teabreak'. Write to 57 Charlton Street, London NW1 1HU, or telephone 01 387 7559.

Employment Relations (Manpower Services Commission). A series of five folders, in this case see Folder 2, 'Employment Facts'. I hesitate to recommend this – most MSC material is essentially an exercise in socialising school leavers into industry, and the role of trade unions is treated as incidental. However, the material could be used selectively and is divided into informative resources – comic-strip modules, etc. – and participative resources, which includes simulations, group exercises and case studies. Write to 62 Hills Road, Cambridge CB2 1LA, or telephone 0223 315944.

Understanding Economics (Economics Education 14–16 Project). See Unit G, 'Wages', for role playing exercise on wage negotiations. Write to Department of Education, University of Manchester, Manchester M13 9PL, or telephone 061 273 4494.

Case studies *(in addition to those cited above)*

Philips, A., and Stuttard, G., *Case in Hand: Cases in Industrial Relations* (Cambridge University Press, 1983). Case studies based on issues, and union roles in decision making on those issues (e.g. sex and race discrimination, redundancy, etc.), together with a set of 'days in the life of . . .' (e.g. shop steward, trade-union official).

Resource centres

Inner London Education Authority (ILEA), Centre for Learning Resources, 275 Kennington Lane, London SE11 5QZ. Reference library and information service: 01 735 8202, general number 01 735 8202. Future uncertain due to ILEA's impending abolition but, for those in the south-east, it provides an excellent resource centre, with a film and video library and a comprehensive catalogue of learning materials.

Understanding British Industry, Sun Alliance House, New Inn Hall Street, Oxford OX1 2QE, telephone 0865 722585. Also has nine regional liaison officers and over fifty satellite resource centres; UBI is a politically independent industrial education resource centre, funded by the CBI Education Foundation. UBI will run, on request, a very up-to-date computer print-out of the direct resources they have available; in addition, the print-out gives information on secondary material, usually reports on the use and value of particular resources.

Education Department, Trades Union Congress, Great Russell Street, London WC1. For interviews, write and arrange in advance, although the TUC does publish a Teacher's Kit, currently being revised, which is useful for basic information. They can also suggest regional union organisers who are helpful in arranging visits.

Audio-visual aids

This subject is an area where AVA are not always the best approach, though there are two reasonable filmstrips:

You and the Unions (published by the TUC and the National Committee for Audio-Visual Aids in Education).

Trade Unions and Society (published by Mary Glasgow Publications, Brookhampton Lane, Kineton, Warwick CV35 0JB, or telephone 0926 640606). The main source of information for audio-visual aids is the British National Film Catalogue, published by the British Film Institute, 127 Charing Cross Road, London WC2H 0EA; they also produce a more concise guide called *Films and Videograms for Schools*, which is essentially a distillation of the main catalogue. Their material is on video post-1979, on 16 mm filmstrip before then. See also the *British Catalogue of Audio-Visual Materials*.

Miscellaneous

There are, of course, many other textbooks available, most of which are quite advanced at the expense of being rather dry. Two that are exceptions are:

Baron, D., *Economics: An Introductory Course*, 2nd edn. (Heinemann Educational Books, 1976) pp. 25–32.

Sanday, A. P., and Birch, P. A., *Understanding Industrial Society*, 3rd edn. (Hodder & Stoughton, 1983) pp. 70–85. Can be used in conjunction with a set of cassette tapes compiled by the same authors. Other textbooks:

Baddeley, J. M., *Understanding Industry*, 2nd edn. (Butterworth, 1983) pp. 90–103.

Davey, M., *Everyday Economics* (Macmillan, 1983) pp. 83–95.

Harbury, C., *Descriptive Economics*, 6th edn. (Pitman, 1981) pp. 161–73.

Harvey, J., *Elementary Economics*, 5th edn. (Macmillan, 1982).

Armstrong, P., and Knights, M., *Trade Unions and Industrial Relations* (Wheaton/Pergamon, 1979).

For revision:

Leeds, C. A., *Basic Economics Revision* (Cassell, 1982) pp. 139–52.

Appendix 19.1

The best method of using the following simulation is to divide the class into two sections – one management, one union – and to distribute the relevant handouts to all students. Each has a copy of sheet 1; the trade union side has a copy of sheet 2, the management side has a copy of sheet 3. Allow each side time to work out its strategy, and then bring the two groups together (see Hints for Teachers below. Sheets 2(a) and 3(a) can be distributed at any suitable time, before or during negotiations. The points that have been noticed during the simulation can then be emphasised and discussed by the class as a whole.

Simulation: 'Essex Raspberry Zooglebar Co. Ltd'

Sheet 1

Essex Raspberry Zooglebar Co. Ltd is a small firm employing twenty-five skilled and semi-skilled operatives to make raspberry zooglebars, largely for export. The firm's premises at Ledsham are about seventy years old, and are in a poor state of repair. They have fifteen expensive machines, and for three years the workforce have frequently complained that the leaking roof, poor heating and dirty conditions have been both unpleasant and dangerous.

In January 1977 there was an accident when water leaking from the roof caused a machine to malfunction, badly burning a woman's hand. Union representations to the management brought a promise to have the premises repaired and modernised.

The work to be carried out was to take about three months, which meant that temporary premises had to be rented at a high cost, and the machinery and offices had to be moved 15 miles further out of Ledsham. This was done by February 1977.

The employers laid on a coach to take their twenty-five workers from the old site at Ledsham to the temporary site 15 miles (30 minutes) away to start work at the usual time of 8 a.m. Then at 5 p.m., the normal time for finishing work, the workers were driven back to the old factory, arriving at 5.30 p.m.

These arrangements brought complaints from the union that they were spending an extra hour a day away from home, through no fault of their own, out of their own time, for no extra pay.

The employers said that with having to pay rent for the new premises, the hire of the coach, the moving of machinery and offices, as well as the repairs to the old premises, they simply could not afford to pay an extra 125 person/hours a week.

Some hints for the teacher

Clearly the way this simulation is organised will depend on the numbers and the conditions involved, and the age of the students. One approach would be to issue the hints given below to the respective protagonists, although it would obviously be of more value if the two groups could come up with these and other points themselves, perhaps with some nudges from the teacher. Also:

1 Some minor points could be highlighted during the simulation, or later; for example, the old management device of not placing chairs on the other side of the negotiating table for the union team, thus the union delegates have to drag some chairs over for themselves and are immediately put at a psychological disadvantage as the management sit impassively behind the table. The ideal union response is to walk out of the room and refuse to return until the management provide chairs for the workers. Incidents such as this will impress upon students the adversarial nature of political arguments over economic issues.

2 It is helpful for each group to anticipate the others' arguments as well as formulating their own.

3 Some attempt at role reversal for, say, known 'anti-union' students could be useful in allocating initial sides.

4 In the discussion following the simulation it could help to highlight, say, the idea of opportunity cost in the workers' time lost by travelling, even though they don't directly pay for travelling. Other concepts can also be drawn out that have relevance for economics in general; for example, the idea of a trade-off between short- and long-run benefits.

Sheet 2: To the trade union

You have a group of members, and you should now call a meeting. At that meeting your group should talk about the situation at work, and how you might be able to do something about it. You should then come up with some ideas about what you want from the management and some arguments in favour of your case. When you have done this, send a representative to the management group to request a meeting with them.

Now elect people to go in and argue your case. Make sure you know exactly what you want, and how far you are prepared to go to get it, that is work-to-rule, strike, selective stoppages, occupation of the factory, etc. Remember this is your first set of negotiations. If you're not sure about something, or if you feel you need further information, the teacher will tell you if this is available.

Sheet 2(a): Some hints for the trade union

In these negotiations you must emphasise the inconvenience of the situation and how unnecessary it all is. The negligence of the employers in this matter might also receive your consideration. The following points may help you to structure your arguments:

1 The repairs should have been done a long time ago.
2 The employers are guilty of negligence and should bear the consequences of their inaction.
3 The workers are being asked to spend longer at work, for no extra pay, with a lot of personal inconvenience.
4 It may be useful to make an allowance in your demands that you are prepared to compromise on – a 'negotiating margin' – that is, you ask for 10 per cent on the assumption that you can compromise down to 5 per cent, which is acceptable.
5 Don't forget you have the power to decide whether or not this factory produces anything.

Sheet 3: To the management

Get your group together and discuss the problem you are faced with; try and come up with some ideas as to what you can do. In a few minutes a team of shop stewards is going to arrange a meeting with you, and you need to anticipate what they want, and what arguments they may use, in order to be able to counter those arguments. When you have discussed this, elect a team of directors to go in and negotiate with the union. Make sure you know what you want, and how much

– if at all – you're prepared to give way. If you're not sure about something, or you feel you need further information, ask the teacher.

Sheet 3(a): Some hints for the management

In these negotiations you must emphasise both the financial consideration and the principle involved. The following points may help you to structure your arguments:

1 The company is spending a lot of money already and cannot afford much more expenditure.
2 The workers are not actually productive during the extra time; they are merely travelling, so why should they be paid?
3 The inconvenience is temporary.
4 It is ultimately for their own benefit – better working conditions, and so on.
5 The company is transporting workers at no extra cost to them – or is it?

Notes and references

1 Crick, B., and Porter, A. (eds) *Political Education and Political Literacy* (Longman, 1978) p. 26.
2 Whitehead, D. J., 'Learning processes and teaching strategies in economics education', *Economics*, vol. XIX, pt. 4, no. 84, winter 1983, pp. 141–8.

20   Money and Banking
David R. Butler

Introduction

Money and banking as a topic is included in most O-level and CSE economics syllabuses as well as related subjects such as business studies and commerce. Money and banking may also be an input to a 'common core' life and social skills course or form part of an 'economic literacy' module in a course for younger students. Too easily this topic can become a rather dry description of banking institutions and their functions. This is a pity as the topic does have the advantage of being 'live' from the students' point of view. They have a very natural interest in money,

they can see the high street banks and will be exposed to their very strenuous advertising campaigns and may well have some form of savings account. Thus the topic lends itself very naturally to a student-centred approach that is also appropriate to a range of ages and ability levels.

Content

Most courses in economics and related subjects at this level require at least some of the following: barter – its problems and the reasons for money; the 'qualities' of money; the development and use of notes, coins, cheques and credit cards; services and functions of commercial banks and other banks (merchant, Giro, savings, overseas); the Bank of England and elementary monetary policy; saving and borrowing.

The topic is wide ranging both in content and in the level of conceptual development required by the student. 'Life and social skills' types of courses tend to place the emphasis on the money management aspects of the topic while 'pure' economic courses tend to be more concerned with the role of financial institutions in the management of the economy.

Teaching methods

1 Barter simulation

Even quite able students rarely understand the purpose and function of money in an economy. A good approach is therefore to start with an economy without money by means of a barter simulation. Divide the class into, say, four groups. Each group produces a different product and has a surplus to barter represented by cards or rulers, rubbers, pens, etc. Start with a simple situation: group (a) wishes to sell to group (b) and group (b) is a willing customer. Even at this stage problems may arise. How is an exchange rate fixed? What if an item cannot be divided up? As each problem occurs it should be noted on the board by the teacher. The barter can then be made more complex, for example, group (c) wishes to trade with group (d) but group (d) does not require group (c) products. This should initiate the student into the problems of multiple exchange rates and a need for a double coincidence of wants. It can then be shown how the use of money can overcome these problems and hence its function in an economy.

2 Hyperinflation case study

Ask the question 'Why is a pound note worth a pound?' Few students will be able to give the correct answer. Many will state that 'it is backed by gold' or 'it has a silver strip in it' or a similar type of answer. This in itself can lead to an interesting discussion. A good approach is to take a really extreme situation such as the German hyperinflation of 1923. This has been well documented in a number of books (see Butler[1]) as well as in several television documentaries. The history department may also be able to assist with documentary evidence.

Example
A 50 mark note in 1919 bought two dozen eggs in Germany. By October 1923 a 10 000 000 000 mark note would not even buy one egg. People used such notes to light their fires and used coal to buy food and clothing.

Questions/discussion
1   Why did eggs cost so much more in terms of marks in 1923 than 1919? (Had eggs become scarce or was it that money was worth less?)

2   Why did coal come to be used as money while mark notes were burnt? (What properties did coal have that mark notes lacked?)
3   Why are modern marks accepted as money? (Do they have intrinsic value or is it trust in their value?)

3 Credit exercise

Students are given alternative methods of purchasing, for example, a stereo system – cash, hire purchase, credit transaction, credit card, loan from bank. (More-able students may be asked to obtain this information for themselves.) Students calculate total cost of methods and consider (i) which method is cheapest (apart from cash)? (ii) what are the advantages and disadvantages of each method? (iii) Why buy on credit when cash is cheaper? (More-able students may be asked to consider the relationship between the rate of interest and the rate of inflation of the item in question.)

4 Bank loans

Ask the local bank manager to come in and talk to the class about the criteria the bank would use for assessing loans. Use this as a lead in to a bank-loan simulation exercise where some students act as managers and others as customers requesting loans. (The Economics 14–16 Project and the Banking Information Service give a published simulation; see Resources on p. 101). A well-briefed bank manager would make such a simulation all the more realistic by providing professional comment on the decisions made by the students.

5 Savings and investment

The National Savings Bank, the Trustee Savings Bank and some of the clearing banks will assist a school in setting up its own bank. This requires staff supervision but students are able to carry out most of the basic functions. Sixth-form students might also help supervise the running of the school bank. Banks can operate both current and deposit accounts and an exciting extension would be to use a microcomputer for holding account details and calculating interest.

A competitive element could be introduced by running an investment game. Students are divided into investment teams each with £10 000 to invest in a variety of ways (e.g. shares, unit trusts, bank deposit, commodities, etc.). This can be done on a short-term basis with the teacher inventing interest rates, share and commodity price movements, etc. as a result of economic changes. It can also be played with real data over a period of, say, three months with students being allowed to adjust their portfolios each month. The winning team is the one that makes the largest gain net of tax. (The Economics Education 14–16 Project gives details of a computer simulation; see Resources on p. 102.)

6 Asset/liability structure

The actual figures can be obtained from bank reviews and

the *Bank of England Quarterly Bulletin*, and can be used as the basis for discussion with more-able students. The class could also be divided into groups, each representing a different clearing bank with an equal amount of assets to divide between cash at the bank, money at call, advances, etc. The game runs for ten years with the teacher allocating different interest rates and special effects (e.g. a cash loss from Barclays to Lloyds, a call for special deposits, etc.). Banks running short of cash have to borrow at a high rate of interest. The winning team is the bank that makes the most profit during the time period of the game.

7 A bank visit

Contact local banks to arrange open evenings when students can visit the bank and see the 'behind the counter' action. A good format is to circulate small groups of students around the various functions (counter, securities, cheque clearing, manager, etc.), each group being given a short talk and demonstration at each stage. It is important to prime the students well before the visit in order to bring out the economic aspects of the visit. (For example, how does the bank know the level of cash to maintain at the branch and how does this vary throughout the year? What determines the level of branch lending?) The visit would relate well to a short project or piece of course work on bank services and the functioning of a local branch.

Areas where students have problems of understanding

1   Barter and the function of money. Less-able students find it difficult to visualise an economy without money. In particular, they do not easily understand the concept of one good having a 'price' in terms of another. The simulation suggested in the above section together with the hyperinflation example may partly help to overcome these difficulties.
2   Some students find it difficult to understand how banks are able to lend money that has been deposited with them by customers. The film *Curious History of Money* (see Resources) gives a good demonstration of the principles of banking and illustrates this particular concept well. A simple classroom simulation can also demonstrate the idea – the teacher nominates students as banks, makes a new deposit at one of them and shows how it is possible for only a small percentage of the deposit to be asked for in cash. The same simulation can also show the idea behind an asset structure for the bank.
3   The control of the economy by the Bank of England. This is quite a frequent O-level question and the problem for the teacher is to simplify the necessary information required without distorting the ideas. (See Resources for texts that make an attempt to do this.) Newspaper headlines such as 'Bank increases interest

rate' or 'Big expansion in bank lending' can help to stimulate discussion and to add interest to what could otherwise be a mere listing of 'functions of the Bank of England'.

Resources

Texts

Most of the standard textbooks include this topic. Many have become understandably out of date (e.g. reference to MLR, the use of special deposits, etc.) and the teacher might well be advised to seek information from the excellent pamphlets produced by the Banking Information Service (see later) which are certainly a great deal more current and are in a better position for being more frequently updated.

Recommended texts include:

Anderton, A. G., *An Introduction to Social Economics* (Heinemann Educational Books, 1984) pt. 1. A lively and well-presented look at banking, building societies, insurance, saving and borrowing, including questions based on articles and other stimulus material. See also Anderton, A. G., *Money Matters* (Collins Educational, 1984). Forty units on all aspects of personal finance including a text, a set of assignments and a case study.

Butler, D. R., *Moneywise* (Harrap, 1981). A guide to money management for 14–16-year-olds including questions, exercises and a variety of stimulus material on personal finance.

Moss, P., and J., *Commerce in Action* (OUP, 1983) chs. 6 and 7. Commercial aspects of money, banking, credit, etc. presented in a lively way with plenty of diagrams and examination questions at the back of the book.

Stanlake, G. F., *Introductory Economics* (Longman, 1983) pt 7. Good coverage of money, banking mechanism, functions of the Bank of England, etc. presented in a straightforward way. Suitable for O-level students.

Other written material

Banking Information Service. A large number of up-to-date booklets, most of which are free of charge. They will send a pack of resources and details of available material on request. See *Bank Loan* simulation in particular.

Understanding Banking. This is a series of three booklets designed for use with average-ability students either in examination work or in general studies. Book 1, *Money Is Our Business*, deals with money in general and how banks, including the Bank of England, use money. Book 2, *Using Your Bank*, outlines the practical functions of banks; how to open accounts, etc. Book 3, *At Your Service*, examines bank services.

Other resources include: 'Banks today' – a wallchart, specimen cheques, paying-in slips, etc.; methods of payment – three booklets; managing money – three charts.

Life Offices Association. Up-to-date material available free of charge. Obviously concentrates upon life assurance but there are some very useful booklets on money, saving and budgeting.

14–16 Economics Education Project (currently undergoing field trials). Consumer section – units on alternatives (meaning and importance of money), budgeting (management of personal resources), paying (relationships between income and spending, saving and borrowing), bank-loan simulation (role play exercise).

Payday, National Girobank (from Resources for Learning Ltd, 19 Park Drive, Bradford, West Yorkshire). Available free of charge in multiple copies. A quarterly magazine for 14–16-year-olds covering a wide range of topics but with an emphasis on money management and personal finance.

Commercial banks. All the main commercial banks produce some useful material that is generally well presented and up-to-date, although naturally biased towards themselves. Local managers are normally very keen to liaise with schools and will supply multiple copies of leaflets. Examples: Barclays Bank, *Working for Yourself* – examples of businesses established by young people and how to finance them; Lloyds Bank, booklet on *Applying for Loans*.

Films

The Curious History of Money (Multilink, free loan). A 20-minute cartoon film from barter to credit cards. Now a little dated but still good entertainment. Rather a rapid commentary which for younger and less-able students requires plenty of teacher support.

Banking Information Service. Films and videos (VHS) – all available free of charge. *Bank on us* (23 mins) – how a branch works; *A simple account* (21½ mins) – banking system and services; *Banking on industry* (19½ mins) – how industry is financed.

Computer programs

Economics 14–16 Project (available from Longman). *Household budgeting* – information is provided on income and expenditure requirements and students have to allocate income between spending and saving. *Stock Market Role Play* – an investment game where teams deal in imaginary shares. *Stock Portfolio Data Retrieval* – a data file of share names, prices and cash holdings.

Notes and references

1 Butler, D. R., *Moneywise* (Harrap, 1981).

21 Employment, Unemployment and Inflation
Paul Clarke

Introduction

Most syllabuses for students up to the age of 16 include the topics of employment and inflation. In the 1980s, students will be aware of the daily headlines featuring debates about employment and inflation policy. It comes as something of a disappointment then to find that many textbooks give some kind of descriptive attention to these topics, an approach that too easily loses the interest of younger students. For example, the emphasis may be placed on describing the differences between types of unemployment rather than examining how the unemployment has been caused. Another difficulty for younger students is that of moving from personal experience of economics to understanding the nature of 'macroeconomic' variables. Students are more likely to see unemployment in terms of personal failings, a supply problem, than, say, a lack of spending in the economy: a demand problem. Similarly, it can be hard to appreciate any connection between the spending habits of an individual and the movement of prices in general.

Content

Syllabus outlines are sparse. The LREB's CSE Economics, for example, has a section called 'Managing the Economy', which covers 'measures to stabilise the economy, prices, incomes and employment'. Exam questions may provide further clues; in this case, a recent LREB economics paper included the following:

What would be the likely economic effects of a large government expenditure for the building of a third London Airport on (a) the area in which it was built, (b) the economy as a whole?

This suggests that students should understand the causes of changes in the level of employment and prices, and puts the topics into a dynamic context.

Teaching method

The following suggestions are all intended to supplement and enliven what may be covered by class notes or textbooks. The suggestions do not necessarily have to be inter-related, but might provide ideas for particular parts of what are otherwise very broad headings.

1 Exercise on why people are employed

(a) Ask someone in the class to suggest a good or service that they would be willing to pay for. Ask the other members of the class to write down all the different people who would be employed in providing this good or service for the consumer. The list of jobs could be extended almost indefinitely, and in trying to group together similar kinds of jobs, students will cover a useful revision of the production process. A flow chart could be used to link together these 'job-chains', providing an attractive wall decoration for the next few lessons.

(b) Where a department has a kit of materials, it is possible to illustrate the production process in a more obvious fashion. Plastic people represent workers, match-box toys can represent transport, boxes for buildings and Lego for materials. This can be an attractive way of illustrating the effects of a marginal change in demand for the goods or services. If the factors of production have been laid out to an agreed pattern, then a slight increase in demand will not necessarily mean a new box (factory) or more plastic people (workers). Students are likely to realise that jobs are linked to demand but also that fluctuations in employment depend on the extent to which consumer demand varies.

2 Factors affecting demand

(a) Photos can serve as effective stimulus material. For example, shoppers in a supermarket, a machine being delivered to a factory, supplies arriving at a school and export goods being loaded at a dockside. These could stimulate discussion on the relative importance of spending by consumers, investors, exporters and government. Students could suggest their own examples and find out their importance for jobs using one of the many tables and pie-charts printed in textbooks showing the distribution of employees across different industrial groups.

It is also quite easy to find illustrations of changes in demand, for example demand for holidays, Christmas goods, new-registration cars, etc. Students could be asked to discuss in groups the likely effects of these changes on jobs and to rank them in terms of the scale and permanence of the change.

(b) Students could be asked to suggest other reasons for changes in demand (e.g. advertising, level of wages, tax rates, hire-purchase restrictions, rates of interest) and asked to illustrate these (perhaps in the form of posters). For example, a poster to illustrate why a person decides to buy a new video-recorder would give scope to imaginative students.

(c) One of the CAL programs from the Economics Education 14–16 Project asks students to consider the changes they would make in the spending of a particular household given some budget restrictions. The program introduces variations in taxes and interest rates, and presents students with unforeseen problems. This is clearly a 'micro' exercise with which students readily identify, but the teacher can direct follow-up discussion towards the overall impact of the 'households' in the class and the likely repercussions on employment.

Another program from the same source represents a production process for supermarket trolleys. The main focus is productivity and the costs of production but the program allows introduction of new technology. It is soon apparent that a higher output is possible with fewer workers and most interesting discussions arise when students are asked for their policies to prevent unemployment. There are several 'production' exercises available in various guises – mainly as games but many can be used in similar fashion to raise questions about the relationships between demand, factors of production and employment.

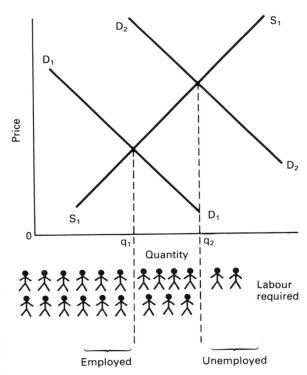

Figure 21.1 Source: McDougall, L., 'Employment, Unemployment and inflation' in Whitehead, D. J., Handbook for Economics Teachers. *(Heinemann Educational Books, 1979).*

(d) Students can tie in conventional supply/demand diagrams with employment. Figure 21.1 represents the supply and demand for houses and the teacher explains that with demand D_1D_1 and supply S_1S_1, then the quantity on the market will be q_1, which requires a certain number of people to be employed building them. If demand increases to D_2D_2 then the quantity on the market will increase to q_2 and this requires more people to be employed in the building industry, thus reducing the number of unemployed building workers.

(e) Case studies have particular merit in that they can familiarise students with causes of unemployment, etc. on a modest scale, before attempting generalisations at a national level. The Mary Glasgow Publications tape/slide sequence on housing (see Chapter 13) covers a wide range of explanations for changes in supply and demand for housing and the related employment figures for the building industry.

A local soft-drinks factory in London proved a worth-while source, not only for a general visit, but also for information on their labour needs. Without any sophisticated economics, it is possible for young students to understand the importance of seasonal fluctuations in demand, of increases in fuel costs for a distributive company, of the choice to install an automatic bottling machine in place of semi-skilled labour, etc.

3 Income and employment

(a) It is not too difficult for students of a young age to grasp the relationship between the level of income and employment using a simple flow diagram (Figure 21.2). The teacher can give values to the different flows. For example, incomes may be £100 and spending £100. This will mean that all the producer's output is being bought. If the government then takes £20 in tax and consumers save £10, how much will producers be able to sell? What happens to the level of employment? The teacher can make this type of diagram as complex or as simple as suits the class by varying the number of flows included in the diagram.

(b) The circular flow can also be illustrated in more concrete fashion with groups in the class taking the roles of producers, households (consumers and workers), savings institutions, etc. and either the teacher or a group acting as government. A card for each group gives brief instruction, for example, each of five households are told they earn £100 by working in a factory and that the house-hold spends £100 on goods and services from the factory. A producer group employs five workers at £100 a week each and can expect orders worth £500 each week. Injections and leakages can be introduced in the guise of taxes, savings, export orders, government spending, etc. Households will find either demand for an extra member of their group to work, or face unemployment and an end to spending. If transactions are to be recorded, then appropriate money tokens and record sheets will be necessary. A multiplier process can be observed if the teacher allows very short periods after any leakage or injection and asks each group to report on their employment or spending. There are likely to be questions

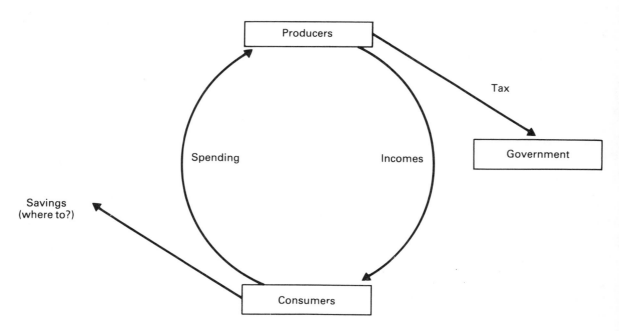

Figure 21.2 Source: McDougall L., 'Employment, unemployment and inflation' in Whitehead, D. J., Handbook for Economics Teachers, (Heinemann Educational Books, 1979).

about some of the most obvious simplifications in this exercise – producers are not making any profit for example; but it does offer some experience of a dynamic rather than a static situation. Also, producers can be asked what effect on employment they might expect if they took a certain profit level and then chose to spend it in this economy.

(c) One or two of Yorkshire Television's 10 × Economics series (1982–3) have very effective illustrations of the multiplier process at work. Programme 1 includes a dramatised sequence showing shops closing down when spending falls following local factory closures. Programme 3 has a section looking at the impact of a council decision to cut spending on council-house maintenance. There are interviews with a private building contractor dependent on such work who has been forced to make redundant the eighteen workers he employed. The mix of documentary evidence, dramatised sequences and imaginative studio graphics make much of these programmes suitable for a wide age range.

4 Types of unemployment

(a) It is often difficult to help a class find out about the different types of unemployment without either telling them or giving them written descriptions. One way of overcoming this is to give the class a long list of people who are unemployed:

> Examples: a building worker in the winter; a former shipyard worker; a Mediterranean tour guide in the winter; a former coal miner; a docker temporarily laid off because of a fall in UK trade; a 50-year-old car worker (due to closure of a plant), etc.

The class is asked to group the list according to the type of unemployment. They could do this on the basis of group discussion, and then perhaps refer to texts for guidance.

(b) A historical case study can be a good way of illustrating how unemployment arises and how it affects particular areas. For example, the development of the docks in London's East End from 1850 to their decline and closure in the 1970s shows how the country's hunger for raw materials created jobs, how other industries developed in the same region, how competition grew and how capital-intensive container methods replaced labour. Finally, it shows how the ancillary industries suffered and how the old industrial heartland of London now stands empty. (Figure 21.3 shows materials typical of those from local papers, census returns and local study groups.)

If the area can provide a graphic picture, then students will appreciate the significance of each stage of development of the industry in their locality. They will then be in a better position to consider other industries at different stages of development.

5 Effects of unemployment

(a) The class is asked how they think different types of people might be affected by unemployment.

> Examples: a boy of 16 who has just left school with no

qualifications; a female graduate with an honours degree in physics; a married woman of 38 with two children; a man of 50 who has been an engineer for twenty-five years, etc.

It is a valuable reminder of the human costs of unemployment and that there is unlikely to be a solution that will fit every case. There are many newspaper extracts that could be used to supplement this theme.

6 Policies to prevent unemployment

Given the difficulties of explaining macroeconomic policy to younger students, these suggestions are intended more as stimulus to discussion than as complete lessons.

(a) Students are given a set of possible measures for dealing with unemployment and are asked to rate them. An important part of the follow-up discussion would be the basis on which the measures were ranked (see Table 21.1).

(b) Cartoons can carry a great deal of economics in deceptively simple form.

(c) Programme 10 in the Yorkshire Television series mentioned above tries to sum up alternative policies that might create more employment. This is one of the more difficult episodes but could be used in short sections.

7 An introduction to inflation – price survey

The class can be asked to find out the current prices of a 'shopping basket' of goods. (Many newspapers publish figures of a representative basket of goods from time to time.) The teacher gives the class the prices of the same goods from one year previously, or the class could generate their own comparative figures by keeping 'price diaries' for a number of months. Calculations of price changes are made and the information presented as bar-charts or, for students familiar with price indices, an index could be constructed based on prices in local shops. The class could discuss the differences in price movements for different goods and possible reasons for the changes.

8 Effects of inflation

(a) Illustrations can convey strong images on a personal level or at a more abstract level. Students could be encouraged to create their own mini-posters. It can be an interesting exercise to follow the many textbook lists of the 'effects of inflation'.

(b) Case studies could be considered in the same way as dealing with the effects of unemployment. The class could be asked to consider how various people would be affected by a period of rising prices.

> Examples: a teenager at school with only pocket money to spend; an unemployed man of 20; a young couple with two children and only the wife working; a couple living on a pension, etc.

This allows the class to appreciate how different types of people may suffer more than others during periods of inflation.

The class can also assess the effects of inflation on less

UNEMPLOYMENT

East End's toll of jobs

Firm	Jobs lost
HACKNEY	
1979	
Bristol Street Motors	73
1980	
M.Levin	78
Quality Shoe Group	254
Elgree Ltd	140
Lesney UK	557
British Cargo Airline	190
Raminax Clothiers Ltd	70
Bonsoir Ltd	85
SHOREDITCH	
1979	
Kelly & Kelly Ltd	56
H.Mono Ltd	120
1980	
M/S W Steel & Co	50
H.Mono Ltd	120
J.Peter & Co.	76
Kelly & Kelly Ltd.	59
Vanguard Raincoats Co. Ltd.	58
1981	
W Steel & Co	165
Multitone Electric Ltd	55
Waterlow Ltd.	165
POPLAR	
1979	
Hestair Toys Ltd	127
Associated Lead Meters.	74
London Graving Dock Co.	457
River Thames Ship Repairers	577
Blundell & Crompton Ltd	116
1980	
River Thames Ship Repairers	231
LRC Products	98
Venest. International Packaging	271
Caplin Profile Group Ltd.	98
Kirk & Kirk Ltd.	64
W. Badger I Ltd.	80
1981	
Southon Horton Labs	50
Sumacon Luralda Packaging	54
Conway Fashions	90
Clean Cut Clothiers	62
1982	
Assoc. Lead Ltd.	105
Avon Lippiatt Hobbs	59
RHM Foods Ltd	70
STEPNEY	
1981	
Truman Ltd	87
Watney Mann Crossman	280
British Pepper & Spice Co. Ltd.	52
Watneys London Ltd	280
B.J.Friends Ltd.	51
Laura Lee Frocks	92
EAST HAM	
1980	
London Co-op Society	50
Associated Adhesives Ltd.	50
1981	
Advance Laundries	87
London Borough of Newham	250
Co-op Retail Service	145
1982	
Biopath Pek Ltd.	74
STRATFORD	
1979	
Bryant & May	268
1980	
Seemeel (Spillers Agriculture)	75
Burrell Colours	72
1981	
Stapleford Kaye Ltd	67
1982	
Robert Porter	79
CANNING TOWN	
1981	
Debenhams Ltd	58
Rank Hovis	110
Dunhill Tobacco	50
Moore Paragon Ltd	321
Hollis Ltd	199
1981	
A.R.Gingell Ltd.	51
Spillers Milling	113
Storemasters	48
1982	
International Paint Co.	50
TOTAL	**8,054**

EAST END NEWS NOVEMBER 1982

'It's an economic scandal'

REPORTS BY IAN RATHBONE

Newham's unemployment problems were highlighted last week in the House of Commons.

The spotlight fell on the borough following questions from Newham North West MP Arthur Lewis.

The DHSS disclosed that more than 25,400 people claimed supplementary benefit in Newham during the past quarter.

The Department of Employment revealed that 16,397 people are now registered unemployed in the borough. This is several hundred more than the number officially claiming benefit.

Of the total number claiming benefit, 11,822 are men, 4,216 are women and well over a thousand of these are under 18 years old.

BENEFIT

DHSS figures show that during the corresponding quarter three years ago 17,200 people claimed supplementary benefit. This has increased by well over 8,000.

Mr. Lewis said he raised the questions to show the Government just how much people in Newham are dependent on benefits.

He also asked Employment Secretary Norman Tebbit what steps were being taken to reduce unemployment in Newham.

"THE unemployed of the East End do not have as far to march as the Jarrow workers of the 1930s. But their plight is increasingly similar" — GLC leader Ken Livingstone in a major industrial and economic report.

"London's unemployment has trebled in three years. About an eighth of London's workforce is unemployed. In Inner London the figure is one in six; in Stepney it is one in three. These figures amount to nothing less than an economic scandal."

The last major industrial employers have all but disappeared from Tower Hamlets. One in five people in Hackney are unemployed — in Poplar, like Stepney, it's one in three.

Factories lie empty, land is unused, machines — often new — are being sold for scrap.

Figure 21.3 Source: Newham Recorder, *2 December 1982;* East End News, *November 1982.*

Table 21.1

Here are some of the ideas which people are suggesting that can either change or end the present situation. Have a think about them, and then give them a 'star rating', 5 stars for the ideas you like best, down to 0.

Scientific and technological growth	**Voluntary early retirement**	**Increased government expenditure**	**A guaranteed minimum income**
More investment is put into areas of high technology and scientific research of a non-military nature which will shape the future. Expansion of universities and other colleges, so that many more people are able to have a high level education. *Rating:*	People are allowed to retire on full pension from the age of 55 if they want to. For this, and some of the other ideas too, people who have jobs will have to pay more in taxation, as their way of 'sharing' in unemployment. *Rating:*	Many more jobs are created, by extra public expenditure, in our hospitals, schools and in all the 'caring' jobs which are so often understaffed at present. More jobs too to rebuild many derelict city areas and to bring wasteland back to life. *Rating:*	Everyone would receive a basic low-level income (supplementary benefit level or higher) from the state. We are then free to work as well, if we want to. No compulsion to work. An end to most of the benefits regulations (also under the 'share out' system next). *Rating:*
Share out the unemployment	**Local economic development**	**Female – male jobsharing**	**Your own ideas:**
Everyone would spend between 10 per cent and 20 per cent of their working lives not working, using the time for personal activities, local activities, education and retraining. This would 'share out' the unemployment in a way that would give people a chance to enjoy it, without fear of not being able to find another job. During our working years, we would have to put aside between 10 per cent and 20 per cent of our income, so that we could have the same standard of living during our years off. *Rating:*	Much more help is given at the local level to people who want to become self-employed or to set up their own small businesses or co-operatives. There is much more investment in new jobs. Capital is made available for local development. Laws are changed, if necessary, to help new small businesses. Schools are encouraged to develop their own small co-operatives, to give young people a chance to learn about them. *Rating:*	A big increase in jobsharing is encouraged, so that women and men are able to share bringing up children and having a job, with two half-incomes coming into the home. More people working from home, as well, with permission to run small businesses from the home. Whole family could take part. *Rating:*	_____ _____ _____ _____ _____ _____

Source: Extract from a CRAC booklet on unemployment (1982).

personal aspects of the economy and so appreciate the wider significance of inflation:

> Examples: a small company with small stocks and low profit margins; a large company with big stocks and a high level of exports; a country's balance of payments; the amount of tax collected by the government.

This type of list can vary in complexity depending on the extent of the class's knowledge of economics.

(c) Sets of cards could be made up to help students understand possible consequences of inflation. Students receive a pack of jumbled cards and have to sort out the most likely chain of events; for example:

increase in world price for rubber	increase in price of UK imports

increase in costs for UK tyre manufacturers	increase in the price of tyres in the UK

increase in prices of new cars	fall in demand for new cars

etc.

With a variety of sets circulating in a class, a large number of consequences could be discussed in a short time. Students could make up their own sets of consequence cards with a little practice, and depending on their knowledge of the economy.

9 Causes of inflation

(a) Demand pull. Students are asked to draw supply/demand diagrams to show the effects of various changes of demand on price:

> Examples: demand is higher for European Cup football matches; demand for houses has risen in the UK; consumers have more to spend owing to tax reductions.

By considering a variety of examples, students should realise that many superficially different situations may have the same basic economic circumstances; namely, that for some reason there has been a rise in demand which has in turn brought about an increase in price.

(b) Cost push. Students choose a product and make a list of all the costs that they think might be involved in the production of that product. They are asked to allocate an approximate percentage of the total cost to each of the costs incurred (for an example, see Table 21.2).

Table 21.2 Production of an ice-cream

	%
Total cost	100 (selling price)
Labour	20
Materials	30
Premises	10
Transport	15
Profit	15
Tax	10

It is less important to be exact with the detailed proportions of the costs than to illustrate the variety of costs involved. Students are then asked to calculate the effect on the selling price of an increase in one of the costs. For example, how would a 10 per cent increase in the cost of materials affect the selling price of the product? They can be asked to suggest ways in which increased costs could be absorbed without passing on any increase to the consumer.

10 Further ideas for teaching about inflation

(a) Statistics exercise. Having discussed possible causes of inflation, it is useful to give students the opportunity to apply the ideas to the actual economy. Time-series data for the changes in the retail price index, import prices, wages and money supply can be drawn up in different colours on OHP overlays. Each possible cause of inflation is matched against the retail price data and students asked about the closeness of the fit. The value of such discussion will depend very much on students' general knowledge about a particular economy, but it is important that they have some opportunity to tackle statistical sources. It is also likely that data-based computer programs aimed at older students can be adapted in use for younger classes.

(b) Goods and money simulation. The main purpose is to provide a simple illustration of the relationship between money supply, output and the general price level. The class is divided into two groups: consumers and producers. There is also a third group – the government – but it is best if the teacher adopts this role to start with until the class becomes more sophisticated in the use of the game. All the members keep a record of each time-period divided into three sections – money supply, output of goods and services, general price level. (More variables could be introduced where necessary.)

The producers are given blocks of wood to sell, the total number of which is fixed at the start of the time-period. The consumers are given money, the total amount of which is controlled by the government. During each time-period the consumers try to achieve as high a standard of living as they can by buying as many goods or services as their money will allow, each block of wood representing a good or service. Consumers and producers haggle with each other to fix the prices, and they soon discover that overpricing will result in unsold stocks while underpricing will reduce profits. At the start of each time-period, the government adjusts either the money supply or the output of goods and services, with everyone in the class noting the totals and effects on the price level during the time-period. Students can try to predict the effects of changes and can suggest means of preventing price rises while still allowing living standards to rise. It is possible to make the simulation more involved by introducing other factors such as income tax, income distribution, savings, spending taxes, and varying rates of economic growth.

(c) Diary of events. A way of developing an awareness of economic events and policies is for students to keep a weekly diary of important issues in the local and national economies. This obviously encourages a general background knowledge of the economy but also encourages students to search for economics in newspapers and television reports. Students could be asked to introduce a diary entry to the rest of the class, explaining its importance. It can be surprising how many policy changes, statistics and new words can be met in this way.

(d) Television programmes. The *10 × Economics* series mentioned above has a very good programme on inflation called *Not worth the paper*. Theories about the causes of inflation are introduced in imaginative fashion and, with careful use, could be used with younger classes.

Problems

Probably the most difficult problem with younger students is introducing them to the language and definitions of these topics in a way that still allows for interest and for students to feel they can contribute something of their own to the discussion. One way of helping them to achieve this is to refer constantly to events in the 'real' economy by record keeping and by references to newspapers and television. Another problem in discussing causes and solutions to unemployment and inflation is the complexity of economic relationships. It is like trying to complete a jigsaw puzzle without having the outside pieces. It is worth spending several lessons at the end of a sequence on employment, unemployment and inflation trying to piece together the significance of individual lessons.

Resources

Books

Anderton, A. G., *An Introduction to Social Economics* (Heinemann Educational Books, 1981). Chapters 25 and 26 give a succinct account of the problems for governments. Some assumed vocabulary is difficult.

Davies, B., and Hender, D., *Production and Trade* (Longman, 1982) ch. 7: 'The government and the economy'. Readable review of the combined problems facing government.

Christie, D., and Scott, A., *Economics in Action* (Heinemann Educational Books, 1977) chs. 15 and 16. Difficult for younger students but still has many useful exercises and examples on running the economy as a whole.

Donaldson, P., *Peter Donaldson's Illustrated Economics* (BBC, 1976). Out of print but still worth looking for old copies as a teacher resource. Chapters 1–5 have some excellent ideas, both visual and written for teaching the topics.

Television programmes

10 × Economics (Yorkshire TV, 1982–3) Programmes 1, 2, 3, 6 and 10 have relevant sections. The accompanying paperback by Donaldson (Penguin, 1983) is helpful, but Yorkshire Television's own workpack to go with the series is the better resource for classes.

Tape/filmstrips

Unemployment and *Inflation* by R. Wilson (Economics Association) provide a useful visual focus but still leave a lot of background to be covered at the class's own speed.

22 International Trade and the Balance of Payments
Robert Paisley

Introduction

One of the major problems of teaching international economics to students in the 14–16 age range is to develop an understanding of the concepts involved in the theory of trade so that they can be used appropriately when studying international trade and payments. Traditionally, a diluted version of the theory of comparative advantage is presented, and then left aside, detached from the realities of 'Britain's trade'. This chapter shows a possible method of presenting the economics concepts involved in such a way that students can make appropriate and confident use of them when studying the more applied aspects of the syllabus. A teaching format is suggested that enables this 'building' process to occur. It begins with theoretical considerations, translating the analysis into less technical terms and introducing the idea of a balance of trade. Building on these basic concepts, UK exports, imports and the balance of payments policies naturally follow. Finally, other aspects of international trading relations are considered.

The theory of trade between countries

This section begins with basic verbal definitions and explanations, shows how they are related to theoretical concepts, and introduces the idea of a balance of trade. This method does not imply that the theory explains fully the nature of international trade, but it does establish an ability to understand and use the basic tools of analysis that economists employ, while at the same time building an awareness of the limits of their adequacy.

To provide an introduction to the most basic concepts of international trade, recent trade figures and a newspaper headline such as 'Britain's trade moves further into the red' can be used. For example, using the April 1984 figures for the balance of trade (so that exports and imports can at this stage be seen as flows of goods), the meaning of 'Britain's trade' (exports = £5.4 billion, imports = £6.2 billion) and 'the red' (X–M = deficit) can be made clear and can be used as a stimulus to examine the question 'Why do countries trade with each other?' or, more parochially, 'Why does the UK trade with other countries?' Discussion of this question can begin at the most basic level, that is, with an explanation that there are some things that the UK needs or wants (e.g. copper, chrome ore for car components, and coffee), but cannot produce. Clearly, the earliest trade between nations took place on this basis, and it can be useful at this point to provide an historical background to trade, how discovery and exploration led to trade with countries possessing previously unobtainable commodities, and how the development of trade has affected the variety of goods available, in both the distant and recent past (e.g. the effect of EEC membership).

Taking this basic level (the origin of international trade) as the starting point, a consideration of the three essential steps to the theory of international trade can be developed. This can be presented by using a single question, 'In what ways can countries benefit from trading?' Three possible explanations can be provided (in this case from the UK point of view), 'translated' into the kind of terminology economists would use, and illustrated using examples and a case study. They can then be analysed for their adequacy. A possible structure for such a format is given below, which can be adapted to the needs of the students concerned.

Question

'In what ways can countries benefit from trading?'

Explanations

1   The UK can benefit from trading with other countries that produce goods the UK cannot.
2   The UK can benefit from trading with other countries in which goods the UK could also produce can be produced at a lower cost.
3   Even if the UK could not produce anything more cheaply than other countries, it could still benefit from trading by specialising in the goods that make the best possible use of the UK's resources.

Translations

1   Resources in country A are unavailable to produce product X, demanded by A, but available in country B. B has an *absolute advantage* in X.
2   Resources in A required to produce X cost more in A than in B. B has an *absolute advantage* in X.
3   The opportunity cost of producing X is lower in B than in A. B has a *comparative advantage* in X.

Illustration

1   Mineral resources can obviously be worked only where they are found; for example, the UK has to import copper for electrical wire and chrome ore to produce hardened steel or chrome-plated components for cars.
2   It is technically possible to produce oranges in this country using greenhouses and artificial heating. However, in Israel, they can be produced using fewer resources and hence at a lower cost.

3   A case study such as Table 22.1 may be used to illustrate the difference between absolute advantage and comparative advantage, and to introduce the idea of a balance of trade. The students are given the role of economic advisers for the Northland government, and their task is to decide in each case whether trade with Southland is desirable. A suggested structure of questions for use with Table 22.1 follows.

Using this material, the students should be able to:

1   *Explain* the economists' case in part A. Absolute advantage is being dealt with here. They should also be able to understand and explain that more resources are needed to produce one million barrels of oil in Northland than in Southland, and this can be compared with the requirement for more resources (and hence higher cost) to produce oranges in the UK, as in the example in 2 under 'Illustration' above.
2   *Explain* that, in part B, Southland has an absolute advantage in both products.
3   For part B, *determine* opportunity costs for each product in each country.
4   *Compare* the consumption of each product in each country before and after trade, and hence show the 'benefit' of trade reflected in the increased consumption of each product in each country after trade.
5   *Complete* the balance of trade sheet for each country (assuming one barrel of oil cost \$10 and one motor vehicle costs \$10 000):

$$\text{Exports (X)} =$$
$$\text{Imports (M)} =$$
$$\text{Balance of trade (X–M)} =$$

This produces a balance of trade equilibrium for both countries (X–M = 0). Students could be asked to describe the effect of a rise in imports or exports in each country on the balance of trade.

It is essential that students are helped to understand the inadequacies of the model, especially that it ignores the immobility of factors of production and the structural effects of transfer of resources from one industry to another (e.g. unemployment and trade-union responses) and it ignores transport costs. Moreover, in spite of the existence of comparative advantages, countries still produce goods that can be produced at a lower opportunity cost abroad, due to the importance of the political and/or social value ascribed to the domestic industry concerned (e.g. for strategic or domestic employment reasons). There may also be an economic value in building up industries for which the growth of demand is high, even though there is no existing comparative advantage (see Eatwell[1] for an elaboration of this point in relation to postwar Japan).

A final point arises from consideration of the case study. Since it involves the students role playing as 'Northland's economists', the case study could be well suited to group work as a simulation, where each group takes on the role of Northland's economic advisers, preparing a report for the government.

Table 22.1   Case study: International specialisation and trade

A   Northland and Southland are two neighbouring islands producing food, clothing and other basic needs from their own resources.

However, the major industries in Northland and Southland are oil and motor vehicles.

Northland's economists have been suggesting for some time that, although Northland produces its own oil, it is very costly to extract and is therefore expensive in Northland. This is affecting the island's motor industry.

Discussions with economists in Southland confirm these views and the two groups publish a joint report advising that trade should take place between Northland and Southland.

They gave the following figures in support of their case:

	One thousand units of resources can produce:		
	Oil (million barrels)		*Motor vehicles* (thousand units)
Northland	2	or	10
Southland	10	or	4

B   Even if the report came up with the following figures, where Southland can produce *both* products at a lower cost, the economists would still have agreed that specialisation and trade should take place as suggested in 1 (assuming 1000 units of resources available to each).

(i)   *Maximum production with complete specialisation*

	Oil (million barrels)		*Motor vehicles* (thousand units)
Northland	4	or	8
Southland	20	or	10

(ii)   *Production and consumption under self-sufficiency*

	Oil (million barrels)		*Motor vehicles* (thousand units)
Northland	2	or	4
Southland	12	or	4

(iii)   *Production and consumption with trade and specialisation*

	Production		*Consumption*	
	Oil (million barrels)	*Motor vehicles* (thousand units)	*Oil* (million barrels)	*Motor vehicles* (thousand units)
Northland	0	8	3	5
Southland	20	0	14	6

Having examined the key concepts of international trade theory, and the nature of a balance of trade, this provides a basis for a more detailed examination of UK exports and imports and the UK balance of payments.

UK exports and imports

UK trade can now be set within the context of the theoretical explanations. Analysis of UK trade statistics lends itself very well to data-response exercises. Key questions here are (i) What are the principal UK imports/exports, and why? (ii) With whom does the UK trade, and why? and (iii) How have these relationships changed over the years? (i) and (ii) can be considered in terms of the theory – for example, distinguishing those goods that are imported because the UK has to import them, those goods that are imported because other countries possess a comparative advantage, those goods

that are exported because Britain has a comparative advantage in their production, and those imports and exports that are not explained by the theory, but by other considerations. More-able students may be asked to consider how and why the UK's comparative advantages may have changed.

Data required for the consideration of these questions are analyses by commodity and by geographical area for different years. These are available in *UK Balance of Payments*, published annually by the CSO. For example, the figures for 1972 and 1982 can be used to analyse the effects of EEC membership and North Sea oil on the analyses by commodity and geographical area. Various methods of presentation can be used, but the greatest visual impact is probably provided by pie-charts. An example of such presentation is provided in Figure 22.1, together with a data-response exercise suitable for CSE level. Another useful, well-presented source suitable for class use is the chapter entitled 'Earning our keep' in *Industry in Perspective* (see Resources on p. 118.)

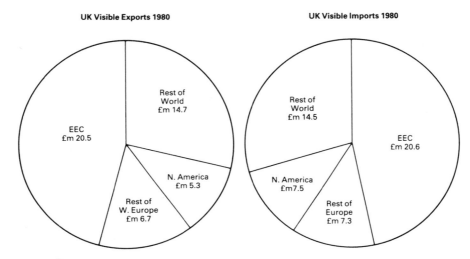

UK Visible Exports 1980

UK Visible Imports 1980

A22. Study the charts above and then answer the questions which follow.

(a) From which area did we buy the greatest share of goods?
(b) To which area did we sell the greatest share of goods?

(c) What is the value of our trade balance with North America?
(d) What is our overall balance of trade for 1980?

Figure 22.1 Source: Taken from LREB CSE Examination, summer 1984.

The balance of payments

Thus far, only visible trade has been considered, and imports and exports have been seen simply as flows of goods into and out of the UK respectively. However, with the examination of invisible trade, it becomes important to show clearly the link between the flow of goods and the flow of money, for example using a diagram like that shown in Figure 22.2.

The key concepts involved in teaching the balance of payments are (i) visible and invisible trade, (ii) exports and imports, and (iii) the current account (dealing with goods and services) and the capital account (investment and capital flows). It is also important to

emphasise that capital inflows and outflows appear as debits and credits on the capital account, while interest and returns on foreign investment, such as profits and dividends, appear on the current account as invisibles. For example, a loan to a foreign firm by a UK firm appears as a debit on the capital account, but the interest on that loan appears as a credit on the current account. Understanding of the meaning of 'surplus' and 'deficit', introduced with the examination of basic trade concepts, also needs to be reinforced.

Familiarisation with the required terminology demands extensive use of worked examples and classification exercises. A possible method using these two strategies is to use a worked example of a typical UK balance of

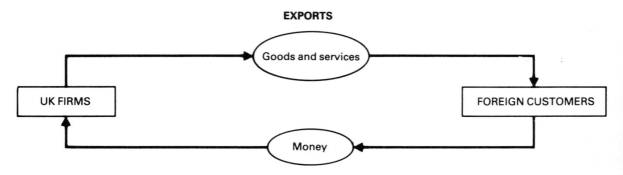

EXPORTS

Goods and services

UK FIRMS

FOREIGN CUSTOMERS

Money

Figure 22.2

Table 22.2   *UK Balance of payments 1983*

		(£million)
Current Account		
(i) Visible Trade		
	Exports	60 658
	Imports	61 158
A	**Balance of Trade (Visible Balance)**	**– 500**
(ii) Invisible Trade (net)		
	Government	– 824
	Sea transport	– 800
	Civil aviation	+ 428
	Travel	– 599
	Financial services	+ 2590
	Other services	+ 3423
	Interest/profits	+ 1363
	Transfers	– 2267
B	**Invisible Balance**	**+ 3424**
C	**Current Balance = A + B**	**+ 2924**
Capital Account (Investment and other capital flows)		
Foreign investment in UK private and public sectors		+ 5698
UK private investment overseas		– 10864
Official long-term capital		– 562
Other capital transactions		+ 1865
D	**Balance on the Capital Account**	**– 3863**
E	**Balancing item**	**+ 123**
F	**Balance for Official Financing (TCF) = C + D + E**	**– 816**
	Transactions with the IMF	0
	Other short-term borrowing (+) and lending (–)	+ 213
	Changes in reserves (additions –, drawings on +,)	+ 603
G	**Total Official Financing**	**+ 816**

Source: Economic Trends, June 1984.

payments account, and classification exercises to apply and reinforce the students' understanding.

To demonstrate such a worked example, Table 22.2 shows the UK balance of payments with presentation adapted specifically to make clear the terminology, and the relationships between the different concepts. It is essential to point out the meaning of the plus and minus signs in each case, particularly in relation to invisibles, capital flows and official financing. The latter two are included in O-level syllabuses, although the detail in Table 22.2 may be reduced for lower-ability students where necessary, especially in relation to the capital account and official financing. The use of contrasting colours to distinguish the different elements of the balance of payments is also advisable. Table 22.2 can be used as an exercise by leaving the key items (the figures for A–D, F and G) blank for the students to work out.

Table 22.3 shows two classification exercises that could be used to apply and reinforce understanding of balance

of payments concepts. They also help to overcome difficulties presented by the direction of money flow, where the correct answer can be found by considering 'where the money ends up'.

Table 22.4 shows a suitable data-response exercise for O-level which tests understanding of the concepts involved in the analysis of both the composition of UK trade and the balance of payments.

Having examined the components of the balance of payments, the significance of deficits and surpluses and their relationship to the economy as a whole can be considered.

The abridged newspaper article in Table 22.5 provides an introductory stimulus for this area. It could be used in conjunction with a tape recording of a news broadcast dealing with the latest balance of payments figures, which could be analysed in a similar way. An exercise based on an article such as this is a prime example of the kind that promotes economic literacy, since it mentions all the major balance of payments terminology, and uses it in different ways (e.g. 'trade in goods and services', to be distinguished from 'trade in goods').

The exercise shows how month-to-month variations can be set in the context of much longer-term variations, probably best depicted on a line graph. These will be familiar from textbooks, but one problem is that when such graphs are plotted at current rather than constant prices over a long term, they can give a distorted picture showing increasing fluctuations in the balance of payments as the general level of prices increases (although more-able students may be able to recognise this). Thus for analysis of the trend since 1975, current prices may be appropriate, whereas for a longer period (which could be used to illustrate the effect of the 'stop-go' cycle) constant prices may give a more accurate picture. Such a diagram is provided in NEDO,[2] which also contains some useful data and charts on UK competitiveness.

The trend can now be analysed, and explanations of the trend – 'stop-go', the effect of inflation, rising oil prices, North Sea oil, and lack of competitiveness as causes of underlying weakness. Having examined possible explanations, possible solutions to balance of payments problems can now be considered.

Economic policy and international trade

Given an awareness of the problem of correcting a deficit, the basic tools of balance of payments policy can be examined.

1 Exchange rates

Exchange rates can give rise to considerable problems of understanding, particularly the relationship between exchange rates and the prices of goods. With this in mind, a stimulating introductory exercise with which many students will be able to identify could be a simple case study recounting the 'story' of a young British couple

Table 22.3

4   State whether the following are visible or invisible and whether they are exports or imports.

	Visible	Invisible	Export	Import
a) British car sold to the USA				
b) French cheese sold in Britain				
c) a British tourist holidaying in Spain				
d) British Airways buying a plane from Boeing (USA)				
e) the United States Air Force maintaining a cruise missile base in East Anglia				
f) British Intelligence paying a spy in East Germany				
g) Ford UK repatriating profits to its parent company in the USA				
h) a Polish ship hired by a British company				

7   Indicate whether each of the following would be put on the current or capital account and whether each is a credit (i.e. given a plus sign) or a debit (i.e. given a minus sign).

Current account Debit –	Credit +		Capital account Debit –	Credit +
		a) a ship sold by a British shipyard to Poland		
		b) a loan given by the British Government to Kenya		
		c) Sony (Japan) setting up a factory in Britain		
		d) Midland Bank (UK) buying computer equipment from IBM (USA)		
		e) interest paid by Kenya on a British loan		
		f) Saudi Arabia banking oil money in the City of London		
		g) Barclays Bank (UK) buying a bank in Texas (USA)		
		h) an American businessman buying London Bridge to rebuild in his back garden in California		

Source: Anderton, A. G., *Economics Study and Revision* (Collins, 1983) pp. 14.2–14.3.

Table 22.4

2   Study the tables below and then answer all the questions which follow.

Table I

United Kingdom Balance of Payments, 1970 *and* 1980

	1970 (£ million)	1980 (£ million)
Visible exports	8,150	47,389
Visible imports	8,184	46,211
Invisible exports	5,082	25,167
Invisible imports	4,269	23,581
Investment and other capital flows (net)	+ 545	− 1,418

Table II

Structure of United Kingdom visible exports, 1970 and 1980 (percentages)

Commodity	1970	1980
Manufactured goods	50	44
Semi-manufactured goods	34	30
Fuels and lubricants	3	14
Others	13	12
Destination		
European Community	30	44
Other West European countries	16	14
North America	15	11
Other developed countries	11	6
Oil exporting countries	6	10
Rest of world	22	15

(Source: United Kingdom Balance of Payments, 1981, HMSO.)

(a) What was the current account balance in 1970? **(2 marks)**
(b) To which of the categories given in Table I would the following transactions belong?
   (i) An American on holiday in Europe pays for his stay at a London hotel. **(1 mark)**
   (ii) J. Brown, a British resident, purchases shares on the New York Stock Exchange. **(1 mark)**
(c) What major economic development led to the change in the visible balance between 1970 and 1980? **(1 mark)**
(d) What was the value of United Kingdom exports of manufactured goods in 1970? **(1 mark)**
(e) The section called 'Total Official Financing' has been omitted from Table I.
   (i) Why is this section necessary? **(2 marks)**
   (ii) Name *two* items that would normally appear in this section. **(2 marks)**
(f) With reference to Table II:
   (i) Describe the changes in the structure of the United Kingdom's visible exports between 1970 and 1980. **(4 marks)**
   (ii) Explain the causes of these changes. **(6 marks)**

Source: University of London O-level, summer 1984.

Table 22.5   Fear for interest rates as deficit reaches £588 m

---

Britain's worst ever deficit on trade in goods and services of £588 million in April was announced yesterday against the background of an imminent rise in interest rates. The current account deficit represented a £611 million deterioration since March, of which £400 million was due to reduced exports and increased imports of oil. Part of the higher oil imports was due to the effects of the miners' strike, which has prompted the electricity authorities to burn more fuel oil in oil-fired stations.

If interest rates do not rise, the danger is that investment funds will leave Britain for New York and other financial centres, thereby depressing the value of the pound.

The current account deficit was the result of a record deficit of £838 million in trade in goods offset by a £250 million surplus on 'invisibles' like banking and tourism.

Exports in April amounted to £5.4 billion and imports were a record £6.2 billion. In the most recent three months, export volume (excluding erratic items) has risen by 2 per cent while imports have gone up by 4 per cent.

Using the passage above, answer the questions below:
1 What was the value of:
   a) the current balance in April 1984   b) the balance of trade (April)
   c) the invisible balance (April)   d) the current balance in March 1984?
2 Explain the causes of the worsening in the current balance since March 1984.
3 Why is a rise in interest rates 'imminent'?
4 Using current UK balance of payments statistics and the article above, describe the main trends in the balance of payments since 1975. Sketch a graph showing this trend.

Source: Abridged from the *Guardian*, 30 May 1984.

spending money abroad, and the effect of changes in the exchange rate on the prices paid and on their spending and budgeting. This could be reinforced by bringing in actual coins from different countries, and discussing with students how much they are worth in pounds sterling, in conjunction with the list of tourist exchange rates from a daily newspaper. Copious examples of the effects of changes in the exchange rate on the price of British goods abroad, and on prices of overseas goods in Britain can be provided.

To examine the determination of an exchange rate, simple supply and demand analysis can be used most effectively, once the relationship between the demand for pounds and UK exports (or inflows), and between the supply of pounds and UK imports (or outflows), has been established. Fixed and floating exchange rates can also be distinguished within this framework, where the Bank of England buys (demands) or sells (supplies) pounds to keep the exchange rate within a very narrow 'band' if the exchange rate is fixed, or within a wider band if there is a 'dirty' or managed float. An exercise of this type can be found in Anderton.[3]

To evaluate devaluation as an instrument of balance of payments policy, its effect on UK imports and exports needs to be examined in more detail. At the simplest level, the more price elastic import and export demand is, the more effective devaluation will be. The merits and draw-backs of devaluation can be examined within this context, along with the possible inflationary implications, particularly for essential raw materials, the demand for which is often relatively price inelastic.

Some very useful data were provided by Jaguar cars in their offer for sale prospectus (July 1984) using the company's results for 1983 adjusted for different levels of the exchange rate, as shown in Table 22.6.

Table 22.6

Average Exchange rate £1 = $	Operating profit/(loss) £m
2.00	(5)
1.80	15
1.60	38
1.40	70
1.20	112

This clearly shows the beneficial effect of devaluation on industries whose exports are highly sensitive to price changes. It could be most usefully employed in conjunction with prices of a Jaguar car in the USA at different exchange rates. For example, at the current rate (£1 = $1.30) a Jaguar 4.2 costs approximately $33 000, that is, approximately £25 000. At £1 = $2.00 a price of $50 000 is equivalent to £25 000. Pictures of the same Jaguar car with different price tags could provide a visual stimulus here.

2 Deflation

The teaching objective here is to promote an understanding of the meaning of deflation, and its relationship with the balance of payments. It is important to distinguish clearly between deflation, reflation and inflation – this is also likely to be a useful revision exercise. Particularly important here is the effect of reduced government spending (aggregate demand) and hence less money available to spend on imports. The relative merits of the use of deflation as a long-term strategy can be examined using a simple case study of the 'stop-go' cycle – which could be used in conjunction with a trend graph of the balance of payments. The effect of stop-go on competitiveness could also be considered, as well as the reasons why the balance of payments has been relatively stable in the 1980s, with such a consistently low level of aggregate demand.

3 Restrictions on imports

Once the idea of 'barriers' or a 'wall' restricting imports has been established, attention can be turned to distinguishing the different types of control (e.g. tariffs, quotas, subsidies, exchange controls, and other 'informal' discriminatory regulations). To reinforce distinguishing features of each type, a list of examples can be provided to be classified according to type (e.g. a 20 per cent customs duty on video recorders, a limit of 100 000 on car imports, etc.). Such an exercise is provided in Anderton.[4] Recent developments, particularly the increased use of informally negotiated quotas, and technical standards that are particularly favourable to domestic producers, need to be emphasised. For example, the French requirement that imported video recorders should pass through a particularly small border customs station inevitably slows up the absorption process. A useful source for further examples of the 'new' protectionism (although its actual content is more suited to A-level students) is Cairncross and Keeley.[5]

The traditional arguments for and against import controls are described in the major textbooks. However, a more stimulating method could be to devise a typical example from which the students can assess its costs and benefits (long term and short term; economic, social and political). For example, adapting from an exercise in Cairncross and Keeley:[6]

A country imports 50 000 family saloons each year at a price of £5000 each. A domestic car plant employs 5000 workers with average annual earnings being £7000. The plant produces family saloons at a price of £6000 each and is threatened with closure because it cannot compete with cheap imports. Pressure is successfully brought to bear upon the government which introduces a tariff on imported cars, the effect of which is to raise the price of these cars to £6000. Imports of the cars fall to 38 000 and the domestic car plant is duly saved.

Questions to consider here are whether the income benefit of protecting the jobs (£35 m) outweighs the loss in spending power (12 000 cars) when the price went up.

Other factors are the social, economic and political benefits of the resultant lower unemployment to be weighed against the possible costs in terms of inefficiency leading to long-term uncompetitiveness.

The General Agreement on Tariffs and Trade was set up in the belief that increasing protectionism had aggravated the interwar depression, and hence that the removal of trade restrictions could help to expand world trade. The work of GATT can thus be more clearly set in context in conjunction with a consideration of the relative merits of free trade and protection.

4 Expanding exports

Clearly, expanding exports offers the best long-term solution to balance of payments problems, but in practice this is difficult to achieve. Increased activity by government export agencies or export subsidies are often cited as possible methods, but the most significant way of achieving increased export demand is by improving competitiveness. Thus an opportunity is provided to recap on the possible reasons for the UK's poor competitive performance (e.g. lack of investment, poor industrial relations) and possible ways that it might be improved. A valuable source for the necessary material here is NEDO.[7]

5 Interest rates

Since a major current issue is whether interest rates should be raised to check the downward trend in the exchange rate, the effect of interest rates on the exchange rate could usefully be analysed at a very simple level, for example in conjunction with Table 22.5. The key phrase in the passage in Table 22.5 is 'If interest rates do not rise, the danger is that investment funds will leave Britain for New York and other financial centres, thereby depressing the value of the pound.'

The terms of trade

Traditionally a 'dry' topic, the terms of trade can be seen to be much more relevant when set in the context of the problems of the Third World, which have been intensified by a general decline in commodity prices, while the prices of manufactures and oil continue to be relatively high. To quote some examples from Cairncross and Keeley[8] (quoting Fidel Castro's speech to the non-aligned countries' summit in 1983):

> In 1960, 6.3 tons of oil could be purchased with the sale of a ton of sugar. In 1982 only 0.7 tons of oil could be bought with the same amount of sugar. In 1959, one ton of copper wire could buy 39 X-ray tubes for medical purposes. By late 1982, only three X-ray tubes could be bought with that same ton.

Thus the significance of the terms of trade can be set within the context of the economics of developing countries.

International economic organisations

The impact of the EEC on Britain's trade can be introduced by means of a data-response exercise using pie-charts based on the analysis of Britain's trade by geographical area discussed above.

The concept of a customs union can then be explained by showing an imaginary 'fence' around the EEC countries which are then listed inside the 'fence', with countries such as the USA and Japan 'outside', signifying free trade within the EEC, and the common external tariff.

Some useful, well-presented information about the EEC is provided by the EEC commission in their pamphlet *The European Community*, although clearly it aims to promote the virtues of the EEC (see Resources on p. 118 for details). The 'Earning our keep' section in *Industry in Perspective* also has some useful material, including diagrams, on the impact of the EEC on Britain's trade. The descriptive nature of much of this topic lends itself well to group project work, particularly where the materials mentioned above are available. The currencies of the EEC countries can also be used as a stimulus and link with work on exchange rates. The arguments about the relative costs and benefits to the UK of EEC membership can probably best be explored by students in groups, acting as 'economic advisers' required to produce a report having weighed up as many costs and benefits as possible, and possibly classifying these as economic, political, social, etc.

Most syllabuses do not require detailed knowledge of the IMF and the World Bank, though it is important that students are able to distinguish their functions, which are quite different. Resource materials are available from both institutions, and details are provided in Resources on p. 118.

Developing countries

Study of the problems of developing countries is becoming an increasingly important part of economics syllabuses. The *Brandt Report*[9] is essential background reading for teachers in this area, particularly the concise summary of the report's recommendations (pp. 282–92).

A wide range of materials are available from the Centre for World Development Education (details below in Resources) including the *World Development Report*, published each August by the World Bank.

Photographic material showing the extent of the disparity of nourishment and living conditions between the Third World and the developed world can provide a graphic stimulus for class discussion.

Resources

Details of textbook coverage of international trade topics can be found in *An Annotated Bibliography of Pupil*

Books, published for the Economics Education 14–16 Project by the Economics Association.

Statistical sources

(These are important for teaching material and for charts in the classroom to provide an 'atmosphere' of the UK's changing position.) Individual students could be assigned to keep each chart (e.g. current balance, exchange rate) up to date.

The UK Balance of Payments (CSO, published annually).

Economic Trends (CSO). Contains useful articles and statistics on the latest UK balance of payments position every March, June, September and December.

Barclays Bank Review, 'UK trade in manufactured goods' (November 1983) and 'World trading patterns' (May 1984). Both these two surveys are presented with useful and stimulating charts and diagrams.

The World Bank Atlas (World Bank, published annually). GNP, GNP per capita, population and growth rates for 189 countries, extremely well presented.

The World Development Report (World Bank, published annually). Detailed information on development trends in the 1980s.

World Bank and IMF publications are available from Microinfo Ltd, PO Box 3, Alton, Hampshire GU34 2PG. World Bank London Office, New Zealand House, Haymarket, London SW1Y 4TE.

Computer program

Anderton, A., *Balance of Payments* (Longman, 1984). Published in conjunction with the Economics Education 14–16 Project. A game where students play the role of Chancellor of the Exchequer and try to solve a balance of payments deficit using deflation, devaluation and import tariffs.

Tape/filmstrip

Audio Learning Ltd tape/filmstrip pack ECO 09: *Theory of Comparative Advantage*.

Other materials

The CWDE (Centre for World Development Education) is a valuable source of a wealth of materials, in particular (i) *The Development Puzzle* (7th edn, 1984), a teacher's source book and handbook on development issues, and (ii) *Cartoonsheets*, a lively presentation of relevant topics (e.g. trade, unemployment, population, LDCS).

Industry in Perspective (published by a consortium of companies with DES Industry Education Unit Support, 1983). Useful charts in section entitled 'Earning our Keep', pp. 8–9.

The GATT Report (published annually). A survey of world trade issues and developments.

Ryba, R., and Wilson, R. (ed.) *Teaching the Economics of the EEC, Vol II* (Economics Association, 1983). (British approaches to the use of teaching resources.) A source book for methods and materials for teaching the EEC.

The European Community. Useful, well-presented pamphlet for students, available from: The London Information Office, Commission of the European Community.

Notes and references

1 Eatwell, J., *Whatever Happened to Britain?* (Duckworth/BBC, 1982) pp. 89–90.
2 NEDO (the National Economic Development Office), *British Industrial Performance* (NEDO, 1983) p. 13.
3 Anderton, A. G., *Economics Study and Revision* (Collins, 1983) p. 14.4, no. 10.
4 Ibid., p. 14.6, no. 14.
5 Cairncross, F., and Keeley, P., *The Guardian Guide to the Economy Vol II* (Methuen, 1983).
6 Ibid.
7 NEDO, op. cit.
8 Cairncross and Keeley, op. cit.
9 Brandt Commission (The Independent Commission on International Development Issues), *North–South: A Programme for Survival* (Pan, 1980).

23 Public Finance

Richard Thorne

Introduction

The public sector, and in particular public finance, is often considered an important area of study within economics courses. Detailed analysis of the topic can involve a mass of statements, definitions, examples and statistics. The problem for the teacher is often one of relating this analysis to the world as perceived by their students.

It is usually unwise to assume, with this age range, a considerable amount of knowledge of the subject-matter. Many students will have little awareness of the world outside the confines of their own experience; others will have a patchy and superficial knowledge which often leads to misconceptions and misunderstandings.

Because the students' knowledge is likely to be limited, it is perhaps desirable to approach the topic from the standpoint of their experiences. By using this approach as a way into the study of public finance, it is hoped that it will make more tangible the data and information with which students are likely to be confronted.

A comprehensive coverage of the subject would probably include:

1 the size of, and reasons for, public finance;
2 government income;
3 government expenditure;
4 local-authority finance.

However, more important than the coverage in terms of detail is the success achieved in putting across the basic reasoning and concepts. A comprehensive unit of work on public finance should consider:

1 Why does the government spend money?
2 Why does the government collect taxes?
3 The link between spending and taxation, including the idea of transfers from one section of the community to another.
4 The provision of public goods.
5 The link between public finance and political decision-making.

Given that any teaching method will, of necessity, be influenced by the time allocated to the topic, the following suggestions are designed to offer some ideas to those who wish to:

(a) relate the subject-matter to the experiences of their students, and

(b) create an environment within which students can consider the rationale underlying public finance decisions.

These suggestions are to be considered either as methods suitable for introducing the topic or as supporting units within a scheme of work. There is considerable scope to develop teaching methods that relate to students' experiences. There is also the danger when dealing with government income and expenditure of becoming list- and fact-oriented.

Some suggestions for units of work

1 Present the students with slides and/or pictures of street scenes, preferably from the local area. These can be used to stimulate a discussion of the various aspects of government involvement depicted in the scenes. From this, students can develop a more general picture of government involvement in the economy. If slides or pictures are not available, then the same effect can be achieved by visualising and discussing the local high street and, from this, gradually developing the key aspects of government.

2 Students could be presented with a list of items of central- or local-government expenditure and then be set a monetary constraint. They then have to discuss and argue the case for certain priorities within the framework they are given (see Table 23.1). A more sophisticated version would involve setting out the various tax changes that could take place in order to finance these expenditure plans (see Table 23.2).

The students have to decide which options should be taken either individually, or in groups. They

Table 23.1

The government has decided to increase expenditure on one of the following. Which should it choose?
A) Pensions
B) Education
C) National Health Service
D) Armed forces
E) Police, law and order

Table 23.2

The government wishes to raise an extra £2000 million in taxation. Which taxes should it increase in order to raise this money? It knows that if it increases the following taxes the effects are:

A   Increasing the basic rate of income tax by 1 per cent raises £1000 million per annum.
B   Raising VAT by 1 per cent brings in an extra £740 million.
C   Raising National Insurance payments by firms by 1 per cent brings in £350 million.
D   Raising the price of beer 1p a pint brings in £95 million.
E   Raising the price of tobacco 1p a packet brings in £35 million.
F   Raising the price of petrol 1p a gallon brings in £50 million.

To raise the £2000 million required it can increase each tax by more than the amount stated above, that is, increase beer by 5p a pint raises £95 million × 5 = £475 million.

(The above figures relate to UK public finance 1984–5.)

should then be prepared to explain and justify their decisions to the class.

3   A survey of the services provided by local authorities could be undertaken. Most councils now send out explanatory leaflets and sources of income. This can prove excellent stimulus material. From this general background, students can be encouraged to find out what services are provided by the council within their local community.

4   A speaker may be invited representing the local authority. This is probably most appropriate after some previous study of the topic, so that students have a reasonable background knowledge upon which to base questions, etc. Rather than organising a general talk, it may prove fruitful to ask the speaker to gear at least part of the session to a discussion of the facilities provided by the council for young people, within the local area.

In order to obtain a speaker, inquiries may be made to the town clerk's or personnel and public relations departments. Alternatively, it may prove possible to obtain the services of one of the school's governing body.

5   Budget Day presents an ideal opportunity to introduce public finance, not so much because of the content of the speech, but more because use can be made of the publicity surrounding the day itself. The extensive media coverage, and the following day's newspapers in particular, can be utilised in classwork. It also gives the teacher an opportunity to obtain up-to-date statistics on government income and expenditure plans.

As there is a budget each March and the date is published well in advance, it may prove practical, when organising a scheme of work, to plan to cover public finance around this period in the academic year. There can be significant trade-offs from the Budget in terms of heightened awareness of the role and importance of public finance, even if the details themselves are not fully covered. It can also provide the stimulus for work on the role of the government within the economy.

6   A local case study. From time to time most local newspapers run articles concerning local issues such as health service provision, OAP homes, education spending, the provision of a new sports centre, etc. These may prove useful discussion points when dealing with the opportunity cost aspects of public finance. They may also prove valuable for those interested in organising role play exercises.

7   Role play. Either as the Cabinet or local council, students can be allotted roles. They may be asked to defend their case in the following examples:
   (a)   The government has decided to reduce their total expenditure. Each student represents a key figure in a department, that is, health, education, defence, etc., who has to justify the level of expenditure within their department.
   (b)   The government/council has to decide priorities in its expenditure programme. Each representative has to justify the expenditure of funds within their allotted department.

The role play can be organised by splitting a class into several groups. Each group of, say, eight students are further divided, with one student in each group representing an area of expenditure. The group argue and discuss among themselves before coming to an overall conclusion.

Alternatively, the class could be divided so that four or five students represent each department. They decide, as a group, upon their arguments and elect a spokesperson to represent their views in the decision-making process in front of the whole class.

If undertaking such role play, two things are particularly important. First, the students need to see clearly the 'point' of what they are discussing. Before the role play begins, the aims and objectives of the exercise should be made very clear. Secondly, they should be able to relate easily to the information provided. They are not going to be able to become 'experts' on a particular area of expenditure. Their role should either be very general, for example to defend expenditure on education, or specific to their experiences, for example to defend expenditure on a local youth club.

8   Work based upon their present or likely future experiences, for example:
   (a)   Discussions based upon the deductions made from pay as seen by studying a sample wage/salary slip.
   (b)   A discussion of the services they already use such as education, health and/or the taxation they already pay, for example VAT.

9   The topic lends itself to research/projects in the local community. A project could either be factual, that is, find out about the ways the local council spends its money, or research-based – for example, surveys of public opinion about such matters as the provision of services in the local community, perhaps relating the questions to a local issue.

Resources

Books

A very useful starting point is *An Annotated Bibliography of Pupil Books* published by the Economics Association (2nd edn, 1984) on behalf of the Economics Education 14–16 Project. It includes a comprehensive survey of relevant literature.

Almost all texts include a section on public finance. Among those that are useful for this age range are:

Stanlake, G. F., *Introductory Economics* 4th edn., (Longman, 1983) ch. 30. A thorough text most suitable for staff reference and the more academic student.

Stanlake, G. F., *First Economics* (Longman, 1983) ch. 25. This is a simpler book than *Introductory Economics*, which appeals to less academic 14–16-year-olds. A variety of questions are included at the end of each section.

Anderton, A. G., *An Introduction to Social Economics*, 2nd edn. (Heinemann Educational Books, 1984) chs. 18–20. As the title implies, this book attempts to place economics topics in a real-world context. It can be used with mixed-ability classes and includes case studies and questions on the text.

Davey, M., *Everyday Economics* (Macmillan, 1983) ch. 18. This chapter offers a concise yet thorough coverage of the topic. It is useful as a reference both for class and homework but would require elaboration by the teacher for all but the more-able student.

Thorne, R., and Leeming, C., *Introducing Economics* (Economics Association, 1981) pp. 34–41. A simple introduction to the topic with cartoons for stimulus and questions on the text. Suitable for younger and less-able students.

Other materials

Given the topical nature of the subject, useful articles can often be obtained from newspapers and magazines. This applies particularly near the time of a Budget when the media's attention is focused on public finance issues. The bi-monthly *Economic Progress Reports*, published by the Treasury, are available free of charge. Local councils often make available free literature on their income and expenditure plans for the following financial year. Finally, the Inland Revenue provide a wide range of forms and documents for use by students, including: *The Taxman, Video and Teacher Resource Pack*.

24   The Welfare State

Alain Anderton

Introduction

The welfare state is a Cinderella topic in economics at O-level. Traditional textbooks and syllabuses carry no reference to it. It may be touched upon when discussing government spending, but it is left to social economics courses, or the CSE courses or the sociologists to discuss the issues involved. Yet, as current national debate on the size and nature of the welfare state illustrates, this topic is of central importance when considering standards of living, distribution of income, economic efficiency, employment and unemployment and the size of the public sector to name but a few areas. With so many of our students likely to find their way into the benefits systems, while the rest pay their taxes grudgingly to support them, it is surely important for all to have an appreciation of the workings of the welfare state and alternative systems.

Content

Many economics CSE and social economics O-level courses require a knowledge of:

1   the national insurance system – the way it finances its operations and the benefits available under the system;
2   the social security system – the benefits available and the conditions under which they are given;
3   other 'situation benefits' available, like child benefit;
4   other aspects of the welfare state like the National Health Service, education provision, housing, social services departments of local authorities, etc.

Skills demanded are often lower-order factual recall skills. However, more enlightened examiners are now demanding higher-order skills such as application and evaluation – the sort of skills that students will need as adults in fact. A knowledge of the welfare state may well occur as parts of questions relating to population ('what are the implications of an ageing population?') or income distribution ('Explain how the state redistributes income in the UK').

Teaching methods

Despite the often heavy emphasis on factual recall in public examinations, the best way to teach this topic is definitely not to dwell upon the knowledge aspect of the topic. *An Introduction to Social Economics* by Anderton and *Social Economics* by Nobbs (see Resources on p. 123) both have sections on the welfare state from which students can take notes if necessary, and which can form the basis of the knowledge required to engage in more interesting and worthwhile activities. One such simple activity is to make a list of various people in need and ask the students to decide which benefits they are each likely to be entitled to. Another is to organise a class discussion around the statistics and case studies to be found in these two books.

On benefits, an activity could be centred round the various leaflets produced by the Department of Health and Social Security and available in class sets from them. They are written in fairly simple language, often with application forms at the end. Students could be asked to make a complete list of benefits available and in what circumstances they can be claimed. They could also be asked to fill in an application form for a benefit, having been given pre-specified information about an imaginary person. Comprehension questions could be set. The benefits could be grouped according to the situation of potential applicants (poor, sick, unemployed, etc.), or according to whether they are national insurance benefits, means-tested benefits or situation benefits.

Newspaper articles are an excellent teaching resource, particularly for generating discussion. Students have strong views – most of which can correctly be described as prejudices – on the social-security system. Some of the more common prejudices are that most immigrants live off the state, workers who are unemployed don't want to work, social-security payments are used mainly for gambling and drinking and most people would be better off on the dole than working. In the light of this, it is very dangerous to provide articles that will reinforce these views. It is far better to pick articles that put over a more balanced viewpoint. Newspaper articles can be used for comprehension as well as to stimulate discussion. In discussion, teachers should have at their fingertips the latest statistics on who is getting what and when. The most recent edition of *Social Trends* is very useful in this context. It contains statistics on benefits and also has good sections on housing, education and health. Newspaper articles are also a good source for material on the health service, housing and education. The never-ending 'cuts' in these areas regularly hit the headlines. Newspapers will also provide comparisons with other countries and they will often suggest that the welfare state abroad has been far better organised than in the UK. This could lead into consideration of alternative ways of financing the system. One simple example that can be used is to discuss 'free' versus insurance health systems. Although this is not specifically related to most syllabuses, it does make students think about what is being provided for them. It is often useful to reproduce accounts from two newspapers of the same story giving two different viewpoints. Political bias can then be discussed.

Cuts in the welfare state can form the basis of a role playing exercise. Students can be given the roles of spending ministers/civil servants who have to cut £2000 million from the budget. A limited number of options would be made available (e.g. one option could be cutting the old-age pension by £2 a week per person, saving £1000 million a year), and students would have to argue the case why their expenditure should not be cut.

There is very little point in organising a visit to a local Department of Health and Social Security office since there is very little to see. Nor do the other topics covered lend themselves to meaningful visits. The local Department of Health and Social Security office will, however, send a speaker or speakers to talk to students. His or her outlook on the system can be quite refreshing to students who think that the whole benefits system is one huge fraud.

Problems

Students find difficulty in distinguishing between national insurance and the social-security system. A good way of distinguishing between the two is to emphasise the insurance nature of the national insurance system, and the means-tested aspect of social security. Only workers who have paid national insurance contributions are entitled to benefits. If you haven't paid in, you can't get anything out. An excellent example of this is relevant to school leavers. A school leaver cannot technically go on 'the dole' when he leaves school because he hasn't paid national insurance contributions. Hence he is unable to obtain unemployment benefit. But he can get social-security payments. If this is emphasised every time a student cracks a joke about going on the dole when he leaves school, the message eventually gets through.

Prejudice has already been mentioned. Teachers in the south of England may find difficulty in convincing students that real poverty does exist in Britain and that the poor are poor despite working hard. In the rest of Britain, poverty is more close at hand. Yet even this closeness may not make the majority of students see poverty as a multi-faceted problem, the worst aspects of which the welfare state attempts to ameliorate. Racial prejudice is the most difficult to combat – comments such as 'they get off the plane and make for the nearest social security office' are all too typical. The citing of statistics, the showing of photographs and discussion of selected case studies can help impress upon students the existence of poverty.

It is difficult to collect resources on the welfare state, because it is not mainstream economics. The places where the economist would normally look first are not particularly helpful. As a result, resources and information have to be dug out of the sort of pool that the man in the street also has to use. In one way this is not such a bad thing. The teacher will have to use the sort of material in his teaching that the students themselves will have to evaluate and interpret if they want to find out about or use the system when they leave school. The traditional textbook approach can be of little value here in preparing students as future citizens.

Resources

Books for students

Anderton, A. G., *An Introduction to Social Economics* 2nd edn. (Heinemann Educational Books, 1984). The chapter on 'The welfare state' contains details of social security benefits as well as a discussion of the health service, education, housing and the work of charities. There are six case studies as well as graphs and statistics.

Anderton, A. G., *Money Matters* (Collins Educational, 1984). Intended for lower-ability pupils, this has sections on benefits, housing and education.

Davey, M., *Everyday Economics* (Macmillan, 1983). Chapter 8 is entitled 'Welfare'.

Nobbs, J., *Economics in Daily Practice* (McGraw-Hill, 1984). This book, aimed at lower-ability students, gives a selective tour of the social services.

Nobbs, J., *Social Economics* 3rd edn. (McGraw-Hill, 1981). An O-level text, this has sections on social security, the National Health Service and housing. Included are three case studies as well as some statistics. Curiously, there is no mention of supplementary benefit.

Books for teachers

CSO, *Social Trends* (HMSO). Published annually, this provides invaluable statistics for the teacher. If the expense is too great £19.95 in 1986), it is well worth a visit to your local public library to photocopy relevant items.

Consumers' Association, *Which?* This publishes regular guides to the benefit system. Look up the index to see the latest survey.

Willmott, P., *Consumers Guide to the British Social Services* (Pelican, 1980).

Leaflets

The Department of Health and Social Security. They produce a wide variety of leaflets, available free from your local office or at post offices. Fifth-formers might well be interested in working on the leaflet for free prescriptions, since after their sixteenth birthday they are only entitled to free prescriptions if they have a certificate of exemption.

Audio-visual material

Both radio and television often carry items of news and current affairs on the welfare state. *World in Action*, *Man Alive* and *Panorama* can provide stimulating programmes for the 14–16-year-old, though video recording is not allowed.

Simulation games

Tenement (Shelter). Players are asked to take the role either of an occupant of a rented house or a worker in a relevant agency like the Rent Tribunal and the Department of Health and Social Security. Role cards explain what each person is trying to achieve. It is a very good simulation that goes down well at this level, covering housing, employment and the social services.

Shirts, G., *Starpower* (Management Games Limited). This powerful game can be used to illustrate the cycle of poverty. Participants quickly realise that the winners and losers of the game were chosen before play even started. How the 'rich' and the 'poor' then react is typical of how the better-off and the poor react to their lot in real life. This game can only be recommended for fairly mature groups.

Part Two
Teaching Economics to the 16–19 Age Range

Introduction to Part Two

'We may not be able to escape the laws of economics but, with luck, we may be able to escape the dogmas of economists.'

Tom Stonier, in *The Wealth of Information*.

Economics teachers are still principally occupied with teaching 16–19-year-olds in most schools and colleges, and this emphasis is reflected in the length of Part Two. Maurice Willatt's survey of syllabus problems is predictably a joy to read. From the philosophical to the pragmatic, Lindsey Collings shows how to compile a study guide, and evaluates the approach. The rate of new product development in software for economics teaching is so fast that it was decided to omit detailed assessment of currently available programs, since such information would be out of date by the time of publication. Instead, Richard Welford examines computer-assisted learning from a deeper perspective, and provides a balanced appraisal. Another innovation of the last decade has been the use of data-response questions in examinations. Roy Wilkinson shows their value in teaching as well as assessment. Great upheavals are currently taking place in courses for non-A-level students in the 16–19 age range. Philip Negus charts recent developments in pre-vocational courses and assesses the contribution of economics to integrated curricula. The school/further education divide is becoming increasingly blurred, but specific problems encountered by economics lecturers in further education, notably the role of economics in BTEC courses, are exposed by Ann Cotterell. A variety of general teaching ideas follows. Ray Jarvis explains his unique development of mini-charts, and Brian Titley his bright idea of 'wipe-able' wall charts. Valuable tips on making overhead projector transparencies are provided by Danny Myers.

The first edition of the *Handbook* had scant treatment of field courses and related ventures. In contrast, we now have two chapters on this theme. Michael Houser describes a variety of possibilities for using London as a resource and Trevor Regan and Nigel Tree assess the benefits and pitfalls of more far-flung field courses.

Mike Morris leads off Section 4 (fifteen chapters on teaching particular topics to 16–19-year-olds) with a thoughtful and stimulating piece on the teaching of supply, demand and price. Alain Anderton follows with the theory of the firm, appending a helpful list of resources. The topic of economic efficiency is gaining wider currency at this level, and Alain Anderton shows how the concept may be applied to a wide variety of teaching topics. The difficult concepts involved in the theory of consumer behaviour are analysed by Andrew Leake, who shows the efficacy of a three-dimensional approach. Richard Powell's expertise is demonstrated by his chapter on population and demography. The fraught topic of industrial relations is dealt with by Stuart Luker, who provides a simulation – among many other possible techniques. Social and environmental economics are increasingly important, as Andrew Leake indicates in his innovative chapter. Another recent syllabus accretion is comparative economics, and Andrew Tibbitt surveys the topic comprehensively.

The problems of teaching money and banking are enumerated by David Butler, who shows how examinations now emphasise different aspects of the topic. Barrie King illustrates the BTEC approach in teaching about sources of capital.

A major chapter by Michael Tighe examines the teaching of national income and the circular flow of income, and the controversial field of macroeconomic policy is carefully described by Nancy Wall. A fascinating piece by Graham Jones on international trade theory provides much food for thought. Keith Marder brings his chapter on government policy up to date, and Stuart Luker ends this section with a new chapter on teaching the economics of the public sector, with special reference to the privatisation controversy and cost-benefit analysis.

Section 3: General Problems

25 Rethinking the Syllabus
Maurice Willatt

Introduction

The path of least resistance for teachers is to 'do as you have been done by', to teach new students what they learnt at school and as much as possible of what they learnt at university. As people mature a good deal between 16 and 23, students attempting undergraduate work in the sixth form tend to grasp some of it, ignore some, and misunderstand the rest. There is a marked premium on precocity. Economics arose from the application of calculus to the simplified Benthamite psychology; it has always tended to gallop off into mathematical structures with little operational use. Marshall continually warned other people of the danger of allowing the theoretical to be separated from the statistical, but when he wrote the best-known textbook of the age[1] he put on the title page *Natura non facit saltum* (roughly translatable as: it is all done by calculus), and put the essential things into mathematical appendices. Schmoller, the best known of the Germans who tried to build on an adequate basis of historical facts, lamented: 'But, gentlemen, it is all so endlessly complicated.'[2] Clapham produced his playful essay 'Of empty economic boxes'[3] in 1922; hatters and hatboxes have gone down the stream of time, but empty pieces of theory are still very evident. The effect at university level is to increase controversy, devised like tournaments to increase the repute of the protagonists and adding to their tally of published works. The effect on the general public is the belief that there is no agreement among economists, who can be ignored or even ridiculed outside money markets. The effect on schools is equally serious. As publishers put out books intended to bring down both undergraduates and sixth-formers at once, academic debates are brought into the classroom. Now the young are eager to find something to memorise; they love the personal and the controversial; like jackdaws they love to collect glittering but not very useful objects. With misplaced zeal they tend to produce what look like savage parodies of all that 'Professor X argues ... but Dr Y argues' stuff. Surely what we want sixth-formers to know is not who said it, but what evidence he produces.

Clearly what is needed is a syllabus that does not ape the less desirable features of many undergraduate courses, steers the students away from the pitfalls of immaturity and towards a body of theory, limited in scope but tied to,

and explaining, a quantity of highly significant observed facts. It can be argued – it has been argued – that a radical solution should be adopted, excluding economic theory from the school curriculum, and presenting a body of factual, non-controversial, descriptive material, selected and packaged to suit the tastes and abilities of the students.

But this is not really possible. To start with, description requires definition and classification. But definition of unemployment, output, money, costs of living, etc. requires complex and important pieces of theory. The selection of topics to be covered rests on theoretical decisions about centrality, stability and importance. Framing of theories is one of the fundamental human activities. A man has a fever. To ask why is an unavoidable reaction. Is it the wrath of some god or witchcraft or excessive use of spices or excess of blood or bacterial infection? The choice is not between theory and non-theory, but between bad theory and better. A non-theoretical syllabus, 'of bias free of every kind', is a delusion.

Everybody above the age of pigtails and short trousers has established, and often pugnaciously defended, economic views. In the famous concluding pages of *The General Theory*,[4] Keynes maintained that 'the world is ruled by little else' than 'the ideas of economists and political philosophers'. 'Practical men ... are the slaves of some defunct economist.' He might have made this plural, for it is quite common to hold two or more conflicting opinions at once, emerging unpredictably from a kind of folk-memory. It seems possible that current support for monetarism and trade-union legislation may owe more to bullionism and the Statute of Artificers than anything else. At least it is clear that the young student comes to the teacher as a multi-palimpsest, not a clean sheet. And teachers must take a definite line about bias and propaganda. Is their role to support the basic myths that hold society together? Or to help to replace them by new and more appropriate ones? Or, as some liberals would have us believe, should they try to keep the field clear for the student to form his own opinion? (In view of students' lack of experience and clarity, and the pressures of family, school, media, etc., can they really do so?) But these are deep waters.

One characteristic feature of nineteenth-century

thinking was the assumption of stability in economic behaviour. Even today, people are surprised when, for example, businessmen, presented with a higher cash flow by a kind government, spend it on foreign investment, takeovers and buying land, rather than in new technology. But just as the origins of our thinking lie in the past, so does the pattern of our behaviour. Every economic question is a historical question. To forestall protest, on the ground that the syllabus is bound to be overloaded already, it should be made clear that the suggestion that more history is needed does not imply covering the whole of economic history. We do not want to be like the girl who began her essay: 'Let us consider the history of mankind from the earliest times.' To take two examples from many: industrial relations, and deindustrialisation. The main problem in the field of industrial relations is to explain why Britain has made such a mess of them. Many teachers spend some time on a potted version of trade-union history and law. But trade unions are a symptom of failure rather than a cause, and trade-union law is probably incomprehensible. Why not go further back, perhaps to the Royal Commission of 1867–69?

> Whether the circumstance is to be regretted or not, the habitual code of sentiment which prevailed between employers and workmen in the times when the former were regarded by both law and usage as the governing class, is now greatly relaxed and cannot be revived. A substitute has now to be found for it, arising from . . . self-interest and . . . mutual forbearance.[5]

Why has such a substitute been found abroad and not here? Consideration of deindustrialisation involves a study of the ingredients of the balance of payments. This becomes much more significant if carried back to the 1880s, thus digging down to the reasons for anxiety. It may be pointed out that, to the pupils and to many teachers, events before about 1970 are already history, so that going a little further back should raise no objections.

Many people have sought to find the ideal school syllabus midway between two extremes. 'Most of the propositions and arguments I have advanced lie between what . . . might be described as "armchair theorising" and "casual empiricism".'[6] Discussion in recent years of the syllabus at higher levels has thrown up a number of suggestions. A review by G. L. S. Shackle[7] of Professor Hutchison's book *The Politics and Philosophy of Economics*, concludes: 'Two themes of the highest practical consequence are convincingly argued and illustrated in Hutchison's book. One is the need to treat economic *history* as our chief source of instruction and understanding. The other is to make case studies, rather than allegedly "general" theories, the vehicle of our thought.' This offers a wide freedom to the deviser of school syllabuses. The doctrine of the Bryce Commission, as long ago as 1895, that the teacher is a discoverer and must be free to experiment, would at last be fulfilled.[8] Case studies have been used for a long time, but mainly as an *aid* to the main course, 'to add verisimilitude to an otherwise bald and unconvincing narrative.' Here the suggestion is that there shall be no main course, but a wide selection of case studies, carefully selected and graded, and students' choice so guided that at the end the students should all have covered both an adequate number of main topics and the theoretical tools needed to deal with them.

The difficulties in organising and managing a syllabus of this kind are simply the difficulties in running systems based on individual 'product' work. To work effectively, they are very expensive in man-power, as experience over the last generation has shown. Collecting an adequate library of pamphlets, journals, cuttings, blue books, handouts, etc. is not necessarily expensive in monetary terms, but very time-consuming. Arranging and grading the material, and issuing to students according to time-tables, based on the abilities of the student and the difficulties of the study, call for very skilled library work. Above all, the teacher must be able to curb without undue nagging both the assiduous yardage-maximiser and the insidious leisure-maximiser. Teachers with little experience of these things should try to visit schools or colleges where they may learn useful models and awful warnings.

Examining might appear to present a serious problem. Here again there is now a mass of experience of special syllabuses, using internal marking and external moderation. On the whole, the maintenance of *standards* has proved less difficult than had been expected. As examinations are increasingly used for purposes of selection, examining bodies have a duty to make clear the *content* of the courses involved. There are too many certificates and diplomas labelled 'economics' that contain little of what is usually implied by the label. Where there may be doubt, an explanatory adjective or phrase should be added. '(Economics (Case Studies))' would be adequate here.

In building any syllabus, the problem is what to leave out. The obvious topic that cannot be treated well through case studies is general equilibrium. This nineteenth-century imitation of eighteenth-century mechanics may well be spared: if static, it is unreal; if dynamic, too difficult. But the nearer the course gets to the great macro-economic topics, the harder it is to frame case studies. Clearly, certain aspects could be separated out: for example, the multiplier, with the changing numerical estimates of the period since 1936 – no general treatment of national income determination. Other examples could be: the measurement and classification of unemployment, 1945–84; price movements, 1914–84; inward and outward migration since 1945; the changes in the numbers of trade unions and trade-union membership since 1914.

It was George III who asked how the apple got into the dumpling. How are items of theory to be selected and processed in order to fit into the hard casing? Traditional teaching here must be modified considerably. Take a simple example – the demand for butter in the local town or suburb. Traditional teaching here creates the impression that something exists called '*the* demand for butter'; indeed, examiners have often sinned in asking why '*the* demand for butter is more elastic than "*the*" demand for margarine'. Whose demand, when and where? Traditionally, students have learnt to expect straight lines that cut both axes. Although they are taught definitions, they persist in assuming that elasticity is the slope of the straight line. Their definition evades them, since percentages are puzzling. For example, they would say that if price changes from 10 to 9 and as a result quantity bought increases from 100 to 110, elasticity is unity and total expenditure is unchanged! Our simple case will present estimated quantities for perhaps half a dozen realistic prices. Nowadays, students may well have acquired some knowledge of sampling and significance, connected perhaps with their geography. They may be able to suggest how many mums and grans must be quizzed about their probable behaviour, how far parents or other relatives of the students can be taken as typical of the local inhabitants, and how a typical type of butter can be selected. It must be stressed that in all interview or questionnaire methods of collecting information, it is very hard to avoid offence; how to avoid trivial or rude answers deserves very careful study.

Another example suitable for beginners might be the pattern of retail trade in a small town or suburb, including the changes in numbers and types of retail outlet over the last ten years or so. Students with some background in geography might use elements of their study of location theory and central-place theory, and their experience of mapping. Direct evidence of relations between output and cost might be hard to obtain by direct questioning, unless students and teachers happen to have some personal or family connections. But figures for differences in prices could be collected easily enough and evidence of monopsony by large national firms. There has been discussion in the press of the reasons for the multiplication of building society branches and their concentration. The study of local planning applications, particularly when rejected, could be informative.

It might be thought that in case studies of this kind much use could be made of what has come over the last fifty years to be known as the theory of the firm. With its array of curves, easily memorised, and attractive especially when drawn in colour, its usefulness is limited, first by the unreal assumptions – one-product, short-period-profit-maximising firms, with predictable, continuous cost and revenue functions – and secondly, by the failure to explain the arithmetical and algebraic derivation of the cost curves. It is all too common to take the whole initial cost of capital equipment and put it in the cost curves of the particular short period, instead of the amortisation and interest charges. The basin-shaped average cost curves require total cost curves at least cubic. They are often drawn, even by examiners, as semi-circles, which would mean a total cost curve beyond belief. Teachers might read J. Robinson's 'Imperfect competition revisited'[9] for the qualms of one of the progenitors of the theory. What is true and essential is the distinction between average and marginal, which can be approached through an initial study of heating a building by various methods, some involving heavy installation costs but low running costs, and others the reverse.

Some possible cases may require difficult theory but offer abundant factual and statistical material. For example, the study of price movements in the UK from 1947 can draw on many statistical tables. The longer, and perhaps more suitable, period 1914–46 offers rather less adequate material. Study must begin with index numbers and their use, in the light of what is called 'the quantity theory of money', which went out of fashion a generation ago but has now returned. The Cambridge or Robertson version is the most suitable. Now students have calculators and can use them, they can examine the construction and pitfalls of index number series and face problems like using official cost of living figures as a measure of P, cash in circulation as a measure of M and official estimates of GNP as a measure of R. Students would need considerable tutorial help, making it hard to stop short of doing the study for them. History students should be grateful if some reference to earlier price movements could be included, for many history books say things like 'Population growth increased the demand for goods and therefore prices rose', which might be true if 'prices' refers only to, say, rye and fuel. Demand is an offer of money: where does the extra money come from?

The family (or household) is an example of a topic very scantily treated in traditional syllabuses, although it provides most of consumption expenditure and the main motive for overtime and saving. Perhaps the so-called 'Protestant work ethic' is really the response to large families in an industrial society. Is there enough material to tackle this topic? Failure to develop shadow pricing of family productive activity is inexcusable. Study of the family suggests further widening of the field. As pointed out above, the tendency of the last century to assume that an economic system established on a tiny part of the world's surface for an infinitesimal part of human history was permanent is astonishing. Why not have a quick look at the structure of some other economies widely separated from us in space and time. In medieval England, for example, the ablest, best-educated and therefore most adaptable section of the population had (officially) no family to provide for: is it an accident that economic progress was slow, and that capitalism developed when and where clergy began to marry? And what about the caste system in India?

Turning to a more obvious topic, generally recognised as important, with similar difficulties occurring in providing clear and generally accepted facts, the effects on Britain of joining the EEC defy measurement. Theory would suggest at least five considerations. First, increased specialisation, with, say, the UK providing small and medium trucks, and medium-small cars, Italy providing motor cycles, and so on. Secondly, movement of factors of production, labour and capital going to meet each other in the most appropriate locations. Thirdly, in industries where the optimum size of firm is too large for the UK market, the removal of tariffs allows growth. Fourthly, where monopolistic positions exist, opening the market to imports tends to remove them. Fifthly, sudden major changes may create structural unemployment. Unfortunately, any measurable changes along these lines seem to have been dwarfed by other processes, such as imports from outside Europe. There were other obstacles to movement apart from tariffs, which could in any case have been reduced by extensions to EFTA and GATT, and evaded by differential pricing. So what happens to this topic as a possible case study?

So far it has been assumed that the end-product is a set of mini-dissertations worked out by the student beavering away at the material with the minimum of help from the tutor and the librarian. But it should now be obvious that the preparation of material by the teacher may require much provision of advice and handouts, which may amount in extreme cases to the giving of classroom lessons with the teacher, in effect, doing the case study. There is scope for any number of possible compromises. But one thing seems quite certain: the intimate and unremitting linkage of verbal or mathematical theory with actual factual material. For example, from the first introduction of the word 'demand', there must be reference to somebody, some precisely described article, in a definite place at a specified time. Within a few minutes of mentioning the multiplier for the first time, students must be given estimates, collected perhaps from the successive editions of Prest.[10] They will understand little of demand management if they are allowed to go away thinking of multipliers of four or more.

Notes and references

1   Marshall, A., *Principles of Economics* (Macmillan, 1890, and later editions).
2   Schmoller, G., quoted in Gay, E.F., 'The tasks of economic history' in *Enterprise and Secular Change*, ed. Lane, F.C. (Allen & Unwin, 1953) p. 411.
3   Clapham, J.H., 'Of empty economic boxes' *The Economic Journal*, vol. XXXII, September 1922, p. 305.
4   Keynes, J.M., *The General Theory of Employment, Interest and Money* (Macmillan, 1936) pp. 383–4.
5   *Thirteenth and Final Report of Royal Commission on Trade Unions 1869,* pp. xvii–xviii.
6   Wilkinson, R., in Whitehead, D.J. (ed.) *Curriculum Development in Economics* (Heinemann Educational Books, 1974) p. 177.
7   Shackle, G.L.S., *The Economic Journal*, vol. XVIII, March 1983, pp. 223–4.
8   *Report of Royal Commission on Secondary Education*, 1895, p. 190.
9   Robinson, J., 'Imperfect competition revisited', *The Economic Journal,* vol. LXIII, September 1953, pp. 579ff.
10 Prest, A.R., *The UK Economy* (Weidenfeld & Nicolson, 1970). Later editions by Prest, A.R., and Coppock, D.J.

26   The Study Guide Approach
Lindsey Collings

Objectives

A study guide can be used for several purposes:
1   To clarify the overall plan of a topic.
2   To provide a structure for the students' own notes.
3   By constructing their own study guide, students learn how to structure their own notes and projects.

Compiling a study guide

1   Collect all likely sources and list suitable chapters. See references section on study guide (Table 26.2, part A).
2   Scan through the chapters listing the sub-sections (Table 26.1).
3   Arrange the sub-sections in a logical sequence with major headings. See the completed study guide (Table 26.2, part B).

Table 26.1

Harvey and Johnson, ch. 5.
Definition of consumption and saving, pp. 58–9.
Consumption and disposable income, p. 59.
The importance of consumption, pp. 59–61.
The long- and short-run consumption functions, pp. 61–3.
And so on.
Stanlake, ch. 5.
Introduction and income and consumption, pp. 41–2 (all on the importance of consumption).
The propensities to consume and save, pp. 43–4.
Graphical representations:
The consumption function, pp. 45–6.
The savings function, pp. 46–7.
Empirical consumption functions, pp. 47–8.
Movements of the consumption function, pp. 48–9.

Table 26.2   Study guide: consumption

References

Lipsey, R. G., *Positive Economics,* 5th edn. (Weidenfeld & Nicolson, 1979) ch. 35.

Harvey, J., and Johnson, M., *Introduction to Macro-Economics* (Macmillan, 1971) ch. 5.

Peston, M. H., *The British Economy* (Philip Allen, 1982) ch. 3, pp. 27–33.

Stanlake, G. F., *Macro-economics: An Introduction*, 2nd edn. (Longman, 1979) ch. 5.

Stonier, A. W., and Hague, D. C., *A Textbook of Economic Theory*, 4th edn. (Longman, 1972) ch. 20.

Note plan

A *Importance of consumption*
Lipsey, p. 513.
Stanlake, pp. 41–2.
Harvey and Johnson, pp. 59–61.

B *Determinants of consumption*
 1 *Income – Keynes's consumption function*
  (a) Introduction: Definition of consumption
   Harvey and Johnson, pp. 58–9.
  (b) APC, MPC and the consumption function
   Lipsey, pp. 513–15.
   Stanlake, pp. 43–6.
   Harvey and Johnson, pp. 66–9.
   Stonier and Hague, pp. 458–61.
  (c) Long-run and short-run consumption functions
   Harvey and Johnson, pp. 61–2.
   Stonier and Hague, pp. 465–8.
   modern criticism of . . .
   Harvey and Johnson, pp. 69–72.
   Stonier and Hague, pp. 468–71.

  (d) Factors underlying the propensity to consume
   Stonier and Hague, pp. 462–5.
  (e) Aggregation problems
   Lipsey, p. 515.
   Harvey and Johnson, p. 72.
  (f) Consumption and national income
   Lipsey, p. 516.
   Harvey and Johnson, pp. 73–4.
  (g) Savings function
   Stanlake, pp. 46–7.
   Harvey and Johnson, pp. 65–6.
  (h) Mathematical expression of consumption functions
   Harvey and Johnson, pp. 74–6.

 2 *Other determinants of consumption – shifts of the curve*
  Lipsey, pp. 516–18.
  Stanlake, pp. 48–9.
  Harvey and Johnson, pp. 63–5.

 3 *Modern theories*
  Permanent income hypothesis and life cycle hypothesis
  Lipsey, pp. 518–22.
  Stonier and Hague, pp. 471–7.

 4 *Empirical evidence*
  Stanlake, pp. 47–8.
  Peston, pp. 27–33.

Table 26.3   A section of the consumption study guide laid out in columns

	Lipsey	Stanlake	Harvey and Johnson	Stonier and Hague
B *Determinants of consumption*				
1 *Income – Keynes's consumption function*				
(a) *Introduction*			pp. 58–9	
(b) *APC, MPC and the consumption function*	pp. 513–15	pp. 43–6	pp. 66–9	pp. 458–61
(c) *Long- and short-run consumption functions*			pp. 61–2	pp. 465–8
modern criticisms of . . .			pp. 69–72	pp. 468–71

The uses of the study guide

1 The guide helps students to follow the development of a topic and enables them to makes notes in parallel with class notes. The resulting notes, which combine the points various authors have made on the same section, are easy to use for reference when writing essays and for revision. Students should use all references at first; later they may use alternatives when they have discovered that certain authors' styles seem to suit them better than others do. Students are also discouraged from copying sections from books, as thought is needed to combine several authors' views. These notes are usually significantly better than when students make when unguided. Notes made without guidance tend to consist of notes from one complete

chapter followed by notes from another. The result is repetition of many points, a confused structure and waste of time in writing and using the notes.

2 The skill of structuring notes and projects can be taught by showing students how to compile a study guide.
   (a) At first students are given a complete guide and use it to make their notes.
   (b) For later topics they can be given the chapters, headings and side headings only, so that they have to insert the page references before making notes.
   (c) The next stage would be to give only the chapters and major headings.
   (d) Finally, only the chapters need be given.

   At each stage, the students could be given a complete guide after they have shown that they can construct their own, so that they can check their work for errors and omissions. If students reach the last stage at the end of an A-level course they will be equipped to write good notes from the kind of references they will be given in further or higher education. This is also a valuable organisational skill which will be useful in work.

3 Students can be encouraged to adapt the approach to their own style of studying (Table 26.3 shows the consumption study guide laid out differently). This second layout is particularly valuable where students cannot obtain all the references simultaneously. The columns can be regarded as a checklist for each text. A separate sheet of paper can be used for notes on each sub-heading, so that the contributions of each author can be added as the books are obtained. The sub-section notes can be rewritten and integrated, where necessary, when all the references are complete.

4 Where students have individual needs, at the extremes of ability or for Oxbridge preparation, more advanced or simpler references can be substituted or added to their guide, being fitted in so that they can be integrated with the appropriate section.

Conclusion: the value of the study guide approach

1 Students find a topic easier to comprehend when they can see the layout of it in a clearly structured study guide.

2 The guide can show where notes should supplement class notes, where class notes only will be necessary, or where the students' own notes will be sufficient.

3 Compiling integrated notes encourages greater understanding or reveals a lack of it, so that students will seek help, if needed. Average and weaker students gain a better understanding while able ones learn good study techniques and read widely.

4 Putting greater emphasis on the making of notes provides an alternative to essays for homework. The notes can be quickly checked in class. Frequent brief checks encourage a disciplined approach to doing references which will be valuable beyond school, and in other subjects.

5 Encouraging such wide reading need not be expensive. For small groups, a few library copies of most texts would be sufficient while in large groups there could be one text and then other books could be shared between three or four. For the cost of two books per student, they could each have access to five texts, each having the central text and one each of the four other books.

27   Computer-assisted Learning in Economics Education
Richard Welford

Introduction

It has been suggested by some writers (e.g. Maddison[1]) that the computer is the most significant new educational tool since the printed book, not only altering the teaching of existing subjects but also creating new ones. In economics education there has been a rapid growth of interest in the use of computers, not least because it enhances the analytical approach which is becoming prevalent in economics teaching, mirroring the work of

the professional, and many academic, economists. The microcomputer is versatile and no more difficult to use than a video recorder. Furthermore, it is interactive and encourages questions of the type 'What would happen if . . .?'

However, the computer should only be introduced as a teaching aid if it is likely to improve the quality of teaching. Distortion of subject-matter to fit a teaching technique will not produce an effective result.

The price of microcomputers means that they are within

the reach of many departments' budgets, but they should not be bought without serious consideration. Remember that the cost of peripherals may be as much as the microcomputer itself.

The experience of others is invaluable when deciding upon computer-assisted learning (CAL) activities. Teachers who have used certain packages will doubtless be aware of any pitfalls that may arise and will be a source of useful advice. Take advantage of computer specialists in schools and colleges, and consult county advisers. A good teacher of computing should be more than happy to help with the 'spread' of CAL into all areas of education.

Successful use of the computer will require considerable effort and in some cases revision of teaching methods to exploit its potential. Rest assured, however, that the teacher will never become redundant because, in the context of computer-assisted learning, the teacher has to be an observer, an adviser and a consultant if all is to run smoothly.

Computer-assisted learning is a tripartite exercise involving the teacher, learner and computer. In some cases, students may be left to use the computer in their own time, but the work will be co-ordinated by the teacher, and students should always be encouraged to report back.

The educational evidence supporting CAL is largely anecdotal. But this is in sufficient volume to be significant. In economics there are strong reasons to believe that the use of the computer can enhance lessons and improve understanding. The reasons for this will now be examined. In what follows CAL covers the whole use of computers in teaching; computer-assisted instruction (CAI) and computer-managed learning (CML) are part of that.

Games, models and simulations

The use of games, models and simulations in economics has been a great success. A characteristic of economics is that we cannot perform controlled experiments, but the microcomputer facilitates the running of quite complex simulations and models in a stimulating way.

Though games and simulations have been used for a long time, the computer has increased their scope and in many cases has removed some of the less enjoyable parts of the exercise by taking over much of the arithmetic involved.

There are a growing number of business games on the market ranging from relatively simple expositions of production theory (e.g. Carter and Greenwood[2]) to more complex games based on oligopolistic interdependence (e.g. BP Educational Service[3]) which even have the facility to store results on a disc file to be analysed at a later date.

The aim of macrosimulations is to help students learn macroeconomics in an interesting fashion, but should not be seen as substitutes for teacher and textbook input. Using a macrosimulation enables students to experience the problems faced by policy-makers, as students are forced to put their understanding of macroeconomics to work in trying to solve these problems. The more complex macrosimulations (e.g. Lumsden and Scott[4]) incorporate a large number of variables and plausible exogenous shocks. The annual Heriot-Watt/Hewlett-Packard 'Running the British Economy' competition for UK schools is becoming a televised event. Schools and colleges are invited to send teams of A-level students to participate in the microcomputer-based simulation exercise. As microcomputers become more widely used in schools and colleges, a growth in the number of participants can be expected.

The major constraint on the use of games and simulations is the time required to use them and follow them up adequately. The important debriefing session can easily be underutilised, with the effect of making the simulation exercise itself just a 'bit of fun'. On the other hand, computers have made the study of complex models and simulations possible. Ten years ago, it would have been impractical to undertake such simulations given the time that would have been involved. In game-like activities, the computer is often able to act as a referee and/or manager and this is useful for the teacher who is then freed to act purely in a teaching role.

The microcomputer can be a great motivator. A fully interactive system will provide continuous feedback on decisions made by students. It is useful to have a 'hard copy' of the feedback so that references can be made to it at a later stage, and for this reason a printer is invaluable. Where a printer is not available, results are best transcribed on to pre-printed record sheets.

A game or simulation is not, however, the best way to learn the fundamental principles of economics.

> If we want students to 'discover' the significance of specific concepts and relationships, such as the MC = MR equality or the nature of the multiplier effect, a more controlled environment has to be created – one where the *ceteris paribus* assumption can be maintained.[5]

However, once concepts have been learned, simulations, models and games have a reinforcing effect. Once the simple Keynesian model $Y = C + I + G + X - M$ has been studied, what could be better than to have a macrosimulation (e.g. Jones[6]) which illustrates, in a simple interactive diagrammatic manner, the effects of changing the parameters of the model and shows the movement of the system towards a new equilibrium.

Simulations, games and models lend themselves to individual, group and, in some cases, class work. Used sensibly, selectively and systematically they will enhance the learning of economics and provide a cost-effective and quick insight into some aspects of the real world.

Data retrieval and databases

Statistical analysis and data manipulation are becoming increasingly important in the study of economics. Examination boards are making increasing use of economic statistics, mainly in the form of data-response questions but also as part of their multiple-choice questions. Data interpretation is an area where many students have had difficulties, for two main reasons. First, many students find numerical work unpalatable, and secondly, the examination time constraint does not allow for the development of skills and practice required to analyse data successfully. The microcomputer can help to overcome both of these problems.

The microcomputer can not only store and retrieve data but it can also carry out complex calculations, sort data, tabulate results and produce graphical displays with great speed and accuracy. While students should not do all their data manipulation and interpretation using the computer (the computer is not allowed in examinations, yet), confidence can be built up by using the computer to handle statistics. Moreover, a wider range of economic statistics are capable of being studied; from regional trends (e.g. Hurd, Banks and Greenwood[7]) to comparative country macroeconomic data (e.g. Lumsden and Scott[8]). An important consideration when buying a database package must be the cost and frequency of updated material. This ought to be available at a small additional cost once the initial package has been bought.

Exposing students to data reveals to them that the real world is far less organised than textbooks would have us believe. Exact relationships do not exist in the social sciences, and econometric problems such as multi-collinearity are a direct result of this. However, the benefits of being able to discover relationships first-hand must outweigh these problems. The student who can be shown the correlation between money supply figures and inflation rates, for example, is likely to be eager to learn about a theory that is capable of explaining this.

Considerable guidance has to be given to students when beginning to work with data. Since teachers do not have the time to use databases exhaustively, students must be expected to do a significant amount of work on their own or in small groups. The teacher must ensure that time is being spent profitably. It is useful to give students data-response-type questions to investigate and answer using the database. A good database package will provide comprehensive and tested data-response questions. Not only can these act as a guide to investigation but they may also be incorporated into the general flow of teaching, using the computer as an electronic blackboard or as a revision aid to consolidate learning.

Data sources such as the *Annual Abstract of Statistics* and *Economic and Regional Trends* are becoming increasingly expensive. A comprehensive database has the advantage therefore of becoming a source of current data. This is available for use by other departments who may even be willing to help out with the initial cost.

There will be far more databases on the market in the future and, like all software, these will become increasingly sophisticated. With experience, the teacher will be able to use such databases in a number of different ways. The greatest advantages of using microcomputers in economics are likely to be gained in this area.

Computer-assisted instruction

Computer-assisted instruction (CAI) is the use of the computer as a teacher substitute where the computer actively teaches the student. CAI programs are of two sorts: one approach is to provide students with information in a similar fashion to a textbook (reading) and the other is to use a programmed learning approach (drill and practice). Some CAI packages contain both (e.g. Attfield and Duck[9]). The boundaries between computer-assisted instruction and other modes of computer-assisted learning are blurred. Some packages will contain simulation and data retrieval elements and others may lean towards computer-managed learning.

The book is a far more flexible tool than the computer, not least because of its portability. Attempts to mirror the textbook with instruction in the form of 'pages' on the computer screen have not been successful. The one benefit with the computer is that diagrams can be built up step by step) which is rarely done in textbooks. It is far more difficult to scan forwards and backwards on a computer as one would do with a book, and what is the equivalent of those pencil notes in the margin? The computer may provide stimulus to the student but the distinction between enthusiasm for the computer and enthusiasm for economics is important to bear in mind.

Programmed instruction is the provision of a sequence of structured questions (based on frames of text) to which the student is expected to respond. The computer has the advantage of providing immediate feedback. When a question is answered incorrectly, the computer gives additional help to the student and the question is posed again. Programmed instruction is best used where topics have to be learned in a systematic fashion, such as national income accounting. It also provides an excellent revision aid. Programmed instruction can be found in books, so the extent to which the computer is used must depend on the quality of the programs available. The computer should only be used if it is seen as a more valuable aid.

CAI packages often provide multiple-choice-type questions. The obvious advantage is that answers can be 'marked' immediately and an appropriate response given. On the whole, however, there is an insufficient number of questions provided.

CAI programs, even more than other software, must be well designed. The computer can expect resistance in this area if CAI is not better than the average teacher. Whereas the use of computers in handling data provides obvious benefits to the economist, the benefits of CAI in the teaching of economics have still to be proven.

The electronic blackboard

Computers make excellent demonstration tools, thus benefiting many students simultaneously. Connected to a large TV monitor, the computer can be used to supplement the blackboard or overhead projector. Although the computer is limited to what has been programmed, one program may provide the equivalent of huge piles of overhead transparencies. Moreover, the computer is able to display programs in a dynamic manner. The traditional monopoly diagram can be built up step by step, or the circular flow of income can be seen to flow (e.g. Jones[10]). The computer used by the teacher as a quick calculating aid is another use of the electronic blackboard, especially when packages are used that can turn those calculations into graphical displays.

The main problem with computer graphics, however, is their lack of accuracy. Even when computers and monitors with high resolution graphics are used, results can be disappointing. Showing accurate tangencies between indifference curves and budget lines is particularly difficult, for example, with the result that students may produce diagrams that are equally poor. Colourful overhead projector slides will produce better results when built up from overlays.

Computer-managed learning

Computer-managed learning (CML) is an administrative tool, selecting what learning should be performed next, testing the student, and reporting back to the teacher. This can release teachers from the management side of teaching.

A CML system will normally operate in modules, deciding which module the student should study next. There will be some basic instruction and references to books and other resources. When the student has finished a module, the computer tests his/her knowledge of it. If students have not mastered certain parts of the module then extra work can be given. The performance of students is recorded by the computer which can subsequently provide a report for the teacher.

It is unlikely the CML will be employed by the typical economics department in schools. In sixth-form and tertiary colleges, however, there may be a significant role.

Practical considerations

Once the economics department has decided to use CAL in principle, its first consideration must be towards the computer itself. Undoubtedly on occasions the computing department will be able to provide a computer, but if it is to be used to any great extent it is worth considering the purchase of one. The cost of a microcomputer is falling to such an extent that it can now be afforded by most departments. Alternatively, the computer could be shared between two or three departments and allocated on a booking system. However, bear in mind that it is not just the computer that has to be purchased. A monitor, disc drive (infinitely preferable to a cassette player), discs, and possibly a printer, and paper will have to be bought, and in some cases this can add up to more than the computer

itself. Once the system is installed, however, the marginal cost of its use is very low.

Most programs used in the department will be bought in. Some may be written by teachers and the county will probably have some form of distribution system for these. Unlike with books, publishers are reluctant to issue inspection copies for fear of 'pirating'. Most software houses are willing to provide demonstrations at conferences and at teachers' meetings. Some will also provide demonstration discs at a small charge, refundable if software is subsequently purchased. Programs should be easy to use and the language appropriate.

Attractiveness is a key consideration. If a computer is capable of colourful displays, then this facility should be used. If the software is flexible, it may well be capable of use elsewhere. Packages on the location of industry, regional problems and population may be purchased jointly by the economics and geography departments for example. Programs designed for 14–16 economics may well be used in social studies lessons. Check that software has been through field trials so that most problems will already be ironed out.

On the whole, software written by a team is of a superior standard to other packages. An expert programmer and an expert economics teacher are likely to produce a better end result than an individual trying to do everything. Software is being produced all the time and older programs are being replaced by more sophisticated ones. The best way to keep up to date with these is to look at the Economics Association's journal where reviews and charts of current availability are provided regularly.

The documentation and teacher materials provided with software packages are important. The computing industry has a tradition of producing unreadable or inadequate manuals. Documentation should be explicit and without jargon, capable of being understood by non-specialists. Teacher materials must be helpful.

Student materials should also be of a high quality. They should be flexible enough to motivate the student to use the software while allowing the student to work independently: experimenting and investigating. The material must be comprehensive and highlight the issues surrounding the subject-matter. This does tend to be neglected. One program on monetary policy, for example, has supporting material that does not mention the word 'inflation'.

Using the computer in the classroom requires additional considerations, especially if the computer is to be moved around. The best way of moving the computer is on a trolley specially designed for the purpose. However, where stairs are involved some other method must be found. Cables should be kept out of the way and checks should be made beforehand that sufficient powerpoints are available. For demonstration purposes, more than one monitor may be needed. When working in groups, size is important. Six members is an absolute maximum with four about optimum. If the CAL involves a competition, bear in mind that lower-ability students may well feel uncomfortable. Where possible, use the computer in a variety of different ways. For practical help, laboratory technicians and older students with experience will be particularly useful.

Finally, it is important to bear in mind the time it takes to set up the computer. Be prepared if something goes wrong and always keep backup copies of software. Publishers generally do not mind copies of discs being made for this purpose.

Economics and computer education

Computers have a tremendous effect on the social and economic structure of countries and all students need to know something of the nature and uses of computers as part of a general education. It is impossible to be fully aware of the working of our society without making reference to the use of computers in government, industry, finance and commerce.

Computer appreciation courses looking at these issues are now widespread in schools. It has been suggested by some (e.g. Welford[11]) that this type of course should be run alongside a social studies/humanities framework in order to establish a firm link between the study of the computer and the social sciences. Thus the economist may well be called upon to accept some responsibility for the computer education in schools. To omit the study of the computer in its broadest sense would be a grave mistake. The connection between the social sciences (particularly economics) and computer education is a strong one. There is a role, therefore, for the active participation of the economics teacher.

Conclusion

Although mainly anecdotal, research evidence on the effectiveness of CAL is encouraging. A study by Wood[12] using a multiplier program[13] found a significant improvement in A-level multiple-choice answers on the concept by students using the package.

The microcomputer can act as a motivator, it enables teachers to focus on particular aspects of an issue and, as more CAL material becomes available, it will be increasingly flexible. It is vital that only robust programs

are used. Oversimplistic approaches, for example, may lead to misrepresentation of the subject-matter. Selectivity is the key to the use of software.

Microcomputers should not be used as teaching aids without serious consideration. They should only be used if they improve the quality of teaching. CAL has nothing to fear from rigorous scrutiny in order to identify those uses of the computer that will be wasteful:

> Such experiments must be made; there is a moral obligation both to the children involved, and to the taxpayer who foots the bill, to provide effective education.[14]

The time is right to be using computers and using the materials being produced. In that way economics teachers themselves can be part of this great educational experiment.

Notes and references

1 Maddison, A., *Microcomputers in the Classroom* (Hodder & Stoughton, 1982) pp. 65–73.

2 Carter, H., and Greenwood, A. G., *Teddy Tales – The Story of a Firm* (Longman, 1984).

3 BP Educational Service, *The Paraffin File* (BP, 1983).

4 Lumsden, K. G., and Scott, A., *Running the British Economy* (Longman, 1982–6).

5 Hurd, S. J., 'Microcomputers in economics education', in Atkinson, B. *Teaching Economics* (Heinemann Educational Books, 1985).

6 Jones, R. H., *An Introduction to National Income Models* (Beecon Educational Software, 1983).

7 Hurd, S. J., Banks, B., and Greenwood, A. G., *Regional Statistics* (Longman, 1984).

8 Lumsden, K. G., and Scott, A., *Macroeconomic Data Base* (Longman, 1984).

9 Attfield, C., and Duck, N., *Economics in Action* (McGraw-Hill, 1984).

10 Jones, op. cit.

11 Welford, R. J., 'Computers in social education', *Computers in Schools,* vol. 6, no. 2, January 1984, pp. 47–9.

12 Wood, K. R. J., 'Case study of computer assisted instruction in economics', *University of London Institute of Education Research Paper in Economics Education* (1983).

13 Randall, K. V., *The Multiplier* (Longman, 1980).

14 Maddison, op. cit.

28 Data-response Questions in Teaching A-Level Economics*

Roy Wilkinson

*An earlier version of this chapter appeared in *Economics*, vol. XVI, pt. 3, no. 71, autumn 1980, pp. 69–73.

Introduction

Although examination boards differ in the importance they attach to data-response questions and in the style of their data-response papers, they all now use such questions. This means that some attention needs to be given by all economics teachers to the problem of coping with what for many is still a very unfamiliar activity.

Books of data-response questions and material continue to appear, but they are of limited value to the teacher for several reasons. On the whole they have the useful but limited educational objective of simply providing practice for examinations. Even in this they give limited guidance to the teacher, usually an indication of the correct approach to an answer, or the correct answer in the case of problems. But an explicit consideration of the skills assessed and how the question examines them is often lacking, and questions covering a wide range of skills, some very elementary, some very complex, get lumped together. Teachers generally lack guidance on how to get their students to the stage where these questions can be used, that is, where they have acquired some skills with handling data.

For many teachers, the data-response question is something to be practised immediately before the examination or, if they devote any teaching time to it, at best it is a technique tacked on to the end of the course. Teachers often complain about the lack of time for teaching when a data-response paper is introduced into the examination syllabus. They see it as something to be added to the course, rather than a different approach which simply calls for a modification of their current practices. In my view, the use of data-response questions offers a different and potentially more stimulating and exciting way of presenting ideas and acquiring knowledge and understanding. By integrating such questions and exercises into the teaching process, it is possible to develop the skills that examiners seek to test.

The purpose of this chapter is to argue the case for using data-response questions as part of normal teaching technique and to offer some guidance on the construction and evaluation of data-response questions.

Types of data-response question

It will help to clarify briefly what I mean by a data-response question. I do not propose to embark on an exhaustive taxonomy, though this can (and doubtless will) be done, but simply to distinguish 'problems' from questions demanding interpretative and evaluative skills. The former are usually based on material specially constructed to lead to a correct answer. Typical of this is the kind of question that provides hypothetical times series data on consumption expenditure and disposable income and asks for the value of the marginal propensity to consume or the multiplier. Such questions are adaptations or developments of textbook examples to illustrate a concept and to fix it in the student's mind. They may be contrasted with, for example, data on fixed capital formation and national income obtained from the *National Income Blue Book* or, say, a piece of prose dealing with disinvestment in a region and its repercussions, each coupled with questions to assess whether or not students can identify the multiplier and apply their knowledge of it.

The questions I shall deal with are of the second variety. They demand of the student the skill (i) to interpret data whether expressed in figures or words, (ii) to 'translate' figures into words or a piece of prose into technical economic terms, (iii) to apply concepts and theories to the data, and (iv) to evaluate the implications of arguments arising from the data.

The rationale of data-response questions

Data-response questions have emerged partly as a result of the desire for greater relevance and reality in the teaching of economics. Increasingly, it is becoming accepted that an A-level course should, among other things, give the student a flavour of real economics and that this is best achieved by giving them some real data to think about. This helps both to focus the attention on particular issues and to provide the context for a little positive economics.

The analysis of problems involves first a process of

observation that leads to the collection of data to illustrate the possible relationship or phenomenon. This automatically leads to speculation on causes and consequences that we call theorising: a process that involves abstraction and simplification. Finally, there is the confrontation between the predictions of the theory and the facts. To acquire the feeling for this process requires the kind of activities that dominate the working lives of economists, namely, using sources, applying (elementary) statistical method, evaluating data, theories and policies and communicating results. These are broadly the kinds of skill that can be assessed by the type of question discussed above.

What does the student stand to gain from this sort of activity? First, it is a different and more interesting challenge than struggling with a textbook, not least for the less 'academic'. Abstraction and the reference to unfamiliar problems or data often encountered in textbooks can lead to frustration and boredom. Secondly, students will discover at first hand that any 'answers' to economic questions have to be qualified by assumptions and are at best provisional. There are no simple 'model' answers to most serious economic problems.

Finally, it is easier for most people to think in terms of a concrete example, and a feeling of relevance and participation can be developed. Thus, the teacher is likely to create a more receptive class. There are, however, costs in terms of the extra work required to develop questions and to integrate them into the existing teaching programme. It is to these problems that we now turn.

Setting questions

It should be apparent from the foregoing that there is more to the construction of data-response questions than finding some interesting-looking statistics or prose passage and, in effect, asking the student to comment on it. Questions need to be related to clear teaching objectives and to be built around an idea of the skills they are intended to test.

Ideally, questions reflect and give practice in the scientific analysis of issues. This involves observation, theory, and verification (of the predictions of theory against factual data). A well-constructed question will involve the student in the whole process. The teacher makes the initial observation and sees the relevance of theory and the nature of the application as well as the wider implications of the analysis. The student can then, in effect, be asked to confirm the observation by describing the main features of some statistics or by summarising a line of argument using the skill of 'translation' referred to above. Then the student can be asked to recognise the piece of theory that underlies the prose or statistics and which can be used to analyse the problem and, finally, to evaluate how well the facts verify the theory and perhaps to speculate about the predictions of the theory.

Although it is not quite true to say that one always starts from a theoretical concept and finds the data to illustrate it, to have this theoretical requirement in one's mind helps in the selection and editing of material. Newspaper articles that do not lead to a reasonably accessible theoretical application are on the whole useless for our purpose. Similarly, it is the concept in mind that is the main criterion used in judging the relevance of a statistical table. Since both prose passages and statistics have been produced for other purposes, it is very unlikely that they will be suitable as they stand. Both can prove daunting to a student unless carefully edited; both may require supplementation from other sources.

Teachers wishing to develop their own data-response questions should find it useful to bear in mind the following points:

1 Start from a theoretical concept or ask what theory is illustrated by the statistics or prose.
2 Confirm that it is within the students' range and will not be found impossibly difficult.
3 Eliminate anything that is not relevant to the questions to be asked, if possible. (i) For prose passages this is relatively straightforward, bearing in mind the theoretical criterion discussed above. (ii) For statistics, the number of observations may need to be reduced so as not to 'outface' the student. Where the intention is to show a trend in something like, for example, the composition of income, it may be sufficient to show one year in two or three rather than the whole series. (iii) A limit may need to be placed on the number of variables. For example, to include in a question tables of all potential influences on the demand for private housing would easily confuse the student. It would usually be sufficient to take price, income, loans and the rate of interest.
4 Give a guide to the source of the data in, at least, a footnote. This is a good practice to instil into the student and, in the case of examination questions, a footnote may contain a clue to the interpretation of the data.
5 Finally, have in mind a time constraint so that the student is not burdened unduly. A long tedious task may kill interest and confidence.

Teaching with data-response questions

Apart from the problem of finding or creating suitable questions, the main problem that faces the teacher is that of integrating data-response questions into the existing syllabus. Since data-response examination questions are intended to test certain skills, it makes sense to begin the development of these skills as soon as possible in a course, since this is an area where improvement and confidence come with experience and practice. This means that some data-response material is required for each part of the course to be used as a means of developing understanding.

The type of question outlined above encompasses three levels of skill, beginning with the descriptive and progressing to the analytical and evaluative. From the very beginning, students can be given exercises in summarising prose passages and sets of tables so that they learn to extract the essential line of argument in either. Such exercises can be supplemented by statistical work designed to give confidence in the use of sources and in manipulating numerical data such as measuring percentage changes, creating indexes, plotting time-series and relating observations of variables on a scatter diagram. In my experience, students are very bad in examinations at distinguishing between relative and absolute changes, and between absolute values and indexes. Data-response questions reveal these deficiencies and data-response questions can be used to remedy them. Students may be given exercises in which they can learn in the context of an economic problem the meaning of indexes, annual percentage changes, etc.

Apart from helping to focus the teaching, practice in relatively straightforward tasks from an early stage can help to avoid the sort of weaknesses that are commonly found in examination candidates. When confronted with a set of tables and being inexperienced in knowing what to look for, candidates commonly resort to a line-by-line, column-by-column recitation of the data or, in the case of prose, an almost verbatim reproduction of the passage. When data are incorporated into teaching, students auto-matically know the context and, in that sense, know what to look for, and they can be taught to look for a pattern and to bring out the essentials from the tables or passage. Quite simple rules need to be instilled such as: (i) check the title of tables, (ii) check the definitions of variables, and (iii) check the footnotes. These may appear rather trivial and obvious things to do but they are vitally important. Good statistical tables and diagrams are the outcome of a process of logic and it is merely a piece of applied logic to check the component parts of a table or diagram. It will also contribute towards making the student more precise and careful in the discussion of data. In summarising a prose passage it is good practice to get the student to underline what they judge to be the key sentences that advance the argument before 'translating' them into their own prose.

The next stage of identifying and applying relevant theory can only come when the student has some grasp of the concepts and analysis. Quite when this should be introduced will depend upon the ability and interest of the class, but in my view these are quite difficult skills and therefore it is important that through writing essays, practising objective questions and solving problems, the student has acquired some familiarity with, and grasp of, concepts. When this stage has been achieved, students can be set the data they have previously used for practising the basic skills, with the instruction to identify the underlying theory and, perhaps, to examine the predictions of the theory that are relevant.

The attempt at analysis and verification merges with evaluative tasks and it may be difficult to maintain this distinction in a teaching context. When data-response questions are being used as a basis for group discussion this may also be unnecessary. The objective of teaching at this stage is to encourage the student to look at the data as the outward manifestation of the operation of an economic theory or model and therefore to learn to approach any data with the automatic expectation that there will be an underlying theoretical principle, such as the investment multiplier, a demand curve, price elasticity, and so on. A second objective, which should reinforce what is gained from essay writing, is that the process of evaluating the predictions of theory rests very much on the assumptions that underlie the analysis and that there are thus no simple or straightforward answers to questions. What matters is the quality of the argument and its supporting evidence.

This then leads to a list of points that students need to have in mind in dealing with data-response questions:

1   When asked to summarise an argument or a set of statistics, do not try to describe everything in minute detail or reproduce the piece of prose exactly. This defeats the object of the question. The purpose is to summarise and this involves being selective and eliminating extraneous material. Look for a pattern in statistical data. Find the purpose and then the conclusion of a piece of prose and concentrate on the main line of argument that connects them.

2   In dealing with statistical tables, read the headings and footnotes carefully. They may give clues to the inter-pretation of the data and perhaps the approach to the question. Make a careful note of the definitions of all variables and categories.

3   The set of tables or prose passage are likely to be based on the assumption of the existence of some kind of economic relationship such as a demand curve, a model of market price determination, etc. Always seek to identify the underlying relationship. The exploration of the implications of a prose argument or a set of tables can be approached by thinking of the predictions of the underlying theory.

4   Remember that the purpose of this type of question is to test skills of observation and particularly the ability to use and appraise economic analysis. Inferences drawn from theory are only as good as the assumptions and arguments on which they are based. There is no single correct answer to these questions. Therefore do not be afraid of exercising judgement and arguing to a conclusion. Assessment of students is based on the quality of argument rather than the conclusion reached.

This sort of information should be given to students when they are being introduced to data-response questions; 1 and 2 apply to the first stage whereas 3 and 4 apply to the more advanced stage. If, as suggested, data-response questions are incorporated at all stages in teaching rather than tacked on to the end of a course, then various 'external benefits' automatically accrue. The student gains experience and confidence as he or she becomes familiar with a range of material and a method of handling it. Some degree of integration of ideas is achieved, especially between 'theory' and 'applied' economics which often seem to be taught out of quite separate economic boxes.

Conclusion

It has been emphasised that the use of data-response questions in teaching requires a particular approach to the subject based on what is generally termed 'positive economics'. The successful integration of data-response into teaching requires there to be clear educational objectives so that the questions can be constructed to reflect them.

An essential part of the process of integration is to introduce easier questions dealing with basic skills early in a course and, indeed, to make it part of the teaching process so that it contributes to the student acquiring new ideas. It is important to pace the introduction of data-response material so as not to reduce the student's confidence. To this end it helps to start with easy questions and progress to more difficult ones (based on the identical material) later on in the course.

Finally, just as it is important that teachers have a clear idea of what they are doing and why they are doing it, the student should be clear about what these questions are intended to achieve. This is often a major stumbling block when approaching examinations. Essays and objective tests are familiar; data-response questions are not. Students are therefore often worried and puzzled as to what is expected of them. It seems reasonable to give them the sort of information listed in 1–4 above when setting exercises, so that they can feel actively involved and able to exert some degree of control over what they do. It is, moreover, important not only for reassurance but as part of the educational process to discuss the precise requirements of a question so that if they are not met it is because of weaknesses in economics rather than misunderstandings about the requirements of the question.

Further reading

Wilkinson, R. K., 'Problems of external assessment in economics', in Lee, N. (ed.) *Teaching Economics* (Heinemann Educational Books, 1975).

Wilkinson, R. K., 'Statistics in sixth form economics', *Teaching Statistics*, vol. 1, no. 1, 1979.

Wilkinson, R. K., 'Examining economics at 18 + ', in Atkinson, B. (ed.) *Teaching Economics* (Heinemann Educational Books, 1985).

List of available data-response books

Anderton, A. G., *Data Response Workpack* (University Tutorial Press, 1982).

Bardsley, J., and Nettleship, J., *Data Response Questions in Economics* (privately published: 24 Woodlands Grove, Preston, 1983).

Dade-Robertson, S. M., *Comprehension Questions for Advanced Level Economics* (Economics Association, 1978).

Livesey, F., *Data Response Questions in Economics* (Polytech Publishers, 1976).

Oliver, J. M., *Data Response Questions in A Level Economics* (Heinemann Educational Books, 1982).

Oliver, J. M., *The Economist: Data Response in A Level Economics* (Collins, 1984).

Walker, S., *Data Response in Economics* (Longman, 1984).

Watts, M., and Glew, M., *Worked Examples in Data Response Questions for A Level Economics* (Heinemann Educational Books, 1982).

29   Pre-vocational Courses

Philip Negus

Introduction

The Certificate of Pre-Vocational Education (CPVE) represents the merging of a series of developments in post-16 education. These developments include:

1   The publication in 1979 of *A Basis for Choice*[1] by the Further Education Unit (FEU).

2   The establishment of the Business Education Council (BEC) and the introduction of their General Certificate/Diploma in Business Studies.

3   The introduction of foundation courses and the Vocational Preparation (General) Certificate by the City and Guilds of London Institute.

4   Similar developments by the Royal Society of Arts with clerical and distribution vocational preparation courses.

All of these developments represent an attempt to provide an education suited to the needs of the 'less-academic' sixth-former or further-education student. As unemployment has risen and as the structure of the job market has changed, so the 'new sixth' has expanded. Traditional educational practice and single-subject academic examinations were seen to be inappropriate as were many of the traditional craft courses in further education. As the vocational preparation courses have spread so the single-subject alternative, the Certificate of Extended Education, has stagnated and the Keohane Report[2] been forgotten.

A Basis for Choice

A Basis for Choice (ABC) does not lay down a syllabus nor does it specify detailed means of assessment. It sets out a curriculum framework within which pre-vocational courses can develop. A key element of the framework is that 60 per cent of a student's time should be devoted to a core of numeracy; communications; economic, social and environmental studies, while the remaining 40 per cent should be divided between a general study of a broad vocational area and training in the skills required for a particular job.

An influential aspect of the ABC framework is a statement of twelve aims for the core studies. Although they have been modified in later editions of ABC and in the mass of supporting documents that have appeared, they give a clear indication of the flavour of pre-vocational courses. It is perhaps possible to define pre-vocational courses as courses that meet the aims of ABC. Table 29.1 sets out the aims in an abbreviated form. Each aim is illustrated by a range of objectives. 'To bring about an informed perspective as to the role and status of a young person in an adult society and the world of work' is broken down into such specific objectives as:

1 'Describe a typical organisational structure of at least two different types of workplace.'
2 'Visit a place of work, relevant to the student's interests.'[3]

Aims and objectives imply a content. Thus although ABC does not claim to be a syllabus, courses pursuing ABC aims do tend to display similarities. More important than the implications for content are the implications for process. Some aims, number 8 for example, imply a method of delivery. They imply use of experiential learning, negotiation and counselling to a much greater degree than traditional subject-based, content-determined qualifications. Recognising this shift of emphasis from content to process, the FEU has produced a series of reports dealing with the implications of pre-vocational courses, the two most useful of which are *ABC in Action* (September 1981) and *Vocational Preparation* (January 1981). All of the reports are available direct from the FEU.

Because of the nature of the content and process it is

advocating, ABC also has implications for questions of assessment. Single-subject end-of-year written examinations are inappropriate for pre-vocational courses and for the types of student who are likely to be attracted to such courses. ABC suggests that a system of formative profiling should be an integral element of pre-vocational courses. Accurate profiling requires accurate assessment and this in turn raises technical questions of norm and criterion-referenced tests. Those courses that come closest to ABC philosophy lay great stress on profiling, on course assessment and graded tests that may be taken when the student feels ready.

Table 29.1   Aims of the common core in pre-vocational courses

1	To bring about an informed perspective as to the role and status of a young person in an adult society and the world of work.
2	To provide a basis from which a young person can make an informed and realistic decision with respect to his or her immediate future.
3	To bring about continuing development of physical and manipulative skills in both vocational and leisure contexts, and an appreciation of those skills in others.
4	To bring about an ability to develop satisfactory personal relationships with others.
5	To provide a basis on which the young person acquires a set of moral values applicable to issues in contemporary society.
6	To bring about a level of achievement in literacy, numeracy and graphicacy appropriate to ability, and adequate to meet the basic demands of contemporary society.
7	To bring about competence in a variety of study skills likely to be demanded of the young person.
8	To encourage the capacity to approach various kinds of problems methodically and effectively, and to plan and evaluate courses of action.
9	To bring about sufficient political and economic literacy to understand the social environment and participate in it.
10	To bring about an appreciation of the physical and technological environments and the relationship between these and the needs of man in general, and working life in particular.
11	To bring about a development of the coping skills necessary to promote self-sufficiency in young people.
12	To bring about a flexibility of attitude and a willingness to learn, sufficient to manage future changes in technology and career.

Pre-vocational courses

GCE and CSE boards have not been very active in developing pre-vocational courses. The initiatives have come from bodies associated with post-16 education and training, like BEC, RSA, and City and Guilds and, of course, the Manpower Services Commission. Examining bodies are rather like oligopolies and one of their objectives is to increase their market share. Competition has been keen and has resulted in a confusing range of courses. However, despite this profusion of new courses, it is possible to pick out common features, most of which derive from the same type of educational thinking that produced ABC.

Some common features

1 The published guidelines are couched in terms of aims and objectives rather than content. Teachers are free, subject to external moderation, to design a content that reflects local needs and abilities.
2 Courses are designed to provide progression to further education, training or work.
3 There tends to be a basic structure of an integrated core plus options. Some schemes allow for other examinable subjects to be 'bolted on' to the basic course package. The Business Education Council, now merged with the Technician Education Council to form BTEC, is far less happy with the idea of adding additional subjects to its courses than is the City and Guilds, and there is no doubt that 'bolting on' options examined by another body does undermine the integrated nature of pre-vocational courses.
4 Pre-vocational courses are integrated courses. They are designed 'for young people who will benefit from broad-based integrated courses or training programmes'.[4] The organisation of such courses 'requires careful integration of material if needless duplication is to be avoided and students are to receive a coherent package of studies.'[5]
    The importance of integration is stressed in two ways. Within the core, the skills of numeracy, communications and problem-solving must be integrated with the investigation of substantive areas such as business organisation, pollution, unemployment and housing. The aim is to give reality and meaning to what can be regarded by students as meaningless exercises as well as to avoid duplication. It is also important to integrate the core and the vocational options. The teacher of a vocational skill such as typewriting is also a teacher of basic numeracy and communications.
5 Learning is experiential, participatory and student-centred. Although some pre-vocational aims tend to imply a narrow concern with training, the overall philosophy of courses like Vocational Preparation (General) and of the CPVE lies in the liberal-progressive tradition of Rousseau and Dewey.
6 The curriculum is a matter for negotiation between the participants in the course, including the students themselves.
7 Pre-vocational courses include real or simulated work experience.

8 Various assessment methods are used rather than just a single end-of-course examination. BTEC courses, for example, make considerable use of assignments.
9 Use is made of formative and summative profiling.

Not all pre-vocational courses display these characteristics to the same degree. They range from the radical, potentially subversive City and Guilds Vocational Preparation (General) to the more traditional BTEC General Certificate/Diploma which is made up of subject-based modules. Interested teachers should contact the various examining bodies for more specific details of each course.

The certificate of pre-vocational education (CPVE)

Although a number of pilot schemes were run during 1984–5 the CPVE only became readily available to all 16+ students during 1985–6. Documents issued by the Joint Board for Pre-vocational Education show that to be acceptable to the Board, CPVE schemes must incorporate many of the views espoused by the Further Education Unit.

The aim of the CPVE is to provide a framework, within which courses suited to local needs can be developed. To satisfy the Joint Board a CPVE programme must include:

1 core, vocational and additional studies;
2 appropriate learning strategies;
3 negotiation, profiling and guidance.

Core and vocational studies must be co-ordinated so that students experience them as a coherent whole. The Joint Board classifies vocational studies into five categories: Business and Administrative Services; Technical Services; Production; Distribution; Services to People. Each category is broken down into 'clusters' of occupational roles that may be simply 'explored', or studied to a 'preparatory' stage that may in turn provide progression to an existing vocational course.

Anyone who has the good fortune to become involved in CPVE developments will need to obtain the *CPVE Handbook* from the Joint Board. It contains useful advice on how to set up and run a CPVE programme as well as reports on the initial pilot schemes.

Some practical issues

The contribution of economics

When considering their contribution to pre-vocational courses, it is easy for economists to concentrate on those aims that stress economic, social and political literacy. Clearly, the content of economics is important in meeting these aims and it is possible for any teacher of economics to draw up a list of knowledge and concepts necessary for such 'literacy'. For the economist to adopt this approach is, however, to devalue the subject. Economics has a much wider contribution to make to the general education of adolescents.

Pre-vocational courses are as much concerned with skills as with knowledge. A quick look at any document dealing with this area will produce references to: problem-solving; coping skills; social skills; manipulative skills and 'effective participation'. Academic economics in schools has become increasingly concerned with problem-solving and with the application of concepts to practical issues. There has been a growing stress on the understanding of data such as official statistics and reports. The challenge for the teacher of economics is to develop teaching strategies that will expand this approach so that it meets the needs of less academic students and enables them to develop the skills needed for economic survival in an industrial society. Table 29.3 gives an indication of some of the aims the economics teacher should be thinking of meeting.

Integration

There are degrees of integration. At its lowest level it might mean little more than dividing the week into four or five blocks of time with a member of staff responsible for each block. A regular team meeting then ensures that the content of each block is kept in step (Figure 29.1). Thus in a particular week there may be separate but related lessons on, for example, hire purchase, calculating percentages, understanding advertisements, and consumer protection.

BTEC General courses operate at a slightly higher level of integration. Although each module may be taught by different teachers in periods clearly labelled 'World of Work' or 'People and Communication', courses are integrated around periodic cross-modular assignments. One of the aims of such assignments, which are supposed to satisfy objectives drawn from each of the core modules, is to 'help the student integrate the knowledge, understanding and skills acquired in the core studies by applying them to practical business problems'.[6] An example of such an assignment is one that asks part-time students to draw up a description of their job and of the firm for which they work to be circulated to applicants for a position shortly to be advertised. Additional tasks could include drafting letters of invitation for interview; preparing a map and directions for interviewees; calculating travelling expenses to be paid to inverviewees. This assignment is based on reality and involves practical tasks. It meets objectives from all three core modules and involves a range of skills.

A fully integrated scheme does away with subject labels and divisions. All that will appear on timetables is 'Core Studies'. Basic skills in numeracy, communication and problem-solving are developed through practical projects set in a range of contexts. Some examples of integrated projects appear in Table 29.2 and Figure 29.2.

The first step in moving towards an integrated scheme is for the subject specialist to 'match' the content of his specialism and the teaching/learning strategies adopted to the aims listed in Table 29.1. Table 29.3 suggests the form

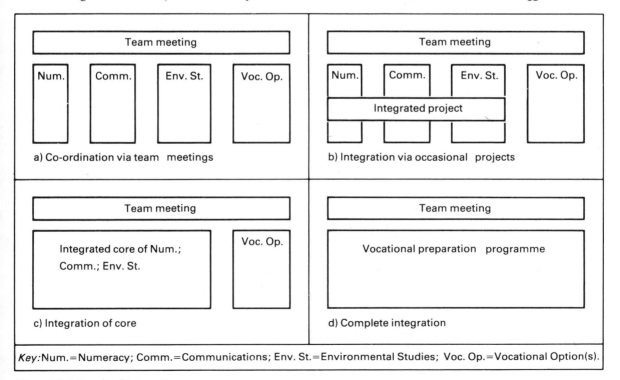

Figure 29.1 Levels of integration

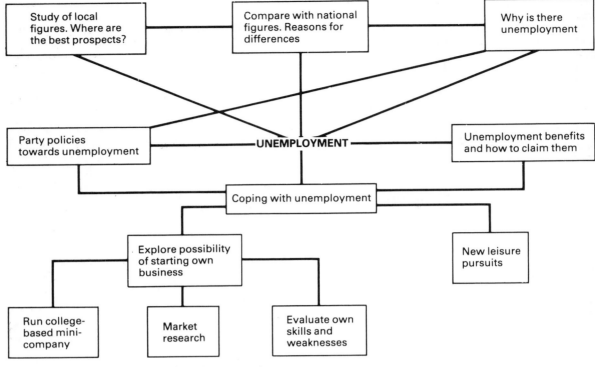

Figure 29.2 An integrated theme based on unemployment

Table 29.2   An integrated scheme of work (layout reflects that suggested by the City and Guilds of London Institute)

Aims	Content	Method/activity	Assessment
1, 6, 11	Finding accommodation a) Buying a house	Discuss case studies of four different ages.	
		Students select a case and two possible properties from local newspapers.	Suitability of properties selected in terms of cost, location and design.
		Obtain full details by visiting estate agent.	
		Students research problems that may arise in older houses. Use copies of surveyors' reports, personal experience.	Students compile guide for house buyer listing items to look for. List assessed for comprehensiveness and clarity.
		Visit local environmental health office for information on grants.	Produce material advertising grants. Assess for accuracy and impact.
		Talk by building society manager followed by completing a mortgage application form.	Students write letter of thanks to manager. Assess for legibility, layout, grammar, spelling.
			Assess completed form for accuracy.

Note: Numbers refer to the aims in Table 29.1

this exercise might take. Following from this 'matching' exercise it may be necessary to consider how far economics can be 'modified' to meet aims and objectives so far not attained. This 'modification' is as likely in the field of teaching/learning strategies as it is in that of content.

Table 29.3   Matching exercise

ABC Aim	Economist's commentary
1	Economist can provide information on the labour market and wage differentials. Can also offer explanations.
6	Economics can offer a range of source materials to be used as a basis for numeracy and communications work, e.g. bank statements, employment figures.
8	There is already a growing emphasis in economics teaching on applying concepts and principles to the solution of problems, e.g. opportunity cost, cost-benefit analysis.
9	This has always been an aim of economics teachers.

After these initial steps the course team may find that although some pre-vocational aims are attained many times over, others are not covered and perhaps cannot be covered no matter how much 'modification' takes place. Once the team recognises this problem it is ready to take a third step towards integration, namely 'extension' (Table 29.4). This step involves injecting something new into the course structure either by one subject area expanding or by the introduction of an interdisciplinary theme or activity. An example of such an activity is the establishment of a college-based 'mini-company'. Many schools and colleges have set up such companies and found that they offer excellent scope to develop problem-solving and social skills as well as involving practical numeracy and communications work.

Table 29.4   Steps to an integrated curriculum

Matching	Asking to what extent the content and teaching of one's own subject is already meeting the aims and objectives of ABC.
Modification	Adapting the subject, as it has been traditionally understood, to fit with the aims and objectives of a more integrated curriculum.
Extension	Identifying curriculum areas which could not be covered by existing subjects and adopting a more interdisciplinary approach to these areas.
Assimilation	Merging the individualism of subjects in a thoroughly integrated approach.

Source: Based on a framework set out in Further Education Unit, *Common Core-Teaching and Learning* (FEU, 1984).

Experiential learning

'This involves learning strategies building on experience and knowledge that students bring to the classroom and devising or simulating experiences to develop that knowledge, rather than relying solely on the student's experiences being selected to illustrate the teacher's curriculum.'[7] Experiential learning is thus not simply 'learning by doing' with the teacher deciding what is to be done. It is the student's background experience that provides the starting point for the activity. The skill of the teacher is to develop the activity beyond the starting point so that desirable learning takes place.

Pre-vocational courses differ in their acceptance of this view of learning. BTEC has a conservative approach to experiential learning, seeing it basically as involving the use of teacher-designed assignments to develop practical and problem-solving skills. The guidelines published by the City and Guilds for Vocational Preparation (General) are much more radical. Taken at face value their literature suggests that a large proportion of a course should be designed with the student as an equal partner in the process. Constraints, however, are imposed mainly by the content of the City and Guilds profile which forms part of the course and by the level of detail required in submissions for course approval.

Although the Further Education Unit sets great store by experiential learning it is questionable how far it can be taken. Students, especially less-able students, take a long time to formulate realistic objectives and they need almost constant support. There is also the question of the nature of the student's experience outside college. A suggested aim for the CPVE is for 'young people both to become aware of their creativity and to develop their powers of critical judgement by experiencing, originating and participating in a range of creative and expressive activities'.[8] Can the restricted experiences of some students outside college really provide the starting point to meet such an aim or should the teacher take the initiative?

Negotiation, counselling and guidance

The learning that takes place will no longer be entirely controlled by the teacher, if it ever was. The teacher must now listen to the expressed needs of the student and agree a set of activities with him. The form of assessment to be used may also be a matter for negotiation. One of the aims of negotiation is to give the student greater responsibility for his own learning. Through the profiling process, the student becomes more aware of his own strengths and weaknesses and of appropriate remedial action. Supporters of profiling claim that it boosts student motivation.

If negotiation with individual students and profiling is to take place, there are clear implications for the organisation of the course. Time has to be found for these activities and this normally means managing the classroom so that individual students can be seen in a reasonable degree of privacy. This plus the fact that students will be following individually negotiated programmes means that the classroom is replaced with a learning workshop, and formal instruction is replaced with individualised learning schemes and the resources to support them.

Resources

For the subject specialist encountering the world of pre-vocational education for the first time, a number of Further Education Unit publications can be regarded as essential reading:

A Basis for Choice (1979).
Active Learning – A Guide (1979).
Vocational Preparation (1981).
ABC in Action (1981).
Common Core Teaching and Learning (1984).

The City and Guilds of London Institute have produced a number of 'Explanatory Notes' giving practical examples of the ways in which each of their foundation courses might be developed. A useful Schools Council publication is *Planning One-year 16–17 Courses*. Each section ends with a list of issues to be decided and an agenda for action, making it an ideal document for a course team to study together in the early stages of developing a course. Like the FEU publications, it is available free of charge. Carroll, S., and McQuade, P., in *The Voc. Prep. Manual* (Framework Press, 1984), provide a range of materials and ideas that should be considered by any course-planning team. The Economics Association has produced a number of items to assist the economics teacher involved in pre-vocational courses. These include the *Working Party Report on the 17+* and the materials produced by the Economics Education 14–16 Project.

Work experience is an important element in pre-vocational courses. The Schools Council Industry Project has produced a very practical booklet called *Schools Industry Practice*. The Project in co-operation with Project Trident has also produced *Work Experience in the School Curriculum*. An alternative to real work experience is a simulated experience on college premises. *The Mini Company Kit* available from the Longman Group provides a package of ideas and materials for teachers who want to set up their own mini-companies.

Notes and references

1   Further Education Unit, *A Basis for Choice* (FEU, 1979).
2   HMSO, *Proposals for a Certificate of Extended Education* (HMSO, 1979).
3   Further Education Unit, *A Basis for Choice*, 2nd edn. (FEU, 1982) p. 30.
4   Royal Society of Arts Examination Board, *Vocational Preparation Courses* (RSA) p. 5.
5   Business and Technician Education Council, *BTEC General Awards in Business Studies* (BTEC, 1983) p. 9.
6   Ibid., p. 11.
7   Further Education Unit, *Common Core-Teaching and Learning* (FEU, 1984) p. 14.
8   Joint Board for Pre-Vocational Education, *Certificate of Pre-Vocational Education: Appendices to Consultative Document* (Joint Board for Pre-Vocational Education, 1984) p. 40.

30   Economics in Further Education

Ann Cotterrell

Introduction

Debates that concern the future of further education have particular relevance for economics teachers. The age of voluntarism in further education is at an end. The politics of curriculum development have expanded beyond the boundaries of the colleges and academically oriented examination and validating boards. Non-advanced further education is now in competition with skill centres for resources, which are likely to be increasingly controlled by the Manpower Services Commission rather than the local education authorities. The control of curriculum development is becoming more centralised, but at the same time it involves a wider range of parties representing a variety of interests.

Vocational relevance is increasingly emphasised as a criterion in evaluating courses. The future of economics education in colleges of further education is likely to depend on the extent to which it is perceived to be vocationally relevant. One of the central problems in the evaluation of courses is the choice as to whose criteria should be used. Vocational relevance, even if it is accepted as a valid criterion, is not necessarily identifiable by objective and unambiguous means. The lecturers, the students, current employers, and local and central government agencies may all have different perceptions of vocational relevance. Economics is particularly affected by this debate because the status of economics in the curriculum and the approaches that are adopted to teaching it depend very much on the particular view of vocational relevance that is adopted and the constituency of students in the colleges at any time.

The population of students has changed in character, thus imposing new demands on the curriculum and teaching approaches. There are therefore pressures for change that derive from the student population and pressures from the various interested groups and coalitions of interested parties which influence developments in further education. A wider variety of agencies is taking an active part in the determination of the content of the curriculum and teaching approaches, including the Manpower Services Commission (MSC) and the Business and Technician Education Council (BTEC). Increasingly, the curriculum must be negotiated with these agencies and at the same time there is growing pressure to make courses attractive to students in order to retain viable classes.

The students

The new further-education student, compared with the typical student a few years ago, is more likely to be under 18 and full time.[1] Although the number of full-time students has increased, there has been a fall in the numbers of overseas students, and this has particularly affected the London colleges which used to attract a disproportionate share of the overseas students.[2] There have therefore been some important changes in the character of the students in further education. The new student is more likely to present challenges in terms of motivation and control, and the new curriculum developments for these students are likely to involve economics teachers both at the pre-vocational and vocational levels. The largest increase in student numbers has been in the CPVE and BTEC General level courses which do not require a four O-level entry qualification.[3]

There is some convergence taking place between the types of students in schools and in non-advanced further education, particularly with the spread of TVEI, CPVE and BTEC courses in schools. In further education however, it is still not uncommon to have a wide range of ages and experience in one class, even if the majority are young, and this can be used as a basis for the development of learning strategies using the experience of the class. *Adults Learning*[4] by Jennifer Rogers contains some interesting ideas and suggestions for teaching adults which can also be used with classes of mixed age groups.

There appears to have been little written discussion of the economics curriculum in a multi-ethnic society, both in schools and in further education. However, there is probably growing awareness that colleges need to look at their textbooks and teaching materials and approaches at all levels to avoid bias on grounds of race or sex. A recent report, *The FE College in a Multi-Ethnic Society*,[5] discusses some of the issues in multi-ethnic education but there remains the need to relate these issues to economics teaching.

In the case of part-time students, there has been a fall in total student numbers.[6] It is difficult to identify those courses that involve economics and much of the fall has obviously been in the traditional engineering apprentice-ship area. However, even in the case of BTEC National level courses, there has been a fall in part-time numbers so that full-time students now constitute 41 per cent of the total compared with 23 per cent in 1979–80.[7] A large proportion of part-time BTEC students are employed in the public sector or the financial sector, and students from the financial sector have declined from their peak numbers in 1980. Of the part-time students, an increasing proportion attend evening classes rather than day-release courses. The approaches to teaching these different groups of students have to vary with their differing needs. In the case of the part-time vocational students, it is important to relate the course to the work the students do, and this is encouraged by the BTEC approaches to learning strategies and assessment.

For the evening students, the strategies have to take account of the fatigue and lack of time for private study that affect many of these students. In some cases, a very high level of motivation is found among evening-class students, and the average age of the class tends to be higher than for day-release classes. This tends to mean that classes are more likely to be missed through domestic and work commitments. In the case of many students on vocational courses, which involve attending evening classes for up to seven hours per week in addition to private study, a very high level of motivation is required and must be fostered by the lecturers and course tutors if the students are to survive the course. The needs of increasing numbers of these students are likely to be met in the future by various distance learning systems, including developments in the Open Tech. At present it seems that the orientation of Open Tech courses will be in the direction of new skill development and the education and training of mature adults, but the impact on economics teachers (in so far as they can be distinguished from teachers of management or new technology) is uncertain at present. (See, for example, news and articles in the *NATFHE Journal* (especially Tolley[8]) or the reports from the Open Tech Unit of the Manpower Services Commission).

Although part-time students may bring their own business experience to the class, assignments related to other organisations are useful to broaden their experience. The increasing proportion of young full-time students makes it even more necessary to look to local industry for support, in the form of visits or visiting speakers, or in allowing their staff time to talk to groups of students visiting the organisation. Although many schools are increasing their links with local industry, these links are particularly important for further-education vocational courses such as BTEC National. Some courses include industrial placements which have to be negotiated with local industry and public-sector organisations. There will probably be an increasing need for teachers in further education to renew their industrial and commercial experience, and a personal view is that the current structures of salary scales and increments do not give sufficient incentive to this kind of mobility.

Part of the problem of adapting the curriculum to the changing student population is the problem of predicting change. The future fall in the 16–18 age group is predictable, and is leading to various changes in educational systems, including possibly more tertiary colleges and increasing links between school sixth forms and further-education colleges. The proportion of 16-year-olds remaining in education, either as full-time self-financed students or on MSC courses, is much harder to predict, and must depend on the economic situation. The balance between full-time and part-time students, the level of academic qualifications, and the choice of courses of future intakes are difficult to predict, so that the changing requirements of the students and of the validating or examining bodies require increasing flexibility from economics teachers. The traditional economics syllabus, with the 'threat' of the external examinations, remains for professional and GCE courses, and the main discretionary area for teachers on these courses is in the learning strategies adopted. However, increasing numbers of students in the next few years are likely to be on Manpower Services Commission courses, and on BTEC courses, where the curriculum may be negotiated with, but more commonly on behalf of, the students, as discussed by Alan Harrison.[9]

Perhaps there is unlikely to be a community of interest between industry, government, students and lecturers regarding the curriculum in colleges, except in so far as students wish to equip themselves better to obtain jobs, and lecturers wish to retain their jobs by meeting student demands and by acquiring resources. If this identity of interest does not exist, or if it is not objectively identifiable by all parties, there is scope for negotiation of the curriculum by the parties involved.

The curriculum

The role of economics in the further-education curriculum was reviewed by Leslie Potts in a useful article[10] that surveys the main courses with substantial economics components. The main areas in which the economics teacher plays a major role are the GCE and professional courses, which are externally examined, and the BTEC courses, which are assessed internally, partly through continuous assessment, and externally moderated. In Scotland there have been developments under the Scottish Business Education Council.[11] Future developments that are likely to affect economics teachers include the 17 + Certificate of Pre-Vocational Education which is still in its development stage.[12]

The role of economics in BTEC and CPVE is discussed by Philip Negus in Chapter 29. The extent to which teachers on these courses regard themselves as 'economics teachers' in the traditional sense is questionable. Economic concepts on the BTEC business studies courses are mostly introduced through the module 'The

Organisation in its Environment', but the objectives of this module include the political, social and legal context of business, and lecturers are expected to teach through student-centred assignments using case studies, role playing and other means that introduce concepts without using disciplinary boundaries. This module may be taught by a multi-disciplinary team (or, quite commonly in practice, an economist and a lawyer), or by an individual, but in either case this module has to be integrated with other modules such as Numeracy and Accounting, People and Communications, through team-work. The evolving requirements of BTEC increasingly necessitate a movement away from lectures or seminars within closed classrooms and instead favour experience-based learning and tutorials on assignment-based learning. (See, for example, the BTEC *Fifth Annual Review of Standards*[13] and the *Discussion Document on Educational Policy*.[14])

The problem is not only one of flexibility of teachers or even development of teachers, but of introducing these new strategies in buildings where the traditional classrooms are ill-equipped for the new teaching/learning strategies. This problem is, however, common to both schools and further education.

A more important problem concerns the fundamental aims of an economics education. According to the BTEC *Discussion Document*: 'The Council's fundamental aim is that students develop the necessary competence for success in their careers in their own, their employers' and the national interest.'[15]

The balance between work-related and general education is very difficult to define and identify. There is a dilemma concerning the extent to which the aim is to improve the economic and political literacy of future citizens and the extent to which the main aim is to concentrate on the immediately vocationally useful. The question of the time scale of the future benefits and the kind of manpower development exercise on which colleges are engaged becomes relevant: whether they are trying to improve the current skills and effectiveness of the labour force or are taking a longer-term view of vocational usefulness. There may also be a choice between the concentration on the development of problem-solving skills and the development of the potential to handle abstract concepts and to engage in the rigorous analysis of traditional economic argument. These questions are crucial for the determination of the economic objectives that must be covered in a business education.

The question of the relevance of further education courses, and of economics in particular, to the needs of industry and commerce has been investigated by a number of writers, and the issue of vocational relevance remains unresolved.

There is the problem of finding out what industry and commerce want from further education both at national and local levels. These problems of vocational relevance are discussed by Bob Challis[16] who reported the results of interviews that two colleges undertook with employers of part-time students. The interviewers found that job-related learning was rarely mentioned, but that the course was expected to provide the students with qualifications and to improve communication skills, personal development and general knowledge. Challis deduced that the idea of vocational relevance is highly ambiguous and its practical realisation not straightforward.

The issue of vocational relevance has important implications for the approach that is likely to be adopted to economics in further education in the future. An interesting study by Alan Pittwood investigated the perceived need by a sample of employers for economic concepts. His empirical work was based on all employers whose students were attending the Buckinghamshire College of Higher Education for the BEC National Certificate course. He found a significant difference between the banks and other organisations in their identification and specification of the need for economics and this was possibly related to the perceived need for economics in preparation for the Institute of Bankers' examinations. However, in the case of other employers, he found that employers have difficulty in identifying and expressing their needs for education and training for their young employees.[17]

The issue of what is vocationally relevant therefore remains in doubt, and economics can claim an important role in vocational education if account is taken of the long-term requirements of the student and the development of the student in ways that are less easily assessed and identified than the development of skills in, for example, numeracy or accounting. It is possible that there is not sufficient awareness generally of the skills that are developed through the study of economics, including the development of the student's ability to organise and evaluate information from a variety of sources, and the ability to use abstract concepts and to explore relationships between concepts. There is also the long-term need for the students to understand the economic environment in which they and their organisations operate, particularly as they progress in the management or trade-union organisation.

Conclusion

The only certain development in the economics curriculum is that it will be part of a process of considerable change as the age distribution of the students and the needs of industry change.

Developments in further education are discussed in the Coombe Lodge Report *The 'New' FE*.[18] In this report Anthony Woollard identified the characteristics of the new FE and suggested that, 'at its best the FE college is an open institution, responsible to the needs of a changing economy'. Several writers in this report pointed to the need to break down institutional barriers. The implications for economics teaching are that teachers are likely to find themselves members of multi-disciplinary teams, and that they will find themselves required to develop an increasing range of skills in their students and themselves through the teaching strategies they use.

The future place of economics in the FE curriculum depends on an awareness on the part of a range of employers and government agencies of the significance of economics education as part of a broad-based vocational education, giving students greater opportunities for personal development and adaptation essential to the needs of a changing economy.

Economics teachers are likely to be required increasingly to act as members of a team developing communication, numeracy and social skills in their students and introducing them to developments in technology. The importance of economics education in developing conceptual or analytical ability, as well as imparting information, has probably been underestimated by parties in the curriculum debate. Economics teachers will increasingly need to be involved in negotiating their role in the curriculum both nationally and within their colleges.

Notes and references

1 DES 15/83, *Statistics of Further Education in England and Wales* (HMSO, 1983) tables 3 and 4.
2 DES 7/84, *Statistical Bulletin; Students from abroad in Great Britain in 1982–3 and provisional information for 1983–4* (HMSO, 1984).
3 BEC, *Annual Report 1982–1983* (1983).
4 Rogers, J., *Adults Learning* (Open University Press, 1977).
5 Coombe Lodge, *The FE College in a Multi-ethnic Society*, The Further Education Staff College, Coombe Lodge Report, vol. 16, no. 2, 1983.
6 DES, 15/83, op. cit.
7 BEC, op. cit.
8 Tolley, G., 'The Open Tech is open for business', *NATFHE Journal*, vol. 8, no. 6, November 1983, pp. 14–17.
9 Harrison, A., 'Negotiating the curriculum', *NATFHE Journal*, vol. 9, no. 4, May/June 1984, pp. 20–3.
10 Potts, L., 'Economics in further education', *Economics*, vol. XX, pt. 2, no. 86, summer 1984, pp. 69–75.
11 SCOTBEC, *Business Education Guide 1984/85;* and SCOTBEC, *Annual Report and Accounts 1982/83*.
12 Economics Association Working Party Report on the 17+, *Economics,* vol. XX, pt. 2, no. 86, summer 1984.
13 BTEC, *Report to Centres Following BEC's Fifth Annual Review of Standards* (January 1984).
14 BTEC, *Discussion Document on Educational Policy* (January 1984).
15 Ibid.
16 Challis, R., 'Questions of relevance', *Educa*, no. 43, May 1984, pp. 10–11.
17 Pittwood, A., 'The provision of economics in the Business Education Council National awards curriculum, and the demand for economics understanding by industry', *Research Papers in Economics Education* (University of London Institute of Education, 1984).
18 Coombe Lodge, *The 'New' FE,* The Further Education Staff College, Coombe Lodge Report, vol. 16, no. 3, 1983.

31 The Use of Mini-charts

Ray Jarvis

Introduction

During the period 1976–8, interest rates first rose to a record 15 per cent then fell back again, reaching 5 per cent in mid-1977. Towards the end of the year, the Chancellor raised interest rates again. In class discussion, the two members of the economics department at this school took the lead in arguing for and against the move. At the end of the session, the main arguments were polished, expanded and noted down: the first mini-chart was born. Diagrams had been used in the school before, of course, but this was the first time a systematic attempt had been made to bring together ideas in chart form. Since then well over fifty charts have been developed.[1]

The ideal formula is an interplay between teacher and students resulting in a written (diagrammatic) summary of the issues concerned. The objective is not to cover the whole syllabus or to obtain a file full of diagrams as such (although doing so would not be unhelpful), but rather to develop a way of thinking about a problem: a technique that is of value in a whole range of areas including other subjects (e.g. history, biology and geography to mention a few crying out for the treatment), school administrative problems and, of course, economics. Charts are well known in this school: the 'mini-chart approach' could be valuable in other institutions. How it could be valuable in tackling problems will be shown below.

The role of charts

Wall charts/charts/diagrams are not new. Their use hitherto, however, has been rather restricted. It is true that some of the wall charts produced in the past have been unimpressive; but frequently, too, there has been a failure to exploit their potential fully. In the case of wall charts, this is probably because of their inaccessibility. Note-taking and desk use is rather difficult. Too often wall charts have been used for decoration rather than education. Perhaps it is no coincidence that many modern wall charts are accompanied by either 'teacher's notes' to encourage a fuller use of the charts, or a miniature version to accompany the main chart.

A second problem with wall charts (and indeed mini-charts) is that effective charts are not easy to produce. On the one hand, the achievement of a clear, easy-to-read chart with visual impact may require over simplification in the analysis. On the other hand, greater depth of treatment may make the charts too complex and difficult to follow. As one writer has pointed out, 'it has clearly proved difficult to convey content and level, and many charts are too slight for use with students of sixteen and over'.[2] Diagrams of various sorts (including graphs) form an important part of many new textbooks. Indeed some books are based specifically on a 'diagrammatic approach'.[3] Mini-charts are a related method of presentation.

Most charts spring from ideas developed in class. Clearly the students involved can receive some benefit from participating in the process. Indeed, on many occasions students have actually demanded a copy of the final version. Their enthusiasm has been most encouraging.

A one-side summary of joint action has a double advantage over ordinary handouts. It is brief, and the students have had a hand in it. Carefully presented and well drawn,[4] it is also likely to be attractive. Give the chart a name and students can associate quite readily with the content. Titles such as 'Equalisers' (comparing equilibrium in supply and demand analysis with that in national income analysis), 'Side-effects' (showing that action taken in one direction, usually by governments, can have repercussions elsewhere, often in the opposite direction), and 'Growth Engines' (highlighting the roles of specialisation and capital accumulation in economic growth) assume a special meaning.

Aims of mini-charts

1 The mini-chart technique is essentially *a method for exploring particular aspects of a problem*. As problems have many dimensions, this particular approach leads on to other questions. For example, the chart 'Beggar My Neighbour' began life as the class question. 'What is meant by the term "exporting unemployment"?' Given the variety of views expressed and given the misunderstanding surrounding the notion of the related 'exporting inflation', it seemed appropriate to focus attention on the interdependence that exists in the modern industrial world. The general framework seemed obvious – the international monetary system. Add in the foreign trade multiplier, a 'no-entry' sign to symbolise interference with trade flows, include a reference to OPEC as a modern example of a major destabilising influence, and many of the ingredients of 'beggar-my-neighbour' type actions are assembled.[5]

2 Charts can be used to demonstrate *an important*

economic mechanism or to explore an important issue. Equally they can be used to investigate some of the more obscure or hidden areas of economics – areas that are relatively neglected in textbooks. In all cases, the aim is to encourage the development of an analytical approach. Such an approach may take the form of a full exposure of the costs and benefits of alternative courses of action; or a revelation of the likely implications of a particular change in the economy; or merely a summary of a particular mechanism. But at all times the intention is to encourage students to think as economists[6] and not simply regurgitate textbook material. Such a sharpening of analytical method should be reflected in a better structured and more probing essay style.

Charts are not unique in encouraging an analytical approach, but their merit is that they force student and teacher alike to establish a framework within which the main elements of a problem can be considered.
3 Once prepared, *the charts can be used as revision aids* (particularly where mainstream syllabus material is concerned). Clearly the advantage of working together with students in formulating a chart will be lost once a chart has been established, but new groups will stimulate new ideas and old charts can be reactivated with a little thought and preparation beforehand. Various charts have been used time and again both as a basis for class discussion and as a revision aid. 'Winners and Losers', 'Equalisers', 'Price Mechanism', 'Target Practice', 'Equilibrium Macro-style' are a few examples.

A mini-chart in the making: Circles (Part 1)

This arose out of a class analysis of the role of exchange rates. Was a depreciation likely to help or hinder the UK economy and in particular the UK balance of payments? A related question had been set as an essay the previous week. Various references had been given, including p. 118 in *10 × Economics*.[7] Not every student was convinced of the beneficial effects of devaluation and wanted to argue for either a 'move down market' with adverse long-term effects, or for an inflationary impact nullifying the devaluation effects on relative import and export prices. These alternative views were happily contained in Circles, Part 1 and Part 3. Class analysis generated the chart (see Figure 31.1) and the chart stimulated further and clearer thinking.

After further thought the chart eventually emerged in the form shown in Figure 31.2. The possible implications of a rising pound were left for another chart (Circles, Part 2).

A further example: Beggar-my-Neighbour

This is one of the earliest charts (1978–9), but has been recently updated. Some of the background thinking to this chart (see Figure 31.3) is explained in an earlier section (see 'Aims of mini-charts').

The mini-chart approach

Mini-charts are normally produced on one side of A4 paper suitable for inclusion in student files. The 'master' chart can be photocopied in quantity although originally charts were produced using Banda masters. They were very colourful but had a very limited production run. Using Gestetner heat stencils overcame this handicap, but colour had to be sacrificed. Using Rotring Micronorm nibs of various sizes in preparing the (chart) master copy facilitates the use of emphasis (important items in thick black writing) which can be reinforced using capitals and underlining where appropriate. An alternative method (not explored at this school, although adopted elsewhere) might be the use of OHP transparencies.

The most important characteristic of the chart-making process is the selection of the central theme (frequently indicated by the title). Ideas flow at an uneven rate and there is no exact formula for devising charts: teachers need to be ready and willing to respond where appropriate (often the same evening while ideas are fresh). It may be a summary of a 'for and against debate' (e.g. 'Should the government abandon lame ducks?'); or the linking together of similar ideas across various aspects of the subject (e.g. 'Equalisers'); or the further development of a comment made in class (e.g. 'Can the government do it?').

Normally it is class analysis → chart → class analysis although with established charts it is largely chart → class analysis.

Conclusion

There are various types of mini-chart ranging from mainstream A-level syllabus material to more obscure topics. When developed with a group of students, they all have some value in encouraging and developing analytical skills. Some have direct course relevance either in demonstrating an economics mechanism or highlighting a policy issue. Later, such charts can be used as revision aids.

The charts were originally developed for A-level use. Since then some have been adopted for pre-O-level and O-level classes with revisions in some cases but not in others. With careful preparation, the structure of a problem can be seen by all.

Notes and references

1 Some of the titles are referred to in the chapter. A full list is available from the author at Simon Langton Grammar School, Canterbury, Kent.
2 Noble, P., in Lee, N. (ed.) *Teaching Economics* (Heinemann Educational Books, 1975) p. 228.
3 Kapoor, S., and Finlayson, B., *Dynamic Approach to Economics* (Holmes McDougall, 1976); Wates, C.J., *A Visual Approach to Economic Analysis* (Longman, 1969). Both books are 'diagrammatic' in approach. Other books using plenty of diagrams include Horsman, J., *Graphic Economics* (Longman, 1983); Sapsford, D., and Ladd, J.,

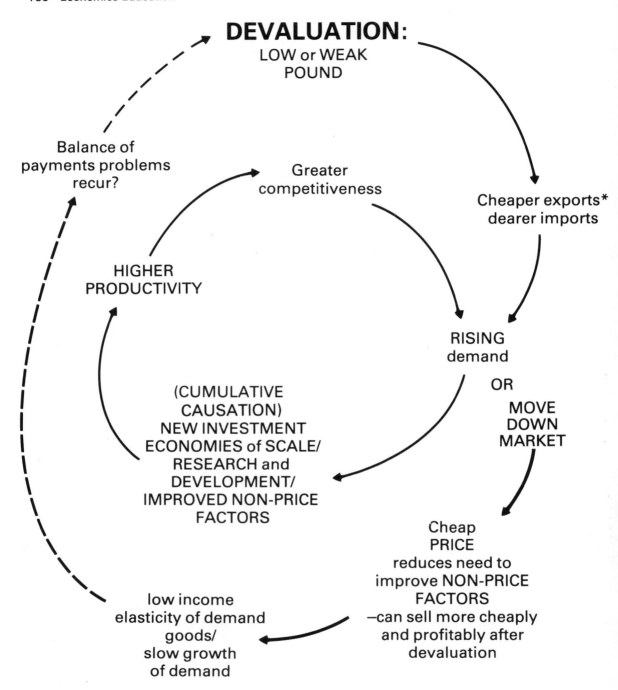

DEVALUATION:
LOW or WEAK POUND

Balance of payments problems recur?

Greater competitiveness

Cheaper exports* dearer imports

HIGHER PRODUCTIVITY

RISING demand

OR

MOVE DOWN MARKET

(CUMULATIVE CAUSATION) NEW INVESTMENT ECONOMIES of SCALE/ RESEARCH and DEVELOPMENT/ IMPROVED NON-PRICE FACTORS

Cheap PRICE reduces need to improve NON-PRICE FACTORS —can sell more cheaply and profitably after devaluation

low income elasticity of demand goods/ slow growth of demand

*Ignores possible INFLATIONARY effects either because economy at or near full employment and/or because cost-push pressure that is unleashed. To the extent that there will be SOME inflation some of the devaluation effects on competitiveness will be reduced.

Figure 31.1

CIRCLES (Part 1)

Based on an original idea/diagram in P.Donaldson's *10 × ECONOMICS* (Penguin, 1982) p. 118.
Other references: 'Moving down market', *Guardian*, 28 April 1977; J. Eatwell, 'Whatever Happened to Britain?',
The Economics of Decline, (BBC and Duckworth, 1982).

OPENING ECONOMIC SITUATION. Balance of payments on current account persistently
in deficit→ UK goods/services uncompetitive as it suffers a higher rate of
inflation than most of its trading partners. In other words, unfavourable price
factors are causing the problems in this hypothetical case.[1]
Will a fall in the value of the exchange rate help or hinder?

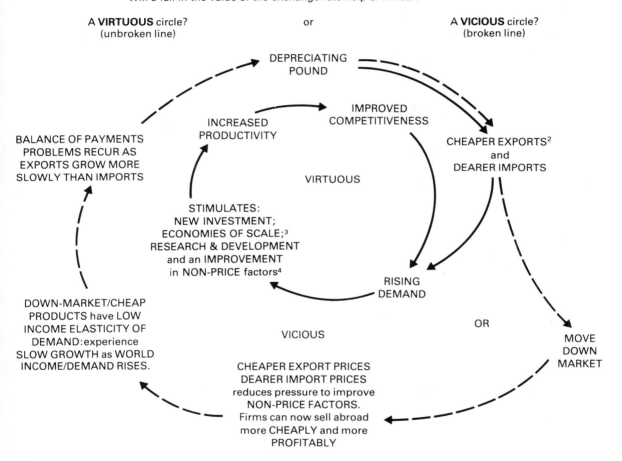

Notes:

1 Other main causes of UNCOMPETITIVENESS include (a) unfavourable NON-PRICE factors;
   and (b) an OVER-VALUED CURRENCY (see circles, Part 2).
2 Falling pound is likely to cause some INFLATIONARY pressure because (i) capacity of economy
   cannot cope with extra export and import substitute demand and/or (ii) cost-push pressure
   unleashed as, for example, unions try to maintain real living standards threatened by depreciation.
   To the extent that there will be some inflation, some of the effects on competitiveness will be reduced-indeed it
   is possible to show another VICIOUS CIRCLE→depreciation→domestic inflation→depreciation (see circles part 3)
3 Eatwell discusses this process–'cumulative causation', in 'Whatever Happened to Britain?' (BBC) see p. 91.
4 NON-PRICE FACTORS include DESIGN, RELIABLLITY, DELIVERY DATES, AFTER SALES, etc.

   Circles (part 2) deals with a RISING POUND; Circles (part 3) deals with INFLATION and EXCHANGE RATES.

Figure 31.2

BEGGAR–MY–NEIGHBOUR

Remember the CRUCIAL role of SPECIALISATION–and therefore TRADE and an effective INTERNATIONAL MONETARY SYSTEM–in determining WORLD PRODUCTION LEVELS and indirectly WORLD LIVING STANDARDS.

AN EFFECTIVE INTERNATIONAL MONETARY SYSTEM ⟶ ALLOWS/ENCOURAGES TRADE ⟶ makes INTERNATIONAL SPECIALISATION possible ⟶ (N.B. Law of Comparative Advantage)

⟶ INCREASED WORLD PRODUCTION LEVELS ⟶ increased INCOMES to spend on increased production ⟶ WORLD LIVING STANDARDS RISE (may be unequally distributed)

So why IMPEDE/ INTERRUPT/ REDUCE this beneficial process? why 'BEGGAR MY NEIGHBOUR'?

Simply INDIVIDUAL COUNTRIES see their own NATIONAL INTEREST over-riding any WORLD COMMUNITY INTEREST–in the short run, at least.
(In the long run some reduction may prove to have been useful if, for example, an infant industry has thereby been allowed to develop–provide the world economy with a viable, effective new industry....)

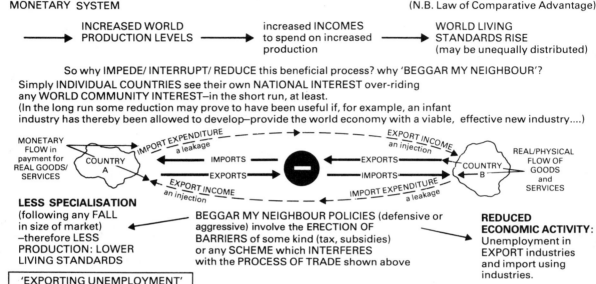

MONETARY FLOW in payment for REAL GOODS/ SERVICES

COUNTRY A

IMPORT EXPENDITURE a leakage

IMPORTS

EXPORTS

EXPORT INCOME an injection

EXPORTS

IMPORTS

EXPORT INCOME an injection

IMPORT EXPENDITURE a leakage

COUNTRY B

REAL/PHYSICAL FLOW OF GOODS and SERVICES

LESS SPECIALISATION
(following any FALL in size of market) –therefore LESS PRODUCTION: LOWER LIVING STANDARDS

BEGGAR MY NEIGHBOUR POLICIES (defensive or aggressive) involve the ERECTION OF BARRIERS of some kind (tax, subsidies) or any SCHEME which INTERFERES with the PROCESS OF TRADE shown above

REDUCED ECONOMIC ACTIVITY: Unemployment in EXPORT industries and import using industries.

'EXPORTING UNEMPLOYMENT'

1. REDUCE AGGREGATE DEMAND AT HOME
Especially important if the country involved is the USA, WEST GERMANY or JAPAN– demand for imports fall i.e. LESS EXPORTS from other countries are demanded–unemployment in their export industries.

2. PROTECTION
Various devices-but NET EFFECT is to SHUT OUT IMPORTS (e.g. 1930's) and/or SUBSIDISE EXPORTS (e.g. EEC + Steel 1979). In BOTH CASES demand for FOREIGN PRODUCTION falls -unemployment in their EXPORT industries.

3. DEPRECIATION/DEVALUATION
Makes exports cheaper and imports more expensive. If elasticities are appropriate and if PRICE COMPETITIVENESS matters (non-price factors?) then EXPORT sales rise and IMPORT spending falls -domestic employment rises.

'EXPORTING INFLATION'

1. EXPAND AGGREGATE DEMAND AT HOME
By fiscal policy (cutting tax and/or raising public spending) and/or by lax money supply policy. If domestic economy NEAR FULL CAPACITY and/or has a HIGH PROPENSITY TO IMPORT then imports will be sucked in-injects demand into the world economy via the foreign trade multiplier (e.g. USA in the late 60's)

2. PROTECTION
Dismantling various import controls/export incentives?

> INTEREST RATE WARS e.g. 1980–'82
> Dollar price of oil rising in this period—oil importers (Japan, W.GY, Switzerland) raised interest rates to prevent own currency falling against the dollar—thereby keeping inflation at bay. 1982 USA interest rates rising...

3. APPRECIATION/REVALUATION
Forces up EXPORT PRICES, forces down IMPORT prices-assuming elasticities are appropriate then demand for and SALES of FOREIGN GOODS rise and SALES of domestic goods fall (also price of UK goods in foreign shops now higher)

EXPORTING UNEMPLOYMENT and INFLATION AT THE SAME TIME: the OPEC case.

METHOD: Impose a large price increase on an important commodity with inelastic demand e.g. OIL.

Severe **DEFLATIONARY affect** in USER countries-big transfer of PURCHASING POWER (aggregate demand) to OPEC countries-in effect an 'OPEC TAX'; an improvement in OPEC's terms of trade; OPEC take a greater slice of world production/living standards. (The effect is moderated by a transfer back of demand when OPEC members buy imports. REAL resources-exports will then flow from OIL USER countries to OPEC countries).

Plus a THIRD PROBLEM: How to deal with the MASSIVE BALANCE OF PAYMENTS DEFICITS and accompanying CAPITAL FLOWS

Severe **COST INFLATIONARY** effect in user countries-price elasticity of demand is very low-therefore demand little changed (until recently)-big increase in COSTS accepted but reflected in RISING PRICES (oil has many direct and indirect effects) and RISING WAGES as consumers tried to protect their standard of living (will all this go into reverse as OIL PRICES FALL?)

Figure 31.3

Essential Economics (Hart Davis Educational, 1982); and *Fred Learns Modern Economics* (Continua, 1975). Usborne Publishing Company produce many excellent booklets in all subjects based on a 'diagrammatic approach' (Usborne Publishing Ltd, 20 Garrick Street, London WC2E 9BJ.

4   If it is felt that too much information has been crammed in, then it would be possible to extend coverage to a second side of A4 paper ('a twin sheet'). This has been tried here, as has the idea of a 'family of charts' and also a series of connected charts (parts 1, 2 and 3, etc.). How much is included is a question of judgement. Two basic ingredients of effective mini-charts are structure and judicious choice of content.

Perhaps readers can make their own assessment of how crowded the charts in this chapter are.

5   The full version of the chart appears later in this chapter.

6   In a recent article such thinking was described as the acquisition of 'an economic perspective'. See Thomas, L., 'Economics for all', *Times Educational Supplement*, 2 February 1984, p. 37.

7   Donaldson, P., *10 × Economics* (Penguin, 1982).

32   The 'Wipe-clean' Wall Chart
Brian Titley

Introduction

Too often the wall chart or poster is relegated to a position on the back wall of an economics classroom. The aim of this chapter is to demonstrate that it is in fact a versatile instrument, and indeed an essential part of the teacher's repertoire. Not only does the wall chart bring welcome variety to a lesson, but it has visual impact and thus proves an efficient and effective means of conveying information.

Professionally produced wall charts from industry and various commercial institutions are generally available for use in the classroom. But these are of necessity rather general. Teachers of economics may therefore wish to design and produce their own charts and posters in order to achieve certain specific objectives and in accordance with their own needs, student needs and syllabus requirements. Of course, it may be argued that wall charts will prove unusable in the larger classroom as students will be unable to read them clearly. This should not prove to be a great problem in the case of purely diagrammatic posters, but clearly any written information must be carefully designed and should above all be brief. As most people are shown to scan from the top of any layout, this should guide the designer to place necessary wording above any diagrams, etc. A bright background, for example yellow, will also help to make the written work, and indeed diagrams, stand out.

While poster paper and coloured pens should prove inexpensive, the cost in time to produce charts is likely to be an inhibiting factor, but the teacher needs to make a comparison with possible alternatives (e.g. the OHP slide, class handouts, etc.) and also take into consideration the stream of possible future benefits from the re-use of such charts. With this in mind it is wise to avoid designing wall charts that need constant revision and updating, for example graphs of current time-series, and to make the charts as simple as possible. Wall charts of a fairly 'static' nature could encompass purely theoretical constructs from demand and supply diagrams to simple circular flow of income models; historical time-series graphs (e.g. Peacock and Wiseman's 'displacement effect' of the two world wars on government expenditure, the European currency 'snake' before sterling's departure in 1972); or clearly defined structures such as the UK balance of payments accounts, bank assets, the counterparts of the sterling M_3 monetary aggregate, and so on.

What is clear, however, is that many economic relationships are by nature dynamic. It is therefore necessary to provide up-to-date, or even contrasting, statistical data, to illustrate and reinforce such relationships. Data can of course be written up on a blackboard or reproduced at great expense as class handouts. On the other hand, bar-charts, pie-charts and pictograms, etc., widely used to communicate differences or changes in situations, are natural display material. In both cases wall charts can be used, there being considerable advantages involved: for example, ease of transport from room to room.

One way the provision of up-to-date statistical data in the economics classroom may be achieved is to provide an area on a wall chart that can be wiped clean of any water-based felt-tip pen markings. Thus, the teacher may, for example, explore the UK balance of payments accounts of 1979 and write up statistical data relevant to the three main sections, and the corresponding sub-divisions of the accounts, to provide students with quantitative information and to make the whole framework of the account more concrete (see Figure 32.1). The teacher may then wipe clean the column of figures from the wall chart and explore the accounts of, say, 1982, when the balance of visible trade moved into surplus and the balance for official financing showed, for various reasons, a negative sum rather than a positive figure.

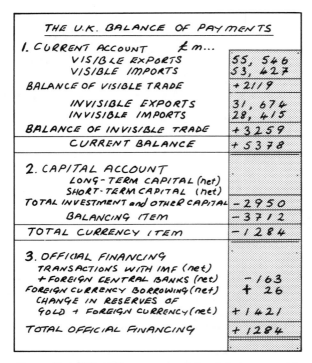

Figure 32.1 (Wipe-clean area on right of chart to provide contrasting statistical data).

Clearly, the 'cleanable' wall chart can take many forms and represent numerous economic relationships, but what all will have in common is a relatively strong plastic cover, preferably clear or light in colour, which is fixed to an appropriate area of any such chart. Plastic of a suitable nature can often be found protecting new furniture, and so a visit to a furniture warehouse or wholesaler may be profitable. The teacher may even wish to obtain a more professional, but therefore more expensive, finish by having the entire chart laminated. Contact adhesive plastic can also be used. In this way a wall chart can be employed for more general purposes, for example drawing graphs on pre-drawn axes.

Figure 32.2 illustrates a chart that employs the graphical representation of accelerator theory as used by Robins.[1] Three pairs of axes are employed to show fluctuations in the growth of output, the capital stock and net investment. Comparison can then be made of different patterns of growth in output, and between naïve and flexible accelerator models, simply by cleaning the chart and plotting new situations. Figure 32.3 in turn illustrates a simple circular flow of income model where the 'wipe-clean' method may also be employed to explore various situations of disequilibrium between injections into, and withdrawals from, the flow. As such, charts of this nature should prove reusable on many occasions until such a time as wear and tear or economics have got the better of them.

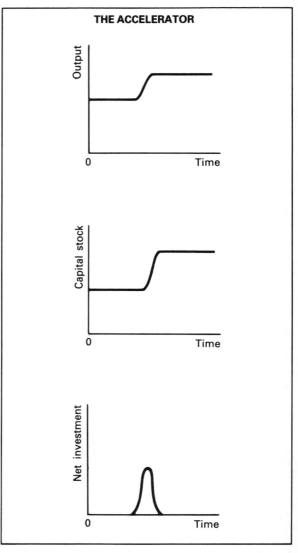

Figure 32.2 'Wipe-clean' chart with pre-drawn axes

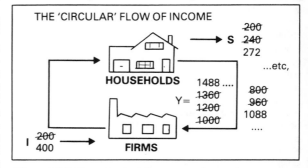

Figure 32.3 Hypothetical figures can be used to illustrate the multiplier

It is hoped that for those teachers who have not considered the profitable use of wall charts in the classroom, this chapter will be a practical push in the right direction.

Notes and references

1 Robins, P., 'The accelerator principle – development and evidence', *Economics*, vol. XX, pt. 1, no. 85, spring 1984, pp. 3–5.

33 Making and Using Overhead Transparencies

Danny Myers

Introduction

Visual imagery forms an important part of many lessons. Attracting the students' attention through eyes and ears at the same time makes a bigger impact. It is certainly true that a picture talks louder than words. Consequently, the development of a personal set of overhead transparencies is a good long-run investment. The artwork needs only to be produced once; the finished products can be highly professional; class contact time is used more effectively; lesson planning becomes more efficient; and you no longer have to tolerate 'chalk dried skin'.

The following suggestions may prove useful to both the postgraduate Certificate of Education student and the experienced teacher – as the OHP is at present often overlooked as a versatile teaching tool.

Equipment

All schools have OHPs. However, should you be fortunate enough to buy a new one, the Elite 2000,[1] the Fordigraph 90[2] and the 3M[3] models are all good buys. Useful optional extras include: scroll attachments, wide-angle lens (for projecting over short distances) and filter shields (to enable you to work with the projector without blinding yourself). This final extra is a bonus if you are going to use the OHP all day – they fix to the machine and cost approximately £5. Next you will need an acetate roll, acetate sheets and various pens. It should be noted that the quality of these latter items varies immensely and it may well be worthwhile going to an art shop and making a local purchase in preference to having hands tied by consortium arrangements. For example, 'Artcel' make a very high-quality heavy duty acetate for special presentations, while Cellofilm provides a cheap substitute at the other end of the price range. Also Staedtler, Rotring and Faber-Castell all make ranges of 'super-fine' pens which,

although marginally more expensive than the standard ones, last twice as long, since they don't go 'fat' and 'furry'.

Making of OHP transparencies

Production possibilities range from simply paper clipping a diagram to the acetate and tracing those features that you wish to copy, to using a process camera (which some FE institutions have) loaded with the new Agfa Copycolor film[4] which produces a high-quality coloured visual ready for use on the OHP. The production techniques discussed below will range between these two extremes.

1 Overlays

Using a series of acetates enables one to build up a complex visual, discussing each stage as the presentation proceeds. This is particularly useful when analysing graphs relating to the market mechanism or theory of the firm; especially as different colours can be used which are often crowded out of texts due to expense. The starting point is to determine how many overlays you'll need and sellotape them together before commencing. This will help with accurate production and presentation. The alternative method of lining up dots or crosses on each consecutive sheet is rather fiddly.

2 Cartoons

Looking through the weekly press provides the frustrated artist with many ideas to modify (with Tippex) and photocopy.

3 Banda

Another time-saving device is to produce a Banda master on acetate so that the final duplicated sheets, when distributed to a class, can be discussed and consolidated on the screen. To produce these, kits are available boxed in 100s, from Audio-Visual Productions,[5] cost £12.75.

4 Printed

Because an OHP magnifies the original acetate, a neat production can be made by typing – preferably with a Golf ball or jumbo typewriter – on to plain white paper and then photocopying from there on to acetate. This is particularly useful for making tables relating to national income, balance of payments, population and employment (e.g. experiment with Table 33.1). Similarly, Letraset can be employed, especially as their products are not limited to lettering only.

Use of OHP transparencies

Many conscientious teachers have spoilt the impact of their overhead transparency by delivering it all at once.

Uncovering each piece stage by stage directs students' visual attention to each important aspect as it unfolds.

Another spoiling element that even the most experienced seem to suffer, is writing all over their carefully prepared visual. If one must indulge in this, prepare the base in permanent inks and use only water-soluble pens in class. An easier and neater solution is to place the acetate under the roll attached to the OHP, thus avoiding any markings on the original. Getting into the habit of placing the original acetate under the roll will also prevent the acetate from curling while you talk.

So far, the uses detailed have lent themselves to aiding the expository part of a lesson. However, other types of teaching can also employ OHPs. Students enjoy using the OHP when involved in reporting back on work they've researched. Data-response questions are often best stored and presented on an acetate, as the marking can then be discussed by the relevant section/figures being pointed

Table 33.1   OHP master produced with a jumbo typewriter

Jobless – the great divide Official total: 3 094 000 (November 1983)			
Left-wing critics ADD:		*Right-wing critics SUBTRACT:*	
Unemployed over-60s (no longer required to register)	199 000	School leavers	168 000
Short-time working	43 000	Claimants who are not really looking for jobs	490 000
Students on vacation	27 000	Severely disabled	23 000
Effect of special employment measures	395 000	'Unemployables' – mentally or physically incapable	135 000
Unregistered unemployed	490 000	'Job changers' – out of work for four weeks or less	360 000
		'Black economy' – workers illegally claiming benefit	250 000
Total additions	1 154 000	Total subtractions	1 426 000
Total unemployed	4 248 000	Total unemployed	1 668 000

Source: Sunday Times, 6 November 1983, p. 62.

out. Moreover, distributing questions in this way often means that items lifted from books with answers incorporated are now isolated as separate entities, until such a time as the framework answers need to be considered. Similarly, flow-diagrams can be discussed and constructed as part of a class activity – with the students proceeding from a basic framework projected on the OHP.

Storing and collecting

Different teachers use different methods. Some frame the finished visual in purpose-built frames which can then be stored in a cardboard box or LP record case. Others use washing lines with bulldog clips threaded on from which the finished products hang. I find it easiest to use A4-size transparencies and paper clip them to the related lesson notes (for those who use ring binders acetates can be hole-punched).

Commercially produced acetates are not common owing to the high production costs set against the limited market. However, professional organisations in Britain have experimented with a few limited editions. The Economics Association produced some on the location of

industry, the theory of the firm, and comparative costs – although most of these are now out of stock. The ICFC produced some to support their Understanding Industry course, and the Banking Information Service are toying with the idea of producing some soon. Abroad, in Holland and Australia, they have been slightly more adventurous, producing prototype overhead transparencies on paper which once purchased can be photocopied on to acetate – but only in black and white. An innovating publisher may commission someone to fill this gap – but until then you'll have to make your own. I hope the above comments will set you off in the right direction.

Addresses

1   Elite Optics Ltd, 354 Caerphilly Road, Cardiff CF4 4XJ.
2   Fordigraph, Ofrex Ltd, Fordigraph Division, Ofrex House, Stephen Street, London W1A 1EA.
3   3M, 3M House, PO Box 1, Bracknell, Berkshire RT12 1JU.
4   Agfa Copycolor AGFA-Gevaert Ltd, Mac Systems Division, 27 Great West Road, Brentford, Middlesex TW8 9AX.
5   Audio-Visual Productions, Hocker Hill House, Chepstow, Gwent NP6 5ER.

34   'Actuality' in Economics Education: London-based Experience Courses*

Michael Houser

*An earlier version of this chapter appeared in *Economics,* vol. XVIII, pt. 3, no. 79. autumn 1982, pp. 108–13.

Economics of the real world

The vast majority of today's educators, like generations before them, learned their economics in the classroom. In today's world, however, it is neither the only nor by any means the best place in which to teach it.

Particularly in the case of sub-degree examination classes, what usually results is an awkward distinction between classroom economics on the one hand, and the economics of the real world on the other. The distinction is not merely awkward for those who teach economics; it cannot be allowed to continue if the remarkable growth in popularity that economics has enjoyed during the past decade and a half is itself to continue.

And it need not. Teachers in Britain often overlook the lack of institutional constraints that characterise our

teaching environment: no tightly controlled centralised curriculum, no officially 'approved' texts, no unwieldy classes averaging forty-five to fifty pupils. Freedom to innovate outside the classroom is a tremendous asset.

The constraints on getting out of the classroom and into the 'real' world tend to be personal rather than institutional: the common lack of previous experience working in industry and commerce is perhaps the greatest inhibitor, though lack of personal contacts or practical experience in, and confidence gained from, organising extra-curricular study schemes restrains many as well.

Once the benefits of studying and experiencing economics in the real world are fully appreciated, the potential for innovation and variety is almost limitless. The use of London as a base for residential short courses lasting from two days to a week is only one of any number of possibilities. However obvious it may seem as a venue, given its strategic role in the British economy with respect to industry, finance and economic policy-making, coupled with its international importance in trade, finance and services, the possibilities are more plentiful, more diverse and often more interesting than is commonly imagined.

London: walk before trying to run

In every sense, the first rule of thumb in course planning is: nothing succeeds like success. Begin as you mean to go on – and as if you mean to go on; London-based courses should be developed gradually from modest first efforts into week-long annual events which may become the high point of the teaching year. The more successful first efforts are, the more organisational momentum is built up for subsequent courses, the greater are student expectations and interest and the easier it is in future to secure the combined support of heads worried about covering for absent staff, colleagues who prize the free periods they will lose taking your classes, and parents who may have to foot the bills.

The first attempts require the most effort and until the various skills required begin to come naturally, organising residential courses requires no little amount of commitment. Allowing sufficient lead-time for planning, organising and preparing for these courses makes it much easier to fit the additional workload and any necessary fund raising projects into what is likely to be an already busy work day.

Courses of this nature are bound to be voluntary, which means that they must project a balanced image of relevance and interest in order to attract sufficient numbers. For a variety of reasons, courses are markedly more successful if you can define and then exceed a break-point or threshold level of participation: economies can be achieved in the costs of transport, accommodation and board, and you achieve a better effort–benefit ratio since extra numbers add only marginally to the effort required. At the same time, a teaching group that is split down the middle between those who can afford it and want to go and those who can't or don't is an awkward propositon best avoided. Substantial numbers will also encourage institutions you wish to visit to take your proposals more seriously, and student responses during sessions tend to be better where there is strength in numbers. Experience suggests that the optimum level lies between ten and fifteen as far as individual sessions go, although double or triple this number is feasible altogether, provided that within the overall programme several visits are running at any one time.

This may in fact mean several separate programmes operating simultaneously within one course, which is an option worth considering for courses of three or more days in which two or more schools work together, or where the range and type of students is quite varied: for example, where O-level and second-year A-level economics students find themselves together as a group with commerce and business studies students. A judicious mixture of students from different course levels, subjects and institutions can produce exceptional performance, and generally adds an element of excitement to the learning process.

Timing is important right from the start. Longer and more ambitious courses, which require more prior negotiation, need longer lead-times. Much time can be saved and unnecessary effort spared by doing a feasibility study first: timing must avoid mock examination periods as well as clashes with commitments already entered on the institutional calendar – cruises, overseas visits, major sports events, drama productions, public holidays. Periods of likely bad weather, peak tourism and any forebodings of possible industrial action that could affect your plans should be considered as well. To use evenings productively and in an interesting way, you may wish to take your groups to a national newspaper to see it being put together, or join the audience of a live television broadcast: both are quite feasible and well advised (even if they deviate somewhat from the theme of the course) but their popularity – being gratis has much to do with this – means that you must book at least six months in advance to be successful.

Before going 'public' with a prospective course, you will need to work out costings (travel, board, lodging, course materials), decide on the length and timing of your course – it's worth thinking about offering two different sets of dates, one during term, the other in term holiday time – and then settle on the most popular choice if there is enough support over all (see Figure 34.1). Apart from the obvious disadvantages, running courses during term holiday periods can actually simplify matters administratively. Whatever dates you decide upon, present your proposals in the form of a written prospectus that outlines your aims, the benefits to be gained from the course, and general details about the programme and costs. In time, you might be able to promote the idea by including references to previous courses along with any press cuttings or other media attention you may have managed to attract. Be sure to get in return a clear indication in writing of support for what you are proposing.

Once you determine that sufficient numbers make your proposed course viable, you will want to obtain accurate costings – partly in order to decide whether fund raising and appeals to your governors or LEA (either of whom may help defray costs from their contingency funds if they are impressed by your proposals) will be necessary. You may also want to consider opening an account to receive instalment payments: interest can be earned for a course 'float' in this way, and an instalment system for payments tends to keep greater numbers committed from the beginning.

Fund raising should be considered as a major part of the planning. If you don't wish to compete with other sponsored fund-raising events, consider a series of weekend car washes held at your school, or organised social events such as discos and bake and jumble sales; the

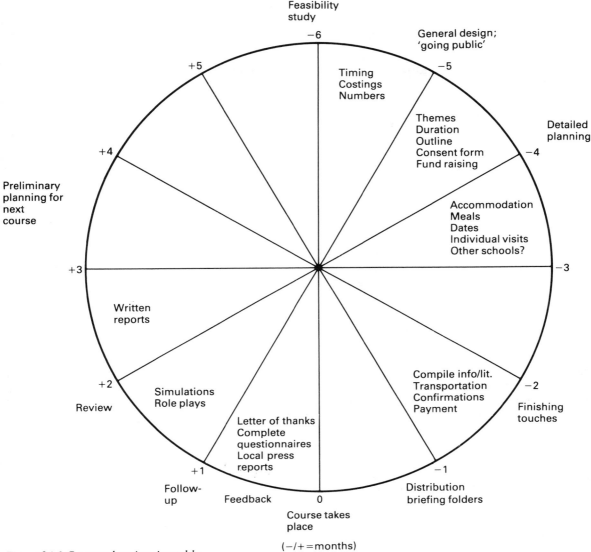

Figure 34.1 Course planning timetable

money raised can be used in instances where the costs would otherwise impose hardship on particular families, and to provide a level of subsidy for others.

With numbers, costs and timing settled, you can turn your thoughts to the heart of the course, the individual visits. One way to begin is to work out an overall theme for your course, one that will probably reflect particular interests you or your groups have (regional policy, structural decline, comparative advantage, interest rate determination, and so on), along with what you feel London can best provide that you can't provide in your own classroom. A theme for each day can then be worked out which enables you to build gradually towards the general theme of the whole course.

Picking your spots

The precise choice of visits requires a balance of practicality and genuine interest. While there is little point in going to the Stock Exchange merely because it is there and accommodating, the same applies equally to visiting an obscure exchange because of intrinsic but unspecified interest. Visit places that can teach you and your groups something they are interested in and need to know. Your planning should also take into consideration the possible careers in which students have begun to show some interest. There may also be scope during longer courses to visit an economics department of a polytechnic or London

Table 34.1   Sample course possibilities

Two-day course — FOCUS: Key issues in economic and industrial policy		
	a.m.	p.m.
DAY I	Treasury Department	Bank of England
DAY II	British Railways Board	National Union of Railwaymen

Three-day course — FOCUS: Trade, finance and industrial relations		
	a.m.	p.m.
DAY I	Department of Trade	HM Customs and Excise
DAY II	Intelligence Unit: Brokerage house	Merchant bank
DAY III	Industrial Society	Trades Union Congress

Five-day course — FOCUS: The mixed economy, the international economy, the economy in theory		
	a.m.	p.m.
DAY I	Consumers' Association	Office of Fair Trading
DAY II	Monopolies and Mergers Commission	Marks & Spencer
DAY III	Building Societies Association	Head Office: major clearing bank
DAY IV	American Overseas Bank	Japanese General Trading Company (*Sogo Shosha*)
DAY V	Institute of Economic Affairs	Policy Studies Institute

University college with those considering degree-level study in economics.

A sound strategy is to select venues that are capable of dealing with difficult questions and issues within the course you are teaching. It is also sensible to try to examine issues from different points of view in the same (see Table 34.1) day: Treasury policies presented in Whitehall in the morning will be seen rather differently in the afternoon at *The Economist*, a 'think tank' or pressure group. Pairing the NUR with British Rail, BP with the Department of Energy, the Bank of England with a Merrill-Lynch economist tends to produce another equally important sense of balance.

The choice of venue will also to some extent depend upon the type of visit you are looking for, as well as its content. At one extreme, institutions like the Stock Exchange (and the Bank of England to a lesser extent) are so accustomed to public visits that their response has been standardised into tours of limited relevance to serious students. At the other extreme, busy foreign exchange dealing rooms and brokerage houses, some of the nationalised industries and smaller organisations generally tend to shy away from all but the most artfully conceived, carefully and persistently presented visit proposals. For the great majority of visits, however, you get what you ask for.

This requires that you know what you're after and what is available (see Table 34.2). Tours of limited duration within a visit can be useful, but seminars with question and answer sessions are invaluable; public relations efforts are unavoidable to some extent, but with delicate footwork they are best sidestepped.

Since the organisation in question is doing you a favour, help them to help give you the individually tailored programme you want by providing them with your aims and clearly stated objectives, a fairly precise indication how long you wish to stay (2–3½ hours is optimal), what your numbers are likely to be and at what level they are studying. Pre-viewing of films and audio-visual programmes is ideal, but not always possible.

Since you could unexpectedly find yourself in a boardroom with several high-powered executives or in a 'think tank' or government department with a specialist unused to communicating with non-specialists, or in a pressure group with a highly politicised speaker, be wary of allowing your opposite number in an organisation to overestimate – or underestimate – your group's potential. For courses lasting more than two days, be especially careful to build variety into each session, breaking up lectures and the question and answer periods with short tours, tape-slide or film programmes. Handouts should be obtained before the course begins if possible, for inclusion in the course briefing folder (see Table 34.3). If you can manage to extend your visit over lunch, a more relaxed but very useful atmosphere for discussions often develops.

Experience is important in this regard. It helps to teach you whether the film Shell wishes to show will enlighten your group on the current account, whether British Airways' tape-slide programme is relevant to the interesting session you had planned on airline economics, whether the Industrial Society's management game can capture sufficient interest.

Whatever the mode of presentation, discussion and follow-up after the course are vital, not to mention *your*

Table 34.2   Directory of possible visit venues

Venue	Rating	Comments
CITY		
Banking		
British clearing banks	1/2	Contact 'Schools Liaison Divisions' and Bank Education Service
American-Japanese Overseas Bank	2/3	American/Japanese banks number 1 and 2, with CITI Bank and Bank of Tokyo recommended
Discount houses	2/3	Possible link between Lloyds Bank and LABCO, Lloyds Discount house
Merchant banks	3	
Bank of England	1	Book early! Ask for ample discussion time with bank staff
Exchanges		
Foreign currency	2/3	Possible link between National Westminster and NatWest World Money Centre
Baltic Mercantile & Shipping	1	
Lloyds of London	1	Limited time; ask for discussion time with a member
Insurance/assurance	1	Contact British Insurance Association
Commodity/metal	2	Sugar, rubber, coffee/cocoa recommended
Stock Exchange	1	Follow-up at a brokerage house
Miscellaneous		
Building societies	2	Link with Building Society's Institute
National Giro Centre	2/3	Possible link with Post Office visit
National savings movement	2	Arrange through local/regional office
Brokerage houses	3	
Japanese General Trading Companies (*Sogo Shosha*)	2/3	
PUBLIC SECTOR		
Government departments		
Treasury departments	2	Contact Information Division; possible link with Bank of England visit
Inland Revenue	3	Link with Treasury and Institute of Fiscal Studies visits
HM Customs and Excise	3	
Department of Trade	2	
British Overseas Trade Board	2	Link with JETRO visit
Exports Credit Guarantee Dept	2/3	Link with foreign exchange/overseas bank visits
Ministry of Overseas Development	2/3	Link with Oxfam/Christian Aid visits
Industry Department	2	Link with NEDO visit and later with visit to firms in specific Development Areas
Public corporations		
British Airports Authority	2	Link with British Airways visit
British Airways Corporation	2	
British Railways Board	2	Link with NUR/ASLEF visits
London Transport Board	2/3	Link with BR visit
British Steel Corporation	2	Link with NEDO/industry visit
Post Office Corporation	2	Link with National Giro visit
National Coal Board	2	Link with NUM visit
REGULATORY BODIES, PRESSURE GROUPS (Including media) AND 'THINK TANKS'		
Advertising Standards Authority	2/3	
Centre for Policy Studies	2	
Consumers' Association	2	
Economist newspaper	2	Plan for early in the week and request specific journalist if possible
Financial Times	2	
Institute for Economic Affairs	2	
Institute for Fiscal Studies	2/3	
Japan External Trade Organisation (JETRO)	2/3	Link with BOTB's 'Exports to Japan' Unit and with Trade Department visit

Table 34.2 (cont.)

Venue	Rating	Comments
Monopolies Commission	2/3	
National Institute for Economic and Social Research	2/3	
Office of Fair Trading	2/3	Link with Consumers' Association visit
Patent Office	2/3	
Policy Studies Institute	2	
INDUSTRY, COMMERCE and MANAGEMENT		
Arbitration, Conciliation and Advisory Service	3	Link with visits to TUC, CBI, specific trades unions and British Institute of Management
Confederation of British Industry	1/2	Link visit with issues raised with trades unions; link with TUC visit
Industrial Society	1/2	
British Association for Commercial and Industrial Education	1/2	
Institute of Personnel Management	2	
Design Centre	1	Link with visits to British Standards Institute and with BOTB
British Standards Institution	2	
National Economic Development Organisation	2/3	
Trades Union Congress	1/2	
Major trades unions	2	Link with visits to specific firms or public-sector corporations
ICI	2	Britain's largest manufacturer
Marks & Spencer	2	Emphasis on retailing and on reasons for overseas successes
British Petroleum/Shell-Mex	1/2	
Institute of Directors	2/3	
EVENING VISITS		
National newspapers	1	Visits by parties limited generally to 8–15, booking required nine months in advance, production facilities visited 3–4 hours required
Audience participation in live TV broadcasts	1	Participation in programmes such as *Question Time* can be particularly valuable
House of Commons debates	1	Contact local MP to see if any special arrangements can be made
London University/college/NUS	2	An opportunity to visit the facilities, meet student leaders, officials from Registrar's Office

Rating: 1 = pre-arranged public visits in existence; 2 = accessible to educational parties without difficulty; 3 = unaccustomed to 'outside' visits; initiative required.

responsibility. Students need to be encouraged to get involved to be taken seriously at some venues; they need to be carefully briefed before each visit as well as advised as to how to prepare themselves generally for the course over all. Prior to departure, each visit should be profiled in writing on a briefing paper (see Table 34.3). Explain the programme in detail, say why this particular venue was selected, and what the purpose of the visit is. It is helpful to provide suggested reading and a set of the sort of questions you want the visit to answer, the implication being that they can be asked in discussion if not otherwise dealt with during the session.

Briefing papers, along with maps, instructions, information for general reference and background literature obtained from various venues in advance, can then be combined in a course briefing folder which should be given to each participant up to a fortnight prior to departure as required reading. Time should be set aside

each evening or morning to review the next day's visits in some detail during the course itself. Sending copies of the briefing paper to each visit organiser before arrival says a great deal about your group's commitment and preparation and has the added advantage of reconfirming your interpretation of the agreed visit programme.

A successful visit increases the likelihood that you will be welcomed back again in the future; an unresponsive, uninterested group may dissuade the organiser from repeat performances. Maintaining good contacts with these organisers is important: notes of thanks, copies of relevant press cuttings, reports on project follow-up or possible career interest that has been generated are much appreciated. You may wish to have your own business cards printed to exchange with each organiser during visits in order to have your growing lists of contacts carefully on file; following the same procedure with various speakers may enable you to carry on subsequent correspondence on

Table 34.3 Model outline of 'briefing paper' to accompany individual visits

---

London economics course

VISIT TO: (full name of venue)	**CONTACT:** (organiser within venue)
DATE: (day/month)	**TELEPHONE:** (in case of separation)
TIME: (duration agreed with organiser)	**NEAREST TUBE STOP:** (ease of travelling and in case of separation)

Nature: 1–2 paragraphs on the philosophy and purpose behind the choice of this particular venue and the nature of the programme arranged. Should include themes to be covered during the programme and expected benefits to the participants.

Programme: specific details agreed with the organiser. To include names of speakers and their subjects, mention of films or audio-visual presentations, possible places to be visited, some indication of when discussion time will be available.

Specimen questions: 4–5 carefully considered questions, presented to the students. Intended to provide food for thought when preparing for the visit (for example, in directing preliminary reading), to act as a springboard for exchanges during question-and-answer sessions (when, initially, many students may be tempted to retreat into silence) and also as a structure for notes taken during the course of the programme.

Required reading: highly selective and highly relevant sections, to be chosen from reference library. This can be supplemented with inclusions in the briefing dossier, such as newspaper photocopies, material produced by the institution to be visited (generally available in bulk, if requested). Students could also be requested to purchase, in groups, *The Economist* and *Financial Times* for the week of the visit and to read accordingly.

Suggestions for course briefing dossiers

A document wallet, appropriately labelled, distributed 3–4 weeks prior to departure and filled with thoughtfully considered carefully assembled materials, can make or break such a course. The following inclusions represent a basic but essential core for such dossiers:

400–500 word course outline: a statement of the organisers' philosophy and objectives behind the course. Useful when sent to each visit organiser and to arouse local media interest in the course before and after.

Course aims and terms of reference: spells out in detail what is expected of participants and enables them to know what freedoms they will have throughout.

Hotel brochure/information sheet

Underground/bus maps

Map sheets of City, Westminster, Central London

Briefing sheet for each individual visit

Supplementary visit handouts (fact sheets, photocopied articles).

Materials provided by individual institutions

Course questionnaire: to be completed during and after (1 week) the course, intended to focus student attention on course details and to act as feedback for future planning.

Appendix A

Pro forma parental consent form

_____ School/College

A Course Taking Place in _____

From _____ to _____ 19____

To the Course Organiser(s):

I wish my son/daughter, _____, to be allowed to take part in the above-mentioned course programme and, having read the information sheet*, agree to his/her taking part in any or all of the activities described.

I understand that, while the staff in charge of the party will take all reasonable care of the children (students), they cannot necessarily be held responsible for any loss, damage or injury suffered by my son/daughter arising during or out of the journey or course programme.

** My son/daughter does not suffer from any condition requiring regular treatment.

** My son/daughter suffers from _____ requiring regular treatment. (If your child suffers from a particular complaint, please enclose a letter from your own doctor giving details of the complaint and its treatment.)

His/her National Health Service Medical Card number is

_____

I consent to any emergency medical treatment necessary during the course of the programme.

Signature of Parent
(or Guardian) _____

Date _____

*A 400–500 word Course Synopsis, containing this kind of material, should accompany this consent form when distributed.

**Delete appropriately.

N.B. While this form is essential in courses of this nature, it is important to remember that it has no formal legal standing and cannot guarantee any protection or grant any immunity to staff operating such courses.

a specialist topic and enable you to widen your range of contacts and increase your knowledge in a specialist field. You may even find yourself invited to subsequent conferences and presentations that deal with an area in which you clearly have an academic interest.

After visiting a particular venue several years in succession, you may feel confident enough to include a careers element within your programme, one which could include the participation of your local careers officer who might also wish to organise visits to London colleges and polytechnics, meetings with NUS leaders and possibly even group interviews in various economics faculties if the timing is appropriate.

Conclusion

Thoughtfully conceived and sensibly run, the catalogue of benefits from this type of activity is considerable – and cheap at the price. If, as is hoped, the annual economics residential course does become the centrepiece of the year's work, it can concentrate student minds in areas of research and preparation beforehand, and on your return you have a wealth of potential follow-up possibilities. It might be worth thinking about structuring individual visits with follow-up simulations and role play exercises

clearly in mind. Individual students can be asked to prepare financial and economic news reports based upon sessions that occurred during the course itself, while other pre-selected groups could prepare detailed reports or critiques on visits of greatest substance and relevance – for duplication later if suitable.

Even during a three-day course, contact time between you and your groups is up to five to six times what it would have been in the classroom, with appropriate learning economies following on from the intensity and concentrated nature of the course. Opportunities for informal discussion and improved personal relationships are great both within groups and with you. This increases when courses are jointly run by several schools.

The value of personal experience of the real world where economics happens is incalculable; students think in less one-dimensional terms and begin to appreciate abstractions and models apart from economic reality more clearly. Thoughts about future careers and about higher education are more clearly focused and students generally gain a much greater sense of purpose and see more relevance in their own work.

If asked to give the most important motivation behind all of the effort required to get this type of course off the ground, I would reflect on that traditional Japanese proverb that goes: 'few are born wise, but many may become wise'.

35   Economics Tours Abroad*

Trevor Regan and Nigel Tree

*An earlier version of this chapter appeared in *Economics*, vol. XIX, pt. 2, no. 82, summer 1983, pp. 67–68.

Introduction

Most teachers will have had experience of organising industrial visits or economics field studies within the UK, and will have realised the value of gaining an insight into our economy through first-hand experience. Economics tours allow students to obtain and collate information and make observations directly, instead of indirectly through the medium of the teacher.

Having established the virtues of field studies within the UK, why should economics teachers consider taking their students abroad? While tours within the UK provide a

valuable insight into the workings of the UK economy, they cannot provide a comparative economic perspective of the UK's performance relative to others.

Tours abroad provide a number of specific advantages. They put the UK in an international context and show us something of the world that Britain is trading and competing in. Secondly, they give us a picture of cultural and political differences that sometimes generate economic and social targets which may be different from our own. Finally, they open up a range of industries and production methods which we cannot observe in this country.

Planning and organisation

The first decision to be made is of course the choice of country to be visited. This will depend upon the type of economic system chosen to be studied, but this choice may well be tempered by logistical considerations. These will include the location of the school or college, availability of transport, time available for the tour, and of course budget constraints. Although location and budgets will vary, common problems will be experienced over transport and length of visit.

Since April 1978 we have organised seven economics tours abroad to Denmark, Greece, Norway, Switzerland, West Germany, Sweden and Hungary. We have made three tours by air and four by school mini-bus and have found the mini-bus tours superior for their flexibility in allowing us to see a good cross-section of the economy we are visiting.

However, when taking a mini-bus there are a number of administrative duties to attend to, such as the need to obtain Green Card insurance, breakdown insurance, the maintenance of a tachograph record, warning triangle, headlight deflectors, and so on.

Duration of visits will vary from trip to trip but we would suggest an average of seven to ten days to allow three or four days for visits and the remainder for cultural and social activities and general sightseeing.

As far as accommodation is concerned, we have found that youth hostels are cheap and generally satisfactory. If teachers have an International Leader's Card, students do not need to be individual members of the Youth Hostels Association.

Perhaps the major problem is that of arranging visits. Many organisations offer standard visits but these should generally be avoided since they are aimed at the general public rather than the economist. Teachers should attempt to make specific arrangements with the organisation or institution that they wish to visit.

The visits should be a representative cross-section of the structure of the economy concerned. To establish contact one can firstly approach the Commercial Attaché in the British Embassy in the country concerned who will usually be able to supply a list of useful addresses. This could be followed by similar requests to the representatives of the country concerned in the UK. More localised help may be available through chambers of commerce in the areas to be visited. Finally, contact with academic institutions may also be helpful in organising the programme and/or providing an initial talk on the economy concerned.

Many of these points are illustrated in the tour we made to Hungary in 1982:

Programme of visits for the Royal Grammar School, Newcastle, in Budapest, Hungary

Monday	10.00 a.m.	Hungarian Chamber of Commerce
	1.00 p.m.	Address by Professor of Economics at the Karl Marx University of Economics
	3.00 p.m.	Hungarovin – wine-producing company
Tuesday	9.00 a.m.	Ikarus bus factory
	2.00 p.m.	Talk with chief economist at the National Bank of Hungary
Wednesday	8.00 a.m.	Obuda co-operative farm
	10.30 a.m.	Central Statistical Office
	2.30 p.m.	Globus food-canning factory at Debrecen

When approaching firms or organisations for visits, it is advisable to be as specific as possible and give details of the party, including an indication of their level of economic understanding.

The advantages of economics tours abroad

One of the major advantages from the staff point of view is that we end up with a number of interesting stories and anecdotes which can enliven classroom teaching.

For example, the chairman of the nationalised Norwegian coal industry told us about the situation when they wish to order new equipment. He said that they write to suppliers in England, the USA, France and Germany, asking what they have to offer. From England they get a long letter back explaining why the British product is best. From the USA they get a glossy brochure explaining why their product is superior. From the French they never hear again – and the Germans have two men in his office the next day trying to clinch the deal. Stories like this give a new slant to export figures!

Some of the experiences may not even be directly related to the visits. For instance, in Hungary we found that our hotel would not accept payment in their own currency until the Central Bank came to our aid.

A second advantage for teachers is that the comparative knowledge gained abroad can give a fresh perspective on our teaching of the British economy. For example, our visit to the comprehensive apprentice training centre at Krupps in Essen gave us a deeper appreciation of the current debate on youth training.

Thirdly, teachers can gain specific knowledge which is not available in the textbooks. We can ask the questions we always wanted to ask. At GATT headquarters in Geneva, we were able to discuss with one of their economists the implications of the Tokyo Round; at the German TUC headquarters we looked in some detail at the German system of worker representation and could then contrast this with our own Bullock Report; and finally, complex areas such as foreign exchange markets come alive when you stand in the dealing room of a Swiss bank.

As far as the gain to students is concerned, they can see the problems and advantages of other economies and so become more informed, and perhaps balanced, in their viewpoints. The opportunity to sit in the boardroom of a Swiss bank and pass around a gold bar worth £¼ million which has been brought up from the vaults just for us, is worth any number of chapters on the Gold Standard! In Hungary students were able to discuss the problems of international currency convertibility facing a communist country with the chief economist of the National Bank.

Economics tours abroad involve months of hard work and frustration, but in providing students and teachers with specific economic insights and a broader understanding of other economies, they are essentially worthwhile and highly recommended.

Section 4: Ways of Teaching Particular Topics

36 Supply, Demand and Price
Mike Morris

Introduction

The core of microeconomics is the understanding of what constitutes the return from consuming or using a particular commodity or resource and the cost of offering those items to the market. Where one draws the line, so to speak, between extreme hypothesis (*ceteris paribus*) and the reality, which accommodates the influence of all factors, depends upon one's level of study. Though we may recognise the existence of a full Walrasian general equilibrium analysis, at A-level we are still dealing with relatively simple equations with few variables to determine new equilibria.

Therefore, a vital skill required in the teaching of microeconomic theory is to lead the students step by step along the road from one laboratory situation to another without allowing them to glimpse reality too soon and become confused by its complexity. At the same time there is in this section of the course a tendency to throw too many equations and calculations at them in the early stages, so that they are engrossed in excessive detail and lose the sense of adventure that is vital if they are to regenerate interest in the subject. The message is familiar – compromise!

Inevitably, some groups will be more mathematical and will revel in the intricacies of graphical analysis, while others with weak numeracy need earlier development of the wider implications of the diagrams they are straining to master, in order to encourage them to persist in their labours. The speed of their progress and the emphases put on the different processes will, therefore, be dependent upon the shrewd estimation of the students' propensities by the teacher. While bits of the course are easily programmable, the overall pace must be supervised carefully and each student's reactions taken into account. Economics is a social science in more ways than one and, unless the students are sorted with great precision into computerised blocks like robots, even the teaching of something as seemingly mechanical as supply and demand analysis cannot be left entirely to a computer program. The basic diagrams and equations will need greater or less

development, and feedback from the student must be dealt with to avoid frustration. What is more, it is amazing how fresh minds can bring to life even the most watertight of accepted graphical sequences. Over-reliance on a fixed sequence and timetable of individual learning can lead to stultification and stagnation on all sides.

Timing

Once the rudiments of supply and demand analysis and the interlinking effects of changing prices are understood, the other topics can be organised in a clearer fashion. Nationalised industries' pricing policies, effects of taxation on government revenue and the consequential restraints on action to reduce or increase public expenditure, regional multipliers and the costs of regional aid in terms of subsidies, international trade and the results of changing exchange rates, interest rates, investment, European Community 'mountains', OPEC oil prices – the list is extensive. These are all more easily explained, once it is possible to analyse the major factors and assemble them into a diagram, however simple it may be initially. For these reasons, most textbooks begin with a fairly detailed exposition of supply and demand, usually following it immediately in logical fashion with an analysis of the theory of the firm (see Chapter 37).

There are a few authors who leave the diagrammatic presentation of price determination until later in the course.[1] After a brief discussion of scarcity and choice they move on to more descriptive topics before returning to expound the basics of microeconomics. This approach may well appeal to the less numerate students, in that it does not immediately present them with a difficult hurdle to jump, but, since the examinations require a detailed knowledge of how market forces determine price, not least the multiple-choice papers, an early attack has a great deal to commend it. It gives students a longer overall time to master the more difficult sections. It presents them with something different and challenging, while they are still enthusiastic about starting a new subject. If they have already done O-level economics or some related course, then the foundations of the microeconomic theory will already have been laid, and there would be no advantage in delaying the next steps. Finally, as mentioned above, a visual presentation of the forces at work will often accelerate the understanding of a structural or applied topic.

It is tempting to deal first with the more interesting 'macrocosm', so that major issues of the day can be examined in an economic format and the students can achieve speedy success by using jargon in discussion with their peers.[2] However, the teacher will frequently be itching to use the tools of microanalysis, especially elasticity, but will also find that the students are aware of too many influencing factors on these topics, so that abstraction becomes difficult. Microeconomics is much more amenable to investigations under laboratory conditions. Moreover, it is much better for the pacing of the course to leave macroeconomics as the carrot to pull them through the less exciting price theory. The Greeks had a phrase for it – 'do nothing in excess' – and Socrates may well have been thinking of the teaching of economics when he attempted to reach the universal definition of 'justice' by first defining 'the just man'. Micro then macro.

Method

1   It was suggested above that the teacher should be ready to compromise. Teachers who begin the course with supply and demand analysis realise that slabs of micro theory for week after week can quickly dismay the bright-eyed student, let alone the cynical one. Some leaven must be put with the dough: a suitable concomitant is the study of the development of a firm from sole proprietorship through to joint-stock company. This fits in well with market theory, of course, and by making the students start up a hypothetical firm and taking them through the various stages of expansion, the teacher can involve them personally in the learning process and correlate with concepts like equilibrium price and elasticity. Consideration of the joint-stock company naturally leads on to the complexities of share prices and the Stock Exchange. Interrelationships between the determination of share prices and the micro theory abound at this stage, with the added advantage that costs of production need not be covered in detail.

2   Though essay writing is vital in the course in general, in the initial stages of supply and demand, instructive questions, which can test the ability to organise and develop an answer in essay form, are difficult to devise. At the same time, rapid learning of the relationships and how to draw the diagrams is essential. Hence short answer tests with definitions and graph drawing are more suitable. After each section, the students should become used to quick tests, on which they should expect to achieve almost full marks. A high success rate at fairly frequent

intervals has several advantages. It means that most diagrams will be drawn at least twice in the first term. Also, the students become accustomed to examination conditions and are less likely to suffer from nerves at a later date. Finally, as with all teaching, psychology is very important. Success, on however small a scale, breeds confidence and enthusiasm, which breeds further success.

3   Many problems are brought about by unequal progress in a class. If there is a cumulative gap between the slowest and the fastest learners, both extremes suffer. The slowest begin to lose hope and the fastest lose interest. Once the trend has set in, it is very difficult to reverse it. Thus an attempt must be made to keep the class working together. Joint note-taking and graph drawing from the blackboard, overhead projector or whatever, may be slow, but is very useful in the early stages. It teaches students how to make notes, how to draw the graphs (the teacher has time to go round and check on neatness and accuracy while the work is being done) and sorts our misunderstandings on the spot.

Once the majority are making presentable notes, photocopies of notes and diagrams or some basic textbook can be used for class discussion with rough additions being made on particular points. Each student can then make a neat version of the notes later in his own time. As an intermediary stage, photocopied notes could be distributed, with gaps where diagrams are needed. These could be filled in in class and copied up neatly later. However it is done, the aim should be to keep everyone moving at approximately the same speed, so that at any time the teacher can move the group on to a new topic or recapitulate an important concept.

4   Normally the A-level course covers two years. If one reserves what is available of the last term for revision, there are, therefore, only five terms, in which to steam through an extensive syllabus. Speed is essential. A reasonable target should be to complete supply and demand analysis by the end of the first term and the theory of the firm by the end of the second. However, the process described in 3 above can easily become turgid and lose momentum. A snappy rate of progress needs to be set right from the start. Short periods of constructive relaxation will be necessary to increase overall productivity. These can take the form of reference to topical events, which show the power of market forces, though prior research and planning is vital to avoid a clumsy explanation, which might cloud the main point under review and dispel some of the authority of the teacher. The creation and disposal of European Community food mountains is a good example, as long as the discussion is not allowed to spill over into politics at this stage. Similarly, the influence of OPEC on oil prices provides a telling illustration of the effect of a change in price on both the demand and the supply curves. Some books of collected items are to be found.[3]

Content

There is a wide range of textbooks available on which to base the teaching. Most follow a scheme similar to the following: 1 A general introduction with a definition of economics and its basic constituents, pointing out that resources can be allocated by an infinite variety of methods between the two extremes of the command economy and the purely free-enterprise economy. All economies are 'mixed'. 2 Having explained that the price mechanism of allocation (Adam Smith's 'invisible hand') is the prime subject for investigation at this level, move quickly on to the demand schedule and the drawing of a demand curve. 3 Explain the derivation of the supply curve. 4 The determination of market price and the effects of shifts in demand and supply curves. 5 Elasticity – PeD, YeD, XeD and PeS. 6 The basis of demand – utility, income and substitution effects, perverse demand curves, the law of equimarginal utility and consumer equilibrium. 7 The basis of supply – law of diminishing returns, costs of production, economies and diseconomies of scale. 8 Applications – taxation, subsidies, cobweb theorem, joint supply, etc.

Most of the above list is a generally accepted sequence, though the basis of supply 7 inevitably overlaps and is a vital foundation for discussion of the theory of the firm. The justification for including it here is that it balances 6 and also clears the decks ready for introductory notes on specialisation and the production function before attacking the theory of the firm proper. One can certainly afford to make the survey of the basis of supply relatively quick, since most of it will be investigated again in full in the context of pricing and output decisions of the firm. More detailed suggestions follow for the treatment of the sections listed above.

1 Introduction to microeconomics

It is vital that the students do not get the impression that there are only two methods of allocating resources in an economy, the price mechanism (capitalism) and the command system (socialism). In this respect a diagram showing a spectrum of mixtures between the two extremes (with capitalism on the right, of course) makes the point clear, and by asking students to fill in where they think different countries lie on the spectrum, the teacher can involve them at an early stage. Stanlake has a good chapter on this point.[4]

2 The demand curve

Although in the early lessons learning may be accelerated by treating the situation as buyers strolling through a physical market with sellers competing to sell their goods and services, the teacher should make it clear that the market is not necessarily a particular location in economics. As long as there is some kind of communication between buyers and sellers, a market exists. When a demand curve has been plotted, preferably by the students themselves, great emphasis must be laid on the

assumptions underlying it: homogeneous goods, unchanged income, fixed prices of substitutes and complements, no change in information and conditions (i.e. consumers' tastes constant) and no change in population. Get students to use abbreviations in their notes straightaway – tell them to be economical! As these things are discussed, shifts in the demand curve will naturally be evolved. Insist on neat and correctly labelled diagrams from the start.

To avoid becoming involved in non-normal goods at this stage, it is probably better to direct the class to safe examples like eggs or bread. The former is useful in that their unit price is quite low and therefore the arithmetic involved is relatively easy. Once an individual consumer's demand curve (ICD) has been drawn, the class can more easily construct a market demand curve by horizontal summation of the ICDs.

Students will see that there can be a wide range of individual tastes, but the market demand curve is usually a fairly regular shape. At this point it is appropriate to point out one of the basic assumptions for all of the theory – rationality of both consumer and producer. In this instance the demand curve is downward sloping. If challenged, tell students that upward sloping curves will be dealt with in the very near future. To prevent giving the impression that the teacher has been caught out and is merely delaying, be quick to praise the questioner for anticipating a future stage in the course.

3 The supply curve

Both 2 and 3 are dealt with very clearly in Lipsey.[5] Stanlake is good but deals with the theory in a slightly different order.[6] Hanson[7] introduces inferior goods early (as does Stanlake); these are probably best left until the discussion of elasticity. However, Hanson does develop the topic clearly and produces a large number of very useful graphs. A lively explanation is put forward by Harvey, also using eggs as an example, though the transition to applications of demand and supply curve analysis is probably too early.[8] Work needs to be done on elasticity and the basis of supply first.

It is very important that students understand the precise definition of supply – the 'quantity offered for sale per unit time at different prices', that is, not 'the quantity produced . . .'. This may help them to accept that the supply curve is generally upward sloping. A teaching tip is to begin the drawing of the supply curve by considering zero price first and then gradually increasing price and asking what would be the reaction of the entrepreneur. If one starts with the top of the supply curve and reduces price, the student is not always clear what the entrepreneur would do. The avoidance of 'what if . . .' questions can save a great deal of time. Once the basic processes have been set up, those questions can be dealt with very succinctly or, more usually, become redundant.

In the first part (1) the main definitions should have been attempted, including opportunity cost. This concept is usually explained with reference to the consumer. In this section the choice of the entrepreneur can be explained in terms of opportunity cost. If entrepreneurs can plant either strawberries or raspberries, they will choose the one with the higher market price. Thus, as the price of raspberries rises (all other factors being unchanged – *ceteris paribus*), more entrepreneurs will switch from whatever they are producing to raspberries, and vice versa. The supply curve is upward sloping.

The treatment of costs, which are the basis of supply, is best left until later (section 7) in order than an early description of equilibrium can be achieved (section 4). Similarly, the distinction between short run, very short run and long run is explained more satisfactorily after the examination of elasticity (section 5).

4 Market price

This section has a natural attraction, a kind of milestone. Once the equilibrium has been explained, it is immediately possible to see how much of the preceding sections has been misunderstood by asking the students to show the effects of changes in any of the factors. Insist on a precise answer, so that a systematic routine is instilled in them, which will save them a great deal of time, especially in multiple-choice tests. Save the applications of this analysis until section 8, if possible, though, as with all teaching, one must judge the mood of the class and their ability to move quickly. A short discussion of the effects of subsidising a product may be sufficient to satisfy their inquisitiveness.

5 Elasticity

The teacher must beware of putting off the non-numerate student in this section. Students should prepare a clear and well-ordered set of notes, culling the best bits from a range of books.[9] A suggested sequence is as follows:

(i) *PeD* (price elasticity of demand)

  A Definition and drawing of the limiting cases (see Figure 36.1).

  B Demonstration that the slope of *DD* is not the same as *PeD* (see Figure 36.2).

     e.g. A drop from 25p to 20p results in an increase of 5 units demanded on both demand curves. However, on D_1D_1, 5 units is a doubling of demand (very responsive), whereas on D_2D_2 it represents an increase of only about 3 per cent.

  C Measurement – Marshall's formula: $\dfrac{\%\triangle QD}{\%\triangle P}$ which can be translated into $\dfrac{P\cdot\triangle Q}{Q\cdot\triangle P}$. Point out that the smaller the change in price the greater the accuracy. Since the elasticity over the same arc will be different, when measured with price rising or price falling, the average formula is more satisfactory for *PeD* over a price range. Leftwich gives a clear explanation of this, as he

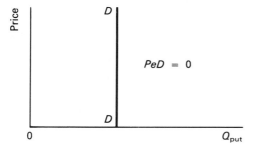

Figure 36.1

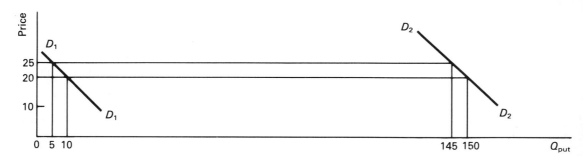

Figure 36.2

does of the whole topic. Relate the change in total revenue to elasticity, and show how to calculate point elasticity.

Draw the rectangular hyperbola with *PeD* = 1. Show the importance of this point, especially in multiple-choice questions.

D Factors affecting elasticity. Note Lipsey's comment on this.

E The significance of the concept – to the entrepreneur and to the government. Some diagrams showing the effects of subsidies and taxation with curves of different elasticity may be appropriate here, even though a formal examination of price elasticity of supply (*PeS*) has not yet been covered. Once again, it depends on the class. With the average or slower than average class it is probably better to leave these applications until section 8, and merely talk about these points in general terms here.

(ii) *YeD* (income elasticity of demand)
A Definition, explanation of the sign – positive for normal goods and negative for inferior.
B Factors affecting *YeD* – existing level of income, time period, luxury or necessity, availability of substitutes.

(iii) *XeD* (cross-elasticity of demand)
Definition, explanation of signs – positive for substitutes, negative for complements. Figure 36.3 is useful as a visual prompt.

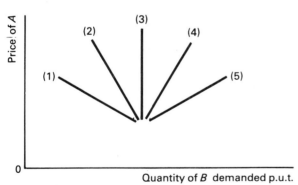

1 Negative, therefore *A* and *B* are complements. Very elastic therefore they are close complements.
2 Complements, but not very close.
3 Zero elasticity, therefore independent goods.
4 Positive, therefore substitutes.
5 Positive and high elasticity, therefore *A* and *B* are close substitutes.

(iv) *PeS* (price elasticity of supply)
A Definition, explanation of sign.

Figure 36.3

B Factors affecting *PeS* – time-period and cost of attracting factors from alternative employment. A diagram showing the supply curve in different time periods is appropriate here.

6 The basis of demand

A reasonable order for this section is: utility, total utility and marginal utility (the paradox of value), law of diminishing marginal utility (LDMU), principle of equimarginal utility (PEMU), income and substitution effects, perverse demand curves, indifference curve analysis (ICA). Following this system the method of explanation would be by the 'revealed preference theory' – the consumer is assumed to be rational and reveals his or her preference consistently in the demand curve rather than as a result of a hypothetical indifference map. This approach is more direct and testable (see Stonier and Hague[10]). However, ICA is gaining favour. Multiple-choice questions increasingly require the use and understanding of indifference curves. It is true that they give an apparently rigorous dissection of income and substitution effects, show the LDMU in terms of diminishing marginal rate of substitution, and can more clearly relate demand to a given budget. Stigler,[11] whose book is the 'bible' for price theory (probably best left as a resource for the teacher at this level), and most other authors concentrate on ICA.[12] Teachers must make up their own minds where to put the emphasis, though certainly at some point in the course indifference curves have to be explained and their use in combination with the budget line developed.

Perverse demand curves are usually easily accepted by A-level students as rare exceptions, and can be learned as such. Lipsey deals with them in this way and points out that factual evidence of their existence is difficult to obtain.[13] As with all empirical studies, it is almost impossible to filter out the effects of extraneous factors.

7 The basis of supply

This section should not impinge on the theory of the firm in terms of determining an output and discussing profits. It is primarily an expansion of the difference between short-term and long-term costs. It involves therefore an explanation of the law of diminishing marginal returns (LDMR) which applies in the short run, when there is a fixed factor. Then follows the derivation of the long-run average cost curve with a discussion of internal and external economies and diseconomies of scale. Lipsey deals with this as the theory of costs.[14]

Students usually find this relatively straightforward, though the drawing of graphs to show average total costs, average variable costs, marginal costs, etc. provides problems, until they plot marginal costs half a unit early. Then marginal costs cut through minimum average costs and the logical justification for it can be explained.

When explaining LDMR, it is a natural progression to talk about producer equilibrium, which will only be achieved, if marginal output does eventually decrease, as employment of the variable factor increases. The equilibrium for the principle of least cost combination with the marginal output of each factor divided by its price being equal, should remind the students of PEMU which determines consumer equilibrium. The distinction between product markets and factor markets is a good one to present early in the course, so that factor pricing is not such a difficult hurdle when it comes.

8 Applications

Probably by this time the teacher will have already been lured into real-life examples by eager devotees. Here is a list of suggested applications:

(a) Indirect taxes – with differing elasticities for demand and supply curves, noting the effect of VAT as opposed to excise duties on the supply curve.[15]

(b) Subsidies – similar to (a). The distribution of benefit between consumer and producer will depend on *PeD*.

(c) Direct taxes – noting the distinction between normal and inferior goods.

(d) Price fixing – below equilibrium,[16] producing a shortage and possible 'black market'; above equilibrium, as with European Community farm prices, producing surpluses.

(e) The importance of elasticity in determining the effects of devaluation with fixed exchange rates: since elasticities will tend to be low in the short run, the implications for the balance of trade (the 'J' curve).

(f) The effects of sudden changes in demand (e.g. government reflationary policies) on inflation even with high unemployment.

(g) The 'cobweb' theorem, applying especially to agricultural produce, whereby a change in demand may spark off an 'explosive' price fluctuation, if the *PeS* is greater than *PeD*.[17]

(h) Competitive demand – where an increase in demand for one good reduces the demand for another (e.g. beef and lamb).

(i) Complementary (joint) demand – where an increase in demand for one good increases the demand for another (e.g. freezers and electricity).

(j) Joint supply – where the increase in demand for one good induces more to be supplied of that good and another, which is produced with it almost as a by-product (e.g. coke and town gas or mutton and fleeces; an interesting example).

(k) Derived demand – where an increase in demand for a good leads to an increase in demand for the producer or servicer (e.g. cars and mechanics).

Resources

There is a need to keep in touch with the latest publications and ideas. This can be simply done by joining the Economics Association. Reviews of newly released books and material on the teaching of economics are

presented along with stimulating articles on the subject-matter of the course. Regular reading of the 'heavy' newspapers and journals, like *The Economist*, will provide good examples for analysis (e.g. the extending of VAT to hot take-away foods in the UK 1984 Budget caused a considerable amount of speculation on the elasticity of demand for those goods and the derived demand for the suppliers).

Data-response questions are mostly useful for students after they have finished the theory of the firm. However, multiple-choice questions are ideal for testing their understanding of supply, demand and price.[18]

Increasingly, computer programs are being devised for this topic in the course, though the majority of programs are still for macroeconomics. The teacher should do thorough research of the material available. Once again, the Economics Association is very helpful.[19] Remember the proviso that the teacher should monitor the students' reactions carefully and keep the learning process a two-way operation (see the last paragraph of the Introduction).

Notes and references

1   Paish, F. W., *Benham's Economics* (Pitman, 1971).
2   Nobbs, J., *'A' level Economics*, 3rd edn. (McGraw-Hill, 1983).
3   Rees, R., and Baxter, R. E., *Readings in Economics* (Collins Educational, 1984) Book One.
4   Stanlake, G. F., *Introductory Economics*, 3rd edn. (Longman, 1980) pp. 9–20.
5   Lipsey, R. G., *Introduction to Positive Economics*, 6th edn. (Weidenfeld & Nicolson, 1983) ch. 7.
6   Stanlake, op. cit., ch. 14.
7   Hanson, J. L., *Textbook of Economics*, 4th edn. (Macdonald & Evans, 1969) p. 160.
8   Harvey, J., *Intermediate Economics*, 4th edn. (Macmillan, 1983) ch. 2.
9   For example, Lipsey, op. cit.; Stanlake, op. cit.; Manchester Economics Project, *Understanding Economics* (Ginn, 1972); Leftwich, R. H., *The Price System and Resource Allocation*, 6th edn. (Dryden Press, 1976) pp. 41 ff.
10 Stonier, A. W., and Hague, D. C., *A Textbook of Economic Theory*, 4th edn. (Longman, 1972) ch. 4.
11 Stigler, G., *Price Theory*, revised edn. (Macmillan, 1964) p. 70.
12 For example, Leftwich, op. cit.; Stanlake, op. cit.; Manchester Economics Project, op. cit.; Lipsey, op. cit.; Nevin, E. T., *Textbook of Economic Analysis*, 5th edn. (Macmillan Education, 1981) ch. 3.
13 Lipsey, op. cit., pp. 184 and 197.
14 Lipsey, op. cit., pp. 200–34.
15 Manchester Economics Project, op. cit., pp. 163–5.
16 Harvey, op. cit., ch. 26.
17 Lipsey, op. cit., pp. 131–3.
18 For example, Harbury, C. D., *Workbook in Introductory Economics*, 2nd edn. (Pergamon Press, 1974); Oliver, J. M., *Multiple Choice Questions for 'A' level Economics* (Butterworth, 1983); Stanlake, G. F., *Objective Tests in Economics* (Longman, 1974); Chapman, J. M., and Smith, J. C., *Multiple Choice Questions in Economics for A level*,

3rd edn. (Heinemann Educational Books, 1984). See also Robinson, R., *Study Guide to Accompany Samuelson's Economics*, 9th edn. (McGraw-Hill, 1973); Manchester Economics Project, op. cit.; Livesey, F., *A Textbook of Economics*, 2nd edn. (Polytech Publishers, 1982).

19 Cotterrell, A., 'Computer programs for teaching economics', *Economics*, vol. XIX, pt. 1, no. 81, spring 1983, p. 16; Wood, K. R. J., *Computer Assisted Learning in a Sixth Form Course*, research paper circulated by the Department of Economics and Business Studies, University of London Institute of Education, 1983.

37   The Theory of the Firm
Alain Anderton

Introduction

Since their inception, A-level economics syllabuses have required a knowledge of the theory of the firm. Traditionally this referred to the neoclassical models of perfect competition and monopoly, first propounded in the nineteenth century. Then students began to be asked about the neoclassical theory of monopolistic competition and were expected to display an awareness of oligopolistic markets. It is only recently that oligopoly theory has received any prominence – a prominence that it surely deserves given that most output in this country is generated in oligopolistic industries. However, the neoclassical theories of perfect competition and monopoly remain at the core of teaching in this area.

The following is a summary of the main content areas in this topic:

1 Cost and revenue curves, including marginal, average and total.
2 The assumptions underlying any theory of the firm – the goals of firms, number of firms in the industry, knowledge, extent of freedom of entry to the market and the degree of product homogeneity.
3 How different firms reach price and output decisions in equilibrium – for instance, in perfect competition firms will produce where $MC = MR = AC = AR$ whereas in monopoly they will produce where $MC = MR$ and price according to the average revenue curve. Equilibrium decisions for the main types of competition are covered in any standard textbook.
4 What happens in disequilibrium – what happens if a perfectly competitive firm is making abnormal profits or a loss? Why is it that for a monopolist to produce where $AC = AR$ would be going against one of the assumptions of the neoclassical theory of the firm?
5 Interesting corollaries of neoclassical theories – an excellent exposé of these can be found in Lipsey's

Positive Economics. They include why all perfectly competitive firms in equilibrium must have identical cost curves, how monopolists can profitably split markets, and why monopoly is accused of being less efficient than perfect competition.
6 The main criticisms of the neoclassical theories – does it really matter that firms in real life don't know their marginal cost and revenue curves? Are the assumptions of 'perfect knowledge', etc. realistic and, if not, does it affect the validity of the theory? Is it important that evidence shows that AC curves are L-shaped and not U-shaped?
7 An appreciation of alternative theories of the firm. No particular theory is specified in any current syllabuses or demanded in any current examination papers. However, it would be difficult to tackle some of the essay questions without some knowledge of at least one alternative theory to the neoclassical theory of the firm.

Essential to any critical examination of the theory of the firm is a grounding in applied economics in this area.

Methods

The neoclassical theory of the firm is particularly difficult for students to understand. When asked about what sections of the course they have found difficult, students will almost invariably mention this area, and for two main reasons. First, the theory is not intuitively obvious to them. The teacher can work through the theory, and the students may understand each step, yet they will often turn round at the end and say they don't understand. They don't seem to be able to see the wood for the trees. Secondly, the theory is taught mathematically and many students have a block about mathematics in general and graphs in particular. They see the mathematics as an (impossible!) end in itself, not as a means of understanding economics.

One of the best ways to increase understanding of traditional theory is to get the students to use it in individual questions. All the workbooks published at this level have sections on the theory of the firm. Working through these individually, students will be much more likely to understand the theory. Multiple-choice question books are also very good sources of these questions.

Workbooks do not solve the problems of exposition, and most teachers probably approach this topic using chalk and talk. The textbooks usually take the following path through the minefield: cost curves, perfect competition, monopoly, imperfect competition. Strewn along the way there usually is work on the short and long run. As mentioned above, it is very important for students to have an overall picture of what they are doing at all times. What follows is one possible way of guiding them through the exposition with this in mind.

At this level, the theory tries to find out three things:

1 At what price will the firm sell its goods?
2 What quantity will it produce?
3 How much profit will it make?

At the start, students should be made to realise that pricing, output and profit all depend on costs and revenue. Average, total and marginal can then be introduced. The relationship between average, total and marginal tends to present comparatively few difficulties. Plenty of practice from a workbook is advisable, though. If a student is failing to understand, always go back to a simple example, such as 'If you buy three apples at 5p each, what is the total cost to you?' or 'If a firm buys three sacks of material, one priced at £3, one at £4, and the last at £5, what is the average price paid per sack?' The shape of total, average and marginal cost curves should then be explained. The law of diminishing returns gives rise to the upturn in the average variable cost curve. From average cost data, the marginal cost curve can be derived via total costs. A useful introductory exercise is to get the students to construct the cost curves from just the average cost data. Small points, like the fact that the MC curve cuts the AC curve at its lowest point, should be briefly explained. It is not worth spending a great deal of time explaining the mathematics of this since it tends merely to confuse the students. It is far better to press on and to return later once they have an overall view of the mechanism. It should be emphasised that these cost curves apply to *all* firms.

Revenue curves can now be introduced. For all firms, output in equilibrium is where $MC = MR$. As with many proofs on this topic, the easiest way to approach it is to show what would happen if $MC \neq MR$. $MC = MR$ is a crucial landmark and every student should, when asked 'Where does a firm produce in equilibrium?', immediately reply 'where $MC = MR$'. Once output is known, price is known, because of the demand curve facing the firm. Work out the shape of the demand curve facing the firm, show that it is also the AR curve and then derive the MR curve from it. The differing assumptions for each type of competition will have to be introduced here. Profit is simply total revenue minus total costs. Students experiencing difficulties with profit should be taken back to an easy example of how to calculate total revenue and costs, and then asked to apply it graphically. Equilibrium output, price and profit depend on the freedom of entry assumption. If there is freedom of entry, no abnormal profits will be made in the long run. Students then work out what this means in terms of MC, AC, MR and AR curves. The concept of long and short run will have to be introduced here, if it has not been explained before. Finally, the corollaries for each type of competition can be proved, preferably by the students.

All the time, the simplicity of the mathematics involved, the similarities between the differing forms of competition and what is ultimately going to be proved by the theory should be emphasised. If the students have a clear idea of where they are going, the exposition will not get bogged down in time-consuming minor points which merely clutter up and obscure the argument. The finer details can be set in place once the broad outline has been established. Table 37.1 could perhaps be written on a wall chart for constant reference.

Table 37.1

Landmarks
1 We want to find out (a) output;
(b) price;
(c) profit.
2 Remember that standard cost curves apply to all firms.
3 Output for all firms will be where $MC = MR$ if profits are maximised.
4 Using the demand curve, output will determine price.
5 Total profit = total revenue − total costs.
6 Equilibrium: if there is freedom of entry, it will be where no abnormal profit is made; if there are barriers to entry, it will be where there is maximum abnormal profit.

Teachers can considerably improve their exposition by attention to teaching skills. A very common source of misunderstanding arises from the use of poorly drawn graphs. Many textbooks are guilty of this. But, more important, teachers may draw hasty diagrams on the blackboard which they can understand but the struggling student cannot. One simple way to improve the quality of a diagram is to use coloured chalk – using a different colour for each curve; or one colour for total cost and revenue curves and another for marginal cost and revenue – or perhaps putting all cost curves in one colour and all revenue curves in another. What system of colour is used depends on the purpose of the exposition. Carefully drawn curves and straight labelled axes should always be the rule, however quick the sketch. Simple drawing rules should be observed and passed on to the student. For instance, the MC curve cuts the AC curve at its lowest point. A downward sloping marginal revenue curve bisects the distance between the $x = 0$ line and a linear average revenue curve. One particularly difficult diagram to draw is the equilibrium position in monopolistic competition where the AC or MC curves should be drawn last remembering that the MC curve cuts the AC curve at its lowest point and that $AC = AR$ and $MC = MR$.

One way to get round drawing difficulties is to produce a set of overhead transparencies, each transparency carrying a different curve. These can then be built up as overlays to produce whatever situation is desired. Once completed in permanent ink, these transparencies can be used year after year.

How to teach alternative theories of the firm is perhaps even more beset with problems than how to teach the neoclassical theory of the firm. The neoclassical theory of the firm demands intellectual rigour and a logical presentation, but at least it is fairly clear what examination boards expect teachers to teach. When it comes to alternatives, however, teachers have to ask themselves whether or not they should present the neo-Keynesian theory of the firm, look at Baumol's model of sales maximisation, consider behavioural and managerial theories, teach games theory, study Galbraith's *The New Industrial State* or, indeed, present other theories.

A few general guidelines can be given. First, no board expects students to have the same amount of knowledge of a particular alternative theory as they do of the neoclassical theory of the firm. Certainly a formal mathematical treatment, of, say, the neo-Keynesian theory of the firm is not required. Secondly, broad knowledge of several different theories is likely to prove more beneficial to students than an in-depth knowledge of one particular theory. Students will benefit from appreciating that economists are concerned with making their models mirror the real world of business and will realise that different economists explain the same world in different ways. Thirdly, it is valuable reinforcement with regard to the neoclassical theory of the firm to be constantly comparing the alternative theory under discussion with neoclassical theory.

Resources

Textbooks

All A-level textbooks (apart from Livesey's *A Textbook of Economics*) contain a satisfactory outline of neoclassical theory. Two texts in particular are worth mentioning:

Lipsey, R. G., *An Introduction to Positive Economics*, 6th edn. (Weidenfeld & Nicolson, 1983). This provides the most thorough outline of neoclassical theory likely to be accessible to A-level candidates. Also included is a spirited defence of neoclassical theory.
Stanlake, G. F., *Introductory Economics* 4th edn. (Longman, 1983). Contained in this book is a clear and

simple explanation of the neoclassical theory, accessible to all A-level candidates.

Both of these books, however, have the serious fault of implying that the neoclassical theory of the firm really is the best model available. More modern textbooks are adopting a more impartial approach. Worth mentioning in this respect are:

Anderton, A. G., *Economics: A New Approach* (University Tutorial Press, 1984). This has a complete chapter on alternative theories of the firm.
Burningham, D., *et al., Understanding Economics* 2nd edn. (Hodder & Stoughton, 1984). The chapter entitled 'Oligopoly' provides a well-balanced view of alternative theories.

A book that is openly critical of the neoclassical approach, to the point of providing the barest of outlines of it, is:

Livesey, F., *A Textbook of Economics* 2nd edn. (Polytech Publishers, 1982). Instead of adopting the neoclassical approach, Livesey concentrates almost exclusively on the neo-Keynesian model.

Other books

Some specialist texts exist in this area. These are:

Davies, J., and Hughes, S., *Pricing in Practice* (Heinemann Educational Books, 1975). This provides a summary of theory and a down-to-earth analysis of how firms price (and hence determine the output of) their products.
Galbraith, J. K., *The New Industrial State* (Penguin, 1967). This is a masterly attack on neoclassical economics and an attempt to build a realistic model of the firm. It is one of the few books that has had a significant impact upon economics, and which can be read and understood by A-level students.
Pass, C. L., and Sparkes, J. R., *Monopoly*, 2nd edn. (Heinemann Educational Books, 1980). Although concentrating on the control of monopoly, this does contain a good section on monopoly theory.
Utton, M. A., *Industrial Concentration* (Penguin, 1970). This is for the good A-level candidate and covers how concentration can be measured, as well as concentration in British industry.

Case studies

All data-response books contain case studies on the firm. Anderton's *Economics: A New Approach*, and Livesey's *A Textbook of Economics*, contain case studies in the text. Two specific relevant case-study books are:

Barker, P., *et al., Case Studies in the Competitive Process* (Heinemann Educational Books, 1976).
Blois, K., *et al., Case Studies in Competition Policy* (Heinemann Educational Books, 1975).

Audio-visual materials

Audio Learning Tapes, *Monopoly and Competition, Issues in Monopoly Policy* (ECA 001); *The Growth of the Firm, Growth and Business Concentration* (ECA 015); *Industry, Competition and Monopoly – Forms of*

Competition and Market Structures, Policy Considerations (ECA 051). Audio Learning Cassette/filmstrip programmes, *Production – Fixed and Variable Costs of Production* (ECO 003), and *The Law of Diminishing Returns* (ECO 010).

38   Economic Efficiency
Alain Anderton

Introduction

Economic efficiency is one of those topics that is gradually creeping into examination papers, not only because it is being seen as an important concept in itself, but also because 'efficiency' has been one of the favourite words in political speech-making since Margaret Thatcher's government came into office in 1979.

That bell-wether of textbooks, Lipsey's *An Introduction to Positive Economics*, illustrates the growing interest in efficiency. In the fourth edition (1975), efficiency was not important enough to include in the index. By the fifth edition (1979), efficiency was being discussed in the context of public goods and externalities. In the sixth edition (1983), the distinction between productive and allocative efficiency is made and is used to analyse monopoly and oligopolist markets.

The concept of economic efficiency can be applied to a wide number of teaching topics, such as social and environmental economics, comparative economic systems, government policy, nationalisation and economics of the public sector. These topics are dealt with elsewhere in the *Handbook*, so this chapter will be particularly concerned with considering economic efficiency in relation to market structures. Anyway, this is likely to be the context in which economic efficiency will be introduced to A-level students.

Content

An A-level student should be aware of:

1   the distinction between productive (or cost) efficiency, allocative efficiency and distributive efficiency;
2   the application of the concept of efficiency to the comparison of different types of market. Perfect competition versus monopoly is the most common comparison made;

3   the application of economic efficiency to the question of state versus private ownership of the means of production. The relative merits of privatisation have come to replace questions on the desirability of nationalisation on examination papers;
4   economic efficiency, externalities and social and private costs and benefits;
5   economic efficiency and market imperfections. In particular, A-level students will need to be familiar with UK legislation covering monopolies, mergers and restrictive practices (although examination boards are fortunately setting fewer and fewer questions that require a knowledge of the minutiae of the law), the broad principles that determine competition policy, and a knowledge of some (preferably recent) cases to illustrate the workings of legislation in practice. For the rest of this chapter, we shall be particularly concerned with 1, 2 and 5 above.

Methods

Students find it relatively easy to understand the distinction betweeen productive, allocative and distributive efficiency. Productive efficiency presupposes a knowledge of cost curves if a diagrammatic treatment is used. It is useful to point out here that a perfectly competitive industry in equilibrium will be productively efficient (because each firm is producing at the lowest point on its average cost curve), while a short-run profit-maximising monopolist will be productively inefficient (because economies of scale remain unexploited where $MC = MR$). It is also important to point out that the standard textbook case against monopoly, involving monopolising a perfectly competitive industry or vice versa, often cannot be translated into real-market situations. It is simply impossible to turn the electricity supply industry or the health industry or the rail industry into perfectly competitive industries. A better comparison therefore would be between productive efficiency in a monopoly and an oligopoly, or an oligopoly and mono-politically competitive industry. These comparisons of course fail to show that greater competition necessarily leads to greater productive efficiency.

Allocative and distributive efficiency can also be illustrated by the monopoly versus perfect competition debate. Monopolists may exploit their market through selling inferior products at a high price and in reduced quantities compared to a perfectly competitive industry. On the other hand, the dynamic advantages of monopoly put forward by economists such as J. Schumpeter and J. K. Galbraith should also be outlined. These relate to the necessity of market security and abnormal profits to encourage innovation. It is possible to show, on a standard monopoly diagram (see Figure 38.1), that innovation could not only lead to greater allocative efficiency owing to the production of new goods, but also greater productive efficiency as the cost of these goods declines.

If students find little problem in grasping the concept of efficiency, they do find difficulty in applying that concept. As with other economic concepts, such as the margin, or the multiplier, or elasticity, it is only repeated practice that enables students to turn an abstract concept into a workable tool for analysing real-life economic problems. The topic of market imperfections provides an ideal vehicle for the reinforcement of the concept of efficiency.

Teaching market imperfections didactically is unlikely to motivate students. There is a great temptation to feel that students should spend their time in class writing down every detail of monopolies and mergers legislation, to have notes on at least three restrictive practices cases which went before the Court, understand the historical background to resale price maintenance legislation, etc. A better approach is either for teachers to produce a set of notes to distribute to the class, or for students to make notes from whichever applied economics textbook they have been given (all applied textbooks have suitable sections on this staple topic). That leaves time in class to adopt a case-study approach. Case studies not only generally interest students but also force them to apply what they have learnt about efficiency and the workings of UK legislation. Case studies may be used in a variety of ways:

1 Students can be asked to read a particular case study and the teacher can use that as a basis for whole-class discussion.

2 The teacher can set questions on a case study and students can work out a solution to produce written answers to those questions, that is, students work

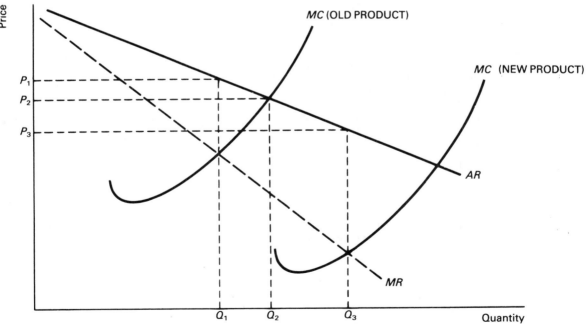

$P_1 Q_1$ = Price and output in monopoly for old product.
$P_2 Q_2$ = Price and output in perfect competition for old product.
$P_3 Q_3$ = Following innovation, price and output in monopoly for new product.

Figure 38.1

through a data-response question. This may or may not be followed by a whole-class discussion.

3 The class can be asked to engage in role play. One way to do that is to split the class into three groups – one representing the firm or group of firms under investigation, the second representing investigators from the Office of Fair Trading, the third the Monopolies and Mergers Commission, or the Restrictive Practices Court. The first two prepare cases that suit their interests, the third researches the case in the light of the relevant legislation. The first two groups then put their case to the third group, who finally deliver a judgement. The initial material given to the class should preferably not contain details of the actual outcome of the case. It is interesting, though, for students to be able to compare their judgement with the real-life outcome at the end of the role play.

4 A debate could be organised on an issue of topical interest, for example, 'This House believes that the proposed merger between company X and company Y is detrimental to the interests of the economy, and should be forbidden'.

5 For teachers who regularly collect newspaper material, a very worthwhile exercise is simply for students to spend a double lesson reading through recent articles reporting monopoly cases, etc. A good student will read between ten and fifteen articles in such a session. This activity has the added advantage that teachers show their students that wide reading is important – important enough to allocate time in class for it.

Case studies should be chosen to illustrate the way in which efficiency is impaired through monopolistic or restrictive practices (practices such as the establishment of fighting companies, pooled tenders, full-line forcing, collective boycotts, price discrimination, resale price maintenance), the sources of monopoly power (natural monopolies, barriers to entry, cartelisation, etc.), and the forms that government intervention might take if markets are to be made more efficient (from making monopolies and restrictive practices illegal to encouraging both).

Resources

Books

Most textbooks do not have an adequate treatment of efficiency. Two books that cover the topic extensively are:

Anderton, A. G., *Economics: A New Approach* (University Tutorial Press, 1984).

Burningham, D., *et al.*, *Understanding Economics*, 2nd edn. (Hodder & Stoughton, 1984).

Also worth reading are the relevant sections in:

Lipsey, R. G., *An Introduction to Positive Economics*, 6th edn. (Weidenfeld & Nicolson, 1983).

Livesey, F., *A Textbook of Economics*, 2nd edn. (Polytech Publishers, 1982).

All applied economic textbooks cover the area of competition legislation. For instance:

Harbury, C., and Lipsey, R. G., *An Introduction to the UK Economy* (Pitman, 1983).

Prest, A. R., and Coppock, D. J., *The UK Economy*, 10th edn. (Weidenfeld & Nicolson, 1984).

Three books that deal specifically with competition policy are:

Pass, C. L., and Sparkes, J. R., *Monopoly*, 2nd edn. (Heinemann Educational Books, 1980).

Stanlake, G., *Monopolies and Restrictive Practices*, 3rd edn. (Ginn, 1980).

Watts, N. R., *Competition, Monopoly and Public Policy* (Longman Resources Unit, 1982).

There are a large number of published case studies that teachers can use. Both Anderton's *Economics: A New Approach*, and Livesey's *A Textbook of Economics* (cited above), contain case studies. All data-response question books contain relevant material. One book that contains a particularly large number of items is:

Livesey, F., *Data Response Questions in Economics*, 2nd edn. (Polytech Publishers, 1979).

Two books contain much longer case studies. These are:

Barker, P., *et al.*, *Case Studies in the Competitive Process* (Heinemann Educational Books, 1976).

Blois, K., *et al.*, *Case Studies in Competition Policy* (Heinemann Educational Books, 1975).

The quality newspapers always have detailed articles on Monopolies and Mergers Commission reports as well as Restrictive Practices Court judgements.

Audio-visual material

Audio Learning Ltd, *Monopoly and Competition, Issues in Monopoly Policy* (ECA 001); *Industry, Competition and Monopoly – Forms of Competition and Market Structures, Policy Considerations* (ECA 051); Sussex Tapes, *Competition in Firms, Multinationals* (E 17).

39   Teaching the Theory of Consumer Behaviour
Andrew Leake

Introduction

How valuable it would be for us all as economics teachers to sit down together and be taught a lesson in advanced astro-physics! For one of the most difficult parts of teaching is to put oneself in the position of the student. This leap of the imagination is especially important to the teaching of pure economic theory. Teachers, presumably, understand their subject, and value it. The student has a quite different perspective.

It is possible, however, that trained economists are able to recall their first impressions of the theory of consumer behaviour more than for many other topics. I for one can still remember a feeling of astonishment at what I then saw as an obscure and contrived exercise in logic – not so much 'pure', as 'mere' theory.

There may be some A-level boards that continue to feel the same way. All boards include such major topics as demand curves and elasticity in their syllabuses. These I see as part of the broader area of supply, demand and price (see Chapter 36). But only one in three A-level candidates is required by their examination board (Cambridge, Oxford, Oxford and Cambridge, Welsh, Northern Ireland) to have studied the theory of consumer behaviour in any depth. For some of these candidates, this may amount to little more than a statement of the results of utility and indifference curve analysis, such that they can answer the more predictable forms of multiple-choice questions. A small minority of candidates may be taken far beyond this, to a detailed, almost degree-level, study of the same theories. How can their teachers best help them in these tasks?

Theories of consumer behaviour seem to present the typical A-level student with more than their fair share of difficulties. I suggest that there are three in particular of which teachers should beware. These are the students' fear, confusion and resistance. The fear, albeit unreasonable and unjustified, is of abstract mathematical theory, such as that which demonstrates the theories of utility and indifference curves. The confusion is of the different and difficult ideas that go to make up the theory. And the resistance is towards artificial theoretical ideas with which students find it difficult to identify. But these difficulties can all be overcome, by even the less-able among A-level students, with a suitable teaching approach.

A common-sense approach

Priority must be given to overcoming the fear of less mathematical students. The analysis of consumer behaviour, as with much standard A-level theory, is inherently mathematical in nature. It involves ratios, marginal values and equilibrium. It is expressed in equations or diagrams. It is understood readily by mathematical students in terms of differentiation, tangents and gradients. But non-mathematical students cannot understand it at all, in these terms, and are likely to become so discouraged that they will not understand the theory in any other terms either! How can we combat this?

I believe that the best approach is to balance and to precede this rigorous mathematical analysis with a common-sense approach. Consumer behaviour is, after all, about everyday matters, such as what you buy, how many you choose, and how well off you are. The same acts of analysis seem easier to the student if they are expressed in everyday terms: 'extra' for 'marginal'; 'value for money' for the 'ratio of marginal utility to price'; 'matching up' for 'equilibrium'. Clearly the analysis cannot stop at this level if it is to be rigorous, but it can at least start there, for even the weakest student.

Two examples, taken from each end of the 'story' of consumer behaviour, may serve to illustrate this approach. A good way to start is in terms of real-world problems by asking how a family makes its decisions on what to buy in order to make the most of its limited income. We could each do something similar, and perhaps produce some interesting contrasts in class between students, or between teacher and students. Already this suggests the major questions that guide the analysis: Why one purchase rather than another? Why no more of each type of product?, etc.

At a more advanced stage in their analysis, students meet the distinction between substitution and income effects of a price change. Some succeed in understanding these concepts, but often in visual terms only, as movements that can be identified and applied to an indifference curve diagram. Some students do not understand the issues at all. It is valuable to both categories of student, therefore, to see the concepts first, and perhaps foremost, in accessible, everyday terms. All can understand substitution as a switch from a more costly to a

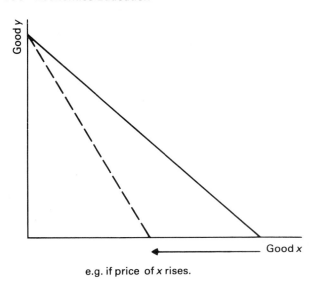

e.g. if price of x rises.

Figure 39.1 Consumption possibilities (budget lines)

e.g. if goods x and
y are substitutes.

*Figure 39.2 Consumption preferences
(indifference curves)*

cheaper alternative, and changed real income as a move to higher or lower satisfaction. Further progress is then possible towards the more difficult effect of a change in price of a good on its consumption, on substitutes and on complements.

Structured ideas

One reason why most A-level examination boards avoid the theory of consumption may be because it is thought too difficult for students at this level. Certainly, this is a view shared by some of the students that do study it, and by some of their teachers. As with much of economic theory, however, this problem is less with understanding individual concepts and relationships, than with fitting all those parts together into a complete theoretical framework. How can teachers help students to overcome likely confusion of different and difficult ideas?

The first step is to explain each step in the argument clearly, in terms that the student understands. Next, that understanding must be reinforced with practical exercises, applications to economic problems and discussion in groups. But the last step is as important as all this, and that is to establish a structure of ideas that students can appreciate and retain. This allows them to preserve a clear and distinct understanding, and relate points accurately to one another and to analytical issues. Teachers can establish this structure as a matter of routine. We can devote each lesson to an identifiably distinct stage in the analysis. We can interrupt the argument deliberately with discussion and exercises at the end of each stage.

One of the most important themes in the theory (and one of the most common confusions) is between value and price. We can state that value is a subjective assessment, measured in terms of utility, expressed in terms of

indifference curves, and that relative price is an objective, market rate of exchange. We can illustrate with examples how an individual's valuation of units of a product is determined, and how this is decided independently of price. But many students may still find it difficult to retain their understanding of this distinction in a way that will guide them through A-level examination questions. We can at least express this distinction in our teaching – spending a number of lessons on satisfaction, utility and personal value, *then* proceeding to consider prices and budgets, *then* relating the two separate ideas in terms of consumer equilibrium.

A similar approach is well suited to the teaching of indifference curve analysis (see Figures 39.1–39.4). First we establish the patterns of consumption possibilities, in terms of the budget line. We apply this, and practise our understanding of it, in terms of price and budget changes. Then we teach consumer preferences and tastes in terms of indifference curves. We describe possible patterns of values, and how the goods may be related as complements or substitutes in the consumers' minds. *Finally*, we combine the two separate parts of the model to derive and employ consumer equilibrium. This approach helps students avoid many of the standard confusions in understanding the model.

To go further, a three-dimensional view of indifference curve analysis can help all students achieve a fuller understanding of the true nature of the model. My own version of this model was constructed quite simply from a dozen polystyrene ceiling tiles. The bottom square represents the axes of the standard indifference curve diagram. Successive layers are built up on that, cut to form a quarter-hemisphere, to represent greater levels of satisfaction. The exercise is especially worthwhile as the least mathematical of students appreciates indifference curves as 'contours on a hill' of satisfaction, and substi-

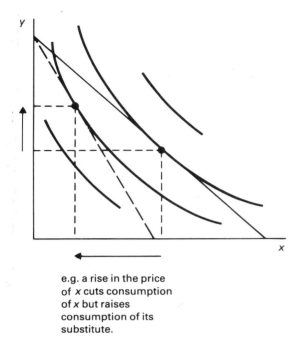

e.g. a rise in the price
of *x* cuts consumption
of *x* but raises
consumption of its
substitute.

Figure 39.3 Consumer equilibrium

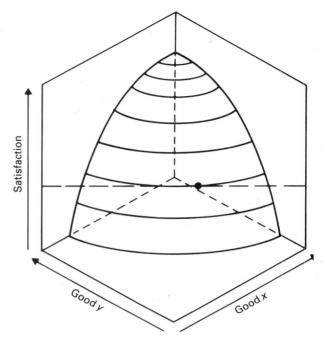

'Plan' appears as Figure 39.3,
'side elevations' appear as
total satisfaction curves for
goods *x* and *y*.

Figure 39.4 The complete model – in 3D

tution and income effects as physical movements either around or up/down the 'hill' respectively. They can observe the 'hill' from above, to see the standard indifference curve diagram, or from either side to see rising total satisfaction (and declining marginal utility) curves for each good. This cannot help but preserve a 'structured' view of the model, and in physical, tangible form.

Explaining behaviour

I have already expressed sympathy for students who resist studying 'merely artificial, abstract' theory. This comes often from those who chose the subject out of genuine enthusiasm, in order to study real-world problems or, as Keynes more romantically expressed it, in 'order to do good'. If we are to succeed in teaching even such a topic as the theory of consumption, we must first motivate our students, and show that the exercise has genuine purpose and value. This comes at two levels.

First we must show that theoretical argument does relate to real-world experience. This follows naturally from the common-sense approach that I advocated earlier.

We are all consumers, and consumption decisions were for most of us our first experience of economic behaviour. Sensible consumers are economists, and it should not be too difficult for us to reach theoretical principles of consumption behaviour with reference to interests and activities beyond the classroom, outside the conventional textbook.

Unfortunately, it is more difficult for consumption theory than for many other topics. Economic theory always argues in terms of hypothetical plans, but real-world experience is seen in terms of actual outcomes. In many cases, we can find clues to *ex ante* decisions, and the forces that lead towards equilibrium, which would otherwise be all we could observe directly, *ex post*, in the real world. But consumer satisfaction is determined only in the mind, and actual behaviour is no more than a final expression of equilibrium. The most useful teaching examples of consumption behaviour, therefore, are those we find from personal viewpoints – within the classroom, perhaps.

The study of pure theory can of course be justified on a more fundamental level as well, and this is particularly necessary for consumption theory in view of its only partial inclusion in A-level work. The theories of utility and indifference curve analysis allow us to explain demand curves and elasticity in depth. Teachers can justify the topic to their students in terms that have already been learnt, as a way of fully understanding ideas that students already know to be important.

This justification can be incorporated into our teaching approach. Consumption choices develop the principle of opportunity cost, marginal utility parallels the concept of marginal productivity; balancing value for money is

Table 39.1

A rational consumer spends a fixed budget on just two goods, *x* and *y*, which may be related as:	Unrelated goods	Substitutes	Complements
If the price of x rises			
1 then the quantity bought of *x* falls to some degree, raising MU_x, tending to restore consumer equilibrium $(\frac{MU_x}{P_x} = \frac{MU_y}{P_y})$	Q_x *falls* proportionately	Q_x *falls more* than proportionately	Q_x *falls less* than proportionately
2 so total revenue spent on *x* may change ($TR = P \times Q$)	TR_x does *not* change	TR_x *falls*	TR_x *rises*
3 and price elasticity of demand for *x*, *PeD* =	1	greater than 1	less than 1
4 but the quantity bought of *y* may also change, altering MU_y to restore consumer equilibrium	Q_y does *not* change	Q_y *rises*	Q_y *falls*
5 so total revenue spent on *y* may change	TR_y does *not* change	TR_y *rises*	TR_y *falls*
6 and the cross-elasticity of demand for *y* with respect to the price of *x*, *CeD* =	0	positive	negative

similar to balancing marginal productivity to marginal cost in a least-cost combination of factors; indifference curve analysis employs the same concepts and expresses the same equilibrium as the theory of utility. We guide students towards the final conclusions of the theory, to show how demand curves derive from changes in consumer equilibrium, how price and cross-elasticity derive from substitution and income effects. Students appreciate that they can relate the new ideas to familiar ones, preferably as a way to understand more fully the ideas over which they have suffered in the past. Table 39.1 shows one way to relate all these results to one another, to make our teaching of theory coherent, and to give students a greater sense of purpose as they grapple with it.

Resources

Begg, D., Fischer, S., Dornbusch, R., *Economics* (McGraw Hill, 1984) ch. 5.

Heertje, A., and Robinson, B. R. G., *Basic Economics* (Holt, Rinehart & Winston, 1982) ch. 8.

Hewitt, G., *Economics of the Market* (Fontana, 1976) ch. 4.

Lipsey, R. G., *An Introduction to Positive Economics* (Weidenfeld & Nicolson, 1983) pt. 3.

Leake, A. M., *Consumption and Production – Casebooks on Economic Principles* (Macmillan Education, 1983) section 2.

Computers in the Curriculum Project, *Equi-marginal Utility* (Longman, 1983).

Hardwick, P., Khan, B., Longmead, J., *An Introduction to Modern Economics* (Longman, 1982) ch. 4.

40   Population and Demography
Richard A. Powell

Introduction

Population is an important component of economics courses and syllabuses at school and college level. The main consideration here is with the position that population and demography take in the teaching and examining of economics at A-level. The explicit reference to population in the A-level syllabus can be illustrated by the following extracts.

The JMB syllabus includes, in the section on subject-matter, under the heading 'The generation of production and income': 'The sources of production: natural resources; population and manpower'.[1] The University of London syllabus includes the topic in Section A of the syllabus for Advanced Economics as: 'Changes in the size and composition of the population: its occupational and geographical distribution. Mobility of labour.'[2] These are examples from two of the current A-level economics syllabuses; similar references to the subject may be found for the other examination boards.

Population, of course, also appears implicitly elsewhere in other topics and parts of the syllabus. Discussion of standards of living, comparisons between countries, the problems of development and underdevelopment, the public sector and collective goods, are just a few of the topics that inevitably involve some consideration of, and direct involvement with, demographic factors.

Although population is clearly a main element of the A-level, what is not so obvious is the amount of time and emphasis given to the topic in A-level teaching and in the structure of courses. Population can be referred to directly as an important core element of the syllabus from which discussions of welfare and standards of living, problems of the Third World, the role of the public sector in collective provision of goods and services, and other substantive areas naturally follow. The rationale for this is that a knowledge and understanding of demographic factors provides a context and framework to underpin the analysis and evaluation of the problems of allocation and distribution in the national and international economy.

Why study population?

The justification for devoting time on the A-level course to demographic analysis can be explained to the student as follows:

> The study of population is important to the economist in two ways. Population figures provide information basic to an understanding of the workings of the economy. The economic functions of production and consumption are related through the population which provides both producers and consumers. The supply of labour or producers in the economy is determined initially by the size of the population, before other factors come into play, such as education and training, length of the working week, skills and abilities, social attitudes to employment and the relative level of wages. The distinction being made is one between the quantity and quality aspects of the supply of labour. The demand for labour is derived from the level of demand for goods and services. The population, as consumers, determines the level of output in the economy and through this, the level of employment. Changes in population have an impact on both producers and consumers in the economy, not simply in terms of the absolute numbers involved, but also in the age structure, occupational distribution, geographical location and so on. Patterns of consumption alter as a result of changes such as these, and consequently lead to variations in production.[3]

The justification lies not simply in the context of the topic in relation to other subject matter of the syllabus. The aims of the A-level syllabus include the development of abilities as well as testing knowledge. Abilities such as the comprehension and understanding of economic information and data in numerical and graphical form as well as verbal; the ability to make generalisations and inferences from data; the ability to interpret and present data in the form of diagrams and statistics – all of these may be fostered by the use and application of population data. These skills and abilities are also encountered in other aspects of the work on the A-level course. However, population presents not just the opportunity for such skills to be developed but also introduces a general context for other parts of the course.

Approaches to teaching population and demography

It is perhaps useful to make a distinction between teaching population of the UK (or any other single country) and teaching world population. The distinction is useful in terms of the context for discussion and analysis and also for building from demographic factors to wider considerations. As examples of this division and the development to other areas, it is possible to see work on the UK population leading to a better understanding of the constraints on economic and social policies and an appreciation of world population changes as relevant to an understanding of problems of the Third World, differences in rates of economic growth and in standards of living.

Population study inevitably begins with census statistics and data. Working with data and handling the statistics is a valid enough exercise in its own right. An understanding of the components of population change and the factors affecting these changes takes on more relevance and immediacy when elicited by the students themselves working directly from actual data. The historical development and pattern of the population from census statistics is an appropriate starting point.

Obtaining relevant statistics for the UK population is relatively easy through many different sources, though the *Annual Abstract of Statistics* is probably the most accessible. Here the first problem with handling data, that of classification, becomes apparent. A-level students given the task of researching the annual population of the UK from 1801, quickly find that separate tables are available for Great Britain, England and Wales, UK home population, Scotland, etc., and it becomes a useful exercise in itself to consider the different bases for the figures and how they can be related to each other. Which set of figures proves to be most suitable depends on the particular purpose in mind. If it is intended to show the changes involved in the components of population growth over time and to illustrate the natural changes involved, then statistics for England and Wales from 1801 are the most useful. (Political changes since 1801 concerning Ireland within the UK, before partition, make attempts to produce comparable UK figures very difficult and problematic.) Statistics for UK birth rates and death rates can also be obtained from the same general source and these three sets of data provide ample opportunities for follow-up work and exercises (see Tables 40.1, 40.2 and 40.3).

Population statistics provide a source of material for different types of exercise – the interpreting of tables, drawing graphs, calculating relative and absolute levels of population growth. Each of these approaches can be adopted with the appropriate data. A convenient introduction to population analysis is provided by the model of the demographic transition for England and Wales (see Figure 40.1).

Table 40.1 UK population 1801–2011 ($\times 1 000 000$) projected after 1981

			Absolute increase %	Relative increase %
1801	10.5			
1811	12.0	1801–1811	1.5	14.3
1821	15.4	1811–1821	3.4	28.3
1831	17.8	1821–1831	2.4	15.6
1841	20.1	1831–1841	2.3	12.9
1851	22.2	1841–1851	2.1	10.4
1861	24.7	1851–1861	2.5	11.3
1871	27.3	1861–1871	2.6	10.5
1881	31.2	1871–1881	3.9	14.3
1891	34.2	1881–1891	3.0	9.6
1901	38.2	1891–1901	4.0	11.7
1911	42.0	1901–1911	3.8	9.9
1921	44.0	1911–1921	2.0	4.8
1931	46.0	1921–1931	2.0	4.5
1941	47.9 est.	1931–1941	1.9	4.1
1951	50.2	1941–1951	2.3	4.8
1961	52.7	1951–1961	2.5	5.0
1971	55.5	1961–1971	2.8	5.3
1981	56.4	1971–1981	0.9	1.6
1991	56.3	1981–1991	−0.1	−0.2
2001	56.9	1991–2001	0.6	1.0
2011	57.9	2001–2011	1.0	1.7

Source: CSO, *Annual Abstract of Statistics.*

Table 40.2 UK births, 1901–1983, annual averages or calendar years

	Total ($\times 1000$)	Birth rate/1000
1900–2	1095	28.6
1910–12	1037	24.6
1920–2	1018	23.1
1930–2	750	16.3
1940–2	723	15.0
1950–2	803	16.0
1960–2	946	17.9
1963	990	18.5
1964	1015	18.8

Table 40.2 contd.

	Total ($\times 1000$)	Birth rate/1000
1965	997	18.4
1966	980	18.0
1967	962	17.6
1968	947	17.2
1969	920	16.7
1970	904	16.3
1971	902	16.2
1972	834	14.9
1973	780	13.9
1974	737	13.2
1975	698	12.5
1976	676	12.1
1977	657	11.8
1978	687	12.3
1979	734	13.1
1980	754	13.4
1981	731	13.0
1982	719	12.8
1983	721	12.8

Source: CSO, *Annual Abstract of Statistics.*

Table 40.3 UK deaths, 1901–1982, annual averages or calendar years

	Death rates per 1000 population	
	Males	Females
1900–2	18.4	16.3
1910–12	14.9	13.3
1920–2	13.5	11.9
1930–2	12.9	11.5
1940–2	n/a	n/a
1950–2	12.6	11.2
1960–2	12.5	11.2
1970–2	12.4	11.3
1971	12.2	11.1
1972	12.6	11.5
1973	12.5	11.5
1974	12.4	11.5
1975	12.3	11.4
1976	12.5	11.8
1977	12.1	11.3
1978	12.4	11.5
1979	12.5	11.7
1980	12.1	11.4
1981	12.3	11.6
1982	12.0	11.5

Source: CSO, *Annual Abstract of Statistics.*

Stage 1 High birth and death rates, the level of population fluctuates, overall growth rate is slow.

Stage 2 Death rates decline but birth rates remain at or near previously high levels, population expands rapidly.

Stage 3 Birth rates begin to decline but are still higher than death rates, population growth continues but at a slower rate.

Stage 4 Low birth and death rates, population growth rate slows considerably and may lead to population levels stabilising.

Stage 5 Advanced industrial economies at the present time appear to be moving into a further stage where the levels of birth rate have continued to fall below the level of death rate, so that the prospect of an absolute decline in population is likely.

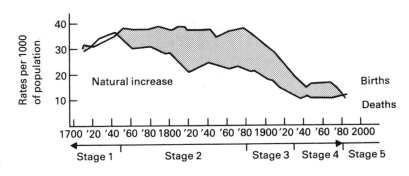

Figure 40.1 England and Wales: birth and death rates, 1700–1981 Source: Powell, R.A., Population, *Longman Economic Studies (Longman, 1982), p. 12.*

The comparison of the level of birth rates and death rates for the UK can be looked at alongside the level of total population for the same time-period and with the rates of population growth between census dates. Introducing the concept of stages of population growth provides a ready stepping off point for further work on economic growth and development. Natural increase or decrease in a population is immediately highlighted by graphical presentation (see Figure 40.1).

The historical basis to population growth is brought into the analysis by consideration of the birth and death rates over time and the factors that contribute to the changes in these rates. Additional information and data develop the analysis. Infant mortality figures (for England and Wales) can be used to draw attention to both the changes in the numbers of births and in deaths as components of total growth.

Any survey of causes of population change in Europe in the nineteenth and twentieth centuries must incorporate, at an early stage in the analysis, the effects of migration, whether it be intra-national or international. Movements of people within the UK in the nineteenth century can be closely related to the growth of industrialisation and the social changes in lifestyle brought in its wake. International migration not only led to colonial expansion overseas but also eased population pressures in the home country.

Analysis of net migration statistics is particularly relevant and appropriate in economics courses to help counter the general misconception and misinformation and interpretation that is, at times, faced by the student. Many students express surprise and disbelief at the actual figures for the UK net migration outflow in the postwar period. Moreover, the historical and political contexts for migration flows are essential for a genuine understanding of demographic changes resulting from migration. A particularly useful approach that can be adopted is to attempt a cost–benefit analysis of the effects of migration and also to relate immigration to different international situations. (An example of this exercise can be found in *Investigating Economics*.[4])

Data for world population, actual and projected, provide a useful means of introducing topics of economic development, the Third World, the North–South debate, etc. on an A-level economics course, as well as providing very suitable stimulus material for practice in data-response exercises. Table 40.4, showing data giving the distribution of world population by area (1950–2025), is a

Table 40.4   World population – actual and projected – 1950–2025

% distribution by area	1950	1980	2000	2025
Eastern Europe and the USSR	10.6	8.5	7.1	5.9
North America	6.6	5.6	4.8	4.2
North, west and south Europe	12.0	8.4	6.4	4.8
East Asia	26.7	26.5	24.1	20.9
South Asia	28.4	31.7	33.9	34.4
Africa	8.7	10.6	13.9	18.8
Latin America	6.5	8.2	9.3	10.6
Oceania	0.5	0.5	0.5	0.4
Population total (billions)	2.52	4.43	6.12	8.19
% share of world population by level of economic development (as defined by the UN in 1980)				
More developed countries	32.9	25.5	20.7	16.8
Less developed countries	67.1	74.5	79.3	83.2

Source: Barclays Bank Review, vol. LIX, no. 1, February 1984.

typical example of the type of information readily available.

Material such as this lends itself to a number of different teaching approaches and applications. As was outlined earlier, the A-level student is expected to be able to interpret data and make generalisations and valid inferences from data. What is also particularly valuable from information such as that contained in Table 40.4, is the use of projections for population numbers. These can be used by the teacher to bring out the difficulties involved in making such projections; the assumptions involved, the extrapolation of present trends and the degree of accuracy and reliability that can be given to such exercises.

The comments made here have only touched upon the ways in which population and demography may be brought into A-level economics lessons. Many other areas for teaching have not been directly referred to, such as the age distribution, occupational and geographical distribution, social statistics (e.g. marriage and divorce rates, average family size, dependency ratios). The use of population statistics to demonstrate the effects of diminishing returns, the concept of optimum population, the effects of an increasing or decreasing population, are also obvious areas of population study to include in the A-level course. Material relating to these aspects of population issues is available from a wide range of sources although they are not always dealt with in economics textbooks. Articles in newspapers and journals, notably in *The Economist*, and books from other disciplines in the social sciences will provide ample classroom resource material for the economics teacher.

Resources

'World Population 1950–2025' *Barclays Bank Review*, February 1984.

'British Population Trends and their economic implications' *Barclays Bank Review*, February 1985.

Bowen, I., *Population* (Nisbet/Cambridge University Press, 1966).

Clarke, J. I., *Population Geography*, 2nd edn. (Pergamon, 1974).

Cipolla, C. M., *Economic History of World Population*, 6th edn. (Penguin, 1974).

CSO, *Annual Abstract of Statistics*, no. 114 (HMSO, 1977).

CSO, *Annual Abstract of Statistics*, no. 116 (HMSO, 1980).

CSO, *Social Trends*, no. 10 (HMSO, 1980).

'The reproduction function', *The Economist*, 8 January 1977.

'Going for growth', *The Economist*, 3 February 1979.

'The people bulge', *The Economist*, 10 February 1979.

'Forecasts of the future', *The Economist*, 12 May 1979.

'Is Malthus dead?' *The Economist*, 29 December 1979.

'Employing China's millions', *The Economist*, 16 February 1980.

'Ending the world's baby boom', *The Economist*, 16 February 1980.

Elkan, W., *An Introduction to Development Economics* (Penguin, 1973).

Galbraith, J. K., *The Age of Uncertainty* (BBC/André Deutsch, 1977).

Hey, J. D., *Britain in Context* (Basil Blackwell, 1979).

Britain: An Official Handbook, (HMSO, 1980).

Lowry, J. H., *World Population and Food Supply* (Edward Arnold, 1970).

Manley, P. and Sawbridge, D., 'Women at work', *Lloyds Bank Review*, January 1980.

McEvedy, C. and Jones, R., *Atlas of World Population History* (Penguin, 1978).

McGraw, E., *Population Today* (Kaye & Ward, 1979).

Osborn, F. (ed.) *Our Crowded Planet – Essays on the Pressures of Population* (George Allen & Unwin, 1963).

Papps, I., *For Love or Money? A Preliminary Economic Analysis of Marriage and the Family* (IEA, 1980).

Powicke, J. C., Iles, D. J., and Davies, B., *Applied Economics* (Edward Arnold, 1972).

Reddaway, W. B., 'The economic consequences of zero population growth', *Lloyds Bank Review*, April 1977.

Williams, R. M., *British Population* (Heinemann, 1972).

Notes and references

1   GCE Regulations and Syllabus 1984, JMB, Manchester, p. 86.
2   University of London GCE Syllabus, Advanced Economics.
3   Powell, R. A., *Population*, Longman Economic Studies (Longman, 1982) p. 4.
4   Hocking, A., and Powell, R. A., *Investigating Economics* (Longman, 1984) p. 152.

41   Industrial Relations

Stuart Luker

Introduction

Industrial relations is a topic that is often neglected by teachers of A-level economics. Yet relationships between employers, employees, trade unions, firms and the state have a significant effect upon how successfully a society achieves its economic objectives. An understanding and appreciation of industrial relations is of value to all young people. Industrial relations is an important topic in A-level business studies and sociology as well as A-level economics. It is also part of the O-level syllabus for business studies, economics and social economics. The topic may feature in careers education and as part of complementary or general-studies lessons.

When teaching industrial relations as part of an A- or O-level course, the syllabus requirements must be considered and specific attention given to the appropriate theoretical background. The teaching of wage determination under various market structures should not be divorced from the realities of wage determination, and thus must necessarily involve an appreciation of the structure of collective bargaining and the nature of industrial relations in the UK. The integration of theory and practice is very difficult to achieve, but should be attempted. It will inevitably lead to a consideration of where existing theory is inadequate, and the teacher should be prepared for this. An understanding of the operation of the labour market is now regarded as increasingly important in the debate surrounding the causes of unemployment and inflation.

For students on general-studies courses, detailed analysis is not needed, but there is more opportunity for wider coverage. Materials can be included which would be considered beyond the scope of an O- or A-level economics syllabus.

Industrial relations is an area where there is likely to be considerable student interest, and it is important that the teaching methods adopted take advantage of this. There is quite a lot of basic factual material which must be learnt by students taking economics exams, and one way in which this can be made more interesting is to relate it to current industrial-relations problems; there is usually something of relevance in the news. However, the temptation to look at industrial relations solely as a current affairs subject, or to deal with it in a purely descriptive way, should be avoided.

A further consideration of general significance that arises from the nature of the topic is that the majority of students will approach the subject with a number of preconceived ideas, which are unlikely to be based on objective information or understanding. It would be unrealistic to suggest that there will be a major change of attitude on the part of the student as a result of studying industrial-relations practices and problems, but it is important to get them to recognise their own prejudices. A recognition of the fact that industrial-relations problems are unlikely to be solved by purely rational analysis is sometimes difficult to get across but is nevertheless important. Some of the participative exercises suggested are designed to generate 'feeling' in the classroom, and follow-up discussion can be used to emphasise the role of attitudes. This is an area of the economics course where value judgements play a big part, and it may be worthwhile to look, in a general context, at the relationship between normative and positive economics using this part of the course to illustrate some of the problems of treating economics as a science.

Content

The materials and teaching approaches suggested have been selected taking into account the requirements of a typical A-level economics syllabus, but this was not the only criterion. The following industrial-relations topics have been included, and it is probable that they would form the major part of any A-level economics course:

1 The structure and organisation of the trade-union movement.
2 Employers' organisations.
3 The structure and nature of collective bargaining in the UK.
4 Industrial disputes.
5 The government and industrial relations.

Teaching methods

1 The structure and organisation of the trade-union movement

This aspect of the topic involves the teacher in imparting factual information, some of which should be backed up by recent statistics. It can be achieved by dictation, the preparation of a handout which is distributed to each student, the use of previously prepared overhead projector slides, or by asking the students to make their own notes from a textbook. One or more of these methods is likely to provide the main way of teaching this section of the course. However, it is well worth while reinforcing this with a set of short-answer questions to test whether or not the student has grasped the essentials.

It is also a part of the course where the students' ability to interpret simple statistical information can be developed. Since most examination boards, at all levels, now include data-response questions, this approach is to be recommended. The ability to identify trends and relationships within the figures and to interpret what is discovered are valuable skills that can be improved with practice. The following approaches may be adopted:

(a) The teacher may provide a table of statistics describing, for example, the number of trade unions, the size of the working population and trade-union membership. The *Annual Abstract of Statistics* will provide this type of data in a ten-year series. Questions can then be asked that are designed to enable students to discover for themselves the main trends and important features of the present structure of the trade-union movement. Much more difficult questions involving judgement and interpretation can be asked, for example:

(i)   Describe the changes that have occurred in the last ten years in the percentage of the working population that belongs to a trade union.
(ii)   Outline some of the possible reasons for these changes.
(iii)   How might the significance of some of these changes be interpreted, and what other information would you want before coming to any conclusions?

(b) Instead of providing the statistics, the teacher could provide the sources of information and ask the students to find out for themselves:

(i)   What is the total number of unions in the UK?
(ii)   How has this changed since 1975?
(iii)   What has happened to the average size of trade unions?
(iv)   How many unions have less than 1000 members?

Answers to these and other questions can easily be obtained from various publications, such as the *Annual Abstract of Statistics*, TUC pamphlets and the *Department of Employment Gazette*.

(c) Now that computers are becoming more readily available in schools, the students could be asked to construct, or at least use, a data base on the structure of the trade-union movement. Software packages such as *Micro-Query* or *Quest* would be very suitable for this purpose. Once the original data have been input, it is a fairly easy matter to update them each year. A data base of this sort can, of course, be invaluable for other syllabus topics as well.

(d) The occasional newspaper or periodical article on the structure and organisation of the trade-union movement can be duplicated and given to students with a list of questions.

(e) Information sheets are also available from the TUC; these could be used instead of teacher-produced handouts or dictated notes.

2 Employers' organisations

Information on the role of the CBI and the activities of employers' organisations is not as readily available as for the TUC and the trade unions. Nevertheless, it is necessary to outline their activities. Without some explanation of the employers' associations, it is impossible for the students to understand the structure and process of collective bargaining in the UK. The CBI publishes information on its functions.

3 The structure and nature of collective bargaining

Again, for this part of the syllabus there is some basic factual material that has to be covered. It is necessary to outline the different types of collective-bargaining arrangement, distinguishing between national and local negotiations. The normal procedures will have to be explained and terms such as conciliation and arbitration discussed. Several of the standard textbooks do this fairly well. It can be useful to represent the process diagrammatically, as shown in Figure 41.1. This figure also attempts to avoid the common misunderstanding amongst students, concerning what happens when negotiations fail.

It does not suggest that conciliation and arbitration are sequential, while emphasising that, even in the most protracted dispute, negotiations will have to take place and a settlement be reached.

However, the collective-bargaining process is particularly suitable for participative exercises of various kinds. The following role playing exercise has been used successfully on several occasions and can easily be amended to fit in with the circumstances at the time. It can also be extended to include other aspects of the collective-bargaining procedure. Role playing exercises that are devised by the teacher have the advantage that they can be constructed to include up-to-date examples and to illustrate issues that the teacher considers need reinforcing.

A role playing exercise

Adequate preparation is vital, but once this has been done the exercise can be carried out in a double lesson.

Materials: Three duplicated information sheets:

1   General background to the negotiations.
2   Instructions for the employer's representatives.
3   Instructions for the union negotiators.

Sheet 1 is given to all the participants, but sheets 2 and 3 are only to be distributed to those who are negotiating on behalf of the employer and trade union respectively.

Sheet 1 General background to the negotiations
1 The firm makes components for the main car producers and is situated in Coventry.

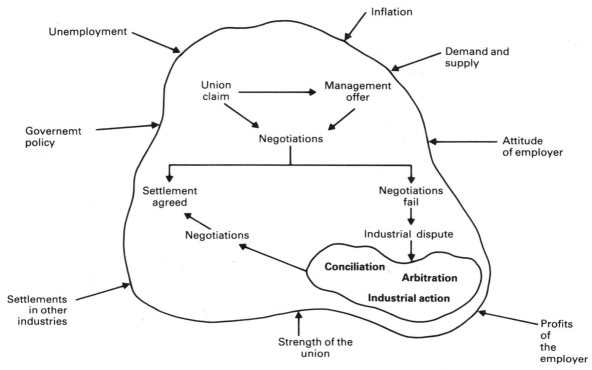

Figure 41.1 The economic and industrial environment

2 The workers who are involved in the negotiations are toolmakers who belong to the AUEW.

3 Inflation is estimated to be about 5 per cent and the government predicts that it will fall to about 4 per cent the following year. The government is also confident that within the next few years a zero inflation rate will be achieved.

4 Table 41.1 shows what has happened to prices and average earnings for industrial workers, in comparison with your firm over the last few years.

Table 41.1

Year	Your wage rise	Increase in RPI	Increase in industrial earnings
	%	%	%
1979	17	11	18
1980	14	18	14
1981	0	10	8
1982	4	8	7
1983	3	5	6

5 A similar group of workers in Birmingham have recently negotiated an 8 per cent wage rise.

6 Unemployment in the Midlands was about 6 per cent of the working population but now stands at about 15 per cent and is still rising slowly.

7 The car industry has seen a year of record sales and demand is still buoyant, although import penetration is approaching 60 per cent.

8 The government has ruled out an incomes policy, but it continues to emphasise the need for moderation in wage rises if unemployment is to be reduced. It has also imposed a 3 per cent cash limit on the public-sector wage bill.

9 In 1980 the company was close to bankruptcy and since that time the workforce has been cut back by 25 per cent. There were compulsory redundancies. After making losses between 1980 and 1982, the firm made a small profit in 1983. In recent years there has been substantial investment in machinery embodying new technology. The unions have agreed to changes in working practices and, as a result, productivity has risen by over 30 per cent in four years.

Sheet 2 Instructions for employer's representatives
1 The company's profit forecast for the following year is £6 million, but this assumes that output and sales will increase by about 5 per cent. Demand for the product is very price sensitive because there is a lot of competition. Wage costs were £40 million in 1983 and the profit forecast assumes that they will increase to £41 million in 1984.

A profit of £6 million is still considered to represent an unacceptably low rate of return on capital employed. Lower profits are likely to affect the dividend that can be paid to shareholders and the amount of new investment that can be financed.

2 You have recently received a large contract, but as yet neither the employees or the union are aware of this. The order would keep the current workforce fully employed for the next eighteen months. However, the contract is conditional on delivery dates, which have been specified, being met. The first consignment is due in two months' time. Should this contract be lost, it is probable that there will be further redundancies and profits will be reduced.

3 Any prolonged strike action will threaten the survival of the firm.

4 You would prefer that any wage increase is tied to a productivity deal which would help to meet the cost of the settlement. Demarcation is still a problem and more flexible working practices would improve efficiency.

Decisions to be made:

(a) The offer you are willing to make in response to the union's claim.

(b) The maximum you would be willing to pay as a straight percentage.

(c) You need to discuss the various proposals you would be willing to make, should your initial offer be rejected.

(d) You should also discuss the strategy you will adopt during the negotiations and try to anticipate union action under various circumstances.

Sheet 3 Instructions for the union negotiators

1 Your members are very disgruntled. They are disillusioned with the union for allowing their standard of living to fall significantly over the past few years. They have also seen many redundancies and have accepted changes that have enabled the company to make profits again. They may well take unofficial action if they don't receive a substantial increase this year.

2 You have heard that your company has recently received a large contract which should ensure your members' jobs for the next eighteen months. However, you are concerned that further changes in working practices would result in a smaller workforce. Consequently, you are not very keen on a productivity deal. The mood of the men is such that they will fight against any further loss of jobs, and the union does not want to lose members.

Decisions to be made:

(a) The initial claim that you are going to submit to the management, before negotiations begin. It is obvious that a very substantial settlement is needed to restore your members' standard of living to its 1979 level.

(b) Discuss the minimum offer you would be willing to accept.

(c) Discuss the general strategy to be adopted during the negotiations.

(d) Consider the action you would be willing to take should the negotiations fail (e.g. work-to-rule, strike, demand arbitration).

The Procedure

The sheet outlining the general background to the negotiations should be given to the participants in the previous lesson and they should be asked to read it for homework. At the start of the lesson, the teacher needs to 'set the scene' and to emphasise the important elements in the situation, indicating how the various parties are likely to feel about the circumstances in which they find themselves. The class should be divided into groups of about six to eight, half of whom are to be the employer's representatives and the other half, union representatives. Alternatively, one group may be used with the rest of the class being used as observers, or perhaps employees of the company. If they act as employees it becomes possible for the union negotiators to consult their members, perhaps holding a mass meeting with a show of hands vote.

The other handouts now need to be given to the negotiators, and the parties separated. It is far better if the employer's representatives are sent out of the room to carry out their preliminary discussions. The teacher should spend a few minutes briefing each of the groups, stressing the need for adequate preparation prior to the negotiations. Adequate time must be allowed for each group to prepare its general strategy before the bargaining session begins.

The game starts with the union negotiators formally submitting their claim to the management. The management are allowed a few minutes before they come back with their offer; at this stage, the bargaining session begins. If during the negotiations either side want an adjournment to discuss their position in private, this should be allowed.

The game can be extended by providing for the possibility of conciliation and arbitration. If industrial action is taken, the teacher could explain how the situation develops, before negotiations are resumed and each party would have to take this into account.

The game is fairly open-ended, and it is difficult to predict what will happen, but it usually proves an enlightening experience for those involved, providing the basis for follow-up discussion. Reviewing what actually happens is very important. When selecting the students for various roles, it is often worthwhile to select the trade-union representatives from those with 'right wing' views and vice versa.

Case studies

It is fairly easy to find materials that can be used as case studies, either from publications such as the *Department of Employment Gazette* or articles in newspapers. Case studies can be attempted by the student working on his own, but it is probably better for them to work in small groups of about three or four. Each group can be asked to present their answer to a particular question to the class, and this can provide the basis for general discussion. An

Table 41.2

WENDY BERLINER on the teachers' pay talks

The class war heats up

THOUSANDS of children throughout England and Wales will miss school this afternoon as their teachers walk out in protest at the local authority employers refusal to increase their 3 per cent pay offer or go to arbitration.

Since the pay talks broke down last week the teachers unions have shown surprising unanimity of anger. Battle trenches unused for years are being dusted off and there is now a very real threat of disruption to public examinations this summer.

Negotiations began in late February and five meetings later on he was still sticking officially to a 3 per cent offer and warning that any settlement over that meant lost teachers' jobs.

This was despite a 4.5 per cent offer to Scottish teachers, a 4.5 per cent settlement for local authority manual workers and the teachers' claim that they have fallen 31 per cent behind in the salary stakes since the Houghton Report on teachers pay gave teachers a giant leg up the comparability stakes 10 years ago.

In fact the three per cent offer is a phoney one. In what are known in Burnham terminology "behind the chair" talks — a description for a tiny nucleus of employers and teachers being separated from the unwieldy main committee for private talks with the independent chairman — the employers have been suggesting anything from 3.45 per cent and four per cent.

Arbitration has been avoided like a plague by the employers because of the notorious practice of arbiters splitting the difference between the two sides in a pay dispute. In the past the employers believe the teachers have usually got the tastier end of arbitration lollipop.

However, if the teachers had put a lower figure on their claim they may well have been in business for arbitration last Tuesday when a breakthrough appeared likely. But the NUT argued in the teachers' panel for 12.5 per cent to be put to the employers. The other unions suggested ten per cent was probably a more reasonable figure to get talks going. The employers had in mind 7.5 per cent.

After a wearying day of non-talks at London's Piccadilly Hotel, with most of the activity taking place "behind the chair", the 12.5 per cent suggestion caused a sharp intake of breath all round the management seats.

Even the Labour employers who had been arguing for a 4.5 per cent offer to be made felt this was too much to take. "How on earth do they expect us to pay that," said one angry management official leading the exodus from the talks.

Management sources say that a 12.5 per cent settlement would cost 63,000 lost teaching jobs. Mr Meridale maintains that the biggest ever re-structuring of teachers' pay, which is currently under discussion in separate talks between both sides, is far more important than this year's settlement.

The employers argue that these pay structure talks which could bring a big pay bonus to teachers next year are now in jeopardy. Decisions on whether to put extra money in the rate support grant for teachers pay will be taken by the Cabinet in June and, although Sir Keith Joseph, the Education Secretary, is sympathetic to the idea of pay restructuring, it is thought the Cabinet will not be if it meets against a background of chaos in the schools.

So far the teachers have dismissed the distant sunshine of pay re-structuring money as "jam tomorrow". Even if it does come it may not be enough to satisfy them. The local authorities have not quantified how much extra their ideas may add to the overall pay bill but there is little doubt the percentage would be a single figure one. In no way could it compensate for the salary depression since Houghton.

A slightly higher offer is thought likely but by Friday the teacher trenches may have been dug so deep that there will be little room to peer over the sides. All the unions report unrelenting anger from their members.

But the employers have a trench too. It was dug for them by the Conservative government in the form of rate capping. Three per cent was built into the rate support grant for pay settlements this year. In education the biggest single expenditure — some 70 per cent — is on teacher salaries. If they get more, the services gets less and in parts of the country it is already threadbare.

Source: Guardian, April 1984.

overhead projector could be made available where appropriate.

Table 41.2 reprints an article from the *Guardian* on the 1984 teachers' pay negotiations. This provides suitable material for a short case study, provided some of the points are explained first (e.g. the Houghton award).

1 Explain the following terms as used in the passage: (a) arbitration; (b) comparability; (c) the Burnham Committee; (d) behind the chair talks; (e) pay restructuring.
2 Why do you think that the teachers' pay talks broke down, with the result that industrial action was taken?
3 What forms of industrial action are available to teachers?
4 (a) Why were the employers reluctant to go to arbitration?
(b) Do you consider that arbitration is a good way of resolving industrial disputes?
5 What are the arguments for and against 'comparability' as a basis for wage negotiations?
6 Management sources claimed that a 12.5 per cent pay claim would cost 65 000 teachers' jobs. What was the basis for this assertion?
7 To what extent do you consider that market forces influence the wages of teachers?

One advantage of case studies for A-level is that they provide examples that can be used in essays. It is a knowledge of the real world and an appreciation of the relevance of economic theory to events that is most difficult to get across in the classroom. They do, of course, also illustrate some of the limitations of economic theory and the teacher must be prepared for this.

Industrial relations discussion questions
It is a relatively easy task for the teacher to make up a number of short examples of industrial-relations situations which can be used as discussion questions. They are probably best used with small groups. The following examples are intended to highlight some fairly common industrial-relations problems:

1 You work for a firm employing 100 men on the factory floor. Ninety-seven of them belong to the union, paying a weekly subscription of 60 pence.
(a) You are a member of the union and would like to see the union negotiate a closed shop with the management. Explain why.
(b) You are one of the non-union members. Explain why you think that the closed shop would be wrong.
(c) Do you think that it should be illegal to have closed-shop agreements?
2 You are the supervisor responsible for a group of twenty-five men in a factory making shoes. You are on the day shift and it has been a very hot day. At 12 o'clock, the shop steward comes up to you and says that at 2.30 p.m. the men are going out on an unofficial stoppage. This is likely to disrupt the factory's production. Outline the course of action you would take.

3 You are the shop steward representing the workers in a factory employing 200 men. One of the assembly line workers, who is a member of the union, swore at a foreman and has been sent home. You have not been consulted or officially informed about the incident. Rumour has it that the management are going to dismiss him as an example to the rest of the men. What would you do?

These last two examples illustrate day-to-day industrial-relations issues. It is easy to overlook such issues, which take up a lot of the time of shop stewards and first-line supervisors.

Films and TV programmes
There are a number of films that deal with collective bargaining and industrial relations. Some of these can be borrowed free of charge. Films are useful because they introduce an element of realism. Some films can also be used as case-study material and have the added advantage that they involve student participation. Two of the programmes in the Peter Donaldson series *10 × Economics* (Yorkshire TV) are useful when considering incomes policies, the question of new technologies and the possibility of redundancies.

Visiting speakers
It is usually possible to get speakers from both sides of industry to talk on a variety of industrial-relations topics. For students to come into contact with first-hand experience of industrial-relations problems and collective bargaining has obvious advantages.

4 Industrial disputes

Most of the methods suggested in the previous section can be used to teach this particular topic. Role playing exercises, case studies and the use of visiting speakers are particularly appropriate. Current information and stimulus material can easily be found in newspapers and periodicals such as *The Economist*. Once more, there is a certain amount of factual material to be imparted, and again data-interpretation questions can be used to supplement the usual methods. Statistics can be presented on factors such as:

(a) The main causes of industrial disputes in the UK.
(b) International comparisons of working days lost as a result of industrial disputes.
(c) Time-series data on days lost as a result of industrial disputes in the UK.

Questions can then be asked that bring out the relevant points. If the information is stored on a computer data base, it can easily be updated and directly interrogated by the students themselves.

5 The government and industrial relations

The ways in which the government is involved in industrial relations can usefully be categorised as follows:

The government is a major employer and must take a view regarding wage settlements in the public sector. In recent years this has been achieved largely through the imposition of cash limits.

Government agencies, in particular ACAS, are involved in trying to promote good industrial-relations practices and help settle industrial disputes.

There is a framework of laws that determine the rights of the various parties involved in industrial disputes and limit their freedom of action. During the last twenty years, the role of the law has been a major political issue.

The government may wish to use incomes policies as one of its macroeconomic policy instruments.

The teacher is likely to want to consider some or all of these areas of government involvement. This section of the course can be related to the role of government in a mixed economy and can be used to consider some of the links between macro- and microeconomic policy. Some of the issues provide interesting topics for a formal debate. Alternatively, one of the students could be asked to give a prepared talk which would provide the stimulus for a fuller discussion of the topic. At this stage, most of the students will have sufficient background knowledge to make discussion worth while. It is also an area where a visiting speaker may have something interesting and controversial to say.

Other teaching methods

There are a number of other methods that can be used to teach industrial relations which have not been mentioned so far. These include:

1 Topic or project work, which enables the individual student to cover some of the work in more detail than might otherwise be possible.
2 Pre-recorded tapes can be used for individual study or played to a class. If the school has a language laboratory, it is possible to use pre-recorded tapes much more effectively in the following way. First, the tape should be played through the control and recorded on each of the individual tape-recorders. This means that each individual student now has a copy of the tape which can be played back as required. The students can then be given an assignment to complete at their own pace.
3 The Industrial Society will arrange a two-day conference for fifth- and sixth-formers. The conferences deal largely with industrial-relations issues. The students are divided up into groups of about eight or ten and the Society recruits a number of managers and union representatives to act as group leaders. The two days consist of talks, films, case-study exercises and small-group discussions. They are well organised and, in the author's experience, enjoyed by all those who take part. The cost is usually between £150 and £200, depending on the number of students. The Society will also help schools to arrange their own conferences.

Resources

Books

The coverage of industrial relations in standard textbooks is often limited. There are, however, several smaller specialist books which can be used with an A-level group. I have found the following useful:

Stanlake, G. F., *Introductory Economics,* 4th edn. (Longman, 1983). Chapter 18 covers the basic theory of wage determination and some aspects of industrial relations. However, it is limited in scope and depth of analysis.

Lipsey, R. G., *An Introduction to Positive Economics*, 6th edn. (Weidenfeld & Nicolson, 1983). Provides an in-depth analysis of the basic economic theory of wage determination.

Prest, A. R., and Coppock, D. J., *A Manual of Applied Economics*, 9th edn. (Weidenfeld & Nicolson, 1982). This book, which is published in alternate years, is valuable for up-to-date information and statistics.

Williamson, H. *The Trade Unions*, 7th edn. (Heinemann Educational Books, 1977). A book in the 'Studies in the British Economy' series, so has been written with A-level students in mind and is short enough to be read by interested students. This book provides up-to-date coverage of recent industrial-relations laws and includes some case studies.

Grant, R. M., *Industrial Relations*, 2nd edn. (Heinemann Educational Books, 1977). A Manchester Economics Project satellite text, providing a useful account of the British system of industrial relations, suitable for A-level students.

Vincent, M., *Introduction to Industrial Relations* (Heinemann, 1983). This book does not attempt to cover the economic theory of wage determination, but it is very well presented and is full of good ideas. Although written for BEC students, it is to be recommended to the A-level teacher.

Hawkins, K., *Trade Unions* (Hutchinson, 1981). This book adopts an historical approach and might be considered as background reading for the teacher.

Other resources

The TUC and ACAS publish quite a lot of information for students, some of which can be obtained free. The TUC will also provide names and addresses of local trade-union officers who are willing to give talks to schools and colleges.

Information can also be obtained from the Industrial Society, the Understanding British Industry project, SCIP, HMSO and CRAC. There are many films available and two programmes in the Peter Donaldson series *10 × Economics*, entitled 'One more try' and 'Work without workers', are worth considering.

42 Social Economics

Andrew Leake

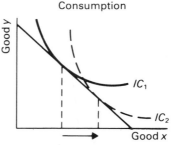

A change in tastes in
favour of good x raises
consumption of x.

Introduction

The importance of social and environmental issues to our
teaching of introductory economic principles comes from
two main sources. One is that the study of social issues
requires the student to assemble many different parts of
the subject. Teachers welcome this as a way to reinforce
and revise students' understanding of both consumption
and production, products and factors, private and public
sectors, by application to new types of problems. Students
find that they must understand basic concepts such as
opportunity cost, efficiency, externalities and positive/
normative analysis, but mainly in order to *use* that understanding to approach real-world issues. Their preliminary
work in economics acquires a greater sense of direction
and gives purpose to their revision.

There is, however, another more important source of
value in the topic. Social and environmental issues allow
students to approach directly the important and
controversial policy questions that interest them most.
Many of us respond to this interest in our teaching when
we discuss important news of the day, as a sideline to our
standard coursework. Social economics allows us to teach
more systematically and in greater depth, and to
encourage students to use their economics training in a
'practical' way. And the choice of topics is limitless – from
privatisation, taxation, and cost–benefit studies, to
national and local, social or environmental questions.

This is an opportunity that most teachers are quick to
take, in order to extend the curriculum and meet the
interests of students. Not all examination boards take the
same line, however, for social questions are often more
difficult to examine.

Factual evidence is topical and changeable, arguments
are often difficult to substantiate, and students are prone
to include political and social comment and subjective or
impressionistic judgement, alongside the positively
economic. But all this is, after all, the main source of
appeal in the topic.

Teachers must decide, therefore, whether to prepare
their students directly for examinations or to look beyond
that goal. In either case, they will need to prepare some
work on social economics, and must decide when, what
and how to teach.

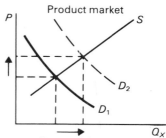

Demand rises, so
raising equilibrium
price of x.

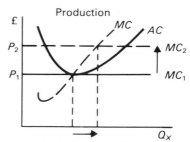

A typical, competitive
firm raises output of x.

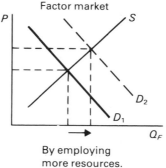

By employing
more resources.

When to teach?

Social and environmental issues such as rail closures,
nuclear power, and pollution are always around, and the   *Figure 42.1*

intelligent student's interest is likely to be aroused at all times. Teachers must decide when and how they will respond to this interest, and I for one can offer no strong guidance. In the difficult, opening stages of a course, for example, it is wise to allow students to tackle the issues that perhaps first led them towards the subject. And a topical cost–benefit study, or something along similar lines, does succeed in raising the fundamental questions and using the basic concepts that are generally introduced more conventionally at this level. But such an early treatment must inevitably lack rigour. However well the teacher expresses ideas to the student, those ideas cannot be fully understood until they have been studied in the context of the full introductory course.

For this reason, many teachers prefer to concentrate on social questions towards the end of their microeconomics teaching, as a conclusion, summary and even revision of earlier work. In this way, they can lead the student to relate the areas of microeconomics, previously studied separately over a long period, and understand the complete operation of the market system.

Figure 42.1 shows one way in which this can be done. Each diagram summarises in students' minds a body of work and an area of understanding: the theories of consumption, market behaviour, production and distribution respectively. Now they can relate each part to the others, and return to a fuller analysis of how the market system accommodates the fundamental economic problem of scarcity. A change in tastes, for example, affects consumption, market, production and distribution decisions and so causes a reallocation of resources. A second look at this sequence of events shows, further, how imperfections in the market system can arise and result in a misallocation of resources. This leads in general terms towards the study of particular imperfections and possible public responses to them, which is the heart of social economics.

What to teach?

Teachers will want their students to learn how to analyse problems of social economics in whatever form they arise, and not just one or two particular problems that have been met in coursework. It is important, therefore, to teach an understanding of general, basic principles, and to practise applying those principles to a range of issues. Students must be taught to distinguish private from social effects, and cost from allocative efficiency. They must know how externalities arise, for public and merit products in particular. They must know the different ways in which the authorities can overcome free-market imperfections, and so achieve the efficient allocation of resources. All this is fundamental, and common to all A-level and equivalent courses. But it gives rise to two particular teaching problems, in deciding how far to take the analysis.

Introductory courses, including those at A-level, concentrate upon free-market economics. Social

Table 42.1

Seat belt law cuts deaths by 25%

By Michael Baily
Transport Editor

The compulsory wearing of seat belts saved 350 lives and prevented 4,500 serious injuries in the first eight months of the new legislation, the Department of Transport disclosed yesterday.

The percentage of front seat passengers wearing seat belts rose from 40 to 95 between February and September last year; and the death and serious injury rate dropped by 25 per cent.

But this may have been achieved at the expense of other road users. Aware that car drivers may be less cautious when wearing seat belts, the department found that the number of pedestrians and cyclists hit by cars and vans increased 3 per cent, while those hit by motorcycles and other vehicles declined 20 per cent.

There could be other reasons for this and the trends will continue to be monitored, the department said.

The Automobile Association, said last night: "We always said compulsory wearing of seat belts would be the one single road safety measure with the most dramatic effect, and we are pleased. But one cannot overlook the disturbing upward trend in cycle casualties."

Source: The Times, 13 January 1984.

---

questions can enter this framework only in a certain form, by asking what prevents the free-market system from working well, and how can government intervention in a fundamentally free system help to improve matters? To some teachers, this appears as one-sided, weighted analysis. They would prefer to give greater weight to the behaviour of planned economies, and to policies of direct

Table 42.2

▰▰▰ *HEALTH* ▰▰▰

COST OF THE BAD LIFE

SHOULD people who eat, drink and smoke too much—and even love unwisely—pay a special Health Service premium?

A levy has been suggested to compensate the healthier members of society who make fewer demands on doctors, hospitals and the national drug cupboard.

Few would doubt that too many fags, too much booze, too many chips, and too much of La Dolce Vita can, when added up, put a sizeable burden on Health Service resources.

The latest Government estimate is that coping with smoking ailments costs the Health Service £100 million a year.

Alcohol abuse costs the country another £350 million in treatment and lost working time, but this is not broken down to show just how much of that burden the NHS bears.

There are now 13,000 NHS beds coping with those with drink problems.

Chuck in another £70 million a year for the treatment of dental decay that could be avoided by more sensible diet.

Add as much again for the treatment of the over-weight, and you come up with something in the £350 million a year bracket. Slimming drugs alone cost £3,500,000 a year.

And promiscuity has increased Health Service payment for sex-disease clinics.

Source: Daily Mirror, 9 May 1978.

state control. The constraint of preparing candidates for public examination naturally makes it difficult to justify such an approach. But also, it may be unnecessary if there are other ways to open students' eyes to both sides of a case.

There are many social and environmental questions that can prompt students to consider alternative lines of approach within the framework of conventional market courses. The extract shown on seat belts (Table 42.1) suggests such an example. Many similar cases are readily available. Students can be invited to identify the different social costs raised in each case. They can contrast the economic effects of direct legal control with those of taxation. They can discuss alternative treatments of each problem and additional social considerations not mentioned in the text. They can use their analysis of the market system in order to see both what it can and cannot do.

But should teachers aim to go further? Should they treat the study of social issues as an introduction to the types of welfare argument that are normally studied only in the later stages of a degree course? To an extent, these issues cannot be avoided, of course. Students must assess social questions in terms of their impact upon economic efficiency, and hence national welfare; on the distribution of income between groups even as broad as simply producers and consumers; on the search for a second-best policy when the ideal of perfect market behaviour is clearly impossible. But A-level textbooks and A-level examination boards suggest no more than this, and there does not yet seem to be any satisfactory introductory source to welfare economics for the 16–18-year-old.

How to teach?

Social economics can draw on any number of topical and controversial examples, illustrated by a wealth of resources. Teachers can draw their own material from the media, or use some of the many published case studies. The topic is among those best suited to a teaching approach that relates economic principles to real-world events. These sources can be used for reading, followed by discussion, for exercises in class, perhaps even role playing in small groups or visits to investigate local environmental issues. With such opportunities open to them, it is *almost* impossible for teachers to go wrong in their approach to the topic – but not quite.

Table 42.2 is offered as a typical example of the type of material that is available. But this material can be presented to students in different ways, and leave them with very different lessons learnt. To a large extent, the success of teaching from applied material depends on whether students are asked to argue from the general to the particular, or vice versa. Confronted by this extract, for example, some students may end up being expert in health matters. Such expertise may be commendable in some respects, but it is not likely to transfer at all well when the same students are asked to consider different social issues – such as lighting all motorways, or supporting British Airways.

It is important, therefore, to teach students to see the wood, and not the trees, and to use particular examples only as illustrations of, and not instead of, general economic principles. I suggest that students should consider, for example, the theoretical case for privatisation, and its likely effects on both private costs of operation as well as social efficiency, before turning to particular examples. There is clearly room for flexibility in all this, but the overriding aim should be kept in view – that students should be able to learn, understand and apply general principles to any practical example of social economics.

Perhaps the best teaching approach, therefore, is one that relies upon neither text-and-talk instruction, nor on an extended and detailed case study. Instead, the teacher should guide students through three areas of social economics in turn, illustrating each major principle with relevant examples. First is the complete operation of the free market system, when all conditions for its efficient use of resources are met. Then comes a survey of major imperfections, as they arise in the real world – the lack of knowledge, motivation and freedom that prevent markets clearing; the externalities – economies of scale, social costs and social benefits – that prevent individual decisions from achieving an optimum allocation of resources. Finally, there is the role for government, and its main methods of intervention: by buying, selling and holding stocks, by imposing taxes or subsidies, or by acting directly as producer and consumer in public enterprise. Here the wheel finally comes full circle, as the state ensures an adequate provision of public and merit goods, matches private to social values, and achieves the allocation of national resources that satisfies as many wants as possible. Each principle can be illustrated by examples, but established clearly in general terms. In this form, it is available for use by the student in different circumstances, for future problems and under examination conditions.

Resources

Begg, D., Fischer, S., Dornbusch, R., *Economics* (McGraw Hill, 1984) pt. 3.
Gowland, D. H., *Modern Economic Analysis 2* (Butterworth, 1983) chs. 8–11.
Lipsey, R. G., *An Introduction to Positive Economics* (Weidenfeld & Nicolson, 1983) pt. 7.
Leake, A. M., 'Government and markets', in *Casebooks on Economic Principles* (Macmillan Education, 1983).
Institute of Economic Affairs, *Hobart Papers* and *Occasional Papers* on various topics.
Computers in the Curriculum Project, *Cost Benefit Analysis* (Longman, 1983).
Hewitt, G., *Economics of the Market* (Fontana, 1978), chs. 11 and 12.
Hardwick, P., Khan, B., and Longmead, J., *An Introduction to Modern Economics* (Longman 1982) ch. 12.

43 Comparative Economics
Andrew Tibbitt

Introduction

Increasingly, it is being recognised that there is value in introducing a world perspective into A-level economics courses. This trend is also reflected in several examination syllabuses which now include a comparative element. For example, Section D of the Applied Economics paper of the Oxford and Cambridge examination board requires students to be able to:

1 make comparisons between various features of the British economy with those in a chosen, centrally planned, developing country, or another developed country;
2 explain the main economic features of the European Economic Community;
3 analyse the significance and operation of international economic institutions such as the International Monetary Fund (IMF), the World Bank and the General Agreement on Tariffs and Trade (GATT).

Comparative material can be incorporated in A-level courses in three ways:

1 As part of the introduction – to bring about the awareness that, although countries may face a common economic problem, the economic system they use to provide a solution to that problem varies from country to country.
2 As a comparative element to core topics throughout the course – for example, in the study of the interpretation of data generated from national-income accounts, in analysing the factors that contribute to economic growth and in the determination of the pattern of international trade flows.
3 As separate topics in their own right, which could be: (i) country based (e.g. Brazil, Russia or Japan) or (ii) theme based (e.g. the world debt crisis, the role of national planning).

This chapter will include some material developed for use in all three approaches. Traditional textbooks devote very little space to comparative topics, and with limited finance it is unlikely that there will be enough specialised books for classroom or individual student use. However, once basic principles have been established, there is much material in periodicals and booklets (such as *The Economist*, the *British Economy Survey*, and the *Economic Review*) that can be adapted for use as the basis for discussion or as data for a worksheet response.

In general, teachers should consider carefully before deciding to teach the comparative element through one or two specific countries. On a practical basis there is likely to be insufficient coincidence of experience of teachers and students of a particular country, and on an educational basis the better examples of international issues that affect and highlight aspects of the British economy in operation may come from a variety of countries.

It is, perhaps, even more important to have clear objectives in mind when introducing comparative topics than when teaching other aspects of A-level courses. There is much information available of a general nature which allows only a broad appreciation of the economic situation of a country, but less information of a specific nature dealing with key issues at a level appropriate to the A-level student. Much of the information available is not written for such students, but rather for businessmen and bankers.

When dealing with topical issues, whether domestic or international, it is important to keep up to date but at the same time retain sufficient detachment from day-to-day developments to obtain a longer-term perspective. This is much harder for overseas developments than for those at home.

Teachers should not, however, be discouraged from attempting to introduce a comparative element into their courses. Although a little knowledge might be considered to be a dangerous thing, much can be achieved from a highly selective and limited approach to a study of the economies of parts of the rest of the world and their economic problems that either affect the British economy or help put its performance in perspective.

An introduction to different economic systems

1　The objectives of introducing a comparative element during the early stage of the A-level course are threefold:

(a) Students should appreciate that the economic systems employed by different countries vary, and what elements of economic systems give them their character.

(b) They should understand some of the issues involved in an evaluation of the various economic systems.

(c) They should understand some of the advantages and disadvantages of different systems, and why most countries in practice opt for a mixture of free market and centrally planned allocation of resources.

2　A simple data-response exercise (see Exercise 1 on p. 200) with subsequent discussion should allow the teacher

to bring out the key elements of economic systems.

3　These can be based on the idea of systems built on 'building blocks' as suggested by Ian Ward.[1] He suggests three pairs of blocks, namely:

(a) those describing the ownership of the means of production as a basis for distinguishing between capitalist and socialist systems;

(b) those describing the means of co-ordination as a basis for distinguishing between market and centrally administered (non-market) systems;

(c) those describing the degree of centralisation or decentralisation to highlight the involvement of central authorities in decision-making.

4　An enlightening exercise can be set to get students to produce the structure of the economic systems of specified countries (or, at the risk of exposing the limitations of one's own knowledge, chosen countries of the students). Some results might appear as in Figure 43.1.

5　A more detailed profile of a country can be developed by asking your students to research and complete an appropriate information grid. Some discussion as to possible responses for your chosen column headings will help channel their efforts.

Some suggested headings might include:

(a) General classification of economic system (e.g. centrally planned, market socialist, etc.).

(b) Priority goals (e.g. industrial development, equality of wealth).

(c) Major strengths (e.g. minerals, skilled labour).

(d) Major problems/weaknesses (e.g. lack of infra-structure, dependence on imported oil).

(e) Current government policies (e.g. deflation according to IMF guidelines, a five-year plan).

(f) Standard of living.

(g) Performance on standard macroeconomic objectives (i.e. employment levels, price stability, economic growth and balance of trade).

(h) Strength of currency (e.g. its trade weighted effective exchange rate).

6　Before any attempts are made to evaluate the various economic systems operating throughout the world, there will have to be some discussion of the criteria to be used for such an evaluation and the level of importance that is to be attached to each of these criteria. Graeme Taylor[2] suggests asking a question such as 'What is the best car?' to get over these ideas. A similar topical question within the experience of most A-level students might be 'What micro-computer is best?'

7　Graeme Taylor suggests using the following criteria for evaluating an economic system:

(a) The distribution of incomes and wealth. In general, the distribution will be less equal in capitalist economies than in socialist economies, although Russia and post-Mao China now see a role for income relativities.

(b) The allocation of resources. In capitalist economies resources are mostly allocated to satisfy consumer wants, whereas in planned economies resources are

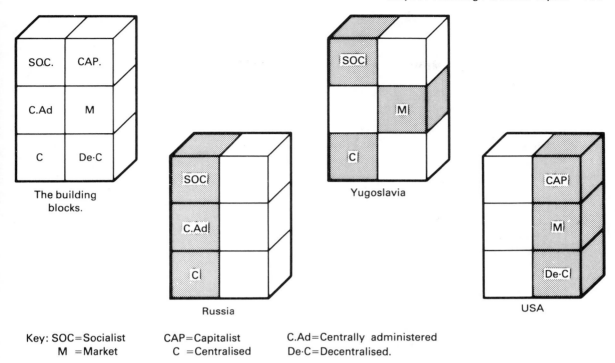

The building blocks.

Russia

Yugoslavia

USA

Key: SOC=Socialist CAP=Capitalist C.Ad=Centrally administered
M =Market C =Centralised De·C=Decentralised.

Figure 43.1

allocated to achieve the targets of the national plan.
(c) The rate of economic growth. Even allowing for problems of comparing statistics between the West and East, it does appear that economic growth in centrally planned economies has been higher than that achieved in market economies.
(d) The degree of individual economic security. That is, should individuals be protected from personal misfortune such as loss of job, accident or illness, as in socialist economies, or is some insecurity necessary to 'keep people on their toes', as in market economies?
(e) The degree of stability of prices and employment. Market economies are subject to greater fluctuations in prices and employment than centrally planned economies, although the queues, rationing and low levels of productivity in centrally planned economies are symptoms of suppressed inflation and under-employment.
(f) The distribution of economic power. That is, who is it that takes the economic decisions? How much power should individuals have to influence economic activity? In planned economies, freedom is clearly limited.
8 Group discussion work based on a question such as 'What features would you consider important in an economic system? List the components such a system would require' will reinforce these and other points.
9 Countries are, of course, not free to pick any economic system as if from a supermarket shelf. They are bound in their choice by constraints such as:

(a) their history and tradition;
(b) the stage of their economic development;
(c) the level of the standard of living;
(d) their relationships with the rest of the world.
* Ask your students which systems might be most appropriate (e.g. for less developed countries, or for those with low standards of living).
* There are examples of countries that have undergone radical changes in the form of their economic systems. Your students may be able to provide some examples from their O-level history studies (e.g. Russia under Lenin and Stalin, Britain during wartime), from knowledge of current affairs (e.g. Grenada), or be told of others (e.g. Yugoslavia).
* Do your students think that the 1986 Conservative government in Britain, through its policy of privatisation, is trying to remould the British economic system?
10 Most standard economics textbooks have descriptions of the advantages and disadvantages of the two main forms of economic system; free market and centrally planned economies. The main problems

associated with the operation of free market economies include:

(a) the under-production of public and merit goods;
(b) the over-consumption of demerit goods;
(c) the problems of externalities;
(d) the basic instability of certain markets (e.g. in agriculture);
(e) the fluctuations of prices and employment;
(f) the inequalities of incomes and wealth;
(g) the need to protect national strategic considerations.

The disadvantages of centrally planned economic systems include:

(a) bureaucracy;
(b) inflexibility;
(c) lack of consumer choice;
(d) lack of positive incentives.

These points can be brought out from data-response exercises such as Exercise 2.

Exercise 1 An appointment in Prague

Following the 1st leg European soccer cup match in Watford where nearly 20000 fans saw Watford defeated 2–3 by Sparta Prague, the team, officials and press corps arrived in Czechoslovakia for the second leg.

'We were directed to a press conference in the airport lounge. Elton John (Watford FC chairman) is very big news in Prague. His Russian tour was such a success that he has the rubberstamp of Big Brother's approval throughout the Soviet bloc. He is rated the number one pop star. He was big enough on the black market before that tour but he is rated a superstar now.

'Tickets for the match have all been sold. Party members, government officials, sports club members and "best factory workers of the month" have first choice. It is almost impossible for the ordinary Czech fan to obtain a ticket unless he falls into one of those categories.'

Questions

A Who, or what, decided that Elton John's music should be made available in Czechoslovakia? Who, or what, would make that decision in Britain?

B What is a black market? Do you get black markets in Britain?

C Contrast the ways that tickets may have been allocated for the matches in Britain and Czechoslovakia.

D Why are 'best factory workers of the month' selected in Czechoslovakia? How are factory workers rewarded in Britain?

Source: Tibbitt, A., *A Guide to A-level Economics* (Nelson, 1986).

Exercise 2 Speech to Communist Party Central Committee

In a speech written by the late Mr Andropov to the Communist Party Central Committee in December 1983, he called for 'tighter discipline by the labour force to fulfil the current five year plan'.

'People have been working with greater desire. In general, a change for the better in the national economy has begun to show . . . the most important thing now is not to lose the tempo. In the conditions of the present international situation which has been sharply aggravated through the fault of the aggressive imperialistic circles, the strict implementation of the state plan becomes not just an obligation but also a patriotic duty of every Soviet person. There has to be proper order in meeting the planned targets. Bottlenecks have to be eliminated.'

In demanding better consumer goods, the speech revealed that, 'Soviet trade organisations had rejected as sub-standard 50000 TV sets, 115000 radios, almost 250000 cameras, 1500000 clocks and watches and 160000 refrigerators offered by factories for retail in 1984.'

The state's retail buyers refused to purchase because of 'the disparity between the quality and assortment of these goods and the demands made by the consumers'.

Questions

A What would be contained in 'the current five year plan'? Does Britain have a five year plan?

B How would bottlenecks be removed in Russia? How would they be eliminated in Britain?

C What do you think is the function of the state's retail buyer in Russia? Has the consumer any choice as to the goods and services he or she buys in Russia?

D What might happen to factories producing sub-standard goods in Russia? What would happen to firms producing sub-standard goods in Britain?

E Are there similarities between the Russian and British economies?

Source: Tibbitt, A., *A Guide to A-level Economics* (Nelson, 1986).

The comparative element of core topics

1 Several of the traditional core topics of an A-level course lend themselves to the introduction of additional comparative material. An obvious example would be to introduce some of the problems experienced by less developed countries into the area of interpretation of national income accounts.

2 Statistical data can be used to stimulate early discussion (see Table 43.1).

Table 43.1 Estimates of GNP per head in $US (1977)

Kuwait	12 270
Switzerland	9 970
Sweden	9 250
USA	8 520
Japan	5 670
UK	4 420
USSR	3 020
India	150

Source: Marsden, C., Adams, S., and Crewdson, J., *An Introduction to Comparative Economics* (Heinemann Educational Books, 1980) p. 2.

(a) What can be inferred about the standard of living of people in the countries shown from this data (Table 43.1)?

(b) Does the average Indian really live on less than 5 per cent of what the average Briton consumes (Table 43.1)?

3 Additional statistical data comparing the level of incomes and consumption in India and the UK can be introduced later (see Table 43.2).

Table 43.2 India and UK income and consumption compared (1975)

	India	*UK*
National Income		
National income	£42.2b	£92.8b
Population	598m	56m
National income per head	£71	£1657
Physical indicators		
Calories/hd/day	1990	3250
Proteins/hd/day	49	90
Steel consumption/hd/day	14	385
Electricity consumption/hd/ year (KWH)	132	4490
Telephones/1000 people	3	379
Letters posted/hd/year	12	166
Net industrial output/hd/year	£5	£578

Source: Marsden, C., Adams, S., and Crewdson, J., *An Introduction to Comparative Economics* (Heinemann Educational Books, 1980) p. 71.

(a) What do the statistics in Table 43.2 tell you about the relative standard of living in India and the UK?

(b) Can anything be inferred from Table 43.2 about future standards of living in the two countries?

4 The main points to emerge would include:

(a) The problem of exchange rates. Should the national figures be converted at official exchange rates or at a rate that reflects purchasing power parity?

(b) Different consumption patterns. Purchasing power parity loses some relevance if consumption patterns differ between countries for reasons such as climate, culture, geographical factors, defence commitments, political needs, and so on.

(c) The use of different statistical bases. For example, Russia does not include the output of service industries in her accounts; much economic activity in less-developed countries goes unrecorded.

(d) Non-marketed output. That is, the goods and services provided by collective action of families and villages in less-developed countries which are not paid for in any measurable way.

(e) The distribution of income. This tends to be more unequal in less-developed countries, and subject to differences between regions, and between rural and urban areas.

5 Donaldson's story of 'Innocentia' in the *Economics of the Real World*[3] fully explores the factors 'behind the growth index'.

Topics in comparative economics

There are a number of opportunities to teach separate comparative economics topics within an A-level course. As stated in the introduction, a thematic approach is likely to be more rewarding than one based on a single country. An idea of the material available can be seen from the following approach to teaching aspects of the current world debt or international banking crisis. The development of the crisis can be traced with the aid of a simple flowchart (see Figure 43.2).

Data relating to changes in the level of oil prices, and hence the import bills of less-developed countries, non-oil commodity prices, and hence the export revenue of less-developed countries, the spiralling debts of the oil importers, and the rates of growth in economic activity in the developed and less-developed world, can be provided (see Figure 43.3) and turned into a data-response exercise with the addition of appropriate questions.

For example:

1 Describe the trends in oil prices since 1972.

2 In which years have there been falls in the prices of non-oil primary commodities?

3 What is the relationship between the rate of growth of output in countries and the level of current account balances?

4 Describe the trends in the levels of OPEC surpluses. How have the OPEC countries applied these funds?

5 Why have developed countries been able to correct the current account deficits caused by oil price rises but not the less-developed countries?

The problems can be highlighted by reference to the experience of a particular country (e.g. Brazil). It does not matter if neither teacher nor students are experts in Brazilian economics, as it is quite easy to build up a file (or

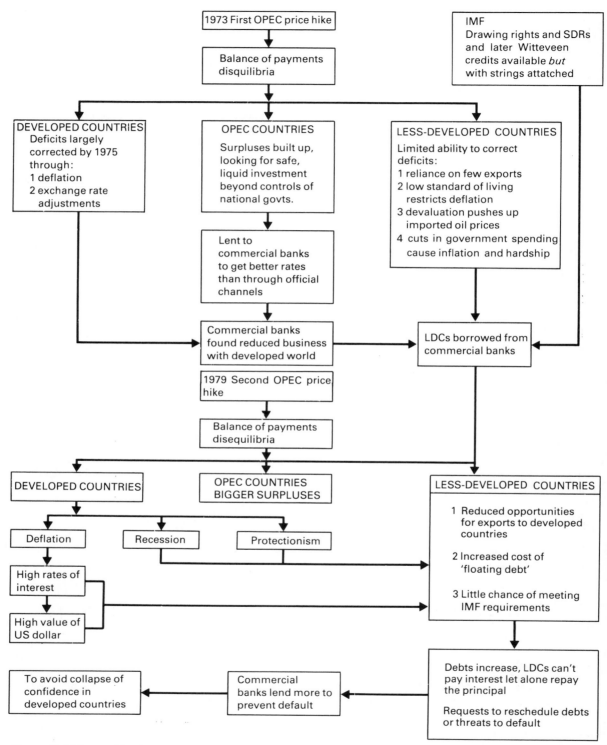

Figure 43.2 The world debt crisis Source: Tibbitt, A., A Guide to A Level Economics (Nelson, 1986).

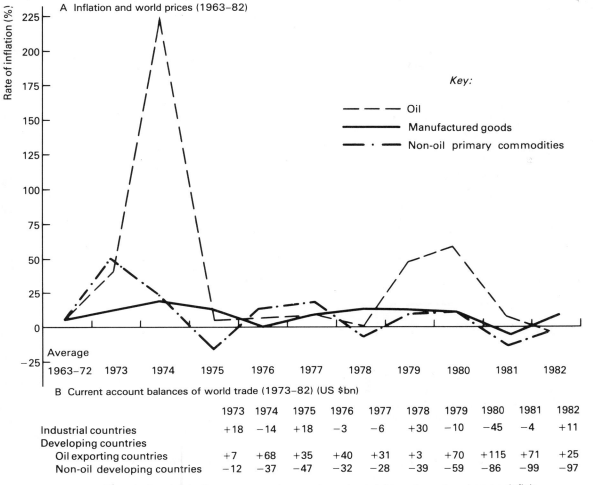

A Inflation and world prices (1963–82)

B Current account balances of world trade (1973–82) (US $bn)

	1973	1974	1975	1976	1977	1978	1979	1980	1981	1982
Industrial countries	+18	−14	+18	−3	−6	+30	−10	−45	−4	+11
Developing countries										
Oil exporting countries	+7	+68	+35	+40	+31	+3	+70	+115	+71	+25
Non-oil developing countries	−12	−37	−47	−32	−28	−39	−59	−86	−99	−97

*Note:*A plus sign indicates a current account surplus, while a minus sign shows a deficit.

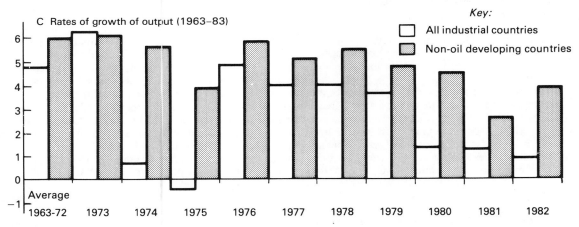

Figure 43.3 Sources: Treasury and Civil Service Select Committee Report on International Lending by Banks *(1983) pp.xiv, xv, xliv and xlv*

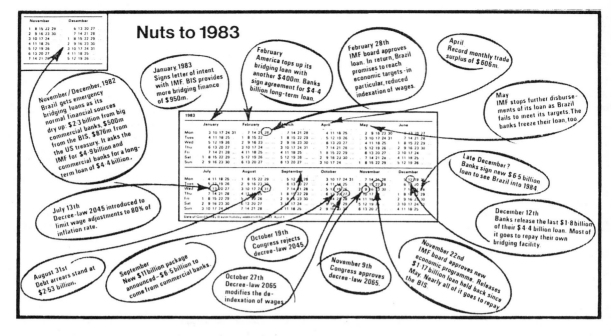

Figure 43.4   Source: The Economist, 17 December 1983.

for the students to develop a scrap book) from regular reading of the journals and newspapers familiar to all teachers. An example of material suitable for classroom use is provided in Exercise 3 and Figure 43.4.

Exercise 3   A Diary of a debtor nation

By the end of 1984 Brazil estimates it will have accumulated foreign currency debts of over $100 billion. Interest payments during the year will be $18.7 billion. The aim is to find this money by achieving a balance of payments surplus of $9 billion, renegotiating the rates of interest charged on their loans, rescheduling some of their debts and raising new loans for about $5 billion.

However, there are signs that Brazil cannot tolerate much more recession. Although the goals agreed with the IMF are being met, it seems politically impossible for Brazil to keep on course much longer. Inflation shows no sign of falling from the 10 per cent per month, 200+ a year level. Average per capita income has shrunk by 12.6 per cent in the past four years. Imports are being held down to last year's very low levels which cannot be managed much longer.

The cruzeiro is being devalued by at least the rate of inflation so that exports become more competitive abroad, but this means that imports become more expensive. Utility prices have been raised to keep pace,

and food subsidies have been removed, to reduce the government's borrowing requirement.

There are signs that the foreign trade success may be short-lived. Extra exports are nearly all to the USA, but in the States there are calls to protect industry against 'dumping' from Brazil.

Source: The Times, 10 May 1984.

Questions

A   Explain the following: (i) rescheduling debts, (ii) bridging loans, (iii) letter of intent, (iv) wage indexation, (v) Bank of International Settlements (BIS), (vi) devaluation.

B   Why were commercial banks prepared to lend currency to Brazil? Why was Brazil prepared to borrow from the commercial banks?

C   Why do you think that wage indexation was such a crucial issue for the IMF? Have the measures insisted on by the IMF brought about a reduction in the rate of inflation in Brazil?

D   Why was it important for Brazil to achieve a balance of payments surplus? What problems did Brazil experience in trying to achieve this surplus by (i) deflation, (ii) devaluation, (iii) expanding exports.

E   Even with all the measures, Brazil's debts were still increasing during 1984. What could be done to ease her debt problems?

Further reading

Economic systems

Dalton, G., *Economic Systems and Society* (Penguin, 1983).

Coleman J., *Comparative Economic Systems – An Inquiry Approach* (Holt, Rinehart & Winston, 1968).

Halm, G., *Economic Systems – A Comparative Analysis* (Holt, Rinehart & Winston, 1970) chs. 14, 18 and 22.

Specific countries

Hutchings, R., *Soviet Economic Development* (Blackwell, 1982).

Nove, A., *The Soviet Economic System* (Allen & Unwin, 1980).

Goldman, M., *USSR in Crisis* (Norton, 1983).

Nove, A., *Economics of Feasible Socialism* (Allen & Unwin, 1983).

Allen, G., *The Japanese Economy* (Weidenfeld & Nicolson, 1981).

Taylor, G., 'Yugoslavia – building blocks and performance', in Burke, G., and Nottle, R. (eds.) *The Economy in Operation 3* (VCTA, Melbourne, 1978) ch. 6.

Vaughan-Williams P., *Brazil* (University Tutorial Press, 1981).

Specific issues

Cairncross, F., and Keeley, P., *Guardian Guide to the Economy Vol. 2* (Methuen, 1983) chs. 4 and 5.

McQueen, M., *Britain, EEC and the Developing World* (Heinemann Educational Books, 1982).

Maunder, P. (ed.) *Case Studies in Economic Development* (Heinemann Educational Books, 1979).

Donaldson, P., *Worlds Apart* (Penguin, 1978).

Brandt, W., *North:South – A Programme for Survival* (Pan, 1980).

Brandt, W., *Common Crisis – North:South Cooperation for Economic Recovery* (Pan, 1983).

Pratt, M., *A Guide to the International Financial System* (Banking Information Service, 1984) chs. 6 and 7.

Periodicals

A number of periodicals contain regular articles of relevance to comparative economics.

The Economist is a mine of information each week, articles being found in its Finance, World Business, International or Economic Indicator sections. Specific articles worth chasing include 'Russian agriculture' (15 November 1980) and 'The Third World's overdraft' (14 April 1984). The *Schools Briefs on the World Economy* published in 1979, and now in separate booklet form, are useful.

The *British Economy Survey* (OUP) regularly includes articles on comparative topics. See particularly, Dawkins, S., 'A crisis in world banking', vol. 13, no. 1, autumn 1983; Jones, W., 'The UK and the world economy (USSR)', vol. 13, no. 2, spring 1984.

Finance and Development is published quarterly by the IMF and World Bank and is available from IMF, Washingon DC, 20431, USA (specify the English language version, and why you want it sent to you).

Look also for:

Reddaway, W., and Oppenheimer, P., 'World recession and world debts', *Midland Bank Review*, spring 1983.

'The labour market in the Soviet Union', *New Society*, 10 April 1980.

Broadsheets

Economic Reports on individual countries are produced by the National Westminster Bank Overseas Department (e.g. on Brazil (March 1984) and on Comecon countries (April 1984)). Inquire at your local branch.

TV programmes

Material on market and mixed economic systems is contained in the series by John Eatwell, *Whatever Happened to Britain?*, especially in programmes 1, 2 and 8. There are regular documentaries examining life in other countries that can be adapted for use in teaching comparative economics.

Notes and references

1 Ward, I., 'Economics: problems, systems, performance', in Burke, G., and Nottle, R. (eds.), *The Economy in Operation 2* (VCTA, Melbourne, 1975).

2 Taylor, G., 'Evaluating an economic system', *Economics*, vol. XVI, pt. 3, no. 71, autumn 1980, p. 65.

3 Donaldson, P., *Economics of the Real World* (BBC/Penguin, 1983) p. 130.

44 Money and Banking
David R. Butler

Introduction

Money and banking features in all A-level economics syllabuses and in many other courses, such as BTEC National. It is a wide-ranging topic including not only the banking system but also aspects of macroeconomic policy and international economics. Some of these aspects are dealt with elsewhere so this chapter will limit itself to a consideration of the teaching of the development of money, the banking system, and UK monetary policy. Clearly, many aspects of this topic cannot be taught in isolation from the rest of macroeconomic theory but it is necessary to impose some restrictions on the scope of this chapter.

Content

Ten years ago many A-level questions on this topic concentrated very heavily upon the institutional aspects of money and banking and students were expected to have a detailed knowledge of the intricacies of the London money market. More recently, the emphasis seems to have shifted very much more towards theory and policy as monetarism has become increasingly important in the management of the economy. At the same time, it may be argued that at least some knowledge of institutional arrangements is important for a real understanding of the theory. The following 'checklist' on money and banking may be useful to teachers, especially those embarking on the teaching of this topic for the first time. Teachers need to check their own examination syllabuses and past papers carefully to see where the particular emphasis is placed within this topic.

Checklist

Money: What is it? Its functions and development.
Monetary theory: Credit creation, monetarism, Keynesian monetary theory, Interest rate theory. Monetary policy and practice.
Financial institutions: Commercial banks, central banks, merchant banks, discount houses, IMF.

Student problems

1 Credit creation

There is a good deal of confusion as to how banks create credit and what assumptions there are in the credit-creation model. Students will often be under the misapprehension (reinforced by some textbooks) that a bank is able to loan out, say, ten times its deposits. Possibly the best explanation of credit creation is still that given in Lipsey's *Positive Economics* (see Resources on p. 208). A computer or paper simulation, such as that described under 'Teaching Methods and Aids', will also be very valuable here and add interest to the topic.

2 'The rate of interest'

Because textbooks and the media refer to 'the rate of interest', students often gain the impression that there is a single rate of interest or confuse this with rates advertised by banks. The student needs to know that there are a number of different but interrelated interest rates. The following type of question may help students to think about this area.

Interest rates (June 1984) *Savers.* Clearing banks deposit account, 6% (taxable), Finance Houses, 10% (taxable), Local Authority bonds, 3–5 years, 11% (taxable).
Borrowers Personal bank loan, 8.5%–10.5% (flat), mortgage rates, 10.5%.
Questions: (a) Explain the pattern of interest rates given above.
(b) What are the relationships between these rates of interest?
(c) How would you expect these rates to change if the bank rate rose? Distinguish between (i) the immediate effects, (ii) the effects if the bank rate continued to rise over a period of several months.

3 The quantity theory

Students sometimes experience problems in grasping the basic theory here. A good explanation of this that could very easily be developed into a classroom simulation is contained in Nobbs's *Advanced Level Economics*, p. 184. Having grasped the fundamental notions behind the theory students are too often uncritical and accept its implications for monetarism unequivocally. Programme 2, 'Not Worth the Paper', in the TV series *Ten × Economics* is excellent both in outlining a simple monetarist model and also in explaining why it might not work.

Teaching problems

There are three main problems facing the teacher with this topic. First, when and where to include it in the syllabus.

As indicated above, the topic is wide ranging and does not fall neatly into any particular 'slot' in the syllabus. The integrated nature of economics makes this true of other syllabus areas but the many-sided aspect of this topic makes the problem particularly acute here. Should it be taught before or after the main body of macroeconomics? Should the quantity theory be tackled here or as a separate section? There are no entirely satisfactory answers to these questions and the teacher may well find it best not to teach this topic in its entirety but to return to it throughout the course as other interrelated aspects of theory are introduced.

A second major problem in teaching this topic is for the teacher to keep up to date with what is a continually and rapidly changing area. It is perhaps true to say that changes tend to occur more frequently here than with any other syllabus section. Many textbooks are inevitably out of date almost as soon as they are printed. It is also a particular problem for the teacher actually to find out what the changes are because they are not normally introduced through any form of legislation. Thus 'minimum lending rate' has become obsolete and we are back to 'bank rate', the 'corset' has been quietly dropped and new forms of bank assets arrive almost overnight. Clearly, the financial press and the bank reviews are useful here but the busy teacher may find even this valuable source of current information too much to cope with at times. Fortunately, the Banking Information Service (see Resources) are now providing a very valuable updating service in their occasional papers on banking and other financial topics. The same organisation will also provide speakers who are experts in this field and have access to research facilities (see Resources).

A third problem is that this topic can in part prove to be a little 'dry' for the student. This is perhaps less true today with the switch in emphasis away from the institutional arrangements to the theory and policy considerations. The teacher is also being helped by the growth of computer simulations, videos, and much more interesting written material (see Teaching Methods and Aids, and Resources), all of which will help to make this topic more alive and interesting.

Teaching methods and aids

1 The use of newspaper articles and data response

This is one syllabus area where there really is a wealth of 'live' material available from the financial press. Frequent announcements about the money supply, interest rates and inflation provide the teacher with ideal data with which to examine monetary interrelationships. Figure 44.1 and the following questions provide an example of the type of material that might be used to promote discussion and to test understanding.

Questions
1 What is meant by the terms 'real national income' and 'real money stock'?

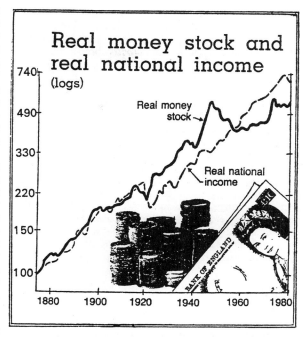

Figure 44.1 Source: Guardian, 15 December, 1983.

2 Discuss whether or not Figure 44.1 supports the monetarist case.

For some excellent published data-response questions, see Anderton, A.G., *Data Response Workpack in Advanced Level Economics* (UTP, 1982), particularly workcard number 29, the Demand for Money.

2 Games and simulations

This is a good area to experiment with simulations to bring realism into the classroom. A simple simulation to demonstrate some basic banking principles can be set up by having groups of students represent different banks. Each bank has to allocate its assets within broad guidelines. The teacher then initiates various transactions within the economy and introduces 'shocks' to the system, such as interest rate changes. Banks running short of 'cash' are penalised while investments earn an appropriate rate of interest. (For a published version of a competitive game, see the 1979 edition of the *Handbook*, Chapter 38.)

Students can also try their hand at being investment experts by taking part in the locally and nationally run 'Stockpiler' game (contact local chamber of commerce for details). See also Chapter 20 for details of some computer simulations in this area which could be used with older students.

3 Outside speakers and visits

The Banking Information Service will provide lecturers to

give talks on topical issues in banking and monetary policy. Speakers need to be well briefed and made aware of the level of ability of the students and their previous knowledge of the subject area. Most branch banks will arrange visits either to a local office or to a head office on request, and again it is important to stress the purpose of the visit and the students' particular interests. National Westminster Bank will arrange a 'City Day' which could include visits to one of the main City institutions such as the Stock Exchange, a tour of a City bank branch, and playing a management simulation game. There is understandably a considerable waiting list for such visits and plenty of notice is required. The London Stock Exchange has a free public gallery and shows the film *My Word Is My Bond* at regular intervals throughout the day. The Stock Exchange likes to have notice of parties of students in advance. Regionally, stockbrokers are often very prepared to give talks on the Stock Market or other related topics. The Treasury may also be prepared to arrange a visit and provide a speaker.

Resources

Most of the standard texts cover this area in terms of the theory and a selective list is given below. Textbooks rapidly become out of date in terms of policy and institutional arrangements and the teacher is strongly urged to refer to some of the non-textbook material mentioned to supplement sources of information.

Books

Lipsey, R. G., *Positive Economics*, 6th edn. (Weidenfeld & Nicolson, 1983) pt. 9, ch. 38, 'The money supply', and ch. 39, 'Monetary equilibrium'. Good and accurate explanation of credit creation in a multi-bank system.

Powell, R., *Advanced Level Economics* (Letts, 1983) ch. 16, 'Money'. A student guide and study aid.

Stanlake, G. F., *Macroeconomics – An Introduction*, 3rd edn. (Longman, 1982) ch. 11, 'Money', ch. 12, 'Structure of banking', ch. 13, 'Demand for money and liquidity preference', ch. 14, 'Control of money supply', and ch. 15, 'Quantity of money and price level'. Well-presented, and its easy-to-read style is appreciated by students.

Nobbs, J., *Advanced Level Economics*, 3rd edn. (McGraw-Hill, 1981) section 4: Money. A popular and well-presented book giving a simple introduction to the quantity theory and monetarist debate.

Prest, A. R., and Coppock, D. J., *The UK Economy – A Manual of Applied Economics* 9th edn. (Weidenfeld & Nicolson, 1982) Section 2: Monetary, Financial and Fiscal Systems. Current discussion with reference to recent statistics.

Livesey, F., *A Textbook of Economics*, 2nd edn. (Polytech Publishers, 1982) ch. 12, 'Monetary policy'.

Burningham, D., *Understanding Economics*, 2nd edn. (Hodder & Stoughton, 1984) ch. 15, 'Money and banking', and ch. 16, 'Control of monetary system'.

Donaldson, P., *10 × Economics* (Penguin, 1983) ch. 2, 'Not worth the paper'. Based on a television series of the same name. Good explanation of quantity theory.

Pamphlets

Banking Information Service. Excellent series of current and up-to-date booklets available free of charge. See, in particular *Guide to International Financial System, Guide to Monetary Policy, Guide to British Financial System*. These are being constantly revised and new titles added so the teacher is advised to contact the Banking Information Service to obtain the most recent publications list.

Bank Reviews. Published quarterly by Barclays, Lloyds, National Westminster, Midland, The Bank of England and the Three Banks. Available free (except *Bank of England Quarterly Bulletin*) through local branches. Contact head offices to be put on regular mailing lists. Lloyds Bank also provide a very useful 'briefing' sheet on current developments.

Films/videos

Banking Information Service, *'It doesn't grow on trees...'*, Money and the UK monetary system. Covers functions of money, creation of money and monetary policy. Also, *Banking on Industry*. An introduction to how banks help to finance industry by looking at a small ceramics business being set up.

45 Teaching on BTEC National: Sources of Finance

Introduction

The term economics, even when presented as part of the integrated Organisation in its Environment module, is likely to conjure up in the minds of many BTEC National level students all manner of popular misconceptions and prejudices regarding its assumed lack of relevance to their personal and working lives. Obviously such a view, even when only mildly expressed, presents the teacher of economics with a challenge in motivating the students and in successfully managing the learning experiences that are provided.

The challenge posed by this antagonism is the need to convince those holding the prejudiced view of the advantages that the pursuit of economics understanding may bring them. Teachers may see the value of economics education in terms of the opportunity it provides to extend the student's repertoire of skills and knowledge, to assist in the development of an economics understanding, and to establish a basic structure on which further knowledge and understanding may be built. But the student is unlikely to possess such a clear vision.

One approach that may be adopted by the teacher in attempting this task is to establish an appropriate business context from which it is possible to identify and 'work back' to key economic concepts. This could provide day-release and evening-class students with a recognisable framework to which they are able to relate and, above all, accept as meaningful and relevant.

If economics is 'the analysis of choice'[1] and if it may be seen to provide the tools with which to analyse situations that require choices to be made, then what better place to start than by identifying the major choices likely to be faced by an organisation or firm – for example, which sources of short-term finance are open to it and how much should it borrow and from where?

Economics understanding facilitates choice, and hence the all-important decision-taking process, because it develops the ability to identify the particular variables involved in a problem and to make predictions regarding the behaviour of these variables given the making of particular choices. For students to acquire such abilities it is inevitable that they will need to be exposed to the techniques of the economist. Model-building and theories are important techniques that are of direct relevance to the students, if only as a basis of generalisation, given the vast complexity of the business world.

However, care must be taken to avoid any over-emphasis on abstraction, for models may tend to obscure the role of human choice and values, and the reality may well be that choice is not a clinical and scientific procedure. Furthermore, an acknowledgement of the existence and importance of perspectives other than an economic one (e.g. accountancy) is essential, given the perceived needs of the BTEC National students. This should be self-evident to the teacher, who is required by the BTEC approach to move outside his/her own discipline and to work as a member of a team.

An acknowledgement of the importance of the normative aspects of management and decision-making does not mean, however, that the teaching of the Organisation in its Environment unit must be solely concerned with the provision of factual and descriptive details about matters and institutions broadly identified in its general objectives and indicative content.

The use of the BTEC-recommended problem-solving approach appears to have much to offer, both in meeting the calls for relevance and in maintaining a vehicle for the development of meaningful economic awareness. It is possible to adopt a method that seeks to identify some of the important choices faced by an organisation and to work through them to the basic core of economics understanding, pausing to develop appropriate models and theories *en route*. Inevitably this approach requires an acceptance that the logical arrangement and systematic view of economics is something that may be aimed for but cannot be assumed to exist initially, or that it may be readily achieved using a traditional approach.

Starting with the problem and establishing alternative approaches may be thought by some teachers to create difficulties because of the inevitable loss of a detailed structure and well-regulated sequence. The aim must, however, be to establish the link between business activity and the underlying economic theory.

A descriptive approach that seeks to describe the working environment of the businessman or woman may be boring and tedious to the students. Nor is it satisfactory to be content to plough through the traditional theoretical basis of economics, leaving students to make their own links with reality. Either approach, with or without any student antagonism, is unlikely to lead to learning that is anything more than patchy at best. Certainly, economic theory is likely to be seen as irrelevant, if not misleading, to business activities.

An example of a more relevant and direct approach may be provided by reference to the work of D. Swords at

Barnfield College (Luton) who sought to introduce BTEC National Certificate and Diploma students to the relevance and necessity of an economics perspective in the examination of the topic of short-term finance available to business organisations.

The teaching strategy adopted involved three distinct stages:

1 List, categorise and describe the types of finance available to the organisation

In the case of BTEC National Certificate students, this would appear to be a prime example of a topic about which the students are likely to possess at least some prior knowledge and therefore one that may benefit from the technique of 'brainstorming'. Brainstorming has been described as an appropriate strategy, 'when you want to produce quickly a plethora of ideas or alternatives about a particular subject or problem. The object is to stimulate the pupils' imagination and creativity'.[2]

The possible outcome of this exercise, which may be oral, written, collective or individual, might concentrate on the distinction between internal and external sources of finance. An alternative to this might be as shown in Figure 45.1.

2 The measurement of the cost of each potential source

Again, the technique of brainstorming may be of value as the students are likely to have some prior knowledge and understanding, for example familiarity with interest charges. Bank loans attract interest and there is obviously a price to pay, but what of a policy of cash discounts, the use of retained profits and so forth?

Essential economic concepts such as opportunity cost may be introduced or highlighted at this stage. Additionally, effective links may be made between the Organisation in its Environment and other units, such as Numeracy and Accounting, in consideration of the concepts of cost, profit, value added, etc. In fact, and always assuming that sufficient time is available, much could be made of the practical link with accountancy if the

approach is based on a set of accounts from an existing business organisation. Follow-up work might be thought appropriate and might possibly take the form of a discussion with a visiting speaker, preferably a business person from a similar organisation.

3 How does a businessman or woman choose which source(s) of short-term finance to use?

This step offers much scope for the development of an economic perspective while at the same time acknowledging that non-economic factors may influence the choice. This perspective will involve imparting the concept of the margin, that is in respect of how the cost of each source of short-term finance varies as the amounts are increased, relative costs and the ideal of borrowing from each potential source up to the point where marginal costs are equal. Obviously there are no right or wrong answers, merely an acknowledgement of the factors involved and an attempt to establish an economic perspective given the particular objectives of the organisation in question.

This three-stage approach starts with the positive advantage of a real business-world phenomenon, which students may experience, and follows through with the development of some economic analysis relevant to the operation of their own organisations in practice.

Significant benefits may be claimed for this type of approach compared with one of a more traditional nature. It has been found to stimulate interest particularly with part-time day and evening-class students. The treatment genuinely challenges their understanding, yet at the same time encourages them to impart their existing knowledge. They are at no time launched into abstraction for its own sake. As a result, it may be felt to aid student understanding. It may also contribute to the process of dismantling existing blocks to learning generated by the popular antagonism to economics and its propagators.

Perhaps even more importantly, the students may have learned, by virtue of the concepts they have been taught

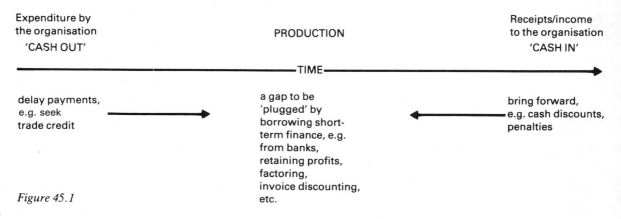

| Expenditure by the organisation 'CASH OUT' | PRODUCTION | Receipts/income to the organisation 'CASH IN' |

TIME

delay payments, e.g. seek trade credit

a gap to be 'plugged' by borrowing short-term finance, e.g. from banks, retaining profits, factoring, invoice discounting, etc.

bring forward, e.g. cash discounts, penalties

Figure 45.1

and the methods of analysis undertaken, an economics skill that can be used in other topics or transferred to their own future experiences. The structure that is presented also accommodates developments in the business world. Given new forms of business finance for example, students may be able to classify them and have a view on how they may affect the organisation.

Notes and references

1 Gowland, D. L., *Modern Economic Analysis* (Butterworth, 1979) p. vi.
2 Whitehead, D. J., 'Learning processes and teaching strategies in economics education', *Economics*, vol. xix, pt. 4, no. 84, p. 144, winter 1983.

46 National Income: An Introduction to Macroeconomics
Michael Tighe

Introduction

For many years the study of national income and the basic elements of macroeconomics have been relegated in most economics courses to a position near to the end of the first year, since it is thought that such topics are too complex and difficult to comprehend without the earlier study of the more basic building blocks of microeconomics. Certainly the macro approach uses different analytical techniques and the concepts themselves are also often more sophisticated than those involved in microeconomics. However, where microeconomics is often concerned with a rather unrealistic static model of partial equilibrium, macroeconomics involves the use of dynamic models in producing a general equilibrium theory.

The decision on when to introduce macroeconomics, and to what depth the analysis should be pursued, must be left to the individual teacher, who will be governed by the nature of the students involved in terms of maturity and ability to comprehend a series of interrelationships simultaneously. Traditionally microeconomics has tended to be covered before macroeconomics, and many of the standard introductory texts used by teachers have tended to reflect this. The latest edition of Stanlake's book, for example, does not introduce national income until part six has been reached,[1] although the same author has recognised the need for a more concentrated approach to macroeconomics to assist both student and teacher, and has produced a separate macroeconomics text.[2] Other authors have also produced specialist macroeconomics texts, including Harvey,[3] whose *Intermediate Economics* will be familiar to many teachers. One particularly useful text that attempts to bridge the gap between standard general elementary textbooks and more advanced specialist macroeconomics texts is that of Aston and

Rickard.[4] The first four chapters are of great value in providing a sound analysis of national income theory, but later chapters on policy are now rather dated.

Some textbooks have attempted to start with macroeconomics[5] so that the economic information received by the student in everyday life can be related to the study of the subject more readily. Macroeconomic events such as changes in the rate of inflation and levels of unemployment, the balance of payments and changes in fiscal and monetary policy are mentioned daily in newspapers, on radio and television. One of the intrinsic attractions of the subject of economics is its concern with the real world.

An important problem faced by any teacher in introducing basic macroeconomics is to present an objective approach in the light of recent controversial developments in macroeconomic theory. Most of the textbooks currently available concentrate almost exclusively on the Keynesian analysis but barely mention alternative views on the working of the economic system. One of the main developments in the past ten years, for example, has been the incorporation into macroeconomics of the rational expectations hypothesis. Some indication needs to be given of the relationship between the new macroeconomics and the earlier classical and Keynesian synthesis. The controversy in macroeconomics between the two main schools of thought, Keynesians and monetarists, need not be a dry academic argument but one related to the real-world economy. The argument can be used to demonstrate the considerable measure of agreement between economists on certain matters in contrast to the vehement disagreement on policy issues. One recent macroeconomic text[6] may well be of assistance to the teacher in dealing with such controversies and, although there is some evidence of monetarist bias (despite the authors' claim otherwise), the book does present alternative views of macroeconomic policy in a clear manner.

In presenting an explanation of national income theory, textbooks tend to deal first with the concept of national income, followed by the measurement of its value, and finally the determination of its value. Although the topic can be conveniently divided in this way, it is arguably preferable to leave the technical difficulties of measurement until after students have a better understanding of the concept and the factors that affect it. National income accounting does create problems for students, particularly when large quantities of statistics are presented in the form in which they appear in the *National Income and Expenditure* 'Blue Book'.[7] It is possible for students to understand and use the concept of national income without being able to follow the precise technical problems involved in measurement. In addition, with the wider availability and use of microcomputers in schools and colleges, the mathematical complexities of calculation can be accomplished by the computer and thus aid student understanding of the basic concepts. There are a variety of approaches available to the teacher in introducing this topic but generally a mixture of techniques would be advisable. It is possible to start with a historical introduction, contrasting the classical view with the Keynesian and the context in which Keynesian macroeconomics developed. A useful non-mathematical text is that by Stewart.[8] An early introduction of the national income flow diagram is also helpful in presenting the overall view of national income. This can later be modified to assist with both determination and measurement. Depending on the skills of the group, some numerical, algebraic or graphical methods can also be used. Again, the use of a computer program can make this approach much more acceptable to the less numerate student.[9]

The meaning of National income

It is a standard pedagogic technique to relate theory to the students' own experience, and this should be possible at almost any level. With A-level students, however, it is possible to refer to incomes fairly realistically in terms of pocket money and the earnings from part-time employment, and then to abstract to the idea of aggregate income by summing all individual incomes. Students should also be aware that incomes are not only received from the provision of the factor of production labour, but also from land, capital and enterprise. There are many simulation exercises that can be devised to illustrate the contribution of the various factors of production to national output using resources readily available in the school, such as paper, scissors and labour which can be used to create paper loaves and fishes or any other product. On a more sophisticated level, it is possible to introduce such concepts by means of a computer business simulation such as 'Fillet and Billet'[10] in which the participants have to produce brown plastic mouldings from red and green raw materials using a given quantity of capital and labour (see Figure 46.1). The simulation also takes account of certain exogenous shocks that students have to incorporate into their future production plans. The simulation also helps the students distinguish between stocks and flows of goods and the importance of making provision for capital depreciation as well as investment for future growth of production. Thus it is possible to emphasise the distinction between gross and net capital formation. The red and green raw materials must be ordered well in advance of production and held as stocks until needed. One of the shocks involves the loss of one supplier so that stocks must be run down more quickly in order to maintain production. The problem of financing future investment also illustrates the importance of the savings/investment relationship and prepares the way for a discussion of equilibrium. There are now several business games available that can perform similar functions to those described above.[11] Textbooks tend not to be very helpful in describing the meaning and significance of national income, so the teacher has to look further afield for assistance. Business games and computer programs are now useful additional resources in this area.

The significance and usefulness of national income can be emphasised as a measure of the standard of living and some comparisons can be made between economies in

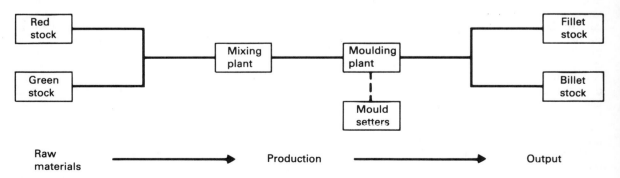

Figure 46.1 The production of fillets and billets

order to illustrate the difficulties of using national income statistics with different population sizes and rates of inflation as well as the more obvious difficulties of cultural differences and disparities in methods of calculation. One particularly useful text here is Marsden, Adams and Crewdson.[12]

National income determination

The circular flow model may now be reintroduced as a tool of economic analysis. From a very simplified model of a closed economy with no government sector, it is possible to introduce the various injections and leakages that make the model more realistic. It is possible to illustrate both money flows and real flows of goods and services between households and firms which represent consumption and production activities respectively. Traditionally such a diagram can be built up on a blackboard, but the use of an OHP transparency overlay is preferable but and, with the availability of a microcomputer used as an electronic blackboard, the diagram can be built up step by step by the teacher, and realistic numbers may be introduced, having been calculated by the program. One such program is *Circular Flow of Income*.[13] The computer program also helps to overcome the difficulty of explaining the complex interrelationships between producers and consumers that produce eventual equilibrium. Alternatively, the circular flow can be considered

as a hydraulic system in which taps allow leakages to drain income from the flow and pumps inject income into the flow. A detailed presentation of the circular flow model may be found in Lipsey,[14] who contrasts a simple version without injections and leakages with one incorporating saving and investment before analysing the Keynesian model in more detail. The importance of the simplifying assumptions made must be stressed throughout the analysis so that the students may more readily accept greater complexity later. Stanlake's *Macroeconomics*[15] takes several chapters to develop the various injections and leakages in detail, but it should be possible to build a more realistic model by means of overlays on the OHP until a fairly complex diagram such as that illustrated can be produced (see Figure 46.2). Such a diagram can prove useful in illustrating the problems of measurement and in suggesting policy implications.

Some resort to mathematical techniques can hardly be avoided at this stage, but a step-by-step introduction of concepts such as average and marginal propensity to consume and save and then a graphical presentation of the consumption function can usually be understood relatively quickly by the more numerate students. It is useful to introduce some simple, if unrealistic, numbers to begin with so that the various multipliers may be demonstrated. Both Marshall[16] and Prest[17] provide a clear analysis of the multiplier, and the regular updating of the latter text helps provide recent UK values for both propensities to consume and the multiplier. It is usually

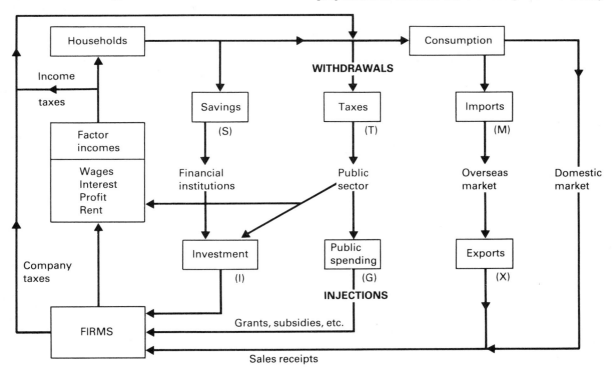

Figure 46.2 The circular flow of income/expenditure

advisable to examine the effect of one change in injections or leakages on national income at a time so that the mathematics remain uncomplicated. It can be shown relatively painlessly that the multiplier effect will be the reciprocal of the marginal propensity to save, import or the marginal rate of taxation. A compound multiplier may then perhaps be attempted.

It is helpful at this stage to examine the factors that produce a particular level of consumption or saving. Aston and Rickard[18] again provide a very comprehensive coverage of the factors influencing the consumption function. It is possible to introduce some alternatives to the Keynesian assumption of a stable consumption function and to look at the permanent income hypothesis supported by Milton Friedman as one example. A common problem for most students is in distinguishing ideas of equality from equilibrium, and the textbooks are not always very helpful in putting forward alternative descriptions for the same relationship. Students find it difficult enough to appreciate how millions of consumption and savings decisions by individuals lead to a particular level of output and investment by firms without the added problem of terminology such as *ex ante* and *ex post* savings and investment. Not all texts link the consumption function to the savings and investment functions, but there are some useful exceptions such as Stanlake,[19] where these functions are presented in the same diagram. This link has the added benefit of making clear the concepts of deflationary and inflationary gaps which again students find difficult to detect and distinguish. One helpful visual aid in this regard is the programme 'Whatever happened to full employment?' in the TV series *10 × Economics* produced by Yorkshire Television[20] where the various components of aggregate demand are represented by wooden packing crates carried by a forklift truck. A similar illustration is provided in the book based on the series written by the presenter Peter Donaldson.[21]

In examining the factors affecting the level of investment, care has to be taken to distinguish between the desired stock of capital and the flow of investment. One possible approach is to use marginal productivity analysis, but this may seem odd if students have not previously encountered this concept in microeconomic analysis. Much depends on what has been taught earlier. It is extremely likely that students will have some familiarity with the concept through the law of diminishing returns introduced in the early stages of most economics courses. Lipsey[22] clearly distinguishes between the marginal efficiency of capital and that of investment, as does Stanlake.[23] The latter text also classifies the different categories of investment in order to explain that investment decisions will be determined by different factors according to the type of investment.

A discussion of the motives for investment enables a number of strands of theory to be brought into the analysis. The profit maximisation assumption suggests that profitability will be the main motive for investment in the private sector. It is interesting, but quite challenging, for the less numerate student to investigate how businessmen or women attempt to measure the expected rate of return on investment. Some actual examples of business practice may be given and the reliance on the 'payback method' given due emphasis. The student needs to be shown that such methods do not provide a true measure of the earning potential of an investment decision because they do not allow for the fact that a sum of money due in the future has a lower present value than the same sum of money due now. In order to estimate more accurately the earning potential of the capital, the businessman or woman must find the present value of the expected receipts and then compare this with the current supply price of the assets. The student can then be introduced to the techniques of 'discounting' and the use of discounted cash flow by the use of a simple numerical example. The apparent accuracy of such a calculation, however, must be tempered by a timely reminder that real-world calculations are based largely on estimates that may themselves be highly inaccurate.

Another difficulty arises in relating the level of planned investment to the rate of interest. It is assumed that an increase in investment will take place if its potential earning power, as measured by the marginal efficiency of capital, is greater than the cost of funds needed to finance the project, that is, the rate of interest. Students need to be aware that investment decisions may not be so heavily dependent on changes in interest rates. This is particularly true of short-term investment projects and investment in stocks in manufacturing industry which are usually financed by trade credit. For a detailed examination of saving, investment and the rate of interest in the 1970s, it is worth consulting the chapter on savings in the UK in *Case Studies in Macroeconomics*.[24] A further difficulty in using Keynesian analysis is the likely instability of the marginal efficiency of capital (MEC). Changes in business expectations will follow moods of either optimism or pessimism about the future progress of the economy. An optimistic view will mean higher expected returns and thus the MEC curve will shift to the right. The reverse will be true for a collapse of business confidence. It is therefore difficult to predict what will be the demand for capital goods at any given rate of interest when the demand curve for capital is unstable.

The expectation of future profits is the factor most likely to influence investment. Where firms are encouraged to invest because of an expected increase in the demand for the final product, the investment is said to be 'induced'. It is this relationship that forms the basis of the acceleration principle which may now be seen as a means of describing the relationship between a small change in income which affects demand for the final product, and changes in investment. It should be made clear that the theory assumes that firms attempt to maintain a constant capital/output ratio, that is, some constant relationship between the level of output and the stock of capital required to produce that output. The importance of changes in technology in determining the capital/output ratio can also be emphasised. The use of a simple arithmetical example can show how small increases in consumer demand are magnified in the demand for capital goods and it is also helpful to demonstrate the importance of capital consumption in the calculation. It should be stressed that it is the 'rate of change' in consumption that determines the amount of induced investment, not just a simple increase in consumer demand. A reduction in the rate of growth of consumer spending, for example, can lead to an absolute decline in orders to the capital-goods industries. It is also necessary to explain that the accelerator effect is dependent on a number of factors, such as the durability of the capital equipment, the proximity of the industry to full capacity, and the belief that the increase in demand is likely to be permanent. If the increase in demand is thought to be temporary, firms will simply run down stocks or lengthen order books.

An increase in demand for investment that coincides with full employment in the capital-goods industries may well lead to rising prices. This could reduce the accelerator effect as the demand for capital decreases and firms seek capital-saving production techniques. This discussion can provide a good foundation for later work on the trade cycle and the theory of economic growth. Students should be aware of the empirical evidence supporting the accelerator theory as well as some contradictory evidence based on individual case studies. A thorough analysis of the accelerator principle and the evidence for its existence is provided by Robins in an article in *Economics*.[25] He comments that providing a convincing presentation of the accelerator to sixth-form students is difficult because, although the simple naïve accelerator is mathematically appealing as an explanation of the instability of invest-ment expenditure, it quickly loses credibility with students once the simplifying assumptions are explained. The article explains the development of accelerator theory and provides a summary of the results of some attempts at empirical application of the accelerator. He concludes that the accelerator principle should not be regarded as a theory of investment in itself, but rather as an analytical structure useful for the testing of different hypotheses about the variables that are most significant in the capital stock adjustment process.

The reaction of sixth-form students to this complex area of analysis varies between individuals, but it is usually possible for them to adjust from an oversimplified model to one more closely approximating reality – though much depends on the skill of the teacher in striking a balance between oversimplification and a confusingly complex real-world situation. Probably the most difficult part of the analysis for the student is the determination of equilibrium national income and the role of the multiplier process. Most texts start with a simple two-sector economy, households and firms, and examine one injection – investment, and one leakage – saving. Equili-brium may then be redefined as leakages equal to injections or planned savings equal to planned invest-ment. If the amount of total output not consumed (saving) is exactly equal to the demands by firms for capital formation (investment), then planned saving is equal to planned investment, total demand is equal to total supply and equilibrium will exist. If, however, consumers plan to save more or less than firms plan to invest, there will be a situation of disequilibrium. The effects of such disparities may be examined by means of a table showing planned output, consumption, saving and investment which can be prepared on an OHP trans-parency or, alternatively, a block diagram or graph may be used. It is helpful to have a transparency prepared illus-trating both the consumption function and the savings/investment functions so that it can be clearly shown that equilibrium national income is achieved where savings equal investment, that is, where the savings and investment functions intersect. By using an overlay, it is also fairly easy to demonstrate the effect on equilibrium of a change in, say, planned investment. Not only does the increase in planned investment lead to an increase in output and income, but it is also quite clear that the resulting change in income is much greater than the change in investment. This is a useful visual explanation of the impact of the multiplier process on national income equilibrium.

The multiplier process shows that changes in spending have a greater effect on national income than the original change in spending. Most texts introduce a relatively simple arithmetical example at this point assuming a change in spending of, say, £100 million on some public-works project such as a hospital or motorway. It is then further assumed that the marginal propensity to consume (MPC) of the community remains constant at 0.8 so that £80 million of the additional £100 million will be spent and £20 million saved. The £80 million spent will provide incomes for those performing services for the first group of workers. They, in turn, will spend 80 per cent of their additional income (£64 million) and so on. The eventual increase in income is the sum of the successive rounds of spending started by the initial change in expenditure. The more mathematically inclined students will recognise this as a geometric series summed to infinity, but for those with pocket calculators, the series can be shown to approach the total of £500 million, indicating a multiplier factor of 5. It can then be shown that the size of the multiplier depends on the value of the MPC. In other words, the greater the amount of income passed on at each stage, the larger will be the eventual rise in total income. It is useful to illustrate other values for the MPC in case the student mistakenly believes that the value is always 0.8 because so many textbooks use the same example. An interesting visual illustration of this example in the form of a block diagram may be found in Stanlake.[26]

Alternative methods of demonstrating the multiplier process may involve role-playing exercises with students using real or 'monopoly' money, but a very useful aid is the computer program MULTSC,[27] based on an original program by Professors Lumsden and Attiyeh. The student is given the task of maintaining aggregate demand as close to capacity as possible. There is control over government expenditure and taxation. Additional stimuli include questions on the value of the investment multiplier or MPC and problems to test student competence. A more up-to-date version of this program is now available as a macroeconomic simulation which is changed each year by the author, Professor Lumsden, as part of an annual nationwide competition for sixth-form students. Once the competition has finished, the program may be obtained from the publishers, Longman, and reduced rates apply where an earlier version has already been purchased.[28]

Macro-simulations help students to learn basic macro-economics in an interesting fashion and provide them with some sense of the dynamics of the macroeconomic system. Students are able to experience the problems faced by the policy-maker and to test their own understanding of the theory in trying to solve such problems. The students' booklet gives a detailed history of the last ten years of the economy and the game can be run for one or more players or teams. Printed results can be obtained (if a printer is available), and each year's results are stored so that the game can be restarted at any stage. This program is of great assistance in promoting student understanding of basic macroeconomics.

The final phase in the explanation of national income determination introduces policy considerations. Having shown how the equilibrium level of output is determined by aggregate demand and that the level of output determines the level of employment, it is now necessary to explain the idea of some desirable level of output that will provide full employment for the labour force. It must be shown that an equilibrium situation in the markets for goods and services does not necessarily produce the desired equilibrium in the market for labour (i.e. full employment). Most texts produce a standard graphical treatment of the deflationary and inflationary gaps but not all show the connection between the consumption function and the savings/investment functions in one diagram. Some texts[29] use the block diagram approach, which may help those students who find graphs difficult to understand.

The measurement of national income

It is useful once again to reintroduce the national income flow diagram so that reference may be made not only to money flows as distinct from real resource flows, but also to each of the three methods of measurement incorporated in the diagram. With a sound understanding of the meaning and the factors affecting the determination of national income, it should now be possible to deal with the difficult area of measurement. It is helpful to make clear at the outset the difference between an equation and an identity arising out of the definitions of national income, output and expenditure and to explain the use of the appropriate signs ' $=$ ' and ' $\equiv$ '. Textbooks are not always consistent in this matter. It should also be made clear that although the term 'national income' appears to be used in a variety of circumstances, it has a more precise meaning

as net national product at factor cost. This point becomes even clearer when using each of the three methods of measurement because the final stage of the calculation will always be net national product at factor cost.

Students are also not helped in their understanding of the problems of measurement by the lack of consistency between textbooks in the definition of terms. It is perhaps worth seeking guidance from a more specialised text such as Edey[30] or Stone[31] or even the *Short Guide*[32] to the *National Income Blue Book*. The major difficulties appear to occur with the expenditure method where statistics are collected from independent sources and do not lead to exactly the same figure as the income method. The difference between the income and expenditure estimates is known as the 'residual error', which can vary considerably from year to year. In 1980, for example, it was £2065 million. This term is often queried by students because it does not appear in the published expenditure totals and this gives the mistaken impression of superior accuracy.

With the income method, the various factor incomes earned in the process of production must be distinguished from 'transfer incomes', such as pensions and student grants, which are not earned from production and which are excluded from the total. A further problem that students find difficult is the idea of 'stock appreciation' involved in both the income and output methods. The value of output in the form of unsold stocks is included in total factor output. The problem arises when the prices at which stocks are valued in the national accounts vary during the course of the year. The value of stocks held will therefore be different at the beginning and the end of the period. The Central Statistical Office attempts to value the physical change in stocks at the average price level during the period.

Alternatively, an estimate of GDP can be derived from data on production but this is only really feasible when a Census of Production is taken. The main problem here is the existence of intermediate output included in the addition of all the outputs of individual firms. This is where one firm's output is used as a raw material in the output of another. Sheet metal from a steelworks, for example, may be used by a firm to make refrigerators so that there is a danger of 'double counting'. The problem is usually overcome by distinguishing between the total or gross output of a firm and its 'value added', the difference between them being the value of intermediate output.

National income statistics are usually calculated at current prices and therefore include an element of inflation that will make it difficult to compare the volume of goods produced in different periods. The *Blue Book*, however, produces estimates of GDP at constant prices based on the prices ruling in 1975. Gross domestic product measured in real terms is the best estimate available of changes in total UK production, but it is important to remind students that all productive work not sold for money is excluded. The statistics ignore, for example, the activities of the housewife, the do-it-yourself enthusiast and what is commonly called the 'black economy', all of which add millions of hours to the total UK production of goods and services.

The presentation of the actual values of national income statistics can either be in tabular form, adapted from the *Blue Book*, or in the form of a block diagram or flow diagram. Different approaches suit different students so that a mixture of techniques will be desirable. Student interest can also be sustained by making historical comparisons of UK statistics or even international comparisons. If the UK national income per head seems low to some students when compared with that of the USA or West Germany, a comparison with India, in contrast, makes the average UK citizen appear extremely affluent.

Finally, an entertaining way of illustrating the difficulties involved in managing the various macroeconomic policies is to use the computer program FISCAL[33]. The student has control over the marginal tax rate and government expenditure in a Keynesian simulation of the UK economy. The objective is to reconcile conflicting policy goals, which include ensuring the re-election of the government in office. There are four 'scenarios' in which the economy presents different problems. Alternatively, teachers may use the 'Keynesian management of the economy game'[34] which does not involve the use of a computer. The game is based on a simple Keynesian model. The full employment capacity of the economy grows over time and its rate of growth is given, that is, in this model it is an exogenous variable and is not affected by government policy. Unemployment depends on the relationship between output and capacity: the closer output is to capacity, the lower the unemployment level. The inflation rate depends on the level of unemployment (a simple Phillips curve relationship) and the balance of payments is affected by the level of demand – directly by its effect on the demand for imports, and indirectly via the effect of inflation on the competitiveness of exports. The student has the responsibility for determining the level of government expenditure, initially the only policy instrument available. In a second attempt the student may impose an incomes policy and/or devalue. The economy is managed for an eight-year period.

Conclusion

The teaching of basic macroeconomics must be carefully structured so that the student can acquire some feeling for the importance of the macroeconomic variables without being confused by the obtrusive effect of national income statistics. There are now many more macroeconomic texts and other resources available to help both teacher and student. The usefulness of computer programs will depend on the availability of microcomputers to the economics department of the school or college. However, some local authorities are establishing economics resource centres including computers, so that teachers may familiarise themselves with both hardware and software before using such resources in their own establishments.

The greater interest and understanding of sixth-form students makes such an effort extremely worthwhile.

Notes and references

1 Stanlake, G.F., *Introductory Economics* (Longman, 1983).
2 Stanlake, G.F., *Macroeconomics: An Introduction* (Longman, 1984).
3 Harvey, J., and Johnson, M., *Introduction to Macroeconomics* (Macmillan, 1971).
4 Aston, D.C., and Rickard, J.H., *Macroeconomics* (Pitman, 1970).
5 Nobbs, J., *Advanced Level Economics* (McGraw Hill, 1984); Livesey, F., *A Textbook of Economics* (Polytech Publishers, 1982). See also Anderton, A.G., *Economics, A New Approach* (University Tutorial Press, 1984).
6 Parkin, M., and Bade, R., *Modern Macroeconomics* (Philip Allan, 1982).
7 *National Income and Expenditure* (CSO, annual).
8 Stewart, M., *Keynes and After* (Pelican, 1972).
9 *Circular Flow of Income* (CIRFLO), Computers in the Curriculum, Phase II (Longman, 1983).
10 *Fillet and Billet Business Game* (BL Systems Ltd, 1982), available from Understanding British Industry.
11 *The Paraffin File* (BP Educational Service).
12 Marsden, C., Adams, S., and Crewdson, J., *An Introduction to Comparative Economics* (Heinemann Educational Books, 1980).
13 *Circular Flow of Income*, op. cit.
14 Lipsey, R.G., *An Introduction to Positive Economics*, 6th edn. (Weidenfeld & Nicolson, 1983).
15 Stanlake, *Macroeconomics*, op. cit.
16 Marshall, B.V., *Comprehensive Economics* (Longman, 1975).
17 Prest, A.R., and Coppock, D.J. (eds) *The UK Economy: A Manual of Applied Economics* (Weidenfeld & Nicolson, 1982).
18 Aston and Rickard, op. cit.
19 Stanlake, *Macroeconomics*, op. cit.
20 *10 × Economics* (Yorkshire Television, 1983).
21 Donaldson, P., *10 × Economics* (Pelican, 1982).
22 Lipsey, op. cit.
23 Stanlake, *Macroeconomics*, op. cit.
24 Maunder, W.P.J. (ed.) *Case Studies in Macroeconomics* (Heinemann Educational Books, 1977).
25 Robins, P., 'The accelerator principle – development and evidence', *Economics*, vol. XX, pt. 1, no. 85, spring 1984, pp. 3–8.
26 Stanlake, *Macroeconomics*, op. cit.
27 *The Multiplier* (MULTSC) Computers in the Curriculum, Phase I 1978 (Longman, 1984).
28 *Running the British Economy and Basic Macroeconomic Models* (Longman Micro Software, 1984).
29 Donaldson, op. cit.
30 Edey, H.C., *et al.*, *National Income and Social Accounting* (Hutchinson, 1967).
31 Stone, Rand G., *National Income and Expenditure* (Bowes & Bowes, 1972).
32 *The National Accounts, A Short Guide* (HMSO, annual).
33 *Fiscal Policy* (FISCAL) Computers in the Curriculum, Phase I 1978 (Longman, 1984).
34 Brownless, C.J., 'Keynesian management of the economy game', *Economics* vol. XX, pt. I, no. 85, spring 1984, pp. 23–6 (reprints available from the Economics Association).

47 Teaching Inflation, Unemployment and the Keynesian–Monetarist Debate*

Nancy Wall

*I would like to thank David Wall for his comments on content and his fortitude at the wordprocessor.

Introduction

When teaching price theory at A-level, we are in the comfortable position of operating well within the frontiers of the subject. We may wish to question some of the assumptions on which standard theory is based but, even if we do this, our debate will have no particular implications as far as government policy is concerned. All of us are in favour of minimising costs of production and prices to consumers, and there is a large measure of agreement on ways of doing this.

Life could hardly be more different when the topic is inflation and unemployment. Both the causes of these problems and their solutions are the subject of intense debate. It is impossible to teach government macro-economic policy without confronting these problems.

If monetarist and Keynesian theories were self-contained approaches, it might be easier. But they are not: monetarist theory builds upon the work of Keynes, to create a logical sequence of ideas that even in its simplest form is rather beyond the scope of A-level. Therefore, we must continue to teach much of the traditional simple Keynesian model. Without it we would be left with no analytical framework for the study of the macroeconomy. Yet as it stands, it is the economics of the 1960s. It cannot cope with stagflation. To provide any sort of explanation of simultaneously increasing unemployment and inflation, we have to introduce new ideas: we cannot avoid some version of a shifting Phillips curve. Then we must tackle the question of whether increased aggregate demand can increase output and employment, or must in the long run lead only to inflation. For it is upon this question that policy differences between the main political parties hinge. Our task is to find a respectable way of clarifying these issues in order that students may be capable of outlining the logic behind government policies, and producing simple analyses of the outcome.

The available resources – textbooks, pamphlets and articles – are in the main unhelpful. Each individual approach seems either to be too complex to start with, or to oversimplify. The need is to introduce ideas in sequence, so that simple beginnings lead to more recent theories and the many-faceted realities. The remainder of this chapter will therefore outline a possible way to deal with these problems, by starting very conventionally and gradually building in new factors until a composite emerges. The disadvantage with this is that a wide range of sources and a considerable teacher input are needed. The advantage is that this approach avoids using technical analyses which are most inappropriate at A-level. This, however, hasn't prevented them from appearing in the literature advertised as appropriate for the A-level market. Inexperienced teachers need to be warned against trying to teach too much, too quickly. Experienced teachers still need to be very careful to build into their analysis recent and current events.

Laying the foundations

Let us assume that the student has studied the simple Keynesian model as described in, say, Stanlake[1] and has mastered the effects of changes in injections and leakages on income, output and employment. For this, Leake's *Casebook*[2] on macroeconomics will be found very useful. The later stages of this learning process will have involved reference to inflationary and deflationary gaps, and to the concept of full-employment output. At this point the student has acquired a logical framework for thinking about changes in the macroeconomy. But the notion of 'full employment output' is so remote from reality that it can and should be eliminated from classroom exposition.

Redefining the old model – simultaneous high inflation and unemployment

First, the diagrams need to be relabelled and the offending concept, full employment output, redefined as, say, 'maximum possible output'. The nature of supply constraints can usefully be explored at this point. One way of doing this is to start with a conventional taxonomy of types of unemployment, and lead on from there to reasons why bottlenecks develop.

But herein lies another problem. A major weakness of most A-level texts is that they devote very little attention to the many and varied causes of unemployment. They are particularly weak on structural unemployment, which has become so important. The literature is very confused about the jargon anyway. Is structural unemployment a subset of frictional unemployment, or does the latter refer solely to temporary, or search, unemployment? The second definition is clearer and preferable but authors often duck this problem by rushing hastily past it. The result is that they miss a marvellous opportunity to redefine the old Keynesian model, simply and explicitly, in a way that makes it once again relevant to the 1980s.

If we define maximum possible output as that at which there is no demand deficiency unemployment, we can account for the simultaneous existence of inflationary tendencies and substantial structural or institutional unemployment. Above this level of output, bottlenecks will be encountered; firms will be prevented from expanding by shortages of scarce skills. So inflation will tend to accelerate long before all resources are fully employed. This analysis fits reasonably well with the situation in the UK in 1978–9. Vacancies increased sharply, inflation accelerated, employment increased, and unemployment was roughly constant. (The labour force was increasing for demographic reasons.)

Introducing expectations – simultaneously increasing inflation and unemployment

The analysis in the model taught so far has stated that unemployment will be falling when the economy is expanding and tending towards inflation, and that as unemployment rises a deflationary gap develops, which will at least decelerate inflation. In other words, it gives us an old-fashioned Phillips curve. We may have redefined the old model to account for the simultaneous *existence* of substantial unemployment and inflation; but we can't yet account for simultaneously *increasing* inflation and unemployment. For this, we must introduce expectations, and show how they affect the short-run trade-off between inflation and unemployment. The squeamish political centrist, or those further to the left, need not be deterred from teaching this theory by Friedman's view that all

unemployment below the natural rate is voluntary. The Wonnacotts[3] and others have shown that employers may well be responsible for the drift back to the natural rate of unemployment, because unexpected increases in costs deny them the expected profits that first induced them to expand. Even Minford,[4] in his address to the Economics Association (March 1984), seems to have abandoned the idea that substantial numbers are work-shy. Having said this, expectations and the Phillips curve are hard to teach, so how do we do it? (See Figure 47.1.)

1 The old Phillips curve (*A*) shows the short-run trade-off between inflation and unemployment. Expansionary policies will add to aggregate demand, improve business prospects and induce firms to expand.

2 Bottlenecks lead to rising wages and prices, there is a move from (i) to (ii).

3 Both costs and prices have risen, profits are disappointing, firms contract again, there is a move from (ii) to (iii). Inflation remains at the new higher level because everyone seeks to preserve real incomes, so that wage demands are at least equal to price increases.

4 Further efforts to reduce unemployment would lead to movement up a new short-run Phillips curve *B*, and a repeat of the events outlined above.

5 If, now, the government pursues contractionary policies in order to control inflation, there will in time be a movement down curve *B* as wage inflation falls and unemployment rises (as in 1982).

Is this what happened?

The shift from the old Phillips curve trade-off to stagflation coincides with the death of money illusion. If you are over the age of 40 you may be able to remember money illusion. If not, you can find out about it by asking grandparents how they feel about today's prices, and encourage students to do the same. 'The pound in your pocket will not be devalued,' said Harold Wilson, in November 1967. The electorate looked carefully at the pounds in their pockets, and wage demands accelerated from that time on. Expectations of inflation became a crucial determinant of the level of wage bargains. Money illusion died. Bearing in mind this and the pressures exerted by exchange rate and commodity price changes, the importance of building expectations into the story is intuitively clear.

Highlighting the divergence of the monetarist and Keynesian views

1 The theory

We have to be able to distinguish the two viewpoints but we are in real trouble if we try to put across the vast

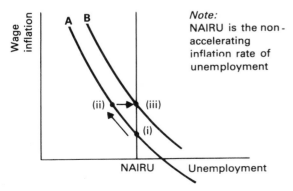

Note:
NAIRU is the non-accelerating inflation rate of unemployment

Figure 47.1

literature: it is too complex. Can it be reduced to a few crucial elements?

It is necessary to describe the transmission mechanism linking the money stock and the price level. Without this, recent monetary policy makes no sense. It is sufficient, however, to do this in the Keynesian fashion. (See Lipsey,[5] which can be supplemented with the diagrams in Stanlake.[6]) It can be shown that if there is inflation, the demand for money function shifts rightwards. If at the same time a tight monetary policy entails holding the money stock constant, then interest rates rise, and the effect on the economy is contractionary, and inflation decelerates. If the teacher then tries to describe a more monetarist view of the transmission mechanism, the need for IS/LM analysis rears its ugly head, something that should never be allowed to happen at A-level. In any case, the Keynesian approach, combined with a thorough understanding of the simple Keynesian model as redefined above, is sufficient for A-level purposes. (At some stage $MV \equiv PT$ can be mentioned since it appears nearly everywhere. But the fact that it is an identity must be emphasised.)

Having done this, we still must try to distinguish the two views. It is possible to point out that the modern quantity theory differs from the Keynesian transmission mechanism in allowing for a more direct link between the money stock and price levels. Excess supply of money is said to increase demand for a wide range of assets. A further central issue is whether output can be increased by increasing aggregate monetary demand. The answer will depend on whether there is underutilised capacity in the economy. In effect, this means that the monetarist and the Keynesian views will depend partly on the protagonists' perceptions of the nature of the existing unemployment. To some extent, this is an empirical question on which there is still insufficient evidence: as was said at the beginning, we quickly reach the frontiers of the subject. Similarly, the effect of monetary policy on prices and output depends partly on whether the velocity of circulation changes in the short run and partly on the interest elasticity of expenditure. Again these are empirical questions on which more evidence would be welcome. At A-level, we cannot do more than draw attention to the desirability of acquiring more evidence on these points, and show that the Keynesian and monetarist views diverge here.

A useful reference for the teacher is Davies.[7]

2 The solutions

In a sense, policies to deal with inflation are just what they always have been: contractionary fiscal and monetary policy, incomes policy, or trade-union reform, or benign indifference with perhaps indexation. The last two are political solutions with economic implications. The monetarist approach rejects incomes policy as distorting, so highlighting the source of the controversy involves examining the two views of how fiscal policy and monetary policy work in practice. It is then possible to show how incomes policy can give the government an additional weapon, if it is willing to use it.

In order to explain the distinction, it is possible to start by outlining a simple version of the rational expectations argument associated with monetarist views. If, the argument goes, unions know that monetary growth will be strictly limited, then they will know that wage settlements in excess of the target rate of monetary growth will lead to job losses. Therefore they will limit wage claims.

At this point, David Worswick's[8] article in *Lloyds Bank Review* still seems to be remarkably helpful. In general, he argues that if demand management policies are earmarked for control of inflation, they cannot be used to deal with unemployment. The particular virtue of the article is that it describes the implications of tight monetary policies for the labour market.

Worswick, outlining the Keynesian criticism of the rational expectations argument with his delightful gravediggers example, shows that individual unions may be uninterested in jobs lost to the workforce as a whole. Therefore a good deal of unemployment may develop, and output be lost, before wage bargainers get the message that tight monetary policies will continue until inflation falls.

In many respects, unemployment policy is much easier to teach. Clearly, a monetarist approach rules out expansionary policies – here again, much depends on the protagonists' views as to the causes of unemployment. In any case, microeconomic measures to reduce unemployment command widespread support. To the extent that they are successful, they will increase 'maximum possible output' (i.e. decrease the natural rate of unemployment). The teacher's only difficulty here is that it isn't too easy to keep up with every development, and excessive detail needs to be avoided. Livesey[9] has about the right level of detail but needs regular updating from *Treasury Economic Progress Reports*.

Government policy, 1979 onwards

The change of government in 1979 brought with it a wealth of interesting events for classroom use. A good discussion for teachers is Llewellyn and Kearney.[10] Suitable props for students are the Collins *Economics Briefs*,[11] and Francis Williams.[12]

General references

It is fair to say that the textbook situation at A-level is still difficult, in that whichever you choose there will be problems with its use. One bone of contention has been removed with Lipsey's sixth edition.[13] There is widespread agreement that it is no longer suitable for A-level. However, chapter 48 is most helpful for teachers wishing to update their own knowledge. Fischer, Dornbusch and Begg,[14] is good both for the ablest students and for teachers. It neatly distinguishes Keynesian from monetarist views in terms of their respective assumptions about market clearing. *Out of work* from Warwick University Economics Department provides a very thorough investigation for rusty minds to work on.

For students, Trevithick[16] is still the greatest help. Hawkins[17] deals with unemployment. Browning[18] is very readable. For weaker A-level students, Livesey[19] is useful, as is Browne,[20] whose chapter on inflation faces the issues bravely. Anderton[21] contains all the main theoretical points.

Conclusion

This chapter has provided no innovative ideas for teaching this topic, but has been confined to describing usable lesson content in an effective order, to be fleshed out with background detail, but containing the vital points. Why can we not be more innovative? The problem is that the basic resources on this topic are frankly deficient and there is therefore a need for the teacher simply to plug the gap.

What about computer programs? As yet, these are based either on too simple or too complex a model. They are useful, but simple ones do not adequately define the problems, and complex ones leave too many questions unanswered. Teachers should use them – but within a framework that takes in as many relevant details as possible, and *after* they have taught the topic.

The purpose of this chapter has been to identify the crucial points, the irreducible minimum needed to make sense of this thorny topic. The strategy has been first to make the old Keynesian model run as far and as fast as it will by adapting it in the light of recent experience. Then the strategy shifts to identifying sources of controversy, and to pigeonholing different approaches in such a way that their similarities and differences are apparent. The aim is to strike a balance between failing to explain current events and confusing the student.

General reading

The Treasury, *Economic Progress Reports,* regular up dates on industrial policy.

Notes and references

1 Stanlake, G.F., *An Introduction to Macroeconomics* (Longman, 1984).
2 Leake, A., *Casebooks on Economic Principles: Macroeconomics* (Macmillan Education, 1982) pp. 6–24.
3 Wonnacott, P., and Wonnacott, R., *An Introduction to Macroeconomics* (McGraw-Hill, 1982) pp. 264–94.
4 Minford, P., 'Unemployment policy', *Economics*, vol. XX, pt. 3, no. 87, autumn 1984.
5 Lipsey, R.G., *An Introduction to Positive Economics*, 5th edn., (Weidenfeld & Nicolson, 1979) pp. 608–21.
6 Stanlake, op. cit., pp. 156–7.
7 Davies, C.P., 'The Keynesian and monetarist models and their implications for key aspects of economic policy', *Economics*, vol. XVIII, pt. 4, no. 80, winter 1982, pp. 129–37.
8 Worswick, D., 'The end of demand management', *Lloyds Bank Review*, no. 123, January 1977, pp. 1–18.
9 Livesey, F., *A Textbook of Economics*, 2nd edn. (Polytech Publishers, 1982) pp. 120–36 and pp. 265–75.
10 Llewellyn, D.T., and Kearney, C., 'The British monetary experiment: a preliminary assessment', *Economics*, vol. XX, pt. 1, no. 85, spring 1984, pp. 15–21.
11 *Economics Briefs* (Collins Educational, 1986). The most relevant is Wall, N., *Inflation and Unemployment.*
12 Williams, F., *The Times on the British Economy* (Collins, 1984).
13 Lipsey, R.G., *An Introduction to Positive Economics*, 6th edn. (Weidenfeld & Nicolson, 1983) pp. 760–77.
14 Fischer, S., Dornbusch, R., and Begg, D., *Economics* (McGraw-Hill, 1984).
15 Cowling, K., *et al., Out of Work* (University of Warwick, 1983).
16 Trevithick, J.A., *A Guide to the Crisis in Economics* (Penguin, 1980).
17 Hawkins, K., *Unemployment* (Penguin, 1984).
18 Browning, P., *Economic Images* (Longman, 1983).
19 Livesey, op. cit.
20 Browne, D.J., *Economics for A-level* (Edward Arnold, 1983) pp. 286–306.
21 Anderton, A.G., *Economics: A New Approach* (University Tutorial Press, 1984).

48　International Trade

Graham Jones

Introduction

While the subject of international economics is an important part of the core syllabus in economics courses, it still tends to be treated as the Cinderella. In many textbooks it is left until the final chapters and for most teachers it is a parcel of theory that is left until late in the course. In many ways this is logical, because the theories employed in the analysis of intranational trade are no different from those already applied in infranational trade. The principles of comparative advantage, the influence of demand flows between sectors, the impact of monetary expansion, and the efficiency of the price mechanism as an equilibrating device are nothing new at that stage in an economics course. The field of international trade should be seen as a specialist area only in so far as geo-political divisions create possibilities for economic chauvinism which, by altering normally unquestioned utility functions, create opportunities for unilateral actions on trade and exchange rates.

The danger is that in a search for uniqueness, comparative advantage, exchange rates and international money are isolated as compartments of some general theory of international trade rather than being seen as further applications of already accepted theories, albeit in a new environment. More worrying about such an isolation, is that the techniques are taught as mechanical devices to be mastered, ready to be paraded for inspection in examinations – a technique encouraged by the constraints of multiple-choice testing. For example, a student needs to master the simple two-country, two-commodity model of comparative advantage; this will earn the mark but not test a wider appreciation of the fundamental economic principle which also explains why his father specialises as a plumber and employs a mechanic to service the car. Payments balances are interpreted as the result of particular exchange rates and much ingenuity goes into the linkage between exchange rates and import/export values with all the micro-economic intricacies of Marshall-Lerner conditions; macroeconomic considerations of import propensities or flows of funds are somehow other parts of the syllabus and left unreconciled. Problems of international money are reduced to historical narratives of institutional arrangements; little is made of the parallels with domestic monetary shortages or expansions and of their impact on price and output levels. The teaching of international trade ought logically to be woven into the fabric of the other parts of the syllabus, recognising that it is not an area or set of techniques *sui generis* but a further application and extension of ideas. We do not require a special theory to accept that an individual will specialise in the work to which he is best suited, that he will sell his product to gain an income, that changes in his product price will alter his income, that his expenditure determines the income of others and that if an expenditure greater than income is financed by credit it may be inflationary. Yet when the individual becomes Utopia, Atlanta, Country P, or one of the other abstractions of international trade, a separate theory is somehow required. McCormick *et al.*[1] have always integrated trade theory with the main body of economics and, in his sixth edition, Lipsey[2] has also moved a long way in that direction.

The model of comparative advantage

The desire of textbooks to rush into an exposition of the Ricardian comparative costs model is almost embarrassing. It is treated as a trick that all students need to be able to pull out of the hat, without a full appreciation of the model or, more importantly, the purpose to which it is to be put (apart from answering examination questions). The purpose of such a model has never been singly defined. It can be viewed, as Ricardo originally used it, as a device to derive theoretical propositions about welfare, or it can be expected to yield testable predictions about the observed patterns of international trade. In that latter role the theory has not offered much beyond such banalities as 'the tropics grow tropical fruits because of the relative abundance there of tropical conditions' (Samuelson). Little time is spent studying the predictive power of international trade theory, despite much interesting (and stimulatingly contradictory) empirical work by MacDougall, Leontief, Keesing and others in the period since 1950.[3]

At the root of the problem is the definition of what leads to differences in comparative costs. For Ricardo the labour theory of value naturally led to an argument based on labour productivity, and it is a nice comment on his inverted chauvinism (or on his Dutch ancestry) that for his famous numerical example he gave Portugal an absolute advantage over the British in both cloth and wine. More modern formulations have followed the line favoured by Samuelson, but bred by Ohlin out of Heckscher, that countries are assumed to have identical production functions but differing proportions of otherwise identical factors of production. This has an intuitive appeal, with the differing factor requirements of different lines of production dictating the specialisation and direction of trade. Over time that specialisation may change, as when British farmers lost their advantage in arable products in the late nineteenth century:

> confronted with a new problem: how were they to hold their own in a treacherous climate on highly rented land whose fertility required constant renewal, against produce raised under more genial skies on cheaply rented soils whose virgin richness required no fertilisers (Lord Ernle).

But when the factor-proportions theory was tested in the 1950s it was found that the USA was exporting labour-intensive products, and the international homogeneity of factors was once again questioned, the USA was apparently exporting goods with high proportions of *skilled* labour. Similarly, the assumption of identical production functions needs questioning when much technology is not internationally mobile. Product life-cycle theories of trade have also been developed whereby exports initially come from an innovating country, but later from other countries where the technology is copied (or sold, or operated by subsidiaries of multinationals) and where factor proportions are more suitable. Such theory explains US exports of electronics being superseded by the specialisation of Far Eastern producers.

Another problem is the neglect of demand factors. Consumers desire a range of differentiated products that leads, for example, to Britain being both an importer and an exporter of cars. To argue, inductively, that Britain has a comparative advantage in the production of Leyland cars and France in the production of Renaults may sound appealing, but it reduces Ricardian theory to the unassailable but sterile status of tautology. What is presented as though it were a predictive theory disintegrates and slips through one's fingers as the vacuous statement that whatever is exported by a country must be a commodity in which that country has a comparative advantage. But if the teacher can press the argument to that point, it gives the precious opportunity to raise the whole question of the use and limiting parameters of any models in economic theory; therein lies a strong argument for treating international trade theory as an entity at the end of a course. Methodology matters but needs perspective.

Given that the teacher is working alongside conventional textbook approaches, the comparative costs model can be used to reinforce lessons about methodology and the handling of theoretico-deductive models. In this context, the model is so neat and well defined that, as Samuelson says, 'if theories could win beauty contests, comparative advantage would certainly rate high in that it is an elegantly logical structure'. A first step is to spell out clearly the assumptions that are made in most presentations, and that can usefully be divided into three categories:

1 Non-substantive expository simplifications

For example, two countries; two commodities.
The relaxation of these assumptions would not alter the predictive thrust of the model, yet students seem to find the unreality of such simplification a barrier to its intuitive acceptance. More can be made of chains of comparative advantage expressed either in terms of a range of goods or a number of countries.

2 Substantive simplifications

It is necessary to reduce the model to some bare essentials, basing it on extreme assumptions which, if relaxed, can intuitively be seen to affect the predictions. Many of these are clearly stated: no transport costs; no artificial barriers to trade, for example. Their significance is easily grasped with a few examples of goods that are not traded: Why is ice not exported from the Arctic to the Gulf? Why are our daily newspapers not printed in Hong Kong? Why are missiles not imported from the USSR?

Other assumptions receive scant attention. The international immobility of factors of production needs emphasis, to show that trade in commodities is a substitute for a trade in factors that the market system would otherwise produce. Perfect internal factor mobility is also assumed and it is the absence of that which provides the major argument for protection – when the opportunity cost of inefficient resource allocation is idle resources. Competitive markets are also necessary if relative prices are to reflect relative marginal costs – the presentation of a model in terms of the opportunity costs of production deflects attention from the distortions possible when prices fail to reflect resource costs (including social costs, another neglected element).

The most important source of difficulty in understanding the model is in the assumption made about returns to scale. Here presentations differ between textbooks, with many looking at production possibility boundaries with constant returns to scale and consequent complete specialisation. Others state the respective outputs of two commodities from 'a man-day of labour' (or the even more indefinite 'unit of resources'). In these cases it needs to be clear whether such productivities are constant at all levels of specialisation, or are relative marginal productivities at a particular and arbitrary pre-trade position on the transformation curve. This latter is certainly more realistic and would help later in specifying the terms of trade, because it clearly implies a rising marginal cost (or supply) curve which is the familiar analytical tool. The case of increasing returns (over some range of output) also needs identification as an important rationale for trade liberalisation between countries with similar factor endowments, production functions and levels of economic development. The potential welfare gains of customs unions can be interpreted from such a theoretical vantage point.

3 Hidden assumptions

The implicit assumptions of a model are always the most dangerous, and should be spelt out if students are to gain a proper understanding of the status of their model. Infant-industry arguments for tariffs are always discussed, but

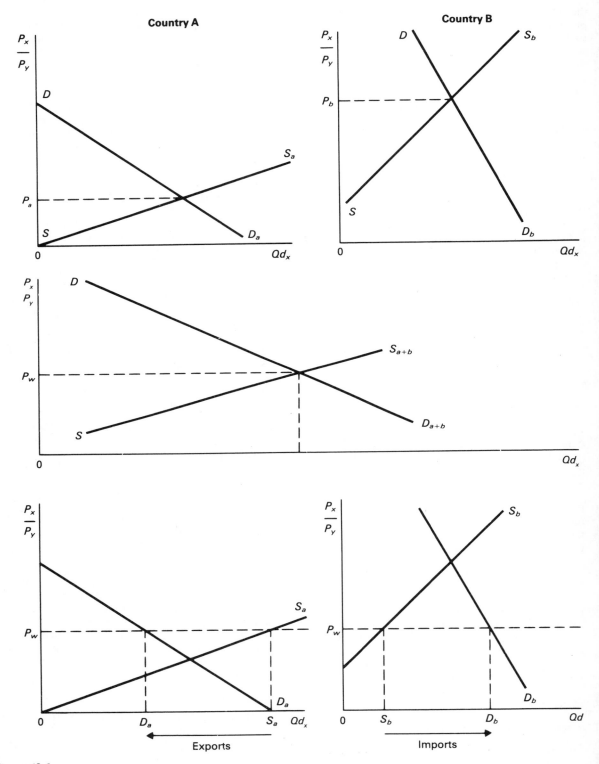

Figure 48.1

should be used to show that the comparative cost model is an exercise in comparative statics. Welfare from existing resources is maximised but countries may set their sights higher than being hewers of wood and drawers of water, and look for the dynamic role of technology and investment in increasing future factor endowments. The more general point is that comparative cost theory is used to show the possibilities of general increases in welfare, but is most vigorously argued by those who gain most. In the first half of the nineteenth century, the free traders who argued so forcefully against the Corn Laws and against import duties were reluctant to see the repeal of the Navigation Acts which protected British shipping from American competition. As Joan Robinson has said, 'the free trade doctrine is just a more subtle form of mercantilism: it is believed only by those who will gain an advantage from it'.[4] She also points out that the Ricardian model was used as the theoretical prop for free trade just at the time when the assumptions of the model were not fulfilled in the real world – massive migrations of labour and international investment, and sufficient unemployment to keep money wages in check.

Another neglected aspect of the theory is the effect of trade on income distribution. Any change in resource allocation will generate a change in income distribution, but the difficulties of interpersonal comparisons of welfare make that too dangerous an area for positive statements – the safest ploy is to sweep the issue under the rug. Nevertheless, an important consequence of trade is the increase in demand for previously abundant factors and the reduction in demand for hitherto scarce factors, with consequent rises and falls in respective prices. Few students are made aware of the equalisation of factor prices between countries (the Samuelson–Stolper theorem) which is an important result of trade – the movement of commodities is merely a substitute for international movement of factors.

Another point that is neglected in simple models is the role of demand in determining specialisation and trade. Comparative advantage models are supply-side theories that say nothing about whether international demand exists for the commodities in which a country may have a comparative advantage. Again, simple examples make the point most clearly: both the Caribbean and the Arctic have comparative advantages in particular types of climate, but the Arctic is yet to develop a tourist industry. The omission of demand factors has also led the exact terms of trade to be left hanging in the air. The terms on which trade actually takes place is some indefinite ratio within the terms of trade bracket formed by the diverging opportunity cost ratios and determined rather vaguely by the 'forces of supply and demand'. An alternative approach to trade theory to enlighten this would be more specific about diminishing returns and follow from simple demand and supply analysis that students already know well.

Figure 48.1 shows the supply and demand conditions for a commodity x in two countries before trade. The vertical axis shows real costs, that is, the price of one commodity relative to another, and the positions of the supply curves (SS_a and SS_b) make it clear that production costs differ between the two countries, but that they rise with output in both cases owing to diminishing returns. The difference between OP_a and OP_b shows the difference in marginal costs at the demand-determined level of production before trade. If trade is opened up, and there are no transport costs, it will be cheaper to buy good x in country A and the converse will be true of the other good y in a simple two-country model. The final price ratio (terms of trade) can be shown to be determined by the horizontal summation of the two sets of demand and supply curves. It can also be seen that at that price ratio there is excess supply in A, but that this is matched by excess demand in B. In other words, A's exports are made equal to B's imports. This approach can also show the effects of shifts in supply and demand on the terms of trade – an increase in B's demand for x will worsen its terms of trade.[5]

Exchange rates and balance of payments

Once the basic theory of international trade has been grasped, it would seem that exchange rates and the balance of payments should present fewer obstacles to understanding in that they are practical issues of almost daily prominence in newspapers. Swings in exchange rates can be followed through newspaper clippings, and reports usually identify forces acting on currency values in terms of supply and demand factors. Monthly trade figures are also prominent, but do require handling carefully and cannot be properly understood until the accounting conventions of visible balances, invisibles, current account, and capital flows have been grasped. Accounts are unfamiliar to many students and one approach is to build up a record of personal transactions to draw a parallel with the nation's transactions – an example of this is Table 48.1, taken from the Banking Information Service's *Guide to the International Financial System*.[6] After that, the detail of some actual accounts may be more digestible.

Another approach is to emphasise the relationship between the balance of payments and the actual dealings on the foreign exchange market, with all credit items leading to a demand for currency just as all debit items generate the supply of a currency. These relationships are particularly well handled in McCormick *et al*[7] where the exchange rate is specifically shown to be the result of both current and capital account transactions. The supply and demand techniques needed for an analysis of the foreign exchange market are relatively simple but give the student a lot of leverage in understanding the supply and demand forces at work on exchange rates. It is also possible to show how fixing the rate at some non-equilibrium level leads to excess demand or supply that has to be accommodated with official selling or buying: the excess represents the difference between debit and credit items on the balance of payments accounts (i.e. the total currency

Table 48.1

Statement of household receipts and outgoings	Balance of payments accounts
Wages or salary	Exports of goods and services
Investment income	Income from overseas investments
Social security benefits	Gifts, etc. from overseas
minus	minus
Expenditure on goods and services	Imports of goods and services
Interest paid on borrowings	Interest, etc. paid abroad
Tax and social security contributions	Overseas aid, etc.
equals	equals
Financial surplus (or deficit) = net financial investment (or net borrowing)	Current account surplus (or deficit) = capital account deficit (or surplus)
equals	equals
Increase in cash balances	Outward investment flows
Investments acquired	Net increase in official reserves
Borrowings repaid	
minus	minus
Reduction in cash balances	Inward investment flows
Investments sold	
Net borrowing	

Source: Pratt, M.J., *A Guide to the International Financial System* (Banking Information Service, 1984) p. 9.

inflow or outflow) and shows the necessary change in foreign exchange reserves or official borrowing. A clear link can be formed between payments disequilibria and official financing.

The danger is that such an emphasis on the foreign exchange market suggests an overriding role for exchange rate adjustments in equilibrating the payments balances. This may have been the conventional wisdom of postwar policy, but 'elasticity pessimism' has recently gained a secure foothold, once 1967 and 1971 made it possible to experiment with exchange rates and test the theory. In terms of balance of payments adjustment policies, changes in exchange rates are overemphasised in text-books compared to the experience of a real world where trade contracts are not easily unscrambled, import elasticities are low, and many countries are price takers for their exports in highly competitive international markets. Balance of payments flows should be more closely integrated with other macroeconomic forces.[8] This can be approached by the use of the foreign trade multiplier or the more general absorption analysis – in both cases, students should be able to interpret balance of payments policy in terms of the standard macroeconomic accounting identity:

$$X - M = Y - (C + I + G)$$

Monetary approaches are more general in that they concentrate on the balance of payments as a whole (rather than just the current account) being the outcome of a difference between the supply of and demand for money. The teaching of monetary policy will emphasise the impossibility of controlling the money supply when exchange rates are not free to float, but the example is seldom incorporated into mainstream teaching on balance of payments determination. The theoretical working of the Gold Standard can be interpreted in this way and would be particularly helpful to students of economic history who, knowing that the nineteenth-century Gold Standard operated only weakly through the conventional effects on price or activity levels, might see the effects on the capital accounts of portfolio shifts occasioned by changes in interest rates.[9]

International trade: the institutions

If the bulk of this chapter has been about the theory of international trade, it may be a reflection of the author's own comparative advantage, but it is also the product of a belief that any learning about economic structures must be firmly rooted in an understanding of the theory. The theory is universal; trade groupings and organisations differ between countries and change over time. Students of economics ought to be provided with the apparatus that allows them not only to interpret and understand the organisation of trade and payments they see currently, but that will allow them to keep abreast of changes during their lifetimes. One problem for the economics teacher is that even when he is not being 'the slave of some defunct economist', he is often the slave of some ancient example or illustration. Events like sterling crises, a 1967 devaluation or a Smithsonian Agreement may be deeply etched on one's own mind but have little relevance to students who did not (at least consciously!) live through the events. If the teaching is to be peppered with topicality rather than littered with fag-ends of memory, the problem is one of keeping up to date. For the economics teacher who is himself interpreting current events in the conceptual terms of economic models, that task will be less difficult: the Japanese invasion of British industry raises questions about the international mobility of factors of production and about the influence of multi-national companies on trade flows; industrial subsidies drive a wedge between price and marginal cost which distorts the pattern of trade from pure comparative advantage; the construction of North Sea oil rigs in the USA shows that capacity constraints limit trade (by raising marginal costs to infinity?); exchange-rate movements show how capital flows are induced by changes in short-term interest rates and expectations about the money supply. Examples should be myriad for the alert teacher; his expertise should be in putting them into the general conceptual context.

If the argument is that the historical detail should not be overplayed, it is not that the broad sweeps of history should be forgotten. Students must be made aware of the changing perceptions and interests of each generation if they are to accept that the climate of opinion is just as likely to change around them in future. In the early 1800s the doctrine of free trade slowly gained its foothold against the vested interests of mercantilism, only to be questioned later when what had been argued to be in the interests of all was no longer in the interests of Britain. The efficacy and neutrality of the Gold Standard was accepted as the means of international exchange; the need for fixed exchange rates was taken for granted in a world that generated such large flows of international capital. The inter-war Depression brought a different story, as each country beggared-its-neighbour in a desperate effort to gain a larger share of the much reduced market. Competitive devaluations shook the stability of exchange rates; tariffs were thrown up and trade huddles formed as countries attempted to export their unemployment. The enlightened attitude of the postwar period was to ensure that no such sillinesses should occur again: exchange rates were fixed and monitored by the IMF; GATT was committed to bring down all those tariff barriers. The steady expansion of trade and international investment seemed to testify to the wisdom of the postwar planners. The new mercantilism of some surplus-hungry countries was tiresome, and regional trade groupings had to be accepted as a second best to free trade, but the *volte face* came in the 1970s when world recession once again sent countries chasing after a bigger slice of the much reduced cake of world demand, and we were plunged into competitive depreciations and covert protectionism. The IMF and GATT could be seen to have been set up to solve the problems of the prewar not postwar period, and as soon as the problems reappeared the institutions were ineffective and redundant.

This is all the canvas against which current events need to be interpreted and it is the job of the teacher to make clear the broad sweeps of history as well as paint in the detail of the present. Each generation needs to be equipped with that appreciation of the historical perspective but, above all, a rigorous knowledge of analytical devices and the confidence and intellectual agility to use them if we are not to sentence our students to be 'madmen...distilling their frenzy from some academic scribbler of a few years back'.[10]

Notes and references

1 McCormick, B.J., *et al.*, *Introducing Economics* (Penguin, 1983).
2 Lipsey, R.G., *An Introduction to Positive Economics* (Weidenfeld & Nicolson, 1983).
3 Bhagwati, J. (ed.) *International Trade* (Penguin, 1969); Findlay, R., *Trade and Specialisation* (Penguin, 1970).
4 Robinson, J., *The New Mercantilism* (CUP, 1966) p. 24. A provocative, short and accessible essay pricking many balloons of free-trade dogma.
5 See Findlay, op. cit. This gives a more rigorous treatment of such an approach.
6 Pratt, M.J., *A Guide to the International Financial System* (Banking Information Service, 1984) p. 9.
7 McCormick *et al.*, op. cit.
8 Gowland, D.H., *Modern Economic Analysis* (Butterworth, 1979) ch. 2. This gives a particularly useful, but condensed, summary.
9 Kenwood, A.G., and Lougheed, A.L., *The Growth of the International Economy 1820–1960* (George Allen & Unwin, 1971) ch. 7.
10 Keynes, J.M., *The General Theory of Employment, Interest and Money* (Macmillan, 1936) p. 383.

49   Government Policy
Keith Marder

Introduction

The role of government extends into almost every part of the economy and there are few items in conventional syllabuses that can be adequately treated without some reference to government policy. It is not possible, within the compass of a chapter, to consider every aspect of policy, and some aspects enter into the subject-matter of other chapters. The aim here is to draw attention to a number of considerations relevant to the teaching of government policy in general and then to suggest possible approaches to selected topics in the broad policy-making areas of public finance, demand management, industrial policy, and external policy.

Introducing government policy

The large proportion of abstract theory in A-level courses can give the impression that the subject-matter has little bearing on the problems of the real economy. Reference to policy is an important way of making economic theory meaningful to students. From this point of view, government policy should be introduced at every opportunity throughout the syllabus rather than being left for treatment as a separate topic towards the end of the course. Students can thus be encouraged, from the beginning, to acquire an interest in public affairs and to follow and understand current economic developments covered by the media. The main strands of government policy can be brought together, and also brought up to date, as a revision topic on completion of the syllabus.

In the important field of demand management, understanding of policy issues must be based on solid foundations of Keynesian and monetarist theories. In this connection many teachers prefer to make the study of national income flows and macroeconomic theory the effective starting point of their courses instead of more traditional approaches through demand and supply analysis or descriptive topics. A great advantage of the macroeconomic approach is that broad movements of the economy associated with inflation and unemployment, and related policy measures, become intelligible to students at an early stage in the course. By the second term, for example, it should be possible for the class to understand developments leading to the spring Budget and then view the Chancellor's objectives and proposals against the background of economic conditions and in the light of relevant theory.

Value judgements

Teaching problems can arise when questions of policy extend beyond the scope of positive economic theory into the realms of political controversy. Government economic policy manifestly cannot be divorced from politics, and students may be confronted with issues involving value judgements reflecting different political viewpoints. This can have the great advantage of stimulating class interest and discussion but imposes a special responsibility on teachers to ensure that the different points of view are fairly represented. It does not necessarily follow that teachers should conceal their own opinions. Sixth-formers and mature students will of course make up their own minds and, in doing so, generally appreciate the opinions of others, including their own teachers. The fundamental principle governing these matters is that conclusions should always be reasoned and seen to be based on a balanced presentation of the arguments.

In connection with value judgements, students sometimes ask if it is acceptable to express personal opinions when dealing with examination questions in which they are required to discuss controversial political issues such as the level of public expenditure or changes in taxation. The answer must surely be that no examiner would penalise a candidate's opinions, even if conflicting with his own, and that reasoned judgements based on relevant and balanced arguments would always be rewarded.

News coverage

Government policy is obviously an area in which frequent updating is needed and standard texts are likely to be inadequate. Much of the burden of keeping material up to date inevitably falls on teachers but students can be encouraged to keep abreast of policy changes through their own efforts. The monthly *Economic Progress Report* published by the Information Division of the Treasury is invaluable, particularly since copies are supplied free and can be ordered in sufficient numbers for every student. Current policy developments are also covered at a level suitable for sixth forms in the *British Economy Survey*, published twice a year by Oxford University Press.

Ideally, students should cultivate the habit of regularly scanning journals and newspapers for relevant items. The teacher can help by displaying cuttings and bringing topical issues to the notice of the class. There are also ways of inducing direct activity:

1 *Economics diaries.* Each student keeps his own record of events in the form of news cuttings and/or jottings, preferably classified under broad headings. This may be regarded as an integral part of the coursework with periods allocated for review of material.

2 *Assignments.* Topics are allotted to cover the broad field of policy and each student is expected to keep abreast of developments in his own sphere. Periodic lessons may be reserved for individual reports to the class as a basis for questions and discussion.

Class discussion

Discussion of government policy enables differing views to be heard, encourages pupils to form and express their own opinions, and uniquely demonstrates the impact of value-judgements on economic decisions. The basis of discussion may be a prepared talk, the report on an individual assignment, or a current news item introduced by the teacher. Tape or video recordings of topical broadcast programmes can also provide fruitful material. If the class is large enough, formal debates can be held, particularly on major policy statements such as a Budget speech or the economic content of the Queen's speech or a party manifesto. For instance, following a Budget, the simple motion 'that this house approves (or disapproves) the Chancellor's proposals' can make an excellent starting point for a debate.

Data response

Government policy provides abundant scope for exercises based on either statistical data or written extracts. The report of a Budget speech or other ministerial statement, an economic debate in Parliament, or publication of a Bill or White Paper, are examples of sources that can provide excellent working material. Students may either read the sources themselves or data may be extracted by teachers. The following is an example of work that might be set after a Budget speech:

Questions on a Budget

1 Comment on the underlying economic conditions and any other factors that might have influenced the Chancellor in preparing his Budget.
2 What are the main Budget objectives?
3 Note the main financial forecasts or targets and explain the reasoning behind them.
4 Outline the Budget measures. To what extent will they help to attain the Budget objectives?
5 Are there any other possible consequences not stated or intended?
6 Note any criticisms and explain your own view of the Budget.

Teaching public finance

The structure of taxation raises difficulties because of the complexity of tax laws and frequency of change. It is unnecessary to memorise technical details or rates of taxation that are subject to annual alteration, but a knowledge of the salient features of the main taxes is required as a basis for comparison and analysis. Students can then attempt to judge the relative merits of particular taxes with reference to recognised criteria such as the following:

1 Revenue-earning capacity including buoyancy in inflation ('fiscal drag').
2 Administrative efficiency including costs of assessment and collection and ease of evasion.
3 Effects on production (via incentives) and resource allocation, for example, affecting investment or exports.
4 Effectiveness in demand management and counter-inflationary policy.
5 Distribution of the burden, for example, progressive or regressive?

Tax controversy usually focuses on the balance between direct and indirect taxation and the degree of progression. Both these issues have been brought to the forefront (under Mrs Thatcher's administration) by policies designed to shift the balance away from direct taxation and, at the same time, reduce the degree of progression.

Comparison between direct and indirect taxes can be based on the criteria outlined above. The economic case against direct taxation and, in particular, against steeply progressive taxation, rests to a large extent on alleged disincentive effects of high taxes on earnings. In considering this question, it is important to distinguish between high *marginal* rates of taxation (which could induce substitution of leisure for income) and high *average* rates which could have opposite consequences. The case for progression must be related to the concept of diminishing marginal utility applied to income.

The expenditure side of public finance used to be a neglected topic but has been brought into the limelight by government attempts to curb its growth. The Budget always attracts attention but students should be aware that the annual public expenditure White Paper is of comparable significance in its effects on production and resource allocation. In connection with expenditure control, a particular point to emphasise is the high proportion of committed or demand-related expenditure – dependent, for example, on the numbers of pensioners, unemployed, or school children – over which governments can exercise no direct control.

Approach to demand management

Government tax and expenditure policies are linked together in the Budget, which provides a logical starting point for the study of macroeconomic policy. The Budget balance, determining the size of the deficit (or surplus), is at the centre of Keynesian-type fiscal policy and, through the medium of the PSBR, also underlies the monetarist strategy of Mrs Thatcher's government. Keynesian and monetarist theories form the subject of another chapter and comment here is restricted to certain policy implications of which students should be made aware:

1 Both are essentially demand-pull approaches relying on demand management policies to control nominal national income.
2 Differing (possibly conflicting) priorities, with Keynesians aiming primarily at full employment and monetarists at price stability. A point to be noted is the monetarist belief that macroeconomic policy can only control inflation and not output or employment, except in the short run; that is, no Phillips trade-off.
3 Reverse emphasis on policy instruments with Keynesians subordinating monetary to fiscal policy while monetarists see fiscal management as a mere adjunct of monetary policy.
4 Keynesians generally accept incomes policy as a means of curbing cost-push inflation. To monetarists, pay restraint is unnecessary if money supply is strictly controlled.
5 Keynesians believe in 'fine-tuning' demand to maintain national income at a satisfactory equilibrium, whereas monetarists advocate a 'fixed throttle' that keeps monetary growth in line with output. Monetarists also

attach importance to fixed monetary targets in moderating inflationary expectations.

The counter-criticisms between the two schools help to explain their different policy prescriptions. Monetarists deny the practicability of 'fine-tuning' with its problems of forecasting and timing, and refer to alleged 'stop-go' policy consequences in the Keynesian era. Keynesians question the assumptions of the quantity theory and the feasibility of either measuring or controlling money supply.

Aspects of industrial policy

Industrial policy embraces a variety of forms of government intervention relating to nationalised industries and privatisation, industrial relations, incomes policy, monopoly or competition policy, regional policy, small firms, industrial training, job creation, and so on. Methods of presentation must vary with the topic. A historical approach is often suitable, particularly in those areas where forms of intervention have evolved largely through legislation. The framework of monopoly policy, for example, can be built up chronologically through an outline of legislation. Chronological treatment is also suitable for regional policy, industrial relations, and incomes policy.

External policy and conflicting objectives

External economic policy relates to trade barriers, trading relationships (including the EEC), exchange rates, and other policies largely concerned with the balance of payments. These topics fall within the scope of Chapter 48 and need not be treated here. However, reference to external policy provides the opportunity to draw attention to the interaction of policies and the possibility of conflict between objectives.

A major area of potential conflict is between domestic and external policy objectives. The problem of reconciliation can be illustrated by a simple diagram (see Figure 49.1). Note the assumption of a trade-off between

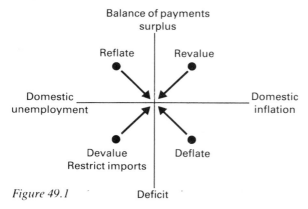

Figure 49.1

unemployment and inflation on the horizontal axis representing the domestic economy. Points can be inserted as illustrated to represent different combinations of domestic and external conditions. Students should suggest appropriate policies to move towards the origin O as an assumed target point of both internal and external balance. It is necessary for them to distinguish between expenditure-changing and expenditure-switching policies. It can be shown that a combination of both kinds may be needed in order to reach the origin or any other chosen location.

Resources

Books

Prest, A., and Coppock, D., *The UK Economy* (Weidenfeld & Nicolson, 1982). Informative on all aspects of policy.

Cairncross, F., and Keeley, P., *The Guardian Guide to the Economy* (Methuen, 1981). Readable account of policy issues including Keynesian-monetarist controversy.

Brown, R., *Monetary Control in Britain 1971–1981* (Banking Information Service, 1981). Useful material for sixth forms, though occasionally too technical.

Vane, H. R., and Thompson, J. L., *An Introduction to Macroeconomic Policy* (Wheatsheaf, 1982). Clear account of theory and practice relating to fiscal, monetary, incomes, and exchange rate policies.

Other publications

Journals, including *The Economist* and political weeklies, comment on current government policies from different viewpoints.

Bank reviews, including the Bank of England's *Quarterly Review* frequently contain relevant articles of high analytical standard.

Britain's Economy Under Strain (*The Economist* Newspaper Limited, 1982). School briefs on macroeconomics. A supplementary booklet, *Macroeconomics in Question*, published by the Economics Association, contains questions on the main policy areas covered by the briefs.

British Economy Survey (OUP, published twice a year). Articles cover current developments in all the main policy areas.

Government publications. The following HMSO publications supply statistical background to government economic policy:

Economic Trends. Monthly commentary, tables and charts on trends in the UK economy.

National Income and Expenditure Blue Book. Annual detailed estimates of the national accounts.

UK Balance of Payments, annual *Pink Book*.

Financial Statement and Budget Report. Income and expenditure tables of central government and economic report including short-term forecast.

Films, tapes, etc.

The following are among films supplied by the Training and Education Film Library: *The Role of the Budget* (16″, 900 8135–2), relating to fiscal policy since the 1960s; *Inflation* (25″, D 101 13), on causes and solutions; *Location of Industry* (25″, 900 8088–9), case study of car industry, examining government influence; *The Balanced Budget* (16″, 900 8131–4), relates to 1930s; *The Phillips Curve* (16″, 900 8134–5), looks at the rate of change of wages and employment.

Discussion tapes on economics are produced by Audio Learning Ltd. Each provides about half an hour's discussion on each track at a standard suitable for A-level students. The following are suitable for revision or consolidation lessons on topics in government policy: no. 7, *Government Finance/Nationalised Industry* by J. Wiseman and A. Peacock; no. 10, *The British Economy – The Nature of the Problems/The Search for Solutions* by J. Hughes and R. Donaldson; no. 26, *Government Responsibility and Industry/Control of Public Expenditure* by V. Bogdanor and W. Waldegrave; no. 28, *Aims of Taxation/Economic and Social Characteristics – Different Taxes in the UK* by G. S. A. Wheatcroft and

A. R. Prest. Also from Audio Learning Ltd, *Monetary Policy* by A. D. Bain and M. H. Miller.

Aspects of government policy are also covered by the following: Sussex Tapes: E1, *Public Finance*, a discussion of taxation and government spending; E8, *Location of Industry*, a discussion of the labour market and regional policy.

Open University, *Taxation* (audio tape, D1O1 13/20). Students Recordings Ltd, *Public Finance* (AVC/144); *The Public Sector* (AVC/30). Colour filmstrips with tape or spool commentaries lasting about 40 minutes. Filmstrip, *Business Cycles and Fiscal Policy* (McGraw-Hill).

Wall charts

Pictorial Charts Educational Trust, four charts: *Rates and Taxes* (D 715). One chart: *Taxation and Spending* (C 32). Shows the average family's taxes and benefits within the framework of government income and expenditure.

Computer programs

Two programs published by Longman, *Basic Macroeconomic Models* and *Running the British Economy*, are in the form of simulations of the real economy.

50 Teaching the Economics of the Public Sector

Stuart Luker

Introduction

The public sector has been a major part of the British economy since the Second World War, yet for a long while suffered from neglect by economists. Certainly it was not until recently that the A-level examining boards started to treat it as a mainstream topic. However, the new AEB syllabus has, for example, caught up with the developments in economic theory that have taken place. Not only has there been a continued growth in the importance of the public sector in the UK, combined with significant developments in economic theory, there has also been a growing controversy over the optimum size and role of the public sector. The orthodoxy of the 1950s and 1960s, which accepted that a truly mixed economy was the best compromise in the interests of the majority, no longer represents the general consensus. The two main

political parties in the UK now represent more divergent opinions about the role of the public sector, while the SDP/Liberal Alliance has taken up the traditional stance as the main supporter of the mixed economy. This change seems to have come about in the early 1970s, when public spending as a proportion of GDP started to increase more rapidly than had occurred during the rest of the postwar period. What is more, the growth was unplanned.

The work of Eltis and Bacon[1] during the mid-1970s, which attributed most of Britain's economic ills to the large public sector, represents a useful focal point for the change in attitudes. Although subject to much criticism, the views of Eltis and Bacon ought to be considered by all A-level economics students. The policies of the present Conservative government and the severity of the recession in the UK have also helped to focus attention on the importance of the public sector. A substantial section of opinion in this country sees a much larger public sector as the only way of achieving a reduction in unemployment, a resumption of economic growth and a fair share in national income for all.

What should we teach A-level students?

Exactly what is taught will obviously be influenced by the syllabus of the examining board and the questions that are being asked on A-level papers. As a matter of principle, I prefer to devote a specific section of my teaching programme to the public sector, because unless this is done, important issues can be neglected, and the influence of the public sector may be underestimated. However, it is essential that the public sector is also explicitly taken into account when other topics are being considered. For example, it would be wrong to look at wage determination and industrial relations, or the determination of the level of investment, without including the role of the public sector. Students should be constantly reminded, as a matter of course, that they should always consider whether or not a distinction should be made between the situation in the public sector and the private sector. Both a separate and an integrated treatment is needed.

Many teachers will no doubt include, as part of their introduction to A-level economics, an outline of the different types of economic system. This will include an overview of the role of the state in a mixed economy. Later in the course, this can be treated in much more depth. At this stage it is necessary to put the subject in perspective by looking at the growth of the public sector in the UK and the rest of the Western world. The work of Wagner, Peacock and Wiseman, Galbraith, and Buchanan and Tullock[2] might usefully be considered. Certainly, data must be used and attention paid to the various ways in which the size of the public sector can be measured. It is very useful to construct a data base on a microcomputer, as this can easily be updated. It also means that the students can interrogate the data base and discover what has happened for themselves, provided the teacher gives appropriate guidance.

At this point, it is necessary to look at the activities of the public sector in more detail. Public-sector accounts can be distributed to the students. When these are being explained, it is possible to introduce some of the important terminology, such as the difference between current and capital spending, the contingency reserve and the difference between direct spending and transfer payments. The students can be asked to interpret the figures, perhaps constructing pie-charts or bar-charts to illustrate the composition of public spending. Students could also be asked to do some simple calculations, such as those involving the use of index numbers to convert current price measures of public spending into constant prices, or to calculate public spending as a proportion of GDP, looking at the changes over time. It will also be necessary to bring out the differences between central-government spending, local-authority spending and the

expenditure of nationalised industries. The way in which nationalised industries are treated in these accounts will need to be explained. The information can be extracted from a variety of sources, such as the *National Income and Expenditure Blue Book*, the annual White Paper, newspaper articles and the *Economic Progress Reports* published by the Central Office of Information. There are always very useful tables of figures in the papers and the *Economic Progress Reports* when the White Paper is published in January or February.

Methods of financing the public sector should probably be outlined at this stage, and it is sensible at least to mention the links between the PSBR, national debt, the money supply, interest rates and macroeconomic policy. These topics are best dealt with in detail elsewhere, but the links between different topics need to be explicitly considered and returned to throughout the course.

The theoretical rationale for a public sector, which has been developed more fully in recent years, is directly linked to the issues of equity, efficiency, resource allocation and the general problems of market failure.

The arguments for the state provision of public goods and merit goods ought to be discussed, together with the problem of externalities and the alternative methods of improving resource allocation when there is a divergence between private and social costs. The major role the government plays in redistributing income, enforcing contracts, promoting competition and attempting to minimise the abuse of private monopoly power also require explanation. The responsibility the state has assumed for the general welfare of the community in the postwar period is very well demonstrated by the use of Keynesian demand management policies. Even though the present government has denied that it has the power to influence the economy in this way, there is no doubt that achieving stability and prosperity remains a vital objective of policy.

Following this development of the theoretical arguments for the public sector, attention could return to its size. The concept of the optimum size of the public sector can be explained in terms of the marginal social cost and marginal social benefit of government activity, and by using the production possibility curve and indifference curves. Appropriate emphasis should also be placed on the distribution of the benefits of economic activity. The potential conflict between the criteria of equity and efficiency comes out very readily in any discussion that takes place between sixth-formers about the role of government in society. The teacher might want to plan a formal debate, or ask one or two of the students to prepare and read a paper that is followed by a discussion. Sufficient time should be allocated, so that the proceedings can be reviewed by the teacher, and the points of disagreement emphasised.

Some teachers may want to spend some time looking at particular aspects of the public sector, such as education, the NHS, or perhaps the system of social security. There is a great deal of literature now available in specialised journals, bank reviews, the publications of the Institute of

Economic Affairs, as well as specialised books. Comparative studies are particularly valuable, because they provide the student with an insight into the various alternatives, and can lead to an evaluation in terms of the theoretical issues that have already been mentioned.

A case-study approach might well be adopted. The class could be divided into different groups and each group would look at a case study on a different area of the public sector. Each group might be asked to present its solutions to the whole class, and in this way a fairly broad coverage could be achieved. An additional benefit is that students would then have some examples that they could quote.

The methods, problems and principles surrounding the raising of finance will represent a major part of any consideration of the public sector. Various types of taxation, the economic effects of different types of taxes and theoretical principles that should be taken into account when deciding whether a tax is good or bad will need to be explained. Most teachers will also want to discuss the various proposals for reforming the tax system, such as negative income tax, changes in local taxation, and the Institute of Fiscal Studies suggestion that we should move towards an expenditure-based system. It is also worth while presenting the students with a statistical breakdown of the way in which revenue is raised in the UK. This, together with the data on the levels and pattern of public expenditure in a given year, could provide the basis for a discussion about the choices facing a government. Again, the students might be asked to work in small groups and to suggest how they would change the pattern of public spending and taxation. They may, or may not, be allowed some flexibility to change the overall level of expenditure. The process that takes place within each group is valuable in itself. During the second part of the lesson, each group should present its proposals to the others, justifying their choices.

Finally, it is necessary to look at the nationalised industries and to give some attention to state intervention and support for industries that are not, strictly speaking, 'nationalised'. It is probably desirable to begin by providing the students with a brief historical background to the government's involvement in industry in the postwar period. The main issues that need to be covered are: the formation of the nationalised industries, the legal structure of public corporations, methods of control and accountability, raising of finance, the general principles of operating the industries as laid down by the various White Papers, aims and objectives, pricing policies and investment policies. A copy of the 1978 White Paper should be available for the students to browse through.

It can be valuable to give each student an assignment to complete on a particular nationalised industry. Information can be readily obtained by writing to the industry concerned. Students may wish to deal with themes such as the history of the industry, why it was deemed suitable for nationalisation, its aims, and the policies it is pursuing.

The privatisation controversy

Nowadays, it must be impossible to discuss the role of the public sector without getting involved in the controversy that surrounds privatisation. A starting point might be an explanation of what exactly is meant by privatisation. This is not at all obvious. It may be useful to adopt the classification suggested by the CLARE Group.[3] They distinguish between three different strands of privatisation policy:

1 Liberalisation. The promotion of competition or competitive behaviour in certain activities that were either reserved to a statutory monopoly or were subject to restricted entry.
2 Transfer of ownership of assests to the private sector.
3 Encouragement of private provision of services that are currently provided collectively. This would include the possible adoption of a voucher system for education and a substitution of private insurance for health and pensions.

Table 50.1 is also taken from the article by the CLARE Group, and shows the major privatisation initiatives that have taken place between 1980 and 1983. It could be updated to include the sale of Enterprise Oil, Jaguar and British Telecom.

One minor point that ought to be explained about the mechanics of the process is that when private capital is introduced into previously wholly nationalised industries, by selling shares, a public joint-stock company is generally created to replace the public corporation. This is a significant organisational change and can be a source of confusion for the students.

There are many recent articles in the bank reviews that tackle the privatisation issue. These can usually be obtained in 'bulk' from the banks, so that they can be used with a whole class. The publications of the Institute of Economic Affairs are also extremely useful. The IEA has since its formation been publicising the benefits of the free market and promoting privatisation in various forms. Publications such as *Experiment with Choice in Education* and *Over-ruled on Welfare* are useful when considering particular privatisation proposals. In addition, the teacher should read Littlechild's *Fallacy of the Mixed Economy*.[4]

In current circumstances, it is very easy to get carried away explaining the more recent arguments surrounding the present government's policies and to neglect the traditional arguments for public ownership and the public provision of services. Arguments such as those relating to natural monopolies, control of the 'commanding heights of the economy', and the distribution of wealth, income and power should not be ignored. However, it is also appropriate to ask questions that are being raised about the concept of a benevolent, all-knowing government. The recent work on the *Economics of Politics* is an interesting if peripheral area for A-level students and teachers.[5]

Privatisation undoubtedly represents an area of the

Table 50.1   Some major privatisation initiatives

1   Liberalisation

Transport Act 1980: deregulated express coach services and relaxed other transport regulations.

Telecommunications Act 1981: permits connection of approved equipment to BT network, allows licensing of Mercury.

Electricity supply: greater opportunities for resale of privately generated electricity.

Civil aviation: Minister overturns CAA's refusal of British Midland's application to operate Heathrow–Scotland services.

Optical services: proposals to permit sales other than through registered opticians.

Shop hours: Committee of Inquiry appointed.

London Transport: private minibuses to be permitted.

2 Transfers of ownership	Proceeds
1980–1	**(£m)**
British Aerospace (51%)	43
Auction of oil licences	210
Motorway service areas	28
Sales of local authority land and dwellings	752
1981–2	
Cable and Wireless (50%)	182
Oil stockpiles	63
Amersham International	64
Local authority land and dwellings	1351
1982–3	
Britoil (51%)	548
Associated British Ports (49%)	22
Local authority land and dwellings	1815
British Rail hotels	35

3   Private production replaces public

Private provision explored or implemented in:
— refuse collection
— municipal parks and gardens
— government office cleaning
— street cleaning
— hospital laundries
— hospital catering

Source: The CLARE Group, 'The new industrial policy. Privatisation and competition'. *Midland Bank Review,* Spring 1984.

syllabus that is most suitable for formal debate. Usually there are varying opinions within the class, and it can arouse passionate controversy. A debate allows prejudices to be exposed and can force individuals to think why they hold certain views. Students could be asked to consider a particular industry or public-sector activity and to outline the various ways in which it could be privatised, perhaps relating their suggestions to the classification mentioned earlier. After considering the various options open, they should attempt to evaluate their own proposals. It can be interesting to ask one group to come up with the proposals for privatisation, but to ask others in the class to comment on their suggestions.

Cost–benefit analysis

It is often erroneously assumed by both the layman and the new student of economics that economists' main concern is with profit or loss. A study of cost–benefit analysis provides an opportunity to dispel this misconception. It also gives the teacher another chance to look at and reinforce a range of topics that have been covered previously, or that will be met later in the course. For example, it is inevitable that time will be spent talking about income distribution and equity, the optimum allocation of resources, externalities and discounting.

The use of cost–benefit analysis in the public sector is increasing and there are many resources that are available. A case-study approach is obviously appropriate for this topic. However, it is also possible to allow the students to carry out a highly simplified cost–benefit analysis of their own. The building of a short motorway link, an airport, or a new underground line in a major city would be obvious projects to take. One of the first important steps in any cost–benefit analysis is to identify the likely consequences of the project, who will be affected, how and when. This can easily be attempted by the students. The next stage is to ask them to discuss the various ways it might be possible to place a money value on the costs and benefits they have identified. They should also be asked to identify the drawbacks of the suggestions they make. It is possible for the teacher to 'invent' the information needed to enable the students to quantify the costs and benefits in money terms, but this may prove difficult and time-consuming. However, they have already learnt a great deal. They should have discovered the relative ease with which 'planners' can find ways to quantify the costs and benefits that have a market value, as opposed to those that are not traded in the market-place.

Their understanding can be extended by using an example of the kind shown in Table 50.2. Time savings have been chosen but there are of course many other possibilities.

It is assumed that time savings for people in their leisure time are only 50 per cent as important as for a man travelling on business. The time horizon chosen to evaluate the project is ten years and the planners are using a rate of discount of 10 per cent to evaluate the various costs and benefits.

Table 50.2   New motorway link

	Traffic per week	
	Nos of journeys	Av. time saving per journey
Year 1		
Lorries	20 000	15 minutes
Cars on business	10 000	10 minutes
Cars on pleasure	5 000	10 minutes
Year 2		
Lorries	25 000	15 minutes
Cars on business	15 000	10 minutes
Cars on pleasure	10 000	10 minutes
Subsequent years		
Lorries	30 000	15 minutes
Cars on business	15 000	10 minutes
Cars on pleasure	15 000	10 minutes

Note: Average wage per lorry driver: £8 per hour.
Average wage per businessman: £10 per hour.

Question
Quantify the money value of the time saving to be used in the cost–benefit study.

It will be necessary to provide the students with discount factors for each of the ten years. Some teachers may feel that to teach discounting is not appropriate for their group. This part of the question can easily be left out. although a general discussion of the principle involved should probably be attempted.

Stimulus-type questions may also be used; the following example is taken from the June 1984 A-level examination:

The following passage is adapted from a *Social Cost-Benefit Study of Two Suburban Surface Rail Passenger Services*, by C. D. Foster

Several studies have been done to estimate the social worth of retaining railway passenger services that are financially unprofitable. What distinguishes this study is that it is one of the first
5   which seeks to justify the retention of rail passenger services because of road congestion in urban areas. The essential case, if proven, must be that the traffic the railways divert from the roads reduces congestion by an amount sufficient to
10   justify the rail subsidies required. Underlying this is the proposition that users of city roads pay less through taxation for using them than covers the real costs of their use.

15   Road users in cities pay substantially less than the costs they occasion. The greater the congestion, the truer this is. The extra cost or, as economists would call it, the marginal social cost, of an extra vehicle coming onto a road is quantifiable.

20   Wherever there is congestion, the marginal social cost will be greater than the actual cost to the individual road user (often called the marginal road user) since the costs to him of using the road are his vehicle costs and his time. He does not have
25   to take into account the costs he imposes on other road users–and on pedestrians.

On the other hand, if rail transport in cities is required to cover costs, it will then be over-priced
30   relative to users of urban roads, since rail users will be required to cover all the real costs they give rise to, while road users will not. The effect of this difference in pricing policy is an inefficient distribution of traffic between road and rail. Less
35   traffic travels by rail, especially in the peak, than is efficient.

One way of getting prices right would be to raise the price of urban road use until both public and
40   private road transport covered its real costs. But if we accept that it is politically imprudent or undesirable to raise the cost of using roads to a level where marginal social costs are covered, one can attempt to get the correct relationship between
45   road and rail by the opposite course of action; that is by keeping rail fares lower than they would be if the railways charged what the market would bear rather than raising road prices. This is the essence of the case for rail subsidies.

(a)   What is meant by the term 'marginal social cost' (line 18)?   *(3 marks)*

(b)   Why is the marginal social cost of an extra road user on a congested road greater than the cost to the marginal road user (lines 20–26)?   *(3 marks)*

(c)   Why was the existing system of prices for road and rail transport considered to be inefficient?   *(6 marks)*

(d)   Describe and discuss the relative merits of the two policy options outlined in the passage that would improve the allocation of traffic between road and rail.   *(8 marks)*

Source: Associated Examining Board

Also, a more recent development has been the publication of a computer program on cost-benefit analysis by Longman.[6]

Resources

Hardwick, P., Kahn, B., and Langmead, J., *An Introduction to Modern Economics* (Longman, 1982). Although this book was written with first-year polytechnic students in mind, parts of the book are very useful for A-level. Chapters 11, 12, 13 and 14 are particularly worth while for this topic.

Stanlake, G. F., *Introductory Economics*, 4th edn. (Longman, 1983).

Trotman-Dickenson, D. I., *Public Sector Economics* (Heinemann Educational Books, 1983). A book in the Made Simple series, which provides a comprehensive coverage of the topic.

Greenaway, D., Westaway, A., Smith, D., and Weyman Jones, T., *Case Studies in Public Sector Economics* (Heinemann Educational Books, 1982).

Barker, P., and Button, K., *Case Studies in Cost-Benefit Analysis* (Heinemann Educational Books, 1975).

Perrott, R. F., *Industry in the Public Sector*, 3rd edn. (Heinemann Educational Books, 1980). A Manchester Economics Project Satellite Text.

The State Executioner, from the *10 × Economics* series (Yorkshire TV) by Peter Donaldson.

Various Economic Progress Reports.

Lloyds Bank Economic Bulletin, *Privatisation's Progress*, December 1983.

Stanlake, G. F., *Public Finance* (Longman, 1982). This is one of the booklets in the Longman Economic Studies series. It is fairly short, and is therefore of some use as a background reader. It also contains some short questions that the student can be asked to complete. Perhaps too much of the booklet is devoted to taxation.

The following articles, taken from the *Economic Review* (published by Philip Allan), are worth giving to the students to read, as well as being of interest to the teacher: *Privatisation and the Welfare State*, by R. Robinson, vol. 1, no. 1; *Practical Cost-Benefit Analysis*, by R. Sugden, vol. 1, no. 1; *Deregulation of UK Telecommunications: Some Economic Aspects*, by S. C. Littlechild, vol. 1, no. 2; *Privatisation and the UK Energy Industries*, by M. G. Webb, vol. 1, no. 4.

Notes and references

1 Eltis, W., and Bacon, R., *Britain's Economic Problem: Too Few Producers* (Macmillan, 1975). Recommended reading for the teacher.

2 Buchanan, J. M., *et al.*, *The Economics of Politics* (The Institute of Economic Affairs, 1978); Tullock, G., *The Vote Motive* (IEA, 1976); both for the teacher.

3 Innumerable bank review articles, for example, *Midland Bank Review*, 'The new industrial policy. Privatisation and competition', by the CLARE Group, spring 1984.

4 Institute of Economic Affairs, *Over-ruled on Welfare* by R. Harris and A. Seldon; *Experiment with Choice in Education* by A. Maynard; *Wither the Welfare State* by A. Seldon; *The Fallacy of the Mixed Economy* by S. Littlechild. These are useful for the teacher and more-able A-level students.

5 Buchanan, op. cit.; Tullock, op. cit.

6 Schools Council Computers in the Curriculum, *COSBEN*, a computer program on cost–benefit analysis (Longman, July 1984).

Part Three
Resources, Assessment and Organisation

Introduction to Part Three

'The purpose of studying economics is not to acquire a set of ready-made answers to economic questions, but to learn how to avoid being deceived by economists.'

Joan Robinson.

Since the first edition of this *Handbook*, Robert Wilson has been a prolific originator of tape/slide programmes. His enormous practical experience in teaching economics lends credence to his chapter on their use and value. Probably the largest expenditure in departmental budgets is on textbooks. All currently available textbooks and related publications may be viewed at the National Textbook Collection and the Economics Research and Curriculum Unit, both at the London University Institute of Education. But for teachers who are unable to use these research collections, Claire Minogue and Nigel Carr provide a substitute in the form of short reviews of each textbook coupled with up-to-date comparative information.

Linda Thomas's chapter on internal assessment plots the move towards criterion-referenced tests and appends an experiment in profiling by Malcolm Scriven. Frank Livesey is a very experienced examiner, and his résumé of current modes of examination is buttressed by varied examples.

The Economics Education 14–16 Project has worked extensively with teacher groups in the preparation and dissemination of exemplar materials. Keith Wood's considerable experience of convening such groups is valuable for other potential innovators.

Many economics teachers are still the only teacher of the subject in their school, and are often *de facto* Head of Department. Lindsey Collings's great experience of running a large department is shared in a detailed and comprehensive chapter. Alain Anderton adds suggestions on how to organise economics resources, and students will appreciate his ideas on how to use libraries. Robert Wilson's practical tips on storing and retrieving ephemeral material are simple yet effective, and Bob Fryer notes that economising economists may find alternative sources of textbooks. The list of over 200 addresses was correct at the time of going to press. It might be advisable to transfer the addresses on to a card index so that alterations may easily be made.

Section 5: Miscellaneous

51 Some ways of Enhancing the Use and Value of Audio-visual Aids
Robert Wilson

Introduction

Teaching and learning aids that combine visual display with sound reproduction are of four main types: filmstrip or slide projector linked to tape or cassette recorder or record player; film projector; television (off-air or linked to a VCR); and computers (which are outside the scope of this chapter). It is highly likely that the great majority of teachers have access to at least some audio-visual equipment, and their place of work probably is also able to supply, directly or indirectly, quantities of commercially produced programmes. It is not uncommon for both the equipment and the programmes prepared for it to remain under-used and their full potential unrealised. In this chapter, a few ideas are offered on how teachers might make more effective use of what is available to them.

Filmstrips are much cheaper to produce commercially than mounted transparencies, but they are inflexible in use and fairly easily damaged. If a filmstrip is exclusively in 35 mm full-frame horizontal (or landscape) format, cutting and mounting the individual frames is easy, comparatively cheap and highly beneficial. With no detriment to their use for their original purpose, the slides are released for use in other syllabus areas, in different ways and with other age/ability levels. For example, set out below is an exercise prepared in order to test students' grasp of terminology relating to types of goods and services. It has been used successfully with senior students, making use of slides borrowed from a set that were originally intended to help more junior classes learn about factors of production.[1] The slides are an integral part of the exercise: few questions can be tackled without reference to them. Once prepared, the exercise can be used over many years.

Types of goods and services
Production is divided between goods and services.
Consumers fall into three main groups: (i) individuals, (ii) private-sector firms, (iii) public sector – government and government agencies.
Goods can be divided into *Capital goods* and *Consumer goods*.

Goods may be suitable for use on only one occasion – *single use*; or for use many times over – *durable*.
Services may be offered (i) to individuals, (ii) to industry and commerce, (iii) to government. Some goods and services are purchased from abroad: these are *imports*. Some goods and services are sold to overseas customers: these are *exports*.

SLIDE

4
1. Write down the names of three items of capital that you can see being used in this picture to help with the operation of the transport service.
2. The firm that built the tram assembled it from bits and pieces largely provided by other firms. These bits and pieces are known as *components*. Write down the names of five manufactured components that have been used in assembling the front of the tramcar.
3. Name five consumer durable items that can be seen in the picture.
4. Name two items of capital owned by the local council *other than* items directly connected with the tramcar service.
5. Name three consumer single-use goods that might well be on sale very close to the scene shown here.
6. Name three other services that might well be on offer to the general public in the vicinity of the scene shown here.
7. Write down three items seen in the picture that are fairly common UK imports.
8. Write down three things seen in the picture that make a contribution to UK export earnings.
9. The lady about to board the tram was heard to ask the driver a non-economic question. Write down your guess at what the lady actually asked the driver.
10. Name two other service industries on which the tram service depends heavily for the success of its own service.

Having converted all available filmstrips into slides, the slides need to be numbered. A catalogue can then be prepared with entries that look something like the following:

Slide number	Depicting	Topic areas
217	Coal-fired power station on greenfield site.	Location of industry, capital-intensive industry, land use, fuel and power, nationalised industries, externalities.

A second catalogue can then be prepared, in which slides are identified on a topic basis. For example:

Topic	Slides
Economies of scale	41, 29, 16, 85, 7, 103, 24, 28, 26, 27, 38.

The numbering reflects an effort to put the catalogue entry in a suggested sequence of use with a class. As computers and data-processors become more commonplace in educational institutions, the construction of this type of catalogue should become less time-consuming. By referring to the catalogue, programmes are quickly compiled.

Small slide-viewers are now cheap enough for one or more to be available to a class as part of workshop activity. Towards the end of a course, individual slides can be used to test understanding across wide areas of a syllabus. For example, set out below is a workcard prepared to be used in conjunction with slide 28 taken from the filmstrip *Factors of Production* mentioned earlier.[2]

Workcard: general revision

1 Explain the link between the picture and 'factor mobility'.
2 Identify two occasions on which the local authority of that area might have had good reason to take an interest in the fate of the building shown.
3 What link can be established between the vehicle seen in the picture and the fate of the building?
4 What evidence is contained in the picture of the practice of (a) division of labour, (b) regional specialisation and exchange?
5 What factors would influence the market value of (a) the vehicle, (b) the building?

The workcard is suitable for use with senior classes on either an individual or a group basis. It makes use of a slide that was obtained in the first instance as part of a programme aimed at considerably younger students. Many slides lend themselves to this kind of process. They can then be used more broadly and more frequently. There is a limit to the number of times that a student will tolerate making use of a particular picture, but it is very seldom that diminishing returns set in after only the first viewing.

Given the comparative cheapness and ease of use of modern SLR cameras, teachers are well placed to produce their own slides and commentaries to accompany them. Every environment has its own intrinsic and possibly peculiar interest and, having converted filmstrips into sets of slides, it is easy to supplement the commercially produced programme with locally photographed slides that heighten the relevance and sharpen the point of what is being covered. Supplementing a programme in this way renders the original accompanying taped commentary unusable, but is seldom any great hardship as, once a programme's logic is absorbed by a teacher, a 'live' commentary can be substituted to advantage for even the original programme. One example of a programme that lends itself to being supplemented is the Audio Learning tape–slide programme on economic aspects of advertising.[3] Many of the points raised in the programme can be enhanced by the introduction of local examples – for example, of branding and of sponsorship. A supplemented version of the slides has been used in courses in media studies and in business studies/ commerce courses. They have even featured in a primary school project, and have been borrowed for use on language courses too. In these ways, the potential of a programme can be more fully realised.

There are usually gaps to be found in commercial provision, and slides and tapes are among the easiest audio-visual aids for teachers to produce for themselves. For example, a locally produced tape–slide programme would serve well to teach about the nature and causes of economic change. The following approach has enjoyed considerable success in introducing students to the dynamic nature of an economy. A set of slides is prepared depicting various local scenes of potential economic interest – for example, the main shopping centre, a pedestrian precinct, an industrial estate, a new housing estate, the local bingo hall, the railway station, etc. The next step is to prepare an accurate account of what the scene depicted looked like, say, thirty years previously, together with a description of the sort of economic activity that was taking place at that location at that time. If the teacher is too young to remember such information personally, libraries are usually able to establish contact with appropriate people willing to recall the past. The same avenue is open to teachers who are not 'local'. The tape can be given coherence by producing a narrative based on the life of a family to which the pictures are linked. The narrative should be in the present tense.

Bringing the tape and slides together produces a programme in which, contrary to the students' usual experience, the commentary is frequently at odds with the slides being shown. For example, one version of this type of programme[4] has the following commentary to accompany a recently taken picture of a busy crossroads on a dual carriageway:

Billy comes here most evenings to visit a friend who lives in the big house in the middle of the picture. The main road is narrow at this point, and lorries struggle up the steep hill only to have to wait their turn to enter the roundabout, their drivers cursing the silent nimbleness of the ubiquitous trolley-buses that always seem to be occupying the road.

This is an accurate account of the scene at that spot some thirty years previously, but in the 1980s picture being looked at by the class, the narrow main road has become a dual carriageway, the roundabout has been replaced by traffic lights, the gradient of the road has been eased and the fine big house has been demolished. The ubiquitious trolleybus has vanished too.

The programme consists of a series of slides linked to a tape, and with each slide students are given the task of looking at the scene, listening to the tape, and jotting down all the discrepancies they notice between what they see presented and what they hear described. Depending on the speed and density of oral presentation, this can be a very demanding task for students, and so it is preferable for the series of slides to be constructed in a sequence that offers natural break points. Having shown some of the programme, the students' observations can be collated and checked for accuracy and completeness. The next stage is to bring some coherence to their findings. This can be done by concentrating on particular themes within the programme. For example, students may be asked to cite the evidence contained in the programme to support the view that people's standard of living has changed over time. They can also be asked to produce evidence from the programme of changes in the pattern of retailing, in the location of industry, in patterns of leisure and entertainment, etc. Once the main trends have been identified, attempts can be made to suggest reasons for the trends. Many of the reasons will have a significant economic dimension. In many parts of the world, environmental change has taken place at such a pace and on such a scale that there will be no shortage of material available for use. Once the slides have been assembled and a general outline established, the programme can be used with a wide range of ability groups, provided that the teacher is willing to adjust the length of the commentary and the language and syntax used.

Tinkering with slides and tapes is much easier than fiddling about with films. With a film the picture sequence is determined, and the commentary cannot easily be dispensed with, given that the pace of presentation is linked to the pictures. Maximising the benefits from showing a film is therefore confined to supporting it in some way: by preparing a preamble, by producing activity sheets to be completed while viewing it, or by providing follow-up exercises. There is a tendency for film-makers to pack more information into a script than can be absorbed at one hearing, and being required to look and listen can make heavy demands on a student. One way around this difficulty is to prepare questionnaires that relate to specific small sections of the film and to allocate tasks to individual groups, so that no person has to look, listen and make notes for more than perhaps five minutes. The workcards need to be constructed with a view to minimising the amount of writing undertaken while the film is in progress. An example of a workcard is given below:

The Stock Exchange

1 How many jobbers were approached by the broker?
2 What was the highest price quoted? ....
3 What was the lowest price quoted? ....
4 Why did the broker telephone his client before selling the shares?

....

5 Why did the broker approach more than one jobber?

....

Preparing this type of work can be time-consuming. It is not worth the effort if a film is of such transient interest that it is unlikely to be used by a teacher on more than one occasion. Films that deal principally with economic principles (rather than with specific economic institutions) tend to have a lifespan long enough to justify the effort.

In the case of television programmes, the effort of preparing support materials is compounded by the tendency of producers to offer a series of related programmes. In urban areas with high densities of population, it is often possible to organise a consortium of economics teachers who share out the task of preparing support material between them. A communal viewing of television programmes can be a pleasant social event as well as a useful forum for an exchange of views. In addition to the support materials indicated above, it is useful for teachers to have summaries of the programmes as an *aide memoire* for future use. These can be prepared on the basis of just one viewing of a programme, and might take the following form:

Unemployment: 30 mins

REF	Item/location	Description
1	Shipyard	Demolition following closure
2	Newspaper headline	Loss of 200 office jobs – computer
3	Street interview	Redundant steelworker on his prospects
4	Studio	Graph of unemployment trends

This type of summary is different from the summaries provided by the publishers of the programme. Where a programme is used only rarely, a synopsis of visual content can prove very useful to a teacher who does not have time to watch the programme through prior to re-using it. It can become the basis of the teacher's preamble.

Teachers' views differ on the wisdom of assigning tasks to students in relation to a television programme that is being viewed. Where the programme is didactic, there seem to be arguments in favour of helping students to maximise their learning from it. Asked simply to 'make notes on the programme' as it progresses, many students will produce little or nothing of value. It is often helpful to students to be given guidance on what to look for. This may well be offered in the form of a set of structured questions, an example of which is given below:

Unemployment

1 Which three industries were used to give examples of structural employment?

....

2 State two of the reasons given for a decline in demand for coal.

....

3 What reasons were given by the steelworker for his reluctance to move to another steel-producing area?

....

4 What factors had led to the closure of his local steelworks?

....

For some students, the answers that they provide to these questions may well serve as their main or only record of the programme, but for others in a group there is no reason why such skeletal notes should not be used as the basis for more extended writing.

All this preparation takes time, and where copyright law precludes the use of a television programme beyond a very limited timespan, the teacher may well feel that the effort is not worth the stunted reward. This line of argument will not stand up in relation to a great deal of audio-visual material already in existence and which in many instances represents an underutilised scarce resource.

Notes and references

1 Wilson, R. D., *Factors of Production* (Economics Association, 1978).
2 Ibid.
3 Wilson, R. D., *Advertising* (Audio Learning, 1983).
4 Wilson, R. D., *Change and Decay*, unpublished.

52   14–16 Textbooks – an Evaluation

Claire Minogue

Introduction

Perhaps the most striking feature of this evaluation is that it will become obsolete even more rapidly than any of the texts it attempts to review. However, until a new generation of textbooks is published with GCSE in mind, teachers will have to make the best use of the resources available.

As most of the textbooks have been aimed at O-level or CSE students, they have been evaluated on this basis. Other criteria include coverage in terms of specific syllabuses, layout and presentation, price, how up-to-date the text is and inclusion of 'special features' such as data-response questions or a detailed index. A summary of the textbooks evaluated here is given in Table 52.1.

Table 52.1

Anderton, A. G., *An Introduction to Social Economics*, 2nd edn (Heinemann Educational Books, 1984) 176pp, limp, ISBN 0435331418, £3.95.

Baron, D., *Economics: An Introductory Course*, 2nd edn (Heinemann Educational Books, 1976) 160pp, limp, ISBN 0435840452, £3.60.

Christie, D., and Scott, A., *Economics in Action* (Heinemann Educational Books, 1977) 140pp, limp, ISBN 0435847961, £3.25.

Davey, M., *Everyday Economics* (Macmillan, 1983) 288pp, limp, ISBN 0333324943, £3.95.

Davies, B., and Hender, D., *Production and Trade*, 2nd edn (Longman, 1979) 105pp, limp, ISBN 0717505421, £3.25.

Davies, F., *Starting Economics*, 5th edn (Hulton, 1979) 144pp, limp, ISBN 0717505421, £2.85.

Harbury, C. D., *Descriptive Economics*, 6th edn (Pitman, 1981) 306pp, limp, ISBN 0273017330, £6.95.

Harvey, J., *Basic Economics* (Macmillan Education, 1981) 352pp, limp, ISBN 0333279859, £3.50; Workbook, 64pp, £1.95.

Harvey, J., *Elementary Economics*, 5th edn (Macmillan Education, 1983) 433pp, limp, ISBN 0333336119, £4.95; Workbook, 68pp, £2.75, or with answers £3.25.

Harvey, J., *Mastering Economics* (Macmillan Education) 352pp, limp, ISBN 0333304772, £2.95.

Hobday, I., *Economics: A First Course* (Edward Arnold, 1983) 272pp, limp, ISBN 0713173092, £4.25.

Iwuji, E., and Turner, P., *First Course in Economics for West Africa* (Nelson, 1982) 160pp, limp, ISBN 245536450, £3.50; Teachers' Guide, 24pp, free.

Lobley, D., *Economics: A New Introduction* (John Murray, 1983) 272pp, limp, ISBN 0719539056, £3.75.

Table 52.1 contd.

Marder, K. B., and Alderson, L. P., *Economic Society*, 2nd edn (OUP, 1981) 280pp, limp, ISBN 019913267, £3.75. *Stimulus Questions For O-level Economics* (OUP, 1981) 48pp, limp, ISBN 0199132720, £2.50.

Nobbs, J., *Social Economics*, 3rd edn (McGraw-Hill, 1981) 264pp, limp, ISBN 00708464X, £5.95.

Nobbs, J., and Ames, P., *Daily Economics* (McGraw-Hill, 1982) 246pp, limp, ISBN 070944393, £4.25.

Powicke, J., and May, P., *An Introduction to Economics*, 4th edn (Edward Arnold, 1984) 272pp, limp, ISBN 0713173092, £4.25.

Sanday, A. P., and Birch, P. A., *Understanding Industrial Society*, 3rd edn (Hodder & Stoughton, 1983) 159pp, limp, ISBN 0340287357, £4.75; Teacher's Guide, £6.95.

Sapsford, D., and Ladd, J., *Essential Economics*, 2nd edn (Hart-Davies, 1982) 228pp, limp, ISBN 0247132667.

Stanlake, G. F., *First Economics* (Longman, 1982) 354pp, limp, ISBN 0582223350, £4.95; Answerbook, £1.35.

Thomas, D. J., *A First Course in Economics*, 2nd edn (Bell & Hyman, 1981) 297pp, limp, ISBN 0713510938, £3.95.

Wardle, H. T., *Introductory Economics: A Comprehensive Study Text* (Wheaton, 1982) 144pp, limp, ISBN 0080241468, £4.25.

An Introduction to Social Economics (A. G. Anderton)
This is a visually exciting book which cleverly presents materials in a digestible form for a wide ability range. Its pages are large and liberally covered with cartoons, diagrams, graphs, charts and keywords picked out in bold type. Chapters are usually followed by questions and there are stimulating case studies spread throughout. It is designed to cover materials for the AEB O-level Social Economics and CSE Social Economics syllabuses and to be used in mixed-ability situations – ambitious aims, which it comes close to achieving. The second edition provides an updated and polished version of the very successful first edition.

Economics: An Introductory Course (D. Baron)
This book is aimed at a wide ability range as it is designed to serve the requirements of both O-level and CSE students. It includes a greater spectrum of resource material and student activities than one usually finds in a traditional O-level text. Care has been taken to make the text visually attractive by using illustrations, diagrams and photographs. The treatment is suitable for CSE/O-level candidates; however, the coverage may not be sufficient for many courses. It states that the central theme is 'the interdependence of the parts of the economy with each other'

Economics In Action (D. Christie and A. Scott)
The main aim of this book is 'to help students to understand the economic environment within which we exist' by introducing them to economic analysis. When first published in 1977, it was original and innovative – making considerable use of case-study material and taking great care to make it visually attractive. However, it no longer has such a fresh and original look.

It is divided into seven sections, the emphasis being on the theoretical elements, with a bias towards microeconomics. Although it does not provide the detailed information on the UK economy that some syllabuses require, it is a good introduction to economic concepts for more able O-level students.

Everyday Economics (M. Davey)
This text aims to provide material suitable for those candidates entered for 'Social and Personal Economics . . . or General Studies courses'. It is suitable for CSE students following a social economics syllabus. It is reasonably attractive, with many diagrams, flow charts, graphs, tables, pie-charts and illustrations. It sets out definitions clearly, and interspersed throughout the text there are a great many short exercises, suggestions for projects (variable quality) and discussion points. As well as providing a great deal of information (often well presented), it gives 'useful addresses and sources' so that these can be updated. The economic content, however, is rather weak.

Production and Trade (B. Davies and D. Hender)
This is a descriptive text aimed at CSE students: it covers broad aspects such as production, foreign trade, price determination, the economic role of the government, and banking. A set of exercises is included at the end of each chapter and 'ideas for further work'. A glossary of terms and a short bibliography of teaching materials are useful additions. An updated edition would be welcomed.

Starting Economics (F. Davies)
An introductory text designed for students aged 13–16 years. It explores economic concepts through a series of fictional situations. These include: factor resources and payments, rich and poor, specialisation, supply and demand, money, taxation, trade, and economic problems. The text has little visual appeal, despite numerous line drawings and some graphs and tables. Each chapter has a concluding summary and student exercises based on the chapter.

Descriptive Economics (C. D. Harbury)
The aim of this text is to provide O-level candidates and above with an account of the chief characteristics of the British economy as it enters the 1980s. It includes clear and straightforward descriptions of population, industrial organisation, the structure of industry, commerce and trade unions and deals with matters relating to national income, the role of the government, money, banking, and the international economy. The sixth edition has been

updated to incorporate changes since the mid-1970s, such as North Sea oil, membership of the EEC and monetarism. There is a comprehensive index which aids the use of this text considerably.

Elementary Economics (J. Harvey), *Basic Economics* (J. Harvey), and *Mastering Economics* (J. Harvey)
Harvey is a long-established author of traditional introductory economics textbooks. Few concessions are made to lower-ability students by way of illustrations and layout. However, for O-level students, *Elementary Economics* provides a comprehensive, reliable and up-to-date textbook. It has a good index and there is an accompanying workbook as there are no questions within the textbook itself. The workbook includes multiple-choice questions on the text, practical projects, points to discuss and past papers.

Basic Economics is similar to *Elementary Economics*: it is a comprehensive traditional introductory text. It differs slightly in the level of treatment – being suitable for more-able students. It is perhaps between O-level and A-level. There is also a companion workbook that enlivens the use of the text considerably. It is worth while in its own right as it contains a variety of activities.

Mastering Economics covers similar ground, in a similar style as part of the 'mastering' series. The treatment is approximately O-level.

Economics: A First Course (I. Hobday)
This book is aimed at both O-level and CSE students. Although the text is mainly descriptive and reasonably well illustrated, it is unlikely to be successful with such a broad ability range and is only suitable for O-level students. In sixteen chapters, it covers the syllabus of most O-level courses in detail. It sets out information in note-form rather like a crammer. The information is reasonably up to date and there are questions at the end of chapters. There is a detailed index which is a useful addition.

A First Course in Economics for West Africa (E. Iwuji and P. Turner)
A text specifically designed to meet the requirements of O-level candidates in West Africa; it is a traditional-style text with relevant O-level questions incorporated.

Economics: A New Introduction (D. Lobley)
Lobley has designed his book to cater for 'modern' O-level syllabuses. This is not to say that the coverage is not orthodox, but an attempt has been made to address the current economic issues and it provides data-response questions that some 'modern' examinations include. The treatment is lively and examples are often original. It is well suited to O-level candidates, although in places the language is a little difficult. Each chapter is followed by assignments of the short-answer variety (no answers provided). It is well presented with many diagrams, tables, photographs and a good glossary of terms.

Economic Society (K. B. Marder and L. P. Alderson)
This is an unexceptional standard O-level textbook. It is fairly well presented; there are many graphs and tables. For an applied economic textbook, it is reasonably up to date. Each chapter ends with sample O-level questions. More stimulating exercises may be found in "Stimulus Questions For O-Level Economics" by the same authors. It provides 43 exercises on a variety of data (often constructed data) which is particularly useful for some syllabuses.

Social Economics (J. Nobbs)
Nobbs has produced a very attractive O-level text which is particularly suitable for the AEB O-level Social Economics. The addition of data-response questions enhances an already successful publication.

Daily Economics (J. Nobbs and P. Ames)
This is a lively and visually attractive text which is suitable for CSE students following a social economics syllabus. The chapters are numerous and relatively short. Each chapter includes questions and 'activities' that are useful for this level. The text develops the theme of young person finding a job to 'young person in the wider economy'.

An Introduction to Economics (J. Powicke and P. May)
This is an O-level text that is fairly traditional in style and content. Coverage includes: the economic framework, the financial framework, the price mechanism, social accounting and economic policy. Although it is not very descriptive, information is up to date. The treatment is suitable for able O-level students. There are exercises at the end of each chapter to test comprehension.

Understanding Industrial Society (A. P. Sanday and P. A. Birch)
The aim of *Understanding Industrial Society* is to provide a text specifically for the AEB O-level syllabus and similar CSE syllabuses. This economics-related course is designed to make full use of role-play, case-study/fieldwork approaches in teaching. The text reflects this philosophy in its design and structure in an attempt to provide the necessary resources required.

It is split into three parts: starting a small firm; expanding the firm; allocating resources – the choice before us. The twenty-three chapters are made up of case studies and questions that supplement a small amount of text. There are a good number of photographs, illustrations and diagrams spread throughout. The third edition does not provide any parallel chapters for both O-level and CSE requirements as earlier editions did. However, apart from updating some case studies, little has changed since the first edition in 1976. It is disappointing that the latest edition does not include more stimulating material which is available from other sources (e.g. *Understanding Industry* by Baddeley (Butterworth); *Learning About Trade Unions* (TUC)). Many of the exercises are of a variable quality; some are too demanding for CSE candidates, and sometimes they are not related to the text from which the answers could be gleaned. Part 3 is rather inadequate in terms of treatment required for both O-level and CSE.

However, the teacher's guide is a very useful aid for any teacher trying to build up suitable resources, and this will help overcome some of the shortcomings of the students' text.

Essential Economics (D. Sapsford and J. Ladd)
This text is designed to meet the needs of O-level candidates. The text is enhanced by an excellent pictorial/diagrammatic dimension. The coverage is comprehensive, including an up-to-date chapter on 'current issues'. There are assignments at the end of each chapter and multiple-choice questions. The index of definitions is helpful and for very able students there is suggested further reading that would stretch the brighter O-level candidates.

First Economics (G. F. Stanlake)
Stanlake has produced a comprehensive and thorough text that teachers have come to expect from this long-established and very successful author (and teacher). Although unexciting, it is dependable and consistent. In thirty chapters the book covers the typical O-level syllabus. There are eleven test papers comprising short answers, true-/false- type questions, multiple-choice and data-response questions (answer book available). The microeconomic theory is quite advanced for O-level, but generally the level of treatment is suitable for O-level candidates, with an extremely clear treatment of comparative advantage and terms of trade. The index is very comprehensive.

A First Course in Economics (D. J. Thomas)
A comprehensive O-level text with a detailed narrative style. There are a small number of graphs and tables. There are questions at the end of chapters based on the text and some sample O-level examination questions (GCE, RSA, LCC), and suggestions for practical work which are sometimes rather vague.

Introductory Economics: A Comprehensive Study Text (H. T. Wardle)
The aim of this text is to provide a self-tuition format and hence it has many more exercises incorporated in the text than traditional textbooks. The twelve chapters are not as comprehensive as some O-level courses require. Each chapter is concluded by a range of comprehension exercises, multiple-choice questions and past examination questions (answers are provided).

53   An Evaluation of A-level Textbooks
Nigel Carr

Introduction

The problem of deciding upon which textbook or textbooks to use must surely be one of the more difficult tasks for the teacher, especially when facing a limited budget, since he or she will probably have to use the books for three or four years before they can be replaced. The choice is made increasingly difficult as the number of available textbooks on the market increases. Some start from first principles while others assume a substantial degree of knowledge; some are essentially theoretical while others favour an applied approach; some are non-mathematical while others assume that the reader has considerable numerate skill.

The average teacher is unlikely to have access to all the various books available or the time to consider more than a very few in depth. This chapter attempts to ease the burden by evaluating the main books in use at present. Given the limitations of space, it is impossible to assess all the material on the market, and thus attention has been devoted to those books that are in most common use and also those books that have only recently appeared or that have been substantially amended in the latest edition.

The factual information presented in economics textbooks with an applied content will gradually become outdated. This is inevitable with a subject such as economics, and teachers must be prepared to update their textbooks regularly, using sources such as *Economics Progress Reports* and newspaper cuttings. Therefore only books that are seriously deficient in this respect have been criticised. Furthermore, the date of publication is given in Table 53.1 so that teachers can assess how much they will have to do in this field. The summary table at the end also contains details of the number of pages, whether there are questions in the text, whether there is a bibliography, whether the book is primarily theoretical or applied, and whether it is for first- or second-year A-level students, or is suitable for both.

In using the following descriptions of the textbooks on offer, teachers must first decide what it is that they want from a textbook. Is it something that merely summarises the main points of a lesson or is it to be a means whereby the student, when reading it, will be developing his or her economic understanding as well as simply learning material? The reader of the books reviewed here will find that many of them are largely identical in the material they

Table 53.1

Title and author	Questions	1st/2nd year?	Bibliography	Publisher	Price	Pages	Date	Theory/applied?
Economics: A New Approach (Anderton)	✓	Both	X	University Tutorial Press	£6.00	314	1984	Both
Economics: A Student's Guide (Beardshaw)	✓	Both	✓	Macdonald & Evans	£8.95	698	1984	Both
Economics (Begg, Fischer and Dornbusch)	✓	Both	X	McGraw-Hill	£9.95	808	1984	Theory
Economics For A-level (Browne)	X	1st	✓	Edward Arnold	£5.95	328	1983	Both
Understanding Economics (Burningham (ed.))	✓	1st	✓	Hodder & Stoughton	£3.95	398	1984	Both
Introduction to Economics (Cairncross and Sinclair)	X	Both	X	Butterworth	£7.95	466	1982	Theory
Economics: An Integrated Approach (Creedy *et al.*)	✓	2nd	X	Prentice-Hall	£10.95	448	1984	Theory
A Textbook of Economics (Hanson)	✓	Both	✓	McDonald & Evans	£6.25	604	1980	Both
Economic Behaviour: An Introduction (Harbury)	X	1st	X	George Allen & Unwin	£4.95	265	1980	Theory
An Introduction to the UK Economy (Harbury and Lipsey)	X	Both	X	Pitman	£4.95	240	1980	Applied
Intermediate Economics (Harvey)	✓	Both	✓	Macmillan	£4.95	446	1983	Theory
Modern Economics (Harvey)	X	Both	X	Macmillan	£5.95	547	1983	Theory
Basic Economics (Heertje and Robinson)	✓	1st	✓	Holt, Rinehart & Winston	£4.95	323	1982	Both
Investigating Economics (Hocking and Powell)	✓	Both	X	Longman	£6.95	432	1984	Both
Economics and the Economy (Jeffreys)	✓	2nd	X	Longman	£5.95	317	1985	Both
An Introduction to Positive Economics (Lipsey)	X	2nd	X	Weidenfeld & Nicolson	£8.95	790	1983	Theory
A Textbook of Economics (Livesey)	✓	2nd	X	Polytech Publishers	£5.50	515	1982	Both
Success in Economics (Lobley)	✓	Both	✓	John Murray	£3.95	400	1984	Both
Understanding Economics (Manchester Economics Project)	✓	Both	X	Heinemann Educational Books	£8.95	331	1976	Theory
The Fundamentals of Economics (Morrice)	✓	1st	X	William Heinemann	£6.95	230	1982	Theory
A Textbook of Economic Analysis (Nevin)	X	2nd	✓	Macmillan	£6.95	525	1981	Theory
Advanced Level Economics (Nobbs)	✓	Both	X	McGraw-Hill	£5.50	225	1983	Both
Approaching Economics (Perry)	✓	Both	✓	Hutchinson	£8.50	448	1985	Both
The UK Economy (Prest and Coppock)	X	2nd	X	Weidenfeld & Nicolson	£6.50	336	1982	Applied
Introductory Economics (Stanlake)	X	Both	X	Longman	£4.25	502	1983	Both

Notes:
1 The number of pages given includes the index and bibliography where applicable.
2 The date given refers to the latest edition or revision, rather than the latest reprinting.

cover, the way it is treated and the level of exposition. Choice between such books is purely a matter of personal preference on the part of the teacher. However, there are a small number of books that are different, either in their approach or in the general style adopted. It is to be hoped that readers of this chapter will not reject such books just because they are not what they are used to. Indeed, the new approach that they bring to the teaching of certain areas of the syllabus would be a welcome breath of fresh air in the average economics A-level classroom. On a purely practical level, the teacher has to decide whether the book is to last for both years of the A-level course, or whether one is looking for a theoretical approach in the first year and therefore a more applied work in the second year, and also whether the textbook is to be completely self-contained or whether one is prepared to supplement it with books of questions and more applied material. Answers to questions such as these will be instrumental in narrowing down the teacher's choice of textbooks.

In what follows, all the books have been considered solely in terms of their suitability for A-level economics students although, in terms of the preface in many of the books, they are supposed to be suitable for a far wider readership – first-year undergraduates, students for accountancy examinations, banking examinations and BTEC courses. Furthermore, they have been reviewed with the school-age reader in mind; books where the approach, language used or content are not suitable have been criticised, although they might be suitable for other types of student or examinations.

Economics: A New Approach (A. Anderton)

The author's ambition, as stated in the preface, is to provide a textbook that is suitable for A-level economics, but also provides an insight into the current state of the science of economics today by considering the various competing theories currently propounded. These aims are achieved with almost total success. As a standard A-level textbook, it scores very highly, being excellently presented with an easy-to-read double-column layout. The text is well spaced out, with a large number of diagrams, all being clearly explained. There are also a number of photographs and cartoons, all helping to reinforce the arguments presented in the text. Chapters are interspersed with data-response questions, which besides testing the reader's understanding, also provide much useful factual information about the UK economy. Chapters also contain a brief summary at the end, essay questions, and a list of key terms. In terms of content, the book is also very impressive, providing an evaluation of such current controversies as the monetarist debate, the role of supply-side economics and the problems of the LDCs. Also worthy of special mention is the way care is taken to provide practical examples, often via the data-response questions, of theoretical areas of the syllabus. It should be noted, however, that the treatment of some areas of the syllabus is brief, and weaker students might find it a little difficult to comprehend without extra explanation. However, this is a book that is to be wholeheartedly recommended for use during some or all of an A-level course.

Economics: A Student's Guide (J. Beardshaw)

This is a book which will appeal strongly to all those teachers looking for a standard approach to the teaching of the subject. It is very well written and is pitched at the level appropriate to the average A-level student, who will find it one of the more readable textbooks on the market. This is due not only to the author's clear and concise use of language, but also to the subdivision of the material into short sections, with the key points emphasised in heavy type. In addition, each chapter contains a summary and a number of questions. Throughout the book there is a good blend of theoretical and applied material, with references between the two where necessary. The book is highly topical with much of the data relating to 1983 and 1984. The standard A-level course is covered although there is nothing on economic development. Teachers using the book might wish to cover the material in a slightly different order, but, since each chapter is self-contained, this would present no difficulty. The chapters on the theory of distribution, that on mathematical techniques and the case study on agriculture are especially good. In conclusion, this is definitely a book worth careful scrutiny by teachers.

Economics (D. Begg, S. Fischer and R. Dornbusch)

This is a book that is new on the British market, and one that is worthy of attention from all teachers. Although based on a US book, it has been substantially revised for the UK reader. It is very well presented, with definitions in red type and clear diagrams. Each chapter concludes with a list of key terms and a number of questions and, throughout, there are many examples to illustrate the concepts considered. In general, the micro sections are of a higher quality than the macro, the latter being explained in such a way as to be more closely geared to the more able student. Teachers using the book would need to supplement it with some form of applied material; however, this is a book that is a serious rival to Lipsey's *An Introduction to Positive Economics* and, in many ways, is more suitable for the A-level student than is the latest edition of Lipsey's work. Although it is slightly more expensive, the average student will find it far more readable.

Economics for A-level (D. Browne)

This book aims to cover the whole syllabus at a standard suitable for the average student. The approach is non-mathematical and the language and the level of exposition are well geared to this purpose, making it generally clear and easy to read. Diagrams are well explained and there are a number of tables of current data although, too often, little reference is made to them in the text. Chapters conclude with a brief summary of the main points, but those emphasised by the author are not always the ones others might regard as being the most important. However, it is in terms of content that some deficiencies in the author's approach are to be found. The standard is too low for it to be used, unaided, in the second year; many areas are explained insufficiently, and concepts such as equilibrium are used and then explained in later chapters. The ordering of topics would probably not suit the majority of teachers and there are also a number of minor errors in the text. No questions are provided (despite the suggestion to the contrary on the cover). However, there are two sections that would make its purchase worth while for the library: those dealing with regional policy and international trade.

Understanding Economics (D. Burningham (ed.))

This book might be better known under its alternative title of *Teach Yourself Economics*. It is intended for the general reader as well as for people studying for examinations in economics. Because of its wide readership, it is written in an easy-to-understand manner that the average A-level student will find appealing. However, a disadvantage associated with this is that in some areas it is too brief, with a tendency for the authors to make statements that are not adequately explained. In general, the more-able student would find this book insufficiently rigorous. An exception to this is the section on oligopoly which is far better than that usually found in A-level textbooks. Chapters terminate with a summary of the main points and questions from A-level boards and professional bodies' examinations. There is also a detailed list of further reading.

Introduction to Economics (A. Cairncross and P. Sinclair)

This book was first written in 1944 and is now in its sixth edition. It aims to provide a comprehensive introduction to the subject and, in most areas of the theoretical side, it does this admirably. There are only two notable exceptions to this, these being the discussion of income and substitution effects and indifference curves, and the general introduction to the macroeconomic framework. There are also weaknesses on the applied side, where the book would need to be supplemented, – especially with respect to recent macroeconomic developments. Exceptions to this criticism of the applied area are the sections concerning the growth of firms and small and large firms which are first class. It is certainly worth a place in libraries for these two sections alone, and also for its general non-mathematical treatment which will appeal to the less numerate student.

Economics: An Integrated Approach (J. Creedy, L. Evans, B. Thomas, P. Johnson and R. Wilson)

This is not strictly an A-level economics textbook, in that it is written by a team from Durham University for first-year undergraduates. However, teachers with a number of very able students might consider using it as an alternative to such books as Lipsey's *An Introduction To Positive Economics*. It covers all the material necessary for A-level and, indeed, certain sections and techniques, such as the Edgeworth Box, can be omitted. The language used and its slight mathematical bias would take it out of the reach of the average student, although the diagrams and their explanations are especially clear and could well be adapted by teachers for more general teaching.

A Textbook of Economics (J. L. Hanson)

Although this book has been slightly revised, it is essentially the same as the seventh edition, published in 1977, and certain sections are now a little dated. The section on money is in need of substantial revision and there is, for example, no discussion of the modern monetarist views or even a mention of Milton Friedman in the index. The emphasis is too heavily weighted towards economic history and ignores many of the developments that have taken place in the economy in recent years. A book that lists the 1949 sterling devaluation under 'recent international monetary developments' and spends twenty-five pages dealing with the history of exchange rates is not really suited to a modern A-level course.

Economic Behaviour: An Introduction (C. Harbury)

This book is intended, according to the preface, to provide an introduction to the subject for those who are looking for a brief survey of the subject and also to provide a base for those taking it at A-level. The book is deliberately restricted to the theoretical elements of the syllabus and would therefore need to be supplemented with a more applied book such as *An Introduction to the UK Economy* (reviewed next). The approach is non-mathematical, although there are notes at the end of those chapters where mathematical details might be useful. However, a teacher looking for a standard A-level approach would be disappointed – there is a very good section on economic methodology but only one line on oligopoly and three on government control of monopolies. In general, the material is not advanced enough for a complete A-level course – there is no explanation of indifference curves for example – but it would be a useful book for the teacher who is seeking a basic theory textbook for the first year of the course.

An Introduction to the UK Economy (C. Harbury and R. Lipsey)

This book, by two well-established authors, is intended to supplement their respective theoretical works, and there are references at the start of chapters to the appropriate sections of Lipsey's work to aid the reader. The book is also intended as an updated alternative to Harbury's *Descriptive Economics* (which has therefore not been considered here). As an example for prospective textbook writers on how to present material, it is very good; key words are in bold type, it is well laid out with headings in the margin, figures are well explained and sources are given to facilitate further research, and the language used is at an appropriate level for the average sixth-form student.

The main method of presenting information is through diagrams and there are very few tables of data or detailed figures given in the text. Therefore, although the diagrams are very good for showing relative sizes, trends, areas and proportions, they are of little use for the reader looking for detailed information who would have to look elsewhere. Good though the diagrams are, possibly there are too many of them at the expense of other methods of presenting information – 104 in 225 pages. Furthermore, some areas of the subject, such as prices and incomes policies, monopoly control and recent monetary changes, not susceptible to diagrammatic treatment, are considered only briefly and would need to be supplemented. This is not a textbook of applied economics, nor does it attempt to be; it is purely descriptive but useful for reference.

Intermediate Economics (J. Harvey)

For teachers searching for a good, well-tried, basic text-book, this is one that they should seriously consider. It covers the A-level syllabus in a straightforward way without any frills. However, in order to achieve this, it does oversimplify some of the more contentious (and perhaps interesting) areas of the subject. Topics are divided into short sections and then subdivided further. This aids the student's ability to take notes but does not necessarily facilitate his ability to operate as an economist. To compensate for this, the teacher must be prepared to develop certain sections of the book in class discussion and to recommend wider reading – as must also be done for some of the applied areas of the syllabus. Chapters conclude with a large number of questions, with answers at the end of the book; these are very useful, as are the many diagrams throughout the text which are all explained clearly, especially in the first-class section on demand and supply.

Modern Economics (J. Harvey)

Many of the comments that were made about the author's *Intermediate Economics* apply equally well to this textbook. Indeed, some parts of the former reappear here. As with the above book, one is obtaining a well-tested product that is easy to understand, making relatively few demands upon the student and, with the exception of needing more material on the applied aspects and on the more advanced theoretical areas, is adequate for a two-year course. However, such books are obtained only at the expense of also obtaining something that is, in places, inclined to be both predictable and unexciting. This book is possibly better suited to the student working on his own since, although there are no questions at the end of each chapter, there is an accompanying workbook and a student's notebook. In terms of the level of the two books *Modern Economics* comes slightly below *Intermediate Economics*, but substantially above the author's O-level publications.

Basic Economics (A. Heertje and B. R. G. Robinson)

This is an extremely good basic textbook which would be suitable for the first year of a two-year course, but does not contain enough material to suit those looking for one textbook to last them throughout the course. It is well organised and divided into a large number of self-contained sections which helps the reader understand the

concepts being developed before moving on to new material. Visually, it is one of the better books on the market, being exceptionally well set out with a large typeface and the use of an alternative colour to reinforce key points and for tables and diagrams. The material contained is typical of conventional textbooks except that, possibly because of its authorship, it has a more inter-national flavour than most of its competitors, with sections on the EEC and centrally planned economies as well as a large number of internationally oriented examples. There are questions at the end of each chapter, together with a summary of the main points, a very useful glossary of terms, and a bibliography at the end. There is also a student's work-book and an extremely useful teacher's handbook to accompany the textbook. The latter contains reading for both teacher and student, guidelines for the teacher, and a scheme of work as well as advice on visits, etc.

Investigating Economics (T. Hocking and R. A. Powell)

This was originally an Australian textbook which has been modified to cater for the A-level economist. The authors aim for a problem-solving approach to the subject, emphasising the importance of methodology rather than factual material. As a result, teachers using the book might find it necessary to supplement it in the latter area. This is especially the case with recent material since, although published in 1984, much of the data provided dates back to 1978 and 1979. The book is well-presented, with topic headings in the margin, key points italicised, summary sections, a generous inclusion of cartoon illustrations and photographs, together with diagrams of a high standard, clearly set out and explained. Chapters contain a number of imaginative questions which are generally above the standard found in most similar books. Many of these are integral to the student's understanding and it would be necessary for teachers using the book to ensure that the appropriate points are learned from them. The topics covered satisfy standard A-level syllabi although the sections on monopoly legislation, the methods of achieving economic growth and current methods of monetary control would have to be supplemented. There are, however, a number of particularly useful sections on areas of current interest, such as the CAP, privatisation, economic development and the costs of economic growth.

Economics and the Economy (D. Jeffreys)

The author's intention in writing this book (aimed at A-level and first year university economists) was to provide a textbook which developed the techniques – both theoretical and applied– used by economists. Its approach is thus fundamentally different from the standard A-level textbook. Indeed, *Economics and the Economy* is intended to be used in conjunction with an additional textbook in order to provide the basics needed by students. Even with this proviso, it is only for very able students, e.g. those who are able to take such techniques as IS-LM analysis in their stride.

The approach is concept-based with opportunity cost and the multiplier stressed at the micro- and macro-levels respectively. Section 1, (An Introduction to Applied Economics), introduces these concepts as well as looking very successfully at the question 'What is Economics?'. The second section, (Applied Economics) contains six chapters on the structure of industry, the public sector, distribution, the monetary system, the balance of payments and finishes with a chapter on current disputes in economics. A feature of these sections is the way both micro- and macro-economics methods of analysis are combined. Chapters contain exercises for the reader as well as a number of stimulating questions for discussion. It is an exceptionally well-written addition to the stock of textbooks already on the market and is definitely worth a place in school economics libraries. Given the level at which it is pitched, I suspect that this will be the most common use made of it in schools.

An Introduction to Positive Economics (R. G. Lipsey)
Lipsey's book is likely to be known to most economics teachers, possibly because they used it themselves when studying, use it now for their students, or have rejected it because of its positivist stance. However, with each new edition, it has become less useful for the A-level student and aimed more at the undergraduate market. The latest edition is no exception. As a class text it would have to be used very sparingly since there is much here that is beyond the A-level syllabus. Indeed, the macro section of the latest edition, which relies heavily upon IS-LM analysis, will be beyond most A-level students. Furthermore, given its price and the need to supplement it with a source of applied material, it is likely that the main place where it will be found in future is in departmental libraries. There students will be able to make use of its many excellent sections without having to rely upon it too heavily.

A Textbook of Economics (F. Livesey)
The second edition of this textbook, by an experienced A-level examiner, is thoroughly recommended as a textbook for the second year of a two-year course. It is exactly geared to the appropriate level, providing enough material for the more-able student while managing to explain difficult sections in a manner that the weaker students would find comprehensible. A key feature of the book is the way in which economic theory is related to the real world and this is reinforced by the large number of data-response questions in each chapter. There are also a number of multiple-choice questions at intervals throughout the book. Answers to both types of question can be found in the accompanying teacher's manual. I would not think that this book is suitable for a whole course since students commencing the subject might find that the pace is too fast. However, for the second year, this would be admirable for a teacher searching for a book that combined both a sound theoretical approach with an attempt to provide applied information, relate it to the relevant theory and give students, through the large number of questions, practice at applying their knowledge.

Success in Economics (D. Lobley)
The first edition of this *Handbook* recommended Lobley's book as being very good value for money. The second edition of *Success in Economics* is even more highly recommended. It has been updated to cover the events in the British economy throughout the 1970s. It is thus one of the few textbooks available on the market that is suitable for both the applied and the theoretical aspects of the course. Furthermore, the content and the level of exposition make it suitable for use throughout a two-year course. The second edition has questions and exercises at the end of each chapter, with answers provided for the latter. There are also data-response questions at the end of the book together with suggestions for further reading.

Understanding Economics (Manchester Economics Project)
This has been the core textbook for the Manchester Economics Project from the early 1970s and is written in such a way as to be especially useful to those studying on their own. The two-column layout of the text, combined with the large number of diagrams and clearly presented definitions, make it very easy to read. Each chapter contains a large number of questions with answers at the end of the book. The theoretical material is well explained but the book can be criticised for concentrating almost exclusively on this aspect of the course. This can be avoided by the use of the eleven satellite texts on such topics as 'monopolies and restrictive practices'. However, since these retail at £2.25 each and the textbook itself is £7.95, it is likely to be too expensive for most potential users. Indeed, it is not clear what advantage using the core book plus the additional material would have for the average teacher who is comparing it with the more commonly used combination of a theoretical and an applied textbook. The only case for its use would appear to be for the teacher who wishes to adopt the individual teaching style at which the book is aimed.

The Fundamentals of Economics (A. Morrice)
The book is the economics component of the publisher's Accountancy and Administration Series and is thus not written primarily for A-level students, although the author suggests that it might serve as a preliminary text for them. However, such students are likely to find the style a little unappetising. It is not visually exciting; the layout and presentation seem more suited to an older age group than to school-age readers – even the paper used is drab. The book covers, in a non-mathematical way, the theoretical, descriptive and applied elements of the course although it would need to be supplemented slightly with respect to the more advanced theory in the A-level syllabus and also for a discussion of the UK's current economic situation. There is, for example, as much time spent on unemployment during the 1930s as there is on the unemployment of the 1970s and 1980s. Its possible use would be as a first-year textbook, combined, for example, with Livesey's *A Textbook Of Economics* in the second year. Even for first-year use, there are a number of

problems for the teacher. One of these is the frequent use of summary tables throughout the text, where the degree of compression is such that there is a risk of oversimplification. Another feature is that topics are subdivided to a considerable degree. This obviously assists the reader when he comes to revise, but it is questionable whether it facilitates his understanding of economic concepts.

A Textbook of Economic Analysis (E. Nevin)

Average students would possibly find this a difficult book but it would be ideal for one's more-able students, especially if they have a mathematical background. It is essentially a theoretical book and, on the basic micro-economic material in the A-level course, it is one of the best on the market. However, since many of the tables of data are now a little out of date (e.g. central government expenditure and revenue in 1978), it would have to be supplemented with much applied material. This is most noticeable in the macro-economic sections which are generally a little less effectively treated than the microeconomic material. Although there are no questions at the end of chapters, there is an accompanying workbook and suggestions for further reading appear at the end of each chapter. Even if not adopted for class use, this would be an invaluable book for the teacher who can draw upon it for his teaching.

Advanced Level Economics (J. Nobbs)

The third edition of this textbook has been substantially revised and is a considerable improvement on the previous editions. Many of the attractive features (e.g. the attractive and easy-to-follow layout) have been retained, but this has been combined with a substantial review of the topics covered and the way in which they are presented. As a result this must now be considered to be one of the more suitable of the textbooks on the market for a two-year A-level course and is a serious rival for the prominent position previously held by Stanlake's *Introductory Economics*. The only criticisms are that there are a small number of errors or misprints and also that, as with Stanlake's book, it needs to be supported with a little additional material of a current nature regarding the state of the economy. However, for a teacher who is looking for a book that will provide a thorough basic coverage of the syllabus for the first year, this is recommended.

Approaching Economics (A. Perry)

This book, which started as a Flexistudy course for the National Extension College, is very different from the usual A-level textbook on the market. Each chapter covers a particular topic and, at the start, there is a statement of aims – the various things which the reader should be able to do and to understand by the end. In order to assist in achieving these, each chapter contains a large number of self-assessment questions, together with comprehensive answers. Although teachers might find a few of these a little simplistic – listing the goods and services one provides or filling in missing words in a passage – their general standard is very high. Especially good are the graphical exercises where the reader is asked to plot the relationship between variables such as unemployment and the percentage change in the Retail Price Index, using data provided, in order to deduce for themselves the Phillips Curve. In addition, each chapter concludes with a selection of past A-level essay questions and some suggestions for further reading.

The author's conversational style, helped by a large number of examples, makes the book easy to read. It is well-presented, with frequent references to relevant material from previous sections, and is divided up into short, easy-to-follow sections, with the key points numbered, thus facilitating revision. The content is suitable for all standard A-level courses and tackles many of the current issues of importance, such as the monetarist–Keynesian debate in a clear and not overtly theoretical manner. For many teachers, the clarity of exposition will more than compensate for the need to supplement the material provided in a few areas.

The UK Economy (A. R. Prest and D. J. Coppock (eds.))

At the time of writing, the latest edition of this publication that is available is the ninth, published in 1982. However, if the publishers continue with their policy of producing a new edition biennially, then the next one should be available by the end of 1984 or 85. It is not intended as a textbook but more as a guide to the British economy, and any teacher attempting to use it as a textbook would find it was necessary to be continually inserting various theoretical explanations. However, it is widely used as a source of applied material in conjunction with a more theoretical textbook, especially in the second year of the course – this being the way the authors intend it to be used. It has five sections, all written separately so that the teacher has to cross-reference where necessary. The sections are 'The economy as a whole', 'The monetary, financial and fiscal systems', 'Foreign trade and the balance of payments', 'Industry' and 'Labour', plus a statistical appendix at the end which provides almost all the information that a student might require.

Introductory Economics (G. Stanlake)

The latest edition of this much used textbook, the fourth, has been substantially updated and amended so that it is now definitely an A-level textbook rather than one that would be suitable for both O- and A-level students. Its coverage of the syllabus is very thorough and there are only a very few areas where the teacher might wish to reinforce the treatment. Examples of these would be in the author's treatment of, or omission of, certain advanced theoretical topics (e.g. indifference curves) and in the lack of examples in some of the applied areas (e.g. monopoly control). It is a very readable book and its non-mathematical approach makes it suitable for all students. There are no questions (although the author is the joint author of a suitable workbook) nor is there a bibliography. However, it is to be well recommended and those who rejected earlier editions are urged to examine Stanlake's latest offering.

54 Internal Assessment
Linda Thomas and Malcolm Scriven

Introduction

This chapter critically examines the techniques of assessment that are available for the purpose of internal, diagnostic assessment and argues that the case for the development of criterion-referenced tests is overwhelming.

What techniques of assessment are available?

Sally Brown[1] begins her account of developments in the field of assessment by listing some of the reasons for its existence. She suggests that assessment is perceived as a motivational tool, as a means of gathering information that is useful to other agencies and as a diagnostic instrument. This list bears a marked similarity to the one that appeared in the first edition of this *Handbook* in 1979, and the rationale that it represents is well established. Assessment of student attainment is the conventional way to answer a variety of questions, such as:

1   Which of these A-level economics students should be selected to fill the places available to study economics at university?
2   Which of these PGCE economics-method students have achieved a sufficient level of proficiency to be awarded qualified teacher status?
3   Should this student be introduced to the notion of comparative advantage in international trade or should he or she be given more opportunity to consolidate his/her understanding of the notion of absolute advantage?
4   What can be said about this student's attainment that will assist his/her future employer?

The variety of uses of assessment is not in question; controversy arises only because it is not matched by a similar variety in forms of assessment. Norm-referenced assessment, designed to facilitate selection processes, is universally applied because of the lack of alternative forms (exceptions cover areas of skills development such as car driving, typewriting, piano playing and swimming). The following two examples may help to demonstrate the dangers that arise from exclusive reliance on one form of assessment:

1   Some multiple-choice papers in A-level economics are under attack. It is claimed not that they fail to provide useful information about a student's attainment, but

that they do not discriminate sufficiently well between candidates. In future, even if they are retained, they will probably play a less important part.
2   The practical element in the PGCE examination assesses a student's skills as a teacher. The pervasiveness of norm referencing ensures that even in this situation it is possible for some students to be graded on a four-point scale not in terms of what the grades signify with respect to performance, but as a means of comparison across the student population.

Despite such anomalies, all assessment (both internal and external) in economics continues to be dominated by methods that are designed to do no more than establish a candidate's relative status. Teachers are, of course, accustomed to using norm-referenced forms of assessment in an economics classroom in order to familiarise students with examination processes and pressures and to provide some indication of levels of expectation. In this case it is important to ensure that they have some general knowledge of what the various grades at A, O and CSE economics signify. Some examination boards and universities are now paying considerable attention to this matter. The *Economic Review*[2] contains a question and answer section that sets out what may be described as model answers. *Examinations in Economics*[3] includes a range of student answers, the grades awarded and the examiner's comments.

Given the ready availability of norm-referenced test items, it is tempting to make further use of them as a matter of routine practice. Indeed, they could be said to represent a systematic attempt to assess student understanding and to provide objective data for diagnostic purposes. Many teachers would consider as invalid the use of their own subjective and intuitive assessments of students based on informal observation. On the face of it, this is a powerful defence of the use of norm-referenced tests for diagnostic purposes, so it is important to consider the kind of information that they provide. Norm-referenced tests exist because of the need to make comparisons between individuals. In economics the information usually takes the form of written answers and responses to essay, data-response, stimulus material, short-answer questions and multiple-choice items. What can be inferred about the type and quality of the information provided by such tests?

First, does the information contained in the answers or responses show whether or not the writer has given a successful answer?

In some cases, for example multiple-choice items and

some short-answer questions, answers are either right or wrong and as long as the incidence of guessing is ignored, it can be deduced that the student who answers correctly is successful. It is more difficult to specify precisely what a successful answer to an essay question must contain. For example, Peter Smith, in the *Economic Review*,[4] attempts to answer the essay question:

Explain the operation of the multiplier in a closed economy without government. What effect does the introduction of government and foreign trade have on the operation of the multiplier?

He comments as follows:

Had I not been working to this deadline, there are aspects of the essay which I would have treated differently. For instance, the 'it can be shown that' phrase which introduces the multiplier formula could be replaced with an explanation; the formula in the expanded model could be derived more carefully. My next choice for lingering would be the role of the rate of interest, with an explanation of how changes in the rate of interest may affect the position of the D function through its impact on investment and consumption. No doubt other tutors would choose to emphasise different aspects (p. 23).

In addition, the fact that many essay questions at A, O and even CSE levels are interchangeable does not inspire confidence in the notion of an absolute or objectively determined 'successful' answer and student. What this means is that, in the case of a substantial number of test items, it is possible to categorise an answer as successful only by reference to an agreed marking scheme at a particular level. This is related to the preferences of those chief examiners and teachers who determine the scheme and level.

Secondly, does the information contained in the answers or responses show whether a writer who is judged as relatively unsuccessful has given a 'fairly good', 'competent', 'mediocre' or 'incompetent' answer?

In the case of items where answers are either right or wrong, such information is not provided, although it must be noted that choice of distractor in a good multiple-choice item may give some clues. Furthermore, in the case of essay or data-response questions, such information is not easily accessible for the following reasons. First, as is argued above, the objectivity of the standard against which all relatively unsuccessful responses are measured is not always securely established. Second, the problem of compensation occurs. Does one sentence containing a brilliant piece of creative argument compensate for lack of breadth and, if so, to what extent? Does a 'neat argument' or 'more assurance' compensate for omissions or errors and, if so, to what extent?

Examinations in Economics[5] inadvertently provides some support for this point. In an evaluation of the use of data-response questions, it notes that:

Research into the use of stimulus material has now convinced the Board that the setting of a single, open-ended question on a given set of data may invite such a wide variety of responses from candidates that co-ordination of marking standards is made considerably more difficult than it need be (p. 6).

This does little to dispel doubts about the best way of categorising responses to open-ended essay questions.

Thirdly, does the information contained in the answers or responses convey much about what students know and understand?

It may be possible to deduce what a 'successful' student understands and knows but it depends on the ability to state what any one item is attempting to test and to agree on the characteristics of a 'successful' answer.

It is more difficult to identify what relatively unsuccessful students know or understand because what their answers show most clearly is their *lack* of knowledge or understanding. And this is, of course, what test constructors intend. It is a salutary and frustrating experience to take part in a group discussion of particular answers if the aim is not to grade the answer but to reach agreement on what the evidence means in terms of understanding. Local groups who wish to take up Keith Wood's suggestion in Chapter 56 of this *Handbook* and attempt this kind of exercise, should be aware that it is not an easy task.

The problem is that the information contained in most answers is inaccessible and imprecise. It is possible to argue that this is an inevitable by-product of a process that attempts to assess higher-order skills such as 'planning, organisation and development of an extended argument in a logical way, the selection and marshalling of a range of facts, concepts and relationships into a coherent discussion'.[6] But is this true? Consider the question that was examined in detail in the *Economic Review*:[7]

The Treasury is proposing further cuts in expenditure when output and employment are falling fast. It is the recession itself which is responsible for the increase in expenditure through increased unemployment benefit which, by automatic stabilisation, counteracts the fall in private sector income. This form of public spending, together with the related falls in tax revenue, must mean that the public sector borrowing requirement should be allowed to fluctuate with the trade cycle. The PSBR should never have a fixed target value (*The Times* Newspapers Ltd).
Explain why you agree or disagree with this statement.

This question is probably a perfect norm-referenced instrument since it tests students' ability to marshal their material so as to construct a coherent and relevant answer while ensuring that the material itself is wide ranging and complex, both in terms of theory and policy. It is possible to predict that most answers will be amorphous, relaying very little information either about what students know in terms of the material or about what they can do in terms of higher-order skills. This is the inevitable result of a process that is extremely efficient in determining what they cannot do. A teacher attempting to test if students can apply higher-order skills would aim to remove all barriers to effective demonstration, by students, of their understanding, knowledge and skills, by including additional questions such as the following:

1   Who, in your opinion, is more likely to have written this – a Keynesian or a monetarist?

2 How can you tell?

3 In general, do Keynesians and monetarists differ with regard to their views of the causes of the recession, the effect of government spending, the composition and influence of the PSBR and the demand for money?

These questions should give a more precise account of the extent of understanding.

Fourth, does the information contained in the answers or responses provide any clues as to why students fail to give a successful answer?

The comments made by an examiner in *Examinations in Economics*[8] on a student answer to the question:

> What are externalities in economics? If an externality has an adverse effect how might it be controlled?

shows that it is sometimes possibly to do this:

> The candidate obviously had some difficulty with terminology and this probably explains the lack of a full, clear-cut definition (p. 37).

However, even in this case, nothing can be deduced about the *reason* for the difficulty with terminology. The possibilities are many – inability to classify an externality; inability to identify the characteristics of an externality; lack of knowledge of the full range of externalities; inability to articulate, in writing; inefficiency of recall mechanisms. Unfortunately, the evidence is inconclusive.

In conclusion, it may be argued that the information provided by norm-referenced tests does not help teachers to identify what the majority of students can do, and it does not assist in the diagnosis of learning difficulties.

An alternative form of assessment?

If teachers are not to be expected to rely on their own haphazard and informal 'hunches' about students' achievements, tests need to be constructed that provide:

1 valid and reliable information about what students know, understand and can do;

2 precise information about what students cannot do;

3 information that aids diagnosis of causes of failure.

In short, the need is for criterion-referenced assessment.

The construction of criterion-referenced tests is dependent on our ability to conceptualise the attainments to be assessed. This involves two processes, at least. First, it is necessary to examine the nature of the knowledge and abilities that define what it means to have a grasp of economics. This concern is also shared by norm-referenced test constructors who wish to design valid tests of economics knowledge and understanding.

Second, it is also necessary to relate the results of the analysis of the nature of economics knowledge to students' behaviour, since criterion-referenced assessment must rely on behavioural indicators of the knowledge that students possess. In other words, we are also concerned to find ways of translating our interpretation of what economics

is about into behavioural criteria. Two problems must be faced at this stage.

First, it is easier to do this in relation to single skills or the kind of simple behaviours that are appropriately defined in terms of 'mastery'. For example, it is not difficult to list those skills that students must master if they are to calculate elasticities correctly; consequently, it is not difficult to state the criteria for judging a successful 'use of the formula for elasticity' performance in operational terms, that is, in terms of well defined, easily recognisable behaviours. But is it adequate to conceptualise all of what we mean by economics understanding as a domain of simple behaviours? Is it possible to describe an understanding of the significance of elasticity and an appreciation of the circumstances in which it may appropriately be used in terms of a hierarchical accumulation of basic skills? Is possession of all identifiable prerequisite skills, such as the ability to compute, to measure, etc., sufficient to guarantee understanding? If the answers to these questions are negative, 'mastery' may be a less useful concept in the context of most economics behaviour than the notion of 'more or less'. This makes the construction of criterion-referenced tests more difficult, since what must be done is to find ways of translating the *development* of complex knowledge and abilities into operational terms. But the problem must be faced unless the criteria against which student attainment is assessed are merely to define those economic behaviours that are capable of being mastered.

Unfortunately, attempts to deal with this difficulty may generate a second problem, because the kind of discussion that is entailed will almost of necessity be at a rather abstract level. The danger is that its product will also be couched in abstract terms rather than in terms of the subject content and skills that are reflected in normal classroom work. In order to ensure that tests are not only valid expressions of economics competence but also of use to the teacher, the design process should incorporate an attempt to investigate the way students behave in relation to classroom material. The kind of relationships on which students focus, the way in which they take account of the influence of more than one variable, the way they handle data, the way they represent organisations and processes, the way they classify and construct models, the way they quantify, etc., should have an influence on the specification of criteria, and eventually on test construction.

What are the implications of the use of criterion-referenced tests for diagnostic purposes?

The tasks that are involved in designing criterion-referenced tests in economics have yet to be fully mapped and it is still not possible to say whether or not the programme described above is a complete description. It is possible, however, to infer that their use will have certain implications. Full implementation of criterion-referenced assessment demands action by teachers and/or students in response to diagnosis of its results. Advocates of criterion referencing should point out that it may imply the need to allocate different work to different students. It may also take far more time than informal class-questioning techniques.

One of the most demanding tasks associated with the introduction of criterion-referenced accounts of student achievement is that of devising sufficiently succinct summary statements that show the complexity of their attainments in the different aspects of economics. Graded tests, which group and label a set of comparable tasks, may provide one answer. The greater use of the profile, one example of which is given in Appendix 54.1, may also lead to the development of more efficient and sophisticated techniques.

Conclusion

It is argued above that techniques of assessment should be appropriate for the purpose of assessment. The move towards the development of criterion-referenced tests in economics may reflect an increasing dissatisfaction with an enforced reliance on norm-referenced instruments.

Appendix 54.1: Peel College – Economics Department profile (Malcolm Scriven)

The department's involvement in profiling began in September 1983 following some experience of the City and Guilds 365 profile.

There were misgivings about our system of record keeping. The simple recording of a mark was really an inadequate guide to a student's strengths and weaknesses; secondly, it became clear that some skills and abilities required for the A-level exam were being assessed in a haphazard and unreliable fashion.

We decided to amend our recording system and institute a more formal means of communication between teacher and students within the department.

The result was the Student Progress Review (see Table 54.1). The introduction was taken from the AEB syllabus while the ten categories broadly cover the areas in which we assess students' performance.

It was intended that the form should meet four main objectives:

1 Clearly demonstrate the areas in which students are expected to perform.
2 Provide students with a clear statement of the teacher's professional assessment of their exam potential.
3 Provide economics staff with a more detailed picture of each student's strengths and weaknesses.
4 Indicate areas for remedial action.

The form is completed termly and signed by both the teacher and Head of Department. At the first review, the system is explained in some detail to the students and they are made aware that staff expect more effort to be expended in the weaker areas. The completed forms are then distributed and staff are prepared to discuss any uncertainties, doubts, etc. with the students.

It soon became clear that the successful completion of the form depended on fairly accurate staff records. In order to achieve this a card index system was introduced. A card is completed for each economics student and simply contains brief comments on each piece of completed work – data-response, multiple-choice and essays. In this way, learning difficulties should be spotted at an early date and communicated (and/or underlined) to the student via the Progress Review.

We feel that our approach, using the five-box system referenced to the A-level examination, is an appropriate starting point. However, a profile is more than this:

1 Profiling is, essentially, a process that stimulates discussion between teacher and taught. The box scheme represents a teacher's professional opinion relating to exam potential and so is not negotiable.
2 Its scope is entirely academic. The information it records is therefore too narrow in scope to provide sufficient evidence for an UCCA or job reference.

To meet these drawbacks, we have introduced a second side to the profile which deals with the more subjective forms of assessment that teachers are required to make. The questions are drawn from the College's internal report forms that are used as the basis for confidential references. This part of the profile is written in the presence of the student and must be the product of consensus. Where no agreement can be reached, both opinions must be recorded, and the document is then signed by both the teacher and student.

In addition to providing evidence for references, the second side of the profile is designed to explore in more detail the student's performance and suggest reasons for progress or lack of it. We hope that this process will highlight strengths and weaknesses and suggest strategies for improving the student's work.

At present, only the Progress Review is being operated within the department, and students are about to receive their second assessment. It is, therefore, too early to evaluate the scheme. However, student reaction is generally favourable (although a little apprehensive), and several students show signs of increased motivation. An encouraging number have taken positive steps to remedy weaknesses shown in the first review, and there appears to be an increased awareness of the demands of an A-level course. However, the scheme must be executed with care because it is easy to intimidate the weaker student. A higher than usual number of students have considered leaving the course, largely because they are more aware of their weaknesses. It is likely, therefore, that more students than usual will not proceed to the second year of the course.

For the scheme to be fully effective in improving student motivation and performance, the department intend to develop resources (worksheets, exercises, etc.) to assist students to overcome the more common forms of learning difficulty.

Table 54.1

Economics Department
Student Progress Review

Name: _____ T. G. _____ Date: _____

The purpose of this review is to provide you with a clear picture of your strengths and weaknesses with regard to economics and to contribute towards any references that may be written at the end of your course. The skills and attributes included in this review thus reflect the demands of your A-level examination and personal characteristics of interest to universities, polytechnics and employers.

Study this review carefully, discuss it with your teacher, and take action to eliminate weaknesses.

Key $\boxed{1}$ = High standard achieved.

      $\boxed{2} + \boxed{3}$ = Adequate standard achieved for a minimum pass but more work required in this area.

      $\boxed{4} + \boxed{5}$ = Inadequate standard that requires immediate remedial action.

	5	4	3	2	1
1 Factual knowledge					
2 Knowledge of theory					
3 Understanding of theory					
4 Ability to apply appropriate theory to the solution of problems					
5 Ability to construct logical arguments					
6 General presentation and use of English					
7 Ability to understand and interpret data					
8 Ability to understand diagrams					
9 Ability to construct accurate diagrams					
10 Awareness of contemporary economic and political events					

(a) What parts of the course have been well done?
(b) What parts of the course have been badly done, and why?
(c) Level of general interest in the subject.
(d) Ability to persevere and work independently.
(e) Ability to organise work and meet deadlines.
(f) In what ways has the work improved or developed?
(g) Does present standard match ability?
(h) Relationships with staff and students.
(i) What action, if any, needs to be taken?
(j) Other comments.

Student's signature .... Staff signature ....

Notes and references

1 Brown, S., *What Do They Know? A Review of Criterion-referenced Assessment* (HMSO, 1980).
2 *The Economic Review* is produced by the Department of Economics, University of Southampton, and is published by Philip Allan Publishers Ltd.
3 Associated Examining Board, *Examinations in Economics* (AEB, 1984).
4 Smith, P., *Economic Review*, vol. 1, no. 4.
5 Associated Examining Board, op. cit.
6 Ibid.
7 *Economic Review*, vol. 1, nos 3 and 4.
8 Associated Examining Board, op. cit.

55 Economics Examinations at A-level*

Frank Livesey

*An earlier version of this chapter appeared in *Economics*, vol. XIII, pt 1, no. 57, spring 1977, pp. 11–15.

Introduction

In recent years there have been marked changes in the format of A-level (and O-level) examinations, with the introduction of objective-test questions and questions based on data or stimulus material. In this chapter the reasons for these changes are discussed, first in terms of the general advantages and disadvantages of each type of question, and second in relation to particular examples of each question type. Finally, some of the implications of the changes for teaching are explored.

Essay questions

Although some questions are far more open-ended than others, in general, essay questions allow candidates to write what they know; they are less constrained than with other types of question. This freedom would probably be considered by most people to be a strength of essay questions. Another important advantage is 'the scope for assessing higher order skills. These include the planning, organisation and development of extended argument in a logical way, the selection and marshalling of a range of facts, concepts and relationships into a coherent discussion, and the underlying skills of expression in coherent and extended prose.'[1]

Perhaps the most obvious disadvantages of essay questions are that the examination can cover only a limited part of the syllabus, and that variations in marking standards may arise because of subjective factors, that is, because they are marked by people and not by machines!

Objective-test questions

Objective-test questions overcome these two disadvantages of essay questions. It is also claimed that they make it more difficult for candidates to be drilled in 'standard answers', that is, they provide a more genuine test of understanding. (The substantial increase that has occurred over time in the average score on objective-test papers suggests that this advantage may be less marked than once thought.) Furthermore, they penalise more severely than do essay questions candidates whose verbal expression may be poor but who are strong in other abilities (e.g. a good numerical sense). In other words, a combination of essay and objective-test questions allows a wider range of skills and abilities to be tested.

Data-response (stimulus material) questions

While the inclusion of objective-test questions improves an examination in terms of the various criteria mentioned above – syllabus coverage, testing of a wide range of abilities, etc. – there are several reasons for thinking that further improvement has resulted from the introduction of data-response questions.

First, the previous format gave an incomplete and biased view of the nature of economics. The methodology of economics is part deductive and part inductive, whereas examinations comprising essay and objective-test questions have a strong deductive orientation. This is due partly to the fact that the models used or implied (especially in objective-test questions) are mainly deductive, and partly to the fact that it is difficult to set questions using actual observations which form the basis for the inductive process. Data-response questions can help to correct this bias, as shown below.

Secondly, since deductive models tend to abstract from reality while inductive models relate more closely to actual events, data-response questions allow a greater measure of reality to be introduced into examinations. This is a very important consideration in view of the feeling that appears to be growing at all stages of the educational system that economics, as it is taught, is becoming increasingly divorced from the real world.[2]

Thirdly, data-response questions encourage the development of abilities – namely the interpretation and manipulation of data – that are important both to candidates who hope to study economics beyond A-level and to those for whom an A-level course is part of the preparation for 'good citizenship'.

Finally, the inclusion of data-response questions makes the examination more flexible in the sense that it allows examiners to use data that would be too involved for objective-test questions, or quotations that would be too long for an essay paper.[3]

Some sample questions

The main lines of the argument presented above are now illustrated by reference to examples of each of the three types of question. These examples can be seen as representative in the sense that they would be serious contenders for inclusion in an A-level paper.[4] The questions are grouped under the broad headings of microeconomics, macroeconomics and government economic policies.

1 Microeconomics

1 Show how prices are set in (a) perfectly competitive, and (b) monopolistic markets.
2 'A firm maximises profits when marginal costs equal average costs.' Comment.

3 What factors determine changes in the demand for a product? What problems arise in the real world for a firm seeking to estimate demand?
4 Demonstrate, with the aid of diagrams, how buffer stocks might be used to achieve a greater measure of stability in the price of agricultural products.

A number of points can be made about this sample of essay questions. First, and perhaps most obviously, different questions require a different depth of understanding. For example, question 1 could probably be answered satisfactorily by regurgitation of notes, whereas question 2 could not. Secondly, there is a strong deductive bias to the questions. Both questions 1 and 2, despite their differences, require reference to two deductive models. Thirdly, although it is possible to introduce elements of 'reality' (questions 3 and 4), such questions tend on the whole to be answered very badly. This presents a dilemma to the examiner. He may continue to set this type of question, hoping that eventually the standard of answers will improve, but knowing that in the meantime, with a high proportion of poor answers, the questions will fail to discriminate adequately. Alternatively, he may seek to test candidates' understanding of the area in a way that is likely to produce a more satisfactory response. The role of data-response questions in this context is discussed below, but first a number of objective-test questions are examined:

5 The profit-maximising position is that at which:
  (a) average cost is at a minimum;
  (b) marginal cost equals average cost;
  (c) an increase in output would result in marginal revenue exceeding marginal cost, while a decrease in output would result in marginal cost exceeding marginal revenue.
  (d) the profit per unit produced is at a maximum;
  (e) the difference between total revenue and total cost is at a maximum.

6 In Figure 55.1, the profit-maximising output is:
(a) *OA*; (b) *OB*; (c) *OC*; (d) *OD*; (e) OE.

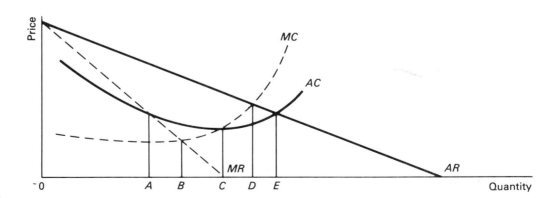

Figure 55.1

7   Profits will be increased as a result of price discrimination between two markets provided that demand is:
(a)   inelastic in at least one market;
(b)   inelastic in both markets;
(c)   more elastic in one market than in the other;
(d)   increasing in both markets;
(e)   increasing in the market in which the higher price is charged.

The advantage of questions 5–7 is that they penalise those candidates who do not *understand* the relevant model (e.g. the 15 per cent who, when the questions were piloted, answered (c) in question 6). Other characteristics of these quesions that may be considered to be less satisfactory are that the models are again deductive and that there is little explicit reference to actual events or situations. In terms of this last point, objective-test questions are less satisfactory than essay questions.

Turning to data-response questions, consider first a question that examines an area also covered by question 4:

8   Further evidence that the whole future of raw material supplies and prices is entering a new era of control by producers, which could be similar to OPEC in oil, has been provided recently in both the copper and tin markets. Rio Tinto-Zinc, the British-based international mining group, has been acting on behalf of a number of leading copper producing countries to deal with the problem of surplus supplies, especially in Japan, depressing copper prices to a level which is below the cost of production for many mines.

The basic idea is to organise a financial consortium to take over, and effectively remove from sale at current prices, the huge surplus of copper supplies in Japan – estimated at some 250 000 tonnes – and also to obtain world-wide agreement to cut back production to levels more suited to the present low demand.

It was the export of surplus copper by Japanese smelters, who refine ore concentrates into copper, when domestic demand plummeted after the oil crisis, that was the major influence in the collapse of world copper prices last year from a peak of £1400 to £500 a tonne in the space of a few months.

The Japanese government, bowing to requests from developing countries dependent on copper for the bulk of their export earnings, banned further exports in November. Since then, however, it has been faced with surplus stocks piling up and threatening to bankrupt the smelters. (*Source*: Extracted from an article in *The Financial Times* 21 April 1975.)

(a)   How would you explain the fact that copper prices had fallen to a level 'below the cost of production for many mines'?
(b)   Can selling copper at this price ever be a sensible policy?

(c)   Assuming that a consortium could be formed that would buy up the surplus supplies of copper, what factors would influence the extent to which such a policy would be commercially successful?
(d)   Indicate in two or three sentences the basis on which a reasonable target price might be determined.

By comparison with question 4, the above question is more helpful to candidates in that it provides guidance, in the second paragraph, as to how a buffer stock system operates. This guidance should make it less likely that candidates would repeat the error that frequently arose in answer to question 4, namely, a confusion of stability of price with stability of income.

At the same time, the question is more demanding in that it tests candidates' understanding of cost concepts. This illustrates another characteristic of data-response questions, namely their ability to span more than one part of the syllabus, and thus to emphasise the interrelatedness of the subject.

9   The Delight Chocolate Co. makes a range of specialist chocolate and sugar confectionery goods, liqueur chocolates, fondants, bon-bons, etc. The company restricts the distribution of its products to a limited number of 'high-class', independent retailers, whose image is consistent with the quality image of the 'Delight' brand name, which the company wishes to foster.

As a very expensive brand, a high proportion of Delight sales are for the gift market. This results in a strong seasonal pattern of sales, with about one-half of orders from retailers coming in the October–December period. This is in turn reflected in a seasonal pattern of production; although the company tries to even out the fluctuations by producing for stock, there is a limit beyond which it feels it would be unwise to go in this respect, since the product has a limited shelf-life. Consequently, during the first half of the year the company operates at below full capacity.

In February of one year, when Delight's level of activity was at about its lowest point, the company was approached by the buyer of a large chain store, which offered to buy a large quantity of Delight's major lines, at a price of £3 a box. The boxes would be labelled not with the Delight brand, but with the brand name of the store, and delivery would be made during May and June.

Delight normally sold this line to retailers at a price of £3.75 a box, the usual retail price being around £4.80. The average cost of production of this line based on the normal volume of sales was calculated as follows:

Direct material and labour	£2.70
General administration	£0.48
Selling and advertising	£0.12
Total cost per box	£3.30

Profit levels in the industry during the previous few years had on the whole been unsatisfactory, mainly because of a fall in the consumption of chocolate and sugar confectionery. Delight had been one of the few companies that had succeeded in maintaining its profits, and this was felt to be due largely to the fact that it produced only high-quality expensive lines. The general view in the industry was that these recent trends were likely to continue.

Should Delight take the order from the chain store?

Question 9 is traditional in the sense that it explores the implications of the split between fixed and variable cost. However, it does require a modification of the traditional model, to take account of the fact that the demand curve is not continuously variable. Incidentally, although the Delight Comapny is, of course, hypothetical, the decision to be made here is one that frequently confronts firms in reality. Another important difference from the more traditional approach is the element of uncertainty inherent in this situation. (It has often been pointed out that under the assumptions of the traditional models, and especially of the perfect competition model, to speak of decision-taking by individual firms is usually a misuse of language.)

2 Macroeconomics

This area can be dealt with rather quickly because most of the points made in relation to microeconomics also apply here. It is suggested that the sample of questions below support the following conclusions. Essay questions may be of varying difficulty but give considerable scope to candidates. Objective-test questions are more specific, but may provide a better test of candidates' understanding of concepts. Data-response questions give scope for the application of traditional models, provide more guidance to candidates, but are more demanding.

10 Examine the role of investment in determining the level of national income.
11 Explain how knowledge of the numerical values of the accelerator and the multiplier could assist the government in its attempt to control the economy.
12 What are the main factors that determine the level of government spending? What are the effects of this level of spending on the economy?
13 Which of the following is most likely to lead to a fall in the value of the multiplier?
(a) reduction in interest rates;
(b) lowering of tariff barriers in the country;
(c) more even distribution of wealth;
(d) more even distribution of income;
(e) reduction in the rate of personal taxation.
14 Given a marginal propensity to save of 0.2, a marginal propensity to import of 0.15, and a marginal propensity to taxation of 0.05, the value of the multiplier would be:
(a) 0.2; (b) 0.4; (c) 0.8; (d) 2.5; (e) 5.0?

15 An investment project generates an additional 100 units of gross income, of which 80 per cent comprises income from employment and 20 per cent income from profits.
Tax is levied at the following rates:

on earned income	25%
on profits	50%
on expenditure (except imports)	20%

The marginal propensity to consume is two-thirds of disposable income. One-quarter of expenditure comprises imports (which are not subject to tax). Companies distribute all their after-tax profits as dividends (not subject to further taxation).
(a) What proportion of the gross income derived from the initial investment is (i) paid as taxation, (ii) saved, (iii) spent on imports?
(b) By how much will income eventually rise following the additional investment?
(c) Describe in a few sentences why the operation of the accelerator might be expected to lead to a rise in income different from that calculated above.

It will be noticed that the model is more fully specified in question 15 than in question 14. (In particular, it is made clear that MPC is related to disposable income.) This need for full specification is emphasised by the fact that in question 14 the number of respondents answering (e) (27 per cent) was greater than the number (25 per cent) identifying the key (d).

3 Government economic policies

This is an area of the syllabus in which data-response questions have a marked comparative advantage. Since examiners do not wish to encourage candidates to memorise large volumes of facts about the reasons for, or the effects of, government policies, they are often forced to set rather routine questions, as follows:

16 What is meant by regional policy? How can it contribute to the future economic development of the UK?
17 Analyse the changes that have taken place in recent years in the methods by which the Bank of England controls the commercial banks in the UK.
18 Examine the economic arguments for and against the sale of council houses to council tenants.

Despite the inclusion of 'analyse' and 'assess', in practice it is often found that such questions test little more than the candidate's knowledge. Nor are things any better with objective-test questions.

19 A collective restrictive agreement may be justified before the Restrictive Practices Court on any of the following grounds, *except* that the removal of the restriction would:
(a) lead to an increase in merger activity;
(b) deny to the public specific and substantial benefits.

(c) cause a substantial reduction in export business;

(d) have a serious and persistent effect on unemployment;

(e) reduce protection to the public against injury.

20 Special Drawing Rights are assets of members of the:

(a) International Bank for Reconstruction and Development;

(b) European Investment Bank;

(c) International Monetary Fund;

(d) European Social Fund;

(e) International Finance Corporation.

By contrast, data-response questions can be set that call for a more searching analysis of government policies.

21 Drawing on the data in Tables 55.1, 55.2 and 55.3, assess the success of regional policy.

22 Concern has been expressed regarding the growth of public expenditure. But in an article in *The Financial Times* (18 June 1981), Samuel Brittan argued that in order to evaluate this growth it is necessary to distinguish between the following categories of public expenditure:

(a) The hard core of goods and services provided by the public sector, such as defence, public health and educational services which are not put through the markets.

(b) Purchases by the public sector of marketable products, mostly from the private sector (e.g. textbooks for use in state schools).

(c) Public-sector provision of marketable outputs, including the output of the nationalised industries.

(d) Private consumption or investment financed by government transfers and subsidies, such as pensions or welfare benefits.

Explain which of the above categories is/are most relevant if one is concerned with (i) the effects of public provision on freedom of consumer choice, (ii) the effect on productive efficiency, including the distribution of labour, (iii) the tax burden and disincentives.

Implications for teaching

All the major examination boards have moved from an A-level examination based entirely on essay questions to a 'suite' of papers incorporating essay, objective-test and

Table 55.2   Rates of unemployment in assisted areas, June 1981

	%
Special development areas	16.5
Development areas	14.2
Intermediate areas	11.3
Unassisted areas	9.0
Great Britain	10.9
Northern Ireland	18.0

Source: Employment Gazette.

Table 55.3   Regional preferential assistance expenditure in Great Britain (£ millions)

1972–3	254	1976–7	717
1973–4	340	1977–8	508
1974–5	473	1978–9	628
1975–6	669	1979–80	567

Table 55.1

	Regional GDP per head *		Index of regional variation** of unemployment		
	1971	1980	1971	1975	1980
North	87.1	92.7	167	141	147
Yorks and Humberside	93.2	92.7	115	96	106
East Midlands	96.5	97.4	87	90	89
East Anglia	93.8	94.4	94	86	79
South East	113.8	115.1	60	70	66
South West	94.7	94.9	97	117	94
West Midlands	102.7	94.7	87	101	104
North West	96.1	95.0	116	130	129
Wales	88.4	87.3	131	136	138
Scotland	93.0	96.0	174	127	139
Northern Ireland	74.3	74.9	227	181	186

*As percentage of UK average.
**Regional unemployment rate as percentage of Great Britain's rate.
Source: Economic Trends.

data-response questions. This change has several important implications for teaching.

First, candidates have to be made aware of a wider range of microeconomic models. Particularly important here is the fact that models of the theory of the firm that involve marginal analysis cannot easily be applied to data-response questions concerned with price or output decisions, especially when the questions relate to actual, rather than hypothetical, situations. Concepts and topics that are often found useful include full-cost pricing, price leadership and decision-taking under uncertainty.

To avoid confusion in the minds of candidates when presented with alternative models, it should be emphasised that the traditional models are intended to throw light on the allocation of resources at the level of the market, while the alternative approach encompasses the procedures and policies of individual firms.

Secondly, data-response questions discriminate fiercely between candidates who understand concepts and realise which concepts are relevant in particular situations and those who have simply learned lecture notes or sections of a book. This implies that teachers need to spend time – in class and/or via homework – helping students to understand how economic analysis can be used to solve problems or illuminate issues, including those arising from government policy.

Thirdly, objective-test questions can be used in a dual function, as practice for examinations and as a means of testing students' understanding. (Asking students why they chose a wrong option is often illuminating, albeit depressing.)

Teachers will, of course, wish to ensure that their students do justice to themselves in the examinations, that they make the best use of their knowledge and understanding of the subject. In this context it is helpful to know what the examiners expect. Many examiners meet teachers at events sponsored by the examination boards, the Economics Association, etc. Guidance is provided on a regular basis in examiners' reports. Finally, boards occasionally publish material that offers more detailed guidance. For example, the AEB publication already referred to contains passages selected from the work of candidates entered for recent examinations. For each question the candidate's answer is accompanied by a commentary from the chief examiner outlining the strengths and weaknesses of the answer and indicating the level of performance. The chief examiners also draw some more general conclusions:

> There is clearly a need for candidates to be familiarised with data in a wide variety of forms in their preparation for the data response paper: time series and cross-sectioned data, tables, charts and graphs, and data in such forms as percentages and index numbers .... It is worth reminding candidates that it is the Board's current policy not to set data-response questions which involve a large amount of calculation. Where a significant amount of numerical data is included in a question, as in this example, it is not there purely for the purpose of calculation. Nevertheless, many candidates wasted time by performing needless calculations.[5]

Notes and references

1 The Associated Examining Board, *Examinations in Economics* (AEB, 1984) p. 3.

2 See, for example, Ward B., *What's Wrong with Economics* (Macmillan, 1972); Worswick, G. D. N., 'Is progress in economic science possible?', *Economic Journal*, vol. LXXXII, 1972; Elkan, W., 'How one might teach economics to undergraduates', *Economics*, vol. XI, pt 4, no. 52, winter 1975; Heathfield, D., and Hartropp, A., 'What economists do', *Economics*, vol. XIX, pt 2, no. 82, summer 1983.

3 Additional flexibility is afforded to examiners when a board adopts a policy 'to set stimulus material questions in which the majority of the marks can be obtained for displaying skills directly to the handling of the data supplied, but with the possibility of inviting candidates also to write answers involving the use of additional relevant material' (The Associated Examining Board, op. cit., p. 6).

4 The essay questions have appeared in recent A-level papers. Other questions are taken from Livesey, F., *Objective Tests in A Level Economics*, 2nd edn (Hodder & Stoughton, 1979); and Livesey, F., *A Textbook of Economics*, 2nd edn. (Polytech Publishers, 1982).

5 The Associated Examining Board, op. cit., p. 27.

56   Teacher Groups For Curriculum Development
Keith Wood

Why teacher groups?

Through the mutual support, shared experience and critical appraisal of each other's ideas that a group of teachers meeting together can provide, it is possible to achieve progress with curriculum development and simultaneously to improve the teaching of economics. This is especially valuable where economics teachers find themselves working alone in the subject and yet are very much aware of the nagging doubts they might have about the exam, the need to introduce a wider range of teaching methods to increase motivation, and the application of economic understanding or the need to make assessment a more effective tool for diagnosis.

Teachers working together on a problem, whether it be the development of materials for teaching, the production of a syllabus or simply pooling of teaching ideas, may provide each other with access to broader experience of teaching situations than one teacher can have, and the possibility of discussing ideas with colleagues that might otherwise remain undeveloped. There is evidence available now from a range of curriculum projects that have used teacher groups,[1] including the Economics Education 14–16 Project,[2] that the formation of teacher groups can be effective in the development of the curriculum. That is not to say that any group of teachers will necessarily be productive, because there are problems associated with motivating, leading and sustaining interest in group work. But examples do exist of successful and innovative groups which are nurtured by economics teachers for the valuable spin-offs that they yield for their own economics teaching.

The curriculum model most suited to teacher group work is one that puts fewest constraints on teachers at the outset. Teachers need to explore areas that they regard as problematic for them and where outcomes are likely to be useful to them. Of course, much of the evidence on teacher groups springs from the experiences of groups that have been established by curriculum projects. In many cases these have attempted to hand down a philosophy and a strategy for action. Where the groups have failed, this may have been part of the reason. The point to be made is that teachers of economics should not await the call but that, if there is perceived need, there is nothing to stop a teacher arranging an exploratory meeting with his/her colleagues in school or, through the local Economics Association branch or activity centre or via the LEA adviser or any other network, arranging a meeting with other teachers to share ideas and to seek advice, guidance and support from others about development work. It may be valuable to involve external agencies where particular expertise is thought to be lacking. The starting point need not be objectives as in curriculum theory, or subject-matter as in traditional curricula, although inevitably each area of the curriculum hinges on another and the problems interlink as Figure 56.1 suggests. All of the dimensions of this model provide starting points for development work.

Teacher groups need not be large to be effective. Indeed, small groups of, say, five members develop more often than not an internal cohesion that leads to regular and constructive inputs and the growth of group loyalty.

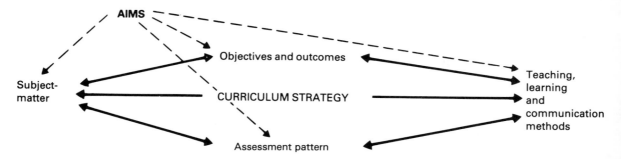

Figure 56.1 Sources: Eraut, M., et al., The Analysis of Curriculum Materials *(University of Sussex Education Area Occasional Paper 2, 1975).*

What areas?

Here are some areas where teacher groups may generate some valuable outcomes.

1 The development of teaching materials and the trialling of new materials in schools and colleges. A good example of teacher group progress in this area has been in the development of CAL materials. Teachers are able to share experience and play an important role in formative evaluation. The Computers in the Curriculum Project has some experience of this, and so has the Economics Education 14–16 Project. Both of these projects' activities have been heavily funded but it is not essential to have a major curriculum development project at the centre to initiate teacher group action. LEAs have facilitated materials development and one of the Economics Education 14–16 Project's groups has worked on materials sponsored by the Banking Information Service on the theme of 'money management'.

2 Ways of teaching particular topics. More ideas like those in this *Handbook* can be shared and developed for use in schools and colleges and, again, evaluation is possible. For example, a group in South Glamorgan has worked on the development of teacher material on how to approach and conduct a case study using local companies. The checklist for teachers preparing to contact local companies generated by this group is immensely valuable, and so is the experience of researching and writing the case studies.

3 Evaluation of published materials (e.g. new texts and CAL units). Linda Thomas[3] has produced an interesting evaluation scheme which might serve as a starting point. Workshops may form the basis of group activity.

4 Appraisal and monitoring of external examinations. Chief examiners are usually willing to discuss exams with teachers at prearranged meetings. Exams often provide vigorous debate and new teachers stand to benefit enormously from discussing exams with more experienced colleagues. Teachers' panels could draw on the views of teacher groups. And teachers can develop Mode 3 syllabuses.

5 Internal assessment techniques designed to diagnose weaknesses in economic understanding are as yet undeveloped. The construction of assessment instruments could be undertaken through teacher group activity, drawing where necessary on external agencies for expertise such as the Economics Research and Curriculum Unit (ERCU) at the London Institute of Education.

6 It may be possible to establish a teacher group to develop and run field studies in economics. The Economics Education 14–16 Project has supported a group working in this area (see the report on the working of the Birmingham Teacher Group[4]).

7 A group may be established to initiate team teaching in a particular school or college or to set up regular area conferences for students. The Education Committee of the Economics Association may be helpful in advising on conference themes and speakers, and the local branch of the Association is likely to have experience of conference organisation.

8 A teacher group may be set up to develop intra-school cross-disciplinary economics teaching. The philosophy and exemplar materials of the Economics Education 14–16 Project would certainly be of interest to such a group.

9 A group might be formed to draw on expertise from external agents such as professional economists and to establish regular updating sessions. Again, the Economics Association may have some experience of this.

In all of the above, new teachers of economics stand to gain from working with more experienced colleagues. And those who have been teaching for some years can be refreshed. This may be reason enough for setting up a group.

Who else can help?

LEA advisers in economics, where they exist (and where they do not, someone must have a responsibility for the subject), could be a starting point for any teacher of economics wishing to establish an initiative. A list of advisers in economics may be obtained from the General Secretary of the Economics Association. Inspectors can be helpful, too. It is in their interest that teachers should be taking active steps to improve the economics curriculum and it is hard to imagine that they would not support a teacher group in some way – if only by providing goodwill, travelling expenses and some limited secretarial help.

The Economics Education 14–16 Project has already been mentioned. It is the major project in economics for this age range and has learned a great deal about operating teacher groups and materials development.

The Education Committee of the Economics Association ought to be able to respond to the needs of economics teachers. The first step may be to contact the local branch or activity centre secretary who will provide a link (see *Economics*, the Association's journal, for a list of names and addresses).

Departments of Education and training institutions may supply expertise and research findings. It needs to be emphasised that it is unlikely that teacher groups will make much headway with educational research without the advice of these external agencies, because the specific expertise required is unlikely to be available within the group, but they may wish to draw on findings to answer questions that crop up in discussion.

Local universities and polytechnics may be a rich source for speakers for teachers' meetings.

The SCDC may be helpful since its predecessor, the Schools Council, supported teacher groups financially for curriculum research and development.

What might be called 'pressure groups' in the context of curriculum development, such as CWDE, BIS and organisations keen to develop schools/industry links, among others, may be supportive of teacher-group initiatives without attempting to influence outcomes.

What are the pitfalls?

At the outset it is important to be clear about the purpose of the group's work – curriculum development, the production of materials, in-service training, dissemination or whatever. Accommodation that meets the group's needs is important. For example, teachers' centres may have more facilities than schools and offer more status. A teacher who is thinking of establishing a group needs to be aware that the teachers who eventually join may come along with a variety of expectations about outcomes, such as access to helpful resources and ideas, contact with colleagues, enhancement of promotion prospects or a break from routine. It is not unusual for teachers to melt away when they realise that they are expected to work on development.

Any outside agencies or experts must not be allowed to dominate because this can disturb the equilibrium of the group and reduce the input of the members. Accepting support may lead to the need for accountability which can be a constraint but may have the positive effect of raising the status of the group, which is important for morale. Later on, there could be problems over copyright of materials.

For the leader of the group there can be some headaches. There is no reason why leadership or co-ordination should not be shared. However, sound leadership is important and requires that the person has a good grasp of the issues involved, can muster sufficient status to draw on the assistance of others, and can motivate the group through structuring tasks, following-up activities and being in a position to determine criteria for assessing progress.

It is essential to be sure about the group's general aims after the first meeting and what the outcomes might be. This first meeting is crucial, for it is from among those attending this meeting that the working group will emerge, if at all. The impact of this initial gathering is so important

that there is much to be gained from having a representative of the LEA present along with any other interested parties. It helps to establish a timetable for activities over the coming weeks, deciding in advance how many meetings will be needed to complete the task and how frequently the group should meet. The time at which the group meets is important, too. If it is to be during school time, members will feel that some recognition is being given to the work, but this may be difficult to arrange. If meetings are to be after school, teachers will be giving up their own time to attend and thus place a higher premium on it. Later on, if the group shows signs of success, it may be possible to arrange secondment for some members.

A teacher group might publish a regular newsletter via the LEA or some other organisation to keep all teachers informed of activities and to enhance the status of the group's work. It is very important that teacher-group members consider that their work is being recognised and that the group can attract new members to sustain its life.

The momentum of the group's work will only be sustained if members are aware that progress towards an outcome is being achieved. The lead is often given by example but leaders should not be indispensable. An effective group will be able to initiate new members and to re-form to take on new tasks as they emerge.

Notes and references

1 Craft, A., *Teacher Groups. Basic Guidelines* (Schools Council, 1980). This publication, which is still available from SCDC, is a must for anyone thinking about setting up a group. It contains a summary of the exprience gained from fifteen projects and provides more detail on the points mentioned above.

2 Smith, D., *An Evaluation Report on the Work of the Project's Stage 2 Teacher Groups* (Economics Education 14–16 Project, 1984). This report summarises the work of the teacher groups set up by the Project. Also available from the Project are separate reports on each of the groups, edited by members. Again these are essential reading for group leaders.

3 Thomas, L., 'An evaluation of classroom materials in economics – a case study', *Economics*, vol. XIX, pt 3, no. 83, autumn 1983.

4 *Economics in General Education. A Report on the work of the Birmingham Teacher Group,* (Economics Education 14–16 Project, 1983).

57 The Head of Department

Lindsey Collings

Introduction

The objective of this chapter is to provide a checklist for a new head of department or for the economics teacher who, although not dignified by the title, has responsibility for the subject throughout the school. The case of the latter may be particularly difficult, as the teacher is likely to be relatively inexperienced, may not have seen a Head of Economics in action, and might be reluctant to seek advice from heads of other subjects. The Economics Association can be especially valuable for someone who is the only economics teacher in a school, and may not even be an economics specialist. Through local meetings, contacts can be made with heads of economics in other schools. If no local branch exists, the local authority adviser can put teachers in touch and self-help groups can be set up.

The work of a head of department is dealt with in depth by Marland,[1] and Marland and Hill.[2] Running an economics department is discussed by Rees.[3] The list of functions of a head of department provided here is not intended to intimidate (although it might well do so!) nor to impress other staff with the amount of work heads of department do (although it seems amazing that this is supposed to fit into perhaps two or three 'free' lessons each week allocated for 'departmental duties'). Rather, the list may help intending heads of department to prepare themselves to undertake these tasks and support newly appointed heads of department who, after their first few months, are certain that they must have omitted some vital aspect of the job!

Characteristics of the head of department

Marland sees the role of the head of department as 'the catalyst and co-ordinator of a team of people [who] is the link between that team and other groups'.[4] He lists the characteristics of a good head of department as:

1 experience of teaching at a variety of levels of ability;
2 wide knowledge of the subject area and of other aspects of education;
3 the knack of relating well to people and of being able to serve their needs and their special qualities;
4 immense energy;
5 a highly developed sense of organisation;
6 the ability to articulate points of view clearly and persuasively.[5]

These are the qualities of any good leader. John[6] has written a great deal on leadership in schools which would be very valuable to a head of department. He has also covered the importance of aims and objectives,[7] and many local authorities see these as being a prime concern of an incoming head of department.

The functions of a head of department

Among the functions listed below are a number of discussion points to encourage new or aspiring heads of department to consider the implications of decisions made in the relevant areas of responsibility. Some of the possible implications arising are noted at the end of the chapter.

1 Staffing

1 *Advise the head* and senior management team on the staffing needs of the department.
2 *Plan ahead* and be aware of the staffing implications of *curriculum change*. Become involved and active in any discussions or working parties on curriculum change to which the department could contribute.
3 Try to appoint staff to build up a *team with complementary skills* but the *same general educational philosophy*.

> **Discussion point A**
> What departmental philosophy would you aim at achieving?
> What are the advantages of such a staffing arrangement and what are the difficulties in trying to achieve it?

4 Write the *advertisement* and *job description* yourself for appointments. Consult and liaise with the senior management team before shortlisting and interviewing. If possible, be open-ended in both until the appointment is made, to take greatest advantage of the skills offered. Too tight a description might deter a suitable candidate who might fit in differently from the way originally envisaged.
5 Develop your own *interviewing techniques* to allow candidates to do most of the talking. Give them open-ended questions with the opportunity to show potential for innovation and suitability for taking responsibility. (Such questions might include solving

an organisational problem or possible content for a non-examined course.)

6 *Allocate subjects and administrative tasks* between staff. Staff need a variety of teaching and non-teaching experiences to maintain their interest and develop their skills. Subjects and tasks can be circulated if the staff have or acquire an overlap of skills and subjects. Also, with an overlap of subjects, a course will not disappear if a teacher leaves.

7 Clearly *delineate duties* of staff, so that they, and others in the school, know who is responsible for what. Confusion over roles prevents jobs from being taken up with enthusiasm. Staff in the department receiving delegated duties may complain that they do not know exactly what they should do, nor do they feel that they have sole responsibility for a particular area. If they can be given some degree of autonomy, then they will feel more valued and their own professional capabilities can develop, leading them on to promotion.

8 The head of department should encourage the right *climate for discussion*, where staff views are heard and innovation encouraged.

9 *Informal contacts* can be very important to help get to know staff and exchange views. Knowledge of the personal circumstances of staff is important in order to understand the outside pressures that may affect their work. Genuine concern and helpful support of others is always appreciated and this does not imply 'prying' or being nosy. Sharing an office or resource area can provide an opportunity for frequent informal contact, but plenty of other occasions may occur, such as during extra-mural activities.

10 *Formal departmental meetings* are also necessary, with an *agenda* and *minutes*. Participation by staff can be on various levels:
   (a) communication – passing on decisions made elsewhere or in the department;
   (b) consultation – asking for the views of others and having a discussion, but the head of department takes the decision without necessarily being bound by the majority view;
   (c) delegation – handing over responsibility for some decisions to others and then being bound by their conclusions;
   (d) participation – where the head of department is prepared to be bound by the decisions agreed on by the majority of staff after a departmental discussion.

Each type of participation may be valuable at different times, or the personal style of the people involved may tend to lead to one form or another. But it is invaluable for the staff to know which kind of situation they are in, otherwise there will be inevitable disappointment if they believe their view is to be final but an opposite decision is taken. When combined with delegation, these formal meetings can encourage an appreciation of general problems and raise the esteem of junior staff who feel that their contribution is valued. Such meetings provide training for future posts of responsibility too. The object of seemingly trivial paperwork can be explained, so that the importance of deadlines and administration may be fully appreciated.

Content of formal meetings. Time is wasted by giving orally general information on dates, where-abouts of resources and other matters needed later for reference. These points are best given out on a printed sheet. Suitable topics for discussion are:
   (a) curriculum planning – discussion of course content and methods;
   (b) evaluation – of courses, methods and materials and revision of each where necessary;
   (c) schemes of work – discussion of progress through courses and order of topics;
   (d) information exchange – on available resources, their use and allocation;
   (e) assessment – of students' standards and progress, moderation of students' work;
   (f) examinations – deciding content of internal examinations and evaluating them, discussion of external examinations and examiners' reports;
   (g) policy – application of the school's policy to the department, discussions requested by senior management;
   (h) courses – reporting back and holding seminars on material covered on courses. Junior staff can often lead here.

11 *Allocation of classes.* Class allocation should *make use of the strengths* of staff but also try to *broaden their experience*. Staff should be familiar with one another's capabilities. This can be achieved by visiting each other's classes and through team teaching.

Discussion point B

What are the objectives of the department? For example, mixed-ability classes? Should teachers have a mixture of classes across the years and ability range or specialise? How should disruptive classes be allocated? Should each difficult class have a different teacher, so that each teacher can find the patience for one class? Should the most senior staff have the most difficult classes? What are the implications of this? Are there staff who are not interested in the academic classes but who have the knack of getting the best from unco-operative students? Should you take advantage of that skill or try to widen the experience of such staff? Should these teachers be sharing their experience and teaching their methods and approaches to the rest of the department, especially new teachers? Which classes should probationers have?

2 Staff development

1 The head of department should *know the aspirations* of the staff and *encourage the development of professional expertise*, through courses and membership and involvement in professional associations. Involvement in extra-curricular activities should also be encouraged. Staff may be unaware of the direction in which they could develop their talents. Discussion, praise, encouragement and support are essential in ensuring high morale and commitment. Heads of department need to ensure their own development too, both within the field of the department and in general school administration to prepare for possible future posts. Records of courses attended should be kept to encourage a coherent programme for each teacher. Evaluation of courses and sharing the benefits is invaluable, especially for in-service training of new staff who can benefit from the acquired experience of courses attended by other teachers. In-service training within the school will become even more important as staff change schools less often and need renewal and remotivation.

2 The head of department should give *kindly support*, tactful discipline and encourage a team approach.

3 *Support new appointees and probationers*:
   (a) letter of welcome after appointment;
   (b) early meeting to discuss syllabuses and resources, and to meet the other members of the department;
   (c) meeting before the start of term to discuss the timetable, class allocation and preparation;
   (d) frequent discussions and moderation to help the new member know the department's standards;
   (e) encourage support for the new teacher from others in the department (who might be more acceptable as confidantes than the head of department).
   (f) encourage visits to permit observation of other classes and teaching styles.

4 *Self-assessment exercises* or, at least, a lengthy discussion on this theme, should take place annually. Staff can be helped to set themselves objectives to achieve a phased development of their careers. They need to consider which parts of their work they enjoy most, which least, and which they need help with. If they need help, what sort would be most appropriate? It is important that these sessions do not turn out to be entirely critical, as no development can occur if the teacher's confidence is destroyed. Preferably, the talk should start and end on a note of praise and encouragement.

5 When staff are ready for promotion to posts of responsibility, the head of department will need *to press for the allocation of salary points for assistants in the department.*

6 Any *report written or reference prepared should be discussed* with the teacher concerned, and if they are not ready for the post they are applying for, this can be a useful step in encouraging appropriate preparation.

7 These points would also apply to helping *student teachers*. Staff should be prepared to take considerable care in training students as the future of the profession depends on them.

3 External relations of the department

1 The head of department is the *public relations officer* for the department. The respect given by others in the school to the department, the amount of resources it receives and the consideration given to its specific needs, all depend on the status of the department, which is created by the head of department.

2 It is necesary for the head of department *to work in a team with other departmental and pastoral heads*. By keeping abreast of their plans, it is possible to be fully aware of changes that will have implications for the department.

Discussion point C

What sorts of changes in other departments might affect economics, for example, in geography, history, careers and other social science subjects?

---

3 *Political skill* is needed in heads of department meetings and where interdisciplinary courses are being organised.

Discussion point D

What might be the penalty of missing or remaining silent during a meeting on the design of the option system? What is the role of the head of economics in discussions on a 'core' curriculum?

---

4 *Liaison with*:
   (a) *the careers staff* – on qualifications for courses and jobs in business and commerce;
   (b) *local employers* – for talks and visits;
   (c) *advisory staff* – of the local authority to ensure full advantage is taken of special funds and courses;
   (d) school *pastoral staff* – they should be informed of academic problems, given copies of communications between the department and parents, and involved in discussions before action is taken in persistent or serious cases. The department can also use the detailed knowledge, held by pastoral staff, of the backgrounds of students in trying to understand their academic progress. The daily contact of tutors with the students can also be valuable if they are willing to help put extra, constant pressure on students who are particularly late in submitting critical pieces of work, such as compulsory projects. Keeping pastoral staff continuously in the picture is important, as a small difficulty that occurs in every subject becomes a large problem, but action can only be taken if pastoral staff are informed. Similarly, serious problems should be communicated before they become disasters. The

head of department will need to talk to heads of year about serious cases, but should also ensure that members of the department pass on information to tutors in minor cases and actually alert the head of department quickly where serious problems are occurring.

5 Departmental *plans must be fully explained to the headteacher* and senior management team. Persuasion may be needed to ensure that the department can carry out these plans, which may affect other parts of the school. It is necessary to show an understanding of the constraints, financial and otherwise, that are affecting the school and how the department could achieve its aims within these constraints.

6 If *disagreements arise*, either between the department and other parts of the school or between individuals in the department and others, then diplomacy will be needed to reach an acceptable compromise while ensuring the continuance of a happy working relationship.

7 A major indicator of the *efficiency of the department* is the way that necessary paperwork is handled. Show an appreciation of the importance of administration by meeting deadlines and ensuring that information is submitted by others in the department on time.

8 The success of students is more likely with *positive parental involvement*. Reports, parents' evenings and communications with parents should all be aimed to achieve this. Parents should know how to help and what the subject involves. Some parents may be overdemanding and others may be uncertain of what the school does. Parents should be helped to feel that they can make a positive contribution to their children's school career.[8] *Tact* will be needed with parents who are aggressive or feel that the school is disrupting family values. Knowledge of family background is needed in helping the student. Care is needed in communications with parents:

(a) reports on individual progress should be constructive;[9]

(b) the reasons for groupings, examination entry, etc. need to be fully explained;

(c) a written description of the commitments needed for the course may be needed;

(d) individual contacts with parents, in person, by telephone or in writing may be needed;

(e) rapid communication of serious problems is necessary, to parents, pastoral staff and to other supportive agencies that may be involved, for example, educational psychologists.

4 Resources

1 The head of department must obtain *funds* for resources. *Capitation* for the purchase of books may be fixed according to a formula for each department, or it may be possible to argue for more funds for new

courses or to overcome particular problems. A good case would have to be made out for more resources as it could mean someone else having a reduction. There may be *separate funds for stationery, audio-visual aids and duplicating*. If money for books is short it may be possible to teach the same topic by using money from other funds (e.g. by using a filmstrip, tape or duplicated notes). There may be money available from the *local authority* for new courses. *Capital equipment and furniture* may also come from other funds. The *Parents' Association* may provide funds for certain items, and in voluntary-aided or private schools the *governors* may have money available too. The *school library* can build up a reference section for the department, or may purchase books for borrowing which can be housed in the department as a departmental library. Departmental libraries are valuable where the library does not have secure borrowing arrangements. If books are likely to disappear from the school library, a secure library in the departmental office will ensure books are widely read and returned. *Students' parents* may fund trips or buy moderately priced leaflets to bring students' notes up to date. *Some resources are free*. A successful head of department will find all the available sources of funds and build up a well-equipped department.

2 *Discuss the allocation of money* with the staff in the department. There will be less cause for complaint if everyone knows that funds are lacking in one area because they have been allocated, by agreement, somewhere else.

3 *Ordering resources.* If you are not on the mailing list of publishers, use the list of Useful Addresses.

(a) Read catalogues as they arrive, mark items of interest and circulate to colleagues.

(b) After comments have been received, keep a list of suitable materials under course headings, ready to be ordered. Note full details of the book, including its ISBN to save looking it up again when ordering.

(c) Order inspection copies of new books as soon as they are available.

(d) If you wish to keep catalogues, store them in a concertina file in alphabetical order. (If you make notes as at (b), you may not need to keep catalogues; they take up a great deal of room.)

(e) Read reviews of resources in the *Times Educational Supplement*, *Economics* (published by the Economics Association) and other journals (if the department includes other social sciences.)

(f) Always look at books brought to the school by visiting publishers' representatives. Discuss new publications with them and give feedback on materials used. Also, make suggestions about new materials needed. Educational publishers are very responsive to comments made in the representatives' field reports.

(g) The teachers' centre may have catalogues of resources, especially in interdisciplinary areas or for younger or lower-ability students. Often, exhibitions are arranged of materials and resource collections.

(h) The Economics Education Project 14–16 has a very useful annotated bibliography of pupil books and is developing a range of materials for the project.[10]

(i) If starting new courses, contact other schools to discuss resources, use examination boards' lists of books, and attend courses where materials may be on display.

(j) When ordering, use all the available information. Check the up-to-date ISBN. This will differ for new editions and paperback editions. If you use a wrong one you will receive the wrong resources, as many LEAs use only the ISBN to order from publishers. To provide a countercheck, include full title, author's name(s) and edition. Check the up-to-date price and if the book is in print (some go out of print in a few months). In some LEAs if the book is out of print you will lose your money, as reordering cannot occur before the end of the financial year and the money will go into general funds, as it cannot be carried forward.

(k) Ask other heads of department or administrative staff to help initially to fill in the order forms.

(l) Keep a record of all orders and check off resources as they arrive.

(m) Keep an account book of actual amount paid on the invoice; prices may change and the discount must be deducted.

(n) Note the running total of money spent and spend it all before the end of the financial year or it may be lost.

(o) Consider covering books with transparent film, or another form of plastic cover: they may last twice as long (see Chapter 26).

4 *Store resources carefully*. Check and *mend damaged books*. Keep a *stock book*, do stock checks annually, and reorder where stocks are low.

5 *Keep careful records of books issued*. Each book should have an individual number and this should be checked on return. All books issued to each student should be recorded, whether on short- or long-term loan. One central file that all staff use when issuing books simplifies the system, as all the records of books issued to one class can be on one loose-leaf sheet. Even if several teachers have issued books to the class and individual students have received departmental library books, the records are together and can be checked off by any available member of the department when returned. It is also easy to see where one particular set of books is, if it is needed by another group. Send letters and try to recover lost books. Often heads of year have a system for recovering books from leavers.

6 Rather than giving a textbook to each student, it may be more flexible to spend the money on a *wide range of alternative books which are shared*. In this way, a group will have access to many texts. This can encourage wide reading at low cost (see Chapter 26). If group sizes change, it allows resources to be more thinly or thickly spread, thus avoiding the need to order more books quickly or leave piles of the standard text unused.

7 *Staff must discipline* themselves to return material and keep records centrally or the system will collapse.

8 *Printed sheets*. Collect sheets prepared by all members of the department. Keep a master file with one copy of all sheets, arranged by topic or class. Class sets can be stored in polythene bags, in box files, or the cheaper cardboard transfer files of the same size. Number the sheets in the master file and in the boxes for ease of retrieval.

9 *Card index*. Keep a card index of non-book resources such as posters, filmstrips, tapes, videos, bank review articles and leaflets, by topic.

10 Keep a bank of *examination papers*, syllabus booklets, examiners' reports, etc. Ensure that changes to the syllabus, etc. are noted and communicated to staff.

11 Keep a stock in the department of *consumables*. Schools have been known to run out of chalk, banda paper or photocopy paper with several months to go before new stock arrives.

5 Content of work

1 *Syllabuses and schemes of work* must be prepared.[11] Exercises to teach *skills* should be incorporated into the scheme of work.[12] Study guides can be used to give the students a scheme of work and to teach note-taking (see Chapter 26). It may be difficult to prepare school syllabuses, as many economics O- and A-level syllabuses are not detailed (see Table 57.1). A study of past papers and attendance at courses, including talks by examiners, can help in drawing up a list of topics. Examiners' reports can show the way topics should be handled. Staff need not follow an internal syllabus slavishly, but it may encourage communication about

Table 57.1 London A-level syllabus extracts

'The functions of the price system' and 'Demand and supply analysis of prices in goods markets, and factor markets, and the application of elementary price theory'. There is no way that the teacher could decide whether these phrases included indifference analysis. For many years no specific questions were asked on indifference curves but suddenly, with no change having been made in the syllabus, questions when indifference analysis was really needed did arise. The only way that the teacher could have decided to include that topic in the internal syllabus would have been by a very careful listing of all topics on examination papers.

the way to tackle a course and provide continuity if staff change. Schemes of work and a plan of the resources needed can be combined into a *year plan* for all classes (Table 57.2). This helps, where there are many classes, to ensure that the same resources are not needed by several classes simultaneously and enables the arranging of visits and administrative tasks over the year so that there is not one frantic period in the year when everything seems to happen at once.

The use of departmental syllabuses and schemes of work makes year-end examinations easier to arrange as classes will be roughly parallel. Schemes can also be used to provide a *record of work*. The head of department should keep in touch with the progress of staff through the course and be aware that in some schools very detailed records of work are kept and may be requested by senior staff.

2 *Keeping up to date with changes in the examination-board syllabuses* is vital. This involves reading communications from the board, attending courses, and even writing to the board for clarification. Keep in touch too with alternative boards. Contacts with staff in other schools is very useful in exchanging information on examinations and especially for

Table 57.2   Year plan

	Third-year economics	Fourth-year personal finance	Fourth-year Brit. Ind. Soc.	Fifth-year Brit. Ind. Soc.	Lower-sixth economics	Upper-sixth economics	Administration
Sept.	Economics 14–16 Project resources on wants and needs	Printed sheets on budget planning	Tape on starting a firm	Book factory visit	TV series *10 X Economics*	Computer game	Record results and analyse
				Discuss drafts of restricted scope projects		Running the Economy	
		Collect interest rates for work on savings	Tape on market research		Computer game on demand and supply		Prepare timetable for student teacher
			Prepare for practice assessment on market research	Trade union talk/video Assessment on trade unions		Collect up-to-date figures for trade	
Oct.	Computer game on demand and supply				Use of class set of workbooks by Stilwell, Lipsey and Clarke*		Prepare examination papers and submit for printing
		Check stocks of blank forms for banking	Arrange talk on loans to firms by bank manager	Factory visit assessment		Give out sets of past papers	
				Marking of assessments		Counsel on UCCA choices	Return projects to students as they are returned by the boards
Half term							
Nov.	Need for notice-board space for display on stages of production	Need for notice-board space for display on bank services	Collect material on retailing survey for assessment	Collect and mark restricted scope projects	Prepare test under exam conditions	Prepare revision exercises for 'mock' A-level	Arrange meetings with student teacher
				Discuss project marks and estimate CSE or O-level entries			Make preliminary bookings for July Challenge of Industry Conference
		Collect rates of interest on consumer credit	Talk/tape/ slides on banking for firms		Counsel students after test		
Dec.	Prepare test papers			Discuss exams and revision exercises			
			Revision tests	exercises			

Source: Stilwell, J. A., Lipsey, R. G., and Clarke, R., *Workbook to Accompany Positive Economics* (Weidenfeld & Nicolson, 1983).

Note: The plan allows a semi-permanent record of commitments to be kept. The actual arrangements can be transferred to a diary when the bookings and dates are known. Where two classes need the same resources in the same time-period, the plan warns of this and allows preparation to avoid clashes. The plan forewarns about busy periods and allows maximum spreading of the load when the actual deadlines are decided and transferred to the diary.

moderating continuous-assessment courses.

3 Syllabuses need to be designed for *non-examined courses*.

> ### Discussion point E
> What might be the criteria for non-examined economics courses?

---

4 Particular problems arise with *writing syllabuses for mixed-ability classes* with some students doing O-level for one board and others doing CSE for another.

5 Records of students' performance must be kept to provide material for *predicted grades*, especially for university entrance, or in order to decide which examination to enter students for.

6 Records of *examination results* must be kept, compared to predicted grades and analysed to see if changes are needed in staffing, grouping, resources or preparation. Most schools now publish results and all staff in the department must be prepared to discuss the published results with parents and students if questions are asked.

7 Moderation of *continuous-assessment work* and the necessary communication with examination boards must be done with extreme care.

8 *Communication* of the content of courses is necessary:
   (a) to heads of year, students, parents and careers staff for option choices;
   (b) to prospective parents in a guide to the school;
   (c) in reports to the governors;
   (d) in reports to meetings of heads of department.

6 Assessment

Assessments can be useful tools in checking whether courses suit student needs or staff skills as well as providing the information needed for prediction.

Assessment of students

1 What system of internal assessment should be used? How will it tie in with the school's existing system? Are there indicators of future performance? How does the student's performance fit in with performance elsewhere, the student's aspirations or what might have been expected? Allocation of a member of the department to be 'tutor' of each class can be valuable. Records can be kept of sixth-formers' other subjects, qualifications, plans and performance, and then individual counselling can be given by the 'tutor'. The head of department will also be able to consult these records to assist students making particularly difficult choices.

2 *Records of attendance at classes* are also needed.

3 Assessments may also be used for the *selection of groups*. What criteria should be used for such selection? Did the choice of group affect student performance? Marland and Hill raise more points on assessment of students.[13]

Assessment of staff

1 The head of department should *set standards* of quality and quantity of work and *ensure common standards* across the department, in line with school policy. Moderation of students' work can ensure this, as can each member of staff marking examination questions across the whole year. Responsibilities for marking should be clearly delineated and should ensure an equitable load.

2 Staff need to be *monitored*.[14] This can be done formally or informally, but the head of department must be prepared to monitor weak teachers formally. Teachers with problems, whether they are aware of them or not, will need to be seen frequently both in class and privately in order to design a programme of help. Ultimately, the head of department must be prepared to discipline weak staff, if all attempts at help are rejected. The headteacher and governors will have a procedure to deal with the most severe cases. A head of department who is very competent in every other field may yet feel reluctant to discipline colleagues. Unhappily, it is necessary on a few occasions, and the penalty for ignoring such problems is that senior staff, parents and students may lose confidence in the department. Some staff may admit that they have problems and seek help, or may welcome it eagerly when they realise that someone understands the difficulties they have been struggling with in silence. The self-assessment exercise mentioned above (p. 267) may be of assistance here in helping staff to appreciate their strengths and weaknesses and the areas where they need to change. If staff will not admit they have problems, then the head of department may still become aware of them – for instance, teaching in a nearby room enables the atmosphere in a classroom to be gauged. Similarly, it is valuable for the head of department to share a sixth-form class with a new teacher (one can teach macro and one micro); comments made by the students may be helpful, for instance, about their work-load or the different methods each teacher uses. In this way, without specifically asking students about the new teacher, a great deal can be learned indirectly and, ultimately, if classes are shared, only half the students' work will need remedial action if the new teacher has problems or if disruption arises due to absence, illness or resignation. Random checks of notebooks of students (easy when covering lessons during staff absence), and even an occasional ear to the keyhole, may be helpful in assessing staff![15]

3 *Staff absences* need to be noted and a check made to ensure work has been set, especially for planned absences. Frequent unplanned absences and difficulties in setting work may be signs of a teacher in difficulties. A stock of 'one-off' exercises, ready prepared for all classes (data-response questions are particularly useful), is valuable, as the head of department is responsible for setting work in emergencies where the teacher responsible has been

unable to set work. The head of department will need to liaise with the staff arranging cover for absence and, if possible, should try to pop in to any class being covered to ensure all is well.

4   The head of department will need to deal with *parental complaints* against staff. These must be discussed with the member of staff and fully investigated. It is important that the head of department loyally supports the teacher, publicly, to the parents. However, such situations may indicate serious problems that warrant careful discussions with the staff concerned, and possibly changes, or a programme of help for the teacher concerned.

5   Collect necessary information on all activities of the staff and be prepared to give an opinion for *internal promotion* or to write a *reference*.

Conclusion

Although the job of a head of department is demanding, it is also one of the most satisfying. The departments carry out the principal function of a school: the teaching of subjects to students. Heads of department have a great deal of autonomy in deciding how to teach the subjects and can therefore feel that they are responsible for the academic achievements of the students.

Surprisingly, very little research work has been carried out on this vital post within a school. Dunham[16] found that there was stress as a result of carrying the heavy administrative load as well as a full teaching timetable. Also, there was role conflict and role confusion. Inter-action with students, colleagues and parents can impose conflicting demands. A school that is well administered can reduce the work-load but the confidence placed in the head of department by the headteacher will be important too. Hughes[17] found in a study of headteachers, that heads will delegate, innovate and allow participation if the governors and the local authority have confidence in them. If, on the other hand, heads do not feel that confidence is placed in them, they will be cautious and defensive. Therefore a head of department can expect to be given autonomy if the headteacher feels trusted. It is likely also that heads of department will not feel able to delegate if they are not allowed to be autonomous. Hughes also found that older staff tend to have a more pastoral approach to their jobs, stressing detailed knowledge of students. On the other hand, young ambitious staff who move rapidly between schools for promotion have a positive leadership role and innovate. Heads of department working for older headteachers and with older senior staff in the school may find it harder to innovate themselves. Also, when appointing within the department, ambitious staff are likely to be those most eager to innovate.

If the head of department is fairly autonomous, then the role is very similar to that of any leader and John's work will be most valuable.[18]

There has been a shortage of opportunities for training in the position of head of department, other than by reading the books referred to in this chapter. Fortunately, many local authorities now run courses on the role of head of department that include simulation exercises (e.g. in interviewing) and, most importantly, they provide the opportunity to discuss all aspects of the job with other heads of department from different schools.

Implications of the discussion points

A   Some philosophical approaches might be to teach the subject in its purest form or, alternatively, to show the interlinkages between economics and other subjects or the practical uses of the subject – such as through courses in personal finance.

A team of staff with different skills may not have the same philosophy. Highly qualified specialist academics may not be happy teaching personal finance or teaching mixed-ability classes. However, if they are all committed to the need to teach economics as widely as possible through the school, then they can train one another to use different skills for the same ends and also attain a professional outlook of understanding and appreciating each other's different but equally valuable skills.

B   There are a great variety of implications of different staff allocations. It is important to realise that if the most experienced and senior staff take the most difficult – and perhaps least-academic – classes, this could leave probationers teaching the A-level and other academic classes. The probationer may feel as overburdened by the large amount of preparation for those academic classes and by the responsibility involved, as by having to prepare interesting work for the most boisterous classes. Also, the school must justify a situation where its ablest students miss the grade for higher or further education or their desired career because of the inexperience of the staff, for the sake of reducing the decibels in the lower school.

C   A few of the changes affecting economics might be:
   (a)   studying the economics of development in geography;
   (b)   handling original sources in history;
   (c)   statistics courses in mathematics;
   (d)   data-response questions in politics;
   (e)   a careers course that encourages more students to consider careers in management, business or commerce, and therefore encourages them to take economics.

D   If economics is blocked in the option system against science and languages, all the ablest children may choose other subjects. Then, if entry to the A-level course depends on the O-level results, the ablest may not get into the A-level class either. Similarly, depending on the other subjects offered, mainly girls or mainly boys may choose the subject. When discussing the 'core', should this include practical aspects of the course that might be a 'survival kit' mainly for non-economists (e.g. personal finance), or the basic principles of the subject (e.g. demand and supply).

E If an economics course precedes O-level option choices, then it can give an idea of the material that will be covered in O-level or CSE courses. A non-examined course for fourth- or fifth-year students may include the skills of money management, trade unions, etc. while sixth-year general studies might cover an appreciation of current economic events.

Notes and references

1 Marland, M., *Head of Department* (Heinemann Educational Books, 1971).
2 Marland, M., and Hill, S., *Departmental Management* (Heinemann Educational Books, 1981).
3 J. Rees in Whitehead, D. J., *Handbook for Economics Teachers*, 1st edn (Heinemann Educational Books, 1979) ch. 54.
4 Marland, op. cit., p. 99.
5 Ibid., p. 98.
6 John, D., *Leadership in Schools* (Heinemann Educational Books, 1980).
7 Ibid., ch. 4.
8 Marland, op. cit., ch. 9.
9 Ibid., p. 84.
10 Economics Education 14–16 Project, *An Annotated Bibliography of Pupil Books* (Economics Association, 1981).
11 Marland and Hill, op. cit., ch. 7.
12 Ibid., chs 8 and 9.
13 Ibid., ch. 6.
14 Ibid., ch. 5.
15 J. Rees in Whitehead, op. cit., ch. 54.
16 Dunham, J., 'Change and stress in the head of department's role', *Educational Research*, vol. 21, no. 1, 1978, pp. 44–7.
17 Hughes, M., 'The role of the secondary school head', unpublished PhD thesis (Cardiff, 1972).
18 John, op. cit.

Acknowledgement

I would like to acknowledge the advice given in preparation of this chapter by Richard Powell, TVEI Adviser (Business Studies), London Borough of Bromley, formerly Head of Economics, Gaynes School, Upminster.

58 Organising Economics Resources
Alain Anderton

Introduction

Cataloguing resources seems a daunting and onerous task to most hard-pressed teachers, and few would admit to having a system of cataloguing and retrieval of resources. The truth is, however, that every teacher engages in this activity. For the majority, the catalogue they keep is a mental one. For instance, they know that the set of multiple-choice books is kept in the cupboard, while the handouts on monopoly are kept in the filing cabinet. For a teacher with few resources, the memory catalogue is perfectly adequate and requires little effort to maintain. However, most teachers do attempt to build up a variety of resources. How many teachers, for instance, have not at some stage collected newspaper articles? Most give up because they cannot retrieve what they want quickly or easily enough, and completely forget that an excellent article suitable for classroom use is in the pile. Here the memory catalogue breaks down and a more systematic approach is needed if resources are to be effectively used. Organising a bank of resources is not difficult or time-consuming, and an effectively organised bank can contribute to effective teaching.

Types of resources

A wide variety of resources exists and much can be acquired free of charge. A large resource bank is likely to contain:

1 Books: textbooks, supplementary reading texts, workbooks of various types, reference books such as *Economic Trends* or the *Annual Abstract of Statistics*.
2 Journals: such as the *Economic Progress Report*, and *Barclays Bank Review*.
3 Teacher-produced paper materials: duplicated notes, exercises, data-response questions, worksheets.
4 Commercially produced leaflets: such as are available from the Banking Information Service.
5 Newspaper articles.
6 Filmstrips, tapes, cassettes and videos.
7 Games and simulations.
8 Wall charts.
9 Overhead projector transparencies.
10 Computer programs.
11 Other resources such as kits and curriculum projects.

Dynamic resources should not be forgotten either. Details of visits or speakers will need to be kept if time is to be saved in the future organisation of such activities.

The target audience

When considering what resources to acquire and how these resources are to be stored and retrieved, it is essential to have a clear idea of who is to use the resource bank. Three possibilities exist:

1   The resource bank will be totally controlled by the teacher. Students who wish to borrow or consult items in the bank will only be able to do so via the teacher. Teachers who keep all their books in a locked cupboard and distribute them as and when needed operate this type of system.
2   There is free access by both teachers and students to the resource bank. An example of this would be where the resource bank contained only books and these were all located in the school library.
3   Some mixture of the above two, that is, some items are freely accessible to students while others are kept for teacher use alone. This is the system most commonly used. In a traditional classroom, teachers will have certain resources locked away in their cupboards while allowing students to 'sign out' books from a departmental library.

The most practical arrangement is likely to be the last. Some items are unlikely ever to be borrowed for individual use by students – simulations are an example. Other items may all too readily go missing if freely available – video tapes, for instance. Yet other items may prove too fragile – some teachers may feel this to be true of filmstrips. However, the bulk of paper-based resources certainly are suitable for open-access use and it seems senseless to have these items locked away when they could be utilised by students. They are only going to use these items, though, if there is a suitable storage system and a good catalogue of the resources.

Storing resources

Resources can be stored in one of two ways, either by topic or by type of resource. If a topic-based approach is decided upon, it is likely that the teacher will use a system of 'tidy' boxes, into which can be placed everything from books to filmstrips to computer programs. The great advantage of storing resources in this way is that the storage system is itself a cataloguing system. It is also easy to set up and easy to maintain. Clear labelling of the contents of the boxes is a great help to effective use. This system can be used either by the teacher alone or on open access by students and teachers. For a small resource bank, it is probably the best system.

However, it does have very important limitations. First, not all resources can be neatly put into one topic area.

Textbooks and bank reviews are two examples. It is possible to start cross-referencing boxes – for instance, leaving a note in the box on 'money' that there is an article on this in December 1983's issue of the *Economic Progress Report* – but already this is destroying the simplicity of the system. Secondly, teachers may not wish to store all their resources in tidy boxes. Textbooks, workbooks and videotapes are three items unlikely to find their way into such a system for differing reasons. We are now talking about two systems: one where some resources are stored by type of resource, and the other where resources are stored by topic. So for a larger resource bank, the teacher will need to consider storing the resources by type and providing a good catalogue.

Some items are easier to store than others. Books can be stored on shelves, worksheets and other paper-based materials in cardboard 'tidy' boxes. Loose filmstrips and cassettes and videos can be stored in boxes too, or simply left on shelves, given that it is unlikely that any single department will have a great quantity of such materials. A filing cabinet can also be used to store items. Anybody using filmstrips in great quantity will probably want to cut them up and mount them as slides. Not only will this increase their life, but it will also allow more flexible use of the materials. Special transparent pages, each holding twelve or more slides, suitable for storing in a filing cabinet, can be bought relatively cheaply. Overhead projector transparencies and wall charts often prove the most difficult items to store. Transparencies are best stored in a filing cabinet. However, if no cabinet is available, it is best to store them flat in large folders. A home-made folder can be made simply by obtaining a large piece of card, folding it in two, and stapling, gluing, or sellotaping up the sides. Special commercially produced storage racks are available for wall charts. These involve suspending the wall charts from battens of wood. However, they are not ideal in that removing one wall chart necessitates removing all the other wall charts on that particular batten. A map chest is far better – and might promote closer relations with the geography department too! Otherwise, carefully folding the wall chart and storing it on a shelf is the only other strategy.

One last important point that needs to be made is that all resources items should ideally be protected from dust, damp and direct sunlight.

Cataloguing resources

Storing resources by topic is a cataloguing system in itself. However, if a moderate number of resources is to be stored by resource, then a catalogue will be needed to make most effective use of the system. If the resource bank is to be used solely by the teacher, then a fairly simple system could be used. The subject-area could be split up into a number of topics and then lists of resources for that topic could be compiled. Topics should correspond to teaching topics, but should not be so large that more than ten items are initially filed under that topic.

Ten items is the maximum number because the list will grow and too great a number of resources on the list will make it difficult to see at a glance what is available. The topic lists would most easily go on to 5″ × 3″ index cards – available from your librarian. The teacher may well wish to include reading references and exercises on this list, for example:

Foreign exchange
Stanlake, *Introductory,* pp. 374–90.
Anderton, *New Approach,* pp. 151–63.
Harbury, *Work book,* p. 120, problem 4.
10 × Economics 'Price of Pounds': Tape 4.
'Have floating rates been a success?' *Economics,* spring 1983.
'Exchange rate fluctuations', *NWBR,* August 1983.
'Wither the pound', duplicated article and questions.

A little more work can produce a catalogue available to both staff and students. A more systematic approach will be needed, but that may not be such a bad thing. The first question to ask is what cataloguing system should be used. There are two main choices, namely: the Dewey decimal system, or developing a personal system. The Dewey system is likely to be the better choice, because it then gives the student practice in using a system that he/she will encounter in public libraries, college libraries, etc. It also is a ready-made system that teachers need only interpret. The disadvantage of Dewey is that it is occasionally inflexible, and difficult to interpret. A list of the Dewey numbers likely to be of interest to economics teachers can be found at the end of Chapter 61.

Next, the teacher will need to prepare a set of 5″ × 3″ index cards or A4 card sheets (card for durability), putting at the top the Dewey number and the title of the category (e.g. 331. Labour Economics). Then all the resources in that category should be listed on the card. Four pieces of information need to be recorded about each item: the title of the item, the nature of the resource (e.g. article, wall chart), where to find the resource, and the date of publication. For instance: 'Four economic recoveries compared', *Economic Progress Report,* May 1984. Another example would be 'Monetary policy', sheet, 339.53, 1982 – indicating a teacher-produced sheet item on monetary policy, stored with other such items in Dewey order (in a box or wallet file perhaps), and written in 1982. It is inadvisable to take short cuts in cataloguing when it comes to entries. Students will become quickly discouraged from using the catalogue if they are unable to work out what the item is or where it is kept. In practice, the main resources used by students when researching for an essay or project are books, journal articles, teacher-produced sheets, and newspaper articles.

For two types of resources, namely newspaper articles and commercial leaflets (such as social security leaflets, or credit card leaflets), the time spent putting each item on the index far outweighs any benefit to be gained. So for these, simply place a catalogue number on each separate item and file them in order so that they are quickly retrievable. Then make some reference on each index card to this set of items – for instance, writing 'newspaper articles' at the bottom of the card. Any important newspaper article can be photocopied, entered on the main catalogue and put into the sheet file.

All this may sound very complicated, but it is only an extension of what every teacher already does with his resources. The time required to maintain a catalogue for a large resource bank amounts to only a few hours each term. Collecting the resources, maintaining them in good condition, and checking on who has got them is far more time-consuming. The advantages of a catalogue are many. For a start, it means that the teacher can see at a glance the resources available on a topic. The catalogue can quickly reveal where there are gaps in resources. It will probably encourage a more varied approach to teaching – how many teachers resort to chalk and talk because they have forgotten the existence of a worksheet they constructed only a year ago, or have mislaid a suitable newspaper article that they cut out six months ago. If the catalogue is constructed with the students as well as the teacher in mind, and it is presented in such a way that they can easily use it, then it makes possible a more student-centred approach to learning. Work could be set based on resources listed in the catalogue. Students could be encouraged to sift through the material available and decide what is useful for themselves. At the very least, it would provide an excellent base for background reading in preparation for an essay.

Whatever happens, they have a guide to resources independent of the teacher. Without a catalogue, most of the resources would essentially be 'dead' because nobody would use them. That is surely justification enough for the work involved in constructing a catalogued resources bank.

59 Constructing a Fugitive File

Robert Wilson

Introduction

An economics teacher's claim to be offering a subject that is exciting, contemporary and relevant to students' lives is suspect whenever reading material is confined to out-of-date textbooks. While it is true that publishers have begun to provide quarterly and annual economic reviews aimed at the schools market, there still remains a gap in provision that is filled (albeit imperfectly) by daily and weekly newspapers, journals and magazines. Maximising the potential value of contemporary newspaper and other sources involves considerable work, but it can also pay handsome dividends. Since enthusiastic economics teachers are regular readers of the economic and financial press in any event, the additional effort lies only in the extraction, filing and recording of relevant material.

The first task is to set up a fugitive file (see Figure 59.1). This need not be outrageously expensive. Since the material is not confidential, there is no need to worry about opting for an entirely accessible system of filing. The filing 'cabinet' needs width and depth in order to avoid folding newspaper articles, etc. The cartons used to transport eggs in bulk to supermarkets are an ideal size, are made from sturdy cardboard, and are available free of charge. They have little aesthetic appeal, but their appearance can be enhanced simply by covering them with coloured paper. Alternatively, a friendly 'knock for knock' agreement with a teacher of woodworking skills can produce a superior product cheaply; an offer to assist with an income-tax return is but one of several marketable commodities that an economics teacher might offer in return! To produce the files, sheets of fairly heavy-duty card are required, size approximately 73 cm × 57.5 cm. These should be folded once, approximately 1 cm from the midpoint of the longer side to produce a file with sides of 36 cm (height or depth) × 57.5 cm (width), with one side having a lip protruding 1 cm high across the length of the file. This can be divided into eight equal parts, and is then trimmed to leave a tab 7.2 cm wide × 1 cm high on which the file name can be written. With each successive file, the position of the tab is moved one place to the right, and the files placed behind each other. In this way, the tab for file 9 is in line with the tab for file 1, the tab for file 10 in line with the tab for file 2, and so on.

The file titles should correspond with the main components of the courses that are taught. Even the smallest system is likely to include titles such as economies of scale, international trade, exchange rates, monetary policy, monopolies and mergers, etc. To keep the miscellaneous file as thin as possible, a minimum of 100 files is recommended. Alphabetical order will suffice, with each file allocated a number also (e.g. 74 TAXATION). This number is required once items begin to be placed in the file. For example, if press coverage is given to a proposed reform of income tax, then any article that it is decided to retain for future use has the reference number 74 added to it before being placed in the file. Under this system, no attempt is made to create a catalogue of what has been filed. Most teachers simply don't have the time to create and maintain an index or catalogue, and few receive administrative assistance in this regard. If a teacher wants to know what articles are available in file 56 on location of industry, then the only action is to extract the file and look. In the course of looking, the teacher can also evaluate the worth of articles currently on file. If time, or superior later material, has rendered some items obsolete or of little value then they are simply discarded – there is no complex procedure of catalogue/index deletion to be observed.

One of the problems with making use of newspaper articles is that they are printed in a wide variety of shapes and sizes. Reducing them to a common format is a long and tedious job – ideal for allocating to some wayward student who is in need of a little corrective attention. It is a scissors and paste job, by and large. Once reduced to A3 or A4 format, the articles are much easier for a class to handle. It should be remembered that duplication of newspaper articles is a matter on which local copyright laws might well have something to say. Where sources are intended to be used regularly, it is politic (and in some countries essential) to contact the owner of the copyright for permission to reproduce. It is not unknown for consent to be given to practising teachers, subject to wholly reasonable restraining conditions.

Once the file has been created, it will soon begin to yield a return on the effort put into its creation. For example, when it is time to teach about merger policy, recent case studies will already be to hand; for a lesson on balance of payments, the previous month's figures will be readily available. Equally important, as the years go by, some articles will earn their keep time and time again – in the UK in the mid-1980s students are no longer exposed to 25 per cent annual rates of inflation, and no longer wake up to find that the pound has devalued by 14 per cent

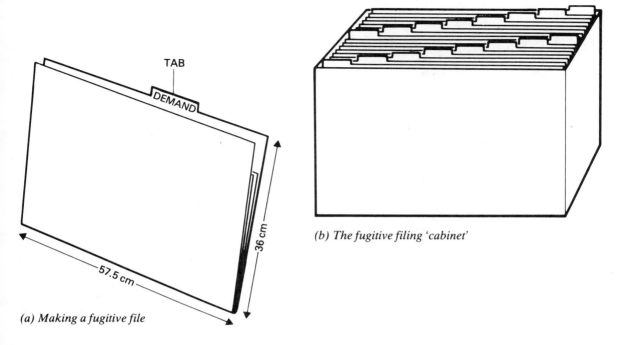

(b) The fugitive filing 'cabinet'

(a) Making a fugitive file

Figure 59.1 A fugitive file

overnight. Newspaper articles written at the time have a freshness and an urgency about them that captures the event better than any subsequent narrative.

Occasionally, articles extracted from newspapers require some editing before making use of them with a class. This involves different skills, which are dealt with elsewhere.[1] Even in their raw state, however, newspapers, etc. will yield sufficient material to make the creation of a fugitive file eminently worth while.

Notes and references

1   Ryba, R., and Wilson, R. (eds) *Teaching the Economics of the EEC, vol. 2: British Approaches to the Use of Teaching Resources* (Economics Association, 1982) pp. 21–38.

60 Economising on Book Purchases*

Bob Fryer

*An earlier version of this chapter appeared in *Economics*, vol. XVIII, pt 2, no. 78, summer 1982, p. 69.

Introduction

While there are many calls upon departmental allowances, probably the largest single expenditure for most is still textbooks. This chapter shows some ways of making that expenditure more economical. This aim is useful, not only because of cuts in real educational expenditure, but also because it permits more spending on other important resources.

The main considerations when buying books are content, presentation, suitability and price. These features can be ascertained from:

1 The several bibliographies and guides published by the Economics Association.
2 Book reviews (e.g. *Economics*, *Times Educational Supplement*, this *Handbook*).
3 Studying inspection copies from the publishers (although these can be expensive to return if they are not bought; check postal charges as it might be cheaper to buy one copy). These books ought to be obtainable from public libraries.
4 Publishers' catalogues – now numerous, generally informative and well presented. If you do not receive these, a note to the publishers will rectify the matter. Be sure that your school communications network sends out all those that arrive.
5 Displays at meetings, etc., and publishers' own travelling displays which will readily come to your school.

My first task in buying is to stocktake, normally in the summer term when most books have been returned and I can find some spare time. The books are then sorted according to condition. Then, with reference to expected numbers of students, I reorder existing texts to maintain stocks. The easy task over, a choice of new items can be made knowing how much money is available.

The choice of new material may be a personal matter, or you may wish to consult colleagues. It is here that priorities for resource allocation must be established.

If, after considering suitability, a choice still exists, then the physical construction of the book can be examined. Hardback books are a strong and resilient product. They are normally quite expensive and, unless large sums are available or the work is so standard as to be

in use for a long time, they might not be worth consideration. Some paperbacks or flexi-covered books are sewn, like hardbacks, and last reasonably well. The unsewn type of paperback has separate pages that are glued together. This type is less hardy in class use, as the spines often break or sections fall out, thus rendering the book useless. If you are in a position to choose among alternatives, then the hardback or gathered paperback would seem to be, to use the Consumers' Association terminology, a 'better buy'. If paperbacks are bought, there are some ways of extending their working life.

I cover paperbacks and 'limp' covered books with 'plastic transparent book covering material', variously called 'Tacky Back' and 'Librafilm'. This protects their outward appearance (which I consider very important to their future life) and strengthens them for the rigours they have to face. The students can easily do this at home, and it makes the book a little more important to them. I have tried a 'division of labour' scheme when a large number of books need covering, but careful choice of students is needed for the final process in order for the finished product to be satisfactory. Try the job yourself first. Flexible plastic dust jackets (at approximately 15p each) will also increase the life of paperbacks, and are, of course, far more convenient to apply than 'Librafilm'. Even so, the life of a paperback is limited, and as economies are made in production, so their quality falls, making maintenance more difficult.

Money can be saved with some effort on your part. It is often easy to buy copies of standard works to complete sets or add to school or departmental libraries at a small fraction of their current price. Even large numbers of recently superseded texts (still very useful in schools) can be found, for example, third-edition Lipsey at £1.50 in 1980, Samuelson in 1981 at £1.50. I write of conditions in London where terms are favourable, but in many cities a similar situation exists and some at least of the following points should be useful:

1 The crucial point is that these economies are usually to be gained outside the normal educational book-buying channels, and it should be cleared beforehand that money can be made available to pay for these purchases. 'Petty cash' is a common route. In (e) below, some shops will accept local purchase orders.

2 Finding the books. I have subdivided the main sources below with some notes.

(a) Remainder bookshops. Many books are 'remaindered', that is, sold off by the publishers as old stock (due to high storage costs, the need to increase 'cash flow' or a new edition of the same work has been recently published), and then sold by remainder shops or sometimes as bargains in established shops.

　　e.g. (i) Booksmith, five branches in London, one in Kingston-upon-Thames, one in Brighton.

　　(ii) Sue Reynolds in London.

　　(iii) Harveys Bookshop in Leicester, Derby, Nottingham, Stafford, Wolverhampton, Birmingham and Leeds.

(b) Secondhand bookshops. There are many throughout the country in which volumes of interest to economists are often cheaply priced. To find them, the local telephone directory is of use, normally under 'Books – Rare and Secondhand', rather than 'Booksellers'. *Shepherd's Directory* (which ought to be available in reference libraries) is a listing of bookdealers operating from shops and private addresses.

(c) Charity shops. These often have secondhand texts. Notable among them are Oxfam and Help the Aged. There are also many local charities that often take over shops for a short period at the end of their lease, so it is a matter of local knowledge to be aware of them.

(d) Students' shops in universities and polytechnics often sell unwanted texts.

(e) Bookshops dealing in new books often have 'sales' or quantities of remainder books (see above) where bargains may be found (W. H. Smith in January and June is noteworthy in this respect).

(f) Library sales. In the London boroughs there are often sales of ex-library stock, presumably as shelf space is limited and some volumes are rarely used. These are advertised but it might be worth while contacting your local library service not only for notification of any forthcoming sales, but also to see if they are discarding any texts of economic interest.

Adoption of at least some of these ideas should make your book purchasing more effective.

61　Using a Library

Alain Anderton

Introduction

Access to a good library is a great help in any academic study. It can provide a wealth of information, open the door to new ideas and lead to the adoption of new values. All too often, however, libraries prove to be most frustrating institutions. How many students and teachers have found themselves:

1 unable to locate the section in the library that contains the books they are looking for;

2 unable to find the book on the shelves even when they know it should be there;

3 unable to find the right information in a book that has been recommended to them;

4 told that the library does not stock the publication they have come miles to consult;

5 a relevant series of statistics whose 'definitional basis changed in . . .' or was simply 'discontinued in . . .'?

In this chapter, we will consider what service a library can reasonably be expected to provide and how teachers and students can best make use of library facilities available in a locality.

Types of library

Teachers and students are likely to have access to a number of different type of library. The smallest library available, and possibly the most used, will be a class library. This will be run by the economics teacher and was discussed in Chapter 58. The way in which this library is set out and administered and the way in which students are instructed to use the library, can have an important influence on the success or otherwise of their use of more complicated libraries. A little time spent cataloguing the books in Dewey order, for instance, is likely to help students understand the organisation of books in a larger collection.

The school library too is likely to be within the sphere of influence of the teacher. It is normal practice for a department to be consulted on the choice of books for its section in the library. Yet all too many teachers fail to provide such lists, or grossly underspend on the amounts suggested. Most librarians are only too happy to discuss library provision in a particular area and implement schemes designed to increase effective library use by students.

The local small-branch public library is unlikely to be of use. It will carry a very small selection of economics books for loan, and many of those will be on topics such as money management or accounting. The reference section will not go beyond the *Encyclopaedia Britannica* – a copy of which should be in the school library. The only important service that a small library can provide will be the inter-library loan service – the service that enables the library to borrow a book from another library. Any serious academic work will need to be conducted either in a very large branch library or in a central public library. These should carry a large stock of books for loan as well as a large reference section.

Students and staff may also be lucky enough to have access to other large libraries. Most commonly, these will be polytechnic or university libraries. Permission for use will need to be obtained beforehand and it may well be that the institution will only grant reference use. However, most such libraries will be of more help than the typical central library.

Finally, teachers may also be able to use authority-based libraries designed to supplement resources in their schools. These facilities may be based at a local teachers' Centre, but are more likely to be linked to the public-library system. Video and film libraries are common, as too is the provision of a selection of books on particular themes. The school librarian should have full details of schemes operating in the local authority.

Services available at a library

Libraries provide a number of different services. These include:

1   The loan of books. Books that are not on the shelves can normally be reserved. If the library does not have a book (or indeed any other type of paper resource), it should be able to obtain it through the inter-library loan service. Note, however, that any books requested in this way are likely to take months to come through. A good school library will be able to order books on inter-library loan.
2   Consultation of books, periodicals and other resources. A well-stocked reference library will provide access to data (e.g. from *Economic Trends* or *Social Trends*), articles in periodicals (e.g. bank reviews, *NIESR Quarterly Bulletin*) and annual

reports (e.g. Inland Revenue, company reports). A reference library is unlikely to carry a large stock of ordinary books. These will need to be obtained from the lending section.
3   Access to non-book materials. These may include wall charts, tapes, slides, films and videos. Every teacher should be aware of loan facilities for such items from the local authorities.
4   Reproduction facilities. Any sizeable library now has a photocopier – a boon if you have discovered material that you want but are not able to borrow the original. However, a library may also have more sophisticated equipment, such as an enlarger, which will enlarge or reduce originals for teachers wishing to use such material.
5   Information from Ceefax, Oracle and Prestel. Of these, Prestel, the Post Office-operated computer information service, has the largest bank of information. A word of warning, however: although it is great fun to go through page after page of information on the television monitor, little practical use is likely to be generated. Ceefax and Oracle are oriented towards the ordinary television viewer while Prestel is very heavily geared to the business user.

How to use a library

A library is a collection of resources. The greater the number of resources, the more useful that library is likely to be to its users, but equally, the more difficult it will be for those users to locate the resources they are seeking. It is virtually impossible to use a large library successfully without knowing something about the information retrieval system in use. Most students unfortunately do not possess such knowledge, and often neither do their teachers. The best piece of advice that can be given to anybody using a library for the first time, or using a familiar library to find unfamiliar information, is 'seek the help of the librarian on duty'. Get librarians to explain how their library works and ask them to help you locate the information you require. Seeking help is not a sign of failure: it is the way to cut the Gordian knot presented by a complex resource bank. Each library will have its own way of cataloguing and storing items. What follows is a list of suggestions for using a typical large public library. It is written so that it could be reproduced and given to students about to use a library for research.

How to use your public library
1   *Prior to the library visit.* Make sure you have any necessary materials such as pens and paper. Take some money in case you wish to photocopy any material. Check the times of opening and closing of the library. If you are in any doubt, check with the library by telephone as to whether it possesses the information you seek. If you wish to borrow books and are not a member of the library, find out, by telephoning the library, whether or not you will be

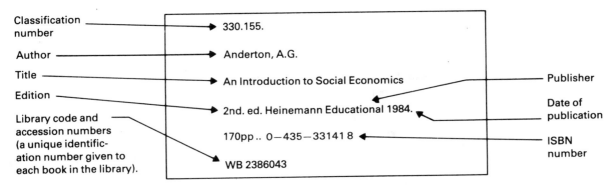

Classification number → 330.155.

Author → Anderton, A.G.

Title → An Introduction to Social Economics

Edition → 2nd. ed. Heinemann Educational 1984.

Library code and accession numbers (a unique identification number given to each book in the library). → 170pp .. 0—435—33141 8

WB 2386043

Publisher

Date of publication

ISBN number

Figure 61.1 A card classified under the Dewey system

able to borrow books on your first visit.

2 *On arrival at the library.* If you have not used the library before or are still uncertain how it is organised, seek help immediately from a librarian. You will save yourself a great deal of time and trouble if you do this.

3 *If you know the title and author of the book(s) you require.* Most libraries use the Dewey decimal system of cataloguing books. This system gives each area of knowledge a specific number between 0 and 999. For instance, economics is given numbers between 330 and 339. However, because knowledge can be grouped in different ways, it could be that an economics book you are seeking has been given a number outside this range. Foreign trade, for instance, is classified in the 'commerce' section under 382. So, the quickest way to find the location of a book is to consult the 'author index'. This may be a card index, or the index may be on microfiche. Figure 61.1 illustrates a typical card.

Having found this card under 'Anderton', the important piece of information to look for is the classification number – in this case, 330.155. You may now proceed to the 330.115 section of books in the library. Do not be surprised if the book is not there. If the library is a loan library, the book may well have been borrowed, in which case you may consider reserving the book: if you can wait a few weeks. If the book is not in the library catalogue, then the library will be able to obtain a copy through the inter-library loan service. However, expect to wait two months on average for the book to arrive.

4 *If you only know the subject that you wish to research.* You will need to locate and use the subject index. This is a list of subjects in alphabetical order which states the classification number of the subject. Once you have the classification number, you can go to that section of the library and browse through the books there, or use the classified catalogue, which is arranged in Dewey order and lists all the books stocked by the library classified under that number. When using the subject index,

try to think of as many different subjects of relevance as possible. For instance, if you are researching 'fiscal policy', you may well find useful books under a wider subject classification such as 'economics', 'macroeconomics', and 'economic policy', or books more narrowly defined such as 'taxation', 'public expenditure', 'public borrowing' or 'income tax'. If you do not find the title of your subject in the index, think how else it might be classified. For instance, the term 'public expenditure' may not be used in the subject index. Instead, the subject may be called 'public spending', or 'government spending' or 'government expenditure' or 'public sector expenditure'. If you are in any difficulty, seek the help of a librarian.

5 *If you are seeking statistics.* You are unlikely to find the statistics you seek by browsing through a typical selection of books in a loan library. A reference library will be of far more help. Just a few publications contain most of the data you are likely to need. These are:

CSO, *Annual Abstract of Statistics* (HMSO) – a yearly publication giving a wide range of data concerning the previous ten years. It is particularly good for information concerning individual industries and population.

CSO, *Economic Trends* (HMSO) – a monthly publication giving the most recent statistics on key economic variables in the UK economy.

CSO, *Economic Trends Annual Supplement* (HMSO) – a yearly publication covering the main economic variables in the economy since 1948.

CSO, *Financial Statistics* (HMSO) – a monthly publication containing the most up-to-date statistics in the financial field.

CSO, *National Income and Expenditure* (HMSO) – a yearly publication giving a detailed breakdown of national income accounts over the past ten years.

CSO, *Monthly Digest of Statistics* (HMSO) – a monthly publication broadly updating data contained in the *Annual Abstract of Statistics*.

CSO, *Regional Statistics* (HMSO) – a yearly publication covering statistics for the eleven standard regions of the UK for the previous year.

CSO, *Social Trends* (HMSO) – a yearly publication particularly useful in areas such as housing, income distribution, population and education.

CSO, *United Kingdom Balance of Payments* (HMSO) – a yearly publication giving a detailed breakdown of the balance of payments account over the previous ten years.

Department of Employment, *Employment Gazette* – a monthly publication giving current employment and unemployment statistics. Articles often contain statistics of interest.

Bank of England Quarterly Bulletin (Bank of England) – quarterly publication containing an appendix with London money market statistics.

The British Economy: Key Statistics 1900–1970 (London & Cambridge Economic Service) – key UK economic statistics over the period 1900–70.

National Institute Economic Review (National Institute of Economic and Social Research) – a quarterly publication. Apart from relevant articles, the *Review* has a statistical appendix detailing key economic variables.

Two last points. First, research takes a great deal of time. You will almost certainly spend far more time finding and utilising resources in a library than you anticipated. Secondly, if you are unfamiliar with a library system, you can speed up search procedures considerably by asking the librarian for help.

Appendix 61.1: The Dewey decimal system

The Dewey decimal system is the system most commonly used to classify books in the UK. Reproduced below are the main Dewey numbers likely to be of interest to an economist. The school librarian might welcome a copy of this list.

330   Economics
    The science of human behaviour as it relates to utilisation of scarce means for satisfaction of needs and desires through production, distribution, consumption
.122   Free-enterprise economy
    Usually synonymous with capitalism
.124   Planned economics
.126   Mixed economies
    Interventionism, welfare-state systems
.153   Classical economics
    School of Smith, Malthus, Ricardo, Bastiat, Say
.155   Miscellaneous schools
    Neoclassicism, welfare economics

.156   Keynesianism
.942   Economic situation and conditions of the British economy
331   Labour economics
    Class here industrial relations
.1   Labour force and market
.118   Labour productivity
.12   Labour market
    Class here supply of labour in relation to demand
.127   Mobility of labour
.128   Placement
    Formal and informal arrangements for matching people and jobs
.137   Unemployment
.21   Wages
.25   Hours and other conditions of employment
.8   Labour unions (trade unions) and labour-management (collective) bargaining
.892   Strikes
332   Financial economics
.024   Personal finance
.041   Capital
    That portion of the stock of economic goods that is used to produce a return
.041 54   Sources of capital
.1   Banks and banking
    Class here comprehensive works on money and banking, on financial institutions and their functions
.11   Central banks
.12   Commercial banks
.15   International banks and banking
.17   Banking services of commercial banks
.32   Savings and loan associations
    Also known as building and loan associations
.37   Industrial banks
.38   Insurance companies
.4   Money
.401   Theories
    Examples: quantity theory, circulation and velocity theory, equation of exchange theory, income and cash balance theories; supply and demand
.41   Value of money
    Class here inflation and deflation
.45   Foreign exchange
.46   Monetary policy
    Class use of monetary policy for economic stabilisation in 339.53
.64   Exchange of securities and commodities
    Buying and selling of securities and commodities; organisation, procedures, activities of organised exchanges
.7   Credit
.8   Interest and discount
333   Land economics
.012   Economic rent
.7   Natural resources
    Class here the environment, raw materials, waste resources

.72 Conservation and protection

334 Co-operatives

.5 Distribution (consumers' co-operatives)

.6 Production

335 Socialism and related systems

336 Public finance

.2 Taxes and taxation

.34 Public borrowing and public debt

.39 Expenditure

337 International economics
Class foreign trade in 382

.142 European Economic Community

338 Production

.01 Factors of production

.04 Entrepreneurship

.06 Production efficiency
Cost-output ratio, effects of technology used. Including automation

.1 Agriculture

.2 Extract of minerals

.3 Other extractive industries

.4 Secondary industry and services

.5 General production economics
Including risk. Class here microeconomics (economics of the firm)

.51 Costs

.516 Profit

.52 Prices
Determination, effects of changes

.521 Price theories
Class here law of supply and demand, theories of value

.521 2 Theory of demand
Including price-demand relationship

.521 3 Theory of supply
Including price-supply relationship

.522 Determination in free markets
Free markets: markets comprising a number of sellers large enough that no individual seller can affect the price, selling either homogeneous, standardised products (pure competition) or similar but not standardised products (monopolistic competition)

.523 Determination in controlled markets
By oligopolies, monopolies

.526 Determination by government regulation

.528 Levels
Statistics, indexes

.542 Business cycles
Causes and effects. Including prosperity, recession, depression, recovery; panics

.544 Business forecasting

.604 2 Location
Proximity to sources of power, raw materials, labour supply, transportation

604 6 Specialisation
Including law of comparative advantage

.61 Private enterprise

.62 Public enterprise

.64 Size of enterprise

.82 Restrictive practices

.83 Mergers and amalgamations

.88 International (multinational) organisations and their activities

.9 Economic development and growth

.91 International development and growth
Foreign economic assistance (foreign aid)

339 Macroeconomics and related topics

.2 Distribution of income and wealth

.3 Measurement and measurements of national income (economic aggregates)
National income: money value of all goods and services produced in a country during a certain time-period. Class here national product, wealth, income accounting.

.41 Income and consumption
Marginal propensities to consume and save at various levels of income, consumer responses to decreases or increases in income

.42 Cost of living (prices)

.43 Savings and investment
Including effect of investment on income (the multiplier), capital formation, relation of consumption and savings

.46 Economic causes and effects of poverty

.47 Consumption (spending)
Class here standard of living, comprehensive works on consumption

.5 Macroeconomic policy
Class here economic stabilisation and growth, incomes policies, full employment policies

.52 Use of fiscal policy

.53 Use of monetary policy

382 International commerce (foreign trade)

.104 2 Specialisation and comparative advantage

.17 Balance of payments
Class here balance of trade, current balance

.173 Capital transactions

.174 Currency movements
Including gold movements, relation of monetary conditions to world trade

.7 Tariff policy
Class here comprehensive works on trade barriers and restrictions

Annotated List of Useful Addresses

David J. Whitehead

Abbey National Building Society, Abbey House, Baker Street, London NW1 6XL. Films, wall charts and booklets on building societies. Local branch managers would be happy to provide a talk.

Accepting Houses Committee, Granite House, 101 Cannon Street, London EC4N 5BA. Speakers may be provided by prior arrangement, and visits arranged to member houses.

Access, 365 Chartwell Square, Southend-on-Sea SS2 5ST. Set of notes outlining the development of the Access credit-card system.

Advertising Association, Abford House, 15 Wilton Road, London SW1V 1NJ. Has a national speakers' panel made up of people from all sides of the advertising business, willing to speak on most aspects and in most areas of the country. Free booklets. An information centre open from 10a.m. to 1p.m. and from 2p.m. to 5p.m., Monday to Friday, to all *bona fide* inquirers. Publications list. List of suggested reading. Leaflet entitled 'Finding out about advertising', available from CRAC Publications, Hobsons Ltd, Bateman Street, Cambridge CB2 1LZ.

Advertising Standards Authority, 2-16 Torrington Place, London WC1E 7HN. The British code of advertising practice, annual reports, case reports, and free leaflets. Two films/videos entitled *A Question of Standards* and *Two Too Many* (from Viscom Audio Visual Library).

Advisory Unit for Computer Based Education, Endymion Road, Hatfield, Herts AL10 8AU. Provides micro-computer software packages. Runs courses for economics teachers in the Chiltern region. Offers advice, and possibly speakers, in the field of CAL in economics.

Alexanders Discount plc, 1 St Swithins Lane, London EC4N 8DN. Booklet explaining the services this discount house provides in financial markets.

Allen & Unwin, 40 Museum St, London WC1. Catalogue of publications.

Edward Arnold, Woodlands Park Avenue, Woodlands Park, Maidenhead, Berks. Catalogue of social science publications.

Associated British Ports, 150 Holborn, London EC1N 2LR. Provides list of port addresses. School and student visits can sometimes be arranged at the discretion of the local port manager.

Associated Examining Board, Stag Hill House, Guilford, Surrey GU2 5XJ. Produces booklet on examining economics.

Associated Lancashire Schools Examining Board, 12 Harter Street, Manchester M1 6HL. Copy of Board's regulations contains list of publications available. Requests for speakers should be addressed to the secretary.

ASTMS, 79 Camden Road, London NW1 9ES. Quarterly economic review; occasional publications and recruitment/promotional material. Field officers sometimes address schools on the role of trade unions.

Association for Teaching of the Social Sciences, 41 Lansdown Place, Hove, Sussex BM3 1HF.

Association of Agriculture, Victoria Chambers, 16/20 Strutton Ground, London SW1P 2HP. Specialist publications, conferences, courses and farm visits.

Association of British Insurers, Schools Liaison Officer, Aldermary House, Queen Street, London EC4N 1TT. *Money Management Review* available free to interested teachers. A lecture on life assurance is offered country-wide. List of publications.

Audio Learning, Unit 1, The Works, 105a Torriano Avenue, London NW5 2RX. Cassettes and cassette/filmstrip programmes with accompanying booklets.

Audio-Visual Productions, Hocker Hill House, Chepstow, Gwent NP6 5ER. List of OHP and related software available. Catalogue of audio-visual publications.

Baltic Exchange, Secretary, 14-20 St Mary Axe, London EC3A 8BU. Film: *The Sea Traders*, from Guild Sound & Vision, Peterborough. Booklet on the Baltic Exchange. Visits to the Exchange are at 11.30a.m. and 12.30p.m. on Wednesdays, Thursdays, and Fridays.

Bank of England, Information Division, Threadneedle Street, London EC2R 8AH. Leaflet listing Bank of England publications. Leaflet listing guide to services, including educational visits, and speakers. Booklets about the work of the Bank of England. A tape/slide programme of the work of the Bank is available on free loan in 16mm film or VHS video format. 'Bank Briefing', a digest of the *Quarterly Bulletin*, is issued free of charge to all secondary schools and is particularly helpful to A-level economics students. A maximum of ten copies per school can be supplied.

Banking Information Service, 10 Lombard Street, London EC3V 9AT. Produces a large range of free resources, such as books, wall charts and specimen bank forms. Five video films available on free loan to schools through the Multi-link Film Library in Peterborough. Leaflet on publications. Leaflet on speaker service.

Barclays Bank, Group Economics Department, 54 Lombard Street, London EC3P 3AH. *Barclays Review* published quarterly. Leaflet about economics information service. Country reports. Commodity surveys.

Barclays Film Library, 12 The Square, Vicarage Farm Road, Peterborough PE1 5TS. Catalogue of films and videos.

BBC Education and Training, BBC Enterprises Ltd, Woodlands, Wood Lane, London W12 0TT. Central reference catalogue. To hire BBC videos, write to BBC Film and Video Hire Library, The Guild Organisation, Guild House, Oundle Road, Peterborough PE2 9PZ.

Beecon Educational Software, 16 Kingrove Avenue, Beeston, Nottingham NG9 4DU. Supplies economics programs for microcomputers.

BP Educational Service, Britannic House, Moor Lane, London EC2Y 9BU. Catalogue of resources for schools and colleges; film catalogue. The Paraffin file computer pack.

BP Film Library, 15 Beaconsfield Road, London NW10 2LE. Catalogue of free-loan films and videotapes.

British Airports Authority, Public Relations Manager, Gatwick Airport, Gatwick, West Sussex RH6 0HZ. Airport timetables and information booklets, summary of public inquiries re. Stansted and Heathrow, airport news, news releases, annual report, Heathrow facts and figures, information sheets on individual airports in UK.

British Association for Commercial and Industrial Education, 16 Park Crescent, London W1N 4AP. Information services are free to members of BACIE. Publications list. *BACIE Journal.*

British Computer Society, 13 Mansfield Street, London W1M 0BP.

British Gas Education Liaison Officer, Room 414, 326 High Holborn, London WC1V 7PT.

British Institute of Management, Management House, Cuttingham Road, Corby, Northants NN17 1TT. Booklet: *The Management Library* – a complete catalogue of publications.

British Insurance Association, Aldermary House, Queen Street, London EC4N 1TU. Brochure of teaching aids on non-life insurance. May be able to provide speakers.

British Insurance Brokers' Association, Fountain House, 130 Fenchurch Street, London EC3M 5DJ. Literature about functions and activities.

British Invisible Exports Council, 14 Austin Friars, London EC2N 2HE. Wallet of cards entitled City Briefs. Annual report. A guide to the services of the City of London. Card of statistics about invisibles.

British Overseas Trade Board, Publishing Unit, Room 224, 1 Victoria Street, London SW1H 0ET.

British Rail Education Services, PO Box 10, Wetherby, West Yorks LS23 6YX. Catalogue of published material on British Rail.

British Shipbuilders, Benton House, 136 Sandyford Road, Newcastle upon Tyne SE2 1QE. A brief guide to British shipbuilders. Most shipyards accept organised visits, but on a limited scale.

British Standards Institution, 2 Park Street, London W1A 2BS. Annual guide for teachers in consumer education.

Available free through local authority advisers. Provides a limited speaker service to groups of teachers, and occasionally to students.

British Steel Corporation, Information Services, 9 Albert Embankment, London SE1 7SS. Leaflet of publications.

British Telecom Education Service, 2-10 Gresham Street, London EC2V 7AG. Publishes an education resources catalogue and a film and video catalogue.

British Tourist Authority, 64 St James Street, London SW1A 1NS. Leaflets on tourism as an industry. Booklet: *Promoting Tourism to Britain.*

British Waterways Board, Melbury House, Melbury Terrace, London NW1 6JX. Lots of booklets about waterways.

Building Societies' Association, 3 Savile Row, London W1X 1AF. Large range of booklets, study packs, wall charts and other materials.

Business Technician Education Council, Central House, Upper Woburn Place, London WC1H 0HH. Booklet on BEC National awards, list of current publications, discussion document on educational policy, information sheets. May provide speakers on a regional basis.

Business Training Services, 2 Drydales, Kirkella, Hull, HU10 7JU.

Butterworth Scientific Ltd, Westbury House, Bury Street, Guildford, Surrey GU2 5BH. Catalogue of publications.

Cambridge Business Studies Project, 22 Nene Crescent, Oakham, Leics LE15 6SG.

Cambridge University Press, The Edinburgh Building, Shaftesbury Road, Cambridge CB2 2RU.

Careers and Occupational Information Centre, Moorfoot, Sheffield S1 4PQ. Seven videos on looking for and choosing a job. Computer simulation on managing a supermarket. Booklets on working in various occupations. Catalogue of resources.

Careers Research and Advisory Centre, Hobsons Press (Cambridge), Bateman Street, Cambridge CB2 1LZ. Catalogue of CRAC publications.

Central Electricity Generating Board, 15 Newgate Street, London EC1A 7AU. *Understanding Electricity: A Catalogue of Resources for Teachers.* Central Film Library, Marketing Headquarters, Central Office of Information; as below.

Central Office of Information, Hercules Road, London SE1 7DU. Leaflet advertising services available to the general public.

Central Statistical Office, Open University Educational Enterprises Ltd, 12 Cofferidge Close, Stony Stratford, Milton Keynes MK11 1BY. OUEE distributes CSO publications. A list of statistical publications is available from this address.

Centre for Alternative Technology, Llwyngwern Quarry, Machynlleth, Powys, Wales. Demonstration Centre, open 10a.m. to 6p.m. Two slide sets: one on the Centre and its work; one on renewable energy for today and tomorrow. Book list. Detailed leaflet about group visits.

Centre for World Development Education, 128 Buckingham Palace Road, London SW1W 9SH. Publishes catalogue of selected resource materials for teachers and students. It lists over 400 items: books, leaflets, photo sets, slide sets and wall charts.

Christian Aid, PO Box No. 1, London SW9 8BH. Booklet: *Real Aid: A Strategy for Britain*. Catalogue of publications and visual aids. Catalogue of schools and youth publications. Trading game.

City and Guilds of London Institute, 76 Portland Place, London W1N 4AA.

City of London, Public Relations Office, PO Box 270, Guildhall, London EC2P 2EJ. Publications about the City. Two films lent on a pick-up/return basis to schools and colleges. A City guide conducts tours of Guildhall, Mansion House and Barbican Estates Office. Four weeks' notice needed.

Commission of the European Communities, 8 Storey's Gate, London SW1P 3AT. Provides details of visits to community institutions. Has a panel of speakers throughout the country to talk about the European Community and its policies. Booklet on the common agricultural policy. Booklet on the historical background to the European movement. Map of Europe with member states.

Commonwealth Development Corporation, 33 Hill Street, London W1A 3AR. Information booklets, report and accounts, wall chart on its activities, film about Mananga Agricultural Centre.

Commonwealth Institute, Kensington High Street, London W8 6NQ. Full range of resources from books to audio-visual materials available for reference and loan. Its education department provides wide and varied services.

Community Service Volunteers, 237 Pentonville Road, London N1 9NJ. Simulation: *Spring Green Motorway*.

Computers in the Curriculum Project, Educational Computing Section, Chelsea College, 552 Kings Road, London SW10 0UA.

Concord Films Council, 201 Felixstowe Road, Ipswich, Suffolk IP3 9BJ. Specialises in documentary and TV programmes about contemporary problems. Film and video catalogue.

Confederation of British Industry, Centre Point, 103 New Oxford Street, London WC1A 1BU. Leaflet of current publications. Booklet about the CBI.

Conservation Trust, c/o George Palmer School, Northumberland Avenue, Reading RG2 0EN. Leaflet about the Trust. Study packs, posters and charts, speaker services. List of publications, including audio-visual programmes.

Conservative Research Department, 32 Smith Square, Westminster, London SW1P 3HH. Publishes a campaign guide before each general election. Fortnightly publication *Politics Today*, some issues of which are sometimes on economics matters. Provides voluntary speakers upon request. The library, reference only, is open to *bona fide* students and researchers.

Consumer Credit Association of the United Kingdom,

Queens House, Queens Road, Chester CH1 3BQ. Directory, code of practice, booklets on consumer credit.

Consumers' Association, 14 Buckingham Street, London WC2N 6DS. *Which?* magazine monthly. Publications list.

Co-operative Bank plc, PO Box 101, 1 Balloon Street, Manchester M60 4EP. Leaflets giving details of the bank's services.

Co-operative Retail Services Ltd, Member Relations Department, 54 Maryland Street, Stratford, London E15 1JE. Schools' pack containing wall charts, pamphlets, booklets and up-to-date notes on all aspects of the co-operative movement. Visiting speakers can be arranged to groups within the trading area of the London region.

Co-operative Union Ltd, Education Department, Stamford Hall, Loughborough, Leics LE5 5QR. Publishes books, booklets, pamphlets and posters, also films and videos on the co-operative movement. School groups may visit the Rochdale Pioneers, Toad Lane, Rochdale.

Corporation of the City of London, PO Box 270, Guildhall, London EC2P 2EJ.

Council for Education in World Citzenship, 19/21 Tudor Street, London EC4Y 0DJ. Pamphlet of United Nations and world studies materials. Brochure describing the work of the CEWC. It offers information broadsheets, organises national conferences and teachers' seminars. Provides speakers for individual schools on any topics of national or international concern. Its London resource centre holds a wide range of teaching materials on world studies, and is open to teachers and students for study and reference purposes. An information service provides a range of services on topics of current or recent international concern. Publishes annual report.

Council for the Securities Industry, 20th Floor, The Stock Exchange Building, London EC2N 1HH. Annual report of the Council.

CSL Vision, Distribution Centre, Chalfont Grove, Gerrards Cross, Bucks SL9 8TM. Film and video catalogues.

Daily Express, Readers Letters Dept, 121 Fleet Street, London EC4P 4JT. Supplies photocopied material on topical subjects contained in library cuttings file. Fee – 40p per selection of articles. Also provides headlines and news stories taken from microfilm, covering most years, fee – 50p.

Daily Mail, Carmelite House, Carmelite Street, London EC4Y 0JA. Write to production department regarding visits.

Daily Mirror, Production Dept (Visits), 33 Holborn, London EC1.

Department for National Savings, Marketing and Information Unit, 4th Floor Charles House, 375 Kensington High Street, London W14 HSD. Booklet on investing in national savings, annual report.

Department of Education and Science, Elizabeth House,

York Road, London SE1 7PH. List of publications. Catalogue of books for schools.

Department of Employment, Public Enquiry Office, Caxton House, Tothill Street, London SW1H 9NF. Students' guide on employment legislation, and list of publications. Applications for booklets and speakers are considered on their individual merit.

Department of Energy, Distribution Unit, Room 1312, Thames House South, Millbank, London SW1P 4QJ. Leaflet of resources for teaching about energy and energy conservation.

Department of Health and Social Security, Alexandra Fleming House, Elephant & Castle, London SE1.

East Anglian Examinations Board, The Lindens, Lexden Road, Colchester CO3 3RL. Social economics syllabus. Provides speakers to groups of teachers. Syllabuses are on commercial subjects.

East Midland Regional Examinations Board, Robinswood House, Robinswood Road, Aspley, Nottingham NG8 3NH. Does not offer economics as a single-examination subject. It does have the 16 + national criteria report for economics.

Economics Association, Maxwelton House, 41–3, Boltro Road, Haywards Heath, West Sussex RH16 1BJ.

Economics Education 14–16 Project, Manchester University Dept of Education, Oxford Road, Manchester M13 9PL.

Economics Research and Curriculum Unit, University of London Institute of Education, 20 Bedford Way, London WC1H 0AL.

Economist Newspaper Ltd, 25 St James's Street, London SW1A 1HG. Booklet cataloguing *The Economist* briefs and books.

Educational Foundation for Visual Aids, Paxton Place, Gipsy Road, London SE27 9SR. Hires 16 mm films and sells filmstrips, slides, multi-media kits and videotapes.

Electricity Council, Understanding Electricity, 30 Millbank, London SW1P 4RD. Catalogue of publications.

Esmée Fairbairn Research Centre, Heriot-Watt University, Chambers Street, Edinburgh EH1 1HX. Supplies economics programs for microcomputers.

Export Credits Guarantee Department, PO Box 272, Aldermanbury House, Aldermanbury, London EC2P 2EL. Leaflets explaining the work of the ECGD.

Fabian Society, 11 Dartmouth Street, London SW1.

Finance Houses Association, 18 Upper Grosvenor Street, London W1X 9PB. Booklets: *Instalment Credit* and *Equipment Leasing*. Publishes annual report.

Financial Times, Bracken House, 10 Cannon Street, London EC4P 4BY. Film: *The FT – a 24 hour day –* available free of charge from Central Film Library. The *Financial Times* is available to both students and teachers at half its regular cover price. To obtain the special application forms for the scheme, write to: The Subscription Dept, *Financial Times* Ltd, Minster House, Arthur Street, London EC4R 9AX. The *Financial Times* can accommodate occasional groups of up to 25–30 sixth-form students to see the film

followed by a presentation/discussion session with staff on specific subjects of interest. 10.30a.m.–12.30p.m. Contact the *Financial Times* at least three months in advance of any proposed trip to London. Write to the Press Office at Bracken House.

Fontana Paperbacks, 8 Grafton Street, London W1X 3LA. Catalogues of publications.

Framework Press, St Leonards House, St Leonardsgate, Lancaster LA1 1NN.

Friends of the Earth Trust Ltd, 377 City Road, London EC1V 1NA. Information sheets. Network of 250 local groups, some of which can provide speakers.

Further Education Unit, Elizabeth House, York Road, London SE1 7PH.

General Agreement on Tariffs and Trade, Centre William Rappard, Rue de Lausanne 154, CH-1211 Geneva 21. Booklets and leaflets relating to GATT. Annual reports on international trade and on GATT activities. Monthly newsletter *GATT Focus*. Accepts visits from student groups.

Government Statistical Service, Press and Information Service, Central Statistical Office, Great George Street, London SW1P 3AQ. Government statistics: *A Brief Guide to Sources*.

Greater London Council, County Hall, London SE1 7PB. For publications, write to The Manager, GLC Bookshop (DG/PRB). For speakers on London's industrial and employment strategies, write to The Director of Industry and Employment and Chief Economic Adviser (DG/DIE).

Greater London Enterprise Board, 63-67 Newington Causeway, London SE1 6BD. Leaflet on London's new enterprise board.

Guild Home Video Ltd, Guild House, Oundle Road, Peterborough PE2 9PZ. Open University Programmes for sale on video and the licensing of these programmes for off-air recording. Also BBC programmes for hire.

Harrap. All Harrap's education list is now distributed by Thomas Nelson (see separate entry).

Heinemann Educational Books Ltd, 22 Bedford Square, London WC1B 3HH. Annual catalogue of economics books and other resources.

HMSO, Publicity Department, St Crispins, Duke Street, Norwich NR3 1PD. Issues a range of leaflets, catalogues and listing of their publication.

Hodder & Stoughton Educational, PO Box 702, Dunton Green, Sevenoaks, Kent CN13 2YD. Catalogue of business studies books.

ICFC, 91 Waterloo Road, London SE1 8XP. This is now a division of Investors in Industry plc. List of booklets available. Also a video on ICFC. Speakers may be obtained via the Business Development Department. Produces annual report and accounts.

ICI (Imperial Chemical Industries plc), School Liaison Section, Group Personnel Department, PO Box 6, Bessemer Road, Welwyn Garden City, Herts AL7 1HD. Booklet on schools liaison, list of video tapes.

ILEA, Learning Resources Branch, Television and Publishing Centre, Thackeray Road, London SW8

3TB. Catalogue of resources.

Independent Broadcasting Authority, 70 Brompton Road, London SW3 1EY. The IBA Code of Advertising Standards and Practice. Leaflets on independent local radio and Channel 4 TV. Booklets on independent broadcasting and advertising control.

Industrial Society, Peter Runge House, 3 Carlton House Terrace, London SW1 5DG.

Industry/Education Unit, Department of Trade and Industry, Gaywood House, 29 Great Peter Street, London SW1P 3LW. Monthly magazine *View*, catalogue of films and videos for schools.

Inland Revenue Education Service, PO Box 20, Wetherby West Yorks LS23 7EH. Leaflet on resources on the Inland Revenue. Leaflet on explanatory booklets.

Institute for Fiscal Studies, 1/2 Castle Lane, London SW1E 6DR. List of publications.

Institute of Chartered Accountants in England and Wales, PO Box 433, Chartered Accountants' Hall, Moorgate Place, London EC2P 2BJ. Careers booklets, and careers film *All Things Business*. Has network of local accountancy careers advisers for visiting schools and attending careers meetings or conventions.

Institute of Economic Affairs, 2 Lord North Street, London SW1P 3LB. Progress report outlining IEA activities. List of publications. May be able to suggest speakers. Films: *Man Uses Markets*; *Adam Smith and the Wealth of Nations*.

Intermediate Technology, 9 King Street, London WC2E 8HW. Book list, *Intermediate Technology News*. Information leaflet.

International Labour Office, 96-98 Marsham Street, London SW1P 4LY. List of publications; speakers can sometimes be provided.

International Monetary Fund, Publications Unit, Room 2/300, 700 19th Street Nw, Washington DC 20431, USA. Publishes a catalogue of all books and periodicals that are currently available. Annual report is free of charge.

Issuing Houses Association, Granite House, 101 Cannon Street, London EC4N 5BA. Free booklet: *British Issuing Houses. The City Code on Takeovers and Mergers* (£1.50).

John Lewis Partnership, 4 Old Cavendish Street, London W1A 1EX. Weekly house journal: *The Gazette*. Booklets about the organisation, reports and accounts. A talk may be arranged on the history, trading policies and democratic structure of the partnership.

John Murray, 50 Albemarle Street; London W1X 4BD. Catalogue of business and management studies books.

Joint Board for Pre-Vocational Education, 46 Britannia Street, London WC1X 9RG. Joint Matriculation Board, Manchester M15 6EU. Examiners' reports and syllabus offprints are circulated free of charge to all JMB centres. The Board will provide organisers of meetings of teachers with suggestions for the names of experienced examiners and committee members who can deal with particular aspects of the Board's examinations.

Labour Party, Information Unit, 150 Walworth Road, London SE17 1JT. Materials on the Labour Party and its policies. Visits and talks at Head Office should be arranged through the Information Unit. The Press Department has a range of films and videos available for hire.

Liberal Party, 1 Whitehall Place, London SW1A 2HE. Issues a number of leaflets on: Liberal economic policy; the Alliance Programme for small businesses and the self-employed; Profit-sharing and employee share ownership. Briefings on trade unions, fighting poverty, international development, rural regeneration. Speakers can be arranged. Visits to the party headquarters: a lecture is given about the party's policies and general principles, with ample time for questions.

Lloyd's of London, Publicity and Information Department, Lime Street, London EC3M 7HA. Booklets, and will answer specific inquiries. Video/film on Lloyd's. Visits may also be arranged.

Lloyds Bank plc, Schools Liaison, Black Horse House, 78 Cannon Street, London EC4P 4LN. Contact and services sheet. Provides nine different talks, a film, four filmstrips, two business games, a work-experience scheme, visits to the local branch, a one-day careers course, and a one-day economics visit for A-level students. Visits to the computer centre, clearing house, and a City branch. Two wall charts. *The British Economy in Figures. An Economic Profile of Britain*, published annually. Two books: *The Economics of International Trade*, *What Goes on in the City*?

London Chamber of Commerce and Industry, Marlowe House, Station Road, Sidcup, Kent DA15 7BJ. An examination board that publishes syllabuses, and *COMLON*, an annual journal.

London Central Markets, London EC1A 9AA. Booklet about Smithfield.

London Commodity Exchange, Cereal House, 58 Mark Lane, London EC3R 7NE. Booklets on the terminal markets. Visits on Tuesdays and Thursdays.

London Discount Market Association, 39 Cornhill, London EC3D 3NU. List of addresses of members of the Association.

London Regional Examining Board, Lyon House, 104 Wandsworth High Street, London SW18 4LF. Past examination papers are made available on request while stocks last.

Longman Group Ltd, Longman House, Burnt Mill, Harlow, Essex CM20 2JE. Catalogue of publications.

Longman Resources Unit, 33-35 Tanner Row, York YO1 1JP. Booklets in economic studies series. 'The Mini Co. Kit' similar to Young Enterprise; economics and politics list of resources and micro software.

Macdonald & Evans, Estover, Plymouth PL6 7TZ. Catalogue of business studies books.

McGraw-Hill Book Company (UK) Ltd, Shoppenhangers Road, Maidenhead, Berks SL6 2QL. Catalogue of publications.

Macmillan Education Ltd, Houndmills, Basingstoke, Hants RG21 2XS. List of economics publications.

Management Games Ltd, 11 Woburn Street, Ampthill,

Bedford MK45 2HP. Sells simulations, e.g. 'Starpower'.

Manpower Services Commission, Careers & Occupational Information Centre, Moorfoot, Sheffield S1 4PQ.

Marks & Spencer plc, The Public Relations Department, Michael House, Baker Street, London W1A 1DN. Company report and accounts.

Metal Box, Education Office, Queens House, Forbury Road, Reading RG1 3JH.

Metal Market and Exchange Company Ltd, Plantation House, Fenchurch Street, London EC3M 3AP. Booklet about the London metal exchange, 75p. Visits to the Exchange may be arranged through Brian Reidy & Associates, Suite 144, Seventh Floor, C Section, Plantation House, Fenchurch Street, London EC3M 3AP. Video about the work of the London Metal Exchange.

Midland Bank plc, Schools Liaison Office, 3 Kings Arms Yard, London EC2R 7BA. Banking handbook. Set of wall charts. Available only to schools in the Greater London area.

Ministry of Agriculture, Fisheries and Food, Whitehall Place, London SW1A 2HH. Catalogue of publications *Look at the Label* booklet and video on labelling and consumer protection.

Mirror Group Newspapers, Production Department (Visits), Daily Mirror, 33 Holborn, London EC1P 1DQ. Applications for group visits, which start at 9p.m., should be made at least four months in advance.

Multi-Link Film Library, 12 The Square, Vicarage Farm Road, Peterborough PE1 5TS.

National Audio-Visual Aids Library, Paxton Place, Gypsy Road, London SE27 9SR. Supplies charts, films, videos, slide/tapes and filmstrips for teachers. Catalogues available on request. Only UK source of American 'trade-offs' series.

National Bus Company, 25 New Street Square, London EC4A 3AP.

National Coal Board, Schools Service, 351 Hobart House, Grosvenor Place, London SW1X 7AE. Set of ten wall charts on Coal Today. Teachers' pack of booklets and leaflets on coal and mining industry.

National Economic Development Office, Millbank Tower, Millbank, London SW1P 4QX. Booklets include *NEDO in Print*, and *British Industrial Performance*. The Office is able to organise occasional visits by small sixth-form groups. These need to be planned well ahead and requests should be addressed to the Head of Communications section.

National Girobank, Bootle, Merseyside GIR 0AA. Money management resource kit. £6. Publishes a magazine called *Over 16*, issued free three times a year. Two films on free loan, 10 minutes each, about National Girobank and the development of money.

National Institute of Economic and Social Research, 2 Dean Trench Street, Smith Square, London SW1P 3HE. Quarterly national economic review: £30 per annum. Leaflet of publications in print.

National Westminster Bank plc, Business Development Division, 41 Lothbury, London EC2P 2BP. Economics reports on particular countries. A wide range of information leaflets for students are available from: Student Liaison Officer, Marketing Dept, National Westminster Bank plc, Domestic Banking Division, 10th Floor, Drapers Gardens, 12 Throgmorton Avenue, London EC2P 2ES. The *Nat West Quarterly Review* and the Annual report and accounts are available from: National Westminster Bank plc, Secretary's Office, 41 Lothbury, London EC2P 2BP. Visits or speakers should be arranged through the marketing department, or the local branch manager.

Nelson (Thomas) & Sons Ltd, Nelson House, Mayfield Road, Walton-on-Thames, Surrey KT12 5PL.

North Regional Examination Board, Wheatfield Road, Westerhope, Newcastle upon Tyne NE5 5JZ. Handbooks on CSE examinations.

Northern Ireland General Certificate of Education Examinations Board, Beechill House, 42 Beechill Road, Belfast BT8 4RS.

Office of Fair Trading, Field House, Bream's Building, London EC4A 1 PR. List of publications.

Office of Population Censuses and Surveys, Census Information Unit, 54 St Catherines House, 10 Kingsway, London WC2B 6JP.

Open University Educational Enterprises Ltd, 12 Cofferidge Close, Stoney Stratford, Milton Keynes MK11 1BY. Provides books, videos, 16mm films and audio cassettes.

OECD, 2 rue André-Pascal, 75775 Paris, France.

Overseas Development Administration, Information Department, Eland House, Stag Place, London SW1E 5DH. Catalogue of publications on overseas development and aid. Wall chart, 'Rich World, Poor World', monthly newspaper *Overseas Development*.

Oxfam, 274 Banbury Road, Oxford OX2 7DZ. Catalogue, with addresses of regional offices and development education centres, and list of education materials for sale to teachers and students. Booklet of publications.

Oxford & Cambridge Schools Examining Board, Brook House, 10 Trumpington Street, Cambridge.

Oxford University Press, Education Department, Walton Street, Oxford OX2 6DP. Catalogue of history and economics publications. Publishes *British Economy Survey*, two issues per annum.

Panel on Takeovers and Mergers, PO Box 226, Stock Exchange Building, London EC2P 2JX. Series of booklets, including the *City Code on Takeovers and Mergers* (£1.50).

Pictorial Charts Educational Trust, 27 Kirchen Road, London W13 0UD. Leaflet of wall charts available.

Pitman Publishing Ltd, 128 Long Acre, London WC2E 9AN. List of publications. The Pitman service department organises one-day and residential conferences for business studies teachers in different parts of the UK at different times. These feature up-to-date topics and frequently lectures of interest to economics teachers; programmes can be obtained from the Pitman service department.

Pitmansoft, Pitman Publishing, Southport PR9 9YS. Various software packages on microeconomics and business simulations.

Polytech Publishers Ltd, 36 Hayburn Road, Stockport SK2 5DB. Provides free inspection copies of textbooks and free teachers' manuals, to teachers of relevant courses.

Population Concern, 231 Tottenham Court Road, London W1P 0HX. Leaflets and books including a yearly world population data sheet; advice on films on population issues, speakers on population and related topics; list of publications.

Port of London Authority, Leslie Ford House, Tilbury Docks, Tilbury, Essex RM18 7EH. Magazine about the Port of London, map of Tilbury Docks. Booklet guide to London's wharves, docks and shipping services. Large photographic leaflet about the Port of London, list of suggested reference books.

Post Office, Schools Officer, St Martin-le-Grand, London EC1A 1HQ.

Routledge & Kegan Paul Ltd, 14 Leicester Square, London WC2H 7PH. Catalogue of books published.

Royal Bank of Scotland plc, Public Relations Manager, Public Relations Office, PO Box 31, 42 St Andrew Square, Edinburgh EH2 2YE. The *Three Banks Review*. Monthly summary of business conditions in the UK. Scotland in figures.

Royal Economic Society, University of York, Heslington, York YO1 5DD. Publishes the *Economic Journal*.

Royal Society of Arts Examination Board, John Adam Street, London WC2N 6EZ.

Sainsbury (J.) plc, Stamford House, Stamford Street, London SE1 9LL. Information sheet, history sheet, annual reports.

School Broadcasting Council for the United Kingdom, The Langham, Portland Place, London W1A 1AA. Annual programme, termly wall chart timetables, publications for teachers and students.

Schools Curriculum Industry Project, Newcombe House, 45 Notting Hill Gate, London W11 3JB.

Scottish Certificate of Education Examination Board, Ironmills Rd, Dalkeith, Midlothian EH22 1BK.

Scottish Curriculum Development Service, Glasgow Centre, 74 Southbrae Drive, Glasgow G13 1SU. Annual newsletter containing list of publications.

Seminar Cassettes, 218 Sussex Gardens, London W2 2UD. International report cassettes from Reuter correspondents. Science in Society audio cassettes. Units on industry, resources in a finite world, energy today and in the future, etc.

Shell Film Library, 25 The Burroughs, Hendon, London NW4 4AT. Catalogue of film and video cassettes.

Shell UK Ltd, Education Service, Shell-Mex House, Strand, London WC2R 0DX. Catalogue of resources for teachers. Annual report, wall chart 'Working for Yourself'.

Shelter, 157 Waterloo Road, London SE1 8XS. Produces simulation called 'Tenement'.

Society for Advancement of Games & Simulations in Education and Training, Centre for Extension Studies, University of Technology, Loughborough, Leics LE11 3TU. List of publications; quarterly journal entitled *Simulation/Games for Learning*; has meetings and conferences, resource list no. 5: Economics.

Society of Motor Manufacturers & Traders Ltd, Forbes House, Halkin Street, London SW1X 7DS. List of publications.

South East Regional Examinations Board, 2–4 Mount Ephraim Road, Royal Tunbridge Wells, Kent GN1 1EU. No Mode 1 examination in economics, but six current Mode 3 courses.

South Western Examinations Board, 23-29 Marsh Street, Bristol BS1 4BP. Mode 1 Scheme of Examinations in Economics, starting 1986.

Southern Regional Examination Board, Avondale House, 33 Carlton Crescent, Southampton SO9 4YL. Booklet of business studies syllabus.

Southern Universities' Joint Board, Cotham Road, Bristol BS6 6BD. Syllabuses for economics examinations. Copies of past papers and examiners' reports.

Stock Exchange, Information & Press Department, London EC2N 1HP. Visits from 10.00a.m.–3.15p.m. Monday to Friday with film and viewing of Exchange; booklet and leaflet about the Exchange and its history, list of publications, booklets on the gilt-edged market and a simple guide to traded options. Wall chart, 'How a Company is Formed and Financed', and 'How the Stock Exchange Works'.

Streetwork, c/o Notting Dale Urban Studies Centre, 189 Freston Road, London W10. Publishes *Bulletin of Environmental Education* (*BEE*). Co-ordinates and promotes urban and local studies. Runs workshops and seminars on urban studies. Information leaflet, and list of available back issues of *BEE*.

Sussex Publications Ltd, Townsend, Poulshot, Devizes, Wiltshire SN10 1SD. Sussex Tapes and Sussex Software. Audio cassettes on economics subjects.

Tesco plc Public Affairs Department, Tesco House, PO Box 18, Delamare Road, Cheshunt, Herts EN8 9SL. Annual report, booklets on urban renewal, and counter-revolution.

Trades Union Congress, Congress House, Great Russell Street, London WC1B 3LS. TUC Guidelines on work experience for schoolchildren. *Learning about Trade Unions*: a book of activities and case studies aimed at teachers. Reading material on trade unions. List of TUC publications. Background notes and statistical information for teachers on trade unions. Booklets on trade-union issues such as health and safety, jobs, racism, equal opportunities, the health service, the social wage.

Treasury, Treasury Chambers, Parliament Street, London SW1P 3AG. Publishes monthly an *Economics Progress Report*, available free in bulk to educational establishments.

Understanding British Industry Resource Centre, Sun Alliance House, New Inn Hall Street, Oxford OX1

2QE. Holds collection of relevant teaching materials. Over fifty satellite resource centres located around the country offer a preview service of the various education materials produced by companies. Annual report, list of UBI regional liaison offices and centres, catalogue of teaching materials.

Understanding Industry, 5 Victoria Street, Windsor, Berks SL4 1EZ. Runs courses at schools, produces booklets in all major areas of management.

Unilever, Education Section, PO Box 68, Unilever House, London EC4P 4BQ.

Union Discount Company of London plc, 39 Cornhill, London EC3V 3NU. Booklets on dealing with a discount house, commercial bills of exchange, certificates of deposit. Group visits may be arranged.

United Kingdom Atomic Energy Authority, 11 Charles II Street, London SW1Y 4QP. Catalogue of publications, a monthly magazine, audio-visual programmes, a photographic library, a resource pack on nuclear energy, mobile exhibitions, and speakers' service.

United Nations, Information Centre, Ship House, 20 Buckingham Gate, London SW1. Many publications. Reference library. Audio-visual aids available on loan.

United Nations Association, 3 Whitehall Court, London SW1A 2EL. List of publications. Provides speakers on any subject relevant to the UN.

University of Cambridge Local Examinations Syndicate, Syndicate Buildings, 1 Hills Road, Cambridge CB1 2EU. Reports on examinations, including analyses of multiple-choice tests and comments from Test Development and Research Unit. Meetings are arranged with schools both nationally and regionally.

University of London Schools Examinations Department, Stewart House, 32 Russell Square, London WC1B 5DN. Lists of suggested reading for O- and A-level. Copies of syllabuses.

University of Oxford Delegacy of Local Examinations, Ewert Place, Summertown, Oxford OS2 7DZ. Supplies book list, past papers and numerical answers, syllabuses, examiners' reports, booklets on the examinations. Will provide speakers to groups of teachers, or visit schools, LEAs or teachers' centres.

University Tutorial Press Ltd, 22 Hills Road, Cambridge CB2 1NG. Lists of books in economics and business studies.

Viscom Ltd, Unit B11, Park Hall Road Trading Estate, London SE21 8EL. Publishes catalogue of low-cost educational and special-interest video programmes, which include the Foundation of Wealth series produced by Video Arts for Esso Petroleum, ICI and Unilever.

Weidenfeld & Nicolson, 91 Clapham High Street, London SW4 7TA. Catalogue of economics publications.

Welsh Joint Education Committee, 245 Western Avenue, Cardiff CF5 2YX. Examines economics at A-, O- and CSE level.

Welsh Office, Economic and Statistical Services Division, Cathays Park, Cardiff CF1 3NQ. List of publications. Booklet on government statistics: *A Brief Guide to Sources*. Films available from Welsh Office film library.

West Midlands Examinations Board, Norfolk House, Smallbrook Queensway, Birmingham B5 4NJ. Has no CSE Mode 1 syllabus in economics.

Williams and Glyn's Bank plc, 20 Birchin Lane, London EC3P 3DP. Publishes *Three Banks Review*.

World Bank, New Zealand House, London SW1. Catalogue of publications; can provide occasional speakers.

World Development Movement, Bedford Chambers, Covent Garden, London WC2E 8HA. Publication list, the EEC and the Third World. Annual report.

Yorkshire and Humberside Regional Examinations Board, 31-33 Springfield Avenue, Harrogate, North Yorkshire HG1 2HW. A subject panel for economics has been set up, and a CSE Mode 1 syllabus is being formulated.

Young Enterprise, Robert Hyde House, 48 Bryanston Square, London W1H 7LN. Provides back-up information about the scheme. Also issues a kit of papers for schools wishing to embark on young enterprise. A number of videos describe its work. Regional directors will talk to teachers, schools and groups of students.

Index